YESTERDAY'S HEROES
Kenneth N. Jordan, Sr.

Also by the author

HEROES OF OUR TIME:
239 Men of the Vietnam War Awarded the Medal of Honor 1964-1972

FORGOTTEN HEROES:
131 Men of the Korean War Awarded the Medal of Honor 1950-1953

YESTERDAY'S HEROES

433 MEN OF WORLD WAR II AWARDED THE MEDAL OF HONOR 1941-1945

Kenneth N. Jordan, Sr.

Schiffer Military History
Atglen, PA

DEDICATION

YESTERDAY'S HEROES is dedicated to all those who sacrificed so much to keep America free. They are all **Heroes.**

Hero: A person admired for courage, nobility, or exploits, especially in war. A person admired for qualities or achievements and regarded as an ideal or model.

ACKNOWLEDGEMENTS

I would like to thank all those who helped me with this book. My wife Louise, son Ken Jr., daughter Kathryn, with a special thanks to my daughter Diane and Kathy Radigan's senior class at the Willoughby Tech Center (Jessica F. Bowman, Francesca A. Bihari, Michelle Renea Davis, Roni Beth DeMeza, Kelly Lynn Gallo, Tammy Gardner, Sharonda M. Kane, Kristina M. Koepp, Sheri L. Malz, Nicole S. Prochaska, Teresa Ann Smoyer, Tiffany Lee Wells, and Tara R. Winkler) who spent many hours helping me with the research and typing of this book. Also to the kind people at the Euclid and Willoughby, Ohio Libraries. Last, but certainly not least, the 433 Medal of Honor recipients.

SOURCES

The Senate Committee on Veterans' Affairs. *Medal of Honor Recipients 1863-1978. Washington, D.C.: U.S. Government Printing Office, 1979.*
The National Archives, Washington, D.C.
The Library of Congress, Washington, D.C.
The New York Times, New York, NY
The Cleveland Plain Dealer, Cleveland, OH
The News Herald, Willoughby, OH

Book Design by Robert Biondi.

Copyright © 1996 by Kenneth N. Jordan, Sr.
Library of Congress Catalog Number: 96-67094.

Printed in the United States of America.
ISBN: 0-7643-0061-X

We are interested in hearing from authors with book ideas on related topics.

Published by Schiffer Publishing Ltd.
77 Lower Valley Road
Atglen, PA 19310
Please write for a free catalog.
This book may be purchased from the publisher.
Please include $2.95 postage.
Try your bookstore first.

CONTENTS

Dedication 4

Acknowledgements & Sources 4

Introduction 7

Chapter 1   1941 9

Chapter 2   1942 26

Chapter 3   1943 72

Chapter 4   1944 158

Chapter 5   1945 438

Summary 614

Index 615

Introduction

T he Medal of Honor is the highest military award for bravery that can be given to an individual in the United States of America. The president may award, and present in the name of congress, a Medal of Honor to a person who, while a member of the Armed Forces, distinguished himself conspicuously by gallantry and intrepidity at the risk of his life above and beyond the call of duty.

American participation in World War II began when the Japanese bombed Pearl Harbor on December 7, 1941 and ended with the Japanese surrender aboard the *U.S.S. Missouri* on September 2, 1945. During that 45-month period over 16,000,000 Americans served in our Armed Forces, of which more than 400,000 were killed, close to 700,000 were wounded, and **433 were awarded the Medal of Honor.**

Yesterday's Heroes is about those 433 men.

From the first Medal of Honor recipient on December 7, 1941 at Pearl Harbor to the last on July 29, 1945, on Luzon in the Philippine Islands, you'll read all 433 actual citations for gallantry above and beyond the call of duty. Included with the citations are official communiques from the battle front for that particular day, interspersed with newspaper accounts of certain battles in which some of these men were involved and many action photographs.

There has never, in our nation's history, been such a dedicated and concerted effort, in fighting and winning a war, as there was in World War II. So to the men and women of that era, whether at the battlefront or on the homefront, you are all heroes.

† **Denotes Posthumous Award**

CHAPTER 1

1941

Note: The following newspaper article appeared in The New York Times on December 8, 1941:

**JAPAN WARS ON U.S. AND BRITAIN;
MAKES SUDDEN ATTACK ON HAWAII;
HEAVY FIGHTING AT SEA REPORTED**

• • •

GUAM BOMBED; ARMY SHIP IS SUNK

• • •

**U.S. Fliers Head North From Manila –
Battleship Oklahoma Set Afire by
Torpedo Planes at Honolulu**

• • •

104 SOLDIERS KILLED AT FIELD IN HAWAII

• • •

**President Fears "Very Heavy Losses" on Oahu –
Churchill Notifies Japan That a
State of War Exists**

• • •

WASHINGTON, Monday, Dec. 8 – Sudden and unexpected attacks on Pearl Harbor, Honolulu, and other United States possessions in the Pacific early yesterday by the Japanese air force and navy plunged the United States and Japan into active war.

The initial attack in Hawaii, apparently launched by torpedo-carrying bombers and submarines, caused widespread damage and death. It was quickly followed by others. There were unconfirmed reports that German raiders participated in the attacks.

Guam also was assaulted from the air, as were Davao, on the island of Mindanao, and Camp John Hay, in Northern Luzon, both in the Philippines. Lieut. Gen. Douglas MacArthur, commanding the United States Army of the Far East, reported there was little damage, however.

[Japanese parachute troops had been landed in the Philippines and native Japanese had seized some communities, Royal Arch Gunnison said in a broadcast from Manila today to WOR-Mutual. He reported without detail that "in the naval war the ABCD fleets under American command appeared to be successful" against Japanese invasions.]

Japanese submarines, ranging out over the Pacific, sank an American transport carrying lumber 1,300 miles from San Francisco, and distress signals were heard from a freighter 700 miles from that city.

The War Department reported that 104 soldiers died and 309 were wounded as a result of the attack on Hickam Field, Hawaii. The National Broadcasting Company reported from Honolulu that the battleship Oklahoma was afire. [Domel, Japanese news agency, reported the Oklahoma sunk.]

Nation Placed on Full War Basis

The news of these surprise attacks fell like a bombshell on Washington. President Roosevelt immediately ordered the country and the Army and Navy onto a full war footing. He arranged at a White House conference last night to address a joint session of Congress at noon today, presumably to ask for declaration of a formal state of war.

This was disclosed after a long special Cabinet meeting, which was joined later by Congressional leaders. These leaders predicted "action" within a day.

After leaving the White House conference Attorney General Francis Biddle said that "a resolution" would be introduced in Congress tomorrow. He would not amplify or affirm that it would be for a declaration of war.

Congress probably will "act" within the day, and he will call the Senate Foreign Relations Committee for this purpose, Chairman Tom Connally announced.

[A United Press dispatch from London this morning said that Prime Minister Churchill had notified Japan that a state of war existed.]

As the reports of heavy fighting flashed into the White House, London reported semi-officially that the British Empire would carry out Prime Minister Winston Churchill's pledge to give the United States full support in case of hostilities with Japan. The President and Mr. Churchill talked by transatlantic telephone.

This was followed by a statement in London from the Netherlands Government in Exile that it considered a state of war to exist between the Netherlands and Japan. Canada, Australia and Costa Rica took similar action.

Landing Made in Malaya

A Singapore communique disclosed that Japanese troops had landed in Northern Malaya and that Singapore had been bombed.

The President told those at last night's White House meeting that "doubtless very heavy losses" were sustained by the Navy and also by the Army on the island of Oahu [Honolulu]. It was impossible to obtain confirmation or denial of reports that the battleships Oklahoma and West Virginia had been damaged or sunk at Pearl Harbor, together with six or seven destroyers, and that 350 United States airplanes had been caught on the ground.

The White House took over control of the bulletins, and the Navy Department, therefore, said it could not discuss the matter or answer any questions how the Japanese were able to penetrate the Hawaiian defenses or appear without previous knowledge of their presence in those waters.

Administration circles forecast that the United States soon might be involved in a world-wide war, with Germany supporting Japan, an Axis partner. The German official radio tonight attacked the United States and supported Japan.

Axis diplomats here expressed complete surprise that the Japanese had attacked. But the impression gained from their attitude was that they believed it represented a victory for the Nazi attempt to divert lease-lend air from Britain, which has been a Berlin objective ever since the legislation was passed and began to be implemented.

Secretary of the Treasury Henry Morgenthau Jr. announced that his department had invoked the Trading With the Enemy Act, placing an absolute United States embargo on Japan.

Robert P. Patterson, Undersecretary of War, called on the nation to put production on a twenty-four hour basis.

A nation-wide round-up of Japanese nationals was ordered by Attorney General Biddle through cooperation by the FBI and local police forces.

Action was taken to protect defense plants, especially in California, where Japanese are particularly numerous. Orders were issued by the Civil Aeronautics Authority to ground most private aircraft except those on scheduled lines.

Fleet Puts Out to Sea From Hawaii

The Navy last night swept out to sea from its bombed base at Pearl Harbor after Secretary of State Cordell Hull, following a final conference with Japanese "peace envoys" here, asserted that Japan's had been a "treacherous" attack. Neither the War nor the Navy Department had been able to communicate with its commanders in Manila.

Secretary of War Henry L. Stimson ordered the entire United States Army to be in uniform by today. Secretary Frank Knox followed suit for the navy. They did so after President Roosevelt had instructed the Navy and Army to expect all previously prepared orders for defense immediately.

United States naval craft are expected to operate out of Singapore as soon as possible in protecting the vital rubber and tin shipments necessary to our national defense program.

Despite these preliminary defense moves, however, it was clear that further detailed discussions would soon take place between officials of the United States, Great Britain, China, the Netherlands and Australia to devise a total scheme of limiting the activities of the Japanese Fleet.

Immediate steps will be taken also to meet the increased menace to China's lifeline, the Burma Road. Reliable information indicates that the Japanese are preparing a large-scale assault on the road in the hope of cutting off American supplies before the Allies can transport sufficient forces into defensive positions.

Censorship was established on all messages leaving the United States by cable and radio.

In Tokyo United States Ambassador Joseph C. Grew obtained a reply to Secretary Hull's early message, according to dispatches from the Japanese capital.

The attack on Pearl Harbor and Honolulu began "at dawn", according to Stephen Early, Presidential secretary. Because of time difference, the first news of the bombing was released in Washington at 2:22 P.M.. Subsequently it was announced at the White House that another wave of bombers and dive bombers had come over Oahu Island, on which Honolulu is situated, to be met by anti-aircraft fire again.

An attack on Guam, tiny island outpost, subsequently was announced. The White House at first said that Manila also had been attacked, but after failure to reach Army and Navy commanders there, President Roosevelt expressed the "hope" that no such attack had occurred. Broadcasts from Manila bore out this hope.

The Japanese took over the Shanghai Bund. Japanese airplanes patrolling over the city dropped some bombs, reportedly sinking the British gunboat Peterel.

Hawaii Attacked Without Warning

Reports from Hawaii indicated that Honolulu had no warning of the attack. Japanese bombers, with the red circle of the Rising Sun of Japan on their wings, suddenly appeared, escorted by fighters. Flying high, they suddenly dive-bombed, attacking Pearl Harbor, the great Navy base, the Army's Hickam Field and Ford Island. At least one torpedo plane was seen to launch a torpedo at warships in Pearl Harbor.

A report from Admiral C.C. Bloch, commander of the naval district at Hawaii, expressed the belief that "there has been heavy damage done in Hawaii and there has been heavy loss of life."

This was subsequently confirmed by Governor Joseph B. Poindexter of Hawaii in a telephone conversation with President Roosevelt. The Governor also said that there were heavy casualties in the city of Honolulu.

At the White House it was officially said that the sinking of the Army transport carrying lumber and the distress signal from another Army ship "indicate Japanese submarines are strung out over that area." Heavy smoke was seen from Ford Island near Honolulu.

In the raids on Hawaii, Japanese planes were shot down, one bomber hitting and bursting into flames just behind a post office on the Island of Oahu. It was reported without confirmation that six Japanese planes and four submarines were destroyed.

The second attack on Honolulu and its surrounding bases occurred just as President Roosevelt was talking to Governor Poindexter at 6 o'clock last evening.

There was no official confirmation of United Press reports from Honolulu that parachute troops had been sighted off Pearl Harbor.

Many Japanese and former Japanese who are now American citizens are in residence in Hawaii.

Saburo Kurusu, special Japanese envoy who has been conducting "peace" negotiations while Japan was preparing for this attack, and Ambassador Kichisaburo Nomura called at the State Department at 2:05 P.M. after asking for the appointment at 1:00 P.M. They arrived shortly before Secretary Hull had received news Japan had started a war without warning. Mrs. Roosevelt revealed in her broadcast last night that the Japanese Ambassador was with the President when word of the attacks was received.

The two envoys handed a document to Mr. Hull, who kept them waiting about fifteen minutes. Upon reading it, he turned to his visitors to exclaim that it was "crowded with infamous falsehoods and distortions."

President Roosevelt ordered war bulletins released at the White House as rapidly as they were received. A sentence or two was added to the story of the surprise attack every few minutes for several hours.

Cabinet members arrived promptly at 8:30 last evening for their meeting in the White House Oval Room. President Roosevelt had been closeted with Harry L. Hopkins in the Oval Room since receiving the first news. He had conferred with Secretaries Stimson and Knox by telephone and also with General George C. Marshall, Chief of Staff. Admiral Harold R. Stark, Chief of Naval Operations, was too busy to talk to the President even by telephone.

The first to arrive was Secretary of Commerce Jesse H. Jones. Secretary Knox came last. Secretary Hull was accompanied by two bodyguards.

Congressional leaders joining the Cabinet in the oval room at 9:00 P.M. included Senator Hiram Johnson of California, hitherto an isolationist and for long the ranking minority member of the Senate Foreign Relations Committee.

Others present were Speaker Rayburn, Representative Jere Cooper of Tennessee, representing Representative John W. McCormack, the House Majority Leader, who was not able to reach Washington in time for the conference; Chairman Sol Bloom of the House Foreign Affairs Committee and Representative Charles A. Eaton, ranking minority member; Vice president Wallace, who flew here from New York; Senator Allen W. Barkley, majority leader; Senator McNary and Senator Warren R. Austin, ranking minority member of the Foreign Relations Committee.

Cheering crowds lined Pennsylvania Avenue to see them arrive, another evidence of the national determination to defeat Japan and her Axis allies which every official is confident will dominate the country from this moment forth.

Senator W. Lee O'Daniel of Texas, of hillbilly band and hot biscuits fame, added a touch of inadvertent comedy to the scene when he arrived uninvited. He said he had come to "try to learn a few things" and "to make sure Texas is represented at this conference", thus ignoring the presence of Senator Connally.

Senator Barkley, who arrived in Washington by automobile about 7:00 P.M., said he did not find out about the Japanese attack until nearly 6 o'clock.

The formal positions of the United States and Japanese Governments toward the war were officially set forth by the release at the White House of the text of President Roosevelt's message of yesterday to Emperor Hirohito and by the Japanese document handed Ambassador Grew in Tokyo.

President Voiced Hope for Peace

The President's message expressed a "fervent hope for peace" and outlined the dangers of the situation.

"We have hoped that a peace of the Pacific could be consummated in such a way that the nationalities of many diverse peoples may exist side by side without fear of invasion," the President told the Emperor.

The President, recalling that the United States had been directly responsible for bringing Japan into contact with the outside world, said that in seeking peace in the Pacific "I am certain that it will be clear to Your Majesty, as it is to me, that both Japan and the United States should agree to eliminate any form of military threat."

The Japanese document, despite the obviously carefully prepared attack on American bases, insisted that:

"On the other hand, the American Government, always holding fast to theories in disregard of realities and refusing to yield an inch on its impractical principles, caused undue delay in the [peace] negotiations."

Late last night, the United States Government announced that all American republics had been informed of the "treacherous attack" by Japan. It was stated that "very heartening messages of support" were being received in return.

The State Department statement on this matter said:

"All the American republics have been informed by the Government of the United States of the treacherous attack by Japan upon the United States. Immediately upon receipt of word of the attacks on Hawaii and other American territories, wires were dispatched to the American diplomatic missions, instructing them to inform the Foreign Offices at once. This government is receiving very heartening messages of support from the other American republics."

Senator Connally, as head of the powerful Foreign Relations Committee, predicted that world-wide war involving this nation probably depended on European developments within the next few days, according to The United Press.

Connally Promises Reply to "Treachery"

As Roland Young, committee clerk, took to Senator Connally's apartment drafts of the war declaration of April 2, 1917, Mr. Connally said:

"Professing a desire for peace and under the pretext that she coveted amicable relations with us, Japan stealthily concealed under her robe a dagger of assassination and villainy. She attacked us when the two nations were legally at peace.

"With rare and tolerant patience our government has striven to adjust our differences with Japan.

"Japan has now declared war upon the United States and on Great Britain. We shall resist this cruel and unjustifiable assault with naval power and all the resources of our country. We shall wreak the vengeance of justice on these violators of peace, these assassins who attack without warning and these betrayers of treaty obligations and responsibilities of international law.

"Let the Japanese Ambassador go back to his masters and tell them that the United States answers Japan's challenge with steel-throated cannon and a sharp sword of retribution. We shall repay this dastardly treachery with multiplied bombs from the air and heaviest and accurate shells from the sea."

Late last night American officers at the Mexican border were detaining all Japanese attempting to enter or leave the United States, according to a United Press dispatch from San Diego.

New York City, Chicago and other police forces acted to control Japanese nationals and with regard to consulates.

James L. Fly, chairman of the Federal Communications Commission and the Defense Communications Board, said further activity by amateur radio stations would be permitted only upon special governmental authorization.

He said he has been in constant touch with heads of all important communications companies with relation to execution of pre-existing plans for cooperation during any emergency.

†BENNION, MERVYN SHARP

Rank and Organization: Captain, U.S. Navy.
Born: May 5, 1887, Vernon, Utah.
Entered Service At: Utah.
Place and Date: Pearl Harbor, December 7, 1941.
Citation: For conspicuous devotion to duty, extraordinary courage, and complete disregard of his own life, above and beyond the call of duty, during the attack on the Fleet in Pearl Harbor, by Japanese forces on December 7, 1941. As Commanding Officer of the U.S.S. *West Virginia,* after being mortally wounded, Capt. Bennion evidenced apparent concern only in fighting and saving his ship, and strongly protested against being carried from the bridge.

†CANNON, GEORGE HAM

Rank and Organization: First Lieutenant, U.S. Marine Corps.
Born: November 5, 1915, Webster Groves, Missouri.
Entered Service At: Michigan.
Place and Date: Sand Island, Midway Islands, December 7, 1941.
Citation: For distinguished conduct in the line of his profession, extraordinary courage, and disregard of his own condition during the bombardment of Sand Island, Midway Islands, by Japanese forces on December 7, 1941. 1st Lt. Cannon, Battery Commander of Battery H, 6th Defense Battalion, Fleet Marine Force, U.S. Marine Corps, was at his command post when he was mortally wounded by enemy shell fire. He refused to be evacuated from his post until after his men who had been wounded by the same shell were evacuated, and directed the reorganization of his command post until forcibly removed. As a result of his utter disregard of his own condition he died from loss of blood.

FINN, JOHN WILLIAM
Rank and Organization: Lieutenant, U.S. Navy.
Born: July 23, 1909, Los Angeles, California.
Entered Service At: California.
Place and Date: Naval Air Station, Kaneohe Bay, Territory of Hawaii, December 7, 1941.
Citation: For extraordinary heroism, distinguished service, and devotion above and beyond the call of duty. During the first attack by Japanese airplanes on the Naval Air Station, Kaneohe Bay, on December 7, 1941, Lt. Finn promptly secured and manned a .50-caliber machinegun mounted on an instruction stand in a completely exposed section of the parking ramp, which was under heavy enemy machinegun strafing fire. Although painfully wounded many times, he continued to man this gun and to return the enemy's fire vigorously and with telling effect throughout the enemy strafing and bombing attacks and with complete disregard for his own personal safety. It was only by specific orders that he was persuaded to leave his post to seek medical attention. Following first-aid treatment, although obviously suffering much pain and moving with great difficulty, he returned to the squadron area and actively supervised the rearming of returning planes. His extraordinary heroism and conduct in this action were in keeping with the highest traditions of the U.S. Naval Service.

†FLAHERTY, FRANCIS C.
Rank and Organization: Ensign, U.S. Naval Reserve.
Born: March 15, 1919, Charlotte, Michigan.
Entered Service At: Michigan.
Place and Date: Pearl Harbor, December 7, 1941.
Citation: For conspicuous devotion to duty, extraordinary courage, and complete disregard for his own life above and beyond the call of duty, during the attack on the Fleet in Pearl harbor by Japanese forces on December 7, 1941. When it was seen that the U.S.S. *Oklahoma* was going to capsize and the order was given to abandon ship, Ensign Flaherty remained in a turret, holding a flashlight so the remainder of the turret crew could see to escape, thereby sacrificing his own life.

FUQUA, SAMUEL GLENN
Rank and Organization: Captain (then Lt. Commander), U.S. Navy, U.S.S. *Arizona*.
Born: October 15, 1899, Laddonia, Missouri.
Entered Service At: Laddonia, Missouri.

Place and Date: Pearl Harbor, Territory of Hawaii, December 7, 1941.
Citation: For distinguished conduct in action, outstanding heroism, and utter disregard for his own safety above and beyond the call of duty during the attack on the Fleet in Pearl Harbor by Japanese forces on December 7, 1941. Upon the commencement of the attack, Lt. Commander Fuqua rushed to the quarterdeck of the U.S.S. *Arizona*, to which he was attached, where he was stunned and knocked down by the explosion of a large bomb which hit the quarterdeck, penetrated several decks, and started a severe fire. Upon regaining consciousness, he began to direct the fighting of the fire and the rescue of the wounded and injured personnel. Almost immediately there was a tremendous explosion forward, which made the ship appear to rise out of the water, shudder, and settle down by the bow rapidly. The whole forward part of the ship was enveloped in flames which were spreading rapidly and wounded and burned men were pouring out of the ship to the quarterdeck. Despite these conditions, his harrowing experience, and severe enemy bombing and strafing at the time, Lt. Comdr. Fuqua continued to direct the fighting of fires in order to check them while the wounded and burned could be taken from the ship and supervised the rescue of these men in such an amazingly calm and cool manner and with such excellent judgement that it inspired everyone who saw him and undoubtedly resulted in the saving of many lives. After realizing the ship could not be saved and that he was the senior surviving officer aboard, he directed it to be abandoned, but continued to remain on the quarterdeck and directed abandoning ship and rescue of personnel until satisfied that all personnel that could be had been saved, after which he left his ship with the last boatload. The conduct of Lt.Comdr. Fuqua was not only in keeping with the highest traditions of the naval service but characterizes him as an outstanding leader of men.

†**HILL, EDWIN JOSEPH**
Rank and Organization: Chief Boatswain, U.S. Navy.
Born: October 4, 1894, Philadelphia, Pennsylvania.
Entered Service At: Pennsylvania.
Place and Date: Pearl Harbor, December 7, 1941.
Citation: For distinguished conduct in the line of his profession, extraordinary courage, and disregard of his own safety during the attack on the Fleet in Pearl Harbor, by Japanese forces on December 7, 1941. During the height of the strafing and bombing, Chief Boatswain Hill led his men of the line-handling details of the U.S.S. *Nevada* to the quays, cast off the lines and swam back to his ship. Later, while on the forecastle, attempting to go to

the anchors, he was blown overboard and killed by the explosion of several bombs.

†JONES, HERBERT CHARPOIT
Rank and Organization: Ensign, U.S. Naval Reserve.
Born: December 1, 1918, Los Angeles, California.
Entered Service At: California.
Place and Date: Pearl Harbor, December 7, 1941.
Citation: For conspicuous devotion to duty, extraordinary courage, and complete disregard for his own life above and beyond the call of duty during the attack on the Fleet in Pearl Harbor, by Japanese forces on December 7, 1941. Ens. Jones organized and led a party which was supplying ammunition to the antiaircraft battery of the U.S.S. *California,* after the mechanical hoists were put out of action, when he was fatally wounded by a bomb explosion. When 2 men attempted to take him from the area which was on fire, he refused to let them do so, saying in words to the effect, "Leave me alone! I am done for. Get out of here before the magazines go off."

†KIDD, ISAAC CAMPBELL
Rank and Organization: Rear Admiral, U.S. Navy.
Born: March 26, 1884, Cleveland, Ohio.
Entered Service At: Ohio.
Place and Date: Pearl Harbor, December 7, 1941.
Citation: For conspicuous devotion to duty, extraordinary courage, and complete disregard of his own life, during the attack on the Fleet in Pearl Harbor, by Japanese forces on December 7, 1941. Rear Adm. Kidd immediately went to the bridge and, as Commander Battleship Division One, courageously discharged his duties as Senior Officer Present Afloat until the U.S.S. *Arizona,* his Flagship, blew up from magazine explosions and a direct bomb hit on the bridge which resulted in the loss of his life.

PHARRIS, JACKSON CHARLES
Rank and Organization: Lieutenant, U.S. Navy, U.S.S. *California.*
Born: June 26, 1912, Columbus, Georgia.
Entered Service At: California.
Place and Date: Pearl Harbor, Territory of Hawaii, December 7, 1941.
Citation: For conspicuous gallantry and intrepidity at the risk of his life above and beyond the call of duty while attached to the U.S.S. *California*

during the surprise Japanese aerial attack on Pearl Harbor December 7, 1941. In charge of the ordnance repair party on the third deck when the first Japanese torpedo struck almost directly under his station, Lt. (then Gunner) Pharris was stunned and severely injured by the concussion which hurled him to the overhead and back to the deck. Quickly recovering, he acted on his own initiative to set up a hand-supply ammunition train for the antiaircraft guns. With water and oil rushing in where the port bulkhead had been torn up from the deck, with many of the remaining crewmembers overcome by oil fumes, and the ship without power and listing heavily to the port as a result of a second torpedo hit, Lt. Pharris ordered the shipfitters to counterflood. Twice rendered unconscious by the nauseous fumes and handicapped by his painful injuries, he persisted in his desperate efforts to speed up the supply of ammunition and at the same time repeatedly risked his life to enter flooding compartments and drag to safety unconscious shipmates who were gradually being submerged in oil. By his inspiring leadership, his valiant efforts, and his extreme loyalty to his ship and her crew, he saved many of his shipmates from death and was largely responsible for keeping the *California* in action during the attack. His heroic conduct throughout this first eventful engagement of World War II reflects the highest credit upon Lt. Pharris and enhances the finest traditions of the U.S. Naval Service.

†**REEVES, THOMAS JAMES**
Rank and Organization: Radio Electrician (Warrant Officer), U.S. Navy.
Born: December 9, 1895, Thomaston, Connecticut.
Entered Service At: Connecticut.
Place and Date: Pearl Harbor, December 7, 1941.
Citation: For distinguished conduct in the line of his profession, extraordinary courage and disregard for his own safety during the attack on the Fleet in Pearl Harbor, by Japanese forces on December 7, 1941. After the mechanized ammunition hoists were put out of action on the U.S.S. *California*, Warrant Officer Reeves, on his own initiative, in a burning passageway, assisted in the maintenance of an ammunition supply by hand to the antiaircraft guns until he was overcome by smoke and fire, which resulted in his death.

ROSS, DONALD KIRBY
Rank and Organization: Machinist, U.S. Navy, U.S.S. *Nevada*.
Born: December 8, 1910, Beverly, Kansas.
Entered Service At: Denver, Colorado.

Place and Date: Pearl Harbor, Territory of Hawaii, December 7, 1941.

Citation: For distinguished conduct in the line of his profession, extraordinary courage, and disregard for his own life during the attack on the Fleet in Pearl Harbor, by Japanese forces on December 7, 1941. When his station in the forward dynamo room of the U.S.S. *Nevada* became almost untenable due to smoke, steam, and heat, Machinist Ross forced his men to leave that station and performed all the duties himself until blinded and unconscious. Upon being rescued and resuscitated, he returned and secured the forward dynamo room where he was later again rendered unconscious by exhaustion. Again recovering consciousness he returned to his station where he remained until directed to abandon it.

†SCOTT, ROBERT R.

Rank and Organization: Machinist's Mate First Class, U.S. Navy.
Born: July 13, 1915, Massillon, Ohio.
Entered Service At: Ohio.
Place and Date: Pearl Harbor, December 7, 1941.

Citation: For conspicuous devotion to duty, extraordinary courage, and complete disregard of his own life, above and beyond the call of duty during the attack on the Fleet in Pearl Harbor by Japanese forces on December 7, 1941. The compartment, on the U.S.S. *California,* in which the air compressor to which Scott was assigned as his battle station, was flooded as a result of a torpedo hit. The remainder of the personnel evacuated that compartment but Scott refused to leave, saying words to the effect "This is my station and I will stay and give them air as long as the guns are going."

†TOMICH, PETER

Rank and Organization: Chief Watertender, U.S. Navy.
Born: June 3, 1893, Prolog, Austria.
Entered Service At: New Jersey.
Place and Date: Pearl Harbor, December 7, 1941.

Citation: For distinguished conduct in the line of his profession, and extraordinary courage and disregard for his own safety, during the attack on the Fleet in Pearl Harbor by Japanese forces on December 7, 1941. Although realizing that the ship was capsizing, as a result of enemy bombing and torpedoing, Tomich remained at his post in the engineering plant of the U.S.S. *Utah,* until he saw that all boilers were secured and all fireroom personnel had left their stations, and by so doing lost his own life.

†VAN VALKENBURGH, FRANKLIN
Rank and Organization: Captain, U.S. Navy.
Born: April 5, 1888, Minneapolis, Minnesota.
Entered Service At: Wisconsin.
Place and Date: Pearl Harbor, December 7, 1941.
Citation: For conspicuous devotion to duty, extraordinary courage, and complete disregard of his own life, during the attack on the Fleet in Pearl Harbor by Japanese forces on December 7, 1941. As commanding officer of the U.S.S. *Arizona,* Capt. Van Valkenburgh gallantly fought until his ship the U.S.S. *Arizona* blew up from magazine explosions and a direct bomb hit on the bridge which resulted in the loss of his life.

†WARD, JAMES RICHARD
Rank and Organization: Seaman First Class. U.S. Navy.
Born: September 10, 1921, Springfield, Ohio.
Entered Service At: Springfield, Ohio.
Place and Date: Pearl Harbor, December 7, 1941.
Citation: For conspicuous devotion to duty, extraordinary courage, and complete disregard for his own life, above and beyond the call of duty during the attack on the Fleet in Pearl Harbor by Japanese forces on December 7, 1941. When it was seen that the U.S.S. *Oklahoma* was going to capsize and the order was given to abandon ship, Ward remained in the turret holding a flashlight so the remainder of the turret crew could see to escape, thereby sacrificing his own life.

YOUNG, CASSIN
Rank and Organization: Commander, U.S. Navy.
Born: March 6, 1894, Washington, D.C.
Entered Service At: Wisconsin.
Other Navy Award: Navy Cross.
Place and Date: Pearl Harbor, December 7, 1941.
Citation: For distinguished conduct in action, outstanding heroism, and utter disregard for his own safety, above and beyond the call of duty, as commanding officer of the U.S.S. *Vestal*, during the attack on the Fleet in Pearl Harbor by Japanese forces on December 7, 1941. Comdr. Young proceeded to the bridge and later took personal command of the 3-inch antiaircraft gun. When blown overboard by the blast of the forward magazine explosion of the U.S.S. *Arizona*, to which the U.S.S. *Vestal* was moored, he swam back to his ship. The entire forward part of the U.S.S. *Arizona* was a

blazing inferno with oil afire on the water between the 2 ships; as a result of bomb hits, the U.S.S. *Vestal* was afire in several places, was settling and taking on a list. Despite severe enemy bombing and strafing at the time, and his shocking experience of having been blown overboard, Comdr. Young, with extreme calmness and coolness, moved his ship to an anchorage distant from the U.S.S. *Arizona,* and subsequently beached the U.S.S. *Vestal* upon determining that such action was required to save his ship.

Note: The following is a front page newspaper summary of the war:

THE INTERNATIONAL SITUATION

• • •

TUESDAY, DECEMBER 9, 1941
The United States yesterday made a formal declaration of war on Japan after President Roosevelt had addressed a joint session of Congress. The Senate approved by unanimous vote while one woman in the House of Representatives dissented.

In the national effort, the Supply, Priorities and Allocations Board mapped expanding production; leaders of organized labor pledged support, and Mayor La Guardia issued a proclamation giving air raid defense instructions.

In San Francisco, two formations of enemy aircraft were sighted over the city, which was blacked out.

White House announcements indicated that the battle of the Pacific was raging with the United States still on the defensive. There were extensive air attacks in the Philippines, raids on Hong Kong, and a Tokyo report that both Guam and Wake had been put under the Japanese flag. The British were mopping up on a Japanese landing party in Malaya, but Thailand had yielded.

The small detachment of United States Marines at Tientsin and Peiping was disarmed and detained by the Japanese, and they closed the United States Consulate in Shanghai. Imperial Headquarters in Tokyo made sweeping claims of victory in the battle of the Pacific, listing great damage to the United States forces.

In London, Prime Minister Churchill announced Britain's declaration of war to Parliament and made a stirring address to the world.

The American nations began to line up behind the United States. A conference will be held, but seven countries have already declared war on Japan, two have broken diplomatic relations and several others are preparing to act. China decided to declare war not merely on Japan but on Germany and Italy as well. The various European governments in exile also supported the United States. Russia's position is obscure.

The United States accused Germany of having egged Japan on; said lease-lend aid would continue.

Berlin gave out word that Winter had stopped the Germans short of Moscow and that the capture of the Russian capital had been put off until Spring.

In Libya, the Axis armored forces were attacked from three directions by the British and what was expected to be a major engagement was eventually merely a rearguard action.

†ELROD, HENRY TALMAGE

Rank and Organization: Captain, U.S. Marine Corps.
Born: September 27, 1905, Rebecca, Georgia.
Entered Service At: Ashburn, Georgia.
Place and Date: Wake Island, December 8 to 23, 1941.
Citation: For conspicuous gallantry and intrepidity at the risk of his life above and beyond the call of duty while attached to Marine Fighting Squadron 211, during action against enemy Japanese land, surface and aerial units at Wake Island, Dec. 8 to 23, 1941. Engaging vastly superior forces of enemy bombers and warships on December 9 and 12, Capt. Elrod shot down 2 of a flight of 22 hostile planes and, executing repeated bombing and strafing runs at extremely low altitude and close range, succeeded in inflicting deadly damage upon a large Japanese vessel, thereby sinking the first major warship to be destroyed by small-caliber bombs delivered from a fighter-type aircraft. When his plane was disabled by hostile fire and no other ships were operative, Capt. Elrod assumed command of one flank of the line set up in defiance of the enemy landing and, conducting a brilliant defense, enabled his men to hold their positions and repulse intense hostile fusillades to provide covering fire for unarmed ammunition carriers. Capturing an automatic weapon during one enemy rush in force, he gave his own firearm to one of his men and fought on vigorously against the Japanese. Responsible in a large measure for the strength of his sector's gallant resistance, on December 23, Capt. Elrod led his men with bold aggressiveness until he fell, mortally wounded. His superb skill as a pilot, daring leadership, and unswerving devotion to duty distinguished him among the defenders of Wake Island, and his valiant conduct reflects the highest credit upon himself and the U.S. Naval Service. He gallantly gave his life for his country.

OFFICIAL COMMUNIQUE:
United States
WASHINGTON, Dec. 23 – War Department Communique No. 24, outlining the military situation as of 9:30 A.M., follows:

1. Philippine theater:
Combat operations are continuing with increasing intensity along the eastern shore
of Lingayen Gulf, north of Damortis. A major engagement is being fought in the
vicinity of Santo Tomas, where defending American Philippine troops have attained some initial successes.

Japanese troops are continuing to land between Agoo and San Fernando. Landing operations are being supported by increasing numbers of bombing and attack
planes.

There were air raids of a minor character over other portions of Luzon.

Fighting is continuing in the vicinity of Davao on the island of Mindanao.
2. There is nothing to report from other areas.

*War Department Communique No. 25, outlining the military situation as of 5
P.M., follows:*

1. Philippine theater:
The commanding general of the United States Army forces in the Far East reports
that fighting on the eastern shore of Lingayen Gulf is increasing in intensity. Japanese invaders are using light tanks in vigorous attacks south of Agoo. Enemy planes
have been particularly active in supporting landing and shore operations.
American Army bombing planes attacked several enemy troop ships off Davao
with undetermined results.
2. There is nothing to report from other areas.

Navy Communique No. 16, covering the situation up to 9 A.M., follows:

Atlantic Theater - There are no new developments to report.
Pacific Theater - Two United States merchant ships were attacked by enemy submarines off the Pacific Coast. Both attacks were unsuccessful.
Central Pacific - Wake Island sustained another strong air attack in the forenoon of
the 22nd. Several enemy planes were shot down. An enemy force effected a landing on Wake the morning of the 23rd.
Far East - Japanese claims of seizure of a large number of American merchant
vessels are without foundation. The only United States merchant vessel known to
have been seized by the Japanese is the steamship President Harrison.

*MANILA, Dec. 23 - Army Headquarters issued this communique at 4:19 P.M.
today:*

Fighting continues on the Northern Front, but there has been no material change in
positions. The enemy has been very active in the air. The situation of Davao is still
obscure.

CHAPTER 2

1942

MacARTHUR, DOUGLAS
Rank and Organization: General, U.S. Army, commanding U.S. Army Forces in the Far East.
Born: Little Rock, Arkansas.
Entered Service At: Ashland, Wisconsin.
Place and Date: Bataan Peninsula, Philippine Islands, late 1941 to early 1942.
Citation: For conspicuous leadership in preparing the Philippine Islands to resist conquest, for gallantry and intrepidity above and beyond the call of duty in action against invading Japanese forces, and for the heroic conduct of defensive and offensive operations on the Bataan Peninsula. He mobilized, trained, and led an army which has received world acclaim for its gallant defense against a tremendous superiority of enemy forces in men and arms. His utter disregard of personal danger under heavy fire and bombardment, his calm judgement in each crisis, inspired his troops, galvanized the spirit of resistance of the Filipino people, and confirmed the faith of the American people in their Armed Forces.

†NININGER, ALEXANDER R., JR.
Rank and Organization: Second Lieutenant, U.S. Army, 57th Infantry, Philippine Scouts.
Born: Gainesville, Georgia.
Entered Service At: Fort Lauderdale, Florida.
Place and Date: Near Abucay, Bataan, Philippine Islands, January 12, 1942.
Citation: For conspicuous gallantry and intrepidity above and beyond the call of duty in action with the enemy near Abucay, Bataan, Philippine Islands, on January 12, 1942. This officer, though assigned to another company not then engaged in combat, voluntarily attached himself to Com-

pany K, same regiment, while that unit was being attacked by enemy forces superior in firepower. Enemy snipers in trees and foxholes had stopped a counterattack to regain part of its position. In hand-to-hand fighting which followed, 2d Lt. Nininger repeatedly forced his way to and into the hostile position. Though exposed to heavy enemy fire, he continued to attack with rifle and handgrenades and succeeded in destroying several enemy groups in foxholes and enemy snipers. Although wounded 3 times, he continued his attacks until he was killed after pushing alone far within the enemy position. When his body was found after recapture of the position, 1 enemy officer and 2 enemy soldiers lay dead around him.

OFFICIAL COMMUNIQUE:
United States
WASHINGTON, Jan, 12 – The following communique, based on reports received up to 9:30 A.M., was issued by the War Department today:

Philippine theatre:
A heavy artillery battle is in progress along the entire front. Ground activity is increasing as fresh Japanese troops move into front-line position. Enemy air attacks are being renewed on defensive installations and fortifications.

General MacArthur reports that Japanese troops occupying Manila are attempting to suppress the use of radio receiving sets by civilians. This apparently is designed to prevent the reception of broadcasts from the United States and England, even though the action also prevents reception of propaganda broadcasts from Tokyo.

There is nothing to report from other areas.

A later War Department communique, as of 5 P.M., said:

Alaska – The War Department was advised today of the destruction by fire in Alaskan waters of the United States transport Clevedon. The ship and cargo were a total loss. All of the personnel are safe. The Clevedon was a combination passenger and freight vessel of 7,314 tons. The cause of the fire is being investigated.
Hawaii – The commanding general of the Hawaiian Department has advised that of the 397 American soldiers wounded in the Japanese attack, fifty-five have fully recovered and have returned to duty. The condition of most of the others is very satisfactory and their early recovery is expected.

There is nothing to report from other areas.

CALUGAS, JOSE

Rank and Organization: Sergeant, U.S. Army, Battery B, 88th Field Artillery, Philippine Scouts.

Born: December 29, 1907, Barrio Tagsing, Leon, Iloilp, Philippine Islands.

Entered Service At: Fort Stotsenburg, Philippine Islands.

Place and Date: At Culis, Bataan Province, Philippine Islands, January 16, 1942.

Citation: The action for which the award was made took place near Culis, Bataan Province, Philippine Islands, on January 16, 1942. A battery gun position was bombed and shelled by the enemy until 1 gun was put out of commission and all the cannoneers were killed or wounded. Sgt. Calugus, a mess sergeant of another battery, voluntarily and without orders ran 1,000 yards across the shell-swept area to the gun position. There he organized a volunteer squad which placed the gun back in commission and fired effectively against the enemy, although the position remained under constant and heavy Japanese artillery fire.

OFFICIAL COMMUNIQUE:

United States

WASHINGTON, Jan. 16 – The War Department issued the following communique today, based on reports received up to 9:30 A.M.:

1. Philippine theatre:
Ground fighting of varying intensity continues all along the front line. Enemy shock troops with special training are attempting aggressive infiltration. Attack planes and dive-bombers are being used incessantly by the Japanese against our front-line troops and artillery positions.

Many reports reaching General MacArthur's headquarters from the occupied areas indicate that the enemy is systematically looting and devastating the entire countryside.

2. There is nothing to report from other areas.

A Navy Department communique, as of 9 A.M., said:

1. Far East-Units of the united States Asiatic Fleet report the sinking of five enemy vessels in Far Eastern waters. They include two large cargo ships, two large transports and one medium-sized transport. These sinkings are in addition to enemy casualties at sea previously reported.

Atlantic Area – The submarine situation along the northeast coast of the United States remains unchanged.

†BIANCHI, WILLIBALD C.

Rank and Organization: First Lieutenant, U.S. Army, 45th Infantry, Philippine Scouts.
Born: New Ulm, Minnesota.
Entered Service At: New Ulm, Minnesota.
Place and Date: Near Bagac, Bataan Province, Philippine Islands, February 3, 1942.
Citation: For conspicuous gallantry and intrepidity above and beyond the call of duty in action with the enemy on February 3, 1942, near Bagac, Province of Bataan, Philippine Islands. When the rifle platoon of another company was ordered to wipe out 2 strong enemy machinegun nests, 1st Lt. Bianchi voluntarily and of his own initiative, advanced with the platoon leading part of the men. When wounded early in the action by 2 bullets through the left hand, he did not stop for first aid but discarded his rifle and began firing a pistol. He located a machinegun nest and personally silenced it with grenades. When wounded the second time by 2 machinegun bullets through the chest muscles, 1st Lt. Bianchi climbed to the top of an American tank, manned its antiaircraft machinegun, and fired into strongly held enemy positions until knocked completely off the tank by a third severe wound.

OFFICIAL COMMUNIQUE:
United States
WASHINGTON, Feb. 3 – The War Department communique, based on reports received up to 9:30 A.M., follows:

1. Philippine theater:
Two Japanese attempts to land troops on the west coast of Bataan were broken up during the night of Feb. 2.

The first raid by the Tatori group of special shock troops was made early in the evening. This was frustrated by our artillery fire.

A second and more serious attempt was made at midnight. A large number of barges under naval escort approached the coast. The raid was discovered by a few of our night flying pursuit planes, which immediately attacked the convoy with light bombs and machine-gun fire.

As the enemy troops approached the shore our beach defense force attacked with artillery and machine guns. The Japanese force suffered heavy casualties in men and boats. On the following morning a number of disabled barges were found along the beaches. Some of these were burning and others were adrift. None of the invading group reached shore.

Ground operations on our left flank were of a minor character. The frontal pressure of the Japanese Sixteenth (Kimura) Division in this sector relaxed.

Some enemy pockets were found where isolated groups of Japanese soldiers are being mopped up.

On our right, where General Nara's Sixty-fifth Division had previously attempted, by a frontal attack, to drive a wedge between our forces, we made a successful counter-attack. Our troops overran three lines of enemy trenches, capturing considerable equipment.

During the past twenty-four hours there has been moderate enemy air activity in support of ground action.

In the recent fighting in the Philippines Brig. Gen. Clinton A. Pierce, United States Army, was slightly wounded in action.

2. There is nothing to report from other areas.

The Navy Department communique, based on reports up to 5 P.M., follows:

1. A motor torpedo boat of Admiral Hart's Far Eastern Command is believed to have torpedoed an enemy warship in night action inside Manila Bay. Although under heavy fire of the warship's guns and in the full glare of her searchlights, the motor torpedo boat managed to fire two torpedoes and to survive the action without being hit.

2. A naval battalion composed of bluejackets and Marines has been organized and is fighting on Bataan Peninsula with General MacArthur's command.

3. The U.S.S. Neches, a naval tanker, has been torpedoed and sunk by an enemy submarine. One hundred and twenty-six members of the crew have reached port safely. Fifty-six men are as yet unaccounted for.

O'HARE, EDWARD HENRY
Rank and Organization: Lieutenant, U.S. Navy.
Born: March 13, 1914, St. Louis, Missouri.
Entered Service At: St. Louis, Missouri.
Other Navy Awards: Navy Cross, Distinguished Flying Cross with 1 gold star.
Place and Date: In the Pacific Theater, February 20, 1942.
Citation: For conspicuous gallantry and intrepidity in aerial combat, at grave risk of his life above and beyond the call of duty, as section leader and pilot of Fighting Squadron 3 on February 20, 1942. Having lost the assistance of his teammates, Lt. O'Hare interposed his plane between his ship and an advancing enemy formation of 9 attacking twin-engine heavy bombers. Without hesitation, alone and unaided, he repeatedly attacked

this enemy formation, at close range in the face of intense combined machinegun and cannon fire. Despite this concentrated opposition, Lt. O'Hare, by his gallant and courageous action, his extremely skillful marksmanship in making the most out of every shot of his limited amount of ammunition, shot down 5 enemy bombers and severely damaged a sixth before they reached the bomb release point. As a result of his gallant action – one of the most daring, if not the most daring, single action in the history of combat aviation – he undoubtedly saved his carrier from serious damage.

Note: Chicago's O'Hare Airport is named after Lt. O'Hare.

OFFICIAL COMMUNIQUE:
United States
WASHINGTON, Feb. 20 – The War Department communique based on reports received up to 9:30 A.M. follows:

1. Philippine Theater:
Positional fighting continues on all sections of the front in Bataan. Enemy airplanes dropped a number of incendiary bombs on installations behind our lines. An examination of these bombs discloses that the Japanese are using white phosphorus as an incendiary filler.
General MacArthur, in behalf of his troops, has acknowledged with appreciation the cordial greeting transmitted to him by 60,000 arsenal employees of the Ordnance Department of the Army in the United States.
2. There is nothing to report from other areas.

United Nations
BATAVIA, Netherlands Indies, Feb. 20 (AP) – A communique from the United Nations Southwest Pacific command said today:

Enemy air attacks on Surabaya Feb. 18 and 19 were intercepted by our fighters which shot down a total of five bombers and five fighters.

Four more fighters were shot down by Allied aircraft which were carrying out attacks on enemy shipping off Bali.

In the course of the attacks three direct hits were scored on one or more enemy cruisers, two direct hits on transport ships and eight near misses on a destroyer.

There also were direct hits with lighter bombs on a cruiser and a transport ship.

All our aircraft returned safely from Far East operations.

†ROOKS, ALBERT HAROLD
Rank and Organization: Captain, U.S. Navy.
Born: December 29, 1891, Colton, Washington.
Entered Service At: Washington.
Place and Date: The Pacific Theater, February 4 to 27, 1942.
Citation: For extraordinary heroism, outstanding courage, gallantry in action and distinguished service in the line of his profession, as Commanding Officer of the *U.S.S. Houston* during the period of February 4 to 27, 1942, while in action with superior Japanese enemy aerial and surface forces. While proceeding to attack an enemy amphibious expedition, as a unit with a mixed force, *Houston* was heavily attacked by bombers; after evading 4 attacks, she was heavily hit in a fifth attack, lost 60 killed and had 1 turret wholly disabled. Capt. Rooks made his ship again seaworthy and sailed within 3 days to escort an important reinforcing convoy from Darwin to Koepang, Timor, Netherlands East Indies. While so engaged, another powerful air attack developed which by *Houston's* marked efficiency was fought off with out much damage to the convoy. The commanding general of all forces in the area thereupon canceled the movement and Capt. Rooks escorted the convoy back to Darwin. Later, while in a considerable American-British-Dutch force engaged with an overwhelming force of Japanese surface ships, *Houston* with *H.M.S. Exeter* carried the brunt of the battle, and her fire alone heavily damaged 1 and possibly 2 heavy cruisers. Although heavily damaged in the actions, Capt. Rooks succeeded in disengaging his ship when the flag officer commanding broke off the action and got her safely away from the vicinity, whereas one-half of the cruisers were lost.

OFFICIAL C0MMUNIQUÉ:
United States
WASHINGTON, Feb. 27 – The text of a War Department communique, based on reports received here up to 9:30 A.M., Eastern war time today, follows:

Philippine Theater - Fighting continues on the Bataan front with light forces engaged on both sides. General MacArthur's troops are holding advance positions which represent gains of from one to eight kilometers along the entire front during the past forty-eight hours. The greatest advance was made on the right of the line north of Pilar. Our troops are being subjected to a relatively light enemy air and artillery attack.

There has been no firing on our fortifications from enemy artillery positions on the Cavite shore for several days.

There is nothing to report from other areas.

The text of another War Department communique, based upon reports received up to 5 P.M., Eastern war time today, follows:

General: In response to inquiries the Secretary of War has authorized the following statement relative to estimated losses inflicted by our Army on Japanese shipping and aircraft:

From Dec. 7, 1941, to date, the American Army Air Force has probably sunk at least nineteen Japanese vessels and seriously damaged thirty-one others. It is particularly difficult to confirm sinking of vessels by aerial action, because the pilots and observers are often at too great an altitude or are flying at too great speed to know in every instance the results of the attack.

In presenting this summary the War Department has included among the vessels probably sunk only those where the observed damage was so great as to leave little doubt as to ultimate destruction. Among those listed as seriously damaged are included only those on which direct hits were scored. It seems likely that some of the vessels so listed were damaged so severely that they might now be considered as lost.

In many cases, near misses were reported during bombing attacks. Some of the resultant explosions may have caused serious damage to ships. However, no estimate of the number of vessels so damaged is included in this report. Many of the enemy transports were sunk before troops had an opportunity to debark, so a heavy loss of life may be presumed.

In addition to the damage inflicted on enemy shipping, our Army Air Force and our anti-aircraft artillery shot down a total of 245 Japanese airplanes. In this total are included only those where the destruction is officially confirmed. Many other airplanes were hit and some of them were last observed smoking and rapidly losing altitude. It seems probable, therefore, that the total enemy losses in aircraft were much greater than the figure given.

It is interesting to note that during the same period the total number of American Army planes shot down by the Japanese was forty-eight. Thus the enemy losses of planes in the air exceeded ours in the ratio of 5 to 1. This is particularly significant in view of the overwhelming numerical superiority of the enemy in practically every encounter. The figures given do not include planes destroyed on the ground. The losses by such destruction were heavy on both sides.

During this same period, the American Volunteer Group serving with the Chinese Army shot down 165 Japanese planes, while losing only thirty-one of their own aircraft. While not officially a part of the American Army, the members of this group are all Americans and are flying American-built planes.

The following is an estimate of losses to enemy shipping inflicted by American Army air attacks:

	Seriously Damaged	Probably Sunk
Battleships	1	1
Cruisers	13	1
Destroyers	2	2
Tankers	0	3
Transports	14	11
Submarines	0	1
Aircraft carriers	1	0
Totals	**31**	**19**

Philippine Theater: General MacArthur has reported to the War Department that he has authorized the expenditure of $10,000,000 in relief finds for immediate distribution to relieve suffering and privation among the families of military personnel in the field. He has set aside the sum of $2,500,000 for the payment of gratuities to widows and orphans of officers and soldiers killed in line of duty, the care and rehabilitation of military personnel permanently disabled, the relief of families of those wounded in action, and of the families of all military personnel who may be in want.

In addition, he has set aside $2,500,000 for gratuities to families of civilians killed or incapacitated by enemy action, the care and rehabilitation of civilians wounded or injured as a result of enemy action, the relief of their families and the reconstruction of homes damaged or destroyed by the enemy.

General MacArthur said his action was inspired by the outstanding loyalty exhibited by Filipinos of all classes, both in occupied and unoccupied areas.

There is nothing to report from other areas.

The text of a Navy Department communique, based upon information up to noon, Eastern war time, today, follows:

Far East: The following submarine commanders have been awarded the Navy Cross in recognition of their especially meritorious conduct during actions with the enemy:

Lieut. Comdr. C.C. Smith, U.S. Navy.
Lieut. Comdr. K.C. Hurd, U.S. Navy.
Lieut. Comdr. W.L. Wright, U.S. Navy.
Lieut. Comdr. M.C. Mumma Jr., U.S. Navy.
Lieut. Comdr. E.B. McKinney, U.S. Navy.
Lieutenant J.C. Dempsey, U.S. Navy.
Lieutenant W.G. Chapple, U.S. Navy.

Citations are not yet available, as the above awards were made in the sphere of action by the commander of United States Naval forces, Southwest Pacific, Vice Admiral William A. Glassford Jr., U.S. Navy.
There is nothing to report from other areas.

ANTRIM, RICHARD NOTT

Rank and Organization: Commander, U.S. Navy.
Born: December 17, 1907, Peru, Indiana.
Entered Service At: Indiana.
Place and Date: Makassar, Celebes, Netherlands East Indies, April 1942.
Citation: For conspicuous gallantry and intrepidity at the risk of his life above and beyond the call of duty while interned as a prisoner of war of the enemy Japanese in the city of Makassar, Celebes, Netherlands East Indies, in April 1942. Acting instantly on behalf of a naval officer who was subjected to a vicious clubbing by a frenzied Japanese guard venting his insane wrath upon the helpless prisoner, Comdr. (then Lt.) Antrim boldly intervened, attempting to quiet the guard and finally persuading him to discuss the charges against the officer. With the entire Japanese force assembled and making extraordinary preparations for the threatened beating, and with the tension heightened by 2,700 Allied prisoners rapidly closing in, Comdr. Antrim courageously appealed to the fanatic enemy, risking his own life in a desperate effort to mitigate the punishment. When the other had been beaten unconscious by 15 blows of a hawser and was repeatedly kicked by 3 soldiers to a point beyond which he could survive, Comdr. Antrim gallantly stepped forward and indicated to the perplexed guards that he would take the remainder of the punishment, throwing the Japanese completely off balance in their amazement and eliciting a roar of acclaim from the suddenly inspired Allied prisoners. By his fearless leadership and valiant concern for the welfare of another, he not only saved the life of a fellow officer and stunned the Japanese into sparing his own life but also brought about a new respect for American officers and men and a great improvement in camp living conditions. His heroic conduct throughout reflects the highest credit upon Comdr. Antrim and the U.S. Naval Service.

BULKELEY, JOHN DUNCAN

Rank and Organization: Lieutenant Commander, Commander of Motor Torpedo Boat Squadron 3, U.S. Navy.
Born: August 19, 1911, New York, New York.
Entered Service At: Texas.

Other Awards: Navy Cross, Distinguished Service Cross, Silver Star, Legion of Merit.

Place and Date: Philippine waters, December 7, 1941 to April 10, 1942.

Citation: For extraordinary heroism, distinguished service, and conspicuous gallantry above and beyond the call of duty as commander of Motor Torpedo Boat Squadron 3, in Philippine waters during the period of December 7, 1941 to April 10, 1942. The remarkable achievement of Lt. Comdr. Bulkeley's command in damaging or destroying a notable number of Japanese enemy planes, surface combatant and merchant ships, and in dispersing landing parties and land-based enemy forces during the 4 months and 8 days of operation without benefit or repairs, overhaul, or maintenance facilities for his squadron, is believed to be without precedent in this type of warfare. His dynamic forcefulness and daring in offensive action, his brilliantly planned and skillfully executed attacks, supplemented by a unique resourcefulness and ingenuity, characterize him as an outstanding leader of men and a gallant and intrepid seaman. These qualities coupled with a complete disregard for his own personal safety reflect great credit upon him and the Naval Service.

OFFICIAL COMMUNIQUE:
United States
WASHINGTON, April 10 – A War Department communique based on reports up to 10 A.M. today said:

1. Philippine Theatre:
General Wainwright reported this morning that all communication between Corregidor and Bataan had been cut off for nearly twenty-four hours. However, it is apparent that fighting on the peninsula has ceased.

The General sent a message to the President in which he expressed his appreciation of the confidence placed in him by his Commander in Chief. He said everything possible had been done to hold Bataan with the limited number of combat soldiers under his command. The overwhelming air and artillery superiority of the Japanese finally overcame the dogged resistance of the hungry and exhausted defenders. General Wainwright declared that our flag still flies on the beleaguered island fortress of Corregidor.

Corregidor was raided frequently throughout April 9 by heavy Japanese bombers. Enemy batteries in Bataan and on the south shore of Manila Bay repeatedly shelled our island forts No material damage resulted. Our guns did not return the fire of the enemy artillery in Bataan, because the exact position of our troops in that area was not known and it was desired to avoid the chance of subjecting them to our own fire.

The enemy apparently is landing troops in Cebu. A fleet of five warships and ten transports is off that island. Our torpedo boats attacked the enemy vessels, sinking a Japanese cruiser.

2. There is nothing to report from other areas.

A Navy Department communique follows:

Philippine area:
Captain K.M. Hoeffel, U.S.N., the senior United States naval officer in the forces defending Bataan Peninsula and Corregidor, acting under the orders of Lieut. Gen. Wainwright, U.S.A., ordered the complete destruction of the previously damaged United States submarine tender Canopus, the Dewey drydock, the minesweeper Bittern and the tug Napa in order to prevent their being of use to the enemy in the event of capture, the Navy Department has been informed. The destruction was ordered when it became apparent that the increasing weight of enemy numbers, combines with the fatigue and exhaustion of our forces, made imminent the fall of Bataan.

These ships and the Dewey drydock were used at and near Corregidor and Bataan Peninsula by the Army, Navy and Marine forces serving under General MacArthur and later under Lieut. Gen. Wainwright in the valiant defense of these vital positions, which control the entrance to Manila Bay.

Southwest Pacific:
A report has just been received that a United States submarine while on patrol in the vicinity of the Celebes Sea sank a large, heavily armed Japanese vessel.

Three torpedo hits were scored on the enemy ship, which is classed either as an auxiliary cruiser or a large tender. This sinking has not been reported in any previous Navy Department communique.

There is nothing to report from other areas.

DOOLITTLE, JAMES H. (Air Mission)
Rank and Organization: Brigadier General, U.S. Army, Air Corps.
Born: Alameda, California.
Entered Service At: Berkeley, California.
Place and Date: Over Japan, April 18, 1942.
Citation: For conspicuous leadership above the call of duty, involving personal valor and intrepidity at an extreme hazard to life. With the apparent certainty of being forced to land in enemy territory or to perish at sea, Gen. Doolittle personally led a squadron of Army bombers, manned by volunteer crews, in a highly destructive raid on the Japanese mainland.

Note: The following is a newspaper account of the preceding battle for which Gen. Doolittle was awarded the Medal of Honor:

MYSTERY IN TOKYO RAID

Flight to Secret China Base After Attack From Carrier Held Possible

The reported bombing of Japan continued yesterday to be a minor mystery of the war, as enemy "explanations" contradicted and modified previous statements and the planes that participated disappeared beyond some "lost horizon" of the Orient.

There seemed to be little doubt that there had been an air raid over Tokyo, Kobe and other cities, although what it had accomplished and how it had been done remained – and may long remain – undisclosed. The Japanese seemed as much confused about the latter point as the American public, and that is one reason why the American public may long remain confused.

For the enemy would give a great deal to know where the bombers came from; if they cannot find out and if the raid should be soon repeated, the bombs dropping on Tokyo might introduce a factor of uncertainty into the calculations of the Japanese High Command.

The first probability – that planes flown from aircraft carriers made the raid – is still a distinct possibility, but later Japanese announcements made it appear that this was no ordinary carrier raid. One Japanese report spoke of three enemy carriers and other naval vessels off the coast of Japan, but at the same time the raiding planes were described – perhaps quite incorrectly –as twin-engine North american B-25 bombers, which are Army planes and are considerably larger and heavier than the single-engine naval bomber types that are operated from carriers.

Three-Carrier Report Doubted

And it seems unlikely that we would, at this stage of the war, risk three carriers in a group on one such operation that could have no decisive effect upon the war's course.

For the United States has a total of only seven regular aircraft carriers (not allowing for possible damaged ships) divided between two oceans; the Japanese probably have at least eight or nine, and hence have clear aircraft carrier superiority in the Pacific.

Moreover, the timing of the attacks – about noon, according to the Japanese announcements – is somewhat later in the day than the usual time of attack by carrier-based planes. ordinarily carrier planes take off at or just before dawn and strike their objective from 200 to 600 miles away in the early morning. Or they attack later in the day, returning to the carrier just before dusk, thus giving the carrier the night hours in which to make good her escape.

But there are bases other than floating ones from which Japan might be attacked. Probably not from the Aleutians; there are no bases on the outer islands, and the hop from Dutch Harbor to Tokyo – 2,835 miles one way, or to Kobe, 3,085 miles – is far too long, unless planes could be refueled at an advanced base somewhere, for a round-trip flight, or even for a one-way flight by planes of the B-25 type.

From Petropavlovsk, Russian base on the Kamchatka Peninsula, to Tokyo, is 1,650 miles; to Kobe, it is 1,830 miles. Vladivostok is within relatively easy bombing range of the same points; it is 680 miles to Tokyo and 650 to Kobe from this russian base in the Maritime provinces. But Russia is not at war with Japan; any air raid from these bases inaugurating war would probably be far heavier than last week's surprise attack appears to have been, and Russian planes, not American, would have participated.

Recalls Secret Bases in China

But the islands of Metropolitan Japan lie on the fringe of a vast and mysterious continent never fully explored. There is room in China and even in Japanese-held Manchukuo for many secret advanced fields, fully as mysterious, fully as well-hidden as those described in James Hilton's "Lost Horizon."

Not long ago the Japanese claimed to have discovered and destroyed at Lishue and Chuhsien in Chungking-controlled China two airfields for long-range bombers, which they claimed were being used by American bombers. These fields are about 1,350 miles from Tokyo and 1,100 from Kobe, but bombers based on them might be able to cut these distances by landing for refueling at improvised advanced bases nearer the coast.

The problem of conducting any continuous raiding from chinese fields would be difficult because of the lack of fighter planes to defend the fields, the lack of anti-aircraft guns, and, above all, the problem of supplying gasoline. China's few oil wells in Kansu and other provinces produce only a slim trickle of the amount of oil needed to supply bomber fleets.

There is another possibility. The B-25 bombers have a wing spread of more than sixty-seven feet, which would mean that they might be able, under certain conditions, to take off from an aircraft carrier, but their considerable weight, their tricycle landing gear and other features would almost certainly prevent them from landing on a carrier's deck.

Carrying a light bomb load, however, they might have been able to take off from a carrier's deck, bomb Japanese cities and wing straight on to secret Chinese bases.

In any case, it seems quite possible that planes based on Chinese fields conducted the first air raid in history upon Metropolitan Japan. If so, it would be retributive justice.

†PETERSON, OSCAR VERNER

Rank and Organization: Chief Watertender, U.S. Navy.
Born: August 27, 1899, Prentice, Wisconsin.
Entered Service At: Wisconsin.
Place and Date: In the Pacific Theater, May 7, 1942.
Citation: For extraordinary courage and conspicuous heroism above and beyond the call of duty while in charge of a repair party during an attack on the U.S.S. *Neosho* by enemy Japanese aerial forces on May 7, 1942. Lacking assistance because of injuries to the other members of his repair party and severely wounded himself, Peterson, with no concern for his own life, closed the bulkhead stop valves and in so doing received additional burns which resulted in his death. His spirit of self-sacrifice and loyalty, characteristic of a fine seaman, was in keeping with the highest traditions of the U.S. Naval Service. He gallantly gave his own life in the service of his country.

WAINWRIGHT, JONATHAN M.

Rank and Organization: General, Commanding U.S. Army Forces in the Philippines.
Born: Walla Walla, Washington.
Entered Service At: Skaneateles, New York.
Place and Date: Philippine Islands, March 12, to May 7, 1942.
Citation: Gen. Wainwright distinguished himself by intrepid and determined leadership against greatly superior enemy forces. At the repeated risk of life above and beyond the call of duty in his position, he frequented the firing line of his troops where his presence provided the example and incentive that helped make the gallant effort of these men possible. The final stand on beleaguered Corregidor, for which he was in an important measure personally responsible, commanded the admiration of the Nation's allies. It reflected the high morale of American arms in the face of overwhelming odds. His courage and resolution were a vitally needed inspiration to the then sorely pressed freedom-loving peoples of the world.

HALL, WILLIAM E.

Rank and Organization: Lieutenant Junior Grade, U.S. Naval Reserve.
Born: October 31, 1913, Storrs, Utah.
Entered Service At: Utah.
Place and Date: Coral Sea, May 7-8, 1942.
Citation: For extreme courage and conspicuous heroism in combat above and beyond the call of duty as pilot of a scouting plane in action against enemy Japanese forces in the Coral Sea on May 7 and 8, 1942. In a resolute and determined attack on May 7, Lt.(jg.) Hall dived his plane at an enemy Japanese aircraft carrier, contributing materially to the destruction of that vessel. On May 8, facing heavy and fierce fighter opposition, he again displayed extraordinary skill as an airman and the aggressive spirit of a fighter in repeated and effectively executed counterattacks against a superior number of enemy planes in which 3 enemy aircraft were destroyed. Though seriously wounded in this engagement, Lt. (jg.) Hall, maintaining the fearless and indomitable tactics pursued throughout these actions, succeeded in landing his plane safe.

†POWERS, JOHN JAMES

Rank and Organization: Lieutenant, U.S. Navy.
Born: July 13, 1912, New York City, New York.
Entered Service At: New York.
Other Navy Award: Air Medal with 1 gold star.
Place and Date: The Coral Sea area, May 4 to 8, 1942.
Citation: For distinguished and conspicuous gallantry and intrepidity at the risk of his life above and beyond the call of duty, while pilot of an airplane of Bombing Squadron 5, Lt. Powers participated, with his squadron, in 5 engagements with Japanese forces in the Coral Sea area and adjacent waters during the period 4 to 8 May 1942. Three attacks were made on enemy objectives at or near Tulagi on May 4. In these attacks he scored a direct hit which instantly demolished a large enemy gunboat or destroyer and is credited with 2 close misses, 1 of which severely damaged a large aircraft tender, the other damaging a 20,000-ton transport. He fearlessly strafed a gunboat, firing all his ammunition into it amid intense antiaircraft fire. The gunboat was then observed to be leaving a heavy oil slick in its wake and later was seen beached on a nearby island. On May 7, an attack was launched against an enemy airplane carrier and other units of the enemy's invasion force. He fearlessly led his attack section of 3 Douglas Dauntless dive bombers, to attack the carrier. On this occasion he dived in the face of heavy antiaircraft fire, to an altitude well below the safety alti-

tude, at the risk of his life and almost certain damage to his own plane, in order that he might positively obtain a hit in a vital part of the ship, which would insure her complete destruction. This bomb hit was noted by many pilots and observers to cause a tremendous explosion engulfing the ship in a mass of flame, smoke, and debris. The ship sank soon after. That evening, in his capacity as Squadron Gunnery Officer, Lt. Powers gave a lecture to the squadron on point-of-aim and diving technique. During this discourse he advocated low release point in order to insure greater accuracy; yet he stressed the danger not only from enemy fire and the resultant low pull-out, but from own bomb blast and bomb fragments. Thus his low-dive bombing attacks were deliberate and premeditated, since he well knew and realized the dangers of such tactics, but went far beyond the call of duty in order to further the cause which he knew to be right. The next morning, May 8, as the pilots of the attack group left the ready room to man planes, his indomitable spirit and leadership were well expressed in his own words, "Remember the folks back home are counting on us. I am going to get a hit if I have to lay it on their flight deck." He led his section of dive bombers down to the target from an altitude of 18,000 feet, through a wall of bursting antiaircraft shells and into the face of enemy fighter planes. Again, completely disregarding the safety altitude and without fear or concern for his safety, Lt. Powers courageously pressed home his attack, almost to the very deck of an enemy carrier and did not release his bomb until he was sure of a direct hit. He was last seen attempting recovery from his dive at the extremely low altitude of 200 feet, and amid a terrific barrage of shell and bomb fragments, smoke, flame, and debris from the stricken vessel.

†RICKETTS, MILTON ERNEST
Rank and Organization: Lieutenant, U.S. Navy.
Born: August 5, 1913, Baltimore, Maryland.
Entered Service At: Maryland.
Place and Date: The Coral Sea, May 8, 1942.
Citation: For extraordinary and distinguished gallantry above and beyond the call of duty as Officer-in-Charge of the Engineering Repair Party of the U.S.S. *Yorktown* in action against enemy Japanese forces in the Battle of the Coral Sea on May 8, 1942. During the severe bombarding of the *Yorktown* by enemy Japanese forces, an aerial bomb passed through and exploded directly beneath the compartment in which Lt. Rickett's battle station was located, killing, wounding or stunning all of his men and mortally wounding him. Despite his ebbing strength, Lt. Ricketts promptly opened the valve of a near-by fireplug, partially led out the firehose and

directed a heavy stream of water into the fire before dropping dead beside the hose. His courageous action, which undoubtedly prevented the rapid spread of fire to serious proportions, and his unflinching devotion to duty were in keeping with the highest traditions of the U.S. Naval Service. He gallantly gave his life for his country.

OFFICIAL COMMUNIQUE:
United States
WASHINGTON, May 8 – A Navy Department communique, based on reports received up to 6 P.M. today, said:

Southwest Pacific:
1. A naval engagement between our forces and those of the Japanese has been in continuous progress in the general area southward of Bismarck Archipelago, in the Coral Sea, since Monday, and there is no indication yet of cessation.
Japanese losses are believed to be:
Sunk – One aircraft carrier, one heavy cruiser, one light cruiser, two destroyers, four gunboats, two transports or cargo vessels.
Damaged – One aircraft carrier, one heavy cruiser, one light cruiser, one seaplane tender, two transports or cargo vessels.
2. Details of losses and damage to our forces are not fully known at present, but no credence should be given to claims that have been or may be put out by Tokyo.
3. There is nothing to report from other areas.

United Nations
AT UNITED NATIONS HEADQUARTERS, Australia, May 8 (AP) – A communique issued here today at 5:53 P.M. [3:53 A.M., E.W.T.], said:

Heavy naval and air fighting continues.
In addition to the previous enemy losses reported our forces have now sunk one enemy aircraft carrier and badly damaged a second, which it is believed will be a total loss.
We have also sunk one heavy cruiser and badly damaged another.
Our own losses are not reported.

Another communique from General MacArthur's headquarters follows:

NEW GUINEA, Louisiade Islands – Allied bombers carried out light attacks on enemy shipping concentrations; one transport was destroyed. Port Moresby – Eight Zero type fighters attacked the airdrome; our fighters intercepted them, destroying one. Lae – Reconnaissance was carried out over the airdrome; our craft were attacked by an enemy fighter, which was shot down.

AT UNITED NATIONS HEADQUARTERS, Australia, Saturday, May 9 – The follwing communique was issued today by General Douglas MacArthur's headquarters:

The great naval and air battle off the northeast coast of Australia has temporarily ceased.

This action represents continued efforts of the Japanese to extend their aggressive conquests toward the south and southeast. First efforts were aimed at expanding Japanese air bases, but our air force consistently and effectively attacked Japanese airfields during the past six weeks, dislocating Japanese plans through destruction of installations and aircraft.

Our reconnaissance, revealed a gradual building up of Japanese naval and transport elements for a coordinated attack by combined forces, which was initiated several days ago.

Our naval forces then attacked in interception. They handled themselves with marked skill and fought with admirable courage and tenacity and the enemy has been repulsed. Our attacks will continue.

†FLEMING, RICHARD E.

Rank and Organization: Captain, U.S. Marine Corps Reserve.
Born: November 1917, St. Paul, Minnesota.
Entered Service At: Minnesota.
Place and Date: Battle of Midway, June 4 and 5, 1942.
Citation: For extraordinary heroism and conspicuous intrepidity above and beyond the call of duty as Flight Officer, Marine Scout-Bombing Squadron 241, during action against enemy Japanese forces in the battle of Midway on June 4 and 5, 1942. When his Squadron Commander was shot down during the initial attack upon an enemy aircraft carrier, Capt. Fleming led the remainder of the division with such fearless determination that he dived his own plane to the perilously low altitude of 400 feet before releasing his bomb. Although his craft was riddled by 179 hits in the blistering hail of fire that burst upon him from Japanese fighter guns and antiaircraft batteries, he pulled out with only 2 minor wounds inflicted upon himself. On the night of June 4, when the squadron commander lost his way and became separated from the others, Capt. Fleming brought his own plane in for a safe landing at its base despite hazardous weather conditions and total darkness. The following day, after less than 4 hours' sleep, he led the second division of his squadron in a coordinated glide-bombing and dive-bombing assault upon a Japanese battleship. Undeterred by a fateful approach glide, during which his ship was struck and set afire, he grimly pressed

home his attack to an altitude of 500 feet, released his bomb to score a near miss on the stern of his target, then crashed to the sea in flames. His dauntless perseverance and unyielding devotion to duty were in keeping with the highest traditions of the U.S. Naval Service.

WAR NEWS SUMMARIZED

• • •

Saturday, June 6, 1942

• • •

United States naval and air forces were apparently victorious in the struggle with the Japanese off Midway Island, but the battle continued, with our forces pursuing the enemy after having inflicted heavy damage on him, Admiral Nimitz announced in his second communique on the action. The Japanese had suffered damage to "several ships" in each of the categories of battleship, carrier, cruiser and transport. American airmen of the three services bore the "brunt of the defense," Admiral Nimitz said. He added that "United States control remains firm in the Midway area."

Far to the southwest, Netherlands and Australian planes under General MacArthur's command sank two and probably three Japanese submarines off Australia's east coast.

An attack by Japanese submarines on British warships in Madagascar's Diego Suarez harbor was acknowledge by the British, but they denied Tokyo claims of damage to a battleship and a cruiser. They said they had suffered no casualties.

The British announced also that the greatest convoy ever sent to India – and possibly the greatest ever to leave Britain – had reached its destination last month without a single casualty.

Behind the walled defenses of Chuhsien, key rail town in Chekiang Province, the Chinese again stood off assaults from three directions by 100,000 Japanese troops and claimed to have inflicted 10,000 casualties in the last two days.

Disclosing that the United States had "authoritative reports" that the Japanese had used poison gas against the Chinese, President Roosevelt warned of American retaliation in full measure if Japan should persist in the practice.

On Europe's western air front, big British bombers were reported to have struck in Germany again last night, after a very heavy daylight offensive by R.A.F. fighters and bombers against Nazi-used ports across the Channel and airfields in France.

On Russia's land front, too, both sides were reported bringing up new forces, while limiting action to local attacks and reconnaissance. But in the air, Soviet dispatches said, russian air forces destroyed at least forty German planes in attacks on Arctic airdromes – bases for Nazi assaults on the supply route to Murmansk.

Germany's reprisal killings for the fatal attacks on Reinhard Heydrich reached a total of 208 with the shooting of thirty more Czechs.

An authoritative source in Washington predicted that the French people would rise in force against their conquerors if a strong second front, led by American troops, should be established in Europe.

†PEASE, HARL, JR.

Rank and organization: Captain, U.S. Army Air Corps, Heavy Bombardment Squadron.
Born: Plymouth, New Hampshire.
Entered Service At: Plymouth, New Hampshire.
Place and Date: Near Rabaul, New Britain, August 6-7, 1942.
Citation: For conspicuous gallantry and intrepidity above and beyond the call of duty in action with the enemy on August 6-7, 1942. When one engine of the bombardment airplane of which he was pilot failed during a bombing mission over New Guinea, Capt. Pease was forced to return to a base in Australia. Knowing that all available airplanes of his group were to participate the next day in an attack on an enemy-held airdrome near Rabaul, New Britain, although he was not scheduled to take part in this mission, Capt. Pease selected the most serviceable airplane at this base and prepared it for combat, knowing that it had been found and declared unserviceable for combat missions. With the members of his combat crew, who volunteered to accompany him, he rejoined his squadron at Port Moresby, New Guinea, at 1 a.m. on August 7, after having flown almost continuously since early the preceding morning. With only 3 hours rest, he took off with his squadron for the attack. Throughout the long flight to Rabaul, New Britain, he managed by skillful flying of his unserviceable airplane to maintain his position in the group. When the formation was intercepted by about 30 enemy fighter airplanes before reaching the target, Capt. Pease, on the wing which bore the brunt of the hostile attack, by gallant action and the accurate shooting by his crew, succeeded in destroying several Zeros before dropping his bombs on the hostile base as planned, this in spite of continuous enemy attacks. The fight with the enemy pursuit lasted 25 minutes until the group dived into cloud cover. After leaving the target, Capt. Pease's aircraft fell behind the balance of the group due to unknown difficulties as a result of the combat, and was unable to reach this cover before

the enemy pursuit succeeded in igniting 1 of his bomb bay tanks. He was seen to drop the flaming tank. It is believed that Capt. Pease's airplane and crew were subsequently shot down in flames, as they did not return to their base. In voluntarily performing this mission Capt. Pease contributed materially to the success of the group, and displayed high devotion to duty, valor, and complete contempt for personal danger. His undaunted bravery has been a great inspiration to the officers and men of his unit.

OFFICIAL COMMUNIQUE:
United States
AT UNITED NATIONS HEADQUARTERS, Australia, Saturday, Aug. 8 – A communique was issued by General Douglas MacArthur's Headquarters today as follows:

Northwestern sector: Allied and enemy air activity was limited to reconnaissance. Northeastern sector:
New Guinea – Lae: Our medium bombers made a strong daylight attack on airdrome dispersal areas with heavy demolition bombs. During the night extended harassing raids continued. All bombs fell in the target area. Direct hits with 2,000-pound bombs were observed on the runway.
Rabaul: Against anti-aircraft fire and fighter interception Allied heavy bombers successfully struck at Vanakanau airdrome. Fifteen tons of bombs hit the target area.

United States
CHUNGKING, China, Aug. 7 – Lieut. Gen. Joseph W. Stillwell's headquarters issued the following communique today:

Yesterday afternoon American bombers with fighter escort attacked the Japanese airdrome at Tienho, near Canton. The Japanese were taken completely by surprise. At least ten aircraft were destroyed on the ground and numerous hits were scored on the runway. All American aircraft returned to their bases. The Japanese attack reported in communique 30 [issued Wednesday] was against Hengyang and not Kweilin.

†THOMASON, CLYDE
Rank and organization: Sergeant, U.S. Marine Corps Reserve.
Born: 23 May 1914, Atlanta, Georgia.
Entered Service At: Georgia.
Place and Date: Makin Island, August 17-18, 1942.

Citation: For conspicuous heroism and intrepidity above and beyond the call of duty during the Marine Raider Expedition against the Japanese-held island of Makin on August 17-18, 1942. Leading the advance element of the assault echelon, Sgt. Thomason disposed his men with keen judgement and discrimination and, by exemplary leadership and great personal valor, exhorted them to like fearless efforts. On 1 occasion, he dauntlessly walked up to a house which concealed an enemy Japanese sniper, forced in the door and shot the man before he could resist. Later in the action, while leading an assault on an enemy position, he gallantly gave his life in the service of his country. His courage and loyal devotion to duty in the face of grave peril were in keeping with the finest traditions of the U.S. Naval Service.

OFFICIAL COMMUNIQUE;
United Nations
HEADQUARTERS, Australia, Aug. 17 – A communique:

Northwestern Sector:
Timor – Our medium bombers attacked an enemy occupied town on the southeast coast. All bombs fell in the target area where a large fire was observed burning. Anti-aircraft fire was encountered. All planes returned to their base.
Northeastern sector:
Kokoda – Patrol skirmishes between small enemy forces and our outguard elements beyond the barrier line of the Owen Stanley range continue.

United States
WASHINGTON, Aug 17 – A Navy Department communique:

South Pacific area:
1. It is now possible to issue some details of the attacks and landing operations which have been in progress in the Solomon Islands since the early morning of Aug 7. (local time).
2. The attacks were a complete surprise to the enemy and eighteen of their seaplanes were destroyed before they could get into action.
3. Transport-borne, amphibious forces of the United States Marine Corps made several landings on islands in the Guadalcanal-Tulagi area. Vigorous enemy resistance was rapidly overcome and a number of Japanese prisoners were taken. The shore positions taken by United States forces have since been developed and are now well established.
4. During these landing operations, cruisers and destroyers were so disposed as to protect our transports and cargo ships as they unloaded troops and equipment.

While thus engaged on Aug. 7 and Aug. 8, our forces were attacked by enemy land-based aircraft. These attacks were driven off and at least eighteen more enemy planes destroyed, while only minor damage was suffered by our forces.

5. During the night of Aug 8-9 an enemy force of cruisers and destroyers attempted to attack supporting forces. This enemy force was intercepted and engaged by our cruisers and destroyers. The heavy fighting which followed resulted in the enemy being forced to retreat before reaching the vessels engaged in the landing operations. The close-range fighting during this night engagement resulted in damage both to the enemy and to our forces. This night action is the only engagement between surface forces which has been fought to date in the Solomon Islands.

6. It is impossible, in night engagements, to determine accurately the damage inflicted on the opposing force. No further statement is made at this time of the extent of damage to our forces because of the obvious value of such information to the enemy.

†BAILEY, KENNETH D.

Rank and Organization: Major, U.S. Marine Corps.
Born: October 21, 1910, Pawnee, Oklahoma.
Entered Service At: Illinois.
Other Navy Awards: Silver Star Medal.
Place and Date: Guadalcanal, Solomon Islands, September 12-13, 1942.
Citation: For extraordinary courage and heroic conduct above and beyond the call of duty as Commanding Officer of Company C, 1st Marine Raider Battalion, during the enemy Japanese attack on Henderson Field, Guadalcanal, Solomon Islands, on September 12-13, 1942. Completely reorganized following the severe engagement of the night before, Major Bailey's company, within an hour after taking its assigned position as reserve battalion between the main line and the coveted airport, was threatened on the right flank by the penetration of the enemy into a gap in the main line. In addition to repulsing this threat, while steadily improving his own desperately held position, he used every weapon at his command to cover the forced withdrawal of the main line before a hammering assault by superior enemy forces. After rendering invaluable service to the battalion commander in stemming the retreat, reorganizing the troops and extending the reserve position to the left, Major Bailey, despite a severe head wound, repeatedly led his troops in fierce hand-to-hand combat for a period of 10 hours. His great personal valor while exposed to constant and merciless enemy fire, and his indomitable fighting spirit inspired his troops to heights of heroic endeavor which enabled them to repulse the enemy and hold Henderson Field. He gallantly gave his life in the service of his country.

EDSON, MERRITT AUSTIN

Rank and Organization: Colonel, U.S. Marine Corps.
Born: April 25, 1897, Rotland, Vermont.
Entered Service At: Vermont.
Other Navy Awards: Navy Cross with Gold Star, Silver Star Medal, Legion of Merit with Gold Star.
Place and Date: Guadalcanal, Solomon Islands, September 13-14, 1942.
Citation: For extraordinary heroism and conspicuous intrepidity above and beyond the call of duty as Commanding Officer of the 1st Marine Raider Battalion, with Parachute Battalion attached, during action against enemy Japanese forces in the Solomon Islands on the night of September 13-14, 1942. After the airfield on Guadalcanal had been seized from the enemy on 8 August, Colonel Edson, with a force of 800 men, was assigned to the occupation and defense of a ridge dominating the jungle on either side of the airport. Facing a formidable Japanese attack which, augmented by infiltration, had crashed through our front lines, he, by skillful handling of his troops, successfully withdrew his forward units to a reserve line with minimum casualties. When the enemy, in a subsequent series of violent assaults, engaged our force in desperate hand-to-hand combat with bayonets, rifles, pistols, grenades, and knives, Col. Edson, although continuously exposed to hostile fire throughout the night, personally directed defense of the reserve position against a fanatical foe of greatly superior numbers. By his astute leadership and gallant devotion to duty, he enabled his men, despite severe losses, to cling tenaciously to their position on the vital ridge, thereby retaining command not only of the Guadalcanal airfield, but also of the 1st Division's entire offensive installations in the surrounding area.

GALER, ROBERT EDWARD

Rank and Organization: Major, U.S. Marine Corps, Marine Fighter Squadron 244.
Born: October 23, 1913, Seattle, Washington.
Entered Service At: Washington.
Other Navy Awards: Navy Cross, Distinguished Flying Cross.
Place: Solomon Islands.
Citation: For conspicuous heroism and courage above and beyond the call of duty as leader of a marine fighter squadron in aerial combat with enemy Japanese forces in the Solomon Islands area. Leading his squadron repeatedly in daring and aggressive raids against Japanese aerial forces, vastly superior in numbers, Major Galer availed himself of every favorable attack

opportunity, individually shooting down 11 enemy bomber and fighter air-craft over a period of 29 days. Though suffering the extreme physical strain attendant upon protracted fighter operations at an altitude above 25,000 feet, the squadron under his zealous and inspiring leadership shot down a total of 27 Japanese planes. His superb airmanship, his outstanding skill and personal valor reflect great credit upon Major Galer's gallant fighting spirit and upon the U.S. Naval Service.

SMITH, JOHN LUCIAN

Rank and Organization: Major, U.S. Marine Corps, Marine Fighting Squadron 223.
Born: December 26, 1914, Lexington, Oklahoma.
Entered Service At: Oklahoma.
Other Navy Award: Legion of Merit.
Place and Date: In the Solomon Islands area, August-September 1942.
Citation: For conspicuous gallantry and heroic achievement in aerial com-bat above and beyond the call of duty as commanding officer of Marine Fighting Squadron 223 during operations against enemy Japanese forces in the Solomon Islands area, August-September 1942. Repeatedly risking his life in aggressive and daring attacks, Major Smith led his squadron against a determined force, greatly superior in numbers, personally shoot-ing down 16 Japanese planes between August 21 and September 15, 1942. In spite of the limited combat experience of many of the pilots of this squad-ron, they achieved the notable record of a total of 83 enemy aircraft de-stroyed in this period, mainly attributable to the thorough training under Major Smith and to his intrepid and inspiring leadership. His bold tactics and indomitable fighting spirit, and the valiant and zealous fortitude of the men of his command not only rendered the enemy's attacks ineffective and costly to Japan, but contributed to the security of our advance base. His loyal and courageous devotion to duty sustains and enhances the finest traditions of the U.S. Naval Service.

Note: The following is a newspaper account of the preceding battle for which Maj. Bailey, Col. Edson, Maj. Galer, and Maj. Smith were awarded the Medal of Honor:

MARINES ATTACKED

• • •

But Foe Loses Twenty Planes in
Three Raids on Guadalcanal
• • •

Allies Blast Buna Base

• • •

Invasion Center in New Guinea Damaged
in Heavy Raid – 17 Aircraft Destroyed

• • •

WASHINGTON, Sept. 12 – Determined Japanese attacks upon United States forces in the Solomon Islands in an effort to recapture positions from which the Americans drove them a month ago were reported in a Navy Department communique issued tonight.

The communique told of heavy attacks by large fleets of Japanese bombers and fighters on American installations in the Guadalcanal-Tulagi area. It told also of heavy toll taken by our own aircraft, a total of twenty Japanese bombers and fighters being shot down during three successive raids by enemy forces on successive days.

[Allied bombers struck one of their heaviest blows in the Pacific by blasting the Japanese invasion base at Buna, Eastern New Guinea, with twenty-six tons of bombs and more than 28,000 rounds of ammunition, a communique reported. At least seventeen enemy planes were destroyed on the ground.]

The attempts of the Japanese to dislodge the American forces obviously have not succeeded but they are continuing with evident strength and ferocity. Naval craft have participated in the enemy offensive, the communique stated, with destroyers shelling our positions at night, but no damage has resulted from naval action.

The extent of damage done by the air raids was not stated. The communique acknowledged the Japanese had been successful in reinforcing their troops in the interior of Guadalcanal, although our Marines, aided by dive bombers and fighters, are engaged in a vigorous campaign against these enemy detachments. Manpower reinforcements and supplies for the Japanese in the interior have been brought ashore in small craft under cover of darkness and the Navy said it "has not been possible to prevent them entirely."

[Detailed accounts of the occupation of islands in the southeastern Solomons by the Marines early in August and of the defeat of the first big Japanese naval counter-attack are contained in delayed dispatches from a correspondent of THE NEW YORK TIMES at sea with the Pacific Fleet, on Pages 46 and 47.]

An attack by American Douglas "Dauntless" dive bombers on Japanese installations on G 120 in the New Georgia group yesterday also was reported. Sinking of a small enemy surface craft was announced and considerable damage to buildings and installations claimed.

The Japanese, the communique said, attacked our positions in the Guadalcanal-Tulagi area in force on Wednesday, Thursday and Friday.

On the first day twenty-six enemy bombers, escorted by Zero fighters, came over our installations at Guadalcanal. American aircraft drove them off, shooting down five bombers and four fighters.

The next day the Japanese returned to the attack, sending over twenty-seven bombers of which our aircraft shot down four.

On the third day the Guadalcanal installations were again the objective of a strong assault by twenty-seven enemy bombers and one fighter.

The American toll of enemy planes officially reported shot down since operations began in the Solomon Islands on Aug. 7 was raised to 143 by the result of the week's raids.

†MUNRO, DOUGLAS ALBERT

Rank and Organization: Signalman First Class, U.S. Coast Guard.
Born: October 11, 1919, Vancouver, British Columbia.
Entered Service At: Washington.
Place and Date: Guadalcanal, Solomon Islands, September 27, 1942.
Citation: For extraordinary heroism and conspicuous gallantry in action above and beyond the call of duty as Petty Officer in Charge of a group of 24 Higgins boats, engaged in the evacuation of a battalion of marines trapped by enemy Japanese forces at Point Cruz, Guadalcanal, on September 27, 1942. After making preliminary plans for the evacuation of nearly 500 beleaguered marines, Munro, under constant strafing by enemy machine guns on the island, and at great risk of his life, daringly led 5 of his small craft toward the shore. As he closed the beach, he signaled the others to land, and then in order to draw the enemy's fire and protect the heavily loaded boats, he valiantly placed his craft with its 2 small guns as a shield between the beachhead and the Japanese. When the perilous task of evacuation was nearly completed, Munro was instantly killed by enemy fire, but his crew, 2 of whom were wounded, carried on until the last boat had loaded and cleared the beach. By his outstanding leadership, expert planning, and dauntless devotion to duty, he and his courageous comrades undoubtedly saved the lives of many who otherwise would have perished. He gallantly gave his life for his country.

OFFICIAL COMMUNIQUE:
United Nations
AT UNITED NATIONS HEADQUARTERS, Australia, Monday, Sept. 28 – A
communique:

Northwestern Sector

Darwin: Two to three enemy aircraft dropped bombs harmlessly in a swamp and in the brush twice during the night.

Northeastern Sector

Buin [Bougainville Island, Solomons]: An Allied medium bomber unit raided the enemy airfield at night with an unknown result.
Rabaul: In night attack against enemy shipping in the harbor an Allied heavy bomber unit scored a direct hit and a near miss on a 15,000 ton merchant vessel. When last sighted, a column of heavy black smoke was seen pouring from the stern and amidship to a height of 300 feet ten minutes after the attack.
Buna-Gona: Allied heavy bombers twice attacked the enemy's base, striking at supply installations, barges and airdrome defenses. Allies fighters strafed enemy supply buildings and sheds with cannon and machine guns, starting fires in the area.
Owen Stanley Area: No change in the ground situation. Allied attack planes bombed and machine-gunned the enemy's supply line with unobserved results.

BASILONE, JOHN
Rank and Organization: Sergeant, U.S. Marine Corps.
Born: November 4, 1916, Buffalo, New York.
Entered Service At: New Jersey.
Other Navy Award: Navy Cross.
Place and Date: Guadalcanal, Solomon Islands, October 24-25, 1942.
Citation: For extraordinary heroism and conspicuous gallantry in action against enemy Japanese forces, above and beyond the call of duty, while serving with the 1st Battalion, 7th Marines, 1st Marine Division in the Lunga Area, Guadalcanal, Solomon Islands, on October 24 and 25, 1942. While the enemy was hammering at the Marines' defensive positions, Sergeant Basilone, in charge of 2 sections of heavy machine guns, fought valiantly to check the savage and determined assault. In a fierce frontal attack with the Japanese blasting his guns with grenades and mortar fire, one of Sergeant Basilone's sections, with its guncrews, was put out of action, leav-

ing only 2 men able to carry on. Moving an extra gun into position, he placed it in action, then, under continual fire, repaired another and personally manned it, gallantly holding his line until replacements arrived. A little later, with ammunition critically low and the supply lines cut off, Sergeant Basilone, at great risk of his life and in the face of continued enemy attack, battled his way through hostile lines with urgently needed shells for his gunners, thereby contributing in large measure to the virtual annihilation of a Japanese regiment. His great personal valor and courageous initiative were in keeping with the highest traditions of the U.S. Naval Service.

PAIGE, MITCHELL
Rank and Organization: Platoon Sergeant, U.S. Marine Corps.
Born: August 31, 1918, Charleroi, Pennsylvania.
Entered Service at: Pennsylvania.
Place and Date: Solomon Islands, October 26, 1942.
Citation: For extraordinary heroism and conspicuous gallantry in action above and beyond the call of duty while serving with a company of marines in combat against enemy Japanese forces in the Solomon Islands on October 26, 1942. When the enemy broke through the line directly in front of his position, Platoon Sergeant Paige, commanding a machine gun section with fearless determination, continued to direct the fire of his gunners until all his men were either killed or wounded. Alone, against the deadly hail of Japanese shells, he fought with his gun and when it was destroyed, took over another, moving from gun to gun, never ceasing his withering fire against the advancing hordes until reinforcements finally arrived. Then, forming a new line, he dauntlessly and aggressively led a bayonet charge, driving the enemy back and preventing a breakthrough in our lines. His great personal valor and unyielding devotion to duty were in keeping with the highest traditions of the U.S. Naval Service.

OFFICIAL COMMUNIQUE:
United Nations
AT UNITED NATIONS HEADQUARTERS, Australia, Monday, Oct. 26 – A communique:

Northwestern Sector

Timor: Allied medium units bombed the airdrome at Koepang at night, starting large fires and dropping their bombs among grounded aircraft.
Darwin: Three enemy aircraft dropped bombs harmlessly near the beach during the night.

Northeastern Sector

Rabaul: In continued support of the general Solomons Islands operations, a strong force of allied heavy bombers again was over this harbor during the (Sunday) night to attack enemy shipping. In the face of intense enemy anti-aircraft searchlight opposition, seventeen tons of bombs were dropped from a low level. A gunboat was seen to sink as a result of a direct hit, and three medium merchant vessels of an estimated aggregate tonnage of 12,000 tons were left listing badly or afire. All were believed to have been destroyed. Fuel barges near wharves were hit and the resultant fires were visible for 100 miles. All our planes returned. This brings the total tonnage by actual observation completely destroyed or badly damaged in this harbor during the past three nights to approximately 80,000 tons. At least 20,000 tons, in addition are believed to have received more or less serious damage.

New Ireland:

Kavieng – In a night attack by allied medium units direct hits were scored on enemy fuel dumps, starting huge fires visible for ninety miles with smoke rising 4,000 feet in the air. Bombs also were dropped on supply dumps, installations and dispersal bays. An enemy four-engine bomber was destroyed on the ground. All our planes returned safely.

New Guinea:

Kokoda – A formation of allied attack planes made a bombing and strafing sweep along the trail north of Isurava. The area south of Wairopi also was bombed. In the Owen Stanley area the situation remained unchanged.

United States
WASHINGTON, Oct. 25 – A Navy Department Communique:

South Pacific

1. During the night of Oct. 22-23 United States long-range aircraft attacked enemy ships in the Shortland Islands area of the Solomon Islands. Bombs and torpedoes inflicted the following damage on enemy vessels:

a. One light cruiser damaged by one direct and one probable torpedo hit.

b. One destroyer damaged by a bomb hit.

c. One heavy cruiser (or battleship) possibly damaged.

All of our planes returned.

2. During the late morning of Oct. 23 our airfield at Guadalcanal was attacked by sixteen enemy bombers escorted by twenty Zero fighters. Our Grumman Wildcats intercepted and shot down one bomber, damaged three others and destroyed the entire fighter escort.

3. During the night of Oct. 23-24, enemy troops, using tanks and heavy artillery barrage, made four attempts to penetrate our western defense lines on Guadalcanal.

Our Army and Marine Corps troops and artillery batteries repulsed each attack and destroyed five enemy tanks.

4. During the early morning of Oct. 24 an additional enemy attack against our western defense lines was broken up by our air-craft and artillery. One United States plane was lost.

5. During the night of Oct. 24-25 United States aircraft attacked an enemy surface force of several cruisers and destroyers about 300 miles northeast of Guadalcanal. One cruiser was reported probably damaged by a torpedo.

6. On Oct. 25:

a. During the morning, troops from enemy transports were landed on the northwest end of Guadalcanal Island. No amplifying report on these operations has been received.

b. During the day Douglas Dauntless dive-bombers from Guadalcanal made three attacks on an enemy force of cruisers and destroyers immediately north of Florida Island. One enemy cruiser was damaged by bombs and the force withdrew.

CASAMENTO, ANTHONY

Rank and Organization: Corporal, U.S. Marine Corps, Company D, First Battalion, Fifth Marines, First Marine Division.
Born: November 16, 1920, Manhattan, New York.
Entered Service At: Manhattan, New York.
Place and Date: Guadalcanal, Solomon Islands, November 1, 1942.
Citation: For conspicuous gallantry and intrepidity at the risk of his life above and beyond the call of duty while serving with Company D, First Battalion, Fifth Marines, First Marine Division on Guadalcanal, British Solomon Islands, in action against the enemy Japanese forces on November 1, 1942. Serving as a leader of a machine gun section, Corporal Casamento directed his unit to advance along a ridge near the Matanikau River where they engaged the enemy. He positioned his section to provide covering fire for two flanking units and to provide direct support for the main force of his company which was behind him. During the course of this engagement, all members of his section were either killed or severely wounded and he himself suffered multiple, grievous wounds. Nonetheless, Corporal Casamento continued to provide critical supporting fire for the attack and in defense of his position. Following the loss of all effective personnel, he set up, loaded, and manned his unit's machine gun, tenaciously holding the enemy forces at bay. Corporal Casamento single-handedly engaged and destroyed one machine gun emplacement to his front and took under fire the other emplacement on the flank. Despite the heat and ferocity of the engagement, he continued to man his weapon and re-

peatedly repulsed multiple assaults by the enemy forces, thereby protecting the flanks of the adjoining companies and holding his position until the arrival of his main attacking force. Corporal Casamento's courageous fighting spirit, heroic conduct, and unwavering dedication to duty reflected great credit upon himself and were in keeping with the highest traditions of the Marine Corps and the United States Naval Service.

OFFICIAL COMMUNIQUE:
United Nations
AT UNITED NATIONS HEADQUARTERS, Australia, Monday, Nov. 2 – A communique:

Northwestern Sector

Buin-Faisi: In continued support of the Solomons operations, two heavy coordinated night attacks were executed by a strong formation of our heavy and medium units against enemy shipping. The attacks were delivered from low altitude in the face of intense anti-aircraft opposition.
Thirty-three tons of bombs were dropped. Accurate observations of the results was difficult, but seven vessels were believed to have been sunk or seriously damaged. One of our planes failed to return.
Lae: Allied medium bombers made a pre-dawn attack on the airdrome, dropping ten tons of bombs areas and dispersal bays, starting fires. A strong force of our attack units, escorted by fighters, was intercepted south of Lae by twenty type Zero fighters. Three enemy fighters were shot down out of control, one by our attack planes and two by our fighters. One of our fighters is missing.
Buna: An Allied medium reconnaissance plane was intercepted by seven Zeros but successfully fought off the enemy fighters without loss.
Port Moresby: Three enemy aircraft lightly raided during the night. There was no damage.
Owen Stanley Area: Our ground forces are continuing the advance and are well beyond Isurava and Abuari.

United States
WASHINGTON, Nov. 1 – A Navy Department communique:

South Pacific

All dates are East Longitude.
1. On Oct. 29:
a. United States aircraft continued attacks on enemy positions on Guadalcanal Island.

b. During minor ground operations two enemy 75-mm. guns were captured west of the Matanikau River.

c. During the late evening a Douglas Dauntless dive-bomber attacked two enemy destroyers near Tassafaronga. No hits were scored but the destroyers were driven westward toward the Russell Islands.

2. On Oct. 30:

a. During the early morning our dive-bombers attacked enemy destroyers in the vicinity of the Russell Islands. Results of the attack have not been reported. One dive-bomber failed to return.

b. During the morning seven Grumman "Wildcats" attacked the enemy at Rekata Bay. Three "Zero" float planes and two biplanes were shot down and building and a fuel dump were strafed and set on fire.

c. During the morning United States surface ships bombarded enemy positions on Guadalcanal. The cannonading lasted more than two hours and some artillery and several buildings and boats were destroyed.

An additional Navy Department communique:

South Pacific

All dates are East Longitude.

1. The first detailed report of the naval air battle which was fought on Oct. 26, to the eastward of the Stewart Islands, was received by the Commander in Chief, United States Fleet, this afternoon from Vice Admiral Halsey, commander of the South Pacific area. In this report the following damage to the enemy was detailed:

a. Four to six heavy bomb hits on an aircraft carrier of the same class.

b. Two medium bomb hits on another aircraft carrier of the same class.

c. Two heavy bomb hits on a battleship of Kongo class.

d. One heavy bomb hit on a second battleship.

e. Five medium bomb hits on a second battleship.

f. Torpedo and bomb hits on a heavy cruiser.

g. Two torpedo hits on a heavy cruiser.

2. Reports indicate the definite destruction of more than 100 enemy aircraft and the probable destruction of fifty others.

3. The above action was first reported in Navy Department Communique No. 169 and subsequent reference was made thereto in Navy Department Communique No. 171.

†CRAW, DEMAS T.
Rank and Organization: Colonel, U.S. Army Air Corps.
Born: April 9, 1900, Traverse City, Michigan.
Entered Service At: Michigan.
Place and Date: Near Port Lyautey, French Morocco, November 8, 1942.
Citation: For conspicuous gallantry and intrepidity in action above and beyond the call off duty. On November 8, 1942, near Port Lyautey, French Morocco, Col. Craw volunteered to accompany the leading wave of assault boats to the shore and pass through the enemy lines to locate the French commander with a view to suspending hostilities. This request was first refused as being too dangerous but upon the officer's insistence that he was qualified to undertake and accomplish the mission he was allowed to go. Encountering heavy fire while in the landing boat and unable to dock in the river because of shell fire from shore batteries, Colonel Craw accompanied by one officer and one soldier, succeeded in landing on the beach at Mehdia Plage under constant low-level strafing from three enemy planes. Riding in a bantam truck toward French headquarters, progress of the party was hindered by fire from our own naval guns. Nearing Port Lyautey, Colonel Craw was instantly killed by a sustained burst of machine gun fire at pointblank range from a concealed position near the road.

WILBUR, WILLIAM H.
Rank and Organization: Colonel, U.S. Army, Western Task Force, North Africa.
Born: Palmer, Massachusetts.
Entered Service At: Palmer, Massachusetts.
Place and Date: Fedala, North Africa, November 8, 1942.
Citation: For conspicuous gallantry and intrepidity in action above and beyond the call of duty. Colonel Wilbur prepared the plan for making contact with French commanders in Casablanca and obtaining an armistice to prevent unnecessary bloodshed. On November 8, 1942, he landed at Fedala with the leading assault waves where opposition had developed into a firm and continuous defensive line across his route of advance. Commandeering a vehicle, he was driven toward the hostile defenses under incessant fire, finally locating a French officer who accorded him passage through the forward positions. He then proceeded in total darkness through 16 miles of enemy occupied country intermittently subjected to heavy bursts of fire, and accomplished his mission by delivering his letters to appropriate French officials in Casablanca. Returning toward his command, Colonel Wilbur detected a hostile battery firing effectively on our troops. He took charge of

a platoon of American tanks and personally led them in an attack and capture of the battery. From the moment of landing until the cessation of hostile resistance. Colonel Wilbur's conduct was voluntary and exemplary in its coolness and daring.

HAMILTON, PIERPONT
Rank and Organization: Major, U.S. Army Air Corps.
Born: August 3, 1898, Tuxedo Park, New York.
Entered Service At: New York, New York.
Place and Date: Near Port Lyautey, French Morocco, November 8, 1942.
Citation: For conspicuous gallantry and intrepidity in action above and beyond the call of duty. On November 8, 1942, near Port Lyautey, French Morocco, Lt. Col. Hamilton volunteered to accompany Col. Demas Craw on a dangerous mission to the French commander, designed to bring about a cessation of hostilities. Driven away from the mouth of the Sebou River by heavy shelling from all sides, the landing boat was finally beached at Mehdia Plage despite continuous machine gun fire from 3 low-flying hostile planes. Driven in a light truck toward French headquarters, this courageous mission encountered intermittent firing, and as it neared Port Lyautey a heavy burst of machine gun fire was delivered upon the truck from pointblank range, killing Col. Craw instantly. Although captured immediately, after this incident, Lt. Col. Hamilton completed the mission.

OFFICIAL COMMUNIQUE:
United Nations
LONDON, Nov. 8 – A joint Air Ministry and United States Air Forces Headquarters communique:

U.S.A.A.F. Flying Fortresses, escorted by Allied fighters, bombed two targets in occupied France during daylight today.

One formation attacked the Fives-Lille steel and locomotive works at Lille and another bombed the enemy airfield at Abbeville.

Good results were observed at Lille, where hits were seen on the works and adjacent marshalling yards.

At Abbeville a heavy cloud made observation of the results difficult. Strong fighter opposition was encountered over both targets and fighting continued until the bombers were recrossing the Channel. In these combats a number of enemy fighters were destroyed by the Fortresses. One fortress and six escorting fighters are missing.

United States
WASHINGTON, Nov. 8 – A War Department Communique:

North Africa

1. Landings by United states forces on the Atlantic and Mediterranean coasts are proceeding according to plan.
2. Several important airfields have been occupied by the United States Army Air Force. Ranger units are participating in the operation.
3. The lack of resistance encountered at most of the beaches in North Africa had no desire to oppose the entry of American troops into this territory.
4. The forces that landed during the night and the early hours of this morning are advancing rapidly, and other landings continue. Resistance appears to have been confirmed mainly to navy and coast defense artillery. Owing to the confused nature of the fighting, precise results are not known.
5. Our naval forces are in control and suffered no losses except for two small ships which entered Oran Harbor.
6. During yesterday one of our transports was torpedoed and disabled. Our troops aboard, under a commander who refused to be idle during the operation, took to their light landing craft and continued toward their objective, 120 miles away, landing there this morning.

†CALLAGHAN, DANIEL JUDSON

Rank and Organization: Rear Admiral, U.S. Navy.
Born: July 26, 1892, San Francisco, California.
Entered Service At: Oakland, California.
Other Navy Award: Distinguished Service Medal.
Place and Date: Off Savo Island, November 12-13, 1942.
Citation: For extraordinary heroism and conspicuous intrepidity above and beyond the call of duty during action against enemy Japanese forces off Savo Island on the night of November 12-13, 1942. Although out-balanced in strength and numbers by a desperate and determined enemy, Rear Admiral Callaghan, with ingenious tactical skill and superb coordination of the units under his command, led his forces into battle against tremendous odds, thereby contributing decisively to the rout of a powerful invasion fleet, and to the consequent frustration of a formidable Japanese offensive. While faithfully directing close-range operations in the face of furious bombardment by superior enemy fire power, he was killed on the bridge of his flagship. His courageous initiative, inspiring leadership, and judicious foresight in a crisis of grave responsibility were in keeping with the finest tra-

ditions of the U.S. Naval Service. He gallantly gave his life in the defense of his country.

†KEPPLER, REINHARDT JOHN
Rank and Organization: Boatswain's Mate First Class, U.S. Navy.
Born: January 22, 1918, Ralston, Washington.
Entered Service At: Washington.
Other Navy Award: Navy Cross.
Place and Date: Solomon Islands, November 12-13, 1942.
Citation: For extraordinary heroism and distinguished courage above and beyond the call of duty while serving aboard the U.S.S. *San Francisco* during action against enemy Japanese forces in the Solomon Islands, November 12-13, 1942. When a hostile torpedo plane, during a daylight air raid, crashed on the after machine gun platform, Keppler promptly assisted in removal of the dead and, by his capable supervision of the wounded, undoubtedly helped save the lives of several shipmates who otherwise might have perished. That night, when the ship's hangar was set afire during the great battle off Savo Island, he bravely led a hose into the starboard side of the stricken area and there, without assistance and despite frequent hits from terrific enemy bombardment, eventually brought the fire under control. Later, although mortally wounded, he labored valiantly in the midst of bursting shells, persistently directing firefighting operations and administering to wounded personnel until he finally collapsed from loss of blood. His great personal valor, maintained with utter disregard of personal safety, was in keeping with the highest traditions of the U.S. Naval Service. He gallantly gave his life for his country.

McCANDLESS, BRUCE
Rank and organization: Commander, U.S. Navy, U.S.S. *San Francisco*.
Born: August 12, 1911, Washington, D.C..
Entered Service At: Colorado.
Place and date: Battle off Savo Island, November 12-13, 1942.
Citation: For conspicuous gallantry and exceptionally distinguished service above and beyond the call of duty as communication officer of the *U.S.S. San Francisco* in combat with enemy Japanese forces in the battle off Savo Island, November 12-13, 1942. In the midst of a violent night engagement, the fire of a determined and desperate enemy seriously wounded Lt. Comdr. McCandless and rendered him unconscious, killed or wounded the admiral in command, his staff, the captain of the ship, the

navigator, and all other personnel on the navigating and signal bridges. Faced with the lack of superior command upon his recovery, and displaying superb initiative, he promptly assumed command of the ship and ordered her course and gunfire against an overwhelmingly powerful force. With his superiors in other vessels unaware of the loss of their admiral, and challenged by his great responsibility, Lt. Comdr. McCandless boldly continued to engage the enemy and to lead our column of following vessels to a great victory. Largely through his brilliant seamanship and great courage, the *San Francisco* was brought back to port, saved to fight again in the service of her country.

†SCOTT, NORMAN

Rank and Organization: Rear Admiral, U.S. Navy.
Born: August 10, 1889, Indianapolis, Indiana.
Entered Service At: Indiana.
Place and Date: Off Savo Island, Oct. 11-12 and Nov. 12-13, 1942.
Citation: For extraordinary heroism and conspicuous intrepidity above and beyond the call of duty during action against enemy Japanese forces off Savo Island on the night of October 11-12 and again on the night of November 12-13, 1942. In the earlier action, intercepting a Japanese Task Force intent upon storming our island positions and landing reinforcements at Guadalcanal, Rear Admiral Scott, with courageous skill and superb coordination of the units under his command, destroyed 8 hostile vessels and put others to flight. Again challenged, a month later, by the return of a stubborn and persistent foe, he led his force into a desperate battle against tremendous odds, directing close-range operations against the invading enemy until he himself was killed in the furious bombardment by their superior firepower. On each of these occasions his dauntless initiative, inspiring leadership and judicious foresight in a crisis of grave responsibility contributed decisively to the rout of a powerful invasion fleet and to the consequent frustration of a formidable Japanese offensive. He gallantly gave his life in the service of his country.

†BAUER, HAROLD WILLIAM

Rank and Organization: Lieutenant Colonel, U.S. Marine Corps.
Born: November 20, 1908, Woodruff, Kansas.
Entered Service At: Nebraska.
Place and Date: In the South Pacific area, May 10 to November 14, 1942.
Citation: For extraordinary heroism and conspicuous courage as Squadron Commander of Marine Fighting Squadron 212 in the South Pacific

Area during the period of May 10 to November 14, 1942. Volunteering to pilot a fighter plane in defense of our positions on Guadalcanal, Lt. Col. Bauer participated in 2 air battles against enemy bombers and fighters outnumbering our force more than 2 to 1, boldly engaged the enemy and destroyed 1 Japanese bomber in the engagement of September 28, and shot down 4 enemy fighter planes in flames on October 3, leaving a fifth smoking badly. After successfully leading 26 planes on an over-water ferry flight of more than 600 miles on October 16, Lt. Col. Bauer, while circling to land, sighted a squadron of enemy planes attacking the U.S.S. *McFarland*. Undaunted by the formidable opposition and with valor above and beyond the call of duty, he engaged the entire squadron and, although alone and his fuel supply nearly exhausted, fought his plane so brilliantly that four of the Japanese planes were destroyed before he was forced down by lack of fuel. His intrepid fighting spirit and distinctive ability as a leader and an airman, exemplified in his splendid record of combat achievement, were vital factors in the successful operations in the South Pacific Area.

WAR NEWS SUMMARIZED

• • •

SATURDAY, NOVEMBER 14, 1942

The battle for possession of Tunisia Started early today when fighting broke out between German troops and the French garrison at Tunis, which was receiving support from the British and American air forces, while the Allied land troops were reported pouring across the border from Algeria. The Germans were said to be using twelve-ton tanks brought in by air, and to have control of the Tunis airport. The Vichy radio reported a large naval battle was taking place off Algiers.

In Libya the British Eighth Army pursuing the Germans occupied Tobruk without opposition. Bardia had fallen the night before.

Admiral Darlan, according to the Vichy news agency, announced he was assuming responsibility for French interests in Africa, saying his action had the full approval of American authorities. Governor General Nogues of French Morocco, "in the name of the Marshal," proclaimed his solidarity with Admiral Darlan.

Swiss reports said there was reason to believe that the larger units of the French Fleet had sailed from Toulon and were operating under Admiral Darlan's orders in Algerian waters.

The German High Command announced that the occupation of the entire south coast of France was complete.

In Washington, President Roosevelt ordered that lend-lease be extended to the North African territories occupied by the United Nations.

In a letter to the Moscow correspondent of The Associated Press, Premier Stalin declared that the North African campaign had turned the tide of war radically in favor of the United Nations, opening the way for the early collapse of Germany and Italy.

In Russia, according to the midnight Moscow communique, German attacks were beaten back in Stalingrad and in the Caucasus. Localized fighting was intense, but Moscow said that the German drives were on a greatly reduced scale.

In the Far Pacific, United States air and sea forces destroyed thirty Japanese planes and thirty large landing boats, silenced a number of shore batteries and started large fires on Guadalcanal. The enemy planes were destroyed when they attacked American naval units subjecting the Japanese shore installations to a bombardment lasting many hours. One Japanese plane fell onto the cruiser San Francisco, killing thirty of her crew.

Allied bombers returned once more to Bougainville Island in the Solomons and scored direct hits on two Japanese cruisers and near-misses on a destroyer and a transport, General MacArthur announced.

VANDEGRIFT, ALEXANDER ARCHER

Rank and Organization: Major General, U.S. Marine Corps, commanding officer of the 1st Marine Division.
Born: March 13, 1887, Charlottesville, Virginia.
Entered Service At: Virginia.
Place and Date: Solomon Islands, August 7 to December 9, 1942.
Citation: For outstanding and heroic accomplishment above and beyond the call of duty as commanding officer of the 1st Marine Division in operations against enemy Japanese forces in the Solomon Islands during the period of August 7 to December 9, 1942. With the adverse factors of weather, terrain, and disease making his task a difficult and hazardous undertaking, and with his command eventually including sea, land, and air forces of Army, Navy, and Marine Corps, Major General Vandegrift achieved marked success in commanding the initial landings of the U.S. forces in the Solomon Islands and in their subsequent occupation. His tenacity, courage, and resourcefulness prevailed against a strong, determined, and experienced enemy, and the gallant fighting spirit of the men under his inspiring leadership enabled them to withstand aerial, land, and sea bombardment, to surmount all obstacles, and leave a disorganized and ravaged enemy. This dangerous but vital mission, accomplished at the constant risk of his life, resulted in securing a valuable base for further operations of our forces

against the enemy, and its successful completion reflects great credit upon Major General Vandegrift, his command, and the U.S. Naval Service.

OFFICIAL COMMUNIQUE:
United Nations
AT UNITED NATIONS HEADQUARTERS, Australia, Wed., December 9 – A communique:

Northeastern Sector

New Britain:
Gasmata: An Allied medium unit bombed and strafed the runway and dispersal areas.
Rabaul: An Allied reconnaissance unit destroyed two enemy fighters attempting interception.
New Guinea:
Lae: A formation of our medium bombers attacked the airdrome, causing large explosions and fires in fuel and ammunition dumps.
Buna-Gona: An enemy counterattack in the Buna area was repulsed with heavy casualties. Our airforce continued harassing attacks on enemy localities. An enemy naval force of six destroyers, attempting for the fifth time to bring relief to their ground troops, was intercepted and attacked by our heavy bombers. Two direct hits with 500-pound bombs were scored on the leading destroyer which was quickly enveloped in flames. The remaining convoy fled.

The enemy's air units have violated the laws of war by repeated attacks on Allied hospital installations, killing doctors, medical personnel, and patients. On Nov. 27 an Australian field ambulance in the Soputa area and an American regimental dressing station were bombed, killing 29 and wounding 31. On Dec. 2 an American field hospital in the Buna area was bombed without damage. On Dec. 7 this same unit was bombed twice in a single day by low altitude dive-bombers, with casualties 7 killed and 30 wounded. In each case the tentage was conspicuously marked and the medical character of the installation was unmistakable.

†BURR, ELMER J.
Rank and Organization: First Sergeant, U.S. Army, Company I, 127th Infantry, 32d Infantry Division.
Born: Neeah, Wisconsin.
Entered Service At: Menasha, Wisconsin.
Place and Date: Buna, New Guinea, December 24, 1942.
Citation: For conspicuous gallantry and intrepidity in action above and beyond the call of duty. During an attack near Buna, New Guinea, on De-

cember 24, 1942, 1st Sgt. Burr saw an enemy grenade strike near his company commander. Instantly and with heroic self-sacrifice he threw himself upon it, smothering the explosion with his body. 1st Sgt. Burr thus gave his life in saving that of his commander.

†GRUENNERT, KENNETH E.

Rank and Organization: Sergeant, U.S. Army, Company L, 127th Infantry, 32d Infantry Division.
Born: Helenville, Wisconsin.
Entered Service At: Helenville, Wisconsin.
Place and Date: Near Buna, New Guinea, December 24, 1942.
Citation: For conspicuous gallantry and intrepidity in action above and beyond the call of duty. On December 24, 1942, near Buna, New Guinea, Sgt. Gruennert was second in command of a platoon with a mission to drive through the enemy lines to the beach 600 yards ahead. Within 150 yards of the objective, the platoon encountered two hostile pillboxes. Sgt. Gruennert advanced alone on the first and put it out of action with hand grenades and rifle fire, killing three of the enemy. Seriously wounded in the shoulder, he bandaged his wound under cover of the pillbox, refusing to withdraw to the aid station and leave his men. He then, with undiminished daring, and under extremely heavy fire, attacked the second pillbox. As he neared it he threw grenades which forced the enemy out where they were easy targets for his platoon. Before the leading elements of his platoon could reach him he was shot by enemy snipers. His inspiring valor cleared the way for his platoon which was the first to attain the beach in this successful effort to split the enemy position.

Note: The following is a newspaper account of the preceding battle for which both Sgt. Burr and Sgt. Gruennert were awarded the Medal of Honor:

BUNA BATTLEFIELD
REFLECTS GRIM WAR

• • •

Devastation and Japanese Dead
Attest to Bitter New Guinea Conflict

• • •

AT A NEW GUINEA BASE, Dec. 21 (Delayed)-The terrain on the Buna front that the Australian and American troops have overrun in the last few days stretches as grim and vivid testimony to the character of the Japanese resistance that has been overwhelmed and the savage intensity of the fighting that has brought the Allied success.

On Cape Endaiadere and westward our men have occupied mainly an area of coconut palms and patchy jungle. The palms are part of a long-untended plantation, and the lanes between the trees are heavily overgrown with tall grass and tangled bush. The area is one that provided ideal conditions for defense.

Adapted to Camouflage

It is higher than the lands surrounding it inland, which are swampy and covered with dense jungle and have only a few narrow lanes of higher ground leading to the Cape Endaiadere district. The grass and shrubbery among the palms made camouflage easy, and the Japanese dispersed their defenses under coverings of dead leaves and fresh coconut fronds, apparently replenished daily, which made them merge completely into the natural surroundings.

The captured area today is an expanse of shell holes, bomb craters, tattered foliage, tree trunks gashed and punctured by mortar fragments and bullets, rotting vegetation and abandoned Japanese gear. Palm log bunkers that constituted strong points in the maze of Japanese defenses rise as scores of little hillocks throughout the area. Nearly every one was a miniature battleground. Scores of unburied Japanese dead around these bunkers today still attest to the fights that were made for their possession.

Allied burial details are only gradually able to clean up the area, and there is still much to be done in the gory business of making the field of the dead fit for the living.

The Cape Endaiadere battle was one in which no quarter was asked or given. The Japanese were fanatically inspired by an order they were told had come from their Emperor to resist to the death. This they generally did.

The troops here see courage as a personal thing, springing from within each man. They cannot understand the Japanese fighting and dying as mere automatons in obedience to some outside will.

The Japanese way of fighting here has made this a battle of extermination. The Japanese have made of the usual procedures of surrender and the few remaining rules of warfare, such as respect for the wounded and for hospitals, tricks to lure the enemy into exposing himself to destruction.

Japanese Pervert War Rules

It is only natural that Japanese treachery has provoked intense bitterness among the Allied troops. No Allied soldier here now expects any humanitarian consideration or fair conduct of the Japanese.

Tanks broke the impasse that held up the Allied ground forces here for a month. Australian-manned General Stuarts went into action last Friday, Dec. 8, in a surprise daylight attack toward Cape Endaiadere.

The Japanese attempted to cling to an especially strong group of bunkers protecting the northern end of the new air strip at the left end of the new Allied line. They planned to use these as bases for a counter-attack. But after two hours of intense tank and infantry combat, these bunkers were captured and the Japanese effort collapsed.

Over a period of days Australian tanks were worked into position for the big attack. The Australian infantrymen who went into the attack with the tanks were veterans of the Middle East. They were specially trained at cooperation with armored vehicles.

The whole Australian force went into battle with irresistible dash and fervor after a heavy ten-minute artillery and mortar barrage.

Tanks with infantrymen close behind plowed straight for the bunkered Japanese positions, shedding storms of rifle and machine-gun bullets from enemy guns inside the defenses. Tank guns drilled the bunkers with armorpiercing shells and then blasted them with high explosive bullets.

Infantrymen followed on, finishing the resistance in the bunkers and the maze of connecting communications trenches with grenades, machine guns and bayonets. Scores of Japanese snipers in the trees peppered the infantry with their fire, but the Australians traded blows with them, leaning up behind palm trees and shooting the snipers out of their perches. Machine gunners in tanks sprayed the bushes as their vehicles advanced.

Some Japanese, demoralized by the tank blasting, were caught by the bayonet-wielding Australians.

The battle had gone on for several hours before the Japanese brought into play any special anti-tank weapons. After a time they began hurling sticky bombs, running up and putting magnetic bombs against the tanks. Flame-throwers were also tried.

The initial tank attack went through the lines of the Americans, who had been battling against the Japanese bunkers for weeks. The Americans joined in wiping out resistance as the tanks overran the bunkers. In the first day's attack the tank effort conquered nearly a hundred Japanese bunkers, formidable shelters for machine gunners and tommy gunners, built up on the surface with many layers of palm logs covered with dirt and camouflaged with dead leaves and palm fronds.

That day's effort broke the back of the Japanese resistance on the Allied right flank. The next day the whole line was pushed another 400 yards inland, with tanks again taking a prominent part.

The following night the Japanese withdrew, except for rear guard forces across Simemi Creek, taking up new positions along the northern edge of the old air strip and the western banks of the creek.

American troops ousted the enemy from his remaining bunkers around the new air strip and completely occupied its environs.

CHAPTER 3

1943

†WALKER, KENNETH N. (AIR MISSION)
Rank and Organization: Brigadier General, U.S. Army Air Corps, Commander of V Bomber Command.
Born: Cerrillos, New Mexico.
Entered Service At: Colorado.
Place and Date: Rabaul, New Britain, January 5, 1943.
Citation: For conspicuous leadership above and beyond the call of duty involving personal valor and intrepidity at an extreme hazard to life. As commander of the 5th Bomber Command during the period from September 5, 1942, to January 5, 1943, Brigadier General Walker repeatedly accompanied his units on bombing missions deep into enemy-held territory. From the lessons personally gained under combat conditions, he developed a highly efficient technique for bombing when opposed by enemy fighter airplanes and by antiaircraft fire. On January 5, 1943, in the face of extremely heavy antiaircraft fire and determined opposition by enemy fighters, he led an effective daylight bombing attack against shipping in the harbor at Rabaul, New Britain, which resulted in direct hits on nine enemy vessels. During this action his airplane was disabled and forced down by the attack of an overwhelming number of enemy fighters.

OFFICIAL COMMUNIQUE:
United Nations
AT UNITED NATIONS HEADQUARTERS, Australia, Wednesday, Jan. 6

Timor: Our attack planes strafed roads along the north coast and the Fuiloro airfield where an enemy fighter and enemy trucks were destroyed.
New Guinea:
Lae: An Allied heavy unit bombed the airdrome.
Salamaua: Our attack planes bombed and strafed enemy installations and enemy-occupied villages in the vicinity.

Mandang: An Allied heavy unit bombed the airdrome.

Sanananda: Our ground troops are closing in one the enemy. Our medium bombers and attack planes bombed and strafed enemy installations.

New Britain:

Rabaul: Our heavy bombers attacked shipping in the harbor. Nine certain and probably ten vessels of an aggregate estimated tonnage of over 50,000 tons were destroyed. A direct hit with 1,000-pound bombs was scored on a destroyer tender with a destroyer tied alongside. Eight other vessels were hit with 1,000-pound bombs and were left either enveloped in flames or sinking. The enemy's fighters attempted interception and six were shot down in air combat. One of our bombers is missing.

Gasmata: An Allied unit bombed the runway.

†FOURNIER, WILLIAM G.

Rank and Organization: Sergeant, U.S. Army, Company M, 35th Infantry, 25th Infantry Division.
Born: Norwich, Connecticut
Entered Service At: Winterport, Maine.
Place and Date: Mount Austen, Guadalcanal, Solomon Islands, January 10, 1943.
Citation: For gallantry and intrepidity above and beyond the call of duty. As leader of a machinegun section charged with the protection of other battalion units, his group was attacked by a superior number of Japanese, his gunner killed, his assistant gunner wounded, and an adjoining guncrew put out of action. Ordered to withdraw from this hazardous position, Sgt. Fournier refused to retire but rushed forward to the idle gun and, with the aid of another soldier who joined him, held up the machinegun by the tripod to increase its field action. They opened fire and inflicted heavy casualties upon the enemy. While so engaged both of these gallant soldiers were killed, but their sturdy defensive was a decisive factor in the following success of the attacking battalion.

†HALL, LEWIS

Rank and Organization: Technician Fifth Grade, U.S. Army, Company M, 35th Infantry, 25th Infantry Division.
Born: 1895, Bloom, Ohio.
Entered Service At: Obetz, Rural Station 7, Columbus, Ohio.
Place and Date: Mount Austen, Guadalcanal, Solomon Islands, January 10, 1942.

Citation: For gallantry and intrepidity above and beyond the call of duty. As leader of a machinegun squad charged with the protection of other battalion units, his group was attacked by a superior number of Japanese, his gunner killed, his assistant gunner wounded, and an adjoining guncrew put out of action. Ordered to withdraw from this hazardous position, he refused to retire but rushed forward to the idle gun and, with the aid of another soldier who joined him, held up the machinegun by the tripod to increase its field action he opened fire and inflicted heavy casualties upon the enemy. While so engaged both of these gallant soldiers were killed, but their sturdy defensive was a decisive factor in the following success of the attacking battalion.

OFFICIAL COMMUNIQUE:
UNITED STATES
WASHINGTON, Jan. 10 – Navy communique 246:

1. On Jan. 8, during the forenoon, Marauder medium bombers (Martin B-26) with Airacobra (Bell P-39) escort bombed the Japanese airfield at Munda on New Georgia Island. Results were not reported.
2. During the night of Jan. 8-9 the United States aircraft again bombed enemy positions in the Munda area. A probable hit on an anti-aircraft battery on Munda Point was reported.
3. All United States planes returned safely from the above missions.

DAVIS, CHARLES W.
Rank and Organization: Major, U.S. Army, 25th Infantry Division.
Born: Gordo, Alabama.
Entered Service At: Montgomery, Alabama.
Place and Date: Guadalcanal Island, January 12, 1943.
Citation: For distinguishing himself conspicuously by gallantry and intrepidity at the risk of his life above and beyond the call of duty in action with the enemy on Guadalcanal Island. On January 12, 1943, Maj. Davis (then Capt.), executive officer of an infantry battalion, volunteered to carry instructions to the leading companies of his battalion which had been caught in crossfire from Japanese machineguns. With complete disregard for his own safety, he made his way to the trapped units, delivered the instructions, supervised their execution, and remained overnight in this exposed position. On the following day, Maj. Davis again volunteered to lead an assault on the Japanese position which was holding up the advance. When his rifle jammed at its first shot, he drew his pistol and, waving his men on,

led the assault over the top of the hill. Electrified by this action, another body of soldiers followed and seized the hill. The capture of this position broke Japanese resistance and the battalion was then able to proceed and secure the corps objective. The courage and leadership displayed by Maj. Davis inspired the entire battalion and unquestionably led to the success of its attack.

OFFICIAL COMMUNIQUE:
UNITED NATIONS
AT UNITED NATIONS HEADQUARTERS, Australia, Wednesday, Jan. 13:

Merauke: Nine enemy bombers raided the town, causing only slight damage.
Timor: Our long-range fighters carried out a low-altitude attack against the airdrome and installations at Fuiloro. One enemy fighter was left burning. The runway, buildings, huts, motor transport, construction equipment and adjacent roads were successfully strafed.
Salamaua: Our long-range fighters and attack planes bombed and strafed the trail to Komiatum, destroying the bridge. Another formation executed a strafing sweep along the coast of Yvto Amboga.
Sanananda: Our ground forces made further gains against the remaining enemy positions.

UNITED STATES
WASHINGTON, Jan. 12-Navy communique 249:

All dates are east longitude.
1. On January 11:
a. A force of Dauntless dive bombers escorted by Wildcat fighters was attacked by twelve Japanese Zeros between Santa Isabel Island and New Georgia Island. Four Zeros were shot down and two others were possibly destroyed. One Wildcat failed to return.
b. A force of Marauder medium bombers with Airacobra escort attacked Japanese positions at Munda. Clouds over the target areas prevented accurate bombing and made observation of results difficult.

FOSS, JOSEPH JACOB
Rank and Organization: Captain, U.S. Marine Corps Reserve, Marine Fighting Squadron 121, 1st Marine Aircraft Wing.
Born: April 17, 1915, Sioux Falls, South Dakota.
Entered Service At: South Dakota.

Place and Date: Over Guadalcanal, October 9-19, 1942, and January 15 and 23, 1943.

Citation: For outstanding heroism and courage above and beyond the call of duty as executive officer of Marine Fighting Squadron 121, 1st Marine Aircraft Wing, at Guadalcanal. Engaging in almost daily combat with the enemy from October 9 to November 19, 1942, Capt. Foss personally shot down 23 Japanese planes and damaged others so severely that their destruction was extremely probable. In addition, during this period, he successfully led a large number of escort missions, skillfully covering reconnaissance, bombing, and photographic planes as well as surface craft. On January 15, 1943, he added three more enemy planes to his already brilliant successes for a record of aerial combat achievement unsurpassed in this war. Boldly searching out an approaching enemy force on January 25, Capt. Foss led his eight F4F Marine planes and four Army P-38's into action and, undaunted by tremendously superior numbers, intercepted and struck with such force that four Japanese fighters were shot down and the bombers were turned back without releasing a single bomb. His remarkable flying skill, inspiring leadership, and indomitable fighting spirit were distinctive factors in the defense of strategic American positions on Guadalcanal.

OFFICIAL COMMUNIQUE:
United Nations
AT UNITED NATIONS HEADQUARTERS, Australia, Saturday, Jan. 23 - The noon communique:

Northwestern Sector

Arafura Sea: Our medium bombers attacked an enemy merchant vessel off Cape van den Bosch with unobserved results.
Merauke: A single enemy float plane dropped two bombs harmlessly in a swamp.
Darwin: Two enemy bombers raided the area after dark, dropping bombs harmlessly in a neighboring swamp.

Northeastern Sector

New Britain - Rabaul: In a predawn attack, our bombers struck heavily at shipping in the harbor. In an extremely low-level strike, four enemy ships of an aggregate tonnage of 24,000 tons were destroyed. Direct hits on a 4,000-ton cargo ship split and sank the vessel within four minutes. An 8,000-ton transport was left burning as a result of two direct hits and later was seen to explode.

A 4,000-ton vessel with a lighter moored alongside was hit and sank within twelve minutes while another 8,000-ton vessel received three direct hits and was left burning with a series of explosions. Two searchlights were extinguished by strafing. All our planes returned safely.

New Guinea - Madang: An Allied heavy unit bombed the airdrome.

Lae: Our medium bombers attacked supply installations, starting many fires.

Salamaua: Our attack planes bombed enemy installations in the town area and made a close sweep along the coast to Bakumbari, strafing barges and small boats.

Sanananda: All organized enemy resistance has been overcome. Mopping up is in progress. Seven hundred and twenty-five enemy dead have been found in addition to those previously reported with many more yet to be counted. A considerable quantity of enemy material and equipment has been captured, including field guns, trucks, and ammunition.

Milne Bay: Three enemy bombers raided under cover of darkness. There was no damage.

United States
WASHINGTON, Jan. 22 - Navy communique 258:

South Pacific

All dates are East Longitude.

1. During the night of Jan. 20-21 United States aircraft carried out several harassing attacks on enemy installations on Ballale Island, off the northeast coast of Shortland Island. Results were not observed.

2. On Jan. 21:

a. A Japanese plane dropped several bombs on the American base on Espiritu Santo Island, in the New Hebrides group. There were no casualties to personnel and our installations were not damaged.

b. During the night of Jan. 21-22 single enemy planes dropped bombs in the vicinity of the airfield at Guadalcanal. Minor damage to installations has been reported and three men were killed and one wounded. Anti-aircraft shot down one enemy plane.

3. United States ground forces on Guadalcanal continued mopping up pockets of enemy resistance and made small advances in some sectors.

DeBLANC, JEFFERSON JOSEPH
Rank and Organization: Captain, U.S. Marine Corps Reserve, Marine Fighting Squadron 112.
Born: February 15, 1921, Lockport, Louisiana.
Entered Service At: Louisiana.

Place and Date: Off Kolombangara Island in the Solomons group, January 31, 1943.

Citation: For conspicuous gallantry and intrepidity at the risk of his life above and beyond the call of duty as leader of a section of 6 fighter planes in Marine Fighting Squadron 112, during aerial operations against enemy Japanese forces off Kolombangara Island in the Solomons group, January 31, 1943. Taking off with his section as escort for a strike force of dive bombers and torpedo planes ordered to attack Japanese surface vessels, 1st Lt. DeBlanc led his flight directly to the target area where, at 14,000 feet, our strike force encountered a large number of Japanese Zeros protecting the enemy's surface craft. In company with the other fighters, 1st Lt. DeBlanc instantly engaged the hostile planes and aggressively countered their repeated attempts to drive off our bombers, persevering in his efforts to protect the diving planes and waging fierce combat until, picking up a call for assistance from the dive bombers, under attack by enemy float planes at 1,000 feet, he broke off his engagement with the Zeros, plunged into the formation of float planes and disrupted the savage attack, enabling our dive bombers and torpedo planes to complete their runs on the Japanese surface disposition and withdraw without further incident. Although his escort mission was fulfilled upon the safe retirement of the bombers, 1st Lt. DeBlanc courageously remained on the scene despite a rapidly diminishing fuel supply and, boldly challenging the enemy's superior number of float planes, fought a valiant battle against terrific odds, seizing the tactical advantage and striking repeatedly to destroy 3 of the hostile aircraft and to disperse the reminder. Prepared to maneuver his damaged plane back to base, he had climbed aloft and set his course when he discovered 2 Zeros closing in behind. Undaunted, he opened fire and blasted both Zeros from the sky in a short, bitterly fought action which resulted in such hopeless damage to his own plane that he was forced to bail out at a perilously low altitude atop the trees on enemy-held Kolombangara. A gallant officer, a superb airman, and an indomitable fighter, 1st. Lt. DeBlanc had rendered decisive assistance during a critical stage of operations, and his unwavering fortitude in the face of overwhelming opposition reflects the highest credit upon himself and adds new luster to the traditions of the U.S. Naval Service.

OFFICIAL COMMUNIQUE:
UNITED NATIONS
AT UNITED NATIONS HEADQUARTERS, Australia, Monday, Feb. 1:

Northwestern Sector

Ambon: Our heavy bombers attacked enemy shipping with unobserved results. Four enemy fighters attempted interception, without success.

Timor: Kupang-Our long-range fighters successfully attacked the airdrome with cannon and machine guns, destroying or damaging eight enemy bombers and a fighter caught on the ground. Hangars and buildings were set on fire, including an apparent ammunition warehouse which exploded violently. Two miles away a motor pool containing twenty vehicles also was strafed. All our planes returned.

Viqueque: Our medium bombers attacked enemy installations.

Tenimber Island: One of our heavy units bombed the jetty on Selatu Island.

Northeastern Sector

New Britain:

Rabaul: Our heavy bombers attacked shipping and harbor installations before dawn, dropping bombs on the docks and among anchored vessels. Haze and searchlights prevented observation of results.

Arawe: One of our heavy reconnaissance units bombed and strafed an enemy cargo ship off Pilelo Island.

Cape Gloucester: One of our heavy units bombed the runway and strafed the area at low altitude.

New Guinea:

Wewak: One of our heavy units attacked the airdrome and shipping, with unobserved results. Anti-aircraft positions were silenced by strafing.

Finschhafen: An Allied night reconnaissance plane strafed buildings in the harbor area.

Markham River: Our long-range fighters executed a sweep down the valley to the mouth of the Waria River, strafing targets of opportunity.

Mubo-Wau: Sporadic ground fighting continues. Our attack planes bombed and strafed the Mubo-Komiatum area.

†**GILMORE, HOWARD WALTER**

Rank and Organization: Commander, U.S. Navy.

Born: September 29, 1902, Selma, Alabama.

Entered Service At: Louisiana.

Other Navy Awards: Navy Cross with one gold star.

Place and Date: In the Southwest Pacific, January 10 to February 7, 1943.

Citation: For distinguished gallantry and valor above and beyond the call of duty as commanding officer of the U.S.S. *Growler* during her Fourth

War Patrol in the Southwest Pacific from January 10 to February 7 1943. Boldly striking at the enemy in spite of continuous hostile air and anti-submarine patrols, Comdr. Gilmore sank one Japanese freighter and damaged another by torpedo fire, successfully evading severe depth charges following each attack. In the darkness of night on February 7, an enemy gunboat closed range and prepared to ram the *Growler*. Comdr. Gilmore daringly maneuvered to avoid the crash and rammed the attacker instead, ripping into her port side at 17 knots and bursting wide her plates. In the terrific fire of the sinking gunboat's heavy machineguns, Comdr. Gilmore calmly gave the order to clear the bridge, and refusing safety for himself, remained on the deck while his men preceded him below. Struck down by the fusillade of bullets and having done his utmost against the enemy, in his final living moments, Comdr. Gilmore gave his last order to the officer of the deck, "Take her down." The *Growler* dived; seriously damaged but inspired by the courageous fighting spirit of their dead captain.

OFFICIAL COMMUNIQUE:
UNITED NATIONS
AT UNITED NATIONS HEADQUARTERS, Australia, Sunday, Feb. 7:

Darwin: One of our fighters intercepted and shot down an enemy bomber on reconnaissance.

Solomons: Bougainville: Our medium bombers executed night raids on airdromes at Buina and Buka. One of our heavy units bombed an 8,000-ton cargo ship approaching Buka passage. The vessel apparently was damaged and reduced speed, with smoke issuing from the bow.

New Britain: Rabaul: Despite extremely poor weather conditions, for the eighth successive night, one of our bomber units again was over the area in a harassing raid lasting three hours.

Open Bay: One of our heavy bomber units scored a direct hit on a 500-ton enemy cargo ship anchored off shore, probably destroying it.

New Guinea, Finschhafen: One of our heavy bomber units scored a direct bomb hit on a 500-ton cargo vessel which was left in flames.

Lae: Our medium bombers attacked the airdrome area, blowing up buildings and silencing an anti-aircraft position.

Mubo area: Our ground patrols were active. An enemy post at Wibaining was surprised and eighteen enemy troops occupying is killed. Our attack planes bombed and strafed the Komiatum track.

Wau: Enemy bombers with strong fighter escort made repeated attempts to attack the airdrome. In a series of air battles lasting throughout the day, the enemy was completely defeated and swept from the air. Forty-one enemy planes were shot down, either completely destroyed or seriously damaged. Thirty-three of these were fighters and eight bombers. Two of the latter were brought down by our anti-aircraft fire. Our losses were negligible.

UNITED STATES
WASHINGTON, Feb. 6- Navy communique 273:

North Pacific

1. On Feb. 4:
a. A United States plane destroyed a Japanese plane during a reconnaissance mission.
b. During the afternoon five enemy float-type planes bombed United States positions in the Western Aleutians. No damage was suffered.
c. During the night of Feb. 4-5 Liberator heavy bombers and Mitchell medium bombers, with fighter escort, bombed Japanese positions at Kiska. Three of the five float-type Zeros which intercepted were shot down. All United States planes returned.

South Pacific

All dates are East Longitude.
2. On Feb. 3:
a. United States planes raided Japanese positions at Munda on New Georgia Island during the evening. Results were not reported.
b. During the morning Dauntless dive bombers, with fighter escort, bombed enemy positions on Kolombangara Island in the New Georgia group.
c. During the night of Feb. 3-4 United States positions on Guadalcanal were bombed twice by single enemy planes.
3. On Feb. 4:
a. A flying Fortress on a search mission was attacked by three Zeros. One Zero was shot down and the damaged Fortress returned to its base.
b. United States troops on Guadalcanal Island continued to advance along the northwest coast of the island. Enemy resistance was weak, and some of our patrols reached points one and one-half miles past Tassafaronga near the Umasani River.

†MATHIS, JACK W. (Air Mission)
Rank and Organization: First Lieutenant, U.S. Army Air Corps, 359th Bomber Squadron, 303d Bomber Group.
Born: September 25, 1921, San Angelo, Texas.
Entered Service At: San Angelo, Texas.

Place and Date: Over Vegesack, Germany, March 18, 1943.

Citation: For conspicuous gallantry and intrepidity above and beyond the call of duty in action with the enemy over Vegesack, Germany, on March 18, 1943. 1st Lt. Mathis, as leading bombardier of his squadron, flying through intense and accurate antiaircraft fire, was just starting his bomb run, upon which the entire squadron depended for accurate bombing, when he was hit by the enemy antiaircraft fire. His right arm was shattered above the elbow, a large wound was torn in his side and abdomen, and he was knocked from his bomb sight to the rear of the bombardier's compartment. Realizing that the success of the mission depended upon him, 1st Lt. Mathis, by sheer determination and willpower, though mortally wounded, dragged himself back to his sights released his bombs, then died at his post of duty. As the result of this action the airplanes of his bombardment squadron placed their bombs directly upon the assigned target for a perfect attack against the enemy. 1st Lt. Mathis' undaunted bravery has been a great inspiration to the officers and men of his unit.

OFFICIAL COMMUNIQUE:
United Nations
LONDON, March 18 - An American communique:

A strong force of Flying Fortresses and Liberators of the United States Army Eighth Air Force heavily attacked the important U-boat yards at Vegesack in Northwest Germany during daylight today.

The weather was clear and many hits were obtained on the large yards, which are principally engaged in the building and repair of submarines.

Heavy opposition from enemy aircraft was encountered and many of them were destroyed and damaged.

Two of our bombers failed to return.

SWETT, JAMES ELMS
Rank and Organization: First Lieutenant, U.S. Marine Corps Reserve, Marine Fighting Squadron 221, with Marine Aircraft Group 12, 1st Marine Aircraft Wing.
Born: June 15, 1920, Seattle, Washington.
Entered Service At: California.
Other Navy Awards: Distinguished Flying Cross with 1 Gold Star.
Place and Date: Solomon Islands area, April 7, 1943.
Citation: For extraordinary heroism and personal valor above and beyond the call of duty, as division leader of Marine Fighting Squadron 221 with

Marine Aircraft Group 12, 1st Marine Aircraft Wing, in action against enemy Japanese aerial forces in the Solomons Islands area, April 7, 1943. In a daring flight to intercept a wave of 150 Japanese planes, 1st Lt. Swett unhesitatingly hurled his 4-plane division into action against a formation of 15 enemy bombers and personally exploded 3 hostile planes in midair with accurate and deadly fire during his dive. Although separated from his division while clearing the heavy concentration of antiaircraft fire, he boldly attacked 6 enemy bombers, engaged the first 4 in turn and, unaided, shot down all in flames. Exhausting his ammunition as he closed the fifth Japanese bomber, he relentlessly drove his attack against terrific opposition which partially disabled his engine, shattered the windscreen and slashed his face. In spite of this, he brought his battered plane down with skillful precision in the water off Tulagi without further injury. The superb airmanship and tenacious fighting spirit which enabled 1st Lt. Swett to destroy 7 enemy bombers in a single flight were in keeping with the highest traditions of the U.S. Naval Service.

OFFICIAL COMMUNIQUE:
United Nations
ALLIED HEADQUARTERS IN AUSTRALIA, Thursday, April 8 - The noon communique:

Northwestern Sector

Dutch New Guinea
Babo: Our heavy units bombed the airdrome and town, causing explosions and fires.
Fak: One of our heavy units bombed the town.

Tenimber Islands
Saumlakki: One of our medium units bombed and strafed the town.

Aruy Islands
Dodo: One of our medium units bombed the town.

Northeastern Sector

New Ireland
Kavieng: One of our heavy reconnaissance units strafed a small enemy convoy consisting of a destroyer and two cargo vessels northwest of Kavieng. An escorting float plane, attempting interception, was driven off damaged.

New Britain

Cape Glouster: One of our heavy units bombed and strafed enemy planes caught on the airdrome.

New Guinea

Wewak: One of our heavy units at midday bombed the harbor.

Saldor: One of our medium bombers executed an intensive sweep along the coast, bombing and strafing the villages of Mur, Savel, Fungair, Wilwilan and Yamai. A succession of fires was started.

Finschhafen: Our heavy units bombed and strafed the town in two separate attacks.

Lae: One of our heavy units bombed the airdrome.

Salamaua: One of our heavy units bombed the town area.

Solomons Sea: One of our medium units attacked an enemy destroyer off the coast of Bougainville, scoring near misses.

UNITED STATES
WASHINGTON, April 7 - Navy communique 336:

North Pacific

1. On April 5, forces of Army Liberator (Consolidated B-23) heavy bombers and Mitchell (North american B-25) medium bombers, escorted by Lightning (Lockheed P-38) and Warhawk (Curtiss P-40) fighters, carried out five attacks against Japanese installations at Kiska and one attack against Attu. Hits were scored on enemy positions.

South Pacific

2. On April 7, a group of Dauntless dive bombers (Douglas SBD) and Lightning fighters attacked Japanese positions at Vila in the Central Solomons. Fires were started.

†BOOKER, ROBERT D.

Rank and Organization: Private, U.S. Army, 34th Infantry Division.

Born: July 11, 1920, Callaway, Nebraska.

Entered Service At: Callaway, Nebraska.

Place and Date: Near Fondouk, Tunisia, April 9, 1943.

Citation: For conspicuous gallantry and intrepidity at risk of life above and beyond the call of duty in action. On April 9, 1943 in the vicinity of Fondouk, Tunisia, Pvt. Booker, while engaged in action against the enemy, carried a light machinegun and a box of ammunition over 200 yards of open ground. He continued to advanced despite the fact that 2 enemy machineguns and several mortars were using him as an individual target. Although enemy artillery also began to register on him, upon reaching his objective he immediately commenced firing. After being wounded he silenced 1 enemy machine gun and was beginning to fire at the other when he received a second mortal wound. With his last remaining strength he encouraged the members of his squad and directed their fire. Pvt. Booker acted without regard for his own safety. His initiative and courage against insurmountable odds are an example of the highest standard of self-sacrifice and fidelity to duty.

OFFICIAL COMMUNIQUE:
United Nations
ALLIED HEADQUARTERS IN NORTH AFRICA, April 9 - A communique:

Pressure was maintained yesterday on the enemy in both North and South Tunisia.

On the Eighth Army front the enemy continued his retreat with our forces in close pursuit.

The total of prisoners captured since the battle of Wadi el Akarit is now over 9,500 on the Eighth Army front alone.

The United States Second Corps continued mopping up operations in the area east of El Guettar. During the past few days many prisoners have been captured in this area.

In the north the First Army continued their attack over very difficult country and yesterday occupied important tactical localities. Since April 7 over 400 prisoners have been taken in this area.

On the night of April 7-8 Wellington bombers attacked communications centers at Sfax and enemy transport columns. A large explosion was caused in the marshaling yards.

Yesterday strong forces of light bombers and fighter-bombers of the tactical air force continued their attacks and many enemy vehicles were destroyed.

Over the rest of the Tunisian front fighters and fighter-bombers attacked enemy positions and communications in the central sector. Enemy transport vehicles were left in flames.

From all these operations seven of our aircraft are missing.

†**NELSON, WILLIAM L.**
Rank and Organization: Sergeant, U.S. Army, 60th Infantry, 9th Infantry Division.
Born: Dover, Delaware.
Entered Service At: Middletown, Delaware.
Place and Date: At Djebel Dardys, Northwest of Dejenane, Tunisia, April 24, 1943.
Citation: For conspicuous gallantry and intrepidity at risk of life, above and beyond the call of duty in action involving actual conflict. On the morning of April 24, 1943, Sgt. Nelson led his section of heavy mortars to a forward position where he placed his guns and men. Under intense enemy artillery, mortar, and small-arms fire, he advanced alone to a chosen observation position from which he directed the laying of a concentrated mortar barrage which successfully halted an initial enemy counterattack. Although mortally wounded in the accomplishment of his mission, and with his duty clearly completed, Sgt. Nelson crawled to a still more advanced observation point and continued to direct the fire of his section. Dying of handgrenade wounds and only 50 yards from the enemy, Sgt. Nelson encouraged his section to continue their fire and by doing so they took a heavy toll of enemy lives. The skill which Sgt. Nelson displayed in this engagement, his courage, and self-sacrificing devotion to duty and heroism resulting in the loss of his life, was a priceless inspiration to our Armed Forces and were in keeping with the highest tradition of the U.S. Army.

OFFICIAL COMMUNIQUE:
United States
ALLIED HEADQUARTERS IN NORTH AFRICA, April 24 - A communique:

On the Eighth Army front yesterday our patrols were very active. A local enemy attack was repulsed.

The First Army made a considerable advance on the whole front between Bou Arada and Medjez-el-Bab. The enemy fought bitterly and launched strong counter-attacks in the sector east of Medjez-el-Bab. These attacks were defeated with heavy loss to the enemy and our forward troops securely held their objectives.

North of Sebkret el Kourzia armored fighting took place. the enemy was forced to withdraw and a number of his tanks were destroyed. In the northern sector American troops made successful attacks, capturing more than 100 prisoners. In several areas advances of many miles were made in difficult hill country.

On the night of April 22-23 light bombers of the Tactical Air Force carried out an attack on enemy communications, motor transport and airfields. Throughout yesterday the attacks were continued on a heavy scale by medium and light bombers and fighter-bombers. Numerous attacks also were made on enemy ground positions, and fighters maintained sweeps and patrols over the battle areas.

Attacks on railway communications and motor transport at Mateur were made by medium bombers of the Strategic Air Force, hits being scored in the target area and on enemy vehicles. B-17 Flying Fortresses attacked two motor vessels off the coast of Sicily. Direct hits were scored on one of the vessels, which was left burning.

During the course of the day's operations eight enemy aircraft were destroyed. One enemy aircraft was destroyed on the night of April 22-23. From all of these operations six of our aircraft are missing.

†MINUE, NICHOLAS

Rank and Organization: Private, U.S. Army, Company A, 6th Armored Infantry, 1st Armored Division.
Born: Sedden, Poland.
Entered Service At: Carteret, New Jersey.
Place and Date: Near Medjez-el-Bab, Tunisia, April 28, 1943.
Citation: For distinguishing himself conspicuously by gallantry and intrepidity at the loss of his life above and beyond the call of duty in action with the enemy on April 28, 1943, in the vicinity of Medjez-el-Bab, Tunisia. When the advance of the assault elements of Company A was held up by flanking fire from an enemy machinegun nest, Pvt. Minue voluntarily, alone, and unhesitatingly, with complete disregard of his own welfare, charged the enemy entrenched position with fixed bayonet. Pvt. Minue assaulted the enemy under withering machinegun and rifle fire, killing approximately 10 enemy machinegunners and riflemen. After completely destroying this position, Pvt. Minue continued forward, routing enemy riflemen from dugout positions until he was fatally wounded. The courage, fearlessness and aggressiveness displayed by Pvt. Minue in the face of inevitable death was unquestionably the factor that gave his company the offensive spirit that was necessary for advancing and driving the enemy from the entire sector.

OFFICIAL COMMUNIQUE:
United Nations
ALLIED HEADQUARTERS IN NORTH AFRICA, April 28 – A communique:

In Tunisia, Allied troops yesterday continued to make steady progress. On the First Army front, fighting in the Medjez-el-Bab sector has been hard, attack being followed by counter-attack throughout the day.

The Second (United States) Corps has made good progress in the hills. French forces operating in the area of Pont du Fahs have made considerable progress through difficult country, advancing more than fifteen miles during the last three days. Contact has been maintained with patrols of the Eighth Army.

SMITH, MAYNARD H. (Air Mission)

Rank and Organization: Sergeant, U.S. Army Air Corps, 423d Bombardment Squadron, 306th Bomber Group.
Born: 1911, Cairo, Michigan.
Entered Service At: Cairo, Michigan.
Place and Date: Over Europe, May 1, 1943.
Citation: For conspicuous gallantry and intrepidity in action above and beyond the call of duty. The aircraft of which Sgt. Smith was a gunner was subjected to intense enemy antiaircraft fire and determined fighter airplane attacks while returning from a mission over enemy-occupied continental Europe on May 1, 1943. The airplane was hit several times by antiaircraft fire and cannon shells of the fighter airplanes. Two of the crew were seriously wounded, the aircraft's oxygen system was shot out, and several vital control cables severed when intense fires were ignited simultaneously in the radio compartment and waist sections. The situation became so acute that 3 of the crew bailed out into the comparative safety of the sea. Sgt. Smith, then on his first combat mission, elected to fight the fire by himself, administered first-aid to the wounded tail gunner, manned the waist guns, and fought the intense flames alternately. The escaping oxygen fanned the fire to such intense heat that the ammunition in the radio compartment began to explode, the radio, gun mount, and camera were melted, and the compartment completely gutted. Sgt. Smith threw the exploding ammunition overboard, fought the fire until all of the firefighting aids were exhausted, manned the workable guns until the enemy fighters were driven away, further administered first-aid to his wounded comrade, and by wrapping himself in protecting cloth, completely extinguished the fire by hand. This soldier's gallantry in action, undaunted bravery, and loyalty to his aircraft and fellow crewmembers, without regard for his own personal safety, is an inspiration to the U.S. Armed Forces.

OFFICIAL COMMUNIQUE:
United Nations
ALLIED HEADQUARTERS IN NORTH AFRICA, May 1 – A communique:

The day was marked by a continuation of exceptionally heavy fighting on the First Army front, especially in the sector east and northeast of Medjez-el-Bab, where the enemy launched repeated counter-attacks against our recently gained positions. In one area, our forward troops were forced to make a slight withdrawal, but elsewhere all our positions were firmly held. All these counter-attacks resulted in heavy losses to the enemy, both in men and in tanks.

In the north, American forces continued their advance over difficult country and captured three more important localities and over 200 prisoners were taken.

On the Eighth Army front, slight local gains were made.

AIR

Yesterday air operations of the Northwest African Air Forces against enemy shipping were continued on an increased scale off the coast of Tunisia. B-25 Mitchell bombers of the Strategic Air Force attacked and scored several direct hits on a destroyer which was left burning. Other medium bombers sank a destroyer and hit a merchant vessel.

The Tactical Air Force also made concentrated attacks on enemy shipping of all types. The Twelfth Air Support Command gave support over the land battle.

Fighter-bombers and fighters of the Desert Air Force put out their full effort against enemy shipping and its heavy air cover, scoring hits on a merchant ship and attacking a corvette, another merchant vessel, an E-boat, an F-boat, a motor ferry and a number of smaller vessels. During these operations eight enemy aircraft were destroyed.

A Beaufighter of the Coastal Air Force while on patrol encountered a formation of five Junkers-52 transport aircraft. The Beaufighter attacked the enemy formation and destroyed all five of them.

On the night of April 29-30 Wellington bombers of the Strategic Air Force attacked enemy air fields in Tunisia and started large fires.

From all these operations seven of our aircraft are missing.

CAIRO, Egypt, May 1 – A United States Air Force communique:

Liberators of the Ninth United States Air Force attacked the harbor of Messina, Sicily, during daylight on April 30.

The burst of heavy caliber bombs caused a tremendous explosion and large fires in the vicinity of the port's power station, and other hits were observed on a ferry terminal and installations.

Our formation was attacked by a concentration of enemy fighters, several of which were damaged.

From this operation one of our aircraft has not returned.

†MARTINEZ, JOE P.

Rank and Organization: Private, U.S. Army, Company K, 32d Infantry, 7th Infantry Division.

Born: Taos, New Mexico.

Entered Service At: Ault, Colorado.

Place and Date: On Attu, Aleutians, May 26, 1943.

Citation: For conspicuous gallantry and intrepidity above and beyond the call of duty in action with the enemy. Over a period of several days, repeated efforts to drive the enemy from a key defensive position high in the snow-covered precipitous mountains between East Arm Holtz Bay and Chichagof Harbor had failed. On May 26, 1943, troop dispositions were readjusted and a trial coordinated attack on this position by a reinforced battalion was launched. Initially successful, the attack hesitated. In the face of severe hostile machinegun, rifle, and mortar fire, Pvt. Martinez, an automatic rifleman, rose to his feet and resumed his advance. Occasionally he stopped to urge his comrades on. His example inspired others to follow. After a most difficult climb, Pvt. Martinez eliminated resistance from part of the enemy position by BAR fire and handgrenades, thus assisting the advance of other attacking elements. This success only partially completed the action. The main Holtz-Chichagof Pass rose about 150 feet higher, flanked by steep rocky ridges and reached by a snow-filled defile. Passage was barred by enemy fire from either flank and from tiers of snow trenches in front. Despite these obstacles, and knowing of their existence, Pvt. Martinez again led the troops on and up, personally silencing several trenches with BAR fire and ultimately reaching the pass itself. Here, just below the knife-like rim of the pass, Pvt. Martinez encountered a final enemy-occupied trench and as he was engaged in firing into it he was mortally wounded. The pass, however, was taken, and its capture was an important preliminary to the end of organized hostile resistance on the island.

OFFICIAL COMMUNIQUE:
United States
WASHINGTON, May 26 – Navy communique 380:

1. On May 23, the small United States auxiliary vessel Niagara was attacked by Japanese planes east of Cape Surville, San Cristobal Island. Considerable damage was inflicted on the vessel which was subsequently sunk by United States forces after members of the crew were taken aboard accompanying naval units.

2. On May 24, Avenger (Grumman TBF) Torpedo bombers and Wildcat (Grumman F4F) fighters bomber and strafed Japanese installations at Ringi Cove, west of Vila on Kolombangara Island.

3. On May 25, Dauntless (Douglas SBD) dive bombers, Avenger torpedo bombers and Wildcat fighters bombed and strafed Japanese installations at Rekata Bay, Santa Isabel Island. Ammunition dumps were exploded and large fires were started.

NORTH PACIFIC

4. On May 24, United States Army ground troops cleared out both sides of Chichagof Valley. An assault was made by combined northern and southern forces along the ridge north of the valley and was reported as continuing. Assisting in the assault were United States Army Air Forces consisting of Liberator (Consolidated B-24) heavy bombers, Mitchell (North American B-25) medium bombers and Lightning (Lockheed P-38) fighters. These planes bombed and strafed Japanese positions in the Chichagof area and started fires.

†SARNOSKI, JOSEPH R. (Air Mission)

Rank and Organization: Second Lieutenant, U.S. Army Air Corps, 43rd Bomber Group.
Born: January 30, 1915, Simpson, Pennsylvania.
Entered Service At: Simpson, Pennsylvania.
Place and Date: Over Buka area, Solomon Islands, June 16, 1943.
Citation: For conspicuous gallantry and intrepidity in action above and beyond the call of duty. On June 16, 1943, 2d Lt. Sarnoski volunteered as bombardier of a crew on an important photographic mapping mission covering the heavily defended Buka area, Solomon Islands. When the mission was nearly completed, about 20 enemy fighters intercepted. At the nose guns, 2d Lt. Sarnoski fought off the first attackers, making it possible for the pilot to finish the plotted course. When a coordinated frontal attack by the enemy extensively damaged his bomber, and seriously injured 5 of the crew, 2d Lt. Sarnoski, though wounded, continued firing and shot down 2 enemy planes. A 20-millimeter shell which burst in the nose of the bomber knocked him into the catwalk under the cockpit. With indomitable fighting spirit, he crawled back to his post and kept on firing until he collapsed on his guns. 2d Lt. Sarnoski by his resolute defense of his aircraft at the price of his life, made possible the completion of a vitally important mission.

ZEAMER, JAY JR. (Air Mission)

Rank and Organization: Major, U.S. Army Air Corps.
Born: Carlisle, Pennsylvania.
Entered Service At: Machias, Maine.
Place and Date: Over Buka area, Solomon Islands, June 16, 1943.

Citation: On June 16, 1943, Maj. Zeamer (then Capt.) volunteered as pilot of a bomber on an important photographic mission covering a formidably defended area in the vicinity of Buka, Solomon Islands. While photographing the Buka airdrome, his crew observed about 20 enemy fighters on the field, many of them taking off. Despite the certainty of a dangerous attack by this strong force, Maj. Zeamer proceeded with his mapping run, even after the enemy attack began. In the ensuing engagement, Maj. Zeamer sustained gunshot wounds in both arms and legs, 1 leg being broken. Despite his injuries, he maneuvered the damaged plane so skillfully that his gunners were able to fight off the enemy during a running fight which lasted 40 minutes. The crew destroyed at least 5 hostile planes, of which Maj. Zeamer himself shot down 1. Although weak from loss of blood, he refused medical aid until the enemy had broken combat. He then turned over the controls, but continued to exercise command despite lapses into unconsciousness, and directed the flight to a base 580 miles away. In this voluntary action, Maj. Zeamer, with superb skill, resolution, and courage, accomplished a mission of great value.

OFFICIAL COMMUNIQUE:
United Nations
ALLIED HEADQUARTERS IN AUSTRALIA, Thursday, June 17 – The noon communique:

NORTHWESTERN SECTOR
Celebes
Kendari: Our heavy units bombed the airdrome after dark with sixteen tons of bombs dropped in the dispersal areas. Numerous explosions occurred among parked aircraft. Fires started were visible for fifty miles. A direct hit was scored on administration installations and on an anti-aircraft battery.

Timor
Kupang: Our medium units in a night raid bombed the town, starting fires.

NORTHEASTERN SECTOR

Solomons
Buka Passage: One of our heavy units on reconnaissance, attacked by fifteen enemy planes, fought its way back to its base in spite of five casualties among the crew.

New Britain
Cape Gloucester: One of our night reconnaissance units bombed the airdrome.

New Guinea
Finschhafen: One of our medium units on night patrol bombed and machine-gunned an enemy powerboat near Hanisch Harbor.
Markham Valley: Our long-range fighters effectively strafed enemy-occupied Boana village and adjacent areas.
Ramu River: Six enemy bombers, escorted by six fighters, attacked the native villages of Kainantu and Aiyura.
Mubo: Our attack planes bombed and strafed enemy territory along Buigap Creek.
Buna: Three enemy bombers raided near Cape Sudest at dusk without damage or casualties.

†VAN VOORHIS, BRUCE AVERY

Rank and Organization: Lieutenant Commander, U.S. Navy.
Born: January 29, 1908, Aberdeen, Washington.
Entered Service At: Nevada.
Place and Date: Greenwich Island, Solomon Islands, July 6, 1943.
Citation: For conspicuous gallantry and intrepidity at the risk of his life above and beyond the call of duty as Squadron Commander of Bombing Squadron 102 and as Plane Commander of a PB4Y-1 Patrol Bomber operating against the enemy on Japanese-held Greenwich Island during the battle of the Solomon Islands, July 6, 1943. Fully aware of the limited chance of surviving an urgent mission, voluntarily undertaken to prevent a surprise Japanese attack against our forces, Lt. Comdr. Van Voorhis took off in total darkness on a perilous 700-mile flight without escort or support. Successful in reaching his objective despite treacherous and varying winds, low visibility and difficult terrain, he fought a lone but relentless battle under fierce antiaircraft fire and overwhelming aerial opposition. Forced lower and lower by pursuing planes, he coolly persisted in his mission of destruction. Abandoning all chance of a safe return he executed 6 bold, ground-level attacks to demolish the enemy's vital radio station, installations, anti-aircraft guns and crews with bombs and machinegun fire, and to destroy 1 fighter airplane in the air and 3 on the water. Caught in his own bomb blast, Lt. Comdr. Van Voorhis crashed into the lagoon off the beach, sacrificing himself in a singlehanded fight against almost insuperable odds, to make a distinctive contribution to our continued offensive in driving the Japanese from the Solomons and, by his superb daring, courage, and resoluteness of purpose, enhanced the finest traditions of the U.S. Naval Service. He gallantly gave his life for his country.

OFFICIAL COMMUNIQUE:
United Nations
ALLIED HEADQUARTERS IN AUSTRALIA, Wednesday, July 7 – The noon
communique:

NORTHWESTERN SECTOR

Timor
Kupang: Our medium units after dark bombed the Penfui airdrome, causing explosions and numerous large and small fires.

Dutch New Guinea
Kaukenau: Our medium bombers bombed the enemy-held village of Keaukwa.
Babo: Our heavy bombers bombed the airdrome at dusk in adverse weather. Results could not be observed.

Arafura Sea
Three enemy float planes and four medium bombers attempted to attack a small Allied convoy shortly before midday, but were driven off by our fighter escort.

Darwin
Twenty-seven enemy bombers, escorted by twenty-one fighters, raided the area at midday and caused slight damage to ground installations. Our intercepting fighters destroyed five bombers and two fighters, probably destroyed two bombers and damaged two others. We lost seven planes. Three pilots were saved and three others were seen to bail out.

NORTHEASTERN SECTOR

New Guinea
Bena Bena: Nine enemy bombers and four fighters ineffectively raided the area during the day.
Lae: Our mediums bombed and strafed enemy installations at Labu Lagoon.
Salamaua: Patrol clashes occurred in the Bobdubi Ridge area.
Nassau Bay: Eight enemy medium bombers and seven dive bombers attacked the area shortly after midday. We sustained no damage nor casualties.

SOLOMONS
(South Pacific Forces)

Buin-Faisi Area
Heavy bombers attacked the enemy airdrome on Ballale Island with twenty tons of high explosives, starting fires. Twelve fighters intercepted, but all of our planes returned.

Kula Gulf
Preliminary dispatches report our naval surface units intercepted an enemy force consisting of cruisers and destroyers in Kula Gulf the night of the 5th. Details are not yet available and a final assessment cannot be made, but it is indicated that six enemy ships probably were sunk and four damaged. We lost one cruiser.

One damaged enemy destroyer beached near Bambari Harbor was attacked by our medium and dive bombers, which scored seven direct hits with 500-pound bombs, resulting in violent explosions and fires. Four of seven intercepting Zeros were downed by fighter escort. One of our heavy bombers on reconnaissance, attacked by five Zeros, shot down two and probably destroyed a third.

†PARLE, JOHN JOSEPH
Rank and Organization: Ensign, U.S. Naval Reserve.
Born: May 26, 1920, Omaha, Nebraska.
Entered Service At: Nebraska.
Place and Date: Sicily, July 9-10, 1943.
Citation: For valor and courage above and beyond the call of duty as Officer-in-Charge of Small Boats in the U.S.S. *LST 375* during the amphibious assault on the island of Sicily, July 9-10, 1943. Realizing that a detonation of explosives would prematurely disclose to the enemy the assault about to be carried out, and with full knowledge of the peril involved, Ens. Parle unhesitatingly risked his life to extinguish a smoke pot accidentally ignited in a boat carrying charges of high explosives, detonating fuses, and ammunition. Undaunted by fire and blinding smoke, he entered the craft, quickly snuffed out a burning fuse, and after failing in his desperate efforts to extinguish the fire pot, finally seized it with both hands and threw it over the side. Although he succumbed a week later from smoke and fumes inhaled, Ens. Parle's heroic self-sacrifice prevented grave damage to the ship and personnel and insured the security of a vital mission. He gallantly gave his life in the service of his country.

†CRAIG, ROBERT

Rank and Organization: Second Lieutenant, U.S. Army, 15th Infantry, 3d Infantry Division.
Born: Scotland.
Entered Service At: Toledo, Ohio.
Place and Date: Near Favoratta, Sicily, July 11, 1943.
Citation: For conspicuous gallantry and intrepidity at the risk of his life above and beyond the call of duty, on July 11, 1943, at Favoratta, Sicily. 2d Lt. Craig voluntarily undertook the perilous task of locating and destroying a hidden enemy machinegun which had halted the advance of his company. Attempts by three other officers to locate the weapon resulted in failure, with each officer receiving wounds. 2d Lt. Craig located the gun and snaked his way to a point within 35 yards of the hostile position before being discovered. Charging headlong into the furious automatic fire, he reached the gun, stood over it, and killed the three crew members with his carbine. With this obstacle removed, his company continued its advance. Shortly thereafter, while advancing down the forward slope of a ridge, 2d Lt. Craig and his platoon, in a position devoid of cover and concealment, encountered the fire of approximately 100 enemy soldiers. Electing to sacrifice himself so that his platoon might carry on the battle, he ordered his men to withdraw to the cover of the crest while he drew the enemy fire to himself. With no hope of survival, he charged toward the enemy until he was within 25 yards of them. Assuming a kneeling position, he killed 5 and wounded 3 enemy soldiers. While the hostile force concentrated fire on him, his platoon reached the cover of the crest. 2d Lt. Craig was killed by enemy fire, but his intrepid action so inspired his men that they drove the enemy from the area, inflicting heavy casualties on the hostile force.

Note: The following is a newspaper account of the preceding battle in which both Ensign Parle and 2d Lt. Craig earned the Medal of Honor:

ALLIES ADVANCE ON 100-MILE FRONT IN SICILY; WIN BATTLES FOR BEACHES, THEN PUSH INLAND, BACKED BY SAVAGE AIR AND NAVAL OFFENSIVE

• • •

FIRST ROUND IS WON

• • •

**Enemy's Coast Defense Shattered –
Men and Guns Pour Ashore**

• • •

WEAKEST SPOT IS HIT
• • •

**New Invasions Hinted in
Washington, London and North Africa**

• • •

ALLIED HEADQUARTERS IN NORTH AFRICA, July 10 – American, Canadian and British troops smashed forward on a 100-mile front in southeastern Sicily today, heralded by a tremendous aerial offensive against enemy communications and airfields.

The first stage of the invasion of Sicily ended successfully at 6 A.M. today, when, after three hours of savage fighting on the beaches and intensive shelling by cruisers, destroyers and gunboats, the Axis coastal defense batteries were shattered and the success of all the landings was assured.

Men and Arms Pour Ashore

By 7:30 A.M., Allied infantrymen, their bayonets bright in the morning sun, were hacking their way inland through the enemy defenses and artillery was rumbling up the beaches to answer the Axis guns barking from the hills. Fierce fighting continued throughout the day. Fresh troops, guns and equipment poured ashore from landing craft and transports of the British and American Navies.

[The Allies landed between Syracuse and Catania, according to a Vichy broadcast recorded by Reuter in London. Other Axis reports, relayed from Berne, told of landings at Cape Boeo and in the Trapani area, in the western part of Sicily, and at Gela, in the southeast.

[Later enemy reports located the main battle area somewhere between Syracuse and Cape Passero, to the south. They said that heavy fighting was going on at Pachino, while the town of Noto had been captured. Reports from France, quoted by The United Press, said that the Allies were in close contact with Axis troops on the inland edge of the plain between Catania and Syracuse.

[In Washington there were hints of an imminent attack on the Italian mainland itself, while London sources, according to The United Press, said that the attack on

Sicily was not to be regarded as "the only landing." An Associated Press dispatch from Allied Headquarters in North Africa said that "other offensives may be in the offing."]

It was apparent tonight that, although Sicily was far from conquered, the Allies had scored a signal success in the first day's operation and that only a very strong and determined counter-attack could halt their steady progress north from the southeastern corner, where they had landed on beaches and landing points extending over 100 miles.

Weather Unfavorable

A heavy swell in the Sicilian Channel, where the landing craft rolled drunkenly, and unfavorable weather conditions in general did not halt the Allied attack. Almost two months after the eviction of the enemy from Africa, Old Glory and the Union Jack were planted on metropolitan Italian soil.

As the landing-craft grated on the beaches, men of the American, British, Indian, Netherlands, Polish and Greek navies sent hundreds of shells over the beaches onto the batteries, pill-boxes and rifle-pits on which the enemy defense of the bridgeheads depended. But the naval operations did not halt with the thunderous support of the landing forces. "Widespread naval operations" are continuing in the central Mediterranean area.

[The Rome radio, heard by The United Press in London, said that Italian naval forces had gone into action off Sicily and that Italian torpedo-bombers had damaged three invasion transports totaling 29,000 tons.]

All the resources of the Allied navies in these waters were thrown into the support of the landing operations. As important, but less glamorous, was the work of the thousands of seamen aboard the transports and landing-craft who brought their ships through a hail of bombs to the appointed places and guided the landing-craft toward the gunfire from the coast.

Most Vulnerable Area

The Allies landed in what is probably the most strongly defended and certainly the most vulnerable corner of Sicily. For not only are the forces landing on the southeastern corner within striking distance of airdromes like Comiso, which is about ten miles from the sea, but they are about sixty miles from Catania, the main port on the eastern coast; roughly fifty-five miles from the mammoth air base at Gerbini – one of the few still in operation – and thirty miles from Syracuse, one of the best ports on the east coast.

The resistance offered to the Allied troops today was stiff. There are a large number of Italian troops, including field and semi-static coastal divisions, and a large number of corps troops, such as coastal defense and anti-aircraft artillery, on the island. These have been stiffened by crack regiments originally intended for Tunisia, but switched to Sicily when the Germans were defeated in Africa.

Despite the fluidity of the tactical situation, it was clear that Anglo-American cooperation in the most difficult of all military operations – a landing on a hostile coast – had denied the enemy the use of Sicily as a submarine and air base and that the Allied troops were driving forward toward the air fields.

The first line of the Sicilian defenses has been pierced. The Germans must now launch counter-attacks strong enough to halt the Allies before they can secure any of the large ports through which the remainder of the huge and varied Allied force can pour.

There is every prospect of harder fighting ahead, especially if the Allies push toward the northeastern corner of the island, which, since its main port, Messina, is closest to Italy, is the most important enemy supply area. Messina is guarded by a mountain chain running from east to west across the northern half of the island, a chain that appears to offer the same difficulties as the Tunisian hills.

At 3 A.M. today, the American, Canadian and British troops, escorted and supported by a strong British naval force and a "token" American squadron and preceded by an armada of Allied planes, began what is believed to be the most important, hazardous and delicate operation yet attempted by the Allies in this war.

Vital to Next Moves

Not only is the invasion of Sicily the first step in the storming of Europe; its possession will give the Allies military advantages without which further operations in the Central Mediterranean area would be almost impossible. The fighting in North Africa, for three years, was a struggle for air bases. This is again true in Sicily. Once Allied bombers are taking off from such fields as Gerbini and Comiso, the air battlefront will extend into northeastern Italy and the Adriatic.

The capture of these airfields would remove any remaining threat from the air to Allied convoys passing through the Sicilian Channel.

Hazards Explained

The Allied offensive that opened this morning is hazardous and delicate for three reasons. First, the enemy has prepared the defenses of Sicily for just such an attack. Second, strategical surprise – that is, surprising the enemy by the invasion of Sicily – was almost impossible after weeks of very heavy aerial bombardment. Third, tactical surprise – that is, fooling the enemy as to the bridgeheads selected – became impossible at dawn.

There are no reports of any accident like the encounter with a German convoy off Dieppe that ended any chance of tactical surprise there. But it is unlikely that the enemy's aerial patrols did not sight the vast armada moving toward Sicily during the night.

First Reports Encouraging

ALLIED HEADQUARTERS IN NORTH AFRICA, July 10 (AP) – Surging ashore from wave on wave of landing craft, American, British and Canadian assault troops opened the invasion of Sicily at 3 A.M. today. In the first critical hours of the operation there were no official details of its progress or even a designation of the landing points and immediate objectives. But, as the hours passed, the feeling of quiet confidence around Allied Headquarters indicated that all was going according to plan and the first eyewitness reports of the attack were optimistic.

Reconnaissance photographs of the first stages of the battle, developed at an advanced airdrome, showed a spectacle hardly paralleled in this war as Allied warships laid down vast smoke-screens and pummeled shore batteries while the troops scrambled onto Sicily's rocky headlands. Barge-load after barge-load of troops drove onto the shore under a withering barrage from the coastal guns, which were also turned against Allied destroyers as they ran close inshore to cover the debarkation from transports to landing craft.

Violent aerial bombardment of Sicilian installations continued today. Allied fliers concentrated on the few airdromes still in use by the enemy, and on roads and other communications. They met little opposition.

The Allied fleet bearing the invasion army was made up of hundreds of ships spearheaded by fast destroyers and heavily armed cruisers, and included a great many of the latest-type landing barges. Many of these latter were understood to be huge tank-landing craft that came over the high seas from Britain or the United States under their own power.

[The Allies completed their initial landings without the loss of any ships. The Associated Press reported. The vessels encountered neither submarine nor air attacks.]

Under the invasion plan, the first troops ashore would be engineers and sappers carrying automatic arms and Bangalore torpedoes, small pipe-like grenades for blasting breaches in the barbed-wire that the Italians were reported to have planted thickly on the Sicilian shores. The proportion of American, British and Canadian troops was not disclosed. Hardened for this battle in prolonged maneuvers in England, the Canadians were believed to include veterans of the bloody clash at Dieppe.

The invasion was a landing operation of a scope unsurpassed in this war or in military history. The Axis invasion of Crete was a thumb-nail venture by comparison, while the overrunning of the Pacific Islands by Japan was far simpler because of the weakness of the Allied defenses.

There were no illusions here that the Sicilian campaign would end in a few hours or without a heavy cost. Some 300,000 of Italy's toughest fighters man the island's defenses, bolstered by a German shock force of uncertain size, but possibly as many as 100,000 men.

WAYBUR, DAVID C.

Rank and Organization: First Lieutenant, U.S. Army, 3d Reconnaissance Troop, 3d Infantry Division.
Born: Oakland, California.
Entered Service At: Piedmont, California.
Place and Date: Near Agrigento, Sicily, July 17, 1943.
Citation: For conspicuous gallantry and intrepidity at the risk of his life above and beyond the call of duty in action involving actual conflict with the enemy. Commander of a reconnaissance platoon, 1st Lt. Waybur volunteered to lead a 3-vehicle patrol into enemy-held territory to locate an isolated Ranger unit. Proceeding under cover of darkness, over roads known to be heavily mined, and strongly defended by roadblocks and machinegun positions, the patrol's progress was halted at a bridge which had been destroyed by enemy troops and was suddenly cut off from its supporting vehicles by 4 enemy tanks. Although hopelessly outnumbered and out-gunned, and himself and his men completely exposed, he quickly dispersed his vehicles and ordered his gunners to open fire with their .30 and .50 caliber machineguns. Then, with ammunition exhausted, 3 of his men hit and himself seriously wounded, he seized his Thompson .45 caliber submachinegun and standing in the bright moonlight directly in the line of fire, alone engaged the leading tank at 30 yards and succeeded in killing the crewmembers, causing the tank to run into the bridge and crash into the stream bed. After dispatching one of the men for aid he rallied the rest to cover and withstood the continued fire of the tanks till the arrival of aid the following morning.

OFFICIAL COMMUNIQUE:
United Nations
ALLIED HEADQUARTERS IN NORTH AFRICA, July 16, - A communique:

GROUND FORCES

Bitter fighting took place, especially in the eastern sector, where the Eighth Army made further progress against German troops, who desperately contested every inch of the ground.

Severe losses were inflicted on the enemy in the western sector. The Seventh Army advanced several miles across the difficult hill country and capture further important positions.

The following towns can now be added to the list of towns captured by the Allied forces: Canicattini, Bagni, Vizzini, Vittoria, Niscemi, Campobello, Palma di Montechiaro, Sortino, Modico, Comiso, Biscari, Riesi and Canicatti.

The speed of the advances is very satisfactory, but transport and supporting weapons are of necessity limited during the present stages. Little damage has been done by the enemy to communications.

†PETRARCA, FRANK J.

Rank and Organization: Private First Class, U.S. Army, Medical Detachment, 145th Infantry, 37th Infantry Division.
Born: Cleveland, Ohio.
Entered Service At: Cleveland, Ohio.
Place and Date: At Horseshoe Hill, New Georgia, Solomon Islands, July 27, 1943.
Citation: For conspicuous gallantry and intrepidity in action above and beyond the call of duty. Pfc. Petrarca advanced with the leading troop element to within 100 yards of the enemy fortifications where mortar and small-arms fire caused a number of casualties. Singling out the most seriously wounded, he worked his way to the aid of Pfc. Scott, lying within 75 yards of the enemy, whose wounds were so serious that he could not even be moved out of the direct line of fire. Pfc. Petrarca fearlessly administered first-aid to Pfc. Scott and 2 other soldiers and shielded the former until his death. On July 29, 1943, Pfc. Petrarca, during an intense mortar barrage, went to the aid of his sergeant who had been partly buried in a foxhole under the debris of a shell explosion, dug him out, restored him to consciousness, and caused his evacuation. On July 31, 1943, and against the warning of a fellow soldier, he went to the aid of a mortar fragment casualty where his path over the crest of hill exposed him to enemy observation from only 20 yards distance. A target for intense knee mortar and automatic fire, he resolutely worked his way to within 2 yards of his objective where he was mortally wounded by hostile mortar fire. Even on the threshold of death he continued to display valor and contempt for the foe; and raising himself to his knees, this intrepid soldier shouted defiance at the enemy, made a last attempt to reach his wounded comrade and fell in glorious death.

MORGAN, JOHN C. (Air Mission)

Rank and Organization: Second Lieutenant, U.S. Army Air Corps, 326th Bomber Squadron, 92d Bomber Group.
Born: August 24, 1914, Vernon, Texas.

Entered Service At: London, England.

Place and Date: Over Europe, July 28, 1943.

Citation: For conspicuous gallantry and intrepidity above and beyond the call of duty, while participating on a bombing mission over enemy-occupied continental Europe, July 28, 1943. Prior to reaching the German coast on the way to the target, the B-17 airplane in which 2d Lt. Morgan was serving as copilot was attached by a large force of enemy fighters, during which the oxygen system to the tail, waist, and radio gun positions was knocked out. A frontal attack placed a cannon shell through the windshield, totally shattering it, and the pilot's skull was split open by a .303 caliber shell, leaving him in a crazed condition. The pilot fell over the steering wheel, tightly clamping his arms around it. 2d Lt. Morgan at once grasped the controls from his side and, by sheer strength, pulled the airplane back into formation despite the frantic struggles of the semiconscious pilot. The interphone had been destroyed, rendering it impossible to call for help. At this time the top turret gunner fell to the floor and down through the hatch with his arm shot off at the shoulder and a gaping wound in his side. The waist, tail, and radio gunners had lost consciousness from lack of oxygen and, hearing no fire from their guns, the copilot believed they had bailed out. The wounded pilot still offered desperate resistance in his crazed attempts to fly the airplane. There remained the prospect of flying to and over the target and back to a friendly base wholly unassisted. In the face of this desperate situation, 2d Lt. Morgan made his decision to continue the flight and protect any members of the crew who might still be in the ship and for 2 hours he flew in formation with one hand at the controls and the other holding off the struggling pilot before the navigator entered the steering compartment and relieved the situation. The miraculous and heroic performance of 2d Lt. Morgan on this occasion resulted in the successful completion of a vital bombing mission and the safe return of his airplane and crew.

SCOTT, ROBERT S.

Rank and Organization: Captain (then Lieutenant), U.S. Army, 172d Infantry Division.

Born: Washington, D.C.

Entered Service At: Santa Fe, New Mexico.

Place and Date: Near Munda Air Strip, New Georgia, Solomon Islands, July 29, 1943.

Citation: For conspicuous gallantry and intrepidity at the risk of his life above and beyond the call of duty near Munda Airstrip, New Georgia, Solomon Islands, on July 29, 1943. After 27 days of bitter fighting, the enemy held a hilltop salient which commanded the approach to Munda Airstrip. Our troops were exhausted from prolonged battle and heavy casualties, but Lt. Scott advanced with the leading platoon of his company to attack the enemy position, urging his men forward in the face of enemy rifle and enemy machinegun fire. He had pushed forward alone to a point midway across the barren hilltop within 75 yards of the enemy when the enemy launched a desperate counterattack, which if successful would have gained undisputed possession of the hill.

Enemy riflemen charged out on the plateau, firing and throwing grenades as they moved to engage our troops. The company withdrew, but Lt. Scott, with only a blasted tree stump for cover, stood his ground against the wild enemy assault. By firing his carbine and throwing the grenades in his possession he momentarily stopped the enemy advance, using the brief respite to obtain more grenades. Disregarding small-arms fire and exploding grenades aimed at him, suffering a bullet wound in the left hand and a painful shrapnel wound in the head after his carbine had been shot from his hand, he threw grenade after grenade with devastating accuracy until the beaten enemy withdrew. Our troops, inspired to renewed effort by Lt. Scott's intrepid stand and incomparable courage, swept across the plateau to capture the hill, and from this strategic position 4 days later captured Munda Airstrip.

OFFICIAL COMMUNIQUE:
United Nation
LONDON, July 28 - A joint American headquarters of the European Theatre of Operations and British Air Ministry communique:
Strong formations of USAAF heavy bombers attacked fighter aircraft factories in central Germany today, while USAAF medium bombers attacked enemy airfields in northern France and Belgium.

The Fortresses bombed an aircraft factory at Kassel and an aircraft assembly plant at Oschersleben near Magdeburg. Bomb bursts were seen in both target areas. the unescorted Fortresses encountered a large number of fighters. Preliminary claims total over sixty enemy aircraft destroyed.

The heavy bombers were covered on their return by squadrons of USAAF Thunderbolts and RAF, Dominion and Allied Spitfires. The Thunderbolts encountered many enemy fighters, nine of which were destroyed.

Other Spitfire squadrons carried out sweeps off the Dutch coast.

While the heavy bombers were attacking targets in Germany, USAAF medium bombers, escorted by Spitfires, bombed the coke ovens at Zeebrugge, and RAF Typhoon bombers, escorted by Typhoons, attacked the enemy airfields at Courtral, Belgium and Merville, northern France.

From all these operations, twenty-three heavy bombers and one fighter are missing.

ALLIED HEADQUARTERS IN THE SOUTHWEST PACIFIC, Thursday, July 29 -A communique:

Northwestern Sector

Dutch New Guinea
Our heavy units bombed the oil field port of Bula, scoring hits on oil storage tanks and supply dumps, among workshops and on the airdrome, causing seven fires.

Timor
Our medium units at night bombed enemy airdrome at Lautem and Cape Chater, scoring direct hits and causing numerous fires.

Tenimber Islands
Our heavy bombers in adverse weather bombed enemy installations on Larat Island with unobserved results.

NORTHWESTERN SECTOR

New Britain
Vitu Islands: One of our heavy reconnaissance unites bombed enemy installations on Unea Island.
Rein Bay: Our medium units bombed and strafed a barge base in the vicinity. Seven barges and two launches were destroyed and hits on fuel dumps inland caused violent explosions and large columns of smoke. Nine of our escorting fighters engaged fifteen enemy fighters attempting interception, shooting down six and probably destroying two more.
Cape Gloucester: An enemy destroyer and a transport or cargo vessel with fighter cover were located by reconnaissance aircraft off Cape Gloucester and later were attacked by our heavy bombers. Direct hits were scored and both ships were left transport aircraft was destroyed on Cape Gloucester airdrome.

New Guinea
Huon Peninsula: Our medium units, in a low-level sweep along the coast from Pommern Bay to Finschhafen, attacked enemy barge hideouts. Eight enemy-occupied coastal villages along the barge route were strafed, starting small fires. Our light surface unites destroyed four large loaded barges off Mange Point during the night.

SOLOMONS
(South Pacific Forces)

New Georgia
Munda: Our torpedo and dive bombers, with fighter escort, dropped forty-seven tons of explosives on enemy positions at Gurasai, Bibolo and Munda Point.

Kolombangara
Our escorted medium units bombed extensively and strafed enemy supply installations at Webster Cove, causing fourteen fires. Our light surface naval craft at night intercepted four enemy barges in Blackett Strait, sinking two.

KISTERS, GERRY H.
Rank and Organization: Second Lieutenant (then Sergeant), U.S. Army, 2d Armored Division.
Born: Salt Lake City, Utah.
Entered Service At: Bloomington, Indiana.
Place and Date: Near Gagliano, Sicily, July 31, 1943.
Citation: On July 31, 1943, near Gagliano, Sicily, a detachment of 1 officer and 9 enlisted men, including Sgt. Kisters, advancing ahead of the leading elements of U.S. troops to fill a large crater in the only available vehicle route through Gagliano, was taken under fire by 2 enemy machineguns. Sgt. Kisters and the officer, unaided and in the face of intense small-arms fire, advanced on the nearest machinegun emplacement and succeeded in capturing the gun and its crew of 4. Although the greater part of the remaining small-arms fire was now directed on the captured machinegun position, Sgt. Kisters voluntarily advanced alone toward the second gun emplacement. While creeping forward, he was struck 5 times by enemy bullets, receiving wounds in both legs and his right arm. Despite the wounds, he continued to advance on the enemy, and captured the second machinegun after killing 3 of its crew and forcing the fourth member to flee. The courage of this soldier and his unhesitating willingness to sacrifice his life, if necessary, served as an inspiration to the command.

†YOUNG, RODGER W.
Rank and Organization: Private, U.S. Army, 148th Infantry, 37th Infantry Division.
Born: Tiffin, Ohio.
Entered Service At: Clyde, Ohio.
Place and Date: On New Georgia, Solomon Islands, July 31, 1943.

Citation: On July 31, 1943, the infantry company of which Pvt. Young was a member, was ordered to make a limited withdrawal from the battle line in order to adjust the battalion's position for the night. At this time, Pvt. Young's platoon was engaged with the enemy in a dense jungle where observation was very limited. The platoon suddenly was pinned down by intense fire from a Japanese machinegun concealed on higher ground only 75 yards away. The initial burst wounded Pvt. Young. As the platoon started to obey the order to withdraw, Pvt. Young called out that he could see the enemy emplacement, whereupon he started creeping toward it. Another burst from the machinegun wounded him the second time. Despite the wounds, he continued his heroic advance, attracting enemy fire and answering with rifle fire. When he was close enough to his objective, he began throwing handgrenades, and while doing so was hit again and killed. Pvt. Young's bold action in closing with this Japanese pillbox and thus diverting its fire, permitted his platoon to disengage itself, without loss, and was responsible for several enemy casualties.

OFFICIAL COMMUNIQUE:
United Nations
ALLIED HEADQUARTERS IN NORTH AFRICA, July 31 – A communique:

Both armies have made good progress.

On the Eighth Army front heavy casualties have been inflicted on the enemy, after successful artillery preparation had been carried out. The Canadian troops have continued to advance.

In the Seventh Army area 941 prisoners, including 500 Germans, were taken. French Moroccan troops (Goums) were in action. The unconditional surrender of the islands of Favignana, Levanzo and Marittimo [off the west coast of Sicily] was reported.

An air communique:

The airfields at Grottaglie and Pratica di Mare in Italy were attacked yesterday by our bombers and hits were scored on the airdrome building, in the dispersal areas, and fires were started. Enemy shipping and the port of Milazzo [Sicily] were attacked by fighter-bombers, one merchant vessel being sunk. Lightning bombers carried out attacks on enemy positions in eastern Sicily.

Sweeps and patrols were maintained during the day by our fighters. In the course of these operations five enemy aircraft were destroyed.

P-40 Warhawks carried out a sweep over southern Sardinia. a number of enemy fighters were encountered and twenty-one of them were shot down.

From all of these operations one of our aircraft is missing.

ALLIED HEADQUARTERS IN THE SOUTHWEST PACIFIC,
Sunday, Aug. 1 – a communique:

SOLOMONS
(South Pacific Forces)

New Georgia
Munda: Our torpedo and dive bombers with fighter escort attacked enemy gun
positions on Bibolo Hill with fifty-two tons of explosives. Thirty enemy fighters
attempting to intercept the bombers were driven off by our fighters. We lost two
fighters. One pilot was saved.

Kolombangara
Vila: Our heavy and medium dive bombers with strong fighter escort made a series of coordinated attacks on enemy camps and positions at Vila airdrome and
Stanmore Plantation, dropping sixty tons of bombs in the target areas. Although
strong anti-aircraft opposition was encountered, all our planes returned.

Blackett Strait
Our light naval craft on night patrol sank a small enemy auxiliary vessel off Mersu
Cove. Two barges were strafed and possibly sunk.

†BAKER, ADDISON E. (Air Mission)
Rank and Organization: Lieutenant Colonel, U.S. Army Air Corps, 93d
Heavy Bombardment Group.
Born: January 1, 1907, Chicago, Illinois.
Entered Service At: Akron, Ohio.
Place and Date: Ploesti Raid, Rumania, August 1, 1943.
Citation: For conspicuous gallantry and intrepidity above and beyond the
call of duty in action with the enemy on
August 1, 1943. On this date he led his command, the 93d Heavy Bombardment Group, on a daring low-level attack against enemy oil refineries
and installations at Ploesti, Rumania. Approaching the target, his aircraft
was hit by a large caliber anti-aircraft shell, seriously damaged and set on
fire. Ignoring the fact he was flying over terrain suitable for soft landing,
he refused to jeopardize the mission by breaking up the lead formation and
continued unswervingly to lead his group to the target upon which he
dropped his bombs with devastating effect. Only then did he leave formation, but his valiant attempts to gain sufficient altitude for the crew to escape by parachute were unavailing and his aircraft crashed in flames after
his successful efforts to avoid other planes in formation. By extraordinary

flying skill, gallant leadership and intrepidity, Lt. Col. Baker rendered outstanding, distinguished, and valorous service to our Nation.

†HUGHES, LLOYD H. (Air Mission)
Rank and Organization: Second Lieutenant, U.S. Army Air Corps, 564th Bomber Squadron, 389th Bomber Group, 9th Air Force.
Born: July 12, 1921, Alexandria, Louisiana.
Entered Service At: San Antonio, Texas.
Place and Date: Ploesti Raid, Rumania, August 1, 1943.
Citation: For conspicuous gallantry in action and intrepidity at the risk of his life above and beyond the call of duty. On August 1, 1943, 2d Lt. Hughes served in the capacity of pilot of a heavy bombardment aircraft participating in a long and hazardous minimum-altitude attack against the Axis oil refineries of Ploesti, Rumania, launched from the northern shores of Africa. Flying in the last formation to attack the target, he arrived in the target area after previous flights had thoroughly alerted the enemy defenses. Approaching the target through intense and accurate antiaircraft fire and dense balloon barrages at dangerously low altitude, his plane received several direct hits from both large and small caliber antiaircraft guns which seriously damaged his aircraft, causing sheets of escaping gasoline to stream from the bomb bay and from the left wing. This damage was inflicted at a time prior to reaching the target when 2d Lt. Hughes could have made a forced landing in any of the grain fields readily available at that time. The target area was blazing with burning oil tanks and damaged refinery installations from which flames leaped high above the bombing level of the formation. With full knowledge of the consequences of entering this blazing inferno when his airplane was profusely leaking gasoline in two separate locations, 2d Lt. Hughes, motivated only by his high conception of duty which called for the destruction of his assigned target at any cost, did not elect to make a forced landing or turn back from the attack. Instead, rather than jeopardize the formation and the success of the attack, he unhesitatingly entered the blazing area and dropped his bomb load with great precision. After successfully bombing the objective, his aircraft emerged from the conflagration with the left wing aflame. Only then did he attempt a forced landing, but because of the advanced stage of the fire enveloping his aircraft the plane crashed and was consumed. By 2d Lt. Hughes' heroic decision to complete his mission regardless of the consequences in utter disregard of his own life, and by his gallant and valorous execution of this decision, he has rendered a service to our country in the defeat of our enemies which will everlastingly be outstanding in the annals of our Nation's history.

†JERSTAD, JOHN L. (Air Mission)

Rank and Organization: Major, U.S. Army Air Corps, 9th Air Force.
Born: February 12, 1918, Racine, Wisconsin.
Entered Service At: Racine, Wisconsin.
Place and Date: Ploesti Raid, Rumania, August 1, 1943.
Citation: For conspicuous gallantry and intrepidity above and beyond the call of duty. On August 1, 1943, he served as pilot of the lead aircraft in his group in a daring low-level attack against enemy oil refineries and installations at Ploesti, Rumania. Although he had completed more than his share of missions and was no longer connected with this group, so high was his conception of duty that he volunteered to lead the formation in the correct belief that his participation would contribute materially to success in this attack. Maj. Jerstad led the formation into attack with full realization of the extreme hazards involved and despite withering fire from heavy and light antiaircraft guns. Three miles from the target his airplane was hit, badly damaged, and set on fire. Ignoring the fact that he was flying over a field suitable for a forced landing, he kept on the course. After the bombs of his aircraft were released on the target, the fire in his ship became so intense as to make further progress impossible and he crashed into the target area. By his voluntary acceptance of a mission he knew was extremely hazardous, and his assumption of an intrepid course of action at the risk of life over and above the call of duty, Maj. Jerstad set an example of heroism which will be an inspiration to the U.S. Armed Forces.

JOHNSON, LEON W. (Air Mission)

Rank and Organization: Colonel, U.S. Army Air Corps, 44th Bomber Group, 9th Air Force.
Born: September 13, 1904, Columbia, Missouri.
Entered Service At: Moline, Kansas.
Place and Date: Ploesti Raid, Rumania, August 1, 1943.
Citation: For conspicuous gallantry in action and intrepidity at the risk of his life above and beyond the call of duty on
August 1, 1943. Col Johnson, as commanding officer of a heavy bombardment group, led the formation of the aircraft of his organization constituting the fourth element of the mass low-level bombing attack of the 9th U.S. Air force against the vitally important enemy target of the Ploesti oil refineries. While proceeding to the target on this 2,400-mile flight, his element became separated from the leading elements of the mass formation in maintaining the formation of the unit while avoiding dangerous cumulus cloud conditions encountered over mountainous territory. Though temporarily

lost, he reestablished contact with the third element and continued on the mission with this reduced force to the prearranged point of attack, where it was discovered that the target assigned to Col. Johnson's group had been attacked and damaged by a preceding element. Though having lost the element of surprise upon which the safety and success of such a daring form of mission in heavy bombardment aircraft so strongly depended, Col. Johnson elected to carry out his planned low-level attack despite the thoroughly alerted defenses, the destructive antiaircraft fire, enemy fighter airplanes, the imminent danger of exploding delayed action bombs from the previous element, of oil fires and explosions, and of intense smoke obscuring the target. By his gallant courage, brilliant leadership, and superior flying skill, Col. Johnson so led his formation as to destroy totally the important refining plants and installations which were the object of this mission. Col. Johnson's personal contribution to the success of this historic raid, and the conspicuous gallantry in action, and intrepidity at the risk of his life above and beyond the call of duty demonstrated by him on this occasion constitute such deeds of valor and distinguished service as have during our Nation's history formed the finest traditions of our Armed Forces.

KANE, JOHN R. (Air Mission)
Rank and Organization: Colonel, U.S. Army Air Corps, 9th Air Force.
Born: McGregor, Texas.
Entered Service At: Shreveport, Louisiana.
Place And Date: Ploesti Raid, Rumania, August 1, 1943.
Citation: For conspicuous gallantry in action and intrepidity at the risk of his life above and beyond the call of duty on August 1, 1943. On this date he led the third element of heavy bombardment aircraft in a mass low-level bombing attack against the vitally important enemy target of the Ploesti oil refineries. Enroute to the target, which necessitated a round-trip flight of over 2,400 miles, Col. Kane's element became separated from the leading portion of the massed formation in avoiding dense and dangerous cumulus cloud conditions over mountainous terrain. Rather than turn back from such a vital mission he elected to proceed to his target. Upon arrival at the target area it was discovered that another group had apparently missed its target and had previously attacked and damaged the target assigned to Col. Kane's element. Despite the thoroughly warned defenses, the intensive antiaircraft fire, enemy fighter airplanes, extreme hazards on a low-level attack of exploding delayed action bombs from the previous element, of oil fires and explosions and dense smoke over the target area, Col. Kane elected to lead his formation into the attack. By his gallant courage, brilliant leadership,

and superior flying skill, he and the formation under his command success-fully attacked this vast refinery so essential to our enemies' war effort. Through his conspicuous gallantry in this most hazardous action against the enemy, and by his intrepidity at the risk of his life above and beyond the call of duty, Col. Kane personally contributed vitally to the success of this daring mission and thereby rendered most distinguished service in the fur-therance of the defeat of our enemies.

Note: The following is a newspaper account of the preceding battle for which Lt. Col. Baker, 2d Lt. Hughes, Maj. Jerstad, Col. Johnson, and Col. Kane were awarded the Medal of Honor:

PLOESTI OIL RAID DAMAGE BIG; PLANE LOSS TOPS 20, FOE'S 51

CAIRO, Egypt, Aug. 2 - American Liberator bombers fought through one of the most heavily fortified areas in the world and shot down at least fifty-one Axis fighter planes to destroy or heavily damage six great refineries and wreck the main pipeline pumping station in yesterday's attack on Rumania's rich Ploesti oil fields, Allied officials announced today

20 of the more than 175 Liberators from the Bomber Command of the United States Ninth Air Force were lost in battles over the target. The enemy, expecting that the allies someday would seek out the fields that provide the Nazi war machines with a third of its petroleum supplies and almost all its high-grade aviation gasoline, had guns barking from haystacks and other concealed positions and clouds of fighter planes aloft.

A number of other Liberators had not yet returned to base, a Middle East Air Command communique said, indicating that some might have been forced down in Neutral or enemy territory.

The reports of the great damage indicated the raid was well worth the price and the weeks of training, during which the 2,000 men who manned the attacking planes on the 2,400-mile round trip practiced against a "ghost" Ploesti built in the Libyan desert. They became so familiar with the reproduction of Ploesti that over the target, some pilots said, it was like flying over their home towns.

Among the planes bagged by the American gunners were many German Focke-Wulf 190s and Messerschmitt 109s and 110s.

A mounting toll of the damage to the Ploesti works was indicated as reports trickled in from the returning crews. The communique said it was a "successful mass raid" and that, in attacks with 300 tons of explosives and thousands of incen-diaries loosed at altitudes from 100 to 500 feet, "distillation plants, a fractionary tower, boiler houses, and tanks received many direct hits."

"Heavy explosions and sheets of flame were observed among oil refinery installations, while many fires were started," the bulletin said.

There are thirteen refineries in the Ploesti region, which lies about thirty miles north of Bucharest. Five of the biggest were damaged by the American bombers and a sixth was destroyed.

The Astro-Romano refinery, largest in all Europe, was heavily damaged by large fires that licked through it after the delayed-action bombs burst. The pumping station on the Giurgiu pipeline, which carries oil some seventy miles south to the Danube River, was battered by many direct hits, followed by heavy explosions.

The Creditul Minier refinery - newest one in the vast fields and producer of large quantities of aviation gasoline - was heavily blasted and it too was ripped by great fires. Vital parts of the Steaua Romano refinery suffered direct hits. The Colarmeo Aquilla refinery, fourth largest in Rumania, suffered direct hits and was set afire.

Formerly Standard Oil Owned

The most heavily damaged was the American-Romano refinery's distillation plant. Before Germany took over the fields the American-Romano was a subsidiary of Standard Oil of New Jersey. The Campini refinery, a large one, twenty miles from the town of Ploesti, was reported completely destroyed.

The returning airmen reported that on the way in to Ploesti they dived their massive bombers into Rumania's rugged ravines as if they were fighter planes.

The plane carrying the commander of the Ninth Bomber Command, Brig. Gen. U.G. Ent, was so low at one time that one wing tipped the middle of a tree. The crews said that, flying to and from the target, farmers and children in Greece and Rumania waved to them.

Lieut. Dan B. Lear of Houston, Tex., said he saw one Liberator on fire just a few seconds before the target was reached.

"But they came in anyway through a crossfire of ack ack and machine-gun bullets and directed their bombs just as they had been told in the briefing sessions," he said. "The pilot couldn't pull up and tried to make a crash landing, but he clipped a wing on a tree and crashed to a flaming halt."

Some pilots missed the target on the first run and turned back through the inferno to try again, the second time successfully.

The low-level bombings with special bombsights was so accurate that it was officially stated the civilian population was believed to have suffered a minimum of harm.

Air Chief Marshal Sir W. Sholto Douglas, chief of the Middle East Air Command, sent a message of praise for General Ent and the bomber crews to Lieut.

Gen. Lewis H. Brereton, commander of the Ninth Air Force and of all United States forces in this area.

Persons strolled in as the attack was in progress and Maj. Norman P. Appold, of Detroit, said:

"It was the darnedest thing ever. While civilians in the streets waved at us, gunners on the house tops were shooting at us."

"The boys took a lesson in street-fighting on this mission," said Maj. Harry T. Bauer of St Louis. "We saw many personal battles between waist and tail gunners and batteries in the fields, roads and roof tops."

Bombers Flew Through Flames

"It was more like an artist's conception of an air battle than anything I ever thought could be," was the comment today of Col. Leon W. Johnson of Moline, Kansas, who led one of the bomber groups over the Ploesti oil target yesterday.

Flight Lieut. George C. Barwell of London, an R.A.F. gunnery expert assigned to the Ninth Air Force, flew with Maj. Norman I. Appold of Detroit. He said the Liberators flew through solid walls of flame and had to bank steeply to avoid explosions at oil installations.

The Liberators swept down as they crossed the Balkan Mountains into the Danube plain of Rumania and dropped fast near the ground. Coming out, the formations, which frequently were scattered by then, scudded 150 miles "on deck" until they hit the Danube River again.

The enemy seemed to be throwing up every pursuit plane he had, said Lieut. Lloyd Holloway Jr. of Washington. Lt. Holloway's gunners accounted for four Axis planes in a running fight on the homeward trip. He said one plane flying ahead of his was flying so low that the open bay doors were ripped off by a corn field fence.

Air Chief Marshal Sir Arthur Tedder, the Allied air commander for the Mediterranean area, traveled from his North African headquarters to attend the briefing of the American pilots before the raid. He congratulated Gen. Brereton and the fliers on the job and said it might help "wobbling" Italy to make up her mind about the war.

†**REESE, JAMES W.**

Rank and Organization: Private, U.S. Army, 26th Infantry, 1st Infantry Division.

Born: Chester, Pennsylvania.

Entered Service At: Chester, Pennsylvania.

Place and Date: At Mt. Vassillio, Sicily, August 5, 1943.

Citation: For conspicuous gallantry and intrepidity at the risk of life, above and beyond the call of duty in action involving actual conflict with the enemy. When the enemy launched a counterattack which threatened the position of his company, Pvt. Reese, as the acting squad leader of a 60-mm. mortar squad displaying superior leadership on his own initiative, maneuvered his squad forward to a favorable position, he caused many casualties in the enemy ranks, and aided materially in repulsing the counterattack. When the enemy fire became so severe as to make his position untenable, he ordered the other members of his squad to withdraw to a safer position, but declined to seek safety for himself. So as to bring more effective fire upon the enemy, Pvt. Reese, without assistance, moved his mortar to a new position and attacked an enemy machinegun nest. He had only 3 rounds of ammunition but secured a direct hit with his last round, completely destroying the nest and killing the occupants. Ammunition being exhausted, he abandoned the mortar, seized a rifle and continued to advance, moving into an exposed position overlooking the enemy. Despite a heavy concentration of machinegun, mortar, and artillery fire, the heaviest experienced by his unit throughout the entire Sicilian campaign, he remained at this position and continued to inflict casualties upon the enemy until he was killed. His bravery, coupled with his gallant and unswerving determination to close with the enemy, regardless of consequences and obstacles which he faced, are a priceless inspiration to our armed forces.

OFFICIAL COMMUNIQUE:
United Nations
ALLIED HEADQUARTERS IN NORTH AFRICA, Aug. 5 - The regular communique:

In spite of enemy resistance our troops continue their advance along the whole front.

The enemy is trying to slow down our advance by leaving behind mines and destroying all installations.

In the Catania plain British troops have crossed the Dittaino and are now in the outskirts of Catania.

The locality of Centuripe is in our hands. Fierce fighting is now going on around Troina.

A special communique:

The city of Catania has been in our hands since 8:30 this morning. It is the British Eighth Army which has entered the town.

An Air communique:

Northwest African Air Force maintained its heavy attacks on the enemy in Sicily throughout yesterday.

Light and medium bombers attacked supply dumps and road communications, while fighter-bombers attacked motor transport and destroyed and damaged many vehicles.

On the night of Aug. 3-4, railway communications at Marina di Catanzaro and Paola were attacked by our night bombers. The attack on these two targets was continued yesterday by medium bombers.

Heavy bombers attacked docks and submarine bases at Naples. The target was well covered by bombs.

A number of enemy aircraft were encountered during these attacks and eleven of them were shot down.

Our fighters maintained sweeps and patrols during the day.

On the night of Aug. 3-4, five enemy aircraft were destroyed.

Last night bombers attacked Messina and railway communications at Battipaglia.

From all of these operations three of our aircraft are missing.

Further reports show six of our aircraft are missing from operations of Aug. 3 in addition to those previously reported.

A naval communique:

The coastal road and railway at Taormina, on the east coast of Sicily, were successfully bombarded by British naval units on Aug. 4.

On the north coast of Sicily cruisers and destroyers of the United States Navy continued to carry out day and night bombardment in support of the Seventh Army. The Army attributes its speed of advance along the coast road to this naval cooperation.

American patrol boats are very active in northeastern Sicilian waters.

The cleaning up of Palermo harbor is proceeding satisfactorily.

In the course of the last few days Allied shipping in the port has been attacked by formations of enemy aircraft several times.

Minor damage was caused before the raiders were driven off by gunfire from ships of the American Navy. In a raid carried out by thirty Ju 88s before dawn on Aug 1, at least seven of the attackers are known to have been destroyed.

†CHELI, RALPH (Air Mission)
Rank and Organization: Major, U.S. Army Air Corps.
Born: San Francisco, California.
Entered Service At: Brooklyn, New, York.
Place and Date: Near Wewak, New Guinea, August 18, 1943.
Citation: For conspicuous gallantry and intrepidity above and beyond the call of duty in action with the enemy. While Maj. Cheli was leading his squadron in a dive to attack the heavily defended Dagua airdrome, intercepting enemy aircraft centered their fire on his plane, causing it to burst into flames while still 2 miles from the objective. His speed would have enabled him to gain necessary altitude to parachute to safety, but this action would have resulted in his formation becoming disorganized and exposed to the enemy. Although a crash was inevitable, he courageously elected to continue leading the attack in his blazing plane. From a minimum altitude, the squadron made a devastating bombing and strafing attack on the target. The mission completed, Maj. Cheli instructed his wingman to lead the formation and crashed into the sea.

OFFICIAL COMMUNIQUE:
United Nations

ALLIED HEADQUARTERS IN THE SOUTHWEST PACIFIC, Thursday, Aug. 19 -A communique:

NORTHWESTERN SECTOR

Celebes
Macassar: One of our heavy reconnaissance units bombed the area after dark.

Borneo
Balik Papan: In the face of extremely adverse weather, our heavy units flew a total of 2,600 miles to attack at night this oil refining center and shipping in the harbor. Descending to masthead height, direct hits were scored on four large vessels, probably tankers, destroying them instantly or setting them ablaze, and two other large ships were seriously damaged. Fires again were started in the refining area, but accurate assessment of such damage was impossible because of poor visibility. All our aircraft returned to base.

NORTHEASTERN SECTOR

New Ireland
Cape Saint George: One of our reconnaissance units bombed a 4,500-ton enemy freighter-transport and damaged one of its four escorting fighters.

New Britain
Cape Bushing: Our medium units on night reconnaissance destroyed or damaged seventeen anchored enemy barges.

New Guinea
Wewak: We have completed the destruction of the remnants of the Japanese air force centered at Wewak. Of 225 planes originally assembled, yesterday's surprise attack destroyed 120 on the ground, three in the air and damaged fifty on the ground, leaving still existent fifty-two undamaged in addition to these fifty damaged. Our attacks in all categories were continued in incessant waves today. The enemy mounted thirty fighters to meet the onslaught and twenty-eight were shot down. The fields were then combed to practical annihilation and only ten planes of the 225 escaped.

The remaining 215 are now gone. We then struck the town and harbor area, setting on fire three medium-sized cargo ships, sinking a number of barges and leaving twenty large fires burning in the supply dump areas. We lost three planes to bring our total to six. This closes the combat.
Salamaua: Our attack planes bombed and strafed villages along the coast and barges and ground installations. Four or five small coastal vessels were hit and a number of previously damaged barges completely destroyed. Fires were started in Lattu Village.

WALSH, KENNETH AMBROSE
Rank and Organization: First Lieutenant, Pilot in Marine Fighting Squadron 124, U.S. Marine Corps.
Born: November 24, 1916, Brooklyn, New York.
Entered Service At: New York.
Other Navy Awards: Distinguished Flying Cross with 5 Gold Stars.
Place and Date: Solomon Islands area, August 15 and 30, 1943.
Citation: For extraordinary heroism and intrepidity above and beyond the call of duty as a pilot in Marine Fighting Squadron 124 in aerial combat against enemy Japanese forces in the Solomon Islands area. Determined to thwart the enemy's attempt to bomb Allied ground forces and shipping at Vella Lavella on August 15, 1943, 1st Lt. Walsh repeatedly dived his plane

into an enemy formation outnumbering his own division 6 to 1 and, although his plane was hit numerous times, shot down 2 Japanese dive bombers and 1 fighter. After developing engine trouble on August 30, during a vital escort mission, 1st Lt. Walsh landed his mechanically disabled plane at Munda, quickly replaced it with another, and proceeded to rejoin his flight over Kahili. Separated from his escort group when he encountered approximately 50 Japanese Zeros, he unhesitatingly attacked, striking with relentless fury in his lone battle against a powerful force. He destroyed 4 hostile fighters before cannon shellfire forced him to make a dead-stick landing off Vella Lavella where he was later picked up. His valiant leadership and his daring skill as a flier served as a source of confidence and inspiration to his fellow pilots and reflect the highest credit upon the U.S. Naval Service.

OFFICIAL COMMUNIQUE:
United Nations
ALLIED HEADQUARTERS IN THE SOUTHWEST PACIFIC, Aug. 29 – A
communique:

SOLOMONS
(South Pacific Forces)

Bougainville
Buin: Our escorted heavy bombers attacked Kahili airdrome and shoreline installations. Fourteen of thirty intercepting enemy fighters were shot down in running combat.

Santa Isabel
Our heavy bombers attacked Rekata Bay causing explosions and fires.

Kolombangara
Our medium torpedo and dive bombers bombed and strafed enemy barge centers on the south coast. Our fighters destroyed a small cargo ship and two barges near Ganongga Island.

Choiseul
Our fighters strafed and destroyed three enemy patrol boats off the coast.

†HUTCHINS, JOHNNIE DAVID

Rank and Organization: Seaman First Class, U.S. Naval Reserve.
Born: August 4, 1922, Weimer, Texas.
Entered Service At: Texas.
Place and Date: Lae, New Guinea, September 4, 1943.
Citation: For extraordinary heroism and conspicuous valor above and beyond the call of duty while serving on board a Landing Ship Tank, during the assault on Lea, New Guinea, September 4, 1943. As the ship on which Hutchins was stationed approached the enemy-occupied beach under a veritable hail of fire from Japanese shore batteries and aerial bombardment, a hostile torpedo pierced the surf and bore down upon the vessel with deadly accuracy. In the tense split seconds before the helmsman could steer clear of the threatening missile, a bomb struck the pilot house, dislodged him from his station, and left the stricken ship helplessly exposed. Fully aware of the dire peril of the situation, Hutchins, although mortally wounded by the shattering explosion, quickly grasped the wheel and exhausted the last of his strength in maneuvering the vessel clear of the advancing torpedo. Still clinging to the helm, he eventually succumbed to his injuries, his final thoughts concerned only with the safety of his ship, his final efforts expended toward the security of his mission. He gallantly gave his life in the service of his country.

OFFICIAL COMMUNIQUE:
United Nations
ALLIED HEADQUARTERS IN THE SOUTHWEST PACIFIC, Sunday, Sept. 5 –A communique:

NORTHWESTERN SECTOR

Amboina: Our heavy bombers attack Ambon, Latha airdrome and the enemy seaplane base at Halong in the late afternoon. Much damage was caused to installations and a four-engine flying boat was destroyed. There was no interception.

NORTHEASTERN SECTOR

New Ireland
Our night reconnaissance units combed and strafed Green Island.

New Britain
Our long-range fighters on a coastal sweep strafed and destroyed fifteen enemy barges at various points along the west coast and at Garove Island and destroyed a

park of motor vehicles at Gasmata. Our medium night reconnaissance units bombed and strafed the jetty and warehouses on Gasmata Island, Arawe and Vitu Island. Our heavy reconnaissance unites bombed enemy villages on Unea Island Tuem Island in Vitiaz Strait.

Cape Gloucester: Our medium bombers with fighter escort made a coordinated attack on airdrome installations, dropping twenty-eight tons of bombs and stafing the area. Fires were started in dispersal areas and medium and light anti-aircraft positions were silenced by direct hits.

New Guinea

Markham Valley: Our escorted medium units bombed and heavily strafed enemy installations at Gabsonkek, Narakapor and Yalu (villages a few miles inland from Lae) starting extensive fires.

Lae: Our escorted heavy bombers attacked enemy installations with eighty-four tons of explosives. Many hits were scored on gun emplacements around the airdrome and on the terrace area. All buildings in the administrative and headquarters area were destroyed. Huge clouds of black smoke rising 1,000 feet covered the area. Intense anti-aircraft fire was encountered.

LOGAN, JAMES M.

Rank and Organization: Sergeant, U.S. Army, 36th Infantry Division.
Born: McNeil, Texas.
Entered Service At: Luling, Texas.
Place and Date: Near Salerno, Italy, September 9, 1943.
Citation: For conspicuous gallantry and intrepidity at risk of life above and beyond the call of duty in action involving actual conflict on September 9, 1943 in the vicinity of Salerno, Italy. As a rifleman of an infantry company, Sgt. Logan landed with the first wave of the assault echelon on the beaches of the Gulf of Salerno, and after his company had advanced 800 yards inland and taken positions along the forward bank of an irrigation canal, the enemy began a serious counterattack from positions along a rock wall which ran parallel with the canal about 200 yards further inland. Voluntarily exposing himself to the fire of a machinegun located along the rock wall, which sprayed the ground so close to him that he was splattered with dirt and rock splinters from the impact of the bullets. Sgt. Logan killed the first 3 Germans as they came through a gap in the wall. He then attacked the machinegun. As he dashed across the 200 yards of exposed terrain a withering stream of fire followed his advance. Reaching the wall he crawled along the base, within easy reach of the enemy crouched along the opposite side, until he reached the gun. Jumping up, he shot the 2 gunners

down, hurdled the wall, and seized the gun. Swinging it around, he immediately opened fire on the enemy with the remaining ammunition, raking their flight and inflicting further casualties on them as they fled. After smashing the machinegun over the rocks, Sgt. Logan captured an enemy officer and private who were attempting to sneak away. Later in the morning, Sgt. Logan went after a sniper hidden in a house about 150 yards from the company. Again the intrepid Sgt. ran a gauntlet of fire to reach his objective. Shooting the lock off the door, Sgt. Logan kicked it in and shot the sniper who had just reached the bottom of the stairs. The conspicuous gallantry and intrepidity which characterized Sgt. Logan's exploits proved a constant inspiration to all the men of his company, and aided materially in insuring the success of the beachhead at Salerno.

OFFICIAL COMMUNIQUE:
United Nations
ALLIED HEADQUARTERS IN NORTH AFRICA, Sept 9 – a communique:

Operations of General Eisenhower's Allied forces which landed at about 4 A.M. (10 P.M. Wednesday, Eastern war time) in the area of Naples are proceeding satisfactorily.

Our troops are in contact with German forces and prisoners have been taken.

Landings were made under the protection and cover of the Royal Navy and United States Navy.

The disembarkation of troops with their guns and vehicles is proceeding according to plan.

All Allied forces on the Italian mainland are under the command of General Alexander and Lieut. Gen. Mark Clark, commander of troops engaged in landing.

A combined Allied Army, Air and Naval communique:

Naval Section: On Sept. 7 gunboats of the Royal Navy continued to support the left flank of the Army operating on the west coast of Calabria.

In the early hours of yesterday, Sept. 8, after light opposition, troops were successfully landed at Vibo Valentia in the Gulf of Sant' Eufemia in landing craft of the Royal Navy supported by warships.

Ground Section: Canadian and British troops of the Eighth Army landed in Italy have moved forward considerably.

The lateral road from Locri on the east coast to Gioia Tauro on the west is now in our hands.

German prisoners have been taken.

Air Section: Heavy bombers of the Northwest African Air Forces made a concentrated attack on German Headquarters at Frascati. There was strong opposition by enemy fighters, twenty-eight of which were destroyed. Medium bombers continued their attacks on bridges and roads at Trebisacce, Lauria and Sapri.

During the night of Sept. 7-8, medium and light bombers attacked the railway yards at Benevento, Metaponto and Potenza.

Fighter-bombers and fighters yesterday attacked enemy troops, gun positions and motor transports in the battle area.

Last night the railway yards at Battipaglia and railway and road targets at Eboli and Foria were attacked by night bombers.

A total of thirty-three enemy aircraft were destroyed during the period. Six of our aircraft are missing.

BJORKLUND, ARNOLD L.

Rank and Organization: First Lieutenant, U.S. Army, 36th Infantry Division.

Born: Clinton, Washington.

Entered Service At: Seattle, Washington.

Place and Date: Near Altavilla, Italy, September 13, 1943.

Citation: For conspicuous gallantry and intrepidity at the risk of life above and beyond the call of duty in action with the enemy near Altavilla, Italy, September 13, 1943. When his company attacked a German position on Hill 424, the first platoon, led by 1st Lt. Bjorklund, moved forward on the right flank to the slope of the hill where it was pinned down by a heavy concentration of machinegun and rifle fire. Ordering his men to give covering fire, with only 3 handgrenades, he crept and crawled forward to a German machinegun position located on a terrace along the forward slope. Approaching within a few yards of the position, and while continuously exposed to enemy fire, he hurled 1 grenade into the nest, destroyed the gun and killed 3 Germans. Discovering a second machinegun 20 yards to the right on a higher terrace, he moved under intense enemy fire to a point within a few yards and threw a second grenade into this position, destroying it and killing 2 more Germans. The first platoon was then able to advance 150 yards further up the slope to the crest of the hill, but was again stopped by the fire from a heavy enemy mortar on the reverse slope. 1st Lt. Bjorklund located the mortar and worked his way under little cover to within 10 yards of its position and threw his third grenade, destroying the mortar, killing 2 of the Germans, and forcing the remaining 3 to flee. His actions permitted the platoon to take its objective.

CRAWFORD, WILLIAM J.

Rank and Organization: Private, U.S. Army, 36th Infantry Division.
Born: Pueblo, Colorado.
Entered Service At: Pueblo, Colorado.
Place and Date: Near Altavilla, Italy, September 13, 1943.
Citation: For conspicuous gallantry and intrepidity at risk of life above and beyond the call of duty in action with the enemy near Altavilla, Italy, September 13, 1943. When Company I attacked an enemy-held position on Hill 424, the 3d Platoon, in which Private Crawford was a squad scout, attacked as base platoon for the company. After reaching the crest of the hill, the platoon was pinned down by intense enemy machine gun and small-arms fire. Locating one of these guns, which was dug in on a terrace on his immediate front, Private Crawford, without orders and on his own initiative, moved over the hill under enemy fire to a point within a few yards of the gun emplacement and singlehandedly destroyed the machine gun and killed three of the crew with a handgrenade, thus enabling his platoon to continue its advance. When the platoon, after reaching the crest, was once more delayed by enemy fire, Private Crawford again, in the face of intense fire, advanced directly to the front midway between two hostile machine gun nests located on a higher terrace and emplaced in a small ravine. Moving first to the left, with a handgrenade he destroyed one gun emplacement and killed the crew; he then worked his way, under continuous fire, to the other and with one grenade and the use of his rifle, killed one enemy and forced the remainder to flee. Seizing the enemy machine gun, he fired on the withdrawing Germans and facilitated his company's advance.

KELLY, CHARLES E.

Rank and Organization: Corporal, U.S. Army, Company L, 143d Infantry, 36th Infantry Division.
Born: Pittsburgh, Pennsylvania.
Entered Service At: Pittsburgh, Pennsylvania.
Place and Date: Near Altavilla, Italy, September 13, 1943.
Citation: For conspicuous gallantry and intrepidity at risk of life above and beyond the call of duty. On September 13, 1943, near Altavilla, Italy, Corporal Kelly voluntarily joined a patrol which located and neutralized enemy machine gun positions. After this hazardous duty he volunteered to establish contact with a battalion of U.S. infantry which was believed to be located on Hill 315, a mile distant. He traveled over a route commanded by enemy observation and under sniper, mortar, and artillery fire; and later he returned with the correct information that the enemy occupied Hill 315 in

organized positions. Immediately thereafter Corporal Kelly, again a volunteer patrol member, assisted materially in the destruction of two enemy machine gun nests under conditions requiring great skill and courage. Having effectively fired his weapon until all the ammunition was exhausted, he secured permission to obtain more at an ammunition dump. Arriving at the dump, which was located near a storehouse on the extreme flank of his regiment's position, Corporal Kelly found that the Germans were attacking ferociously at this point. He obtained his ammunition and was given the mission of protecting the rear of the storehouse. He held his position throughout the night. The following morning the enemy attack was resumed. Corporal Kelly took a position at an open window of the storehouse. One machine gunner had been killed at this position and several other soldiers wounded. Corporal Kelly delivered continuous aimed and effective fire upon the enemy with his automatic rifle until the weapon locked from overheating. Finding another automatic rifle, he again directed effective fire upon the enemy until this weapon also locked. At this critical point, with the enemy threatening to overrun the position, Corporal Kelly picked up 60-mm. mortar shells, pulled the safety pins, and used the shells as grenades, killing at least five of the enemy. When it became imperative that the house be evacuated, Corporal Kelly, despite his sergeant's injunctions, volunteered to hold the position until the remainder of the detachment could withdraw. As the detachment moved out, Corporal Kelly was observed deliberately loading and firing a rocket launcher from the window. He was successful in covering the withdrawal of the unit, and later in joining his own organization. Corporal Kelly's fighting determination and intrepidity in battle exemplify the highest traditions of the U.S. Armed Forces.

Note: The following is a newspaper account of the preceding battle for which Lt. Bjorklund, Pvt. Crawford, and Cpl. Kelly were awarded the Medal of Honor:

BITTER BATTLE RAGES AT SALERNO; BRITISH SWEEP AHEAD IN SOUTH

• • •

ALLIES PUSH INLAND

• • •

Salerno Changes Hands Frequently as Enemy Fights Desperately

• • •

**Eighth Army Takes Crotone and Drives
Onward as British in East Forge Ahead**

• • •

ALLIED HEADQUARTERS IN NORTH AFRICA, Sept. 13 – On and beyond the beaches around Salerno the Allies are engaged today in the entire Mediterranean campaign.

As the unyielding German troops, including the Sixteenth Armored Division, hurled tank-stiffened counter-attacks at the British and American lines and the air over the captured port of Salerno was still streaked with planes in deadly combat, the struggle was said to exceed in intensity anything that Allied troops had experienced in the early stages of either the North African or the Sicilian assaults. Lieut. Gen, Mark W. Clark's steadily reinforced army flung its own tanks at the German armor and repulsed one counter-attack after another.

Germans Fight Desperately

But, taking advantage of their prepared defensive positions, the Germans continued desperately to resist the Allies' hammer-blows aimed at breaking through their positions and sweeping inland.

A front dispatch said that the town of Salerno had changed hands several times yesterday in a violent battle in which allied warships flung their shells into the German troops.]

While the Navy steadfastly protected the landings of reserves and supplies, the consolidations of the beachheads continued within the range of German shellfire.

[The Allies have gained several miles and driven into the German-held mountains, a United Press dispatch from the front reported, but the Germans have counter-attacked deeply the center of the line. The Algiers radio, according to the Associated Press, said that the Allies were fanning out and had captured many towns and villages; and a National Broadcasting Company dispatch from the front told of a battle in progress two miles above Salerno on the road to Naples. All the landing parties have established contact, the dispatch said.]

In the south, however, there were virtually no enemy forces to oppose the British and Canadian units sweeping up the Calabrian Peninsula and the British force fanning out north and northwest from the Taranto-Brindisi line on the heels of the German First Parachute Division's rear guard. The Eighth Army took another useful port, Crotone. This is a town of 10,000 population, with fairly important chemical factories. It has been bombed repeatedly.

The general line of the Eighth Army now cuts east and west from Crotone to a point just south of Amantea. Crotone is thirty-two miles from Catanzaro.

British Pursue Foe

On the Taranto front the British established that there were no enemy forces cut off in the peninsula rimming the Gulf of Taranto on the northeast. They concentrated on chasing the German rear guards.

[The British radio said that Altamura, twenty-two miles southwest of Bari and forty-four miles inland from Taranto, had been captured, the Associated Press said.]

The Taranto campaign has given the Allies a number of useful airfields, presumably including Lecce, about thirty miles east of the city. It was formerly used by the Italians for long-range and torpedo bombers. Grottaglie, nine miles from Taranto, is important primarily as a fighter base.

In the Taranto area, all indicate, not only were Italian civilians cooperative but Italian military and naval personnel was also helpful to the invaders. It is likely that these forces and the Eighth Army will move up to relieve the pressure on the Fifth Army as soon as possible.

Still 120 Miles Away

Despite the rapid rate of the advance, slowed only by demolitions, the minimum distance ahead of the Eighth Army was 120 miles. This would mean that they would require four or five days to reach Salerno at their present speed. But the German forces that have evacuated Calabria and moved northwest through the central part of southern Italy via the important junction of Potenza could conceivably assist the defenders of the Naples area if they could get there though the relentless Allied air attacks on all motor transport within fifty miles of Naples.

The air war over Salerno decreased in savagery only slightly as ninety to 100 German planes traded machine-gun bullets with Lightnings and Spitfires. Four German machines were destroyed here, while in other operations the Allies shot down four other enemy planes. Two Allied planes were lost.

[American pilots are encountering a new problem since the surrender of Italy, The Associated Press said. They must now determine whether the planes that they spot are German-Seized Italian machines. This means recognition at fairly close quarters and possibly a heated dog-fight.]

On Saturday night, after the day when German counter-attacks on land reached a climax, Mitchells and Boston Pathfinders battered the road junctions at Auletta, Corleto and Sapri. Yesterday, Warhawks, Invaders and Baltimores resumed the attack, strafing hundreds of trucks in the same area. Allied airmen have destroyed 375 German trucks in four days. Seventy-eight were shattered yesterday and fifty to sixty were damaged.

Flying Fortresses, Marauders, Mitchells and lesser craft continued their devastating blows. The Fortresses raided the Frosinone airfield, forty miles southeast of Rome.

Other unescorted Fortresses went back to Benevento and Mignano, where important railway bridges and roads were bombed. Two bridges were hit directly at Mignano and left as twisted and pocked as the aircraft parked at Frosinone.

The Marauders struck at Isernia, fifty-five miles above Naples, and went up the coast to Formia, on the Gulf of Gaaeta. Am accurate bomb-pattern straddled the Naples-Rome coastal route.

Mitchells, for the third successive day, went over Casalnuovo, eight miles north of Naples, finding no fighter opposition, in contrast to the previous days. In general. the enemy air resistance was strongest over the area of the land battle.

ITALIAN TROOPS AID ALLIES

An Italian force that has joined the Allies "is fighting bitterly against the Germans near Ponticelli," near Naples, the British radio reported yesterday, according to the Columbia Broadcasting System. An Algiers broadcast, heard by The Associated Press, said that the Germans were battling Italian troops in the hills north and south of Naples.

Note: The following is a newspaper article about Cpl. (now Tech. Sgt.) Kelly and 2d Lt. Childers: ·

COMMANDO KELLY FINALLY IN U.S.; HE AND CHILDERS TELL OF FEATS

• • •

WASHINGTON, April 24 – Commando Kelly, Pittsburgh hero who punched a large hole in the ranks of the German Army at Salerno last September, is home at last.

Winner of the Congressional Medal of Honor, Tech. Sgt. Charles E. Kelly, as he is known to the paymaster, destroyed, single-handed, forty of Hitler's "invincible," with an assortment of weapons.

Today in an interview arranged by the War Department at the Pentagon Building he shared the applause of three Congressmen and 150 reporters with Second Lieut. Ernest Childers of Broken Arrow, Okla., also a winner of the country's highest honor for gallantry against the enemy.

While Pittsburgh and Broken Arrow fretted with impatience to see their native sons, both stopped off here long enough to recount in calm recitals details of their destruction of the enemy in the face of great odds.

The two bronzed and battle-hardened veterans are on twenty-one-day leaves. Neither exhibited the slightest nervousness as they faced interviews and photographers. Each told a story in calm, matter-of-fact tones and when they finished the listeners rose and applauded.

Sergeant Kelly, who summed it all up by saying, "You just take care of Germans" with whatever weapon comes to hand, looked slight of stature beside his companion. Lieutenant Childers, 6 feet 2 and weighing 185 pounds listened with interest as Sergeant Kelly told his story.

The 23-year-old sergeant began his story by observing:

"If you've got enough nerve you soon find out how the gun – any gun – works."

He blushed as he recalled the tight spot in which he found himself on the night of Sept. 13. He was assigned then to protect the rear of an ammunition storehouse to his own lines.

He arrived at the storehouse at the same time as a heavy German attack and remained there all night.

"Toward morning," he related, "when the Jerries came after us hard again, I went to one of the windows and started firing with my automatic rifle. Finally," he added in rueful retrospect, "the gun locked from overheating. I picked up another one and kept firing away until it, too, locked.

"It began to look as if we'd be overrun. I picked up a 60 mm. shell," he said. "but I didn't have any idea how the thing worked. So I pulled a safety pin and threw it, like a grenade. It worked – killed five Germans."

Orders came then to evacuate the position, but Sergeant Kelly volunteered to hang on, while the detachment withdrew.

"I went down into the cellar to find something that would shoot," he continued, "and I found a 'bazooka.' I learned how to load and fire that, too."

While Sergeant Kelly blasted away with this device, his unit withdrew to safety. He prepared to leave, also.

"As I ran," he recalled, " I turned and saw the Germans coming in the front door," but he rejoined his detail "without a scratch," except for some cuts inflicted by shell fragments. An official tally made after the engagement, credited Sergeant Kelly with killing forty Nazis.

Lieutenant Childers, who said he "didn't want to hang around the first-aid station," told how he and eight enlisted men went after three enemy machine-gun nests on a hill near Oliveto, Italy, Sept. 22.

Despite a fractured instep, Lieutenant Childers flanked the nests while the men set up a base of fire at its front.

"I got right along," he exclaimed, "until I was back of the Jerries and started crawling toward them. I had to pass a house which, I soon discovered, had a sniper in it. I saw him peeping out the window. He didn't peep again.

"I waited for a German to raise up out of a fox hole," he said, "but nothing happened and I waited. So did they. I was fresh out of grenades and I couldn't think of a way to get them far enough out of their hole for me to take care of them." At this point an idea came to Lieutenant Childers. He began to throw rocks at the hidden Nazis. This worked fine. The Germans took the stones for grenades and two of them leaped out. "I took care of one of them," said Lieutenant, and, shaking his head ruefully, he added, "One of my men beat me to the other one."

CHILDERS, ERNEST

Rank and Organization: Second Lieutenant, U.S. Army, 45th Infantry Division.
Born: Broken Arrow, Oklahoma.
Entered Service At: Tulsa, Oklahoma.
Place and Date: At Oliveto, Italy, September 22, 2943.
Citation: For conspicuous gallantry and intrepidity at risk of life above and beyond the call of duty in action on September 22, 1943, at Oliveto, Italy. Although 2d Lieutenant Childers previously had just suffered a fractured instep he, with 8 enlisted men, advanced up a hill toward enemy machinegun nests. The group advanced to a rock wall overlooking a cornfield and 2d Lieutenant Childers ordered a base of fire laid across the field so that he could advance. When he was fired upon by two enemy snipers from a nearby house he killed both of them. He moved behind the machinegun nests and killed all occupants of the nearer one. He continued toward the second one and threw rocks into it. When the two occupants of the nest raised up, he shot one. The other was killed by one of the eight enlisted men. Second Lieutenant Childers continued his advance toward a house farther up the hill, and singlehanded, captured an enemy mortar observer. The exceptional leadership, initiative, calmness under fire, and conspicuous gallantry displayed by 2d Lieutenant Childers were an inspiration to his men.

SLATON, JAMES D.

Rank and Organization: Corporal, U.S. Army, 157th Infantry, 45th Infantry Division.
Born: April 2, 1912, Laurel, Mississippi.
Entered Service At: Gulfport, Mississippi.
Place and Date: Near Oliveto, Italy, September 23, 1943.
Citation: For conspicuous gallantry and intrepidity at the risk of life above and beyond the call of duty in action with the enemy in the vicinity of

Oliveto, Italy, on September 23, 1943. Corporal Slaton was lead scout of an infantry squad which had been committed to a flank to knock out enemy resistance which had succeeded in pinning two attacking platoons to the ground. Working ahead of his squad, Corporal Slaton crept upon an enemy machinegun nest and, assaulting it with his bayonet, succeeded in killing the gunner. When his bayonet stuck, he detached it from the rifle and killed another gunner with rifle fire. At that time he was fired upon by a machinegun to his immediate left. Corporal Slaton then moved over open ground under constant fire to within throwing distance, and on his second try scored a direct hit on the second enemy machine gun nest, killing two enemy gunners. At that time a third machine gun fired on him 100 yards to his front, and Corporal Slaton killed both of these enemy gunners with rifle fire. As a result of Corporal Slaton's heroic action in immobilizing three enemy machinegun nests with bayonet, grenade, and rifle fire, the two rifle platoons which were receiving heavy casualties from enemy fire were enabled to withdraw to covered positions and again take the initiative. Corporal Slaton withdrew under mortar fire on order of his platoon leader at dusk that evening. The heroic actions of Corporal Slaton were far above and beyond the call of duty and are worthy of emulation.

OFFICIAL COMMUNIQUE:
United Nations
ALLIED HEADQUARTERS IN NORTH AFRICA, September 22 - A Communique

The Fifth Army continues to regroup and to move forward. San Cipriano, Montecorvin Rovella and Campagna have been captured.
The eighth Army occupied the important town of Potenza.

An air communique:

During the night of Sept. 20-21 light bombers of the Northwest African Air Force attacked roads and enemy transport in the battle area.

Yesterday heavy and medium bombers attacked railways, roads, and bridges at Benevento, Capua and Cancello.

B-24 Liberators of the Eighth United States Air Force, operating under the direction of the Northwest African Air Force, attacked harbor installations at Leghorn and at Bastia, in northern Corsica.

Medium bombers also attacked enemy troop concentrations and gun positions in the battle area. Fighter-bombers attacked enemy transport, while fighters maintained patrols over the battle area, where enemy activity again was on a small scale.

Last night harbor installations at Bastia were attacked by night bombers. From these operations two of our aircraft are missing.

KEARBY, NEEL E. (Air Mission)
Rank and Organization: Colonel, U.S. Army Air Corps.
Born: Wichita Falls, Texas.
Entered Service At: Dallas, Texas.
Place and Date: Near Wewak, New Guinea, October 11, 1943.
Citation: For conspicuous gallantry and intrepidity above and beyond the call of duty in action with the enemy, Colonel Kearby volunteered to lead a flight of four fighters to reconnoiter the strongly defended enemy base at Wewak. Having observed enemy installations and reinforcements at four airfields, and secured important tactical information, he saw an enemy fighter below him, made a diving attack and shot it down in flames. The small formation then sighted approximately 12 enemy bombers accompanied by 36 fighters. Although his mission had been completed, his fuel was running low, and the numerical odds were 12 to 1, he gave the signal to attack. Diving into the midst of the enemy airplanes he shot down three in quick succession. Observing one of his comrades with two enemy fighters in pursuit, he destroyed both enemy aircraft. The enemy broke off in large numbers to make a multiple attack on his airplane but despite his peril he made one more pass before seeking cloud protection. Coming into the clear, he called his flight together and led them to a friendly base. Colonel Kearby brought down six enemy aircraft in this action, undertaken with superb daring after his mission was completed.

OFFICIAL COMMUNIQUE:
United Nations
ALLIED HEADQUARTERS IN THE SOUTHWEST PACIFIC, Tuesday, October 12 – A communique:

Northwestern Sector

Celebes
Macassar: Our heavy bombers struck at the enemy base after dark. Twenty-five tons of bombs dropped among warehouses and fuel tanks near Juliana and Wilhelmina wharves and Fort Rotterdam, starting fires visible ninety miles. All our planes returned.

Kel Islands
Our medium units at night bombed the Langgur airdrome, causing explosions and fires in dispersal areas.

Tenimber Islands
Our medium units raided Saumlakke at night.

Northeastern Sector

New Ireland
Cape St. George: Our reconnaissance units bombed and fired a 6,000-ton freight-transport and sank or seriously damaged a 2,000-ton cargo shop.

New Britain
Our long-range fighters destroyed six enemy barges at Lolobau Island. Our reconnaissance units bombed the Cape Gloucester airdrome and installations on Mundua Island, in the Vitu group.

New Guinea
Ramu Valley: The enemy continues to withdraw under pressure of our forward elements.
Buna: Enemy planes raided the area after dark with minor damage. One plane was shot down by anti-aircraft fire.

Kiriwina Island
Six enemy planes ineffectively raided the island after dark.

†**OLSON, ARLO L.**
Rank and Organization: Captain, U.S. Army, 15th Infantry, 3d Infantry Division.
Born: Greenville, Iowa.
Entered Service At: Toronto, South Dakota.
Place and Date: Crossing of the Volturno River, Italy, October 13, 1943.
Citation: For conspicuous gallantry and intrepidity at the risk of his life above and beyond the call of duty. On October 13, 1943, when the drive across the Volturno River began, Capt. Olson and his company spearheaded the advance of the regiment through 30 miles of mountainous enemy territory in 13 days. Placing himself at the head of his men, Capt. Olson waded into the chest-deep water of the raging Volturno River and despite point-blank machine-gun fire aimed directly at him made his way to the opposite

bank and threw 2 handgrenades into the gun position, killing the crew. When an enemy machinegun 150 yards distant opened fire on his company, Capt. Olson advanced upon the position in a slow, deliberate walk. Although 5 German soldiers threw handgrenades at him from a range of 5 yards, Capt. Olson dispatched them all, picked up a machine pistol and continued toward the enemy. Advancing to within 15 yards of the position he shot it out with the foe, killing 9 and seizing the post. Throughout the next 13 days Capt. Olson led combat patrols, acted as company No. 1 scout and maintained unbroken contact with the enemy. On October 27, 1943, Capt. Olson conducted a platoon in attack on a strongpoint, crawling to within 25 yards of the enemy and then charging the position. Despite continuous machinegun fire which barely missed him, Capt. Olson made his way to the gun and killed the crew with his pistol. When the men saw their leader make this desperate attack they followed him and overran the position. Continuing the advance, Capt. Olson led his company to the next objective at the summit of Monte San Nicola. Although the company to his right was forced to take cover from the furious automatic and small arms fire, which was directed upon him and his men with equal intensity, Capt. Olson waved his company into a skirmish line and despite the fire of a machinegun which singled him out as its sole target led the assault which drove the enemy away. While making a reconnaissance for defensive positions, Capt. Olson was fatally wounded. Ignoring his severe pain, this intrepid officer completed his reconnaissance, supervised the location of his men in the best defense positions, refused medical aid until all of his men has been cared for, and died as he was being carried down the mountain.

OFFICIAL COMMUNIQUE:
United Nations
ALGIERS, Oct. 13 - A communique:

In the Termoli area some further progress has been made and patrols have pushed westward vigorously. In the central sector our forces are moving forward steadily over difficult country. Fifth army patrols have again been active and positions gained have been consolidated.

Light bombers of the Northwest African Air Forces attacked road junctions around Vasto yesterday. Fighter-bombers attacked gun positions around Cercemaglore and destroyed a train loaded with motor transport in the Termoli area.

Heavy and medium bombers were inactive yesterday because of unfavorable weather over target areas.

Last night railroad bridges and yards at Civitavecchia were attacked by night bombers.

None of our aircraft is missing.

†VAN NOY, JUNIOR

Rank and Organizations: Private , U.S. Army, Headquarters Company, Shore Battalion, Engineer Boat and Shore Regiment.
Born: Grace, Idaho.
Entered Service At: Preston, Idaho.
Place and Date: Near Finschafen, New Guinea, October 17, 1943.
Citation: For conspicuous gallantry and intrepidity above and beyond the call of duty in action with the enemy near Finschafen, New Guinea, on October 17, 1943. When wounded late in September, Pvt. Van Noy declined evacuation and continued on duty. On October 17, 1943, he was gunner in charge of a machinegun post only 5 yards from the water's edge when the alarm was given that 3 enemy barges loaded with troops were approaching the beach in the early morning darkness. One landing barge was sunk by Allied fire, but the other 2 beached 10 yards from Pvt. Van Noy's emplacement. Despite his exposed position, he poured a withering hail of fire into the debarking enemy troops. His loader was wounded by a grenade and evacuated. Pvt. Van Noy, also grievously wounded, remained at his post, ignoring calls of nearby soldiers urging him to withdraw, and continued to fire with deadly accuracy. He expended every round and was found, covered with wounds dead beside his gun. In this action Pvt. Van Noy killed at least half of the 399 enemy taking part in the landing. His heroic tenacity at the price of his life not only saved the lives of many of his comrades, but enabled them to annihilate the attacking detachment.

OFFICIAL COMMUNIQUE:
United Nations
ALLIED HEADQUARTERS IN THE SOUTHWEST PACIFIC, Monday, Oct. 18 - A communique:

NORTHWESTERN SECTOR

Activity was limited to reconnaissance.

NORTHEASTERN SECTOR

New Britain
Cape Hoskins: Our medium units at night bombed the airdrome, causing fires, and attacked supply dump areas at Gasmata.
Cape Gloucester: Our attack planes bombed and strafed the airdrome, dispersal area, supply dumps, and anti-aircraft positions. Three enemy bombers and four fighters caught on the ground were probably destroyed or damaged by our attack. There was no interception.
Rottock Bay: Our reconnaissance units sank or wrecked five enemy barges off the coast and destroyed a power launch in John Albert Harbor in the Vitu group.

FINSCHHAFEN

Finschhafen: Our fighters intercepted a formation of fifteen enemy bombers and twelve fighters off the coast, shooting down five bombers and a fighter and probably destroying three fighters. One of our night reconnaissance units bombed and strafed a small enemy vessel off the coast.
Oro Bay: A large group of enemy dive-bombers and fighters attempting to attack our shipping and installations was intercepted by our fighters and virtually annihilated before any damage could by done. Twenty-six bombers and twenty fighters were shot down and eleven other aircraft probably were destroyed. Some of our planes were damaged but all returned.

†**OWENS, ROBERT ALLEN**
Rank and Organization: Sergeant, U.S. Marine Corps.
Born: September 13 1920, Greenville, South Carolina.
Entered Service At: South Carolina.
Place and Date: Bougainville, Solomon Islands, November 1, 1943.
Citation: For conspicuous gallantry and intrepidity at the risk of his life above and beyond the call of duty while serving with a marine division, in action against enemy Japanese forces during extremely hazardous landing operations at Cape Torokina, Bougainville, Solomon Islands, on November 1, 1943. Forced to pass within disastrous range of a strongly protected, well-camouflaged Japanese 75-mm. regimental gun strategically located on the beach, our landing units were suffering heavy losses in casualties and boats while attempting to approach the beach, and the success of the operation was seriously threatened. Observing the ineffectiveness of marine rifle and grenade attacks against the incessant, devastating fire of the enemy weapon and aware of the urgent need for prompt action, Sgt. Owens

unhesitatingly determined to charge the gun bunker from the front and, calling on 4 of his comrades to assist him, carefully placed them to cover the fire of the 2 adjacent hostile bunkers. Choosing a moment that provided a fair opportunity for passing these bunkers, he immediately charged into the mouth of the steadily firing cannon and entered the emplacement through the fire port, driving the guncrew out of the rear door and insuring their destruction before he himself was wounded. Indomitable and aggressive in the face of almost certain death, Sgt. Owens silenced a powerful gun which was of inestimable value to the Japanese defense and, by his brilliant initiative and heroic spirit of self-sacrifice, contributed immeasurably to the success of the vital landing operations. His valiant conduct throughout reflects the highest credit upon himself and the U.S. Naval Service.

†WILKINS, RAYMOND H. (Air Mission)
Rank and Organizations: Major, U.S Army Air Corps.
Born: September 28, 1917, Portsmouth, Virginia.
Entered Service At: Portsmouth, Virginia.
Place and Date: Near Rabaul, New Britain, November 2, 1943.
Citation: For conspicuous gallantry and intrepidity above and beyond the call of duty in action with the enemy near Rabaul, New Britain, on November 2, 1943. Leading his squadron in an attack on shipping in Simpson Harbor, during which intense antiaircraft fire was expected, Maj. Wilkins briefed his squadron so that his airplane would be in the position of greatest risk. His squadron was the last of 3 in the group to enter the target area. Smoke from bombs dropped by preceding aircraft necessitated a last-second revision of tactics on his part, which still enabled his squadron to strike vital shipping targets, but forced it to approach through concentrated fire, and increased the danger of Maj. Wilkins' left flank position. His airplane was hit almost immediately, the right wing damaged, and control rendered extremely difficult. Although he could have withdrawn, he held fast and led his squadron into the attack. He strafed a group of small harbor vessels, and then, at low level, attacked an enemy destroyer. His 1,000 pound bomb struck squarely amidships, causing the vessel to explode. Although antiaircraft fire from this vessel had seriously damaged his left vertical stabilizer, he refused to deviate from the course. From below-masthead height he attacked a transport of some 9,000 tons, scoring a hit which engulfed the ship in flames. Bombs expended, he began to withdraw his squadron. A heavy cruiser barred the path. Unhesitatingly, to neutralize the cruiser's guns and attract its fire, he went in for a strafing run. His damaged stabilizer was completely shot off. To avoid swerving into his wing planes he

had to turn so as to expose the belly and full wing surfaces of his plane to the enemy fire; it caught and crumpled his left wing. Now past control, the bomber crashed into the sea. In the fierce engagement Maj. Wilkins destroyed 2 enemy vessels, and his heroic self-sacrifice made possible the safe withdrawal of the remaining planes of his squadron.

Note: The following is a newspaper account of the preceding battle for which both Sgt. Owens and Maj. Wilkins were awarded the Medal of Honor:

ALLIES ON BOUGAINVILLE
• • •

BIG JUMP IN PACIFIC

• • •

Americans Surprise Foe, Seize Bay
On Largest Solomons Island

• • •

MacArthur Challenges The Japanese Fleet
To Come Out and Fight

• • •

GUADALCANAL, Tuesday, Nov. 2 - Green-clad United States Marines swarmed ashore from landing craft early yesterday against fortified Japanese positions at Empress Augusta Bay on the west side of Bougainville Island in the biggest single allied landing in this theater.

They quickly had the situation "well in hand" and within an hour had established themselves between the two main Japanese forces on the island, which are estimated to total at least 30,000 men.

With American naval vessels standing proudly off after a deafening hour-long bombardment, with white columns of water from Japanese bombs spouting in the bay and with American naval Avenger planes strafing the beaches ahead, the landing craft bearing crack United States fighting men wound their way to shore.

[A spokesman at Allied South Pacific headquarters was quoted by The Associated Press as saying the Japanese planes that tried vainly to interrupt the landing were from Rabaul as all the enemy's Bougainville and Buka fields had been put out of operation by Allied bombings.]

The Avengers twice raced over the beaches, where crashing shells already had ground up the enemy's trenches and gun positions when the landing craft, coming from big transports out at sea, neared their destination.

Then the landing craft fanned out along the shore in movement of sharp precision and the Marines raced through the waves, and across the beaches.

So impressed apparently were Japanese reconnaissance pilots observing not only this but the American naval dispositions through the north Solomons area that a Japanese cruiser force, approaching from the north, turned tail and raced back toward Rabaul. It escaped as our own cruiser force moved swiftly northward.

Direct Threat To Rabaul

ALLIED HEADQUARTERS IN THE SOUTHWEST PACIFIC, Tuesday Nov. 2 - American ground forces captured Empress Augusta Bay in a bold invasion of west-central Bougainville Island at dawn Monday, 260 miles away from Japan's big key base at Rabaul, and Gen. Douglas MacArthur challenged the Japanese Navy to come out and fight.

Cognizant that this big move threatened to unhinge the entire Japanese position in the southwest Pacific and that the enemy must consider counter measures, General MacArthur said:

"If the Jap fleet comes out I will welcome it. I will throw everything we have against it."

This invasion of Bougainville, translating into air, naval, and amphibious action strategy planned by General MacArthur, Admiral William F. Halsey, and other high officials, moved the Allies 200 miles from the scene of their recent victories in the central Solomons.

The attacking force, which achieved its initial landings with such surprise that little opposition was encountered, thus by-passed Japanese positions on southern Bougainville and placed all enemy forces there in peril if they chose to remain.

The Japanese positions on the Shorthand Islands, fifteen miles south of Bougainville and on the newly invaded Treasury Islands and Choiseul also were by-passed.

Explaining the strategy and objectives of the Bougainville operation at a special conference at his headquarters Oct. 31, General MacArthur said repeated heavy air strikes "had neutralized Rabaul but had not prevented the Japanese from syphoning in reinforcements."

The Bougainville invasion followed preliminary - perhaps diversionary - landings last Wednesday on the tiny islands of the Treasury group, 30 miles south of Bougainville and sea-borne American paratroop landings on Choiseul, to the southeast, Thursday.

After his strategy conferences, General MacArthur said on the eve of the

Bougainville invasion, "if my luck and weather are right, Halsey should be able to land without serious losses."

He explained that the by-passing move, in addition to cutting enemy supply and communication lines in the sector, would afford Allies airfields from which fighters could provide cover for bombers raiding Rabaul from the south central Solomons.

"The Jap has been badly beaten and is beginning to lose some of his cocksureness," the general said, but he quickly added:

"The Jap is tough in body, tough in soul.

"Where will we strike next? I'll tell you about that another time."

Whereupon he strode from the conference room.

The American and New Zealand troops who invaded Treasury, meanwhile, captured Japanese mortar guns, as they pinned the enemy against the north coast.

The American paratroops, who landed on southwestern Choiseul, are advancing.

Besides General MacArthur and Admiral Halsey those participating in the strategic plans, now being translated into fiery action, were Lieut. Gen. Millard Harmon, commanding general in the South Pacific, and Maj. Gen. Alexander A. Vandegrift, who led the invasion of the Solomons at Guadalcanal on August 7, 1942. Gen. Vandegrift only recently returned to the South Pacific to lead the marine forces.

Having already bombed out Bougainville's southern air bases and badly smashed the Buka air base on the island's northern tip, fighter-escorted Avenger torpedo bombers and Dauntless dive bombers now have turned their attention to Kieta, on Bougainville's east coast directly across Bougainville from the invasion scene.

Today's communique said the raiders scored hits on the runway, buildings and bivouac areas.

Liberators and Mitchells, with an escort, also went back to Buka.

On Choiseul, the paratroops pushed the Japanese southeastward toward the barge depot of Sangigai.

†THOMAS, HERBERT JOSEPH
Rank and Organization: Sergeant, U.S. Marine Corps Reserve.
Born: February 8, 1918, Columbus, Ohio.
Entered Service At: West Virginia.
Place and Date: Bougainville, Solomon Islands, November 7, 1943.
Citation: For extraordinary heroism and conspicuous gallantry above and beyond the call of duty while serving with the 3d Marines, 3d Marines Division, in action against enemy Japanese forces during the battle at the

Koromokina River, Bougainville Island, Solomon Islands, on November 7, 1943. Although several of his men were struck by enemy bullets as he led his squad through dense jungle undergrowth in the face of severe hostile machinegun fire, Sgt. Thomas and his group fearlessly pressed forward into the center of the Japanese position and destroyed the crews of 2 machineguns by accurate rifle fire and grenades. Discovering a third gun more difficult to approach, he carefully placed his men closely around him in strategic positions from which they were to charge after he had thrown a grenade into the emplacement. When the grenade struck vines and fell back into the midst of the group, Sgt. Thomas deliberately flung himself upon it to smother the explosion, valiantly sacrificing his life for his comrades. Inspired by his selfless action, his men unhesitatingly charged the enemy machinegun and, with fierce determination, killed the crew and several other nearby-defenders. The splendid initiative and extremely heroic conduct of Sgt. Thomas in carrying out his prompt decision with full knowledge of his fate reflect great credit upon himself and the U.S. Naval Service. He gallantly gave his life for his country.

OFFICIAL COMMUNIQUE:
United Nations
ALLIED HEADQUARTERS IN THE SOUTHWEST PACIFIC, Monday, Nov. 8 - A communique:

Northwestern Sector

Amboina - Our medium units at night bombed Ambon Township, causing explosions and fire in the warehouse and barracks area and near the main pier.
Tenimber Islands - Our long-range fighters executed a low-level sweep against targets of opportunity, bombing and strafing Kandar and Lingat villages, Selaru airdrome, warehouses on Itan and Manwaan Islands and surface craft along the Jamdena coast. Four coastal vessels were sunk. Our medium units attacked two small cargo vessels northwest of Selaru and at night bombed Saumlaki, starting large fires.

Northeastern Sector

New Ireland
Cape St. George - One of our reconnaissance units from the South Pacific bombed a destroyer tender.
Kavieng Area - One of our heavy units on reconnaissance bombed an enemy light cruiser on North Mussau Island.

New Britain
Rabaul - Our medium units at night bombed Vunakanau airdrome and dispersal areas, starting large fuel fires. Simultaneously our torpedo bombers attacked shipping, scoring a probable hit on a heavy cruiser in Simpson Harbor and a hit on a cargo vessel in Keravia Bay, resulting in a heavy explosion and fire visible fifty miles.
Gasmata - Our fighters dive-bombed enemy supply dump areas at Anwek River.

New Guinea
Vitiaz Strait - Our light naval craft at night sank four large enemy barges and severely damaged a small barge off Kelana Harbor. One of our air patrols bombed the Bivouac area at Sio. Three enemy planes at night dropped bombs in the sea off Salankaua Point.
Ramu-Markham Valley - Shortly after dawn ten enemy bombers, with fighter escort, raided Nadzab airdrome and four fighters strafed Gusap, causing minor damage. Single enemy aircraft dropped incendiaries near Dumpu after dark.

Solomon Islands
Bougainville - Our medium units on a low-level sweep bombed the Kieta bivouac area, starting fires and destroying or damaging three small coastal vessels and twelve barges.

†GURKE, HENRY
Rank and Organization: Private First Class, U.S. Marine Corps.
Born: November 6, 1922, Neche, North Dakota.
Entered Service At: North Dakota.
Place and Date: Bougainville, Solomon Islands, November 9, 1943.
Citation: For extraordinary heroism and courage above and beyond the call of duty while attached to the 3d Marine Raider Battalion during action against enemy Japanese forces in the Solomon Islands area on November 9, 1943. While his platoon was engaged in the defense of a vital road block near Empress Augusta Bay on Bougainville Island, Pfc. Gurke, in company with another Marine, was delivering a fierce stream of fire against the main vanguard of the Japanese. Concluding from the increasing ferocity of grenade barrages that the enemy was determined to annihilate their small, 2-man foxhole, he resorted to a bold and desperate measure for holding out despite the torrential hail of shells. When a Japanese grenade dropped squarely into the foxhole, Pfc. Gurke, mindful that his companion manned an automatic weapon of superior fire power and therefore could provide more effective resistance, thrust him roughly aside and flung his own body

over the missile to smother the explosion. With unswerving devotion to duty and superb valor, Pfc. Gurke sacrificed himself in order that his comrade might live to carry on the fight. He gallantly gave his life in the service of his country.

OFFICIAL COMMUNIQUE:
United Nations
ALLIED HEADQUARTERS IN SOUTHWEST PACIFIC, Wednesday, Nov. 10
-Today's communique:

Northwest Sector

Dutch New Guinea
Kaimana: One of our heavy reconnaissance units scored a direct hit and two near misses on a 1,500 ton freighter.

Amboina
Ambon: Our medium units at night bombed the waterfront, starting spreading fires near the main pier.

Northeastern Sector

New Ireland
Our patrol units bombed land targets of opportunity.

New Guinea
Ramu: Four enemy fighters strafed Bena Bena and two light ineffective night raids were made on Lae.
Adverse weather interfered with all air operations.

Solomons
(South Pacific Forces)

Bougainville: Our patrol units bombed airdromes at Buka, Kieta, and Kahili.
Empress Augusta Bay: Our medium torpedo and dive bombers and fighters in support of our ground forces bombed enemy gun positions and supply areas southeast of Cape Torokins, destroyed or damaged numerous barges in Atsinima Bay and strafed rear areas. Our ground forces are engaging the enemy to the north near Arsinima Bay.

BRITT, MAURICE L.
Rank and Organization: Captain (then Lieutenant), U.S. Army, 3d Infantry Division.
Born: June 29, 1919, Carlisle, Arkansas.
Entered service at: Lonoke, Arkansas.
Place and Date: North of Mignano, Italy November 10, 1943.
Citation: For conspicuous gallantry and intrepidity at the risk of his life above and beyond the call of duty. Disdaining enemy hand grenades and close-range machine pistol, machinegun, and rifle fire, Lt. Britt inspired and led a handful of his men in repelling a bitter counterattack by approximately 100 Germans against his company positions north of Mignano, Italy, the morning of November 10, 1943. During the intense fire fight, Lt. Britt's canteen and field glasses were shattered; a bullet pierced his side; his chest, face, and hands were covered with grenade wounds. Despite his wounds, for which he refused to accept medical attention until ordered to do so by his battalion commander following the battle, he personally killed 5 and wounded an unknown number of Germans, wiped out one enemy machingun crew, fired 5 clips of carbine and an undetermined amount of M1 rifle ammunition, and threw 32 fragmentation grenades. His bold, aggressive actions, utterly disregarding superior enemy numbers, resulted in capture of 4 Germans, 2 of them wounded, and enabled several captured Americans to escape. Lt. Britt's undaunted courage and prowess in arms were largely responsible for repulsing a German counterattack which, if successful, would have isolated his battalion and destroyed his company.

†LINDSTRON, FLOYD K.
Rank and Organization: Private First Class, U.S. Army , 3d Infantry Division.
Born: Holdredge, Nebraska.
Entered Service At: Colorado Springs, Colorado.
Place and Date: Near Mignano, Italy, November 11, 1943.
Citation: For conspicuous gallantry and intrepidity at risk of life above and beyond the call of duty. On November 11, 1943, the solider's platoon was furnishing machine gun support for a rifle company attacking a hill near Mignano, Italy, when the enemy counterattacked, forcing the riflemen and half the machine gun platoon to retire to a defensive position. Pfc. Lindstrom saw that his small section was alone and outnumbered 5 to 1, yet he immediately deployed the few remaining men into position and opened fire with his single gun. The enemy centered fire on him with machine gun, machine pistols, and grenades. Unable to knock out the enemy

nest from his original position, Pfc. Lindstrom picked up his own heavy machinegun and staggered 15 yards up the barren, rocky hillside to a new position, completely ignoring enemy small-arms fire which was striking all around him. From this new site, only 10 yards from the enemy machine gun, he engaged it in an intense duel. Realizing that he could not hit the hostile gunners because they were behind a large rock, he charged uphill under a steady stream of fire, killed both gunners with his pistol and dragged their gun down to his own men, directing them to employ it against the enemy. Disregarding heavy rifle fire, he returned to the enemy machine gun nest for two boxes of ammunition, came back and resumed withering fire from his own gun. His spectacular performance completely broke up the German counterattack. Pfc. Lindstrom demonstrated aggressive spirit and complete fearlessness in the face of almost certain death.

Note: The following is a newspaper account of the preceding battle for which both Lt. Britt and Pfc. Lindstrom were awarded the Medal of Honor:

AMERICANS PUSH ON
IN DEEP ITALIAN MUD

• • •

Gain Mile At One Point and
Win High Ground as Weather
Slows Up Allied Advance

• • •

NAZI COUNTER-BLOWS FAIL

• • •

ALGIERS, Nov. 12 - The Allied armies in Italy came to a virtual standstill yesterday as the weather worsened and the Germans clung stubbornly to the Garigliano-Sangro line, which prisoners and documents have said the German command intends to hold at least eight weeks.

Lieut. Gen. Mark W. Clark's Anglo-American Fifth Army made local advances up to a mile at one unspecified point and smashed back sporadic counter-attacks. Gen. Sir Bernard L. Montgomery's British, Canadian and Indian forces made limited progress northwest of Isernia but were unable to do much along the south bank of the Sangro except consolidate previously won positions.

The Fifth Army took some prisoners in the course of counter-attacks around Calabritto and repulsed three specific German blows southwest of Mignano but the Nazis still maintained their grip on the town proper.

Americans Win High Ground

American units of the Fifth Army achieved the one-mile advance and also wormed their way up a commanding height in the vicinity of Mount Camino, west of Galluccio between Magnano and Calabritto. Mount Camino is 3,200 feet high.

There was a sharp patrol fight around Acquaviva, which is two and a half miles southwest of Forli del Sannio and six miles north and slightly east of Colli. The relationship of Acquaviva to the day's official line would indicate that the Germans had the initiative in this fray but it was on a small scale and in no sense represented a loss of ground by the Allies.

Mines and demolitions together with bad weather on both Allied Army fronts have combined to make progress difficult. The shortest distance to Rome remained at seventy-five to seventy-eight miles.

As yesterday, the Trans-Italian line crosses the narrowest portion of the Italian boot via the south bank of the Sangro River, Paglieta, Casalanguida Carunchio, Castiglione, Salcito, Rionero, Colli, Montaquilo, the Venafro-Mount Croce region, just outside Mignano, and to the sea via Calabritto and the southernmost loops of the Garigliano River.

Aerial Activity Hampered

The weather that bogged the ground forces in the mud and stiffened troops' fingers with cold also hampered aerial activity just beyond the battlefront.

Spitfires shot down two of fourteen enemy fighters, and Warhawks started many fires near German strong points. Other Spitfires destroyed six trucks on the Eighth Army front while A-36 Invaders blew up an ammunition dump and riddled four trucks near Cassino.

Royal Air Force Bostons and Baltimores cracked down on chemical works at Bussi near Popoli. The latter town is right of the north prong of two roads running through the Apennines from a junction four miles away from the Allies at Rionero. Popoli is thirty-five miles farther up and is important as the junction of a north-south road with the trans-peninsular road to Rome from Pescara on the Adriatic Sea.

Last night Wellingtons struck railway yards at Prato near Florence.

The day's air score was three of the enemy downed, to four of ours missing.

Additional aerial reconnaissance has shown two more ships scuttled at Leghorn while breakwater at Gaeta has been demolished. At Leghorn the north entrances are now completely blocked to shipping.

Photographs of the Savona iron works west of Genoa show that recent aerial blows heavily damaged main buildings and adjoining units.

It was announced today that the following infantry regiments were among the Canadian units in service of the Eighth Army: The Hastings and Prince Edward, from rural districts; the Royal Canadian, from the east coast; and the Carlton and Yorkshire, from the Maritime Provinces.

SCHONLAND, HERBERT EMERY

Rank and Organization: Commander, U.S. Navy, U.S.S. *San Francisco.*
Born: September 7, 1900, Portland, Maine.
Entered Service At: Maine.
Place and Date: Savo Island, November 12-13 1943.
Citation: For extreme heroism and courage above and beyond the call of duty as damage control officer of the U.S.S. *San Francisco* in action against greatly superior enemy forces in the battle off Savo Island, November 12-13, 1943. In the same violent night engagement in which all of his superior officers were killed or wounded, Lt. Comdr. Schonland was fighting valiantly to free the *San Francisco* of large quantities of water flooding the second deck compartment through numerous shellholes caused by enemy fire. Upon being informed that he was commanding officer, he ascertained that the conning of the ship was being efficiently handled, then directed the officer who had taken over that task to continue while he himself resumed the vitally important work of maintaining the stability of the ship. In water waist deep, he carried on his efforts in darkness illuminated only by hand lanterns until water in flooded compartments had been drained or pumped off and water-tight integrity had again been restored to the *San Francisco.* His great personal valor and gallant devotion to duty at great peril to his own life were instrumental in bringing his ship back to port under her own power, saved to fight again in the service of her country.

OFFICIAL COMMUNIQUE:
United Nations
ALLIED HEADQUARTERS IN THE SOUTHWEST PACIFIC, Saturday, Nov. 13 -A communique:

Northwestern Sector

Amboina Island - Our heavy units bombed Ambon at night.
Tenimber Islands - Our long-range fighters bombed and strafed the airdrome and adjacent villages on Selaru Island. Fires were started among supply dumps and in bivouac areas.

Dutch New Guinea - Our medium units executed a midnight attack on Babo, scoring numerous hits in the target area and starting thirteen fires, two of which were visible from thirty-five miles away. One of our reconnaissance units attacked an enemy float plane and shot it down near Cape Valsch. Our medium units raided enemy villages near Wissel Lakes.

Northeastern Sector

New Ireland
Kavieng Area - One of our heavy reconnaissance units bombed an escorted enemy convoy north of Mussau Island.

New Britain
Rabaul - Our medium units during the night bombed dispersal areas at Vunakanau and our heavy bombers dropped more than twenty-five tons of explosives on Lakunai airdrome causing large fires and explosions in the revetment area. Following these night attacks, naval torpedo and dive bombers from carriers with fighter escorts and heavy land bombers from the South Pacific struck enemy vessels in the harbor. The series of attacks was delivered during the morning hours. Pilots report that one cruiser and two destroyers were sunk and probably one cruiser and eleven destroyers were damaged. Twenty-four enemy planes were shot down in air combat.

The enemy later launched four attacks against our naval forces which were successfully repulsed by our carrier and land-based aircraft, ships and anti-aircraft fire. Sixty-four enemy planes were reported shot down. In all these actions we lost seventeen planes and others were damaged. Our carriers, escorting naval vessels, sustained only minor damage and light casualties.
Gazelle Peninsula - One of four night patrols bombed an enemy convoy off Cape Pomas.

New Guinea
Alexishafen - Our attack planes and fighters, coming in at minimum altitude, bombed and strafed airdrome, dispersal areas, gun positions, and fuel dumps, destroying or damaging five bombers and a fighter on the ground. An enemy dive bomber in the air was shot down.

Solomons

Bougainville
Buka - Our escorted torpedo and dive bombers in strength attacked Buka and Bonis airdromes shortly after dawn, scoring heavily on the runway gun positions and

installations. Fires and explosions were caused at both targets. Ack-ack positions at Sohana Island and Chinatown were also bombed, destroying three heavy guns with direct hits and damaging many others. Our medium units at dusk struck at shipping in Matchin Bay, sinking a small cargo vessel and two barges near Tarlena. One of our planes is missing.

Empress Augusta Bay - Our torpedo and dive bombers bombed and strafed enemy positions along the Piva and Jaba Rivers.

Buin - Our medium units bombed Ballale and Kara airdromes with a total of thirty-two tons of explosives, concentrated mainly on the runways. A large fire was started at Kara.

†CROMWELL, JOHN PHILIP
Rank and Organization: Captain, U.S. Navy.
Born: September 11, 1901, Henry, Illinois.
Entered Service At: Illinois.
Other Navy Awards: Legion of Merit.
Place and Date: Off Truk Island, November 19, 1943.
Citation: For conspicuous gallantry and intrepidity at the risk of his life above and beyond the call of duty as Commander of a Submarine Coordinated Attack Group with Flag in the U.S.S. *Sculpin*, during the 9th War Patrol of that vessel in enemy-controlled waters off Truk Island, November 19, 1943. Undertaking this patrol prior to the launching of our first large-scale offensive in the Pacific, Capt. Cromwell, alone of the entire Task Group, possessed secret intelligence information of our submarine strategy and tactics, scheduled Fleet movements and specific attack plans. Constantly vigilant and precise in carrying out his secret orders, he moved his underseas flotilla inexorably forward despite savage opposition and established a line of submarines to southeastward of the main Japanese stronghold at Truk. Cool and undaunted as the submarine, rocked and battered by Japanese depth charges, sustained terrific battle damage and sank to an excessive depth, he authorized the *Sculpin* to surface and engage the enemy in a gunfight, thereby providing an opportunity for the crew to abandon ship. Determined to sacrifice himself rather than risk capture and subsequent danger of revealing plans under Japanese torture or use of drugs, he stoically remained aboard the mortally wounded vessel as she plunged to her death. Preserving the security of his mission, at the cost of his own life, he had served his country as he had served the Navy, with deep integrity and an uncompromising devotion to duty. His great moral courage in the face of certain death adds new luster to the traditions of the U.S. Naval Service. He gallantly gave his life for his country.

OFFICIAL COMMUNIQUE:
United Nations
ALLIED HEADQUARTERS IN THE SOUTHWEST PACIFIC, Saturday, Nov.
20 -A communique:

NORTHWESTERN SECTOR

Dutch New Guinea - Our medium units bombed Babo and Kaimana at night, causing numerous fires. Our heavy units at midday bombed Fak Fak, starting large fires. Our fighters dive-bombed and strafed enemy-occupied Iworep Village, east of Tomoeka, destroying buildings.
Java - Our heavy units at night bombed Surabaya and Tjeope oil refineries, Tandjung-Perak airdrome, and Denpasar airdrome, on Bali, with twenty-seven tons of explosives. Adverse weather prevented observation of results.

NORTHEASTERN SECTOR

New Guinea
Finschhafen - Our ground forces, closing in on Sattelberg from the east and south despite heavy resistance and difficult jungle conditions, are within one mile of the township. Our medium bombers, in direct support, attacked enemy defensive positions and installations with forty-four tons of explosives, causing fire and heavy damage in the target area.

Solomon Islands

Bougainville-Buka - Our medium and heavy units carried out five pre-dawn raids on enemy installations in the passage area, followed in the post-dawn by escorted medium torpedo and dive bombers, dropping a total of seventy-one tons of explosives on Buka and Bonis runways, dispersal points, and gun positions. Our escort shot down two enemy fighters. We lost one plane
Kieta - Our medium units twice bombed the township, damaging installations. One of our fighter patrols, in the late afternoon, strafed targets along the coast to the north.
Empress Augusta Bay - Enemy planes raided our ground positions before daybreak, causing minor casualties. Shortly after dawn our air patrols successfully intercepted a force of escorted enemy torpedo dive-bombers which attacked our shipping without damage. Sixteen enemy planes were reported shot down. We lost two fighters in combat.
Ballale - One of our dive bombers raided the airdrome after dawn.

United States
PEARL HARBOR, Nov. 19 - A communique issued by Admiral Nimitz's Navy headquarters:

Enemy installations on Nauru Island were heavily hit by carrier aircraft Nov. 18. Our planes dropped ninety tons of bombs on the airdrome and shop areas, starting fires and destroying several aircraft aground. One small ship was set afire.
Of seven Zeros which appeared during the later stages of the attack, two were shot down. Accurate anti-aircraft was encountered. All our planes returned. One pilot was wounded.

†BORDELON, WILLIAM JAMES
Rank and Organization: Staff Sergeant, U.S. Marine Corps.
Born: December 25, 1920, San Antonio, Texas.
Entered Service At: Texas.
Place and Date: Tarawa, Gilbert Islands, November 20, 1943.
Citation: For valorous and gallant conduct above and beyond the call of duty as a member of an assault engineer platoon of the 1st Battalion, 18th Marines, tactically attached to the 2d Marine Division, in action against the Japanese-held atoll of Tarawa in the Gilbert Islands on November 20, 1943. Landing in the assault waves under withering enemy fire which killed all but 4 of the men in his tractor, S/Sgt. Bordelon hurriedly made demolition charges and personally put 2 pillboxes out of action. Hit by enemy machinegun fire just as a charge exploded in his hand while assaulting a third position, he courageously remained in action and, although out of demolition, provided himself with a rifle and furnished fire coverage for a group of men scaling the seawall. Disregarding his own serious condition, he unhesitatingly went to the aid of one of his demolition men, wounded and calling for help in the water, rescuing this man and another who had been hit by enemy fire while attempting to make the rescue. Still refusing first aid for himself, he again made up demolition charges and singlehandedly assaulted a fourth Japanese machinegun position but was instantly killed when caught in a final burst of fire from the enemy. S/Sgt. Bordelon's great personal valor during a critical phase of securing the limited beachhead was a contributing factor in the ultimate occupation of the island, and his heroic determination throughout 3 days of violent battle reflects the highest credit upon the U.S. Naval Service. He gallantly gave his life for his country.

†HAWKINS, WILLIAM DEAN

Rank and Organization: First Lieutenant, U.S. Marine Corps.
Born: April 19, 1914, Fort Scott, Kansas.
Entered Service At: El Paso, Texas.
Place and Date: Tarawa, Gilbert Islands, November 20-21, 1943.
Citation: For valorous and gallant conduct above and beyond the call of duty as commanding officer of a Scout Sniper Platoon attached to the Assault Regiment in action against Japanese-held Tarawa in the Gilbert Island, November 20 and 21, 1943. The first to disembark from the jeep lighter, 1st Lt. Hawkins unhesitatingly moved forward under heavy enemy fire at the end of the Betio Pier, neutralizing emplacements in coverage of troops assaulting the main beach positions. Fearlessly leading his men on to join the forces fighting desperately to gain a beachhead, he repeatedly risked his life throughout the day and night to direct and lead attacks on pillboxes and installations with grenades and demolitions. At dawn on the following day, 1st Lt. Hawkins resumed the dangerous mission of clearing the limited beachhead of Japanese resistance, personally initiating an assault on a hostile position fortified by 5 enemy machineguns, and, crawling forward in the face of withering fire, boldly fired pointblank into the loopholes and completed the destruction with grenades. Refusing to withdraw after being seriously wounded in the chest during this skirmish, 1st Lt. Hawkins steadfastly carried the fight to the enemy, destroying 3 more pillboxes before he was caught in a burst of Japanese shellfire and mortally wounded. His relentless fighting spirit in the face of formidable opposition and his exceptionally daring tactics served as an inspiration to his comrades during the most crucial phase of the battle and reflect the highest credit upon the U.S. Naval Service. He gallantly gave his life for his country.

†BONNYMAN, ALEXANDER, JR.

Rank and Organizations: First Lieutenant, U.S. Marine Corps Reserves.
Born: May 2, 1910, Atlanta, Georgia.
Entered Service At: New Mexico.
Place and Date: Tarawa, Gilbert Islands, November 20-22. 1943.
Citation: For conspicuous gallantry and intrepidity at the risk of his life above and beyond the call of duty as Executive Officer of the 2d Battalion Shore Party, 8th Marines, 2d Marine Division, during the assault against enemy Japanese-held Tarawa in the Gilbert Islands, November 20-22, 1943. Acting on his own initiative when assault troops were pinned down at the far end of Betio Pier by the overwhelming fire of Japanese shore batteries,

1st Lt. Bonnyman repeatedly defied the blasting fury of the enemy bombardment to organize and lead the besieged men over the long, open pier to the beach and then, voluntarily obtaining flame throwers and demolitions, organized his pioneer shore party into assault demolitionists and directed the blowing of several hostile installations before the close of D-day. Determined to effect an opening in the enemy's strongly organized defense line the following day, he voluntarily crawled approximately 40 yards forward of our lines and placed demolitions in the entrance of a large Japanese emplacement as the initial move in his planned attack against the heavily garrisoned, bombproof installation which was stubbornly resisting despite the destruction early in the action of a large number of Japanese who had been inflicting heavy casualties on our forces and holding up our advance. Withdrawing only to replenish his ammunition, he led his men in a renewed assault, fearlessly exposing himself to the merciless slash of hostile fire as he stormed the formidable bastion, directed the placement of demolition charges in both entrances and seized the top of the bombproof position, flushing more than 100 of the enemy who were instantly cut down, and effecting the annihilation of approximately 150 troops inside the emplacement. Assailed by additional Japanese after he had gained his objective, he made a heroic stand on the edge of the structure, defending his strategic position with indomitable determination in the face of the desperate charge and killing 3 of the enemy before he fell, mortally wounded. By his dauntless fighting spirit, unrelenting aggressiveness and forceful leadership throughout 3 days of unremitting, violent battle, 1st Lt. Bonnyman had inspired his men to heroic effort, enabling them to beat off the counterattack and break the back of hostile resistance in that sector for an immediate gain of 400 yards with no further casualties to our forces in this zone. He gallantly gave his life for his country.

SHOUP, DAVID MONROE

Rank and Organization: Colonel, U.S. Marine Corps, commanding officer of all Marine Corps troops on Betio Island, Tarawa Atoll, and Gilbert Islands, from November 20 to 22, 1943.

Born: December 30, 1904, Tippecanoe, Indiana.

Entered Service At: Indiana.

Place and Date: Tarawa Atoll, Gilbert Islands, November 20-22, 1943.

Citation: For conspicuous gallantry and intrepidity at the risk of his life above and beyond the call of duty as commanding officer of all Marine Corps troops in action against enemy Japanese forces on Beto Island, Tarawa Atoll, Gilbert Islands, from November 20 to 22, 1943. Although severely shocked by an exploding enemy shell soon after landing at the pier and suffering from a serious, painful leg wound which had become infected, Col. Shoup fearlessly exposed himself to the terrific and relentless artillery, machinegun, and rifle fire from hostile shore emplacements. Rallying his hesitant troops by his own inspiring heroism, he gallantly led them across the fringing reefs to charge the heavily fortified island and reinforce our hard-pressed, thinly held lines. Upon arrival on shore, he assumed command of all landed troops and, working without rest under constant, withering enemy fire during the next 2 days, conducted smashing attacks against unbelievably strong and fanatically defended Japanese positions despite innumerable obstacles and heavy casualties. By his brilliant leadership, daring tactics, and selfless devotion to duty, Col. Shoup was largely responsible for the final decisive defeat of the enemy, and his indomitable fighting spirit reflects great credit upon the U.S. Naval Service.

Note: The following is a newspaper account of the preceding battle for which Sgt. Bordelon, Lt. Hawkins, Lt. Bonnyman, and Col. Shoup were awarded the Medal of Honor:

AMERICANS LAND ON TWO GILBERT ISLANDS COVERED BY MIGHTY SEA AND AIR FLEETS

• • •

BEACHHEADS WON

• • •

Marines and Army Units Get Footing On Makin and Tarawa Atolls

• • •

Fierce Resistance Is Met On Tarawa - Our Bombers Strike in the Marshalls

• • •

PEARL HARBOR, Nov. 21 - American forces have invaded the Gilbert Islands in the central Pacific.

Army troops and Marines, aided by the greatest fleet ever assembled in the Pacific, have established beachheads on Makin and Tarawa atolls and fighting is now going on.

The operation began at dawn Saturday. Amphibious forces, including Marines of the Pacific Fleet and Army units under Lieut. Gen. Robert C. Richardson

Jr., stormed ashore under protection of battleships and other warships bombarding shore installations and throwing tons of steel on enemy defense positions.

Aircraft carriers sent planes roaring over the atolls and at the same time Liberator formations attacked Japanese bases in the Marshall Islands to the north.

Our invading forces met only moderate resistance on Makin, but on Tarawa, main Japanese stronghold in the Gilberts, the enemy fought back fiercely.

Nauru Base Neutralized

The invasion fleet struck furiously after crossing hundreds of miles and following a week-long softening of these and other atolls and islands in the Gilberts and Marshalls by Liberators and carrier planes. The enemy stronghold of Nauru, 500 miles west of the Gilberts, was neutralized by a ninety-ton bomb attack two days ago.

Thus opened the long-awaited offensive in the central Pacific directed at driving the Japanese from the outer defenses of their empire. Gathered from secret bases, our forces are composed both of battle-hardened veterans of the Pacific fighting and troops untried but toughened by long training under General Richardson, who is still here.

Admiral Chester W. Nimitz, commander of the Pacific Fleet, announced the invasion in the following communique:

"Marine Corps and Army forces, covered by powerful units of all types of the Pacific Fleet, have established beachheads on Makin and Tarawa atolls in the Gilbert Islands, meeting moderate resistance at Makin and strong resistance at Tarawa. Fighting continues.

"During these operations Army Liberators made diversionary attacks in the Marshalls."

Enemy Defenses Tested

Since the day when the armadas slipped quietly to sea magnificently formidable, Army and Navy air formations have been testing Japanese strength. They found apparent weakness at least in the air. But the enemy's feeble parrying was no measure of the resistance encountered by our forces on one of the invaded islands.

The invasion thrusts American striking power near to the vital Japanese Marshall bases and toward the Carolines, which include Truk, major enemy stronghold.

Makin is a series of small islands fringing a lagoon about eleven miles wide. A port of entry, it was in pre-war days headquarters of On Chong & Co. copra traders, of Sydney, Australia. The lagoon has two entrances and good anchorages. Tarawa lies below the northern Gilbert group and is a series of islands some twenty-two miles long and has the usual lagoon, to which there is one entrance. It also is a port.

Anchorages and air bases at Tarawa and Makin, while small and limited in character, will afford us needed taking-off places for further extension of the new central Pacific offensive when our positions in the Gilberts are consolidated.

The atmosphere here is one of utmost confidence, and spokesmen appear to have no doubt of the outcome.

It appears likely that this is just the opening phase in a real offensive that will multiply the focal points of pressure against the enemy's encircling line of defense bases.

The main objective in Tarawa is the island of Betio, which has excellent airstrips that have been used many times to good advantage by the enemy.

It is only 292 miles from well-defended Maloelap atoll in the Marshalls, where there is a major airfield on the island of Taroa.

The main island in the Makin atoll is Butaritari, some ten miles long and about 1,000 feet wide at its greatest width.

When Lieut. Col. Evans F. Carlson's marine raiders landed there in August, 1942, they found three piers and a stone wharf, and the island had excellent gun emplacements and defenses. Col. Carlson and his men landed in the middle of the narrow island, and in addition to the immediate tactical achievements of the moment they brought valuable information and sketches that have well served the planners of the present operations. [Lieut. Col. James Roosevelt, then a Major, was one of the leaders in this raid.]

Makin also has a beach suitable for a seaplane base.

Little Cover For Invaders

Since the Japanese on Tarawa had been holding out for twenty-four hours when Admiral Chester W. Nimitz's communique was issued, it appeared that American forces there were up against a win, die, or retreat position.

Both Tarawa and Makin can be strongly defended by a small number of troops concentrating heavy artillery fire on the beaches.

Atolls, coral reefs jutting up from the ocean, afford virtually no protection, either to attacking forces or defenders, except that the latter have had time to dig in, set up artillery positions and gouge out shallow foxholes. Most atolls rise only a few yards above sea level and their palm trees afford little protection.

Landing forces thus face the necessity of wiping out enemy positions quickly or facing the threat of annihilation.

VOSLER, FORREST T. (Air Mission)
Rank and Organization: Technical Sergeant, U.S. Army Air Corps, 358th Bomber Squadron. 303d Bomber Group.

Born: July 29, 1923, Lyndonville, New York.
Entered Service At: Rochester, New York.
Place and Date: Over Bremen, Germany, December 20, 1943.
Citation: For conspicuous gallantry in action against the enemy above and beyond the call of duty while serving as a radio operator-air gunner on a heavy bombardment aircraft in a mission over Bremen, Germany, on December 20, 1943. After bombing the target, the aircraft in which T/Sgt. Vosler was serving was severely damaged by antiaircraft fire, forced out of formation, and immediately subjected to repeated vicious attacks by enemy fighters. Early in the engagement a 20-mm. cannon shell exploded in the radio compartment, painfully wounding T/Sgt. Vosler in the legs and thighs. At about the same time a direct hit on the tail of the ship seriously wounded the tail gunner and rendered the tail guns inoperative. Realizing the great need for firepower in protecting the vulnerable tail of the ship, T/Sgt. Vosler, with grim determination, kept up a steady stream of deadly fire. Shortly thereafter another 20-mm. enemy shell exploded, wounding T/Sgt. Vosler in the chest and about the face. Pieces of metal lodged in both eyes, impairing his vision to such an extent that he could only distinguish blurred shapes. Displaying remarkable tenacity and courage, he kept firing his guns and declined to take first-aid treatment. The radio equipment had been rendered inoperative during the battle, and when the pilot announced that he would have to ditch, although unable to see and working entirely by touch, T/Sgt. Vosler managed to get out on the wing by himself and hold the wounded tail gunner from slipping off until the other crew members could help them into the dinghy. T/Sgt. Vosler's actions on this occasion were an inspiration to all serving with him. The extraordinary courage, coolness, and skill he displayed in the face of great odds, when handicapped by injuries that would have incapacitated the average crew member, were outstanding.

OFFICIAL COMMUNIQUE:
United Nations
LONDON, Dec. 20 – A joint British Air Ministry and United States Army European Theater of Operations communique:

Strong formations of Eighth United States Army Air Force Flying Fortresses and Liberators attacked the important port and industrial city of Bremen today.

Forty enemy fighters were destroyed, twenty-one by the heavy bombers and nineteen by escorting United States fighters. RAF and Dominion fighters flew supporting sweeps and destroyed two enemy aircraft. From these operations twenty-five heavy bombers and eight fighters are missing.

CHAPTER 4

1944

BOYINGTON, GREGORY
Rank and Organization: Major, U.S. Marine Corps Reserve, Marine Squadron 214.
Born: December 4, 1912, Coeur D'Alene, Idaho.
Entered Service At: Washington.
Other Navy Award: Navy Cross.
Place and Date: Central Solomons area, from September 12, 1943 to January 3, 1944.
Citation: For extraordinary heroism and valiant devotion to duty as commanding officer of Marine Fighting Squadron 214 in action against Japanese forces in the Central Solomons area from September 12, 1943 to January 3, 1944. Consistently outnumbered throughout successive hazardous flights over heavily defended hostile territory, Maj. Boyington struck at the enemy with daring and courageous persistence, leading his squadron into combat with devastating results to Japanese shipping, shore installations, and aerial forces. Resolute in his efforts to inflict crippling damage on the enemy, Maj. Boyington led a formation of 24 fighters over Kahili on October 17 and, persistently circling the airdrome where 60 hostile aircraft were grounded, boldly challenged the Japanese to send up planes. Under his brilliant command, our fighters shot down 20 enemy aircraft in the ensuing action without the loss of a single ship. A superb airman and determined fighter against overwhelming odds, Maj. Boyington personally destroyed 26 of the many Japanese planes shot down by his squadron and, by his forceful leadership, developed the combat readiness in his command which was a distinctive factor in the Allied aerial achievements in this vitally strategic area.

OFFICIAL COMMUNIQUE:
United Nations

ADVANCED ALLIED HEADQUARTERS IN NEW GUINEA, Tuesday, Jan. 4
– A communique:
NORTHWESTERN SECTOR

Celebes: Our heavy units bombed the jetty and barracks area at Pomelaa, starting large fires.
Aru Island: Our long-range fighters on a harassing sweep over Terangan Island strafed Meror Village.

NORTHEASTERN SECTOR

New Ireland
Kavieng: Our carrier-based bombers and fighters from the Solomons attacked an enemy force of two heavy cruisers and two destroyers. Both cruisers were hit by bombs and torpedoes and set afire. One of the destroyers was hit by a bomb. Eleven of thirty intercepting enemy fighters were shot down over the target with four others probable. A bomber and another fighter on reconnaissance were later destroyed. Our medium units at night caused explosions and fires in the airdrome, dispersal and supply areas. An air patrol bombed and strafed installations on Mussau Island.

New Britain
Rabaul: Our Solomons-based heavy units with fighter escort bombed Lakunai airdrome at mid-day, starting fires and destroying one enemy bomber on the ground. Eighteen enemy fighters were reported shot down and several others probably destroyed.
Gasmata: Our escorted dive-bombers attacked enemy installations near Government Station, causing fires. Our air patrols bombed Ring Ring and strafed Kalai Plantation in Wide Bay.
Vitu Islands: One of our heavy reconnaissance units bombed and destroyed two barges in Peter Harbor.
Cape Gloucester: Our ground forces are extending their perimeters. Two light enemy air raids under cover of darkness caused no damage.
Arawe: Outpost clashes occurred on the right flank of our position. A minor predawn air raid was ineffective.

New Guinea
Madang: Our escorted medium units bombed enemy supply dumps at Bili Bili and Erima Plantation with fifty-two tons of explosives, causing numerous fires. Our

air patrols carried out several sweeps in this area and along the coast to Hatzfeldt and Uligan Harbors, strafing targets of opportunity.

Saidor: Our ground forces overcame light enemy resistance and secured final objectives. Our heavy units and attack planes with fighter escort bombed and strafed installations at Heimholtz Point, Gumbi Plantation, Biding River and along the coast to Sio. One hundred and twenty-six tons of bombs were dropped, starting fires in targets. Our light naval units at night sank two enemy barges off Vincke Point.

Huon Peninsula: Our ground forces have captured Nuzen and are pushing up the coast toward Wald Bay.

SOLOMON ISLANDS

Bougainville

Empress Augusta Bay: Our torpedo dive-bombers effectively attacked enemy positions along the Torokina River and Mosigetta. Our medium units attacked installations at Kahili and on the northeast coast bombed and strafed an enemy barge base near Numa Numa. Our air patrols on coastal sweeps strafed targets at Queen Carola Harbor on Buka, villages at Matchin Bay and Kieta, and damaged two barges at Tonolei.

Bougainville Straits: Our night air patrols bombed and strafed six barges near Oema Island.

†SPECKER, JOE C.

Rank and Organization: Sergeant, U.S. Army, 48th Engineer Combat Battalion.

Born: Odessa, Missouri.

Entered Service At: Odessa, Missouri.

Place and Date: Mount Porchia, Italy, January 7, 1944.

Citation: For conspicuous gallantry and intrepidity at the risk of his life, above and beyond the call of duty, in action involving actual conflict. On the night of January 7, 1944, Sgt Specker, with his company, was advancing up the slope of Mount Porchia, Italy. He was sent forward on reconnaissance and on his return he reported to his company commander the fact that there was an enemy machinegun nest and several well-placed snipers directly in the path and awaiting the company. Sgt. Specker requested and was granted permission to place one of his machineguns in a position near the enemy machinegun. Voluntarily and alone he made his way up the mountain with a machinegun and a box of ammunition. He was observed by the enemy as he walked along and was severely wounded by the deadly fire directed at him. Though seriously wounded that he was unable to walk, he continued to drag himself over the jagged edges of rock and rough terrain until he reached the position at which he desired to set up his machinegun. He set up the gun so well and fired so accurately that the enemy machinegun nest was silenced and the remainder of the snipers forced to retire, enabling his platoon to obtain their objective. Sgt. Specker was found dead at his gun. His personal bravery, self-sacrifice, and determination were an inspiration to his officers and fellow soldiers.

OFFICIAL COMMUNIQUE:
United Nations
ALGIERS, Jan. 7 – A communique:

In the central sector of the Fifth Army front, our advance through snow-covered mountains is continuing. Bitter fighting is taking place in the town of San Vittore. On the Eighth Army front, Indian troops improved their positions.
Yesterday, bad weather again limited air operations. Gun positions in the Cervaro area and the railway at Fondi were attacked by fighter-bombers.
Two enemy aircraft were destroyed. None of ours is missing.

HOWARD, JAMES H. (Air Mission)
Rank and Organization: Lieutenant Colonel, U.S. Army Air Corps.
Born: Canton, China.
Entered Service At: St. Louis, Missouri.
Place and Date: Over Oschersleben, Germany, January 11, 1944.
Citation: For conspicuous gallantry and intrepidity above and beyond the call of duty in action with the enemy near Oschersleben, Germany, on January 11, 1944. On that day Col. Howard was the leader of a group of P-51 aircraft providing support for a heavy bomber formation on a long-range mission deep in enemy territory. As Col. Howard's group met the bombers in the target area the bomber force was attacked by numerous enemy fighters. Col. Howard, with his group, at once engaged the enemy and himself destroyed a German ME-110. As a result of this attack Col. Howard lost contact with his group, and at once returned to the level of the bomber formation. He then saw that the bombers were being heavily attacked by enemy airplanes and that no other friendly fighters were at hand. While Col. Howard could have waited to attempt to assemble his group before engaging the enemy, he chose instead to attack singlehanded a formation of more than 30 German airplanes. With utter disregard for his own safety he immediately pressed home determined attacks for some 30 minutes,

during which time he destroyed 3 enemy airplanes and probably destroyed and damaged others. Toward the end of this engagement three of his guns went out of action and his fuel supply was becoming dangerously low. Despite these handicaps and the almost insuperable odds against him, Col Howard continued his aggressive action in an attempt to protect the bombers from the numerous fighters. His skill, courage, and intrepidity on this occasion set an example of heroism which will be an inspiration to the U.S. Armed Forces.

OFFICIAL COMMUNIQUE:
United Nations
ALGIERS, Jan. 11, – A communique:

NAVY
During the night of Jan. 7-8, our destroyers in the Adriatic sank three schooners and successfully shelled trains on the coastal railway each side of Divitanova. They also bombarded that place and the railway installations at Ancona. Opposition from a shore battery was ineffectual.

The following night, destroyers in the same area damaged four schooners and left them abandoned, caused interference with railway traffic, and shelled San Benedetto.

ARMY
On the Fifth Army front, the advance continues. American troops consolidated heights previously taken, while British troops pushed forward approximately a mile to seize a hill overlooking a road to Cassino and the River Garigiliano.

On the Eighth Army front there was increased patrol activity.

AIR
Last night a force of night bombers continued the attack on Sofia. Skoplje, important rail center in Yugoslavia, was also attacked by heavy bombers. Many hits were scored in the railway yards.

The port of San Benedetto was bombed by medium bombers. Military installations at Palena and shipping in the harbor at Vela Luka were attacked by light bombers.

Nine enemy aircraft were destroyed during the day and three of ours are missing.

CAIRO, Egypt, Jan. 11 – A Middle East Air communique:

Heavy bombers of the RAF attacked defenses and other targets at Salamis, southern Greece, during the night of Jan. 9. Bursts were seen in the aircraft dispersal area at the Eleusis airfield, and a fire was followed by a heavy explosion.

Bad weather continues to interfere with attacks on enemy shipping in the Aegean and has also diminished the amount of shipping which has been able to put to sea from Greece and the enemy-occupied islands.

From all operations during the period under review none of our aircraft is missing.

McCALL, THOMAS E.

Rank and Organization: Staff Sergeant, U.S. Army, Company F, 143d Infantry, 36th Infantry Division.
Born: Burton, Kansas.
Entered Service At: Veerdersburg, Indiana.
Place and Date: Near San Angelo, Italy, January 22, 1944.
Citation: For conspicuous gallantry and intrepidity at the risk of his life above and beyond the call of duty. On January 22, 1944, Company F had the mission of crossing the Rapido River in the vicinity of San Angelo, Italy, and attacking the well-prepared German positions to the west. For the defense of these positions the enemy had prepared a network of machinegun positions covering the terrain to the front with a pattern of withering machinegun fire, and mortar and artillery positions zeroed in on the defiled areas. S/Sgt. McCall commanded a machinegun section that was to provide added fire support for the riflemen. Under cover of darkness, Company F advanced to the river crossing site and under intense enemy mortar, artillery, and machinegun fire crossed an ice-covered bridge which was continually the target for enemy fire. Many casualties occurred on reaching the west side of the river and organization was imperative. Exposing himself to the deadly machinegun and small-arms fire that swept over the flat terrain, S/Sgt. McCall, with unusual calmness, encouraged and welded his men into an effective fighting unit. He then led them forward across the muddy, exposed terrain. Skillfully he guided his men through a barbed-wire entanglement to reach a road where he personally placed the weapons of his two squads into positions of vantage, covering the battalion's front. A shell landed near one of the positions, wounding the gunner, killing the assistant gunner, and destroying the weapon. Even though enemy shells were falling dangerously near, S/Sgt. McCall crawled across the treacherous terrain and rendered first-aid to the wounded man, dragging him into a position of cover with the help of another man. The gunners of the second machinegun had been wounded from the fragments of an enemy shell, leaving S/Sgt. McCall the only remaining member of his

machinegun section. Displaying outstanding aggressiveness, he ran forward with the weapon on his hip, reaching a point 30 yards from the enemy, where he fired 2 bursts of fire into the nest, killing or wounding all of the crew and putting the gun out of action. A second machinegun now opened fire upon him and he rushed its position, firing his weapon from the hip, killing 4 of the guncrew. A third machinegun, 50 yards in the rear of the first two, was delivering a tremendous volume of fire upon our troops. S/Sgt. McCall spotted its position and valiantly went toward it in the face of overwhelming enemy fire. He was last seen courageously moving forward on the enemy position, firing his machinegun from his hip. S/Sgt. McCall's intrepidity and unhesitating willingness to sacrifice his life exemplify the highest traditions of the Armed Forces.

OFFICIAL COMMUNIQUE:
United Nations
ALGIERS, Jan. 22 - A communique:

In a general attack launched on the Fifth Army front, French troops have advanced westward and captured an important height held by the enemy.

American troops have forced a crossing of the Rapido River under withering enemy fire.

British troops have captured Trimonsuoli and have beaten off enemy counterattacks on several points. Many prisoners have been taken.

Yesterday airfields at Istres-le-Tube and Salon were attacked by escorted heavy bombers. Good coverage was obtained. Railway bridges and yards at Rimini, Porto Civitanova and Pontedera were attacked by other heavy bombers.

On the night of Jan. 20-21, rail facilities at Cecina were attacked by night bombers. Medium bombers attacked railway communications at Orvieto, Foligno and Avezzano.

Fighters and fighter-bombers attacked shipping on the Yugoslav coast and made many sorties in support of ground forces.

On Jan. 20, medium bombers sank a merchant vessel in the Gulf of Genoa.

Twenty enemy aircraft were destroyed yesterday. Five of ours are missing.

A special communique:

British and American troops of General Clark's Fifth Army landed early this morning on the west coast of Italy deep in the rear of the present enemy front-line positions. Naval and air forces are supporting ground troops.

The landing was coordinated with strong attacks by other units of the Fifth Army, including British, French, and American, in the Liri Valley.

The amphibious attacks began before dawn, with Allied troops of the Fifth Army going ashore from landing craft along a beachfront extending several miles from north to south.

British Commandos and American Rangers are participating in this assault. Operations in Italy are under General Alexander, commander of the Allied Central Mediterranean Forces, formerly the Fifteenth Army Group.

†HANSON, ROBERT MURRAY
Rank and Organization: First Lieutenant, U.S. Marine Corps Reserve.
Born: February 4, 1920, Lucknow, India.
Entered Service At: Massachusetts.
Other Navy Awards: Navy Cross and Air Medal.
Place and Date: Bougainville Island, November 1, 1943 and New Britain Island, January 24, 1944.
Citation: For conspicuous gallantry and intrepidity at the risk of his life above and beyond the call of duty as a fighter pilot attached to Marine Fighting Squadron 215 in action against enemy Japanese forces at Bougainville Island, November 1, 1943 and New Britain Island, January 24, 1944. Undeterred by fierce opposition, and fearless in the face of overwhelming odds, 1st. Lt. Hanson fought the Japanese boldly and with daring aggressiveness. On November 1, while flying cover for our landing operations at Empress Augusta Bay, he dauntlessly attacked 6 enemy torpedo bombers, forcing them to jettison their bombs and destroying 1 Japanese plane during the action. Cut off from his division while deep in enemy territory during a high cover flight over Simpson Harbor on January 24, 1st Lt. Hanson waged a lone and gallant battle against hostile interceptors as they were orbiting to attack our bombers and, striking with devastating fury, brought down 4 Zeroes and probably a fifth. Handling his plane superbly in both pursuit and attack measures, he was a master of individual air combat, accounting for a total of 25 Japanese aircraft in this theater of war. His great personal valor and invincible fighting spirit were in keeping with the highest traditions of the U.S. Naval Service.

OFFICIAL COMMUNIQUE:
United Nations
ADVANCED ALLIED HEADQUARTERS IN NEW GUINEA, Tuesday, Jan. 25, –A communique:

NORTHWESTERN SECTOR

Netherlands New Guinea: Our air patrols shot down an enemy bomber and a fighter over Arafura Sea.

Flores Island: Our heavy patrol units bombed enemy barracks at Maumeri and the jetty area at Enden.

NORTHEASTERN SECTOR

New Ireland
Kavieng area: Our night air patrols bombed and damaged a 7,000-ton enemy freighter.

New Britain
Rabaul: Our escorted medium units from Solomons bases bombed Lakunai airdrome. Many hits were scored on the runway and large fires were started. Seventy enemy fighters intercepted. Eighteen were shot down with two probably downed. We lost six planes. During the night, Solomons heavy and medium units dropped incendiary bombs on the town, causing fires visible for seventy-five miles. Two of our planes are missing.
Borgen Bay: Our ground patrols are ranging forward into enemy-held territory. Our attack planes bombed and strafed enemy positions at Natamo.
Arawe: Six enemy aircraft attacked at night, causing slight casualties.

New Guinea
Wewak: Our escorted heavy bombers concentrated 105 tons of bombs on anti-aircraft positions. Eighteen guns were destroyed or seriously damaged. Approximately fifty enemy fighters were waiting at 30,000 feet and intercepted. Our bombers shot down twelve and probably eight more, and our fighters downed twenty-one and probably four more. This made a total of thirty-three definite and twelve probables. We lost five planes and others were damaged. Our night air patrols attacked an enemy destroyer, starting a fire amidships.
Ramu Valley: Our ground forces have driven the enemy from all of his positions in the Shaggy Ridge area and are continuing to advance. Field artillery and much ammunition have been captured.
Rai Coast: Our air patrols on coastal sweeps destroyed three barges at Marakum. Our escorted attack planes bombed and strafed coastal villages and trails from Bonga to Gali, starting fires. At Uligan, our air patrols strafed and damaged enemy barges, and at Madang, our heavy units bombed Amele Mission. We lost one plane.

SOLOMON ISLANDS

Bougainville
Empress Augusta Bay: Our air patrols attacked enemy positions near Motupena Point and Mamagata. One of our light naval units shelled enemy positions on the Rini River.

†GIBSON, ERIC G.

Rank and Organization: Technician Fifth Grade, U.S. Army, 3d Infantry Division.
Born: Nysund, Sweden.
Entered Service At: Chicago, Illinois.
Place and Date: Near Isola Bella, Italy, January 28, 1944.
Citation: For conspicuous gallantry and intrepidity at the risk of his life above and beyond the call of duty. On January 28, 1944, near Isola Bella, Italy, Tech 5th Grade Gibson, company cook, led a squad of replacements through their initial baptism of fire, destroyed four enemy positions, killed 5 and captured 2 German soldiers, and secured the left flank of his company during an attack on a strongpoint. Placing himself 50 yards in front of his new men, Gibson advanced down the wide stream ditch known as the Fossa Femminamorta, keeping pace with the advance of his company. An enemy soldier allowed Tech. 5th Grade Gibson to come within 20 yards of his concealed position and then opened fire on him with a machine pistol. Despite the stream of automatic fire which barely missed him, Gibson charged the position, firing his submachinegun every few steps. Reaching the position, Gibson fired point-blank at his opponent, killing him. An artillery concentration fell in and around the ditch; the concussion from one shell knocked him flat. As he got to his feet Gibson was fired on by two soldiers armed with a machine pistol and a rifle from a position only 75 yards distant. Gibson immediately raced toward the foe. Halfway to the position a machinegun opened fired on him. Bullets came within inches of his body, yet Gibson never paused in his forward movement. He killed one and captured the other soldier. Shortly after, when he was fired upon by a heavy machinegun 200 yards down the ditch, Gibson crawled back to his squad and ordered it to lay down a base of fire while he flanked the emplacement. Despite all warning, Gibson crawled 125 yards through an artillery concentration and the cross-fire of 2 machineguns which showered dirt over his body, threw 2 handgrenades into the emplacement and charged it with his submachinegun, killing 2 of the enemy and capturing a third. Before leading his men around a bend in the stream ditch, Gibson went

forward alone to reconnoiter. Hearing an exchange of machine pistol and submachinegun fire, Gibson's squad went forward to find that its leader had run 35 yards toward an outpost, killed the machine pistol man, and had himself been killed while firing at the Germans.

OFFICIAL COMMUNIQUE:
United Nations
ALGIERS, Jan. 28 – A communique:

ARMY

French troops are continuing their advance to the west several miles north of Cassino despite difficult mountain terrain, determined resistance, and fierce counter-attacks.

American troops are scaling mountains west of the Rapido River in the face of heavy fire from the enemy's prepared positions. One height has been reached and progress has been made toward several others.

British and American troops have further enlarged their beachhead south of Rome. A strong counter-attack was launched against the British, who threw it back, taking many prisoners.

Aggressive patrolling continued on the Eighth Army front.

HAWKS, LLOYD C.
Rank and Organization: Private First Class, U.S. Army, Medical Detachment, 30th Infantry, 3d Infantry Division.
Born: January 13, 1911, Becker, Minnesota.
Entered Service At: Park Rapids, Minnesota.
Place and Date: Near Carano, Italy, January 30, 1944.
Citation: For conspicuous gallantry and intrepidity at the risk of his life above and beyond the call of duty. On January 30, 1944, at 3 P.M., near Carano, Italy, Pfc. Hawks braved an enemy counterattack in order to rescue 2 wounded men who, unable to move, were lying in an exposed position within 30 yards of the enemy. Two riflemen, attempting the rescue, had been forced to return to their fighting holes by extremely severe enemy machinegun fire, after crawling only 10 yards toward the casualties. An aid man, whom the enemy could plainly identify as such, had been critically wounded in a similar attempt. Pfc. Hawks, nevertheless, crawled 50 yards through a veritable hail of machinegun bullets and flying mortar fragments to a small ditch, administered first-aid to his fellow aid man who had sought cover therein, and continued toward the 2 wounded men 50 yards distant.

An enemy machinegun bullet penetrated his helmet, knocking it from his head, momentarily stunning him. Thirteen bullets passed through his helmet as it lay on the ground within 6 inches of his body. Pfc. Hawks, crawled to the casualties, administered first-aid to the more seriously wounded man and dragged him to a covered position 25 yards distant. Despite continuous automatic fire from positions only 30 yards away and shells that exploded within 25 yards, Pfc. Hawks returned to the second man and administered first-aid to him. As he raised himself to obtain bandages from his medical kit his right hip was shattered by a burst of machinegun fire and a second burst splintered his left forearm. Displaying dogged determination and extreme self-control, Pfc. Hawks, despite severe pain and his dangling left arm, completed the task of bandaging the remaining casualty and with superhuman effort dragged him to the same depression to which he had brought the first man. Finding insufficient cover for 3 men at this point, Pfc. Hawks crawled 75 yards in an effort to regain his company, reaching the ditch in which his fellow aid man was lying.

DROWLEY, JESSE R.
Rank and Organization: Staff Sergeant, U.S. Army, Americal Infantry Division.
Born: St. Charles, Michigan.
Entered Service At: Spokane, Washington.
Place and Date: Bougainville, Solomon Islands, January 30, 1944.
Citation: For conspicuous gallantry and intrepidity at the risk of his life above and beyond the call of duty in action with the enemy at Bougainville, Solomon Islands, January 30, 1944. S/Sgt. Drowley, a squad leader in a platoon whose mission during an attack was to remain under cover while holding the perimeter defense and acting as a reserve for assaulting echelon, saw 3 members of the assault company fall badly wounded. When intense hostile fire prevented aid from reaching the casualties, he fearlessly rushed forward to carry the wounded to cover. After rescuing 2 men, S/Sgt. Drowley discovered an enemy pillbox undetected by assaulting tanks that was inflicting heavy casualties upon the attacking force and was a chief obstacle to the success of the advance. Delegating the rescue of the third man to an assistant, he ran across open terrain to one of the tanks. Signaling to the crew, he climbed to the turret, exchanged his weapon for a submachinegun and voluntarily rode the deck of the tank directing it toward the pillbox by tracer fire. The tank, under constant heavy enemy fire, continued to within 20 feet of the enemy pillbox where S/Sgt. Drowley received a severe bullet wound in the chest. Refusing to return for medical

treatment, he remained on the tank and continued to direct its progress until the enemy pillbox was definitely located by the crew. At this point he again was wounded by small-arms fire, losing his left eye and falling to the ground. He remained alongside the tank until the pillbox had been completely demolished and another directly behind the first destroyed. S/Sgt. Drowley, his voluntary mission successfully accomplished, returned alone for medical treatment.

†OLSON, TRUMAN, O.

Rank and Organization: Sergeant, U.S. Army, Company B, 7th Infantry, 3d Infantry Division.
Born: Christiania, Wisconsin.
Entered Service At: Cambridge, Wisconsin.
Place and Date: Near Cisterna di Littoria, Italy, January 30-31, 1944.
Citation: For conspicuous gallantry and intrepidity above and beyond the call of duty. Sgt. Olson, a light machine gunner, elected to sacrifice his life to save his company from annihilation. On the night of January 30, 1944, after a 16-hour assault on entrenched enemy positions in the course of which over one-third of Company B became casualties, the survivors dug in behind a horseshoe elevation, placing Sgt. Olson and his crew, with the 1 available machinegun, forward of their lines and in an exposed position to bear the brunt of the expected German counterattack. Although he had been fighting without respite, Sgt. Olson stuck grimly to his post all night while his guncrew was cut down, 1 by 1, by accurate and overwhelming enemy fire. Weary from over 24 hours of continuous battle and suffering from an arm wound, received during the night engagement, Sgt. Olson manned his gun alone, meeting the full force of an all-out enemy assault by approximately 200 men supported by mortar and machinegun fire which the Germans launched at daybreak on the morning of January 31. After 30 minutes of fighting, Sgt. Olson was mortally wounded, yet, knowing that only his weapons stood between his company and complete destruction, he refused evacuation. For an hour and a half after receiving his second and fatal wound he continued to fire his machinegun, killing at least 20 of the enemy, wounding many more, and forcing the assaulting German elements to withdraw.

OFFICIAL COMMUNIQUE:
United Nations
ALGIERS, Jan. 30, – A communique:

On the main Fifth Army front, French troops repulsed several determined counter-attacks and continued their advance. British troops occupied several important heights. Substantial numbers of prisoners were taken in both sectors.

In the Anzio beachhead, we advanced farther inland at several points.

Eighth Army patrols were engaged with the enemy in many places.

Rail communications yesterday were the main objectives of both heavy and medium bombers. The heavy bombers struck at Ancona, Rimini and Bologna, while the mediums attacked bridges and railways north of Rome and also the harbor of San Benedetto.

Motor transport in the Frosinone area was attacked by fighter-bombers, and over the Anzio beachhead fighters flew many defensive patrols.

On the night of Jan. 28-29, the rail yards at Foligno and Verona were attacked by night bombers.

During these operations, four enemy aircraft were destroyed; three of ours are missing.

It now is known that two of our aircraft reported missing from the operations of Jan. 27, landed safely on our fields.

Mediterranean Allied Air Forces flew over 1,300 sorties yesterday.

ADVANCED ALLIED HEADQUARTERS IN NEW GUINEA, Monday, Jan. 31, – A communique:

NORTHWESTERN SECTOR

Reconnaissance activity only.

NORTHEASTERN SECTOR

New Britain
Our attack planes bombed and strafed enemy bivouac and supply areas near Cape Bushing and east of Natamo Point. Our air patrols were active over coastal sectors, attacking targets at Ubill, Jacquinot Bay, Gasmata and Arawe. One barge was destroyed at Rottock Bay. Minor enemy air raids were reported at Arawe and Cape Gloucester.
Rabaul: Our escorted torpedo dive bombers from the Solomons continued their assault on this enemy air base, probably destroying over twenty planes caught on the ground at Lakunai and damaging others. Twelve effective hits were scored on anti-aircraft positions. In the air, over seventy enemy fighters attempted to halt the attack. Thirty were reported shot down with twelve additional probables. At dusk, our Solomons medium units with escort, struck Tobera from a minimum height, starting fires, destroying a parked aircraft and silencing several gun positions. There was no interception. We lost six planes.

New Guinea
Hansa Bay: Our escorted medium units struck enemy bivouac and supply points at Nubia. Our fighters dive-bombed the dump areas near Sarang.
Ramu Valley: Our fighters and dive bombers attacked enemy positions near Kisa. Our air patrols strafed coastal targets between Cape Iris and Bogadjim, starting fires at Warai.

Solomon Islands
Our air patrols strafed enemy positions in the Shortlands and at Tavelodo Point on Choiseul. Our naval units bombarded shore targets near Mamagata on Bougainville.

KNAPPENBERGER, ALTON W.

Rank and Organizations: Private First Class, U.S. Army, 3d Infantry Division.
Born: Cooperstown, Pennsylvania.
Entered Service At: Spring Mount, Pennsylvania.
Place and Date: Near Cisterna di Lottoria, Italy, February 1, 1944.
Citation: For conspicuous gallantry and intrepidity at the risk of his life above and beyond the call of duty in action involving actual conflict with the enemy on February 1, 1944 near Cisterna di lottoria, Italy. When a heavy German counterattack was launched against his battalion, Pfc. Knappenberger crawled to an exposed knoll and went into position with his automatic rifle. An enemy machinegun 85 yards away opened fire, and bullets struck within 6 inches of him. Rising to a kneeling position, Pfc. Knappenberger opened fire on the hostile crew, knocked out the gun, killed 2 members of the crew, and wounded the third. While he fired at this hostile position, 2 Germans crawled to a point within 20 yards of the knoll and threw potato-masher grenades at him, but Pfc. Knappenberger killed them both with 1 burst from his automatic rifle. Later, a second machinegun opened fire upon his exposed position from a distance of 100 yards, and this weapon also was silenced by his well-aimed shots. Shortly thereafter, an enemy 20-mm. antiaircraft gun directed fire at him, and again Pfc. Knappenberger returned fire to wound 1 member of the hostile crew. Under tank and artillery shellfire, with shells bursting within 15 yards of him, he held his precarious position and fired at all enemy infantrymen armed with machine pistols and machineguns which he could locate. When his ammunition supply become exhausted, he crawled 15 yards forward through steady machinegun fire, removed rifle clips from the belt of a casualty, returned to his position and resumed firing to repel an assaulting German platoon armed with automatic weapons. Finally, his ammunition supply

being completely exhausted, he rejoined his company. Pfc. Knappenberger's intrepid action disrupted the enemy attack for over 2 hours.

OFFICIAL COMMUNIQUE:
United Nations
ALGIERS, Jan. 31, – A communique:

On the main Fifth Army front, hard fighting has taken place. Heights beyond the Rapido bridgehead north of Cassino were captured yesterday and local advances have been made in several sectors.

The Anzio bridgehead is being steadily supplied, enlarged, and strengthened as troops already established ashore fight their way inland and fresh troops and supplies arrive.

Eighth Army patrols are active along the entire front.

Yesterday, the airfields at Villorba, Maniago, Lavarino and Udine, in northeast Italy, were attacked by strong forces of escorted heavy bombers. Bombs were seen to fall among many parked aircraft and among many parked aircraft and on hangers and workshops.

Medium bombers attacked road junctions in the area south of Rome and fighters continued their patrols over the beachhead.

On the Dalmatian coast, enemy shipping was attacked by light bombers.

During the day sixty-two enemy aircraft were destroyed in the air and many more on the ground. Six of ours are missing.

The Mediterranean Allied Air Forces flew approximately 900 sorties.

†ANDERSON, RICHARD BEATTY
Rank and Organizations: Private First Class, U.S. Marine Corps.
Born: June 26, 1921, Tacoma, Washington.
Entered Service At: Washington.
Place and Date: Kwajalein Atoll, Marshall Islands, February 1, 1944.
Citation: For conspicuous gallantry and intrepidity at the risk of his life above and beyond the call of duty while serving with the 4th Marine Division during action against enemy Japanese forces on Roi Island, Kwajalein Atoll, Marshall Islands, February 1, 1944. Entering a shell crater occupied by 3 other marines, Pfc. Anderson was preparing to throw a grenade at an enemy position when it slipped from his hands and rolled toward the men at the bottom of the hole. With insufficient time to retrieve the armed weapon and throw it, Pfc. Anderson fearlessly chose to sacrifice himself and save his companions by hurling his body upon the grenade and taking the full impact of the explosion. His personal valor and exceptional spirit of loy-

alty in the face of almost certain death were in keeping with the highest traditions of the U.S. Naval Service. He gallantly gave his life for his country.

†POWER, JOHN VINCENT
Rank and Organizations: First Lieutenant, U.S. Marine Corps.
Born: November 20, 1918, Worchester, Massachusetts.
Entered Service At: Massachusetts.
Place and Date: Kwajalein Atoll, Marshall Islands, February 1, 1944.
Citation: For conspicuous gallantry and intrepidity at the risk of his life above and beyond the call of duty as platoon leader, attached to the 4th Marine Division, during the landing and battle of Namur Island, Kwajalein Atoll, Marshall Islands, February 1, 1944. Severely wounded in the stomach while setting a demolition charge on a Japanese pillbox, 1st Lt. Power was steadfast in his determination to remain in action. Protecting his wound with his left hand and firing with his right, he courageously advanced as another hostile position was taken under attack, fiercely charging the opening made by the explosion and emptying his carbine into the pillbox. While attempting to reload and continue the attack, 1st Lt. power was shot again in the stomach and head and collapsed in the doorway. His exceptional valor, fortitude and indomitable fighting spirit in the face of withering enemy fire were in keeping with the highest traditions of the U.S Naval Service. He gallantly gave his life for his country.

SORENSON, RICHARD KEITH
Rank and Organizations: Private, U.S. Marine Corps Reserve, 4th Marine Division.
Born: August 28, 1924, Anoka, Minnesota.
Entered Service At: Minnesota.
Place and Date: Namur Island, Kwajalein Atoll, Marshall Islands, February 1-2, 1944.
Citation: For conspicuous gallantry and intrepidity at the risk of his life above and beyond the call of duty while serving with an assault battalion attached to the 4th Marine Division during the battle of Namur Island, Kwajalein Atoll, Marshall Islands, on February 1-2 1944. Putting up a brave defense against a particularly violent counterattack by the enemy during invasion operations, Pvt. Sorenson and 5 other marines occupying a shellhole were endangered by a Japanese grenade thrown into their midst. Sorenson hurled himself upon the deadly weapon, heroically taking the full impact

of the explosion. As a result of his gallant action, he was severely wounded, but the lives of his comrades were saved. His great personal valor and exceptional spirit of self-sacrifice in the face of almost certain death were in keeping with the highest traditions of the U.S. Naval Service.

†DYESS, AQUILLA JAMES

Rank and Organizations: Lieutenant Colonel, U.S. Marine Corps Reserve.

Born: January 11, 1909, Augusta, Georgia.

Entered Service At: Georgia.

Place and Date: Kwajalein Atoll, Marshall Islands, February 1-2, 1944.

Citation: For conspicuous gallantry and intrepidity at the risk of his life above and beyond the call of duty as Commanding Officer of the 1st Battalion, 24th Marines (Rein), 4th Marine Division, in action against enemy Japanese forces during the assault on Namur Island, Kwajalein Atoll, Marshall Islands, February 1 and 2, 1944. Undaunted by severe fire from automatic Japanese weapons, Lt. Col. Dyess launched a powerful final attack on the second day of the assault, unhesitatingly posting himself between the opposing lines to point out objectives and avenues of approach and personally leading the advancing troops. Alert, and determined to quicken the pace of the offensive against increased enemy fire, he was constantly at the head of advance units, inspiring his men to push forward until the Japanese had been driven back to a small center of resistance and victory assured. While standing on the parapet of an anti-tank trench directing a group of infantry in a flanking attack against the last enemy position, Lt. Col. Dyess was killed by a burst of enemy machinegun fire. His daring and forceful leadership and his valiant fighting spirit in the face of terrific opposition were in keeping with the highest traditions of the U.S. Naval Service. He gallantly gave his life for his country.

Note: The following is a newspaper account of the preceding battle for which Pfc. Anderson, Lt. Power, Pvt. Sorenson, and Lt. Col. Dyess were awarded the Medal of Honor:

THE MARSHALLS LANDING

• • •

**Use of Two Divisions Against One 'Atoll
Indicates Hardships Along Road to Tokyo**

•••

The Navy announced the long expected invasion of the Marshall Islands yesterday. A campaign of great importance to the course of the Pacific war has started. Admiral Chester W. Nimitz, Commander in Chief of the Pacific Fleet and of Pacific Ocean Areas, issued a communique at Pearl Harbor revealing that elements of two American divisions had landed on islets of Kwajalein, largest atoll in the Marshall group.

The Fourth Marine Division, hitherto untested in combat, and the Seventh Division of the Army, veterans of the Aleutians, made the landings. That two divisions were used against one atoll and that we made initial landings on adjacent islets and did not attempt the direct storming of the Japanese strongholds in Kwajalein Atoll – Kwajalein Island and Roi Island – are sufficient indications of the magnitude of the task ahead.

Other landings on other important atolls of the Marshall group probably have been, or will be made; the Marshalls campaign will be the greatest we have yet fought in the Pacific. It will be big not only in size but in consequence. If we win the Marshalls, we shall have made our first long step forward on the long, difficult road to Tokyo; we shall have broken through the outer shield of Japan's defenses.

Mystery-Shrouded Islands

The mid-Pacific atolls that American forces are now attacking have been islands of mystery ever since Japan seized them during the first World War. Since then, few foreigners have visited the islands; what visits have been permitted have been limited and guided.

But intelligence reports and aerial reconnaissance have established numerous facts about them; these islands are a network of sea and air bases, far more heavily garrisoned and defended than were the Gilberts, which were, in effect, enemy outposts. In the Marshalls we are assaulting for the first time the first of Japan's main lines of resistance in the Pacific.

The Marshalls consist of more than thirty principal coralline islands, dotted across the blue Pacific, more than 700 miles east to west, 650 miles north to south. They extend from Mili Atoll, 190 miles northwest of Makin, one of the bases we conquered in the Gilberts in November, to Pokaakku Atoll, 304 miles south of Wake. The nearest of the group is 626 miles from Truk, principal Japanese sea-air base in the Central Pacific area, 2,208 miles from Pearl Harbor, 1,242 from Midway and 2,150 from the closest point on the coast of metropolitan Japan. The scene of action in the Pacific, therefore, probably covers an area of island-dotted ocean two or three times bigger than California.

There is, however, very little land surface in this area. There are a great many reefs and islets, but the total land area is only about 100 square miles (not so big as the area of the borough of Queens). The principal groups are of typical atoll formation, a number of low-lying islets, shoals and sand bars connected by and fringed with coral reefs encircling an inner lagoon.

The islands are generally narrow and so low – nowhere more than thirty-three feet above the ocean – that from a distance the coconut palms which about in the Marshalls seem to be growing out of the sea. Sometimes in severe storms, waves wash completely across the islands. For this reason, it has been said, ironically, that the "Marshalls are perfect harbors without land."

No Jungle Areas

Coral sand, covered in some cases by imported top soil or decayed vegetation, covers some of the principal islands; coconut palms, breadfruit trees, bananas, yams, pandanus, taro and other tropical vegetation are found on the larger islands; the smaller ones are barren. None is jungled, in the South Seas sense, and all, though hot and damp, are relatively healthy, with no malaria. February is the driest month, with an average rainfall of about seven inches (it generally rains sixteen days of the month), but it is also the windiest, with a mean wind velocity of seven to eight knots to be expected. The prevailing temperature is between 78 and 87 degrees at this time of the year.

The prevailing winds are from the east and northeast. Generally speaking, the islands on the eastern sides of the coral reefs are the largest. There are two main chains in the Marshalls, which extend northwest and southeast in more or less parallel lines. The eastern group, of which Mili is the southern atoll, is known as the Radak or Ratak, or "sunrise," chain; the western group, 100 miles or more away, is known as the Ralik, or "sunset," chain.

It is in this westernmost chain, on Kwajalein Atoll, that our first announced landing in the Marshalls has been made.

Kwajalein or, as it is sometimes called, Menschikov Atoll, is the heart of the Marshalls. It is composed of some ninety small, flat islands and a number of reefs grouped around a central lagoon, big enough, it has been said, to "hold all the fleets of the world." The atoll is about sixty-six miles long. Kwajalein, principal island of the atoll, is at the southeast, Roi at the northeast corner of the atoll.

Our landings apparently have been made not on Kwajalein and Roi – but on islands near them in the same atoll group.

A thumbnail sketch of atoll follows:

Kwajalein Atoll

About 1,000 inhabitants, mostly Kanakas in 1930, but the Japanese garrison today is probably 5,000 to 10,000 strong. Among the natives, skin disease, so-called "Marshall typhus" and dysentery are prevalent. Fish, copra, breadfruit, pigs and chickens. There are more than twenty entrances to the lagoon, but probably most have been mined or blocked by the Japanese or are commanded by their guns. South Pass, northwest of Kwajalein, had a depth of only three and a quarter fathoms when last surveyed, but may have been dredged since. Gea Channel, farther north, is crooked but deeper.

Mellu Channel, southwestward of Roi Island, seems to have a depth of fourteen fathoms. There are strong currents and dangerous reefs in or near most of these channels. Though speckled in places with coral heads and sand bars, the lagoon has depths of sixteen to twenty-five fathoms. Kwajalein Island, southeasternmost island in the Kwajalein Atoll, is used by the Japanese as a naval station. There is an important anchorage off this island and a seaplane base is maintained here. On Roi Island, northeasternmost of the Kwajalein Atoll islands, the Japanese maintain perhaps their largest airfield in the Marshalls, an important air base with hangars, fuel and ammunition dumps, warehouses, power plants, and radio equipment.

POWERS, LEO J.
Rank and Organization: Private First Class, U.S. Army, 133d Infantry, 34th Infantry Division.
Born: Anselmo, Nebraska.
Entered Service At: Alder Gulch, Montana.
Place and Date: Northwest of Cassino, Italy, February 3, 1944.
Citation: For conspicuous gallantry and intrepidity at the risk of life above and beyond the call of duty. On February 3, 1944, this soldier's company was assigned the mission of capturing Hill 175, the key enemy strongpoint northwest of Cassino, Italy. The enemy, estimated to be at least 50 in strength, supported by machineguns emplaced in 3 pillboxes and mortar fire from behind the hill, was able to pin the attackers down and inflict 8 casualties. The company was unable to advance, but Pfc. Powers, a rifleman in one of the assault platoons, on his own initiative and in the face of the terrific fire, crawled forward to assault 1 of the enemy pillboxes which he had spotted. Armed with 2 handgrenades and well aware that if the enemy should see him it would mean almost certain death, Pfc. Powers crawled up the hill to within 15 yards of the enemy pillbox. At this close range, the grenade entered the pillbox, killed 2 of the occupants and 3 or 4 more fled the position, probably wounded. This enemy gun silenced, the center of the line was able to move forward again, but almost immediately came under machinegun fire from a second enemy pillbox on the left flank. Pfc. Powers, however, had located this pillbox, and crawled toward it, with absolutely no cover if the enemy should see him. Raising himself in full view of the enemy gunners about 15 feet from the pillbox, Pfc. Powers threw his grenade into the pillbox, silencing the gun, killing another German and

probably wounding 3 or 4 more who fled. Pfc. Powers, still acting on his own initiative, commenced crawling toward the third enemy pillbox in the face of heavy machine-pistol and machinegun fire. Skillfully availing himself of the meager cover and concealment, Pfc. Powers crawled up to within 10 yards of this pillbox, fully exposed himself to the enemy gunners, stood upright and tossed the 2 grenades into the small opening in the roof of the pillbox. His grenades killed 2 of the enemy and 4 more, all wounded, came out and surrendered to Pfc. Powers, who was now unarmed. Pfc. Powers had worked his way over the entire company front, and against tremendous odds had singlehandedly broken the backbone of this heavily defended and strategic enemy position, and enabled his regiment to advance into the city of Cassino. Pfc. Powers' fighting determination and intrepidity in battle exemplify the highest traditions of the U.S. Armed Forces.

OFFICIAL COMMUNIQUE:
United Nations
ALGIERS, Feb. 3 - A communique:

NAVAL

During the night of Jan. 31-Feb. 1, light coastal forces in the Adriatic Sea sank two more schooners near Silba Island
On the following night in the Adriatic British destroyers bombarded Porto Recanati and Pedaso, south of Ancona.

LAND

On both the Anzio and main fronts of the Fifth Army there has been hard fighting. The beachhead was enlarged in the face of stiff resistance and counter-attacks were repulsed.
On the main front French and American troops have moved so far through the mountains north of Cassino that the enemy stronghold is seriously threatened. Counter-attacks against the flanks of our troops exploiting the break-through in this sector were thrown back. Eighth Army patrols were active.

†RIORDAN, PAUL F.
Rank and Organization: Second lieutenant, U.S. Army, 34th Infantry Division.
Born: Charles City, Iowa.
Entered Service At: Kansas City, Missouri.
Place and Date: Near Cassino, Italy, February 3-8, 1944.

Citation: For conspicuous gallantry and intrepidity above and beyond the call of duty. In the attack on the approaches to the city of Cassino on February 3, 1944, 2d Lt. Riordan led 1 of the assault platoons. Attacking Hill 175, his command was pinned down by enemy machinegun fire from the hill and from a pillbox about 45 yards to the right of the hill. In the face of intense fire, 2d Lt. Riordan moved out in full view of the enemy gunners to reach a position from where he could throw a handgrenade into the pillbox. Then, getting to his knees, he hurled the grenade approximately 45 yards, scoring a direct hit. The grenade killed 1 and wounded the other 2 Germans in the nest and silenced the gun. Another soldier then cleaned out the enemy pillboxes on the hill itself, and the company took its objective. Continuing the assault into Cassino itself on February 8, 1944, 2d Lt. Riordan and his platoon were given the mission of taking the city jailhouse, one of the enemy's several strongpoints. Again 2d Lt. Riordan took the lead and managed to get though the ring of enemy fire covering the approaches and reached the building. His platoon, however, could not get through the intense fire and was cut off. 2d Lt. Riordan, aware that his men were unable to follow, determined to carry on singlehanded, but the numerically superior enemy force was too much for him to overcome, and he was killed by enemy small-arms fire after disposing of at least 2 of the defenders. 2d Lt. Riordan's bravery and extraordinary heroism in the face of almost certain death were an inspiration to his men and exemplify the highest traditions of the U.S. Armed Forces.

HUFF, PAUL B.

Rank and Organization: Corporal, U.S. Army, 509th Parachute Infantry Battalion.
Born: Cleveland, Tennessee.
Entered Service At: Cleveland, Tennessee.
Place and Date: Near Carano, Italy February 8, 1944.
Citation: For conspicuous gallantry and intrepidity at risk of life above and beyond the call of duty, in action on February 8, 1944, near Carano, Italy. Cpl. Huff volunteered to lead a 6-man patrol with the mission of determining the location and strength of an enemy unit which was delivering fire on the exposed right flank of his company. The terrain over which he had to travel consisted of exposed, rolling ground, affording the enemy excellent visibility. As the patrol advanced, its members were subjected to small arms and machinegun fire and a concentration of mortar fire, shells bursting within 5 to 10 yards of them and bullets striking the ground at their feet. Moving ahead of his patrol, Cpl. Huff drew fire from 3 enemy

machineguns and a 20-mm. weapon. Realizing the danger confronting his patrol, he advanced alone under deadly fire through a minefield and arrived at a point within 75 yards of the nearest machinegun position. Under direct fire from the rear machingun, he crawled the remaining 75 yards to the closest emplacement, killed the crew with his submachinegun and destroyed the gun. During this act he fired from a kneeling position which drew fire from other positions, enabling him to estimate correctly the strength and location of the enemy. Still under concentrated fire, he returned to his patrol and led his men to safety. As a result of the information he gained, a patrol in strength sent out that afternoon, 1 group under the leadership of Cpl. Huff, succeeded in routing an enemy company of 125 men, killing 27 Germans and capturing 21 others, with a loss of only 3 patrol members. Cpl. Huff's intrepid leadership and daring combat skill reflect the finest traditions of the American infantryman.

Note: The following is a newspaper account of the preceding battle for which both Lt. Riordan and Cpl. Huff were awarded the Medal of Honor:

AMERICANS WEDGING INTO CASSINO AFTER WEEK'S BATTLE IN OUTSKIRTS

• • •

Infantry Penetration, Made at Snail's Pace, Threatens to Split Germans in Town From Those on Mountain

• • •

WITH THE FIFTH ARMY, in Italy, Feb. 8 – After a week of extensive in-fighting along the fringe of houses in the outer limits of Cassino and on the craggy ridges above it, American infantrymen began today to make a definite penetration, although at a snail's pace.

They drove forward to edge a wedge between the main German positions on Mount Cassino and those inside the town. Feeling their way cautiously through clouds of powder-smoke that blanketed the area for most of the day, squads worked their way around a hilltop on which a ruined medieval castle stands and established themselves along points from which, if they can hang on, they can much better dominate the town.

It is not yet clear whether any Germans were left in the castle area, from which their machine-gunners especially had been giving trouble. For the past two days, heavy artillery had pounded the ancient fortress, scoring many direct hits and shaking it to its foundations but not destroying it much more than time had already done. This afternoon, however, our guns were laying off this target and the infantry on this prominent feature appeared to be holding its own.

Snipers Impede Advance

As these elements began gradually to punch toward the middle of the enemy positions, other units above them on both sides below the Abbey of Mount Cassino worked their way desperately up the steep slopes, where they wee having much trouble with German snipers hidden among stones and in crevices and with machine-gunners in artfully concealed bunkers. American artillery was shelling cautiously all around the abbey today.

In the town, street-fighting squads achieved a slight advance, obtaining control of a few more houses, but the greater part of the town remained in enemy hands. How long this situation is likely to continue is difficult to predict. Some officers believe that, should the wedge driven over Castle Hill continue forward, the Germans might effect a sudden withdrawal. But, on the other hand, because of the vital strategic important of this bastion blocking the entrance to the Liri Valley, others thought that, despite their disadvantages, the Germans would fight to the end. The town is now a blasted ruin, reeking with the pungent odor of powder smoke and echoing to the continual bark and burr of guns. New reports say that the Americans have installed themselves in approximately one-fourth of Cassino but, as far as this correspondent's observation and knowledge go, this is definitely an exaggeration.

Allies' Bombers Active

Above the battlegrounds, Allied bombers and fighter-bombers, leaving long white vapor streaks in the lower reaches of the cold air, continued to pound the enemy's rear positions and gun emplacements, churning up billows of dust far behind the front. Occasional German planes showed up. One Messerschmitt 109 of a group of three bombing front positions was shot down by ground fire.

One of the difficulties facing the Americans is the German expertness in camouflage. Yesterday artillery observers spotted a self-propelled gun in a house and carefully plotted its position on the map for shelling this morning. When dawn came the house was gone, and today observers were looking all over town for a newly erected stage-setting for the gun.

Both sides did a certain amount of counter-battery work throughout the day. The Germans made an effort to concentrate their fire on rear road junctions, doing little damage.

Within the town an advanced infantry squad knocked out a German tank with a bazooka, the limitations of whose range and efficacy indicate how close the fighting is. So much smoke is lying in a pall over Cassino now that it is even more difficult for the American infantry to locate enemy rifle pits even 200 yards away.

It is apparent now that one of the main attacking efforts is being made around the monastery. If the Germans are forced to abandon their position on top of Mount Cassino, their position within the town may become desperate. The American troops shoving up the slopes are under strict orders not to enter the Abbey building and to regard it as neutral territory unless the Germans should carry the battle within.

GORDON, NATHAN GREEN

Rank and Organizations: Lieutenant, U.S. Navy, commander of Catalina patrol plane.
Born: September 4, 1916, Morrilton, Arkansas.
Entered Service At: Arkansas.
Place and date: Bismarck Sea, February 15, 1944.
Citation: For extraordinary heroism above and beyond the call of duty as commander of a Catalina patrol plane in rescuing personnel of the U.S. Army 5th Air Force shot down in combat over Kavieng Harbor in the Bismarck Sea, February 15, 1944. On air alert in the vicinity of Vitu Islands, Lt (then Lt. Jg.) Gordon unhesitatingly responded to a report of the crash and flew boldly into the harbor, defying close-range fire from enemy shore guns to make 3 separate landings in full view of the Japanese and pick up 9 men, several of them injured. With his cumbersome flying boat dangerously overloaded, he made a brilliant takeoff despite heavy swells and almost total absence of wind and set a course for base, only to receive the report of another group stranded in a rubber liferaft 600 yards from the enemy shore. Promptly turning back, he again risked his life to set his plane down under direct fire of the heaviest defenses of Kavieng and take aboard 6 more survivors, coolly making his fourth dexterous takeoff with 15 rescued officers and men. By his exceptional daring, personal valor, and incomparable airmanship under most perilous conditions, Lt. Gordon prevented certain death or capture of our airmen by the Japanese.

OFFICIAL COMMUNIQUE:
ALLIED HEADQUARTERS IN THE SOUTHWEST PACIFIC, Wednesday, Feb. 16 - A communique:

NORTHWESTERN SECTOR

Reconnaissance activity only

NORTHEASTERN SECTOR

Admiralty Islands
Our escorted medium units attacked Momote airdrome, dispersal and supply areas
with ninety tons of bombs, causing numerous fires and cratering the runway. Returning to base they strafed installations on Pak and Rambutyo Islands.

New Ireland
Kavieng: Our escorted heavy units dropped 113 tons of bombs on Kavieng and
Panapai airdromes, causing heavy damage to installations with many fires. There
was no interception.

JOHNSTON, WILLIAM J.
Rank and Organizations: Private First Class, U.S. Army, Company G,
180th Infantry, 45th Infantry Division.
Born: Trenton, New Jersey.
Entered Service At: Colchester, Connecticutt.
Place and Date: Near Padiglione, Italy, February 17-19 1944.
Citation: For conspicuous gallantry and intrepidity at risk of life above
and beyond the call of duty in action against the enemy. On February 17,
1944, near Padiglione, Italy, he observed and fired upon an attacking force
of approximately 80 Germans, causing at least 25 casualties and forcing
withdrawal of the remainder. All that day he manned his gun without relief,
subject to mortar, artillery, and sniper fire. Two Germans individually worked
so close to his position that his machinegun was ineffective, whereupon he
killed 1 with his pistol, the second with a rifle taken from another soldier.
When a rifleman protecting his gun position was killed by a sniper, he
immediately moved the body and relocated the machinegun in that spot in
order to obtain a better field of fire. He volunteered to cover the platoon's
withdrawal and was the last man to leave that night. In his new position he
maintained an all-night vigil, the next day causing 7 German casualties. On
the afternoon of the 18th, the organization on the left flank having been
forced to withdraw, he again covered the withdrawal of his own organization. Shortly thereafter, he was seriously wounded over the heart, and a
passing soldier saw him trying to crawl up the embankment. The soldier
aided him to resume his position behind the machinegun which was soon

heard in action for about 10 minutes. Though reported killed, Pfc. Johnston was seen returning to the American lines on the morning of February 19 slowly and painfully working his way back from his overrun position through enemy lines. He gave valuable information of new enemy dispositions. His heroic determination to destroy the enemy and his disregard of his own safety aided immeasurably in halting a strong enemy attack, caused an enormous amount of enemy casualties, and so inspired his fellow soldiers that they fought for and held a vitally important position against greatly superior forces.

†DAMATO, ANTHONY PETER

Rank and Organizations: Corporal, U.S. Marine Corps.
Born: March 28, 1922, Shenandoah, Pennsylvania.
Entered Service At: Pennsylvania.
Place and Date: Eniwetok Atoll, Marshall Islands, February 19-20, 1944.
Citation: For conspicuous gallantry and intrepidity at the risk of his life above and beyond the call of duty while serving with an assault company in action against enemy Japanese forces on Engebi Island, Eniwetok Atoll, Marshall Islands, on the night of February 19-20, 1944. Highly vulnerable to sudden attack by small, fanatical groups of Japanese still at large despite the efficient and determined efforts of our forces to clear the area, Cpl. Damato lay with 2 comrades in a large foxhole in his company's defense perimeter which had been dangerously thinned by the forces withdrawal of nearly half of the available men. When 1 of the enemy approached the foxhole undetected and threw in a handgrenade, Cpl. Damato desperately groped for it in the darkness. Realizing the imminent peril to all 3 and fully aware of the consequences of his act, he unhesitatingly flung himself on the grenade and, although instantly killed as his body absorbed the explosion, saved the lives of his 2 companions. Cpl. Damato's splendid initiative, fearless conduct and valiant sacrifice reflect great credit upon himself and the U.S. Naval Service. He gallantly gave his life for his comrades.

OFFICIAL COMMUNIQUE:
ALGIERS, Feb., 19 – A communique:

NAVAL

Gunfire support by our ships has continued in the Anzio area. Patrols of torpedo boats of the United States Navy intercepted enemy destroyers or minelayers approaching north of Capraia during Feb. 17-18. Torpedo attacks were delivered by the PT boats. Results of these were not observed.

ARMY

Troops of the Fifth Army, after hard fighting, took possession of two strongly held crests west of Mount Cassino during attacks on Feb. 17-18. In attacks on this sector of the front, troops of New Zealand and Indian formations are taking part. Attacks against our positions in one other sector of the main Fifth Army front were repulsed.

Against the Fifth Army positions in the Anzio beachhead the enemy continued to hurl troops and tanks. Enemy losses have been heavy. Our lines are intact, and we have launched several successful local counter-attacks.

On the Eighth Army front patrols have been active. Polish troops there have taken German prisoners.

United States
WASHINGTON, Feb. 19 – Navy communique 506:

Pacific and Far East
Two United States submarines recently returned from patrols deep in Japanese Empire waters report sinking thirteen enemy merchant ships totaling 68,200 tons. These sinkings have not been reported in any previous Navy Department communique.

WASHINGTON, Feb. 19 – A Pacific Fleet announcement:

Supplementing the major attacks on Truk and Eniwetok, our forces have continued to neutralize other enemy bases in the Central Pacific area.

On Feb. 16 (West Longitude date)liberators, Dauntless dive bombers and Warhawk fighters of the Seventh Army Air Force attacked four stalls in the eastern Marshall Islands. At one base, Warhawks blew up a fuel dump, damaged a small cargo ship and sank three small craft. On the same day, search planes of Fleet Air Wing Two bombed ground installations at two other areas.

Between Feb. 14-18 our warships repeatedly shelled important enemy positions in the eastern Marshalls.

WASHINGTON, Feb. 19 – A Pacific Fleet communique:

Our forces have captured the enemy air base at Engebi and several other islands in the northern portion of the Eniwetok Atoll. Preliminary reports indicate our casualties have been light.

Assaults on other portions of the atoll are proceeding according to schedule.

LAWLEY, WILLIAM R., JR. (Air Mission)
Rank and Organizations: First Lieutenant, U.S. Army Air Corps, 364th Bomber Squadron, 305th Bomber Group.
Born: August 23, 1920, Leeds, Alabama.
Entered Service At: Birmingham, Alabama.
Place and Date: Over Europe, February 20, 1944.
Citation: For conspicuous gallantry and intrepidity in action above and beyond the call of duty, February 20, 1944, while serving as pilot of a B-17 aircraft on a heavy bombardment mission over enemy-occupied continental Europe. Coming off the target he was attacked by approximately 20 enemy fighters, shot out of formation, and his plane severely crippled. Eight crewmembers were wounded, the copilot was killed by a 20-mm. shell. One engine was on fire, the controls shot away, and 1st Lt. Lawley seriously and painfully wounded about the face. Forcing the copilot's body off the controls, he brought the plane out of a steep dive, flying with his left hand only. Blood covered the instruments and windshield and visibility was impossible. With a full bomb load the plane was difficult to maneuver and bombs could not be released because the racks were frozen. After the order to bail out had been given, 1 of the waist gunners informed the pilot that 2 crewmembers were so severely wounded that it would be impossible for them to bail out. With the fire in the engine spreading, the danger of an explosion was imminent. Because of the helpless condition of his wounded crewmembers 1st Lt. Lawley elected to remain with the ship and bring them to safety if it was humanly possible, giving the other crewmembers the option of bailing out. Enemy fighters again attacked but by using masterful evasive action he managed to lose them. One engine again caught on fire and was extinguished by skillful flying. 1st Lt. Lawley remained at his post, refusing first-aid until he collapsed from sheer exhaustion caused by loss of blood, shock, and the energy he had expended in keeping control of his plane. He was revived by the bombardier and again took over the controls. Coming over the English coast 1 engine ran out of gasoline and had to be feathered. Another engine started to burn and continued to do so until a successful crash landing was made on a small fighter base. Through his heroism and exceptional flying skill 1st Lt. Lawley rendered outstanding, distinguished, and valorous service to our Nation.

†MATHIES, ARCHIBALD (Air Mission)
Rank and Organization: Sergeant, U.S. Army Air Corps, 510th Bomber Squadron, 351st Bomber Group.
Born: June 3, 1918, Scotland.
Entered Service At: Pittsburgh, Pennsylvania.

Place and Date: Over Europe, February 20, 1944.
Citation: For conspicuous gallantry and intrepidity at risk of life above and beyond the call of duty in action against the enemy in connection with the bombing mission over enemy-occupied Europe on February 20, 1944. The aircraft on which Sgt. Mathies was serving as engineer and ball-turret gunner was attacked by a squadron of enemy fighters with the result that the copilot was killed outright, the pilot wounded and rendered unconscious, the radio operator wounded and the plane severely damaged. Nevertheless, Sgt. Mathies and other members of the crew managed to right the plane and fly it back to their home station, where they contacted the control tower and reported the situation. Sgt. Mathies and the navigator volunteered to attempt to land the plane. Other members of the crew were ordered to jump, leaving Sgt. Mathies and the navigator aboard. After observing the distressed aircraft from another plane, Sgt. Mathies' commanding officer decided the damaged plane could not be landed by the inexperienced crew and ordered them to abandon it and parachute to safety. Demonstrating unsurpassed courage and heroism, Sgt. Mathies and the navigator replied that the pilot was still alive but could not be moved and that they would not desert him. They were then told to attempt a landing. After 2 unsuccessful efforts their plane crashed into an open field in a third attempt to land. Sgt. Mathies, the navigator, and the wounded pilot were killed.

†TRUEMPER, WALTER E. (Air Mission)

Rank and Organizations: Second Lieutenant, U.S. Army Air Corps, 510th Bomber Squadron, 351st Bomber Group.
Born: October 31, 1918, Aurora, Illinois.
Entered Service At: Aurora, Illinois.
Place and Date: Over Europe, February 20, 1944.
Citation: For conspicuous gallantry and intrepidity at risk of life above and beyond the call of duty in action against the enemy in connection with the bombing mission over enemy-occupied Europe on February 20, 1944. The aircraft on which 2d Lt. Truemper was serving as navigator was attacked by a squadron of enemy fighters with the result that the copilot was killed outright, the pilot wounded and the plane severely damaged. Nevertheless, 2d Lt. Truemper and other members of the crew managed to right the plane and fly it back to their home station, where they contacted the control tower and reported the situation. 2d Lt. Truemper and the engineer volunteered to attempt to land the plane. Other members of the crew were ordered to jump, leaving 2d Lt. Truemper and the engineer aboard. After observing the distressed aircraft from another plane, 2d Lt. Truemper's

commanding officer decided the damaged plane could not be landed by the inexperienced crew and ordered them to abandon it and parachute to safety. Demonstrating unsurpassed courage and heroism, 2d Lt. Truemper and the engineer replied that the pilot was still alive but could not be moved and that they would not desert him. They were then told to attempt a landing. After 2 unsuccessful efforts their plane crashed into an open field in a third attempt to land. 2d Lt. Truemper, the engineer, and the wounded pilot were killed.

Note: The following is a newspaper account of the preceding battle for which Lt. Lawley, Sgt. Mathies, and Lt. Truemper were awarded the Medal of Honor:

BIGGEST U.S. FORCE BOMBS NAZI FIGHTER PLANTS

• • •

2,000 PLANES MASS

• • •

"Forts," Liberators With Huge Escort Blast 8 Reich Centers

• • •

LEIPZIG IS HIT TWICE

• • •

A UNITED STATES HEAVY BOMBER STATION, in Britain, Monday, Feb. 21 – Employing 2,000 heavy bombers and escorting fighters, the largest American force yet flown against the Nazis, the United States Army Air Forces struck heavy blows yesterday at eight important centers producing aircraft for the Luftwaffe. British, Dominion and Allied fighters flew in supporting forays.

Officially described as an attack to destroy Nazi air power, both "in being" and in process of production, the day's mission was a powerful preliminary to invasion.

[Gen. Henry H. Arnold said at Washington Sunday night the attack "knocked out" 25 percent of Nazi fighter plane output.]

Preliminary reports said at least sixty-one Nazi planes were destroyed by our escorting P-47 Thunderbolts, P-51 Mustangs, and P-38 Lightnings. The number of enemy planes shot down by the gunners of our heavy bombers had not yet been tallied.

The bombing results ranged from "good" to "excellent," returning crew members of the Flying Fortresses and Liberators reported.

[The Germans struck at London again Sunday night. At least three Nazi raiders were downed.]

[At the same time British bombers were reported going out for a new attack on Europe.]

Twenty-two American heavy bombers were missing from the day's big attack. One of our fighters was known to have been destroyed and three others were missing, said a communique from Lt. Gen. Carl A. Spaatz's Strategic Air Forces headquarters.

About eight hours before the multiple attacks by the USAAF, Leipzig, one of the American targets, was blasted by the Royal Air Force. The British bombers dropped 2,575 tons or more of explosives on the city, their target including the Eria component factory, which produces a large proportion of wings and fuselages for the Nazis' Messerschmitt 109 fighters.

The RAF sent almost 1,000 heavy bombers against Leipzig. Seventy-nine planes, the greatest number yet lost in any night attack against Germany, were missing from the Saturday night operations.

Dividing about 1,000 Fortresses and Liberators of the Eighth Air Force's bomber divisions into eight groups of formations, each of which was covered by long-range United States fighters, Gen Spaatz aimed blows at airplane or airplane parts factories in Leipzig, Oschersleben, Gotha, Bernburg, Brunswick, Halberstadt, and Tutow in the Reich, and Posen in Poland.

Besides destroying or damaging the German warplane plants, the American Air Forces heads hoped to spread out and confuse the Luftwaffe fighter defenses to a point of low efficiency.

Judging from the small number of United States planes lost, this plan seems to have worked. When Allied reconnaissance photographs are available and the bombing reports of the crews can be checked, the whole strategic and tactical plan may prove to have been highly successful.

The bombing was visual on many of the targets and well placed by special aiming equipment where there were clouds. Every formation seemed extraordinarily pleased with its bomb pattern.

The RAF's great attack on Leipzig over Saturday night did much to use up and scatter the Luftwaffe's defense forces, besides saturating that German city.

British Mosquito planes made a diversionary attack on Berlin during the night.

The RAF makes no effort to minimize the seriousness of its loss of seventy-nine planes, but, even so, does not hint the price was too costly. Severe icing conditions and the fact the night bombers had to run the length of enemy fighter and flack defenses are seen as the chief reason for the high casualties.

There was absolutely nothing to indicate the Germans employed any new defensive weapons. Rather the Nazis' main reliance was great packs of night fighters, which rained flares to light the air-battle scene. A clear sky above thick clouds also proved helpful to the defending Luftwaffe, according to RAF pilots.

Just one minute before 4 A.M. Sunday, the first of the heavy forces of Halifaxes and Lancasters started bombing Leipzig. On markers dropped by pathfinder planes, the attack developed quickly, although variable winds made the timing of arrivals over the target difficult; and some planes reached it before the zero hour.

When the last of the RAF bombers started home, the glow of fires was visible through the thick cloud layer and smoke was rising to about 22,000 feet.

Widest U.S. Attack To Date

The effort of the United States "heavies" that followed by daylight was their most ambitious to date and apparently one of the most successful. Every target of the "Forts" and Liberators was either an aircraft factory or an airfield on which Nazi planes were parked awaiting transfer to operational fields.

Maj. Louis W. Rohr of Teaneck, N.J., who led one formation over Bernburg, where a Junkers factory was pounded, reported visibility excellent and said scores of Junkers planes were seen hit on the grounds of the plant. He added that the bombing was "right on the nose."

Maj. Marcus M. Elliott of Los Angeles, who led a formation over Leipzig, also reported good visibility, with the general weather conditions "fine." He reported the bombing results extremely good.

Neither of these formations encountered more than perfunctory Nazi fighter opposition and moderate flak. Mustang fighters were at Leipzig with the bombers, but had little work to do.

Some of the crews that bombed Leipzig reported smoke and fires in the northeast section of the city, where the RAF had dumped its load before dawn. They reported the city's defense as feeble.

Bomber crews at other targets reported seeing as many as 100 Nazi fighters at a time and told of many determined attacks. There seemed to be no discernable pattern in the enemy's air opposition. At one point it would be strong; at others, apparently equally important to the Nazis, it was almost non-existent.

Second Lt. Orlando J. Petro of St. Paul, Minn., a Fortress bombardier, said his formation seemed to meet "the entire Luftwaffe" which "came at us twelve at a time." He added that it was "rough over the target area, but a good job of bombing."

Second Lt. William Steele of Mount Kisco, N.Y., a navigator, said Focke-Wulf 190s, making head-on attacks ten at a time, stayed with his formation for nearly three hours.

The formations that went to Posen had one of the longest missions yet made by the USAAF. Those striking at Leipzig had a round trip of about 1,150 miles.

While the interior of Germany rocked and reeled from the blows of the "heavies," Marauder medium bombers of the United States Ninth Air Force, escorted by RAF, Dominion, and Allied fighters, attacked targets, including Nazi airfields, in the Netherlands. No losses were reported from these attacks.

The punishing of the Nazi military targets in northern France was kept up morning and afternoon by British and Australian Mosquito bombers, without loss.

MONTGOMERY, JACK C.

Rank and Organizations: First Lieutenant, U.S. Army, 45th Infantry Division.

Born: Long, Oklahoma.

Entered Service At: Sallisaw, Oklahoma.

Place and Date: Near Padiglione, Italy, February 22, 1944.

Citation: For conspicuous gallantry and intrepidity at risk of life above and beyond the call of duty on February 22, 1944, near Padiglione, Italy. Two hours before daybreak a strong force of enemy infantry established themselves in 3 echelons at 50 yards, 100 yards, and 300 yards, respectively, in front of the rifle platoons commanded by 1st Lt. Montgomery. The closest position, consisting of 4 machineguns and 1 mortar, threatened the immediate security of the platoon position. Seizing an M1 rifle and several handgrenades, 1st Lt. Montgomery crawled up a ditch to within handgrenade range of the enemy. Then climbing boldly onto a little mound, he fired his rifle and threw his grenades so accurately that he killed 8 of the enemy and captured the remaining 4. Returning to his platoon, he called for artillery fire on a house, in and around which he suspected that the majority of the enemy had entrenched themselves. Arming himself with a carbine, he proceeded along the shallow ditch, as withering fire from the riflemen and machinegunners in the second position was concentrated on him. He attacked this position with such fury that 7 of the enemy surrendered to him, and both machineguns were silenced. Three German dead were found in the vicinity later that morning. 1st Lt. Montgomery continued boldly toward the house, 300 yards from his platoon position. It was now daylight, and the enemy observation was excellent across the flat open terrain which led to 1st Lt. Montgomery's objective. When the artillery barrage had lifted, 1st Lt. Montgomery ran fearlessly toward the strongly defended position. As the enemy started streaming out of the house, 1st Lt. Montgomery, unafraid of treacherous snipers, exposed himself daringly to assemble the surrendering enemy and send them to the rear. His fearless, aggressive, and intrepid actions that morning, accounted for a total of 11 enemy dead, 32 prisoners, and an unknown number of wounded. That night, while aiding an adjacent unit to repulse a counterattack, he was struck by mortar fragments and seriously wounded. The selflessness and courage exhibited by 1st Lt. Montgomery in alone attacking 3 strong enemy positions inspired his men to a degree beyond estimation.

OFFICIAL COMMUNIQUE:
United States
ALGIERS, Feb. 22 - A communique:

NAVY

A group of enemy E-boats attempting to approach Anzio during the night of Feb. 20 were driven off by American patrol craft. One E-boat blew up after being hit and a second was believed to have been driven ashore.

ARMY

It was a relatively quiet day on all fronts. Local fighting, however, occurred at three points on the Fifth Army's Anzio front and both our artillery and that of the enemy fired heavy concentrations.

On the main Fifth Army front and on the Eighth Army front patrol activity continued.

†McGILL, TROY A.
Rank and Organizations: Sergeant, U.S. Army, Troop G, 5th Cavalry Regiment, 1st Cavalry Division.
Born: Knoxville, Tennessee.
Entered Service At: Ada, Oklahoma.
Place and Date: Los Negros Islands, Admiralty Group March 4, 1944.
Citation: For conspicuous gallantry and intrepidity above and beyond the call of duty in action with the enemy at Los Negros Island, Admiralty Group, on March 4, 1944. In the early morning hours Sgt. McGill, with a squad of 8 men, occupied a revetment which bore the brunt of a furious attack by approximately 200 drink-crazed enemy troops. Although covered by crossfire from machineguns on the right and left flank he could receive no support from the remainder of our troops stationed at his rear. All members of the squad were killed or wounded except Sgt. McGill and another man, whom he ordered to return to the next revetment. Courageously resolved to

hold his position at all cost, he fired his weapon until it ceased to function. Then, with the enemy only 5 yards away, he charged from his foxhole in the face of certain death and clubbed the enemy with his rifle in hand-to-hand combat until he was killed. At dawn 105 enemy dead were found around his position. Sgt. McGill's intrepid stand was an inspiration to his comrades and a decisive factor in the defeat of a fanatical enemy.

OFFICIAL COMMUNIQUE:
UNITED NATIONS
ALLIED HEADQUARTERS IN THE SOUTHWEST PACIFIC, Sunday, March 5 - A communique:

NORTHWESTERN SECTOR

Reconnaissance activity only.

NORTHEASTERN SECTOR

Admiralty Islands: Shortly after dusk, in a final desperate effort to restore the situation and regain the key Momote airfield, the enemy attacked in a series of continued assaults lasting the entire night. Again and again his forces hurried themselves against our lines in incessant but futile efforts to reach the field. Wave after wave was destroyed before his forces finally recoiled in complete defeat after one of the fiercest encounters of the war. His casualties, dead and wounded, are estimated at 8,000. Seven hundred of his dead were buried by our men on the western perimeter of the field alone. We lost sixty-one killed and 244 wounded. Our troops are preparing to resume the advance. During the day our naval units had bombarded enemy shore installations at Lorenqau and Sea Eagle Harbor. In the air our medium and attack units executed close support missions. One of eight enemy fighters attempting interception was shot down.
New Guinea: Our Solomons air patrol attacked enemy targets at Borpop and along the east coast and enemy positions on New Hanover.

MICHAEL, EDWARD S. (Air Mission)
Rank and Organizations: First Lieutenant, U.S. Army Air Corps, 364th Bomber Squadron, 305th Bomber Group,
Born: May 2, 1918, Chicago, Illinois.
Entered Service At: Chicago, Illinois.
Place and Date: Over Germany, April 11, 1944.
Citation: For conspicuous gallantry and intrepidity above and beyond the call of duty while serving as pilot of a B-17 aircraft on a heavy-bombard-

ment mission to Germany, April 11, 1944. The group in which 1st Lt. Michael was flying was attacked by a swarm of fighters. His plane was singled out and the fighters pressed their attacks home recklessly, completely disregarding the Allied fighter escort and their own intense flak. His plane was riddled from nose to tail with exploding cannon shells and knocked out of formation, with a large number of fighters following it down, blasting it with cannon fire as it descended. A cannon shell exploded in the cockpit, wounded the copilot, wrecked the instruments, and blew out the side window, 1st Lt. Michael was seriously and painfully wounded in the right thigh. Hydraulic fluid filmed over the windshield making visibility impossible, and smoke filled the cockpit. The controls failed to respond and 3,000 feet were lost before he succeeded in leveling off. The radio operator informed him that the whole bomb bay was in flames as a result of the explosion of 3 cannon shells, which had ignited the incendiaries. With a full load of incendiaries in the bomb bay and a considerable gas load in the tanks, the danger of fire enveloping the plane and the tanks exploding seemed imminent. When the emergency release lever failed to function, 1st Lt. Michael at once gave the order to bail out and 7 of the crew left the plane. Seeing the bombardier firing the navigator's gun at the enemy planes, 1st Lt. Michael ordered him to bail out as the plane was liable to explode any minute. When the bombardier looked for his parachute he found that it had been riddled with 20-mm. fragments and was useless. 1st Lt. Michael, seeing the ruined parachute, realized that if the plane was abandoned the bombardier would perish and decided that the only chance would be a crash landing. Completely disregarding his own painful and profusely bleeding wounds, but thinking only of the safety of the remaining crewmembers, he gallantly evaded the enemy, using violent evasive action despite the battered condition of his plane. After the plane had been under sustained enemy attack for fully 45 minutes, 1st Lt. Michael finally lost the persistent fighters in a cloud bank. Upon emerging, an accurate barrage of flak caused him to come down to treetop level where flak towers poured a continuous rain of fire on the plane. He continued into France, realizing that at any moment a crash landing might have to be attempted, but trying to get as far as possible to increase the escape possibilities if a safe landing could be achieved. 1st Lt. Michael flew the plane until he became exhausted from the loss of blood, which had formed on the floor in pools, and he lost consciousness.The copilot succeeded in reaching England and sighted an RAF field near the coast. 1st Lt. Michael finally regained consciousness and insisted upon taking over the controls to land the plane. The undercarriage was useless; the bomb bay doors were jammed open; the hydraulic system and altimeter were shot out. In addition, there was no airspeed indicator, the ball turret was jammed with guns pointing downward, and the flaps would not respond. Despite these apparently insurmountable obstacles, he landed the plane without mishap.

OFFICIAL COMMUNIQUE:
United Nations
LONDON, April 11 - A United States Strategic Air Forces in Europe communique:

Photographs show that three repair works, one assembly plant and four airfields were hit by heavy bombers of the United States Eighth Air Force in attacks on German aircraft industries and installations in occupied Belgium and France yesterday.

B-17 and B-24 gunners reported they shot down seven enemy aircraft, while fighter pilots reported the destruction of eight in the air, one more than previously announced. Many enemy airplanes were damaged or destroyed on the ground by bombs and strafing.

Reconnaissance photographs of engine and airframe repair works at Evere, near Brussels, following the B-17 Flying Fortress attack, show that five workshops were hit. Four of them were still burning when the pictures were made. Two hangars and a small unidentified building were also hit and set afire and two buildings in the barracks area were damaged. Several freight cars in an adjacent railway yard were left burning.

B-24 Liberators heavily damaged the aircraft assembly plant at Bourges, in France, reconnaissance photographs showing three large workshops damaged four bays of an office building , one small unidentified building and nine barracks destroyed. Two unidentified medium-sized buildings and an aircraft shelter also were damaged.

At Vilvarde, near Brussels, one building of an engine repair plant was hit and five buildings of a near-by unidentified factory were damaged. Two of them were left burning. At least five bombs fell on adjacent rail lines at Melsbroek airdrome, also near Brussels. A heavy concentration of combs was spread across two of four main dispersal areas.

The field's largest hangar was severely damaged and one unidentified building after the attack. Two other aircraft shelters were hit. Hits were made on the main workshop, a large hangars and five aircraft shelters at repair works near Dienst, about thirty-five miles east-northeast of Brussels.

Fighter bases near Eccles, ten miles northwest of Ghent, and Florennes, forty miles south-southeast of Brussels also were hit. Two hangars, one of them the largest on the field, were seen burning in pictures made during the attack on an Eccles fighter base. Hits were made on two dispersal areas. Hits were made on a workshop and other bombs fell in the dispersal and barracks areas on the Florennes field.

At a bomber base at Orleans, France, several hits were scored on one of the three main hangars, strike photographs reveal. Barracks and other buildings were damaged.

A later United States Strategic Air Forces in Europe communique:

Very strong forces of B-24 Liberators and B-17 Flying Fortresses today attacked targets deep inside Germany, including aircraft plants at Oschersleben and Bernburg. Fighter escort in very great strength came from P-47 Thunderbolts, P-51 Mustangs and P-38 Lightnings of the Eighth and Ninth Air Forces and RAF Mustangs.

A later United States Strategic Air Forces in Europe communique:

B-17 Flying Fortresses and B-24 Liberators of the Eighth Air Force in very great strength penetrated deep into Germany today to attack successfully aircraft factories at Oschersieben and Bernburg, industrial targets in Germany.

A fighter escort of very great strength, consisting of P-51 Mustangs, P-47 thunderbolts and P-38 Lightnings of the Eighth and Ninth Air Forces and RAF Mustangs of the Second Tactical Air Force provided escort and support for the bombers.

Aircraft factories at both Oschersieben and Bernburg were damaged in attacks earlier this year and today's operations were designed to disrupt reconstruction and inflict new damage. Oschersieben has a Ju 88 component factory and an Fw 190 fighter factory. Bernburg is the location of a Ju 88 plant.

After completion of their escort mission some of our fighters swooped low over enemy airfields, destroying and damaging a large number of enemy aircraft on the ground. Enemy fighter opposition was determined and many serial battles were fought from the enemy coast to the targets.

Our fliers reported the enemy employed all types of single and twin-engine fighters in an unsuccessful attempt to turn our bombers from their objectives.

Fifty-two enemy aircraft were reported shot down in serial combat by our fighters, in addition to the large number reported destroyed or damaged on the ground by strafing. The number of enemy aircraft shot down by our bombers has not yet been evaluated.

Sixty-four of our bombers and sixteen of our fighters are missing.

A later United States Strategic Air Forces in Europe communique:

In today's attack against aircraft factories and other industrial targets in Germany B-17 Flying Fortresses and B-24 Liberators of the Eighth Air Force shot down seventy-four enemy aircraft.

This brings to 126 the total enemy aircraft destroyed in aerial combat by our bombers and their fighter escorts in today's operations.

†SQUIRES, JOHN C.

Rank and Organization: Sergeant (then Private First Class), U.S. Army, Company A, 30th Infantry Division.
Born: Louisville, Kentucky.
Entered Service At: Louisville, Kentucky.
Place and Date: Near Padiglione, Italy, April 23-24 1944.
Citation: For conspicuous gallantry and intrepidity at risk of life above and beyond the call of duty. At the start of his company's attack on strongly held enemy positions in and around Spaccasassi Creek, near Padiglione, Italy, on the night of April 23-24, 1944, Pfc. Squires, platoon messenger, participating in his first offensive action, braved intense artillery, mortar, and antitank gun fire in order to investigate the effects of an antitank mine explosion on the leading platoon. Despite shells which burst close to him, Pfc. Squires made his way 50 yards forward to the advance element, noted the situation, reconnoitered a new route of advance and informed his platoon leader of the casualties sustained and the alternate route. Acting without orders, he rounded up stragglers, organized a group of lost men into a squad and led them forward. When the platoon reached Spaccasassi Creek and established an outpost, Pfc. Squires, knowing that almost all of the noncommissioned officers were casualties, placed 8 men in position of his own volition, disregarding enemy machinegun, machine-pistol, and grenade fire which covered the creek draw. When his platoon had been reduced to 14 men, he brought up reinforcements twice. On each trip he went through barbed wire and across an enemy minefield, under intense artillery and mortar fire. Three times in the early morning the outpost was counterattacked. Each time Pfc. Squires ignored withering enemy automatic fire and grenades which struck all around him, and fired hundreds of rounds of rifle, Browning automatic rifle, and captured German Spandau machinegun ammunition at the enemy, inflicting numerous casualties and materially aiding in repulsing the attacks. Following these fights, he moved 50 yards to the south end of the outpost and engaged 21 German soldiers in individual machinegun duels at point-blank range, forcing all 21 enemy to sur-

render and capturing 13 more Spandau guns. Learning the function of this weapon by questioning a German officer prisoner, he placed the captured guns in position and instructed other members of his platoon in their operation. The next night when the Germans attacked the outpost again he killed 3 and wounded more Germans with captured potato-masher grenades and fire from his Spandau gun. Pfc. Squires was killed in a subsequent action.

OFFICIAL COMMUNIQUE:
United Nations
NAPLES, April 24 - A communique:

Our artillery blew up an enemy ammunition dump in Cassino. Elsewhere along the front activity was limited to patrolling and exchanging of artillery and mortar fire.

Strong forces of escorted heavy bombers yesterday attacked aircraft factories at Wiener Neustadt, Schwechat and Bad Voslau. The north airdrome at Wiener Neustadt also was bombed by heavy bombers.

Tactical Air Force medium bombers attacked bridges in the Attigliano area, the Cecina railyards, Aneona harbor of the battle line.

Light bombers attacked an ammunition dump at Valmontone. Fighter-bombers attacked rail targets northeast of Rome and gun positions in the Cassino and Anzio areas. Riati, Foligno and Perugia airfields also were attacked by fighter-bombers.

Coastal Air Force fighters carried out sweeps against rail targets in San Stefano, Plombino, Genoa and Parma.

The MAAF flew approximately 1,500 sorties. Fifty enemy aircraft were sighted over the battle area during daylight hours yesterday. Twelve or our heavy bombers and five other aircraft are missing. Fifty-one enemy aircraft were destroyed.

SHEA, CHARLES W.
Rank and Organizations: Second Lieutenant, U.S. Army, Company F, 350th Infantry, 88th Infantry Division.
Born: New York, New York.
Entered Service At: New York, New York.
Place and Date: Near Mount Damiano, Italy, May 12, 1944.
Citation: For conspicuous gallantry and intrepidity at risk of life above and beyond the call of duty, on May 12, 1944, near Mount Damiano, Italy. As 2d Lt. Shea and his company were advancing toward a hill occupied by the enemy, 3 enemy machineguns suddenly opened fire, inflicting heavy casualties upon the company and halting its advance. 2d Lt. Shea immedi-

ately moved forward to eliminate these machinegun nests in order to enable his company to continue its attack. The deadly hail of machinegun fire at first pinned him down, but, boldly continuing his advance, 2d Lt. Shea crept up to the first nest. Throwing several hand grenades, he forced the 4 enemy soldiers manning this position to surrender, and disarming them, he sent them to the rear. He then crawled to the second machinegun position, and after a short fire fight forced 2 more German soldiers to surrender. At this time, the third machinegun fired at him, and while deadly small arms fire pitted the earth around him, 2d Lt. Shea crawled toward the nest. Suddenly he stood up and rushed the emplacement and with well-directed fire from his rifle, he killed all 3 of the enemy machine gunners. 2d Lt. Shea's display of personal valor was an inspiration to the officers and men of his company.

OFFICIAL COMMUNIQUE:
United Nations
NAPLES, May 12 - A special communique:

The regrouping of Allied armies in Italy now has been successfully completed without enemy interference.

The operation has been covered by continuous air action and patrol activity along the whole front. Complicated and heavy road and rail movements of men and material have been smoothly carried out.

This has made heavy calls on all administrative services. All formations have been involved.

Despite bad weather and difficult terrain the regrouping has been accomplished on time.

The Fifth and Eighth Armies, directed by General Alexander and supported by the Mediterranean Allied Tactical Air Force, began an attack against the Gustav Line at 23:00 hours (11 p.m.) on the 11th of May.

A later communique:

Patrols and artillery were active along the entire front. Allied coastal forces harassing the enemy supply line off the west coast of Italy engaged two southbound freighters on the night of May 9-10. They sank one of them without themselves suffering either casualties or damage.

Yesterday rail communications again were attacked by medium bombers; bridges at Ficulle, Orvieto, Poggibonsi and Certaldo were hit.

The ports of Plombino and Porto Ferraio also were attacked yesterday and during last night with good result.

Fighter-bombers continued their attacks on road and rail traffic and also attacked shipping off the Dalmatian coast.

No enemy air activity over the battle area in daylight was reported. Eight enemy aircraft were destroyed. One of ours is missing. It now is known we lost two additional aircraft May 10. The Mediterranean Allied Air Force flew over 1,000 sorties.

†**WAUGH, ROBERT T.**
Rank and Organizations: First Lieutenant, U.S Army, 339th Infantry, 85th Infantry Division.
Born: Ashton, Rhode Island.
Entered Service At: Augusta, Maine.
Place and Date: Near Tremensucli, Italy, May 11-14, 1944.
Citation: For conspicuous gallantry and intrepidity at risk of life above and beyond the call of duty in action with the enemy. In the course of an attack upon an enemy-held hill on May 11, 1st Lt. Waugh personally reconnoitered a heavily mined area before entering it with his platoon. Directing his men to deliver fire on 6 bunkers guarding this hill, 1st Lt. Waugh advanced alone against them, reached the first bunker, threw phosphorus grenades into it and as the defenders emerged, killed them with a burst from his tommygun. He repeated this process on the 5 remaining bunkers, killing or capturing the occupants. On the morning of May 14, 1st Lt. Waugh ordered his platoon to lay a base of fire on 2 enemy pillboxes located on a knoll which commanded the only trail up the hill. He then ran to the first pillbox, threw several grenades into it, drove the defenders into the open, and killed them. The second pillbox was next taken by this intrepid officer by similar methods. The fearless actions of 1st Lt. Waugh broke the Gustav Line at that point, neutralizing 6 bunkers and 2 pillboxes and he was personally responsible for the death of 30 of the enemy and the capture of 25 others. He was later killed in action in Itri, Italy, while leading his platoon in an attack.

OFFICIAL COMMUNIQUE:
United Nations
NAPLES, May 13 - A communique:

NAVAL

Yesterday May 12 in support of the Army a British cruiser, escorted by destroyers of the United States Navy, carried out a harassing fire on the Appian Way in the Terracina area and upon the enemy heavy artillery in the Gasta area opposing the

Fifth Army. The result was satisfactory. The area in which the ships operated previously was swept by British minesweepers.

ARMY

The attack by the Fifth and Eighth Armies against the Gustav Line during the night of May 11-12 has driven in the enemy outpost line and heavy fighting is in progress along the whole front which was attacked.

AIR

Yesterday heavy bombers in very great strength attacked many ports and rail centers in north and northwest Italy. In some cases the weather diverted attacks to secondary targets but the result was generally good.

Two of the day's targets, Plombino and Porto San Stefano, were attacked again last night.

Medium bombers and fighter-bombers attacked targets just behind the enemy lines in direct support of the Army, hitting troop concentrations, guns and bridges.

Fighters maintained battle line patrols. One enemy aircraft was shot down the night of May 11. Eighteen of our aircraft are missing from the day's operations. Only one enemy aircraft was sighted in daylight over the battle area. The MAAF flew over 2,700 sorties.

BARFOOT, VAN T.

Rank and Organization: Second Lieutenant, U.S. Army, 157th Infantry, 45th Infantry Division.

Born: Edinburg, Mississippi.

Entered Service At: Carthage, Mississippi.

Place and Date: Near Carano, Italy, May 23, 1944.

Citation: For conspicuous gallantry and intrepidity at the risk of life above and beyond the call of duty on May 23, 1944, near Carano, Italy. With his platoon heavily engaged during an assault against forces well entrenched on commanding ground, 2d Lt. Barfoot (then Tech. Sgt.) moved off alone upon the enemy left flank. He crawled to the proximity of 1 machinegun nest and made a direct hit on it with a handgrenade, killing 2 and wounding 3 Germans. He continued along the German defense line to another machinegun emplacement, and with his tommygun killed 2 and captured 3 soldiers. Members of another enemy machinegun crew then abandoned their position and gave themselves up to Sgt. Barfoot. Leaving the prisoners for his support squad to pick up, he proceeded to mop up positions in the immediate area, capturing more prisoners and bringing his total count to 17. Later that day, after he had reorganized his men and consolidated the newly captured ground, the enemy launched a fierce armored counterattack directly at his platoon positions. securing a bazooka, Sgt. Barfoot took up an exposed position directly in front of 3 advancing Mark VI tanks. From a distance of 75 yards his first shot destroyed the track of the leading tank, effectively disabling it, while the other 2 changed direction toward the flank. As the crew of the disabled tank dismounted, Sgt. Barfoot killed 3 of them with his tommygun. He continued onward into enemy terrain and destroyed a recently abandoned German fieldpiece with a demolition charge placed in the breech. While returning to his platoon position, Sgt. Barfoot, though greatly fatigued by his herculean efforts, assisted 2 of his seriously wounded men 1,700 yards to a position of safety. Sgt. Barfoot's extraordinary heroism, demonstration of magnificent valor, and aggressive determination in the face of pointblank fire are a perpetual inspiration to his fellow soldiers.

DERVISHIAN, ERNEST H.

Rank and Organization: Second Lieutenant, U.S. Army, 34th Infantry Division.
Born: Richmond, Virginia.
Entered Service At: Richmond, Virginia.
Place and Date: Near Cisterna, Italy, May 23, 1944.
Citation: For conspicuous gallantry and intrepidity at risk of life above and beyond the call of duty on May 23, 1944, in the vicinity of Cisterna, Italy. 2d Lt. Dervishian (then Tech. Sgt.) and 4 members of his platoon found themselves far ahead of their company after an aggressive advance in the face of enemy artillery and sniper fire. Approaching a railroad embankment, they observed a force of German soldiers hiding in dugouts. 2d Lt. Dervishian, directing his men to cover him, boldly moved forward and firing his carbine forced 10 Germans to surrender. His men then advanced and captured 15 more Germans occupying adjacent dugouts. The prisoners were returned to the rear to be picked up by advancing units. From the railroad embankment, 2d Lt. Dervishian and his men then observed 9 Germans who were fleeing across a ridge. He and his men opened fire and 3 of the enemy were wounded. As his men were firing, 2d Lt. Dervishian, unnoticed, fearlessly dashed forward alone and captured all of the fleeing enemy before his companions joined him on the ridge. At this point 4 other men joined 2d Lt. Dervishian's group. An attempt was made to send the 4 newly arrived men along the left flank of a large, dense vineyard that lay

ahead, but murderous machinegun fire forced them back. Deploying his men, 2d Lt. Dervishian moved to the front of his group and led the advance into the vineyard. He and his men suddenly became pinned down by a machinegun firing at them at a distance of 15 yards. Feigning death while the hostile weapon blazed away at him, 2d Lt. Dervishian assaulted the position during a halt in the firing, using a handgrenade and carbine fire, and forced 4 German crewmembers to surrender. The 4 men on the left flank were now ordered to enter the vineyard but encountered machinegun fire which killed 1 soldier and wounded another. At this moment the enemy intensified the fight by throwing potato-masher grenades at the valiant band of American soldiers within the vineyard. 2d Lt. Dervishian ordered his men to withdraw; but instead of following, jumped into the machinegun position he had just captured and opened fire with the enemy weapon in the direction of the second hostile machinegun nest. Observing movement in a dugout 2 or 3 yards to the rear, 2d Lt. Dervishian seized a machine-pistol. Simultaneously blazing away at the entrance to the dugout to prevent its occupants from firing and firing his machinegun at the other German nest, he forced 5 Germans in each position to surrender. Determined to rid the area of all Germans, 2d Lt. Dervishian continued his advance alone. Noticing another machinegun position beside a house, he picked up an abandoned machine-pistol and forced 6 more Germans to surrender by spraying their position with fire. Unable to locate additional targets in the vicinity, 2d Lt Dervishian conducted these prisoners to the rear. The prodigious courage and combat skill exhibited by 2d Lt. Dervishian are exemplary of the finest traditions of the U.S. Armed Forces.

†DUTKO, JOHN W.

Rank and Organization: Private First Class, U.S. Army, 3d Infantry Division.
Born: Dilltown, Pennsylvania.
Entered Service At: Riverside, New Jersey.
Place and Date: Near Ponte Rotto, Italy, May 23, 1944.
Citation: For conspicuous gallantry and intrepidity at risk of life above and beyond the call of duty, on May 23, 1944, near Ponte Rotto, Italy. Pfc. Dutko left the cover of an abandoned enemy trench at the height of an artillery concentration in a singlehanded attack upon 3 machine-guns and an 88-mm. mobile gun. Despite the intense fire of these 4 weapons which were aimed directly at him, Pfc. Dutko ran 100 yards through the impact area, paused momentarily in a shell crater, and then continued his 1-man assault. Although machine-gun bullets kicked up the dirt at his heels, and

88-mm. shells exploded within 30 yards of him, Pfc. Dutko nevertheless made his way to a point within 30 yards of the first enemy machinegun and killed both gunners with a grenade. Although the second machinegun wounded him, knocking him to the ground, Pfc. Dutko regained his feet and advanced on the 88-mm. gun, firing his Browning automatic rifle from the hip. When he came within 10 yards of this weapon he killed its 5-man crew with 1 long burst of fire. Wheeling on the machinegun which had wounded him, Pfc. Dutko killed the gunner and his assistant. The third German machinegun fired on Pfc. Dutko from a position 20 yards distant wounding him a second time as he proceeded toward the enemy weapon in a half run. He killed both members of its crew with a single burst from his Browning automatic rifle, continued toward the gun and died, his body falling across the dead German crew.

†FOWLER, THOMAS W.

Rank and Organization: Second Lieutenant, U.S. Army, 1st Armored Division.
Born: Wichita Falls, Texas.
Entered Service At: Wichita Falls, Texas.
Place and Date: Near Carano, Italy, May 23, 1944.
Citation: For conspicuous gallantry and intrepidity at risk of life above and beyond the call of duty, on May 23, 1944, in the vicinity of Carano, Italy. In the midst of a full-scale armored-infantry attack, 2d Lt. Fowler, while on foot, came upon 2 completely disorganized infantry platoons held up in their advance by an enemy minefield. Although a tank officer, he immediately reorganized the infantry. He then made a personal reconnaissance through the minefield, clearing a path as he went, by lifting the antipersonnel mines out of the ground with his hands. After he had gone through the 75-yard belt of deadly explosives, he returned to the infantry and led them through the minefield, a squad at a time. As they deployed, 2d Lt. Fowler, despite small-arms fire and the constant danger of antipersonnel mines, made a reconnaissance into enemy territory in search of a route to continue the advance. He then returned through the minefield and, on foot, he led the tanks through the mines into a position from which they could best support the infantry. Acting as scout 300 yards in front of the infantry, he led the 2 platoons forward until he had gained his objective, where he came upon several dug-in enemy infantrymen. Having taken them by surprise, 2d Lt. Fowler dragged them out of their foxholes and sent them to the rear; twice, when they resisted, he threw handgrenades into their dugouts. Realizing that a dangerous gap existed between his company and the unit

to his right, 2d Lt. Fowler decided to continue his advance until the gap was filled. He reconnoitered to his front, brought the infantry into position where they dug in and, under heavy mortar and small-arms fire, brought his tanks forward. A few minutes later, the enemy began an armored counterattack. Several Mark VI tanks fired their cannons directly on 2d Lt. Fowler's position. One of his tanks was set afire. With utter disregard for his own life, with shells bursting near him, he ran directly into the enemy tank fire to reach the burning vehicle. For a half-hour, under intense strafing from the advancing tanks, although all other elements had withdrawn, he remained in his forward position, attempting to save the lives of the wounded tank crew. Only when the enemy tanks had almost overrun him, did he withdraw a short distance where he personally rendered first aid to 9 wounded infantrymen in the midst of the relentless incoming fire. 2d Lt. Fowler's courage, his ability to estimate the situation and to recognize his full responsibility as an officer in the Army of the United States, exemplify the high traditions of the military service for which he later gave his life.

HALL, GEORGE J.

Rank and Organization: Staff Sergeant, U.S. Army, 135th Infantry, 34th Infantry Division.
Born: January 9, 1921, Stoneham, Massachusetts.
Entered Service At: Boston, Massachusetts.
Place and Date: Near Anzio, Italy, May 23, 1944.
Citation: For conspicuous gallantry and intrepidity at risk of life above and beyond the call of duty. Attacking across flat, open terrain under direct enemy observation, S/Sgt. Hall's company was pinned down by grazing fire from 3 enemy machineguns and harassing sniper fire. S/Sgt. Hall volunteered to eliminate these obstacles in the path of advance. Crawling along a plowed furrow through furious machinegun fire, he made his way to a point within handgrenade range of 1 of the enemy positions. He pounded the enemy with 4 handgrenades, and when the smoke had died away, S/Sgt. Hall and 2 dead Germans occupied the position, while 4 of the enemy were crawling back to our lines as prisoners. Discovering a quantity of German potato-masher grenades in the position, S/Sgt. Hall engaged the second enemy nest in a deadly exchange of grenades. Each time he exposed himself to throw a grenade the Germans fired machinegun bursts at him. The vicious duel finally ended in S/Sgt. Hall's favor with 5 of the enemy surrendered and 5 others lay dead. Turning his attention to the third machinegun, S/Sgt. Hall left his position and crawled along a furrow, the enemy firing frantically in an effort to halt him. As he neared his final

objective, an enemy artillery concentration fell on the area, and S/Sgt. Hall's right leg was severed by a shellburst. With 2 enemy machineguns eliminated, his company was able to flank the third and continue its advance without incurring excessive casualties. S/Sgt. Hall's fearlessness, his determined fighting spirit, and his prodigious combat skill exemplify the heroic tradition of the American Infantryman.

†KESSLER, PATRICK L.

Rank and Organization: Private First Class, U.S. Army, Company K, 30th Infantry, 3d Infantry Division.
Born: Middletown, Ohio.
Entered Service At: Middletown, Ohio.
Place and Date: Near Ponte Rotto, Italy, May 23, 1944.
Citation: For conspicuous gallantry and intrepidity at risk of life above and beyond the call of duty. Pfc. Kessler, acting without orders, raced 50 yards through a hail a machinegun fire which had killed 5 of his comrades and halted the advance of his company, in order to form an assault group to destroy the machinegun. Ordering 3 men to act as a base of fire, he left the cover of a ditch and snaked his way to a point within 50 yards of the enemy machinegun before he was discovered, where-upon he plunged headlong into the furious chain of automatic fire. Reaching a spot within 6 feet of the emplacement he stood over it and killed both the gunner and his assistant, jumped into the gun position, overpowered and captured a third German after a short struggle. The remaining member of the crew escaped, but Pfc. Kessler wounded him as he ran. While taking his prisoner to the rear, this soldier saw 2 of his comrades killed as they assaulted an enemy strongpoint, fire from which had already killed 10 men in the company. Turning his prisoner over to another man, Pfc. Kessler crawled 35 yards, to the side of 1 of the casualties relieved him of his BAR and ammunition and continued on toward the strongpoint, 125 yards distant. Although 2 machineguns concentrated their fire directly on him and shells exploded within 10 yards, bowling him over, Pfc. Kessler crawled 75 yards, passing through an antipersonnel minefield to a point within 50 yards of the enemy and engaged the machineguns in a duel. When an artillery shell burst within a few feet of him, he left the cover of a ditch and advanced upon the position in a slow walk, firing his BAR from the hip. Although the enemy poured heavy machinegun and small-arms fire at him, Pfc. Kessler succeeded in reaching the edge of their position, killed the gunners, and captured 13 Germans. Then, despite continuous shelling, he started to the rear. After going 25 yards, Pfc. Kessler was fired upon by 2 snipers only 100 yards away. Sev-

eral of his prisoners took advantage of this opportunity and attempted to escape; however, Pfc. Kessler hit the ground, fired on either flank of his prisoners, forcing them to cover, and then engaged the 2 snipers in a fire fight, and captured them. With this last threat removed, Company K continued its advance, capturing its objective without further opposition. Pfc. Kessler was killed in a subsequent action.

SCHAUER, HENRY

Rank and Organization: Private First Class, U.S. Army, 3d Infantry Division.

Born: October 9, 1918, Clinton, Oklahoma.

Entered Service At: Scobey, Montana.

Place and Date: Near Cisterna di Littoria, Italy, May 23-24, 1944.

Citation: For conspicuous gallantry and intrepidity at risk of life above and beyond the call of duty. On May 23, 1944, at 12 noon, Pfc. (now T/Sgt.) Schauer left the cover of a ditch to engage 4 German snipers who opened fire on the patrol from its rear. Standing erect he walked deliberately 30 yards toward the enemy, stopped amid the fire from 4 rifles centered on him, and with 4 bursts from his BAR, each at a different range, killed all of the snipers. Catching sight of a fifth sniper waiting for the patrol behind a house chimney, Pfc. Schauer brought him down with another burst. Shortly after, when a heavy enemy artillery concentration and 2 machineguns temporarily halted the patrol, Pfc. Schauer again left cover to engage the enemy weapons singlehanded. While shells exploded within 15 yards, showering dirt over him, and strings of grazing German tracer bullets whipped past him at chest level, Pfc. Schauer knelt, killed the 2 gunners of the machinegun only 60 yards from him with a single burst from his BAR, and crumpled 2 other enemy soldiers who ran to man the gun. Inserting a fresh magazine in his BAR, Pfc. Schauer shifted his body to fire at the other weapon 500 yards distant and emptied his weapon into the enemy crew, killing all 4 Germans. Next morning, when shells from a German Mark VI tank and a machinegun only 100 yards distant again forced the patrol to seek cover, Pfc. Schauer crawled toward the enemy machinegun, stood upright only 80 yards from the weapon as its bullets cut the surrounding ground, and 4 tank shells fired directly at him burst within 20 yards. Raising his BAR to his shoulder, Pfc. Schauer killed the 4 members of the German machinegun crew with 1 burst of fire.

†ANTOLAK, SYLVESTER

Rank and Organization: Sergeant, U.S. Army, Company B, 15th Infantry, 3d Infantry Division.
Born: St. Clairsville, Ohio.
Entered Service At: St. Clairsville, Ohio.
Place and Date: Near Cisterna di Littoria, Italy, May 24, 1944.
Citation: Near Cisterna di Littoria,Italy, Sgt. Antolak charged 200 yards over flat, coverless terrain to destroy an enemy machinegun nest during the second day of the offensive which broke through the German cordon of steel around the Anzio beachhead. Fully 30 yards in advance of his squad, he ran into withering enemy machinegun, machine-pistol, and rifle fire. Three times he was struck by bullets and knocked to the ground, but each time he struggled to his feet to continue his relentless advance. With one shoulder deeply gashed and his right arm shattered, he continued to rush directly into the enemy fire concentration with his submachinegun wedged under his uninjured arm until within 15 yards of the enemy strongpoint, where he opened fire at deadly close range, killing 2 Germans and forcing the remaining 10 to surrender. He reorganized his men and, refusing to seek medical attention so badly needed, chose to lead the way to another strongpoint 100 yards distant. Utterly disregarding the hail of bullets concentrated upon him, he had stormed ahead nearly three-fourths of the space between strongpoints when he was instantly killed by hostile enemy fire. Inspired by his example, his squad went on to overwhelm the enemy troops. By his supreme sacrifice, superb fighting courage, and heroic devotion to the attack, Sgt. Antolak was directly responsible for eliminating 20 Germans, capturing an enemy machinegun, and clearing the path for his company to advance.

MILLS, JAMES H.

Rank and Organization: Private, U.S. Army, Company F, 15th Infantry, 3d Infantry Division.
Born: Fort Meade, Florida.
Entered Service At: Fort Meade, Florida.
Place and Date: Near Cisterna di Littoria, Italy, May 24, 1944.
Citation: For conspicuous gallantry and intrepidity at risk of life above and beyond the call of duty. Pvt. Mills, undergoing his baptism of fire, preceded his platoon down a draw to reach a position from which an attack could be launched against a heavily fortified strongpoint. After advancing about 300 yards, Pvt. Mills was fired on by a machinegun only 5 yards distant. He killed the gunner with 1 shot and forced the surrender of the

assistant gunner. Continuing his advance, he saw a German soldier in a camouflaged position behind a large bush pulling the pin of a potato-masher grenade. Covering the German with his rifle, Pvt. Mills forced him to drop the grenade and captured him. When another enemy soldier attempted to throw a handgrenade into the draw, Pvt. Mills killed him with 1 shot. Brought under fire by a machinegun, 2 machine pistols, and 3 rifles at a range of only 50 feet, he charged headlong into the furious chain of automatic fire shooting his M1 from the hip. The enemy was completely demoralized by Pvt. Mills' daring charge, and when he reached a point within 10 feet of their position, all 6 surrendered. As he neared the end of the draw, Pvt. Mills was brought under fire by a machinegunner 20 yards distant. Despite the fact that he had absolutely no cover, Pvt. Mills killed the gunner with 1 shot. Two enemy soldiers near the machinegunner fired wildly at Pvt. Mills and then fled. Pvt. Mills fired twice, killing 1 of the enemy. Continuing on to the position, he captured a fourth soldier. When it became apparent that an assault on the strongpoint would in all probability cause heavy casualties on the platoon, Pvt. Mills volunteered to cover the advance down a shallow ditch to a point within 50 yards of the objective. Standing on the bank in full view of the enemy less than 100 yards away, he shouted and fired his rifle directly into the position. His ruse worked exactly as planned. The enemy centered his fire on Pvt. Mills. Tracers passed within inches of his body, rifle and machine-pistol bullets ricocheted off the rocks at his feet. Yet he stood there firing until his rifle was empty. Intent on covering the movement of his platoon, Pvt. Mills jumped into the draw, reloaded his weapon, climbed out again, and continued to lay down a base of fire. Repeating this action 4 times, he enabled his platoon to reach the designated spot undiscovered, from which position it assaulted and overwhelmed the enemy, capturing 22 Germans and taking the objective without casualties.

Note: The following is a newspaper account of the preceding battle for which Lt. Barfoot, Lt. Dervishian, Pfc. Dutko, Lt. Fowler, Sgt. Hall, Pfc. Kessler, Pfc. Schauer, Sgt. Antolak, and Pvt. Mills were awarded the Medal of Honor:

AMERICANS CUT APPIAN WAY, SEIZE TERRACINA

• • •

BOTH FRONTS GAIN

• • •

Beachhead Forces Peril Cisterna
and Drive Toward Rome

• • •

NAPLES, May 24 - While the Allies' beachhead forces drove wedges up to 2,000 yards deep into the German defenses in the first hours of the attack below Rome and continued to gain, the Allies' forces on the main Italian front captured Pico, Lenola, and Terracina and were closing in on Pontecorvo after having split the Hitler Line north of the town and punched tanks ahead as far as the Melfa River, it was announced today.

In the American sector near the coast the Fifth Army advanced to Mount Alto, which is only twenty-one miles from the beachhead and twenty-nine miles from the jumping-off point at Minturno. Savagely exploiting the break in the Hitler Line that they achieved north of Pontecorvo, the Canadians have thrust their leading armored elements to the bank of the Melfa five miles from Pontecorvo and only three miles from San Giovanni, which is also threatened from the south by the French at Pico. The surge to the Melfa came after a day of heaving fighting and put the British Eighth Army's vanguard five miles beyond Aquino, which remained in German hands, and seven miles due west of Piedimonte, to which the Germans clung despite the three-quarter encirclement by Polish infantry and tanks.

[A late Associated Press dispatch from the front indicated the Poles had taken Piedimonte.]

[The Americans cut a mile stretch of the Appian Way below Cisterna and severed the railway to Rome, The Associated Press reported, and later smashed through the road on the Rome side of town.]

Moletta Creek Forged

The Anzio offensive is fanning out on a wide front in a generally northeasterly direction and thus far is threatening the vital junction at Cisterna. Beachhead troops on the other flank forged the Moletta Creek with tanks and thus invaded the gully-creased country bounded by Rome on the north and by the Alban Hills on the northeast. The beachhead forces took large numbers of prisoners.

The American and British beachhead forces, with continued air support and renewed bombardment by naval units off shore, crashed across the enemy minefields and through the mazes of barbed wire, which the tanks tore up and ground to shreds. The mines were a knottier problem for a while and caused some delay, but the paths were cleared by mid-morning yesterday and the infantry surged ahead.

On the west flank of the beachhead British armor lurched and splashed into the wooded country through which the suggested Avezzano-Valmontone-Alban

Hills defense line would pass to the coast. In conjunction with the general advance on the Cisterna side, this constituted a double threat to the possible line. Three hundred prisoners have been taken on the beachhead and the total for the whole new offensive has risen to more than 7,500.

Air Effort Kept Up

In view of the known sensitivity of the enemy's beachhead defenses, the first artillery encountered by the assault forces was comparatively light. Some prisoners said that the hour of the attack had come as a surprise.

The air effort in the Avezzano-Valmontone-Frosinone triangle continued last night and today. The First Tactical Air Force called on its full strength to disrupt the enemy convoys either evacuating or bringing down men or supplies between the two fronts. One Invader group concentrating on Valmontone and Priverno destroyed almost 100 vehicles. Priverno is nineteen miles southeast of Cisterna and only four miles from Mount Alto.

Last night Liberators and Wellingtons continued their virtually day-long blows at Valmontone and Ferentino, between it and Frosinone. High explosives streaked down on the Via Casilina, the principal artery linking the Germans in the Liri Valley with Frosinone and Rome.

Two Mountains Taken

The Americans on the main front captured Mount Croce, outside Terracina, and Mount San Stefano, two and a half miles northeast of Mount Croce. But the most sensational drive was the Fifth Army's push to 2,750-foot Mount Alto, which represented a ten mile airline advance in thirty-six hours into the heart of the Volscian Mountains.

[American patrols also moved southwestward from Terracina and approached San Felice, on Cape Circe, only fifteen miles from the beachhead, according to The United Press.]

The mountain advance involved the completion of the occupation of Mount delle Fate, which is four and a half miles northwest of Mount San Diagio as well as the sealing of the four-and-a-half-mile tunnel south of Sonnino, where more than 100 prisoners have already been taken. It was believed that several hundred more Germans might be trapped in the tunnel, whose farther end is only twenty miles from the beachhead perimeter around Borgo Sabotino.

The new Eighth Army offensive begun yesterday in conjunction with the beachhead attack was carried out by the Canadians who cracked the Hitler Line. Tanks and artillery helped them to plow into one of the strongest hubs of the line. The Canadians took more than 150 prisoners in the first phase. The men came from the

Ninetieth Armored Grenadier Division, which has long figured in the Sicilian and Italian campaigns. Recently it was rushed to this front from that south of Rome.

Pico, one of the most important hinges in the Hitler Line farther west, finally fell to the French late on Monday after a two day squeeze from Mount Palinferno to the west and Mount Leucio to the east. The Germans reacted strongly to a further push from the captured town of 3,800 population, a junction only seven miles south of Ceprano, with San Giovanni and the confluence of the Sacco and Liri Rivers between.

Both Monday and yesterday, German tanks, self-propelled guns, and infantry counter-attacked. The French and the Americans not only stood firm, but, in yesterday's coordinated attack, lashed out again along a line northwest of Pico and Mount Leucio. The road from Pico to San Giovanni is relatively level or even downhill, but just beyond the town is the confluence of the rivers, where there is a large dam and a reservoir runs sixty to 150 feet wide, with banks five to twenty feet high.

After the American seizure of Mount Croce, Terracina was dominated from the north and east. Besides taking Mount Croce and Mount San Stefano, the Americans overwhelmed the high ground farther east completely dominating what little of the Appian Way remained in German hands between Mount San Biagio and Terracina. Lenola, which is six miles southwest of Pico and four miles northwest of Fondi fell late on Monday.

The Adriatic sector remained relatively quiet. There were minor clashes around Crecchio and Orsogna and the Germans made small withdrawals around Palena.

NEWMAN, BERYL R.
Rank and Organization: First Lieutenant, U.S. Army, 133d Infantry, 34th Infantry Division.
Born: Baraboo, Wisconsin.
Entered Service At: Baraboo, Wisconsin.
Place and Date: Near Cisterna, Italy, May 26, 1944.
Citation: For conspicuous gallantry and intrepidity above and beyond the call of duty on May 26, 1944. Attacking the strongly held German Anzio-Nettuno defense line near Cisterna, Italy, 1st Lt. Newman, in the lead of his platoon, was suddenly fired upon by 2 enemy machineguns located on the crest of a hill about 100 yards to his front. The 4 scouts with him immediately hit the ground, but 1st Lt. Newman remained standing in order to see the enemy positions and his platoon then about 100 yards behind. Locating the enemy nests, 1st Lt. Newman called back to his platoon and ordered 1 squad to advance to him and the other to flank the enemy to the right. Then, still standing upright in the face of the enemy machinegun fire, 1st Lt.

Newman opened up with his tommygun on the enemy nests. From this range, his fire was not effective in covering the advance of his squads, and 1 squad was pinned down by the enemy fire. Seeing that his squad was unable to advance, 1st Lt. Newman, in full view of the enemy gunners and in the face of their continuous fire, advanced alone on the enemy nests. He returned their fire with his tommygun and succeeded in wounding a German in each of the nests. The remaining 2 Germans fled from the position into a nearby house. Three more enemy soldiers then came out of the house and ran toward a third machinegun. 1st Lt. Newman, still relentlessly advancing toward them, killed 1 before he reached the gun, the second before he could fire it. The third fled for his life back into the house. Covering his assault by firing into the doors and windows of the house, 1st Lt. Newman, boldly attacking by himself, called for the occupants to surrender to him. Gaining the house, he kicked in the door and went inside. Although armed with rifles and machine pistols, the 11 Germans there, apparently intimidated, surrendered to the lieutenant without further resistance, 1st Lt. Newman, singlehanded, had silenced 3 enemy machineguns, wounded 2 Germans, killed 2 more, and took 11 prisoners. This demonstration of sheer courage, bravery, and willingness to close with the enemy even in the face of such heavy odds, instilled into these green troops the confidence of veterans and reflects the highest traditions of the U.S. Armed Forces.

OFFICIAL COMMUNIQUE:
United Nations
NAPLES, May 26 - A communique:

ARMY

Both the Fifth and Eighth Armies have made further progress.

The Eighth Army has now broken the Hitler Line and has established a bridgehead beyond the Melfa River, although some of the enemy offering stiff resistance, are still holding out on the flanks of the advance.

The Fifth Army, after having gained contact with patrols of the Allied bridgehead force, has continued offensive operations on both fronts.

Littoria has been occupied and Cisterna has been captured after heavy fighting.

More than 12,000 prisoners have been taken since the start of operations.

AIR

Yesterday fighter-bombers of the First Tactical Air Force further intensified their onslaught against enemy troop concentrations, guns, tanks and motor transport.

During the operations they destroyed or damaged many hundreds of vehicles. Medium bombers attacked bridges and viaducts in the essential Italian railway system.

In southern France strong forces of escorted heavy bombers attacked important rail centers in the Lyon and Grenoble districts. Other heavy bombers attacked airfields at Placenza, Monfalcone harbor and oil stores at Porto, Santa Margherita.

Last night medium and heavy bombers attacked roads in the Viterbo area. Over eighty enemy aircraft were active during the daylight hours and twenty of them were destroyed. Twelve of ours are missing.

The Mediterranean Allied Air Force flew will over 3,000 sorties.

NAVY

In further support of the armies' thrust, enemy targets in the Anzio area were again bombarded from the sea on May 24 an 25. Good results were reported, fires and explosions were seen, occupied buildings destroyed and gun positions and bivouac areas were covered.

†GALT, WILLIAM WYLIE

Rank And Organization: Captain, U.S. Army, 168th Infantry, 34th Infantry Division.
Born: Geyser, Montana.
Entered Service At: Stanford, Montana.
Place and Date: At Villa Crocetta, Italy, May 29, 1944.
Citation: For conspicuous gallantry and intrepidity above and beyond the call of duty. Capt. Galt, Battalion S-3, at a particularly critical period following 2 unsuccessful attacks by his battalion, of his own volition went forward and ascertained just how critical the situation was. He volunteered, at the risk of his life, personally to lead the battalion against the objective. When the lone remaining tank destroyer refused to go forward, Capt. Galt jumped on the tank destroyer and ordered it to precede the attack. As the tank destroyer moved forward, followed by a company of riflemen, Cap. Galt manned the .30-caliber machinegun in the turret of the tank destroyer, located and directed fire on an enemy 77-mm. antitank gun, and destroyed it. Nearing the enemy position, Capt. Galt stood fully exposed in the turret, ceaselessly firing his machinegun and tossing handgrenades into the enemy zigzag series of trenches despite the hail of sniper and machinegun bullets ricocheting off the tank destroyer. As the tank destroyer moved, Capt. Galt so maneuvered it that 40 of the enemy were trapped in one trench. When they refused to surrender, Capt. Galt pressed the trigger of the

machinegun and dispatched every one of them. A few minutes later an 88-mm. shell struck the tank destroyer and Capt. Galt fell mortally wounded across his machinegun. He had personally killed 40 Germans and wounded many more. Capt. Galt pitted his judgment and superb courage against overwhelming odds, exemplifying the highest measure of devotion to his country and the finest traditions of the U.S. Army.

OFFICIAL COMMUNIQUE:
United Nations
NAPLES: May 29 - A communique:

ARMY

It is evident that the enemy is doing all in his power to resist our advance against the Valmontone-Velletri line south of Highway 6. Despite this, British and American troops of the Fifth Army have made a substantial advance southwest of Velletri against increasing opposition.

French and American troops of the Fifth Army continue to drive the enemy north to the mountains toward Highway 6.

British and Canadian troops of the Eighth Army have made some progress in the Liri and Sacco Valleys while New Zealand troops have advanced in the mountains to the north and occupied Belmonte.

AIR

Yesterday medium bombers struck at railroad bridges and lines in central and northern Italy. Light bombers and fighter-bombers were active against supply dumps, enemy positions, bridges, railways, roads and motor transport in the battle area and elsewhere in central Italy. Other fighters bombed and strafed targets in Yugoslavia, including aircraft on the ground, motor transport, railway trains and enemy concentrations.

Heavy bombers attacked harbor installations at Genoa and railyards at Vercilli. Last night medium bombers attacked objectives at Porto San Stefano.

In these operations four enemy aircraft were destroyed. Three of ours are missing. About fifteen aircraft were sighted over the battle area in daylight. The Mediterranean Allied Air Force flew over 2,000 sorties.

NAVY

Yesterday enemy artillery positions to the north of Anzio were further bombarded by a cruiser of the French Navy. Hostile guns were successfully neutralized. Targets in the same area were also bombarded by a destroyer. Fires and explosions were caused in enemy gun positions while direct hits were obtained on mechanized transport.

Since May 12 in support of the present offensive considerably more than 7,000 rounds have been fired in many bombardments from the sea.

†SMITH, FURMAN L.

Rank and Organization: Private, U.S. Army, 135th Infantry, 34th Infantry Division.
Born: Six Miles, South Carolina.
Entered Service At: Central, South Carolina.
Place and Date: Near Lanuvio, Italy, May 31, 1944.
Citation: For conspicuous gallantry and intrepidity at the risk of his life above and beyond the call of duty. In its attack on a strong point, an infantry company was held up by intense enemy fire. The group to which Pvt. Smith belonged was far in the lead when attacked by a force of 80 Germans. The squad leader and 1 other man were seriously wounded and other members of the group withdrew to the company position, but Pvt. Smith refused to leave his wounded comrades. He placed them in the shelter of shell craters and then alone faced a strong enemy counterattack, temporarily checking it by his accurate rifle fire at close range, killing and wounding many of the foe. Against overwhelming odds, he stood his ground until shot down and killed, rifle in hand.

OFFICIAL COMMUNIQUE:
United Nations
NAPLES, May 31, – A communique:

ARMY

Strong enemy resistance is being encountered by the Fifth Army all along the enemy line from Valmontone to the sea. It is now clear that the enemy intends to hold this line at all costs.

Troops of the Eighth Army are moving steadily beyond the Liri River against strong enemy rearguards who are making the utmost use of demolitions to delay our advance, The towns of Alfedena, Fontana, Stragolagalli, Pofi, Ceccano and Arpino have been occupied.

AIR

Tactical aircraft were active again yesterday against communications and front-line targets. Medium bombers attacked rail bridges in central Italy and road bridges in the Rome area. Light and fighter-bombers also struck at roads, railroads and bridges as well as guns and motor transport in the battle area.

Other light bombers attacked troop concentrations in Yugoslavia, while fighters attacked motor transport and rail traffic.

Medium forces of heavy bombers attacked aircraft and components factories in the Wiener Neuatadt area, an aircraft factory airdrome at Zagreb.

In these operations fifteen enemy aircraft were destroyed. Eight of ours are missing. Approximately fifty enemy aircraft were sighted or encountered over the battle area during daylight hours. The Mediterranean Allied Air Force flew over 2,400 sorties.

Last night medium bombers attacked objectives in the Orvieto area.

†CHRISTIAN, HERBERT F.

Rank and Organization: Private, U.S. Army, 15th Infantry, 3d Infantry Division.
Born: Byersville, Ohio.
Entered Service At: Steubenville, Ohio.
Place and Date: Near Valmontone, Italy, June 2-3, 1944.
Citation: For conspicuous gallantry and intrepidity at risk of life above and beyond the call of duty. On June 2-3, 1944, at 1 a.m., Pvt. Christian elected to sacrifice his life in order that his comrades might extricate themselves from an ambush. Braving massed fire of about 60 riflemen, 3 machineguns, and 3 tanks from positions only 30 yards distant, he stood erect and signaled to the patrol to withdraw. The whole area was brightly illuminated by enemy flares. Although his right leg was severed above the knee by cannon fire, Pvt. Christian advanced on his left knee and the bloody stump of his right thigh, firing his submachinegun. Despite excruciating pain, Pvt. Christian continued on his self-assigned mission. He succeeded in distracting the enemy and enabled his 12 comrades to escape. He killed 3 enemy soldiers almost at once. Leaving a trail of blood behind him, he made his way forward 20 yards, halted at a point within 10 yards of the enemy, and despite intense fire killed a machine-pistol man. Reloading his weapon, he fired directly into the enemy position. The enemy appeared enraged at the success of his ruse, concentrated 20-mm. machinegun, machine-pistol and rifle fire on him, yet he refused to seek cover. Maintaining his erect position, Pvt. Christian fired his weapon to the very last. Just as he emptied his submachinegun, the enemy bullets found their mark and Pvt. Christian slumped forward dead. The courage and spirit of self-sacrifice displayed by this soldier were an inspiration to his comrades and are in keeping with the highest traditions of the armed forces.

†JOHNSON, ELDEN H.

Rank and Organization: Private, U.S. Army, 15th Infantry, 3d Infantry Division.
Born: Bivalue, New Jersey.
Entered Service At: East Weymouth, Massachusetts.
Place and Date: Near Valmontone, Italy, June 3, 1944.
Citation: For conspicuous gallantry and intrepidity at risk of life above and beyond the call of duty. Pvt. Johnson elected to sacrifice his life in order that his comrades might extricate themselves from an ambush. Braving the massed fire of about 60 riflemen, 3 machineguns, and 3 tanks from positions only 25 yards distant, he stood erect and signaled his patrol leader to withdraw. The whole area was brightly illuminated by enemy flares. Then, despite 20-mm. machineguns, machine pistol, and rifle fire directed at him, Pvt. Johnson advanced beyond the enemy in a slow deliberate walk. Firing his automatic rifle from the hip, he succeeded in distracting the enemy and enabled his 12 comrades to escape. Advancing to within 5 yards of a machinegun, emptying his weapon, Pvt. Johnson killed its crew. Standing in full view of the enemy he reloaded and turned on the riflemen to the left, firing directly into their positions. He either killed or wounded 4 of them. A burst of machinegun fire tore into Pvt. Johnson and he dropped to his knees. Fighting to the very last, he steadied himself on his knees and sent a final burst of fire crashing into another German. With that he slumped forward dead. Pvt. Johnson had willingly given his life in order that his comrades might live. These acts on the part of Pvt. Johnson were an inspiration to the entire command and are in keeping with the highest traditions of the armed forces.

Note: The following is a newspaper account of the preceding battle for which both Pvt. Christian and Pvt. Johnson were awarded the Medal of Honor:

AMERICANS OVERRUN HILLS SOUTH OF ROME; CITY'S FALL NEAR, ALLIED COMMAND SAYS

• • •

NAZI LINES CAVE IN

• • •

**Americans Drive Toward Rome
In Pursuit of Fleeing Germans**

• • •

ORDERED TO DESTROY FOE

• • •

Eighth and Fifth Armies Join Forces in Push – Fierce Fighting in Alban Hills

• • •

NAPLES, June 3 – American troops raced through Rome's outer approaches from the south and southeast tonight under orders to destroy the retreating German armies, five of whose eighteen divisions already have been practically annihilated and whose defensive lines have been blasted apart.

With the city's skyline in easy view of the advancing American armor and infantry, it appeared that within a matter of hours, Rome might become the first European capital to be liberated from the Nazis.

[American troops swept down through the Alban Hills to within ten miles of Rome Saturday night while the Allied High Command flashed a dramatic radio warning to the Romans that the fall of the capital was imminent and called upon them to prevent the Germans from putting the city to the torch, The United Press reported.

[The farthest advance toward the capital was believed to be on the northern slopes of the Alban Hills. The capture of Nemi, fifteen miles southwest of Rome on the lake of the same name, was reported in a front dispatch from a United Press correspondent.]

"Destroy Enemy," Clark's Order

Lieut. Gen. Mark W. Clark, commander of the Fifth Army, instructed his subordinates, however, that the immediate task was to pursue and destroy as much as possible of the German Tenth and Fourteenth Armies and that entry into Rome would come afterward.

Besides the five Nazi divisions virtually destroyed since the present Allied offensive began May 11, several others have been battered badly, and front-line dispatches tonight said further progress was being made toward the goal of annihilation.

There was no word as to how many Germans might be caught by the American, British and French troops converging below Rome and be added to the 16,000 prisoners already in the Allied bag.

The belief grew, however, that the Allied forces closing in on a pocket in the northern edge of the Sacco Valley still held by the enemy could hope to trap only a relatively small proportion of the German units which earlier had been reported there.

This was supported by front-line accounts tonight showing that, despite its apparent speed, the German retreat was not a rout.

Edward Kennedy, Associated Press correspondent with the Fifth Army, reported that "there were still many German pockets behind us, raking the road with machine-gun and shellfire, but these were being mopped up."

Germans Pillaging Countryside

He said further that the Germans were taking time in their flight to pillage the countryside and were leaving snipers behind to try to delay the Allies.

Front dispatches indicated clearly that distances of the Allies from Rome were short and growing shorter.

The Americans were thrusting up both the Appian Way and Via Casilina and across open country, while other Allied troops converged on routes leading up to the city.

The British Eighth Army, which had pushed up through the Liri and Sacco Valleys, made a junction with the Americans on the Via Casilina ten miles east of Valmontone shortly before noon Saturday and continued toward Rome on that route.

Fifth Army fighters smashed apart the Germans' last mountainous positions guarding Rome by seizing most of the Alban Hills mass dominating the capital on the south. Descent from the hills would put them within ten miles of Rome's outskirts.

The Berlin radio broadcast that Rome now was "free of armed forces," indicating the possibility that the city might not be defended.

Allied headquarters already had announced that if the Germans chose to fight for Rome, the Allies "will be obliged to take appropriate military measures to eject them."

Fierce fighting continued tonight in the Alban Hills, also known as the Colli Laziali mountain mass, as the Germans struggled desperately to hold off smashing attacks that every hour threatened more and more to engulf their defenses and send the Fifth Army surging down the last few miles to Rome.

The newest breakthroughs, catching the Germans by surprise, jeopardized the entire Nazi position between the Alban Hills and the seacoast, apparently leaving the Germans guarding the Appian Way to Rome faced with alternatives of fleeing or remaining to fight where the retreat route might easily be cut from behind them.

Enemy Defenses Pierced

Ripping the enemy fortress wall from Valmontone to Velletri and beyond, the doughboys seized vital peaks dominating he approaches to the Italian capital. The drive was accompanied by twin smashes westward from the captured strongholds of Valmontone and Velletri on the direct roads to the city.

Fifth Army troops advanced to within fourteen miles of Rome from the southeast, capturing the Alban Hills stronghold of Mount Castellaccio, six miles north of Valletri.

Yard by yard the Americans punched their way through the stubborn defenses. One of these smashes tore through the powerfully held and bitterly defended town of Lanuvio, four miles west of Velletri and sixteen miles from Rome, after several days of blazing battle. Another overwhelmed the village of Labico on the Via Casilina, two miles closer to Rome than Valmontone.

Another slashing American spearhead poked a strong, deep salient northward toward Cave, three miles above Valmontone on the road paralleling the Via Casilina and at the edge of the hills through which the enemy may be forced to withdraw.

To the east, in the Via Casilina area where the Allies effected a junction, there were remnants of four German divisions – the Fifteenth, Twenty-sixth, Twenty-ninth Panzers, and the 305th Infantry. This portion of a dozen enemy divisions that started an offensive on the lower sector of the front twenty-three days ago have been trying desperately to scramble out of the Sacco and Cosa Valley areas northward before the Allies pulled the string closing the bag.

Counter-Attacks Smashed

While the mountain conquerors under General Clark swept into possession of cloud-stabbing Mount Castellaccio, four and one-half miles east-southeast of Frascati and just below Rocca Priors, front-line reports said other Americans were striking vigorously toward Rome along the Via Casilina from Valmontone.

The Allies earlier this week reached a point fourteen miles from Rome along the Appian Way.

Americans charging up the Via Casilina from the Valmontone break-through smashed numerous heavy German counter-attacks and took a bag of more than 1,000 prisoners within twenty-four hours.

Near Lanuvio, just west of captured Velletri, the Germans lost heavily in blistering counter-attacks which were successively turned back. The area of the town of Campoleone, three miles west of Lanuvio, was littered with enemy tanks and vehicles and much equipment was captured.

To the east of this theatre, "the Eighth Army continues to drive the enemy to the north and west," the Allied communique said. "Ferentino and Veroli have been occupied and our advance elements are approaching Alatri."

[The British radio in a broadcast heard by the OWI reported that advance Eighth Army elements had captured Alatri, and that farther west, New Zealand units had pushed ahead beyond Sora in the Liri Valley.]

So hard were the Allies punching along the Italian front despite fierce counter-attacks that German soldiers do not seem to know what has hit them. Many were found so bewildered they were more like stragglers than prisoners when they were rounded up. Some were hiding out in fields of high grain, waiting for the battle to pass by, and others were mingling with Italian civilians and attempting to settle down in Italy.

Germans who have managed to escape the massive Allied traps on the Italian front left little behind in their flight northward except where pursuit compelled them to abandon equipment.

A British security officer reported that the Germans' looting left Frosinone "almost denuded of furniture, fixtures, fittings and even doors and windows." It was clear the Germans were continuing their systematic pillage of the Italian countryside. Once rich Italian farm areas were found completely devoid of live stock by civilians who began straggling timidly back to their homes.

Enemy demolition parties ahead of the advancing Allied forces continued to blow up bridges and culverts. Some of the intended demolition was halted by the close pursuit of the enemy.

†DAVID, ALBERT LEROY

Rank and Organization: Lieutenant, Junior Grade, U.S. Navy.
Born: July 18, 1902, Maryville, Missouri.
Entered Service At: Missouri.
Other Navy Awards: Navy Cross with gold star.
Place and Date: Off French West Africa, June 4, 1944.
Citation: For conspicuous gallantry and intrepidity at the risk of his life above and beyond the call of duty while attached to the *U.S.S. Pillsbury* during the capture of an enemy German submarine off French West Africa, June 4, 1944. Taking a vigorous part in the skillfully coordinated attack on the German U-505 which climaxed a prolonged search by the Task Group, Lt. (then Lt., jg.) David boldly led a party from the *Pillsbury* in boarding the hostile submarine as it circled erratically at 5 or 6 knots on the surface. Fully aware that the U-boat might momentarily sink or be blown up by exploding demolition and scuttling charges, he braved the added danger of enemy gunfire to plunge through the conning tower hatch and, with his small party, exerted every effort to keep the ship afloat and to assist the succeeding and more fully equipped salvage parties in making the U-505 seaworthy for the long tow across the Atlantic to a U.S. port. By his valiant service during the first successful boarding and capture of an enemy man-

o-war on the high seas by the U.S. Navy since 1815, Lt. David contributed materially to the effectiveness of our Battle of the Atlantic and upheld the highest tradition of the U.S. Naval Service.

†VANCE, LEON R., JR. (Air Mission)

Rank and Organization: Lieutenant Colonel, U.S. Army Air Corps, 489th Bomber Group.
Born: August 11, 1916, Enid, Oklahoma.
Entered Service At: Garden City, New York.
Place and Date: Over Wimereaux, France, June 5, 1944.
Citation: For conspicuous gallantry and intrepidity above and beyond the call of duty on June 5, 1944, when he led a Heavy Bombardment Group, in an attack against defended enemy coastal positions in the vicinity of Wimereaux, France. Approaching the target, his aircraft was hit repeatedly by antiaircraft fire which seriously crippled the ship, killed the pilot, and wounded several members of the crew, including Lt. Col. Vance, whose right foot was practically severed. In spite of his injury, and with 3 engines lost to the flak, he led his formation over the target, bombing it successfully. After applying a tourniquet to his leg with the aid of the radar operator, Lt. Col. Vance, realizing that the ship was approaching a stall altitude with the 1 remaining engine failing, struggled to a semi-upright position beside the copilot and took over control of the ship. Cutting the power and feathering the last engine he put the aircraft in glide sufficiently steep to maintain his airspeed. Gradually losing altitude, he at last reached the English coast, whereupon he ordered all members of the crew to bail out as he knew they would all safely make land. But he received a message over the interphone system which led him to believe 1 of the crewmembers was unable to jump due to injuries; so he made the decision to ditch the ship in the channel, thereby giving this man a chance for life. To add further to the danger of ditching the ship in his crippled condition, there was a 500-pound bomb hung up in the bomb bay. Unable to climb into the seat vacated by the copilot, since his foot, hanging on to his leg by a few tendons, had become lodged behind the copilot's seat, he nevertheless made a successful ditching while lying on the floor using only aileron and elevators for control and the side window of the cockpit for visual reference. On coming to rest in the water the aircraft commenced to sink rapidly with Lt. Col. Vance pinned in the cockpit by the upper turret which had crashed in during the landing. As it was settling beneath the waves an explosion occurred which threw Lt. Col. Vance clear of the wreckage. After clinging to a piece of floating wreckage until he could muster enough strength to inflate his

life vest he began searching for the crewmember whom he believed to be aboard. Failing to find anyone he began swimming and was found approximately 50 minutes later by an Air-Sea Rescue craft. By his extraordinary flying skill and gallant leadership, despite his grave injury, Lt. Col. Vance led his formation to a successful bombing of the assigned target and returned the crew to a point where they could bail out with safety. His gallant and valorous decision to ditch the aircraft in order to give the crewmember he believed to be aboard a chance for life exemplifies the highest traditions of the U.S. Armed Forces.

OFFICIAL COMMUNIQUE:
United Nations
LONDON, Tuesday, June 6 – Supreme Headquarters, Allied Expeditionary Force communique 1:

Under the command of General Eisenhower, Allied naval forces supported by strong air forces began landing Allied armies this morning on the northern coast of France.

NAPLES, June 5 – A communique:

Allied armies in Italy have maintained their relentless pressure upon the enemy. Troops of the Fifth Army on June 4th entered the city limits of Rome, where sporadic resistance is being encountered. They control the whole of the Colli Laziali and have advanced in contact with the enemy toward the Lower Tiber. Our troops now dominate Highways 5, 6, and 7, leading into Rome.

Troops of the Eighth Army in contact with enemy rear guards have made considerable progress. The towns of Palestrina, Fiuggi, Piglio, Paliano, Guarcino, and Cave are now clear of the enemy.

The total number of prisoners taken since the start of the attack now exceeds 20,000.

Motor transport, rail yards and bridges, highways and road bridges were attacked by aircraft of the Tactical Air Force north and west of Rome and in central Italy yesterday.

Medium and fighter-bombers as well as fighters also attacked rail and other military targets and shipping in Yugoslavia.

Strong forces of escorted heavy bombers struck at rail yards in northern Italy and important enemy communication lines along the French-Italian border.

From these operations, two enemy aircraft were destroyed and eleven our aircraft are missing. Seven enemy aircraft were sighted over the battle area yesterday during the daylight hours.

It is now known that one enemy aircraft was destroyed and one of ours is missing from night operations during the night of June 3-4.

The Mediterranean Allied Air Force flew approximately 2,000 sorties. Last night, our bombers attacked objectives in northern Italy.

BARRETT, CARLTON W.

Rank and Organization: Private, U.S. Army, 18th Infantry, 1st Infantry Division.
Born: Fulton, New York.
Entered Service At: Albany, New York.
Place and Date: Near St. Laurent-sur-Mer, France, June 6, 1944.
Citation: For gallantry and intrepidity at the risk of his life above and beyond the call of duty on June 6, 1944, in the vicinity of St. Laurent-sur-Mer, France. On the morning of D-day Pvt. Barrett, landing in the face of extremely heavy enemy fire, was forced to wade ashore through neck-deep water. Disregarding the personal danger, he returned to the surf again and again to assist his floundering comrades and save them from drowning. Refusing to remain pinned down by the intense barrage of small-arms and mortar fire poured at the landing points, Pvt. Barrett, working with fierce determination, saved many lives by carrying casualties to an evacuation boat lying offshore. In addition to his assigned mission as guide, he carried dispatches the length of the fire-swept beach; he assisted the wounded; he calmed the shocked; he arose as a leader in the stress of the occasion. His coolness and his dauntless daring courage while constantly risking his life during a period of many hours had an inestimable effect on his comrades and is in keeping with the highest traditions of the U.S. Army.

†MONTEITH, JIMMIE W., JR.

Rank and Organization: First Lieutenant, U.S. Army, 16th Infantry, 1st Infantry Division.
Born: July 1, 1917, Low Moor, Virginia.
Entered Service At: Richmond, Virginia.
Place and Date: Near Colleville-sur-Mer, France, June 6, 1944.
Citation: For conspicuous gallantry and intrepidity above and beyond the call of duty on June 6, 1944, near Colleville-sur-Mer, France. 1st Lt. Monteith landed with the initial assault waves on the coast of France under heavy enemy fire. Without regard to his own personal safety he continually moved up and down the beach reorganizing men for further assault. He then led the assault over a narrow protective ledge and across the flat, exposed terrain to the comparative safety of a cliff. Retracing his steps across the field to the beach, he moved over to where 2 tanks were buttoned up

and blind under violent enemy artillery and machinegun fire. Completely exposed to the intense fire, 1st Lt. Monteith led the tanks on foot through a minefield and into firing positions. Under his direction several enemy positions were destroyed. He then rejoined his company and under his leadership his men captured an advantageous position on the hill. Supervising the defense of his newly won position against repeated vicious counterattacks, he continued to ignore his own personal safety, repeatedly crossing the 200 or 300 yards of open terrain under heavy fire to strengthen links in his defensive chain. When the enemy succeeded in completely surrounding 1st Lt. Monteith and his unit and while leading the fight out of the situation, 1st Lt. Monteith was killed by enemy fire. The courage, gallantry, and intrepid leadership displayed by 1st Lt. Monteith is worthy of emulation.

†PINDER, JOHN J., JR.

Rank and Organization: Technician Fifth Grade, U.S. Army, 16th Infantry, 1st Infantry Division.
Born: McKees Rocks, Pennsylvania.
Entered Service At: Burgettstown, Pennsylvania.
Place and Date: Near Colleville,sur-Mer, France, June 6, 1944.
Citation: For conspicuous gallantry and intrepidity above and beyond the call of duty on June 6, 1944, near Colleville-sur-Mer, France. On D-day, Technician 5th Grade Pinder landed on the coast 100 yards off shore under devastating enemy machinegun and artillery fire which caused severe casualties among the boatload. Carrying a vitally important radio, he struggled towards the shore in waist-deep water. Only a few yards from his craft he was hit by enemy fire and was gravely wounded. Technician 5th Grade Pinder never stopped. He made shore and delivered the radio. Refusing to take cover afforded, or to accept medical attention for his wounds, Technician 5th Grade Pinder, though terribly weakened by loss of blood and in fierce pain, on 3 occasions went into the fire-swept surf to salvage communication equipment. He recovered many vital parts and equipment, including another workable radio. On the 3rd trip he was again hit, suffering machinegun bullet wounds in the legs. Still this valiant soldier would not stop for rest or medical attention. Remaining exposed to heavy enemy fire, growing steadily weaker, he aided in establishing the vital radio communication on the beach. While so engaged this dauntless soldier was hit for the third time and killed. The indomitable courage and personal bravery of Technician 5th Grade Pinder was a magnificent inspiration to the men with whom he served.

†ROOSEVELT, THEODORE, JR.
Rank and Organization: Brigadier Gerneral, U.S. Army.
Born: Oyster Bay, New York.
Entered Service At: Oyster Bay, New York.
Place and Date: Normandy Invasion, June 6, 1944.
Citation: For gallantry and intrepidity at the risk of his life above and beyond the call of duty on June 6, 1944, in France. After 2 verbal requests to accompany the leading assault elements in the Normandy invasion had been denied, Brig. Gen. Roosevelt's written request for this mission was approved and he landed with the first wave of the forces assaulting the enemy-held beaches. He repeatedly led groups from the beach, over the seawall and established them inland. His valor, courage, and presence in the very front of the attack and his complete unconcern at being under heavy fire inspired the troops to heights of enthusiasm and self-sacrifice. Although the enemy had the beach under constant direct fire, Brig. Gen. Roosevelt moved from one locality to another, rallying men around him, directed and personally led them against the enemy. Under his seasoned, precise, calm, and unfaltering leadership, assault troops reduced beach strong points and rapidly moved inland with minimum casualties. He thus contributed substantially to the successful establishment of the beachhead in France.

Note: The following is a newspaper account of the preceding battle for which Pvt. Barrett, Lt. Monteith, Tech. 5th Grade Pinder, and Gen. Roosevelt were awarded the Medal of Honor:

HITLER'S SEA WALL IS BREACHED, INVADERS FIGHTING WAY INLAND; NEW ALLIED LANDINGS ARE MADE

• • •

ALL LANDINGS WIN

• • •

Our Men Are Reported in Caen and At Points on Cherbourg Peninsula

•••

BIG AIR ARMADA AIDS

•••

10,000 Tons of Bombs Clear the Way
– Poor Weather a Worry

•••

Latest Communique:

SUPREME HEADQUARTERS, Allied Expeditionary Force, Wednesday, June 7 - Allied forces continued landings on the northern French coast throughout yesterday and "satisfactory progress was made," headquarters announced today.

United States Rangers and British Commandos formed part of the assault forces, the third invasion bulletin said.

"No further attempt at interference with our sea-borne landing was made by enemy naval forces," it continued.

"These coastal batteries still in action are being bombarded by Allied warships," the bulletin said.

"At twilight yesterday, and for the fourth time during the day, Allied heavy bombers attacked rail communications and bridges in the general battle area, and "there was increased air opposition," the announcement added.

•••

SUPREME HEADQUARTERS, Allied Expeditionary Force, Wednesday, June 7 - The German Atlantic Wall has been breached.

Thousands of American, Canadian and British soldiers, under cover of the greatest air and sea bombardment of history, have broken through he "impregnable" perimeter of Germany's "European fortress" in the first phase of the invasion and liberation of the Continent.

Communique 2, issued to the Supreme Headquarters, Allied Expeditionary Force, before last midnight, reported that all initial landings, which had earlier been located on the coast of Normandy, in northern France, had "succeeded." The Germans told of heavy fighting with Allied air-borne troops in Caen, road and railroad junction eight and one-half miles inland from the Seine Bay coast, and the enemy said there was heavy fighting at several points in a crescent-shaped front reaching from St. Vaast-la-Hougue, on the west, to Havre, on the east.

[The German Transocean News Agency said early Wednesday that the Allies had made "further landings at the mouth of the Orne under cover of naval artillery," according to The Associated Press. The agency said "heavy fighting" was raging.

[A British broadcast, recorded by Blue Network monitors, said Wednesday that "another air-borne landing south of Cherbourg has been reported." Another British broadcast said that Allied bulldozers were busy "carving out the first RAF airfield on the coast of France."]

At last midnight, just over twenty-four hours after the beginning of the operation, these were the salient points in the military situation:

1. Despite underwater obstacles and beach defenses, which in some areas extended for more than 1,000 yards inland, the Atlantic Wall has been breached by Allied infantry.

2. The largest air-borne force ever launched by the Allies has been successfully dropped behind the Atlantic Wall and has attacked a second echelon of German defenses vigorously. The Germans estimate this force at not less than four divisions, two American and two British, of paratroops and air-borne infantry.

3. Most of the German coastal batteries in the invasion area have been silenced by 10,000 tons of bombs and by shelling from 640 naval ships. The shelling was so intense that HMS Tanatside, a British destroyer, had exhausted all her ammunition by 8 o'clock yesterday morning.

4. Against 7,500 sorties flown from Monday midnight to 8 A.M., Tuesday, by the Allied Air Forces during the first day of the invasion and Luftwaffe has flown fifty, and the main weight of the enemy air force in the west, estimated at 1,750 aircraft, has not entered the battle.

5. The first enemy naval assault on the Allied invasion armada was beaten off with the loss of one enemy trawler and severe damage to another.

There is reasonable optimism at this headquarters now, but there is no effort to disguise concern over several factors, among them weather and the shape of the first major German counter-blow.

Navies 100 Per Cent Effective

Admiral Sir Bertram Ramsay, Allied naval commander in chief, declared the Allied navies had "in effect been 100 per cent successful in the task of landing the invasion troops in France. These troops have now become the most important of the fighting services involved in the invasion, for there are indications that the enemy to some extent is withholding reserve formations for a general counter-attack once he is certain yesterday's landings constitute the main threat in northwestern Europe.

The heaviest fighting in a 100-mile battle area appeared to revolve around Caen, according to the German News Agency, DNB. The enemy also admitted the establishment of an Allied bridgehead on both sides of the Orne estuary, and another in the area northwest of Bayeux, and the Germans said an Allied paratroop formation had a firm grip on both sides of the Cherbourg-Valognes road.

A group of light Allied tanks and armored scout cars was placed northeast of Bayeux by the enemy. [Bayeux is about six miles inland from the southwest shore of the Seine Bay.] Earlier Allied tanks had been reported fighting in the area of Arromanches on the south coast of the Seine Bay. This group was attempting to join the main beachhead forces northwest of Bayeux, the enemy said.

A German military spokesman reported fifteen cruisers and fifty to sixty destroyers were operating west of Havre last night covering a large number of Allied landing craft. The two naval task forces that led the invasion were commanded by Rear Admiral Sir Philip Vian, who won fame while commanding the destroyer Cossack early in the war, and Rear Admiral Alan Goodrich Kirk of the United States Navy. The two naval forces plus a third force, which came from the north, included one fifteen-inch gun battleship, the British Warspite; an American battleship, the Nevada, a veteran of Pearl Harbor; the American cruisers Augusta and Tuscaloosa and the British cruisers Mauritius, Belfast, Black Prince, and Orion, and shoals of destroyers flying the Stars and Stripes and the White Ensign.

Steaming through the English Channel, swept by 200 British minesweepers, the men o' war escorted thousands of landing craft, transports, and assault craft bearing Gen. Sir Bernard L. Montgomery's landing forces to the beaches.

Shortly before the first soldiers "hit the beach" three German torpedo boats and an undisclosed number of armed trawlers attacked. They were driven off with withering fire. One trawler was sunk and another severely damaged.

Then the destroyers turned their guns on enemy defenses, while the ships engaged enemy batteries already battered by high explosives dropped from the air.

The large air-borne forces that were dropped and landed in the night were already assembling behind the Atlantic Wall as the first troops scrambled up the beaches. Dawn was the climax of the first phase of the invasion. Wave after wave of American bombers – at least 31,000 Allied airmen were in the air between Monday midnight and breakfast Tuesday – took up the task of flattening the German defenses and silencing guns. Fighters circled over the beachheads on defensive patrol, while fighter-bombers darted inland to attack German troops moving up to attack the air-borne and sea-borne invaders.

So feeble was the German Air Force opposition that one fighter force swept seventy-five miles inland without meeting opposition. In one of the few clashes, 300 Marauders ran into twenty Focke-Wulf 190s, destroying a single enemy plane without loss. A great fleet of more than 1,000 planes, including gliders and towplanes, went almost unmolested when it carried the air-borne force to its objectives, while some Flying Fortress groups reported neither fighter interference nor flak fire.

All day the weather forced medium and light bombers to attack at low level, 300 Marauders bombing from 3,000 feet during yesterday afternoon. Havocs on a similar attack jumped and halted a column of eight German armored cars. Road junctions and railway yards behind enemy lines were bombed repeatedly.

Allied Integration of Arms

Yesterday's operations, the greatest yet undertaken by the Western powers, were marked by a complete integration of all striking arms. Tens of thousands of bombs and shells tore at the German defenses as air force and Navy gave maximum support to the infantrymen struggling ashore or the air-borne forces attacking the "Atlantic Wall" from the rear.

The Bomber Command of the Royal Air Force, the first Allied force to strike at the heart of Germany in this war, had the honor of opening the assault. At 11:30 o'clock Monday night, the first of ten waves of Lancasters and Halifaxes swept in from the sea to begin bombardment of the German batteries along the French coast.

There were more than a hundred bombers in this and subsequent waves, and the total number of "heavies" involved was more than 1,300. Since on such a trip each of these heavies can carry at least five tons of bombs, the batteries were hit by around 7,000 tons of bombs before the sun rose to reveal the great invasion fleet gently rolling on the choppy waters of the English Channel.

The batteries attacked were of two types, with two different functions. There were long-range rifles – mostly 155 mm. and 177 mm. weapons – to engage shipping far out at sea. Equally important to the success of the landing were batteries of heavy howitzers sited on beaches or on areas just off the beaches where landing craft might congregate. Both types of batteries were strongly protected, with most of the 155s in casements of reinforced concrete. The howitzers were in sandbagged emplacements or newly constructed casemates.

The preliminary air attacks appear to have been successful, for reports from the front stressed the failure of German batteries to maintain determined fire. Many of the casemates were blown apart, while some of the howitzers were knocked over by the blasts and their gunpits were smothered with dirt torn up by the bombs.

This destruction was well under way by dawn yesterday, when more than 1,000 Flying Fortresses and Liberators of the United States Eighth Air Force roared out from Britain to maintain the bombing. At the same time, far out at sea gunfire flickered along the decks of battleships, monitors, cruisers, and destroyers as they engaged not only gun batteries but strong-points and blockhouses along the Normandy beaches.

By this time, troop carriers and gliders of the United States Ninth Army Air Force and the RAF had flown paratroops and air-borne infantry to their objectives and the two-sided battle of the so-called Atlantic Wall had begun on the ground as well as in the air and at sea.

All day the big guns roared from the sea to shore and from the shore to sea. All day Liberators, Fortresses, Marauders, Mitchells, Typhoons, Havocs and Thunderbolts of the Allied Air Forces bombed the German coastal defenses and troop concentrations sheltered in the lush orchards of Normandy.

All day Allied fighters patrolled the battle area and spread an air umbrella above the invasion fleet.

Air Chief Trafford Leigh-Mallory, General Eisenhower's deputy commander for air, was so proud of the work done by the Allied air forces that yesterday morning, while the battle was still developing, he congratulated his forces on the "magnificent work done in preparation for the invasion."

As this order was flashed to the far-flung squadrons of the RAF and USAAF, the battle on the ground, where it will eventually be fought and won, was beginning with the first air-borne landings. According to enemy radio reports, these were made "in great depth" in the area of the Seine Bay. British air-borne units were dropped in the Havre area, while Americans floated to earth in the Normandy district.

The enemy has already identified the First and Sixtieth British Air-Borne Divisions and the Eighty-second and the 101st American Air-Borne Divisions, according to Axis broadcasts. Air-borne troops landed at Barfleur, east of Cherbourg; Carentan, five miles from the Seine Bay on the Cherbourg peninsula, and northeast of Caen between the estuaries of the Seine and Orne, the Germans said.

Air and naval losses for the first day were considered remarkably low at this headquarters, although it was emphasized the enemy had not attacked strongly in either element. One American battleship, risking unswept mines and shore torpedo tubes, moved in to short range in order to silence a troublesome battery that was holding up operations with its fire.

The Allied sea-borne landings began to develop along the coast of Normandy at the same time. The Germans placed the first attacks between the mouths of the Seine and the Vire, a stretch of coast about seventy-five miles long, beginning in the east at Trouville and Deauville, once filled with holiday crowds from all over Europe, and reaching to the Bay of Isigny in the west. The stretch of coast is the nearest to Paris and is connected with the capital by good rail and highway communications.

American tanks poured ashore in the area of Arromanches, a small fishing village about fifteen miles northwest of Caen, and Asnelles, in the middle of the Seine Bay south coast, the Germans said, adding that thirty-five tanks had been destroyed in the fighting around Asnelles. What the Germans described as "particularly extensive landings" also were made at the small coastal village of St. Vaast-la-Hougue, close to the tip of the Cherbourg peninsula. The enemy also claimed the Allies had landed on Guernsey and Jersey in the Channel islands, the last bit of the British Empire held by Germany. As the infantry scrambled over the beach obstacles from the sea, air-borne invaders were fighting a hot battle in the district of Caen, according to the enemy reports. Caen lies on the main railroad line running from Cherbourg to Rouen, Evereux and Paris and is a junction of nine highways. Other large air-borne concentrations were around Havre and Cherbourg, and the enemy claimed they had been made in order to seize those ports for the invasion fleet.

The enemy claimed a battleship had been badly damaged and a cruiser and large transport sunk during a duel between shore batteries and the Allied naval escort. The enemy put the escort at six battleships and twenty destroyers, with well over 2,000 landing craft, some of them of 3,000 tons, participating in the landings along the Seine Bay.

Enemy Claims Hits

[President Roosevelt said at his Tuesday press conference that General Eisenhower had reported the loss of two American destroyers and one LST, a land-carrying landing ship.]

Sea-borne landings overcame intricate and elaborate German obstructions, mainly because General Eisenhower took a chance and landed his forces at low tide when naval engineers' parties could deal with underwater obstacles. These included mines moored below the low-water line, beach mines and hundreds of obstacles. The latter included a section of braced fences, concrete pyramids, and wood and steel "hedgehogs."

All these obstacles were extensively mined, either with Teller mines or specially prepared artillery projectiles. But before the invasion armada could reach these defenses some 200 Allied minesweepers manned by 10,000 officers and men had to sweep a passage through extensive minefields with which the enemy had masked the approaches to the beaches.

It was officially called the biggest and probably the most difficult, certainly the most concentrated, minesweeping operation ever carried out. The most delicate and dangerous work was done at night in a cross-tide of two knots.

When dawn came, the landing craft moved slowly toward the beaches through the swept channels, and the minesweepers, were sweeping new areas.

It was through this sort of sea defenses that the invasion ships had to make their way before they grated on continental beaches.

Ashore the engineers and infantry found a variety of new obstacles. The entire beaches were guarded by bolts of wire. The exits from the beaches were blocked by an adaptation of existing seawalls to become anti-tank walls, and steel obstacles were set up. Anti-tank ditches fifty to sixty feet wide were extensively employed and minefields had been laid up to a depth of more than 1,000 yards from shore, while inundations were employed wherever the ground was suitable.

Allied Reinforcements Pour In

SUPREME HEADQUARTERS, Allied Expeditionary Force, Wednesday, June 7 - Allied troops swiftly cleared Normandy beaches of the dazed Nazi survivors of a punishing sea and air bombardment, and armor-backed landing parties ranged inland today in a liberation invasion. Reinforcements streamed across the white-capped Channel.

Some reports reached here that Gen. Sir Bernard L. Montgomery's men had cut at Caen the Paris-Cherbourg railway, a main route supplying Hitler's defense forces in the Cherbourg peninsula.

Prime Minister Churchill first disclosed that Allied troops were fighting in Caen, on the River Orne. He said the invasion was proceeding "in a thoroughly satisfactory manner," and with unexpectedly light casualties.

The German High Command asserted that no Allied troops had penetrated Caen.

Returning RAF pilots said:

"We could easily tell the beaches were secure – we could see our soldiers standing up."

Caen was the only point specifically named here as a scene of fighting, although penetrations as deep as thirteen miles were reported. Nazi-controlled radios, however, reported Allied landings at a dozen points, with the most important on both sides of the estuary of the River Orne.

From west to east along the 100-mile shoreline, Axis accounts said Allied seaborne and air-borne forces struck at:

The port of Barfleur, fifteen miles east of Cherbourg, the fishing village of St. Vaast-la-Hougue, five miles south of Barfleur; both sides of the Valognes-Carentan highway, a section of an important supply road to Cherbourg running five miles inland from the peninsular coast; the twenty-seven-mile-long area between Carentan and Bayeux; the River Orne estuary; a fifteen mile stretch of beaches in the Villers-Trouville region across the Seine estuary from Havre; and the town of Honfleur, on the Seine six miles southeast of Havre.

The German-controlled Vichy radio also said that a vicious fight developed last night north of Rouen, on the Seine, forty-one miles east of Havre, "between powerful Allied paratroop formations and German anti-invasion forces."

†PEREGORY, FRANK D.

Rank and Organization: Technical Sergeant, U.S. Army, Company K, 116th Infantry, 29th Infantry Division.
Born: April 10, 1915, Esmont, Virginia.
Entered Service At: Charlottesville, Virginia.
Place and Date: Grandcampe, France, June 8, 1944.

Citation: On June 8, 1944, the 3d Battalion of the 116th Infantry was advancing on the strongly held German defenses at Grandcampe, France, when the leading elements were suddenly halted by decimating machinegun fire from a firmly entrenched enemy force on the high ground overlooking the town. After numerous attempts to neutralize the enemy position by supporting artillery and tank fire had proved ineffective, T/Sgt. Peregory, on his own initiative, advanced up the hill under withering fire, and worked his way to the crest where he discovered an entrenchment leading to the main enemy fortifications 200 yards away. Without hesitating, he leaped into the trench and moved toward the emplacement. Encountering a squad of enemy riflemen, he fearlessly attacked them with handgrenades and bayonet, killed 8 and forced 3 to surrender. Continuing along the trench, he singlehandedly forced the surrender of 32 more riflemen, captured the machine gunners, and opened the way for the leading elements of the battalion to advance and secure its objective. The extraordinary gallantry and aggressiveness displayed by T/Sgt. Peregory are exemplary of the highest tradition of the armed forces.

†DEGLOPPER, CHARLES N.
Rank and Organization: Private First Class, U.S. Army, Co. C, 325th Glider Infantry, 82d Airborne Division.
Born: Grand Island, New York.
Entered Service At: Grand Island, New York.
Place and Date: Merderet River at la Fiere, France, June 9, 1944.
Citation: He was a member of Company C, 325th Glider Infantry, on June 9, 1944, advancing with the forward platoon to secure a bridgehead across the Merderet River at La Fiere, France. At dawn the platoon had penetrated an outer line of machineguns and riflemen, but in so doing had become cut off from the rest of the company. Vastly superior forces began a decimation of the stricken unit and put in motion a flanking maneuver which would have completely exposed the American platoon in a shallow roadside ditch where it had taken cover. Detecting this danger, Pfc. DeGlopper volunteered to support his comrades by fire from his automatic rifle while they attempted a withdrawal through a break in a hedgerow 40 yards to the rear. Scorning a concentration of enemy automatic weapons and rifle fire, he walked from the ditch onto the road in full view of the Germans, and sprayed the hostile positions with assault fire. He was wounded, but he continued firing. Struck again, he started to fall; and yet his grim determination and valiant fighting spirit could not be broken. Kneeling in the roadway, weakened by his grievous wounds, he leveled his heavy weapon against the

enemy and fired burst after burst until killed outright. He was successful in drawing the enemy action away from his fellow soldiers, who continued the fight from a more advantageous position and established the first bridge-head over the Merderet. In the area where he made his intrepid stand his comrades later found the ground strewn with dead Germans and many machineguns and automatic weapons which he had knocked out of action. Pfc. DeGlopper's gallant sacrifice and unflinching heroism while facing unsurmountable odds were in great measure responsible for a highly important tactical victory in the Normandy Campaign.

OFFICIAL COMMUNIQUE:
United Nations
SUPREME HEADQUARTERS Allied Expeditionary Force, June 9 -
Communique 7:

Allied troops have continued to make progress in all sectors despite further reinforcement of German armor.

Landings have continued on all beaches and by-passed strong points of enemy resistance are being steadily reduced.

During yesterday there was desultory firing from some coastal batteries, which were again silenced by gunfire from Allied warships.

Allied aircraft continued to support naval and land forces yesterday by attacks on a variety of targets. Late in the day the weather over northern France caused a reduction in the scale of the air operations. Our heavy bombers, in strong force, attacked railway targets and airfields beyond the battle areas. Yesterday morning they were escorted by a medium force of fighters. These and other fighters strafed ground targets, shooting down thirty-one enemy aircraft and destroying more than a score on the ground. From these operations three bombers and twenty-four fighters are missing.

Medium bombers attacked a road bridge over the Seine at Vernon and fighter-bombers struck at troop and transport concentrations, gun positions, armored vehicles, railway and road targets behind the battle line.

Fighters patrolled over shipping and the assault area. Twenty-one enemy aircraft were destroyed. Eleven of our fighters were lost but two of the pilots are safe. Rocket-firing fighters attacked German E-boats in the Channel, leaving one in a sinking condition.

Last night heavy bombers in force attacked railway centers at Rennes, Fougeres, Alencon, Mayenne and Pontaubault.

Two bombers are missing. Light bombers struck at railway targets behind the battle area during the night.

SUPREME HEADQUARTERS Allied Expeditionary Force, Saturday, June 10 - Communique 8, announced early today:

American troops are across the Caretan-Valognes road in several places and have cut the broadgauge railway to Cherbourg. Further gains have been made west and southwest of Bayeux.

Fighting is severe in the area of Caen, where the enemy is making a determined effort to stem the advance.

The weight of armor on both sides is increasing and heavy fighting continues in all areas. Enemy strongpoints previously by-passed have now been eliminated.

The weather has deteriorated, but our beachheads are being steadily developed. Poor visibility and stormy weather reduced Allied air activity to a minimum over the battle area today (Friday).

During the twenty-four hours to 8 a.m. forty-six targets were engaged by Allied warships which shelled enemy concentrations and coastal batteries.

Before dawn this morning (Friday) HMS Tartar (Comdr, B. Jones, DSO, DAC, RN), with HMS Ashanti (Lieut. Comdr. J.R. Barnes, RN), HMCS Haida (Comdr. H.G. de Wolf, RCN) and Huron (Lt. Comdr.

H.S. Rayner, DSC RCN), the Polish Blyskawia, HMS Eskimo (Lt. Comdr. E.N. Sinclair, RN) the Polish ship Pioron, HMS Javelin (Lt. Comdr.

P.B.N. Lewis, DSC, RN) in company intercepted a force of German destroyers which had previously been reported off Ushant by Coastal aircraft.

The enemy was sighted and our ships turned toward them, avoiding their torpedoes. In the course of the action, at times conducted at point-blank range, HMS Tartar passed through the enemy's lines. One enemy destroyer was torpedoed and blew up. A second was driven ashore in flames. Two others escaped after receiving damage by gunfire. HMS Tartar sustained some damage and a few casualties but continued in action and has returned safely to harbor.

Unsuccessful attempts were again made after dawn by E-boats to enter the assault area both from the east and the west. They were intercepted and driven off by light coastal forces off Point de Barfleur in a short gun action. Hits were observed on two of the enemy before they escaped.

During the night destroyers under the command of Rear Admiral Don Pardee Moon, USN, intercepted a force of heavily armed enemy craft between the mainland and the Isles St. Marcouf and drove them off.

Spotting for these ships was carried out both by aircraft and military forward observation officers who had been landed with the assault troops.

HMS Belfast (Capt. F.R. Parhan, DSO, RN), wearing the flag of Rear Admiral F.H.G. Dairymple-Hamilton, CB, and HMS Frobisher (Capt. J.F.W. Walter Montford, RN) have done considerable execution on enemy concentrations. This morning (Friday) HMS Frobisher neutralized two enemy batteries and destroyed an ammunition dump.

EHLERS, WALTER D.
Rank and Organization: Staff Sergeant, U.S. Army, 18th Infantry, 1st Infantry Division.
Born: Junction City, Kansas.
Entered Service At: Manhattan, Kansas.
Place and Date: Near Goville, France, June 9-10, 1944.
Citation: For conspicuous gallantry and intrepidity at the risk of his life above and beyond the call of duty on June 9-10, 1944, near Goville, France. S/Sgt. Ehlers, far ahead of his men, led his squad against a strongly defended enemy strongpoint, personally killing 4 of an enemy patrol who attacked him enroute. Then crawling forward under withering machinegun fire, he pounced upon the gun-crew and put it out of action. Turning his attention to 2 mortars protected by the crossfire of 2 machineguns, S/Sgt. Ehlers led his men through this hail of bullets to kill or put to flight the enemy of the mortar section, killing 3 men himself. After mopping up the mortar positions, he again advanced on a machinegun, his progress effectively covered by his squad. When he was almost on top of the gun he leaped to his feet and, although greatly outnumbered, he knocked out the position singlehanded. The next day, having advanced deep into enemy territory, the platoon of which S/Sgt. Ehlers was a member, finding itself in an untenable position as the enemy brought increased mortar, machinegun, and small-arms fire to bear on it, was ordered to withdraw. S/Sgt. Ehlers, after his squad had covered the withdrawal of the remainder of the platoon, stood up and by continuous fire at the semicircle of enemy placements, diverted the bulk of the heavy hostile fire on himself, thus permitting the members of his own squad to withdraw. At this point, though wounded himself, he carried his wounded automatic rifleman to safety and then returned fearlessly over the shell-swept field to retrieve the automatic rifle which he was unable to carry previously. After having his wound treated, he refused to be evacuated, and returned to lead his squad. The intrepid leadership, indomitable courage, and fearless aggressiveness displayed by S/Sgt. Ehlers in the face of overwhelming enemy forces serve as an inspiration to others.

†DeFRANZO, ARTHUR F.
Rank and Organization: Staff Sergeant, U.S. Army, 1st Infantry Division.
Born: Saugus, Massachusetts.
Entered Service At: Saugus, Massachusetts.
Place and Date: Near Vaubadon, France, June 10, 1944.
Citation: For conspicuous gallantry and intrepidity at the risk of his life,

above and beyond the call of duty, on June 10, 1944, near Vaubadon, France. As scouts were advancing across an open field, the enemy suddenly opened fire with several machine-guns and hit 1 of the men. S/Sgt. DeFranzo courageously moved out in the open to the aid of the wounded scout and was himself wounded but brought the man to safety. Refusing aid, S/Sgt. DeFranzo reentered the open field and led the advance upon the enemy. There were always at least 2 machine-guns bringing unrelenting fire upon him, but S/Sgt. DeFranzo kept going forward, firing into the enemy and 1 by 1 the enemy emplacements became silent. While advancing he was again wounded, but continued on until he was within 100 yards of the enemy position and even as he fell, he kept firing his rifle and waving his men forward. When his company came up behind him, S/Sgt. DeFranzo, despite his many severe wounds, suddenly raised himself and once more moved forward in the lead of his men until he was again hit by enemy fire. In a final gesture of indomitable courage, he threw several grenades at the enemy machine-gun position and completely destroyed the gun. In this action, S/Sgt. DeFranzo lost his life, but by bearing the brunt of the enemy fire in leading the attack, he prevented a delay in the assault which would have been of considerable benefit to the foe, and he made possible his company's advance with a minimum of casualties. The extraordinary heroism and magnificent devotion to duty displayed by S/Sgt. DeFranzo was a great inspiration to all about him, and is in keeping with the highest traditions of the armed forces.

OFFICIAL COMMUNIQUE:
United States
SUPREME HEADQUARTERS, Allied Expeditionary Force, June 10 - Communique 9:

American troops have captured Isigny. Despite unfavorable weather conditions, the disembarkation of further men and material was uninterrupted.

Withstanding heavy enemy attacks delivered yesterday morning by infantry and armor, British and Canadian troops stood firm in the Caen area. Our forces have made contact with strong enemy forces near Conde-sur-Seulles. There is continuous fighting in other sectors.

Adverse weather during daylight yesterday confined our air activity to limited patrols over the coastal aircraft operations. An enemy destroyer driven ashore off Bats in the Brest Peninsula earlier in the day by naval surface forces was attacked and left a smoldering hulk.

One enemy aircraft was shot down twenty miles off Brest by anti-E-boat patrols flown over western Channel waters.

Last night a strong force of heavy bombers, eight of which are missing, attacked enemy airfields at Flers, Rennes, Laval, and Le Mans in northwestern France and the railway center at Etampes. Light bombers pounded enemy communications in the rear of the battle zone. Weather conditions remained unfavorable.

Night fighters and intruder aircraft shot down four enemy planes over the beachhead.

Coastal aircraft are cooperating with naval surface forces in a vigorous offensive against U-boats which are threatening to attack our lines of communications in the assault area.

Communique 10:

Allied progress continues along the whole of the beachhead. Trecieres is in our hands.

On the eastern sector severe fighting is in progress against strong enemy armored forces. In the Cherbourg peninsula our advanced patrols are west of the main railway in several heavy fighting continues.

Intensive air operations in support of our ground and naval forces were resumed this morning in better weather. Heavy bombers attacked enemy airfields in Brittany and Normandy. Their fighter escort remained in the zone of operations, strafing enemy armor and transport. Other fighters attacked similar targets over a wide area.

Our medium bombers and their fighter escorts twice attacked targets close behind the enemy. These included road and rail transport, troop and tank concentrations, bridges and communication centers. Widespread air cover was maintained over our beaches and the Channel.

Few enemy fighters were seen but flak was heavy at many points. According to reports so far received three enemy aircraft have been destroyed. Seven of our fighters are missing.

Allied warships have maintained their activity on the eastern and western flanks of the assault area in support of our ground forces.

Last night enemy E-boats operated to the west of the assault area. They were intercepted by light coastal forces under the command of Lieutenant Collins, RN, and a number of brief engagements ensued. Some damage was inflicted on the enemy. Neither damage nor casualties were sustained by our forces.

Enemy patrol vessels heading toward the assault area this morning were attacked off Jersey by our coastal aircraft, which also dispersed a cluster of E-boats.

An unsuccessful attack was made by enemy aircraft on an Allied merchant convoy. One of the enemy was destroyed by gunfire from H.M.S. Wanderer, (Lieut. Comdr. R.D. Whitney, RN). There was no damage to the convoy or its escort.

†COLE, ROBERT G.

Rank and Organization: Lieutenant Colonel, U.S. Army, 101st Airborne Division.

Born: Fort Sam Houston, Texas.

Entered Service At: San Antonio, Texas.

Place and Date: Near Carentan, France, June 11, 1944.

Citation: For conspicuous gallantry and intrepidity at the risk of his life, above and beyond the call of duty on June 11, 1944, in France. Lt. Col. Cole was personally leading his battalion in forcing the last 4 bridges on the road to Carentan when his entire unit was pinned to the ground by intense and withering enemy rifle, machinegun, mortar, and artillery fire placed upon them from well-prepared and heavily fortified positions within 150 yards of the foremost elements. After the devastating and unceasing enemy fire had for over 1 hour prevented any move and inflicted numerous casualties, Lt. Col. Cole, observing this almost helpless situation, courageously issued orders to assault the enemy positions with fixed bayonets. With utter disregard for his own safety and completely ignoring the enemy fire, he rose to his feet in front of his battalion and with drawn pistol shouted to his men to follow him in the assault. Catching up a fallen man's rifle and bayonet, he charged on an led the remnants of his battalion across the bullet-swept open ground and into the enemy position. His heroic and valiant action in so inspiring his men resulted in the complete establishment of our bridgehead across the Douve River. The cool fearlessness, personal bravery, and outstanding leadership displayed by Lt. Col. Cole reflect great credit upon himself and are worthy of the highest praise in the military service.

OFFICIAL COMMUNIQUE:

United Nations

SUPREME HEADQUARTERS, Allied Expeditionary Force, June 11 -Communique 11:

As the result of an armored thrust British troops have reached Tilly-sur-Seulles. Naval guns yesterday lent effective support to our advance in this sector.

Farther west, American forward troops are everywhere south of the flooded areas in the Lower Aure Valley. High ground between Isigny and Carentan also has been taken by American forces.

In the vicinity of Caen, the enemy has made no progress against our positions, despite continuous and vigorous attacks.

To the northwest of Carentan we have crossed the Merderet River, and, overcoming enemy resistance, have made further progress.

Allied aircraft pounded road and rail targets yesterday and last night.

Heavy day bombers attacked airfields and inflicted considerable damage to rolling stock, bridges and armored vehicles. Thirteen enemy aircraft were destroyed.

After escorting the bombers, formations of fighters of fighters attacked road and rail traffic, destroying an ammunition train. From these operations twenty-three fighters are missing.

Medium bombers, sometimes flying at 200 feet in the absence of enemy air opposition, bombed and strafed field guns and armored vehicles. Considerable damage was inflicted in the Falaise and St. Lo areas.

Fighter-bombers and fighters attacked rail yards at ground level. At Avranches armored vehicles and a train were targets. In these operations fifteen enemy fighters were destroyed.

Last night heavy bombers attacked rail centers at Orleans, Dreux, Acheres and Versailles. There was strong opposition, and six German aircraft were destroyed. Twenty bombers are missing.

Our night fighters were active and six German bombers were destroyed five, five of them over the battle area.

Communique 12:

Good progress has been made on the right. Our troops are now fighting in the outskirts of Montebourg. To the southwest of the town we have held enemy counter-attacks attempting to stop our advance west of the main Cherbourg Railway.

American troops have liberated Lison and have advanced several miles southward on a broad front.

In the vicinity of Tilly-sur-Seulles there is heavy fighting. The enemy has strong armored forces in this area and is stubbornly resisting our advance along the River Seulles.

A particularly effective bombardment was carried out in this area by H.M.S. Argonaut (Capt. T. E. W. L. Longley-Cook, CBE, RN) and H.M.S. Orlon (Capt. J.P. Gornall, RN). Allied warships also gave support to the armies yesterday by bombarding mobile batteries and enemy concentrations.

This morning the Allied air force continued their supporting operations in spite of adverse weather. Strong forces of heavy day bombers attacked airfields, bridges, gun positions, and other targets ranging from the battle area to the vicinity of Paris. Objectives in the Pas-de-Calais were also bombed. They were escorted by a strong force tanks and lines of communication.

Medium bombers, fighter-bombers and fighter attacked many targets behind the battle area, including two railway bridges over the River Vire, military trains, railway sheds and yards, armored cars, and troop concentrations, fighters maintained patrols over the battle area and shipping in the opposition in the air, though intense fisk was met at some points.

Seaborne supplies are arriving at a satisfactory rate.

Enemy E-boats were active again during the night and a number of brisk gun actions ensued, during which one of the enemy was destroyed. Several of the enemy were damaged by gunfire before they evaded the pursuit.

Early this morning our coastal aircraft attacked enemy E-boats off Ostend and left two of them on fire.

WISE, HOMER L.

Rank and Organization: Staff Sergeant, U.S. Army, Company L, 142d Infantry, 36th Infantry Division.
Born: Baton Rouge, Louisiana.
Entered Service At: Baton Rouge, Louisiana.
Place and Date: Magliano, Italy, June 14, 1944.
Citation: While his platoon was pinned down by enemy small-arms fire from both flanks, S/Sgt. Wise left his position of comparative safety and assisted in carrying 1 of his men, who had been seriously wounded and who lay in an exposed position, to a point where he could receive medical attention. The advance of the platoon was resumed but was again stopped by enemy frontal fire. A German officer and 2 enlisted men, armed with automatic weapons, threatened the right flank. Fearlessly exposing himself, he moved to a position from which he killed all 3 with his submachinegun. Returning to his squad, he obtained an M1 rifle and several anti-tank grenades, then took up a position from which he delivered accurate fire on the enemy holding up the advance. As the battalion moved forward it was again stopped by enemy frontal and flanking fire. S/Sgt. Wise procured an automatic rifle and, advancing ahead of his men, neutralized an enemy machinegun with his fire. When the flanking fire became more intense S/Sgt. Wise ran to a nearby tank and exposing himself on the turret, restored a jammed machinegun to operating efficiency and used it so effectively that the enemy fire from an adjacent was materially reduced, thus permitting the battalion to occupy its objective.

Note: The following is a newspaper account of the preceding battle for which Sgt. Wise was awarded the Medal of Honor:

NEW GERMAN LINE IN ITALY IS PIERCED

• • •

Impromptu Defense Arc Cut at 3 Points –
Allies Drive On Grosseto and Terni

• • •

ROME, June 14 – The Allies, in hard fighting, having broken through a hastily established German defense arc above Rome at three vital points and are nearing the important highway hubs of Grosseto, 114 road miles northwest of the capital, and Terni, sixty-two road miles north of it, it was announced today.

The attempted German stand from the Tyrrhenian coast around the top of Lake Bolsena was of brief duration, shattered by attacks by Allied armor and infantry. Nor could the enemy hold in the Tiber Valley, the central sector or the Adriatic sector, and front dispatches reported Allied advances all along the 200-mile front.

One break-through was made on the Tyrrhenian coast by American forces. Another, at the northwest corner of Lake Bolsena, was made by British and American units, and the third, southwest of Terni, was made by British troops.

British Eighth Army forces continued their advance on the Adriatic sector, the communique said without giving details.

Our troops were reported to be within eighteen miles of Grosseto, more than half way from Rome to the Rimini-Florence-Pisa line that the Germans may next defend. Northeast of Rome, our forces were "enclosing Narni," the communique said. Narni is only seven miles southwest of Terni, five-way road junction, and twenty-five miles east of Lake Bolsena. The capture of Terni would outflank the important cities of Reiti, Aquila and Teramo, southeast of Terni, and would force the rapid withdrawal of German units facing the Eighth Army on the Adriatic coast.

The most spectacular gain was made by Americans of the Fifth Army driving up the Tyrrhenian coast northwest of Rome along Highway 1. South and east of Orbetello the Germans, dug in on high ground, made a determined stand to protect highway 74, a lateral route vital to the movement of enemy forces.

American infantry, supported by tanks and self-propelled artillery, drove the Germans from these fortified positions and plunged down the northern slopes to take the junction of the two highways about highways about four miles north of Orbetello. From there one group turned east along Highway 74 while the main force advanced north along Highway 1 toward Grosseto, its next objective. [Orbetello was captured, according to a dispatch from the front.]

Highway Cut Above Lake

The Allies' forces fighting their way up the west shore of Lake Bolsena advanced through Latera, four miles north of Valentano, cut Highway 74 northwest of the lake and approached Gradioli, two miles northeast of Latera. On the northeast shore of the lake, the Allies, after very heavy fighting in the past two days, were closing in on the town of Bolsna and on Bagnoregio. The Allies' right flank was driving on Orviento, less than two miles distant. [Agnoregio also was taken, according to front dispatches.]

On the central sector, Eighth Army troops pushing up the Tiber Valley were fighting ten miles northeast of Viterbo. East of the Tiber, Eighth army armor was "several miles" north of Magliano de Sabino, thirty-five miles directly north of Rome. Enemy resistance varied. The advancing British had to contend with many mines and demolitions.

On the Adriatic sector, the Pescara River generally marked the front, although some Eighth Army units had reached and crossed the Saline River, five miles north, near the coast.

Bombers, fighter-bombers and fighter continued intensive assaults on German motor transport, troops on the move bridges, railways and highways, flying more than 2,100 sorties in twenty-four hours. Over the battle areas only two German aircraft were encountered; they were destroyed. Our planes were already attacking the Florence area, the rallying point for the retreating Germans, destroying vehicles on highways and locomotives on railways.

†McCARD, ROBERT HOWARD

Rank and Organization: Gunnery Sergeant, U.S. Marine Corps, 4th Marine Division.
Born: November 25, 1918, Syracuse, New York.
Entered Service At: New York.
Place and Date: Saipan, Marianas Islands, June 16, 1944.
Citation: For conspicuous gallantry and intrepidity at the risk of his life above and beyond the call of duty while serving as platoon sergeant of Company A, 4th Tank Battalion, 4th Marine Division, during the battle for enemy Japanese-held Saipan, Marianas Islands, on June 16, 1944. Cut off from the other units of his platoon when his tank was put out of action by a battery of 77-mm. guns, G/Sgt. McCard carried on resolutely, bringing all the tank's weapons to bear on the enemy, until the severity of hostile fire caused him to order his crew out of the escape hatch while he courageously exposed himself to enemy guns by hurling grenades, in order to cover the evacuation of his men. Seriously wounded during this action and with his supply of grenades exhausted, G/Sgt. McCard then dismantled one of the tank's machineguns and faced the Japanese for a second time to deliver vigorous fire into their positions, destroying 16 of the enemy but sacrificing himself to insure the safety of his crew. His valiant fighting spirit and

supreme loyalty in the face of almost certain death reflect the highest credit upon G/Sgt. McCard and the U.S. Naval Service. He gallantly gave his life for his country.

Note: The following is a newspaper account of the preceding battle for which Sgt. McCard was awarded the Medal of Honor:

SAIPAN TOWN WON IN STREET FIGHTING

• • •

Correspondent With Americans in Marianas Invasion
Says War Resembles Europe's

• • •

ABOARD JOINT EXPEDITIONARY FORCE FLAGSHIP, Saipan, Saturday, June 17 - United States assault troops fought their way inland over the green, rolling hills of southern Saipan in the Marianas today after a street-by-street conquest of the town of Charan-Kanoa, where they landed under the heaviest Japanese fire encountered since Tarawa.

From the bridge of this flagship I saw our first assault waves of loaded "Alligators" claw their way over the Saipan barrier reef and on the beaches, supported by the thundering salvos of naval guns and flaming rockets and automatic weapons operated from LCI's.

Despite the powerful support of the fearsome fleet and aerial preparation, the Alligators battled their way shoreward under a shower of Japanese long-range mortar and artillery fire from the hills rising toward 1,500-foot Mount Apotchau on the left flank of the assault beach.

The Japanese, under naval and aerial bombardment for several days preceding our attack, evacuated the civilians from Charan-Kanoa, a sugar company town estimated to have 3,000 population, but left a strong rearguard, which the Americans cleaned out in the first Pacific fighting comparable to Europe's house-to-house encounters.

Troops Land on Two-Mile Front

Our troops landed on a two-mile front on either side of Charan-Kanoa, which lies along the southwest cost backed by the Lioboone Hills rising toward the sheer cliffs of Magiciennce Bay on the opposite coast.

The units which went ashore south of Charan-Kanoa jumped off on a powerful attack today that carried close to the Aslito Airdrome while the northern forces consolidated the beachhead area below the principal city of Garapan. Those troops set afire the town's oriental buildings, sending up great rolling puffs of flames toward the black and white smoke that shrouded the island.

Casualties are not expected to equal the Tarawa figures but our assault battalions suffered material losses and the Japanese are still throwing mortars-their favorite weapon-into the beachhead area.

The heaviest fighting developed behind Charan-Kanoa in a swampy lake area where the Japanese mounted tank-supported counter-
attacks that were turned back.

The Americans secured the narrow Charan-Kanoa airstrip bordering the beach in the initial attack but as yet it is not out of mortar range.

Thanks to the preparatory strikes against dozens of Japanese bases in the Carolines, the Japanese were unable to send aloft a single plane to interfere with the landing operations and the arrival at dusk of five Japanese torpedo-planes was nullified by an anti-aircraft barrage that forced them to jettison their explosives harmlessly.

Artillery Enfilade Balked

United States naval forces patrolled the two and one-half mile channel separating Saipan and Tinian Islands and effectively prevented an artillery enfilade during the assault by knocking out the Tinian batteries.

We arrived off Saipan exactly on schedule and ships carrying the assault troops were in their prescribed positions within two minutes of the times specified in the plans drawn up weeks earlier.

When the sun came up, the morning light illuminated a sea bobbing with landing craft. Battleships and cruisers had already began roaring reveille with their big guns, and planes swept overhead to drop nearly 100 tons of bombs on the invasion beaches.

The powerful hammering of the beaches apparently forced the Japanese to abandon any plans to defend them with automatic weapons as they did at Tarawa and the assault troops met only mortar and artillery fire as they went in.

The troops going ashore charged forward over the airstrip, by-passing the town and leaving mop-up jobs to following forces, but were forced to slow up and consolidate the gains as mortar fire was intensified.

The Americans occupied Agingan points in the initial attack and found huge sugar mills in flames. An imitation scotch distillery shared the same fate.

As the battle progresses into the more mountainous regions in the center and the north of the island, fighting is likely to become more bitter.

McCAMPBELL, DAVID

Rank and Organization: Commander, U.S. Navy, Air Group 15.
Born: January 16, 1910, Bessemer, Alabama.
Entered Service At: Florida.
Other Navy Awards: Navy Cross, Silver Star, Legion of Merit, Distinguished Flying Cross with 2 Gold Stars, Air Medal.
Place and Date: First and second battles of the Philippine Sea, June 19, 1944.
Citation: For conspicuous gallantry and intrepidity at the risk of his life above and beyond the call of duty as commander, Air Group 15, during combat against Japanese aerial forces in the first and second battles of the Philippine Sea. An inspiring leader, fighting boldly in the face of terrific odds, Comdr. McCampbell led his fighter planes against a force of 80 Japanese carrier-based aircraft bearing down on our fleet on June 19, 1944. Striking fiercely in valiant defense of our surface force, he personally destroyed 7 hostile planes during this single engagement in which the outnumbering attack force was utterly routed and virtually annihilated. During a major fleet engagement with the enemy on October 24, Comdr. McCampbell, assisted by but 1 plane, attacked a formation of 60 hostile land-based craft approaching our forces. Fighting desperately but with superb skill against such overwhelming airpower, he shot down 9 Japanese planes and, completely disorganizing the enemy group, forced the remainder to abandon the attack before a single aircraft could reach the fleet. His great personal valor and indomitable spirit of aggression under extremely perilous combat conditions reflect the highest credit upon Comdr. McCampbell and the U.S. Naval Service.

OFFICIAL COMMUNIQUE:
United Nations
ADVANCED ALLIED HEADQUARTERS ON NEW GUINEA, Tuesday, June 20 - A communique:

NORTHEASTERN SECTOR

Netherlands New Guinea
Biak Island: Our ground forces continued their advance. An additional 165 enemy were killed, bringing the total enemy known dead to 1,820. Thirty-six Javanese, formerly belonging to the Netherlands East Indies Army and prisoners of the enemy, have been freed.

Since, our occupation of Owl Island, five miles south of Biak, eighteen days ago we have constructed an airfield which is now in operation.

British New Guinea
Aitape-Wewak coast: Our medium units, attack planes and fighters dropped sixty tons of bombs in raids on enemy-controlled coastal sectors from Suain to Wewak. Night air and naval patrols bombarded shore targets west of But, silencing enemy guns, and sank or damaged five barges at Kairiru and Mushu Islands.

New Ireland
Our dive-bombers and fighters attacked Kavieng and Selapiu Island. Light naval units off the southeast coast of New Hanover,
causing explosives, and shelled coastal targets south of Borpop.

New Britain
Rabaul: Our heavy, medium and light bombers on the airdrome and defense positions at Ropopo. Vunskanau and Tobera, scoring hits on runways and gun positions. Air patrols started fires in night raids and wrecked fifteen trucks in daylight sweeps. We lost one plane.

Bougainville
Our air patrols swept the coast lines, attacking opportune targets.

Caroline Islands
Truk: Our heavy units, with fifty-five tons of bombs, struck enemy installations on Dublon, Eten and Param Islands. A huge explosion and many fires were seen in fuel storage and airdrome areas, the smoke rising 15,000 feet. Of approximately twenty-five defending enemy fighters, twelve were shot down. Two of our planes failed to return.

WASHINGTON, June 19 - Pacific Fleet communique 56:

Our assault troops on Saipan Island have captured Aslito airdrome and have driven eastward across the island to Magicienne Bay, where we hold the western shore. Two pockets of enemy resistance remain east of Lake Susupe. The enemy continues to counter-attack, but all attacks have been successfully repulsed.

Seabees are at work on the air strips at Aslito.

On June 18 (west longitude date) our carrier task force, providing cover and support for our amphibious force, was subjected to a severe aerial attack which continued for several hours. The attack was successfully repulsed by our carrier aircraft and anti-aircraft fire. Information presently available indicates that only one of our surface units was damaged, and this damage was minor.

It is believed a portion of the enemy planes were carrier-based and used nearby shore bases as shuttle points. However, the effectiveness of this procedure was sharply limited by our systematic bombing and strafing of the aircraft at Guam and Rota.

It is estimated that more than 300 enemy aircraft were destroyed by our forces during this engagement. No estimate is yet available of our own aircraft losses.

†BUTTS, JOHN E.

Rank and Organization: Second Lieutenant, U.S. Army, Company E, 60th Infantry, 9th Infantry Division.
Born: Medina, New York.
Entered Service At: Buffalo, New York.
Place and Date: Normandy, France, June 14, 16, and 23, 1944.
Citation: 2d Lt. Butts heroically led his platoon against the enemy in Normandy, France, June 14, 16, and 23, 1944. Although painfully wounded on the 14th near Orglandes and again on the 16th while spearheading an attack to establish a bridgehead across the Douve River, he refused medical aid and remained with his platoon. A week later, near Flottemanville Hague, he led an assault on a tactically important and stubbornly defended hill studded with tanks, antitank guns, pillboxes, and machinegun emplacements, and protected by concentrated artillery and mortar fire. As the attack was launched, 2d Lt. Butts, at the head of his platoon, was critically wounded by German machinegun fire. Although weakened by his injuries, he rallied his men and directed 1 squad to make a flanking movement while he alone made a frontal assault to draw the hostile fire upon himself. Once more he was struck, but by grim determination and sheer courage continued to crawl ahead. When within 10 yards of his objective, he was killed by direct fire. By his superb courage, unflinching valor, and inspiring actions, 2d Lt. Butts enabled his platoon to take a formidable strong point and contributed greatly to the success of his battalion's mission.

OFFICIAL COMMUNIQUE:
United Nations
SUPREME HEADQUARTERS, Allied Expeditionary Force, June 23 -Communique:

Operations against the fortress of Cherbourg are proceeding satisfactorily. Offensive action and local attacks have effectively pinned down the enemy formations in the eastern sectors.

In preparation for our ground operations, waves of fighter-bombers attacked the strongly fortified German positions encircling Cherbourg during the day and again at dusk yesterday. They went in, often at pistol range, to bomb forts, concrete pillboxes, ammunition dumps, oil stores and troop concentrations. Medium bombers also took part. Our aircraft flew through intense ground fire.

Strong forces of heavy bombers attacked rail and road transport, barges and oil containers between the coast and Paris and the rail junctions of Lille and Ghent. During these operations six enemy aircraft were destroyed. Ten of our bombers and nine fighters are missing.

Light and medium bombers destroyed a steel works near Caen. Fighter-bombers attacked bridges northeast of Paris. In Alderney, one of the Channel isles, gun posts and barracks were the targets for bombers and fighters. During the evening, other formations raided fuel dumps in the Forest of Conches, Bagnoles de Lorne, rail yards at St. Quentin and Armentieres, tracks and full tanks at Dreux and Verneuil.

After dark heavy bombers attacked the rail centers of Reims and Laon in force, thus completing the biggest air effort for some days. Seven bombers are missing.

Rail targets at Lisieux, Dreux and Evreux were the night targets for our light bombers.

Last night our fighters and intruders destroyed seven enemy aircraft over northern France.

Weather over the beachhead has moderated and unloading is proceeding.

Communique 36:

Pressure on the Cherbourg defenses is increasing. Patrols east of Cherbourg are finding little opposition in the sector between Cap Levy and St. Vaast.

Local fighting continues in the Caen and Tilly area.

Early this morning an escorted convoy was intercepted south of Jersey by light coastal forces. One enemy armed trawler was sunk. One of the convoy was left blazing and damage was inflicted on the remainder.

Weather restricted air operations this morning. Fighters and fighter-bombers attacked varied rail targets beyond the battle area, including the yards at Mezidon and the junction north of Le Mans.

The rail lines south of Tours and Orleans have been cut. Bridges and tracks at Nantes, La Roche, Saumur, Niort and east and southeast of Granville were attacked. Locomotives and other rail targets in the Paris and Chateaubriand areas were shot up.

Preliminary reports show eleven enemy aircraft destroyed. Nine of ours are missing.

Heavy day bombers, escorted by fighters, attacked without loss flying bomb installations in Pas-de-Calais.

Coastal aircraft attacked E-boats in the eastern Channel, sinking two, probably sinking three more and damaging several others. A minesweeper also was damaged.

Reconnaissance photographs show much rolling stock was destroyed in the attack by heavy night bombers on rail yards at Laon and Reims last night. The main lines were effectively blocked at many points by direct hits.

†KINGSLEY, DAVID R. (Air Mission)

Rank and Organization: Second Lieutenant, U.S. Army Air Corps, 97th Bombardment Group, 15th Air Force.
Born: Oregon.
Entered Service At: Portland, Oregon.
Place and Date: Ploesti Raid, Romania, June 23, 1944.
Citation: For conspicuous gallantry and intrepidity in action at the risk of his life above and beyond the call of duty, June 23, 1944, near Ploesti, Romania, while flying as bombardier of a B-17 type aircraft. On the bomb run 2d Lt. Kingsley's aircraft was severely damaged by intense flak and forced to drop out of formation but the pilot proceeded over the target and 2d Lt. Kingsley successfully dropped his bombs, causing severe damage to vital installations. The damaged aircraft, forced to lose altitude and to lag behind the formation, was aggressively attacked by 3 ME-109 aircraft, causing more damage to the aircraft and severely wounding the tail gunner in the upper arm. The radio operator and engineer notified 2d Lt. Kingsley that the tail gunner had been wounded and that assistance was needed in checking the bleeding. 2d Lt. Kingsley made his way back to the radio room, skillfully applied first aid to the wound, and succeeded in checking the bleeding. The tail gunner's parachute harness and heavy clothes were removed and he was covered with blankets, making him as comfortable as possible. Eight ME-109 aircraft again aggressively attacked 2d Lt. Kingsley's aircraft and the ball turret gunner was wounded by 20-mm. shell fragments. He went forward to the radio room to have 2d Lt. Kingsley administer first aid. A few minutes later when the pilot gave the order to prepare to bail out, 2d Lt. Kingsley immediately began to assist the wounded gunners in putting on their parachute harness. In the confusion the tail gunner's harness, believed to have been damaged, could not be located in the bundle of blankets and flying clothes which had been removed from the wounded men. With utter disregard for his own means of escape, 2d Lt. Kingsley unhesitatingly removed his parachute harness and adjusted it to the wounded tail gunner. Due to the extensive damage caused by the accurate and concentrated 20-mm. fire by the enemy aircraft the pilot gave the order to bail out, as it appeared that the aircraft would disintegrate at any moment. 2d Lt. Kingsley aided the wounded men in bailing out and when last seen by the crewmembers he was standing on the bomb bay catwalk.

The aircraft continued to fly on automatic pilot for a short distance, then crashed and burned. His body was later found in the wreckage. 2d Lt. Kingsley by his gallant heroic action was directly responsible for saving the life of the wounded gunner.

Note: The following is a newspaper account of the preceding battle for which Lt. Kingsley was awarded the Medal of Honor:

PLOESTI IS BATTERED
BY BIG U.S. BOMBERS

• • •

Italy-Based Craft Strike Blow
– Mosquitos Hit Hamburg

• • •

ROME, June 23 – Strong forces of American heavy bombers raided Rumanian oil installations at Ploesti and Giurgiu today.

Other American Flying Fortresses and Liberators struck deep into southeastern Yugoslavia to bomb the big railway junction at Nish. Thunderbolt and Mustang fighters escorted the four-engine raiders.

Enemy fighters challenged the attacking formations over Rumania and a number of Nazi planes were shot down.

• • •

SUPREME HEADQUARTERS, Allied Expeditionary Force, June 23 –Mosquito bombers last night stung Hamburg. The full sweep of Allied strategic airpower was underlined in tonight's announcement from Italy of renewed attacks on oils refineries at Ploesti and Giurgiu, Roumania, and on rail connections at the Nish communications bottleneck in Yugoslavia.

†EPPERSON, HAROLD GLENN
Rank and Organization: Private First Class, U.S. Marine Corps Reserve, 2d Marine Division.
Born: July 14, 1923, Akron, Ohio.
Entered Service At: Ohio.
Place and Date: Saipan, Mariana Islands, June 25, 1944.

Citation: For conspicuous gallantry and intrepidity at the risk of his life above and beyond the call of duty while serving with the 1st Battalion, 6th Marines, 2d Marine Division, in action against enemy Japanese forces on the island of Saipan in the Marianas, on June 25, 1944. With his machinegun emplacement bearing the full brunt of a fanatic assault initiated by the Japanese under cover of predawn darkness, Pfc. Epperson manned his weapon with determined aggressiveness, fighting furiously in the defense of his battalion's position and maintaining a steady stream of devastating fire against rapidly infiltrating hostile troops to aid materially in annihilating several of the enemy and in breaking the abortive attack. Suddenly a Japanese soldier, assumed to be dead, sprang up and hurled a powerful handgrenade into the emplacement. Determined to save his comrades, Pfc. Epperson unhesitatingly chose to sacrifice himself and, diving upon the deadly missile, absorbed the shattering violence of the exploding charge in his own body. Stouthearted and indomitable in the face of certain death, Pfc. Epperson yielded his own life that his able comrades might carry on the relentless battle against a ruthless enemy. His superb valor and unfaltering devotion to duty throughout reflect the highest credit upon himself and upon the U.S. Naval Service. He gallantly gave his life for his country.

OFFICIAL COMMUNIQUE:
United Nations
WASHINGTON, June 25 – Pacific Fleet communique 63:

On June 24, United States Marines and Army troops on Saipan launched an attack, preceded by intense artillery and naval gunfire preparation, which resulted in advances on our western flank around Mount Topotchau ranging from 500 to 800 yards. Strong enemy opposition continues.

During the evening of June 23 a small flight of enemy planes dropped several bombs in the area occupied by our forces on Saipan. Casualties were very light.

†KELLY, JOHN D.

Rank and Organization: Technical Sergeant (then Corporal), U.S. Army, Company E, 314th Infantry, 79th Infantry Division.
Born: Venango Township, Pennsylvania.
Entered Service At: Cambridge Springs, Pennsylvania.
Place and Date: Fort du Roule, Cherbourg, France, June 25, 1944.
Citation: For conspicuous gallantry and intrepidity at the risk of his life above and beyond the call of duty. On June 25, 1944, in the vicinity of Fort

du Roule, Cherbourg, France, when Cpl. Kelly's unit was pinned down by heavy enemy machinegun fire emanating from a deeply entrenched strongpoint on the slope leading up to the fort, Cpl. Kelly volunteered to attempt to neutralize the strongpoint. Arming himself with a pole charge about 10 feet long and with 15 pounds of explosives affixed, he climbed the slope under a withering blast of machinegun fire and placed the charge at the strongpoints base. The subsequent blast was ineffective, and again, alone and unhesitatingly, he braved the slope to repeat the operation. This second blast blew off the ends of the enemy guns. Cpl. Kelly then climbed the slope a third time to place a pole charge at the strongpoint's rear entrance. When this had been blown open he hurled handgrenades inside the position, forcing survivors of the enemy guncrews to come out and surrender. The gallantry, tenacity of purpose, and utter disregard for personal safety displayed by Cpl. Kelly were an incentive to his comrades and worthy of emulation by all.

OGDEN, CARLOS C.

Rank and Organization: First Lieutenant, U.S. Army, Company K, 314th Infantry, 79th Infantry Division.
Born: May 19, 1917, Borton, Illinois.
Entered Service At: Fairmont, Illinois.
Place and Date: Fort du Roule, France. June 25, 1944.
Citation: On the morning of June 25, 1944, near Fort du Roule, guarding the approaches to Cherbourg, France, 1st Lt. Ogden's company was pinned down by fire from a German 88-mm. gun and 2 machineguns. Arming himself with an M1 rifle, a grenade launcher, and a number of rifle and handgrenades, he left his company in position and advanced alone, under fire, up the slope toward the enemy emplacements. Struck on the head and knocked down by a glancing machinegun bullet, 1st Lt. Ogden, in spite of his painful wound and enemy fire from close range, continued up the hill. Reaching a vantage point, he silenced the 88-mm. gun with a well-placed rifle grenade and then, with handgrenades, knocked out the 2 machineguns, again being painfully wounded. 1st Lt. Ogden's heroic leadership and indomitable courage in alone silencing these enemy weapons inspired his men to greater effort and cleared the way for the company to continue the advance and reach its objectives.

Note: The following is a newspaper account of the preceding battle for which both Cpl. Kelly and Lt. Ogden were awarded the Medal of Honor:

AMERICANS IN CHERBOURG, FIGHT WAY TO DOCKS; NAZIS BLOW UP STORES, GIVE UP BY HUNDREDS

• • •

WARSHIP GUNS AID

• • •

Smash Forts Blocking Advance of Infantry Into Vital Port

• • •

BATTLES IN STREETS

• • •

SUPREME HEADQUARTERS, Allied Expeditionary Force, Monday, June 26 – American infantry drove into the streets of Cherbourg from the east, south and southwest yesterday and a spokesman at headquarters said last night that the city was "almost in our possession."

After five days of the hardest fighting of the campaign, Lieut. Gen. Omar N. Bradley's doughboys were driving the German defenders from house to house and street to street into the interior of the city last evening, and one battalion was only a few hundred yards from the docks.

[A United Press correspondent at the front said some troops even had reached the docks and had surprised Germans in the act of blowing up installations.]

The forces that entered from the south silenced Fort du Roule, last German stronghold in that area, yesterday afternoon, to open their way into the city.

[However, later reports from the front said that some Germans had crawled back into the fort through tunnels and from intact pillboxes were firing at the Americans from the rear.]

Navy Shells Port Defenses

Other forces smashed into the city in the afternoon from the east and southwest after storming German positions on high ground on both sides of the city while the guns of a powerful Allied squadron of battleships and cruisers, commanded by Rear Admiral Morton L. Deyo, flying his flag in the United States cruiser Tuscaloosa, knocked out German guns on the far side of the harbor that had been harassing our advancing troops.

The entry into Cherbourg – France's third greatest port – was a major victory and all signs of such triumph were in evidence yesterday. Hundreds of dazed German soldiers surrendered as tanks rumbled along the cobbled streets and a white flag fluttered from one battered blockhouse.

Some Germans continued to fight to the last. Snipers moved from house to house, trading shots with oncoming American machine gunners, and fired their pieces until their last round or until they died by grenade or bayonet. Whole sections of the city were ablaze and a great pall of smoke hung over the port where the Germans had blown up stores and had fired fuel.

So swift was the American advance in the final phase that bombing by the clouds of fighter-bombers that hung over the city had to be restricted because of the danger to American troops. But the bombers had done their job, for when the troops moved forward yesterday morning German artillery fire was fitful and inaccurate, and prisoners already were coming in from the most heavily bombed fortifications. One infantry unit swept up 300 in its first advance.

Far to the east of the American sector in Normandy the British again hammered their way forward, advancing more than two miles southeast of Tilly-sur-Seulles on what reports from the field described as an eight-and-a-half-mile front. There was fighting around Fontenay-le-Pesnel, two and a quarter miles southeast of Tilly, and the British smashed one strong German counter-attack in the area.

Part of this area will undoubtedly become the main battle sector with the fall of Cherbourg, for it is here that enemy has concentrated his armor, and it is here that a successful offensive would offer him the greatest rewards. The Germans are worried about the Allied attack here. They said a great fleet of transports had disgorged fresh divisions off the mouth of the Orne River during the past two days and predicted that Gen. Sir Bernard L. Montgomery would open an offensive as soon as he had these troops in line. The Cherbourg fight moved at a tremendous pace yesterday, faster than it had since General Bradley hurled his divisions up the peninsula after they had broken through to the sea around Barneville a week ago. Our troops were looking down into the city from some of the high ground to the south by late Saturday, but Fort du Roule still held out during the night.

Yesterday morning, as the field guns resumed their iron clamor, the Americans drove the Germans out of field positions on the high ground and assaulted Fort du Roule.

The advance from the west progressed over high ground west of Equeurdreville. Here again a fort was knocked out and the road from Cherbourg west to Beaumont was cut again – it had been cut farther west Friday – and patrols fought their way into the area just west and south of the naval base in the region of the Municipal Stadium on Rue de la Bucaille.

Other units to the southwest met bitter resistance in the area of St.-Croix-la-Hogue, but these Germans have probably been outflanked by the advance farther north. A few enemy detachments were still reported holding out in the area of Bois du Mont du Roc.

In other areas, prisoners drifted in by twos and threes and sometimes by the dozen. Some complained of lack of ammunition, others of a terrific hammering by American artillery. The enemy suffered heavy casualties. Along the Cherbourg-Valognes road, the dead were so thick that a path had to be cleared through the bodies so that jeeps could pass to the front.

Two German generals have been killed in Normandy since Friday. On Saturday the German radio announced the death of Lieut. Gen. Richter and that of General Stegman, who was killed in action at Cherbourg.

Here and there across the stricken field the Germans fought bravely. German troops were defending the airfield at Maupertus, five miles east of the city, with bitter tenacity. German gunners served their weapons in the port area under the accurate fire of Allied battleships and cruisers until the guns were knocked out.

Except for fighting around Maupertus there was little sign of the enemy in the Barfleur-St. Vaast area. Once occupied, Barfleur, a fishing port with long docks, will be useful for the Allies.

While the infantry, supported by tanks, were cracking Cherbourg's last landward defenses, Allied cruisers and battleships were engaging in a duel with German batteries in the port. One by one the German batteries "Bromm" and "York" under the command of Rear Admiral Henneke, naval commander in Normandy, were knocked out by Allied shells, according to the enemy. Above the forts circled observation planes of the United States and British spotting for warships.

An unofficial but reliable estimate received by this correspondent yesterday said that the capture of Cherbourg would complete the destruction of four German divisions, the Ninety-first, Seventy-seventh, 243d and 109th, the latter under Lieut. Gen. Carl Wilhelm von Schlieban, who also commands the whole Cherbourg garrison. Remnants of these four units, plus German paratroopers and marine and naval units in the city, probably will bring the total Allied bag to about 32,000 effectives.

†AGERHOLM, HAROLD CHRIST

Rank and Organization: Private First Class, U.S. Marine Corps Reserve.
Born: January 29, 1925, Racine, Wisconsin.
Entered Service At: Wisconsin.
Place and Date: Saipan, Marianas Islands, July 7, 1944.
Citation: For conspicuous gallantry and intrepidity at the risk of his life above and beyond the call of duty while serving with the 4th Battalion, 10th Marines, 2d Marine Division, in action against enemy Japanese forces on Saipan, Marianas Islands, July 7, 1944. When the enemy launched a

fierce, determined counterattack against our positions and overran a neighboring artillery battalion, Pfc. Agerholm immediately volunteered to assist in the efforts to check the hostile attack and evacuate our wounded. Locating and appropriating an abandoned ambulance jeep, he repeatedly made extremely perilous trips under heavy rifle and mortar fire and single-handedly loaded and evacuated approximately 45 casualties, working tirelessly and with utter disregard for his own safety during a gruelling period of more than 3 hours. Despite intense, persistent enemy fire, he ran out to aid 2 men whom he believed to be wounded marines but was himself mortally wounded by a Japanese sniper while carrying out his hazardous mission. Pfc. Agerholm's brilliant initiative, great personal valor and self-sacrificing efforts in the face of almost certain death reflect the highest credit upon himself and the U.S. Naval Service. He gallantly gave his life for his country.

†BAKER, THOMAS A.
Rank and Organization: Sergeant, U.S. Army, Company A, 105th Infantry, 27th Infantry Division.
Born: Troy, New York.
Entered Service At: Troy, New York.
Place and Date: Saipan, Mariana Islands, June 19 to July 7, 1944.
Citation: For conspicuous gallantry and intrepidity at the risk of his life above and beyond the call of duty at Saipan, Mariana Islands, June 19 to July 7, 1944. When his entire company was held up by fire from automatic weapons and small-arms fire from strongly fortified enemy positions that commanded the view of the company, Sgt. (then Pvt.) Baker voluntarily took a bazooka and dashed alone to within 100 yards of the enemy. Through heavy machinegun and rifle fire that was directed at him by the enemy, he knocked out the strongpoint, enabling his company to assault the ridge. Some days later while his company advanced across the open field flanked with obstructions and places of concealment for the enemy, Sgt. baker again voluntarily took up a position in the rear to protect the company against surprise attack and came upon 2 heavily fortified enemy pockets manned by 2 officers and 10 enlisted men which had been bypassed. Without regard for such superior numbers, he unhesitatingly attacked and killed all of them. Five hundred yards farther, he discovered 6 men of the enemy who had concealed themselves behind our lines and destroyed all of them. On July 7, 1944, the perimeter of which Sgt. Baker was a part was attacked from 3 sides by from 3,000 to 5,000 Japanese. During the early stages of this attack, Sgt. Baker was seriously wounded but he insisted on remaining

in the line and fired at the enemy at ranges sometime as close as 5 yards until his ammunition ran out. Without ammunition and with his own weapon battered to uselessness from hand-to-hand combat, he was carried about 50 yards to the rear by a comrade, who was then himself wounded. At this point Sgt. Baker refused to be moved any farther stating that he preferred to be left to die rather than risk the lives of any more of his friends. A short time later, at his request, he was placed in a sitting position against a small tree. Another comrade, withdrawing, offered assistance. Sgt. Baker refused, insisting that he be left alone and be given a soldier's pistol with its remaining 8 rounds of ammunition. When last seen alive, Sgt. Baker was propped against a tree, pistol in hand, calmly facing the foe. Later Sgt. Baker's body was found in the same position, gun empty, with 8 Japanese lying dead before him. His deeds were in keeping with the highest traditions of the U.S. Army.

†O'BRIEN, WILLIAM J.

Rank and Organization: Lieutenant Colonel, U.S. Army, 1st Battalion, 105th Infantry, 27th Infantry Division.
Born: Troy, New York.
Entered Service At: Troy, New York.
Place and Date: Saipan, Marianas Islands, June 20 to July 7, 1944.
Citation: For conspicuous gallantry and intrepidity at the risk of his life above and beyond the call of duty at Saipan, Marianas Islands, from June 20 through July 7, 1944. When assault elements of his platoon were held up by intense enemy fire, Lt. Col. O'Brien ordered 3 tanks to precede the assault companies in an attempt to knock out the strongpoint. Due to direct enemy fire the tanks' turrets were closed, causing the tanks to lose direction and to fire into our own troops. Lt. Col. O'Brien, with complete disregard for his own safety, dashed into full view of the enemy and ran to the leader's tank, and pounded on the tank with his pistol butt to attract 2 of the tank's crew and, mounting the tank fully exposed to enemy fire, Lt. Col. O'Brien personally directed the assault until the enemy strongpoint had been liquidated. On June 28, 1944, while his platoon was attempting to take a bitterly defended high ridge in the vicinity of Donnay, Lt. Col. O'Brien arranged to capture the ridge by a double envelopment movement of 2 large combat battalions. He personally took control of the maneuver. Lt. Col. O'Brien crossed 1,200 yards of sniper-infested underbrush alone to arrive at a point where 1 of his platoons was being held up by the enemy. Leaving some men to contain the enemy he personally led 4 men into a narrow ravine behind, and killed or drove off all the Japanese manning that

strongpoint. In this action he captured 5 machineguns and one 77-mm. fieldpiece. Lt. Col. O'Brien then organized the 2 platoons for night defense and against repeated counterattacks directed them. Meanwhile he managed to hold ground. On July 7, 1944, his battalion and another battalion were attacked by an overwhelming enemy force estimated at between 3,000 and 5,000 Japanese. With bloody hand-to-hand fighting in progress everywhere, their forward positions were finally overrun by the sheer weight of the enemy numbers. With many casualties and ammunition running low, Lt. Col. O'Brien refused to leave the front lines. Striding up and down the lines, he fired at the enemy with a pistol in each hand and his presence there bolstered the spirits of the men, encouraged them in their fight and sustained them in their heroic stand. Even after he was seriously wounded, Lt. Col. O'Brien refused to be evacuated and after his pistol ammunition was exhausted, he manned a .50 caliber machinegun, mounted on a jeep, and continued firing. When last seen alive he was standing upright firing into the Jap hordes that were then enveloping him. Some time later his body was found surrounded by enemy he had killed. His valor was consistent with the highest traditions of the service.

†TIMMERMAN, GRANT FREDERICK

Rank and Organization: Sergeant, U.S. Marine Corps, 2d Marine Division.

Born: February 19, 1919, Americus, Kansas.

Entered Service At: Kansas.

Other Navy Award: Bronze Star Medal.

Place and Date: Saipan, Marianas Islands, July 8, 1944.

Citation: For conspicuous gallantry and intrepidity at the risk of his life above and beyond the call of duty as tank commander serving the 2d Battalion, 6th Marines, 2d Marine Division, during action against enemy Japanese forces on Saipan, Marianas Islands, on July 8, 1944. Advancing with his tank a few yards ahead of the infantry in support of a vigorous attack on hostile positions, Sgt. Timmerman maintained steady fire from his antiaircraft sky mount machinegun until progress was impeded by a series of enemy trenches and pillboxes. Observing a target of opportunity, he immediately ordered the tank stopped and, mindful of the danger from the muzzle blast as he prepared to open fire with the 75-mm., fearlessly stood up in the exposed turret and ordered the infantry to hit the deck. Quick to act as a grenade, hurled by the Japanese, was about to drop into the open turret hatch, Sgt. Timmerman unhesitatingly blocked the opening with his body holding the grenade against his chest and taking the brunt of the explosion.

His exceptional valor and loyalty in saving his men at the cost of his own life reflect the highest credit upon Sgt. Timmerman and the U.S. Naval Service. He gallantly gave his life in the service of his country.

Note: The following is a newspaper account of the preceding battle for which Pfc. Agerholm, Sgt. Baker, Lt. Col. O'Brien, and Sgt. Timmerman were awarded the Medal of Honor:

DESPERATE JAPANESE LUNGE
A MILE OUT OF SAIPAN TRAP

• • •

PEARL HARBOR, July 8 – A fierce counter-attack by cornered Japanese troops on Saipan penetrated American lines on the island's western shore and gained more than a mile on Thursday. Several thousand Japanese hurled themselves at out left flank and, at terrific cost in casualties, advanced up to 2,000 yards, reaching the outskirts of Tanapag town, Admiral Chester W. Nimitz stated this morning.

He estimated that 1,500 Japanese troops were killed.

The attempt to relieve the thumb-screw pressure that marines and Army troops applied increasingly throughout the past week began before dawn on Thursday and was not stopped until noon of that day. Our troops then "began to push the enemy back" the communique said.

In the classic Japanese manner, the last-ditch struggle had all the blind fury and damaging effect of an animal's death throes and the communique said the fighting was severe, with numerous casualties. It did not say how much of the ground had been regained.

Admiral Nimitz said earlier in the week that the end of the Saipan battle was near and that there would probably be heavy fighting as the remaining enemy garrison was packed tighter and tighter in the island's rugged northern tip.

It is not improbable that other attempts will be made to inflict as much damage as possible on American forces before the end.

U.S. Troops Near Airfield

As the fighting raged along the western shore our forces on the right flank continued to advance and were at last reports a little more than a mile from the airfield at Marpi Point.

Despite our unquestioned control of the air, the enemy is still able to operate some enemy planes. Small groups of their aircraft raided our positions on the island before dawn Thursday in attacks apparently coordinated with the counter-offensive. They attacked again the following night, dropping bombs near some of our ships. No damage was done.

One enemy plane was shot down.

Shore batteries on Tinian Island, across the channel south of Saipan, opened up on Isely Field, formerly Aslito airdrome, in the southern Saipan area as the counter-attacks began, but destroyers and our own artillery based on Saipan blasted the enemy batteries into silence.

Admiral Nimitz disclosed that the damage we did to enemy bases on Chichi and Haha islands in the Bonins on the 3d of July was even greater than his communique on July 4 indicated.

In addition to the planes shot down that day in the coordinated attacks on island bases, it is now known that thirty-two enemy planes were destroyed on the ground and another ninety-six damaged at the two places.

Nineteen of the planes destroyed and thirty-four of those damaged were twin-engine craft, Admiral Nimitz said, adding that some of them may have been damaged in previous strikes by our aircraft.

In the continuing air forces on Truk, Liberators dropped forty-three tons of bombs at the Bublon Island naval base on Thursday, despite the efforts of a dozen enemy fighters to intercept our force. Five of the enemy planes were shot down and three of our planes received minor damage.

Nauru was bombed by Liberator and Mitchell bombers on Thursday and on the same day fighters and dive-bombers attacked remaining enemy bases in the Marshalls.

†PUCKET, DONALD D.

Rank and Organization: First Lieutenant, U.S. Army Air Corps, 98th Bombardment Group.
Born: Longmont, Colorado.
Entered Service At: Boulder, Colorado.
Place and Date: Ploesti, Romania, July 9, 1944.
Citation: 1st Lt. Pucket took part in a highly effective attack against a vital oil installation in Ploesti, Romania, on July 9, 1944. Just after "bombs away," the plane received heavy and direct hits from antiaircraft fire. One crewmember was instantly killed and 6 others severely wounded. The airplane was badly damaged, 2 engines were knocked out, the control cables cut, the oxygen system on fire, and the bomb bay flooded with gas and hydraulic fluid. Regaining control of his crippled plane, 1st Lt. Pucket turned its direction over to the copilot. He calmed the crew, administered first aid, and surveyed the damage. Finding the bomb bay doors jammed, he used the hand crank to open them to allow the gas to escape. He jettisoned all guns and equipment but the plane continued to lose altitude rapidly. Real-

izing that it would be impossible to reach friendly territory he ordered the crew to abandon ship. Three of the crew, uncontrollable from fright or shock, would not leave. 1st Lt. Pucket urged the others to jump. Ignoring their entreaties to follow, he refused to abandon the 3 hysterical men and was last seen fighting to regain control of the plane. A few moments later the flaming bomber crashed on a mountainside. 1st Lt. Pucket, unhesitatingly and with supreme sacrifice, gave his life in his courageous attempt to save the lives of 3 others.

OFFICIAL COMMUNIQUE:
United Nations
ROME, July 9 – A communique:

Attacks by the Allied armies in Italy are continuing to meet stiff enemy resistance, particularly in increased artillery and mortar fire. However, in the coastal sector troops of the Fifth Army have advanced north of Castellina and to the northwest of Volterra and also south of Poggibonsi.

All counter-attacks against positions of the Eighth Army south of Arezzo have been repulsed and limited progress has again been made in the Upper Tiber Valley.

In the Adriatic sector, where the enemy is trying to stem our advance on Ancona, Fillottrano has been taken by Italian troops. Polish troops have repulsed counter-attacks and have made a further limited advance northwest of Osimo.

Oil installations and airdromes in the Vienna area yesterday were attacked by strong forces of heavy bombers. Escorting fighters also conducted an offensive sweep over the target area.

Tactical aircraft directed their attack on enemy communications and supply lines in northern Italy and in the battle area, striking at roads and railways, transport, shipping, bridges, and ammunition and fuel dumps, gun sites, and other targets. Attacks also were made against shipping in the north Adriatic and objectives in Yugoslavia.

In these operations, fifty-seven enemy aircraft were destroyed and sixteen of our heavy bombers and five other aircraft are missing. The Mediterranean Allied Air Force flew approximately 2,000 sorties.

†ENDL, GERALD L.
Rank and Organization: Staff Sergeant, U.S. Army, 32d Infantry Division.
Born: Ft. Atkins, Wisconsin.
Entered Service At: Janesville, Wisconsin.
Place and Date: Near Anamo, New Guinea, July 11, 1944.
Citation: For conspicuous gallantry and intrepidity at the risk of his life

above and beyond the call of duty near Anamo, New Guinea, July 11, 1944. S/Sgt. Endl was at the head of the leading platoon of his company advancing along a jungle trail when enemy troops were encountered and a fire fight developed. The enemy attacked in force under heavy rifle, machinegun, and grenade fire. His platoon leader wounded, S/Sgt. Endl immediately assumed command and deployed his platoon on a firing line at the fork in the trail toward which the enemy attack was directed. The dense jungle terrain greatly restricted vision and movement, and he endeavored to penetrate down the trail toward an open clearing of Kunai grass. As he advanced, he detected the enemy, supported by at least 6 light and 2 heavy machineguns, attempting an enveloping movement around both flanks. His commanding officer sent a second platoon to move up on the left flank of the position, but the enemy closed in rapidly, placing our force in imminent danger of being isolated and annihilated. Twelve members of his platoon were wounded, 7 being cut off by the enemy. Realizing that if his platoon were forced farther back, these 7 men would be hopelessly trapped and at the mercy of a vicious enemy, he resolved to advance at all cost, knowing it meant almost certain death, in an effort to rescue his comrades. In the face of extremely heavy fire he went forward alone and for a period of approximately 10 minutes engaged the enemy in a heroic close-range fight, holding them off while his men crawled forward under cover to evacuate the wounded and to withdraw. Courageously refusing to abandon 4 more wounded men who were lying along the trail, 1 by 1 he brought them back to safety. As he was carrying the last man in his arms he was struck by a heavy burst of automatic fire and was killed. By his persistent and daring self-sacrifice and on behalf of his comrades, S/Sgt. Endl made possible the successful evacuation of all but 1 man, and enabled the 2 platoons to withdraw with their wounded and to reorganize with the rest of the company.

OFFICIAL COMMUNIQUE:
United Nations
ADVANCED ALLIED HEADQUARTERS ON NEW GUINEA, Wednesday, July 12 –A communique:

Ceram
Our air patrols bombed two small merchant vessels northwest of Bula, forcing them to beach.

Halmahera
Our air patrols scored damaging near-misses on a 10,000-ton enemy tanker off Morotai Island, leaving it dead in the water. Tobi Island to the east was also attacked.

Netherlands New Guinea
Sorong: Our night air patrols bombed and strafed enemy establishments on Middleburg Island.
Sarmi-Maffin: Our heavy units bombed enemy rear areas.

British New Guinea
Aitape - Wewak: Our medium units attack-planes and fighters with twenty tons harassed enemy-occupied coastal sectors from Wewak to Yakamul, starting fires in bivouac and supply areas. Air and naval patrols attacked lines of communication, destroying or damaging six barges.

　　Adverse weather hampered air operations in all sectors.

Palau
Our air patrols by night bombed Peleliu Airdrome and barracks and by day struck installations at the Sonsorol Islands, starting fires.

†HARMON, ROY. W.
Rank and Organization: Sergeant, U.S. Army, Company C, 362d Infantry, 91st Infantry Division.
Born: Talala, Oklahoma.
Entered Service Date: Pixley, California.
Place and Date: Near Casagia, Italy, July 12, 1944.
Citation: Sgt. Harmon was an acting squad leader when heavy machinegun fire from enemy positions, well dug in on commanding ground and camouflaged by haystacks, stopped his company's advance and pinned down 1 platoon where it was exposed to almost certain annihilation. Ordered to rescue the beleaguered platoon by neutralizing the German automatic fire, he led his squad forward along a draw to the right of the trapped unit against 3 key positions which poured murderous fire into his helpless comrades. When within range, his squad fired tracer bullets in an attempt to set fire to the 3 haystacks which were strung out in a loose line directly to the front, 75, 150, and 250 yards away. Realizing that this attack was ineffective, Sgt. Harmon ordered his squad to hold their position and voluntarily began a 1-man assault. Carrying white phosphorus grenades and a submachinegun, he skillfully took advantage of what little cover the terrain afforded and crept to within 25 yards of the first position. He set the haystack afire with a grenade, and when 2 of the enemy attempted to flee from the inferno, he killed them with his submachinegun. Crawling toward the second machinegun emplacement, he attracted fire and was wounded; but he continued to advance and destroyed the position with handgrenades, killing

the occupants. He then attacked the third machinegun, running to a small knoll, then crawling over ground which offered no concealment or cover. About halfway to his objective, he was again wounded. But he struggled ahead until within 20 yards of the machinegun nest, where he raised himself to his knees to throw a grenade. He was knocked down by direct enemy fire. With a final, magnificent effort, he again arose, hurled the grenade and fell dead, riddled by bullets. His missile fired the third position, destroying it. Sgt. Harmon's extraordinary heroism, gallantry, and self-sacrifice saved a platoon from being wiped out, and made it possible for his company to advance against powerful enemy resistance.

OFFICIAL COMMUNIQUE:
United Nations
ROME, July 12 – A communique:

Further limited advances have been made by the Allied army in Italy in many sectors of the front against the same fierce resistance by the enemy.

Between the Upper Tiber Valley and Arezzo troops of an Indian division of the Eighth Army have advanced, taking the village of Mucignano and have established themselves on two hill features nearly two miles to the north.

To the east, the Adriatic sector, Italian troops have taken some ground in the vicinity of the Musone River.

American troops of the Fifth Army have continued their advance and are just behind Castiglioncello on the coast and have driven the enemy from a number of positions in the hills east and west of Lajatico, where heavy fighting is in progress just south of the town.

†CHRISTENSEN, DALE ELDON

Rank and Organization: Second Lieutenant, U.S. Army, Troop E, 112th Cavalry Regiment.
Born: Cameron Township, Iowa.
Entered Service At: Gray, Iowa.
Place and Date: Driniumor River, New Guinea, July 16-19, 1944.
Citation: For conspicuous gallantry and intrepidity at the risk of his life above and beyond the call of duty along the Driniumor River, New Guinea, from July 16-19, 1944. 2d Lt. Christensen repeatedly distinguished himself by conspicuous gallantry above and beyond the call of duty in the continuous heavy fighting which occurred in this area from July 16-19. On July 16, his platoon engaged in a savage fire fight in which much damage was caused by 1 enemy machinegun effectively placed. 2d Lt. Christensen

ordered his men to remain under cover, crept forward under fire, and at a range of 15 yards put the gun out of action with handgrenades. Again, on July 19, while attacking an enemy position strong in mortars and machineguns, his platoon was pinned to the ground by intense fire. Ordering his men to remain under cover, he crept forward alone to locate definitely the enemy automatic weapons and the best direction from which to attack. Although his rifle was struck by enemy fire and knocked from his hands he continued his reconnaissance, located 5 enemy machineguns, destroyed 1 with handgrenades, and rejoined his platoon. He then led his men to the point selected for launching the attack and, calling encouragement, led the charge. The assault was successful and the enemy was driven from the positions with a loss of 4 mortars and 10 machineguns and leaving many dead on the field. On August 4, 1944, near Afua, Dutch New Guinea, 2d Lt. Christensen was killed in action about 2 yards from his objective while leading his platoon in an attack on an enemy machinegun position. 2d Lt. Christensen's leadership, intrepidity, and repeatedly demonstrated gallantry in action at the risk of his life, above and beyond the call of duty, exemplify the highest traditions of the U.S. Armed Forces.

OFFICIAL COMMUNIQUE:
United Nations
ADVANCED ALLIED HEADQUARTERS ON NEW GUINEA, Thursday, July 20 –A communique:

Netherlands New Guinea
Geelvink Bay: Our light naval units shelled coastal targets south of Manokwari and sank an enemy barge to the east of Numfor.
Numfor: Total enemy dead and prisoners at Numfor now amount to 871. Prisoners of the Japanese recovered and freed now number 268.

British New Guinea
Aitape-Wewak: The enemy having been frustrated in his initial frontal attempt at infiltration of the Driniumor River sector, is now attempting to bypass our right flank through foothills of the Torriceli Mountains. Our ground forces report an additional 582 enemy killed. Our medium units and fighters harassed the enemy's rear areas while naval units shelled coastal traffic. Adverse weather hindered air operations in all sectors.

SKAGGS, LUTHER JR.
Rank and Organization: Private First Class, U.S. Marine Corps Reserve, 3d Battalion, 3d Marines, 3d Marine Division.
Born: March 23, 1923, Henderson, Kentucky.
Entered Service At: Kentucky.
Place and Date: Adelup beachhead, Guam, Marianas Islands, July 21-22, 1944.
Citation: For conspicuous gallantry and intrepidity at the risk of his life above and beyond the call of duty while serving as squad leader with a mortar section of a rifle company in the 3d Battalion, 3d Marines, 3d Marine Division, during action against enemy Japanese forces on the Asan-Adelup beachhead, Guam, Marianas Islands, July 21-22, 1944. When the section leader became a casualty under a heavy mortar barrage shortly after landing, Pfc. Skaggs promptly assumed command and led the section through intense fire for a distance of 200 yards to a position from which to deliver effective coverage of the assault on a strategic cliff. Valiantly defending this vital position against strong enemy counterattacks during the night, Pfc. Skaggs was critically wounded when a Japanese grenade lodged in his foxhole and exploded, shattering the lower part of one leg. Quick to act, he applied an improvised tourniquet and, while propped up in his foxhole, gallantly returned the enemy's fire with his rifle and handgrenades for a period of 8 hours, later crawling unassisted to the rear to continue the fight until the Japanese had been annihilated. Uncomplaining and calm throughout this critical period, Pfc. Skaggs served as a heroic example of courage and fortitude to other wounded men and, by his courageous leadership and inspiring devotion to duty, upheld the high traditions of the U.S. Naval Service.

†MASON, LEONARD FOSTER
Rank and Organization: Private First Class, U.S. Marine Corps, 3d Marine Division.
Born: February 2, 1920, Middleborough, Kentucky.
Entered Service At: Ohio.
Place and Date: Asan-Adelup Beachhead, Guam, Marianas Islands, July 22, 1944.
Citation: For conspicuous gallantry and intrepidity at the risk of his life above and beyond the call of duty as an automatic rifleman serving with the 2d Battalion, 3d Marines, 3d Marine Division, in action against enemy Japanese forces on the Asan-Adelup Beachhead, Guam, Marinas Islands on July 22, 1944. Suddenly taken under fire by 2 enemy machineguns not

more than 15 yards away while clearing out hostile positions holding up the advance of his platoon though a narrow gully, Pfc. Mason, alone and entirely on his own initiative, climbed out of the gully and moved parallel to it toward the rear of the enemy position. Although fired upon immediately by hostile riflemen from a higher position and wounded repeatedly in the arm and shoulder, Pfc. Mason grimly pressed forward and had just reached his objective when hit again by a burst of enemy machinegun fire, causing a critical wound to which he later succumbed. With valiant disregard for his own peril, he persevered, clearing out the hostile position, killing 5 Japanese, wounding another and then rejoining his platoon to report the results of his action before consenting to be evacuated. His exceptionally heroic act in the face of almost certain death enabled his platoon to accomplish its mission and reflects the highest credit upon Pfc. Mason and the U.S. Naval Service. He gallantly gave his life for his country.

Note: The following is a newspaper account of the preceding battle for which both Pfc. Skaggs and Pfc. Mason were awarded the Medal of Honor:

INVADERS FIND DEFENSES OF GUAM
BLOWN TO SHREDS BY OUR ATTACKS

• • •

ABOARD A FLAGSHIP AT GUAM, July 21 (Guam Time)-A liberation force of Third Amphibious Corps marines and Army troops thundered ashore at Guam today with the destructive blast of a Pacific typhoon.

The Leathernecks spearheaded two separate beachhead assaults, storming across coral-studded shorelines in the wake of a 17-day sea and air bombardment that reached a stupefying crescendo as landing craft churned into remnants of the Japanese coast defenses.

Casualties were described as "light" for United States forces. The Japanese dead were uncounted.

At nightfall Maj. Gen. Roy Geiger's Third Amphibious Corps troops dug in on perimeters between Adlup and Asan, a point north of Orote Peninsula, and from the shattered town of Agat to Bangi Point, south of the rocky finger of land.

The northern beachhead, where the terrain was most rugged, stretched in an arc several thousand yards. The southern force shoved inland and established its own substantial beachhead. General Geiger is a marine aviator and veteran South Pacific commander.

So effective had been the preparatory barrages that troops flowed ashore with negligible initial resistance and in record time.

Listening to the guns and the roaring planes and watching the landing craft move shoreward, the Japanese already reduced in strength and efficiency by the unrelenting attacks of the preceding weeks, heard and saw the quality of American vengeance. And Guam lies only 1,565 miles from Tokyo and 1,595 from Manila in the Philippines.

In a second communique issued at 2:30 this afternoon Admiral Nimitz told of the stiffening resistance in some sectors and said "good beachheads have been secured."

Artillery Probably Landed

Naval gunfire and serial bombing were employed right up to the moment of the landings and continued afterward to keep enemy artillery batteries neutralized. The smoothness of the initial stages of the assault can be attributed in large part to the weight and precision of the air and gun bombardment of the defenders.

Rear Admiral Richard L. Conolly, who directed amphibious operations against Roi and Namur Islands in Kwajalein atoll early this year, is in command of the Guam amphibious operation.

The expeditionary troops, both Marines and Army, commanded by Maj. Gen. Roy S. Geiger of the Marine Corps, commanding general of the Third Amphibious Corps. One of the outstanding Marine Corps airmen, General Geiger's fighting spirit is known to the Japanese of old. He commanded marine aviation in the early Guadalcanal days when the downward rush of the enemy's Pacific push was stopped. He also was a commander in the invasion of Bougainville.

Capture of Guam will give American forces complete control of the Marianas, for Guam and Saipan were their most important bases. It will give us unquestioned authority over at least the eastern sector of the vast Philippine Sea, where, as Tokyo has already conceded, the outcome of the Pacific war may well be determined.

Terrain Favorable to Enemy

Estimates are that the number of troops involved on both sides approximate the forces that fought out the bloody Saipan engagement from June 14 to July 8, when organized resistance ended.

On Saipan the Japanese had more than 20,000 troops. We had there the elements of three divisions, the Twenty-seventh Army and the Second and Fourth Marines.

Guam's terrain is rugged and mountainous, particularly so in the southern part. The 225 square miles of land offer ideal fighting ground for the Japanese, with plenty of opportunity to take cover in caves and brush areas. Since the island is three times the size of Saipan, the ferreting out of the last remnants may take considerably longer.

The island geologically is in two distinct and dissimilar parts. In the north it is a raised reef with a limestone plateau covered almost wholly by dense low vegetation except where it has been cleared away for growing and defense purposes.

The largest trees are banyans, which sometimes reach a height of fifty or sixty feet. There are some big hardwood trees, many bread fruit trees and plenty of scrubby undergrowth.

Eastern Shore Not So Rugged

In the southern half is a range of volcanic peaks towering at one point to about 1,300 feet. This is Mount Lamlam. On the western shore it drops off abruptly into the sea with short and steep valleys running from the volcanic crests to the rocky shore with beach pockets and jutting headland.

The eastern shore slopes more gently with larger valleys and big streams, none of which are navigable. At the south end the volcanic slope runs right down into the sea and there is a narrow fringing reef. On the west there is a limestone peninsula ending in Orote Point and Agana is north of there.

When the Japanese landed on the night of Dec. 8, 1941, West Longitude date, they picked Agana and Umatae Bay on the southwest, assuming that we had fortified Apra Harbor. They picked the two most difficult landing places.

Guam had been guarded prior to 1922 by 6-inch naval guns but after the signing of the Washington Treaty limiting naval fortifications these guns were removed and the island was not fortified when the enemy landed.

In another respect seizure of Guam is a different task from any attempts before in the central Pacific. For the first time we are assaulting a large land area where the natives may be expected to welcome our forces.

The 1939 census listed about 700 United States residents, mostly naval personnel and 21,500 natives, mostly Chamorros. The native Chamorro islanders have always been friendly to the United States and in the past vainly sought an opportunity to take American citizenship.

They are believed to be definitely unfriendly to the Japanese and there is no reason to think their attitude toward Americans has changed appreciably.

A peace loving and civilized people with many noble characteristics their attitude toward the returning Americans should be vastly different from that of the Saipanese, who were either Japanese themselves or loyal in the majority of cases to the Japanese cause.

The Chamorros have a folk song which has deep implications for the enemy occupation troops now fighting for their existence. It says:

When you cause a person pain, Wait for pain to come to you; Though it may be a very long time, You will pay, as it is a debt.

Admiral Nimitz announced in his second communique that Liberator search planes of Fleet Air Wing 2 had made a second bombing attack on Chichi and Haha

Islands in the Bonin Islands and also struck Iwo in the Volcano Islands on Thursday.

†LOBAUGH, DONALD R.

Rank and Organization: Private, U.S. Army, 127th Infantry, 32d Infantry Division.
Born: Freeport, Pennsylvania.
Entered Service At: Freeport, Pennsylvania.
Place and Date: Near Afua, New Guinea, July 22, 1944.
Citation: For conspicuous gallantry and intrepidity at the risk of his life above and beyond the call of duty near Afua, New Guinea, on July 22, 1944. While Pvt. Lobaugh's company was withdrawing from its position on July 21, the enemy attacked and cut off approximately 1 platoon of our troops. The platoon immediately occupied, organized, and defended a position, which it held throughout the night. Early on July 22, an attempt was made to effect its withdrawal, but during the preparation therefor, the enemy emplaced a machinegun, protected by the fire of rifles and automatic weapons, which blocked the only route over which the platoon could move. Knowing that it was the key to the enemy position, Pfc. Lobaugh volunteered to attempt to destroy this weapon, even though in order to reach it he would be forced to work his way about 30 yards over ground devoid of cover. When part way across this open space he threw a handgrenade, but exposed himself in the act and was wounded. Heedless of his wound, he boldly rushed the emplacement, firing as he advanced,. The enemy concentrated their fire on him, and he was struck repeatedly, but he continued his attack and killed 2 more before he was himself slain. Pfc. Lobaugh's heroic actions inspired his comrades to press the attack, and to drive the enemy from the position with heavy losses. His fighting determination and intrepidity in battle exemplify the highest traditions of the U.S. Armed Forces.

†BOYCE, GEORGE W. G., JR.

Rank and Organization: Second Lieutenant, U.S. Army, 112th Cavalry Regimental Combat Team.
Born: New York City, New York.
Entered Service At: Town of Cornwall, Orange County, New York.
Place and Date: Near Afua, New Guinea, July 23, 1944.
Citation: For conspicuous gallantry and intrepidity at risk of his life above and beyond the call of duty near Afua, New Guinea, on July 23, 1944. 2d

Lt. Boyce's troop, having been ordered to the relief of another unit surrounded by superior enemy forces, moved out, and upon gaining contact with the enemy, the two leading platoons deployed and built up a firing line. 2d Lt. Boyce was ordered to attack with his platoon and make the main effort on the right of the troop. He launched his attack but after a short advance encountered such intense rifle, machinegun, and mortar fire that the forward movement of his platoon was temporarily halted. A shallow depression offered a route of advance and he worked his squad up this avenue of approach in order to close with the enemy. He was promptly met by a volley of handgrenades. 1 falling between himself and the men immediately following. Realizing at once that the explosion would kill or wound several of his men, he promptly threw himself upon the grenade and smothered the blast with his own body. By thus deliberately sacrificing his life to save those of his men, this officer exemplified the highest traditions of the U.S. Armed Forces.

†EUBANKS, RAY E.
Rank and Organization: Sergeant, U.S. Army, Company D, 503d Parachute Infantry.
Born: February 6, 1922, Snow Hill, North Carolina.
Entered Service At: LaGrange, North Carolina.
Place and Date: At Noemfoor Island, Dutch New Guinea, July 23, 1944.
Citation: For conspicuous gallantry and intrepidity at the risk of his life above and beyond the call of duty at Noemfoor Island, Dutch New Guinea, July 23, 1944. While moving to the relief of a platoon isolated by the enemy, his company encountered a strong enemy position supported by machinegun, rifle, and mortar fire. Sgt. Eubanks was ordered to make an attack with 1 squad to neutralize the enemy by fire in order to assist the advance of his company. He maneuvered his squad to within 30 yards of the enemy where heavy fire checked his advance. Directing his men to maintain their fire, he and 2 scouts worked their way forward up a shallow depression to within 25 yards of the enemy. Directing the scouts to remain in place, Sgt. Eubanks armed himself with an automatic rifle and worked himself forward over terrain swept by intense fire to within 15 yards of the enemy position when he opened fire with telling effect. The enemy, having located his position, concentrated their fire with the result that he was wounded and a bullet rendered his rifle useless. In spite of his painful wounds he immediately charged the enemy and using his weapon as a club killed 4 of the enemy before he was himself again hit and killed. Sgt. Eubanks' heroic action, courage, and example in leadership so inspired his men that

their advance was successful. They killed 45 of the enemy and drove the remainder from the position, thus effecting the relief of our beleaguered troops.

OFFICIAL COMMUNIQUE:
United Nations
ADVANCED ALLIED HEADQUARTERS ON NEW GUINEA, Monday, July 24 - A Communique:

Philippine Islands
Our air patrols sank a coastal vessel seventy miles off the coast of Mindanao.

Tenimber Islands
Our heavy units bombed enemy installations at Saumlaki, while fighters strafed the Selaru airdrome, destroying a parked enemy bomber.

Halmahera
Our medium units bombed shipping and villages, destroying a 1,000-ton vessel. We lost one plane to anti-aircraft fire.

Netherlands New Guinea
Timika: Our medium units bombed and strafed the airdrome and attacked small craft near by.
MacCluer Gulf: Our heavy, medium and attack planes bombed the enemy airdrome and supply installations at Babo, Kakas and Fakfak.
Sorong: Our medium bombers attacked the western Vogelkop oilfield area, destroying oil derricks and oil installations, with heavy personnel losses, and setting fire to fuel dumps. A defensive gun battery also was demolished.
Geelvink Bay: Our heavy units bombed the airdrome and defense positions at Manokwari, causing large explosions and fires.

British New Guinea
Aitape-Wewak: Our ground forces repulsed small-scale enemy reconnaissance attacks on our Driniumor River line, where the enemy is apparently still trying to effect a large scale concentration of force. Our medium units and attack planes dropped twenty-seven tons of explosives on bivouac and supply areas near But and coastal roads.

WASHINGTON, July 23, - Pacific Fleet Communique 85:

Substantial gains were made by our forces on Guam during the night of July 22 (West Longitude date). In the northern area all of Cabras Island and Piti town were captured. Attempts made by the enemy during the night of July 21-22 to infiltrate our lines were repulsed in the southern area. Orote Peninsula has been nearly cut off by our forces. Aircraft and naval gunfire are closely supporting our troops.

Our estimated casualties through July 22 are as follows: Killed in action, 348: wounded in action, 1,500: missing in action, 110.

Intense artillery and naval gunfire was directed against Tinian Island on July 21. Enemy gun positions and troop concentrations were principal targets. On the same day, Thunderbolt fighters of the Seventh AAF attacked Tinian and Pagan Islands. At Tinian gun emplacements and pillboxes were bombed. At Pagan the airstrip was bombed and strafed. Intense anti-aircraft fire over Pagan damaged two of our aircraft.

Seventy-five tons of bombs were dropped on airfield and dock areas at Truk Atoll on July 21 by Seventh AAF Liberators. Fires and explosions were observed. Two airborne enemy fighters did not attempt to intercept our force. Anti-aircraft fire was meager.

WILSON, LOUIS HUGH, JR.

Rank and Organization: Captain, U.S. Marine Corps, Commanding Rifle Company, 2d Battalion, 9th Marines, 3d Marine Division.
Born: February 11, 1920, Brandon, Mississippi.
Entered Service At: Mississippi.
Place and Date: Fonte Hill, Guam, July 25-26, 1944.
Citation: For conspicuous gallantry and intrepidity at the risk of his life above and beyond the call of duty as commanding officer of a rifle company attached to the 2d Battalion, 9th Marines, 3d Marine Division, in action against enemy Japanese forces at Fonte Hill, Guam, July 25-26, 1944. Ordered to take that portion of the hill within his zone of action, Capt. Wilson initiated his attack in mid-afternoon, pushed up the rugged, open terrain against terrific machinegun and rifle fire for 300 yards and successfully captured the objective. Promptly assuming command of other disorganized units and motorized equipment in addition to his own company and 1 reinforcing platoon, he organized his night defenses in the face of continuous hostile fire and, although wounded 3 times during this 5-hour period, completed his disposition of men and guns before retiring to the company command post for medical attention. Shortly thereafter, when the enemy launched the first of a series of savage counterattacks lasting all night, he voluntarily rejoined his besieged units and repeatedly exposed himself to the merciless hail of shrapnel and bullets, dashing 50 yards into the open on 1 occasion to rescue a wounded marine lying helpless beyond the frontlines. Fighting fiercely in hand-to-hand encounters, he led his men

in furiously waged battle for approximately 10 hours, tenaciously holding his line and repelling the fanatically renewed counterthrusts until he succeeded in crushing the last efforts of the hard-pressed Japanese early the following morning. Then organizing a 17-man patrol, he immediately advanced upon a strategic slope essential to the security of his position and, boldly defying intense mortar, machinegun, and rifle fire which struck down 13 of his men, drove relentlessly forward with the remnants of his patrol to seize the vital ground. By his indomitable leadership, daring combat tactics, and valor in the face of overwhelming odds, Capt. Wilson succeeded in capturing and holding the strategic high ground in his regimental sector, thereby contributing essentially to the success of his regimental mission and to the annihilation of 350 Japanese troops. His inspiring conduct throughout the critical periods of the decisive action sustains and enhances the highest traditions of the U.S. Naval Service.

Note: The following is a newspaper account of the preceding battle for which Capt. Wilson was awarded the Medal of Honor:

MARINES CLOSE ON GUAM AIRPORT; WIN FOURTH OF TINIAN, WITH STRIP

• • •

PEARL HARBOR, July 26-Japanese forces isolated on Guam's Orote Peninsula are battering desperately at the American Steel ring holding them in, but they are trapped.

On Monday night after the American line on Guam had been pushed into the promontory a few hundreds yards, obviously headed for the airport, Japanese forces made "desperate attempts to escape," Admiral Chester W. Nimitz said in a six o'clock communique tonight.

There was still a way open, a narrow gateway between the northern and southern American beachheads, but our patrols were already pushing across the one and one-half mile escape opening.

Repeated enemy attempts failed and our lines were not penetrated. Then yesterday morning our forces counter-attacked, supported by heavy artillery and naval gunfire. Aircraft roared over and bombed ahead of our advance and the marines drove, in one push, about 3,000 yards up the peninsula.

[The Tokyo radio said yesterday that an American carrier force had struck at Palau, about 500 miles from Mindanao, the Philippines, according to The Associated Press.]

Meantime, American Marines on Tinian, under the supporting fire of the guns of a battleship and land-based aircraft hacked their way across the island to win possession of the entire northern quarter, including the whole of the Ushi Point airfield.

The Americans on Guam are now only 400 yards or so from the airport and approximately the same distance from the town of Sumay and the old headquarters of Pan-American Airways. The advance gave us control of the entire southern or inner half of the peninsula and the remaining enemy defenders, whose strength has not been officially estimated, appeared to be doomed.

The gap in our lines has now been irrevocably closed and the marines and Army forces on the 225-square-mile island now have a beachhead more than nine miles in length.

In their attempt to escape the Japanese lost 400 dead and our marines destroyed at least twelve of their tanks.

With supplies dwindling and their numbers being steadily reduced, their fate is sealed.

When the peninsula is completely in our hands the entire strength of the American forces can then proceed with the reduction of the rest of the garrison.

While the battle has gone well for us there is still hard fighting ahead, particularly so in the region of Agana Town, where the left flank is still anchored as it was after the first day at Adelup Point.

Fierce fighting pressure is being applied to the battered enemy defenders on Tinian Island, and the American forces, forging rapidly ahead, have captured the northern quarter of the island.

Yesterday the Marines plunged forward in a full-scale attack, seizing the whole of the Ushi Point airport. Battleships and aircraft blasted the enemy with shells and fire bombs. They also strafed a rail junction, coastal guns and barracks.

Our troops have counted 1,958 enemy dead.

Admiral Nimitz this afternoon said that our Tinian lines are anchored below Faibus and San Hilo Point on the western coast and extend to Asiga Point on the east coast.

Battleship action during the day came when their heavy guns were called to knock out several camouflaged blockhouses.

Our aircraft are still bombing and strafing targets throughout the island along the hard pressed enemy line and targets to the rear.

Heightening pressure, together with the fact that the enemy has not once been able to meet our attack with anything much heavier than machine gun and rifle fire, excepting one feeble tank thrust that was quickly squelched, indicates that the Tinian landing was either unexpected or that the Japanese were unable to offer real resistance on both Guam and Tinian. It now appears possible that we may attempt an all-out crushing of Tinian as quickly as possible.

Before yesterday's push we had only a deep wedge in Tinian's west shore, and the marines in one day pushed clear across the island, cleared away the northern tip and started driving south along both coasts.

Admiral Nimitz said the fire bomb and strafing attack on the enemy was made by Thunderbolts of the Seventh Army Air Force, and that other Thunderbolts had raided Pagan Island in the northern Marianas, scoring bomb hits on the airfield.

The Guam battle is proceeding against a stiff enemy defense, with carrier planes attacking constantly and also keeping Rota Island neutralized.

Ponape, Truk and Nauru, far behind the battle zone, were also raided.

WHITTINGTON, HULON B.

Rank and Organization: Sergeant, U.S. Army, 41st Armored Infantry, 2d Armored Division.
Born: July 9, 1921, Bogalusa, Louisiana.
Entered Service At: Bastrop, Louisiana.
Place and Date: Near Grimesnil, France, July 29, 1944.
Citation: For conspicuous gallantry and intrepidity at the risk of life above and beyond the call of duty. On the night of July 29, 1944, near Grimesnil, France, during an enemy armored attack, Sgt. Whittington, a squad leader, assumed command of his platoon when the platoon leader and platoon sergeant became missing in action. He reorganized the defense and, under fire, courageously crawled between gun positions to check the actions of his men. When the advancing enemy attempted to penetrate a roadblock, Sgt. Whittington, completely disregarding intense enemy action, mounted a tank and by shouting through the turret, directed it into position to fire pointblank at the leading Mark V German tank. The destruction of this vehicle blocked all movement of the remaining enemy column consisting of over 100 vehicles of a Panzer unit. The blocked vehicles were then destroyed by handgrenades, bazooka, tank, and artillery fire and large numbers of enemy personnel were wiped out by a bold and resolute bayonet charge inspired by Sgt. Whittington. When the medical aid man had become a casualty, Sgt. Whittington personally administered first aid to his wounded men. The dynamic leadership, the inspiring example, and the dauntless courage of Sgt. Whittington, above and beyond the call of duty, are in keeping with the highest traditions of the military service.

OFFICIAL COMMUNIQUE:
United Nations
SUPREME HEADQUARTERS, Allied Expeditionary Force, July 29 -Communique 107:

Coutances is now clear of the enemy, and Allied armored forces have reached the sea south of the estuary of the Sienne River. Areas of enemy resistance north of the town are being rapidly cleared.

Further progress has been made by a thrust southwest from Notre Dame-de-Cenilly.

In support of ground operations yesterday fighter-bombers attacked an ammunition distribution point, enemy gun positions, enemy reserves and vehicles.

Other fighter-bombers and long-range fighters on armed reconnaissance over northwest France attacked locomotives, rolling stock and road transport.

Targets for our medium and light bombers were eight rail bridges northwest of Paris, an important ammunition dump in the Foret de Senonches, near Chartres, and rail centers north of Bernay. Last night light bombers attacked eighteen trains and many road targets in northern France.

Coastal aircraft attacked were shot down over the beachhead last night.

Communique 108:

Allied armored columns in the western sector continue to advance against stiffening resistance. One column has reached the coast west of Coutances and has taken the town of Pont de la Rouque.

Another column has reached Hyenville south of Coutances. Pockets of resistance at Cerisy-la-Salle and Montipinchon have been mopped up.

The salient between Villebaudon and St. Denis-Le-Gast has been cleared of the enemy. The town of Hambye has been taken.

Enemy forces are astride the Vire south of Tessy.

South of St. Lo Allied forces have advanced several kilometers.

German military buildings near Morlaix were attacked by fighter-bombers this morning.

†OZBOURN, JOSEPH WILLIAM

Rank and Organization: Private, U.S. Marine Corps, 4th Marine Division.
Born: October 24, 1919, Herrin, Illinois.
Entered Service At: Illinois.
Place and Date: Tinian Island, Marianas Islands, July 30, 1944.
Citation: For conspicuous gallantry and intrepidity at the risk of his life above and beyond the call of duty as a Browning Automatic Rifleman serving with the 1st Battalion, 23d Marines, 4th Marine Division, during the battle for enemy Japanese-held Tinian Island, Marianas Islands, July 30, 1944. As a member of a platoon assigned the mission of clearing the remaining Japanese troops from dugouts and pillboxes along a tree line, Pvt. Ozbourn, flanked by 2 men on either side, was moving forward to throw an armed handgrenade into a dugout when a terrific blast from the entrance severely wounded the 4 men and himself. Unable to throw the grenade into

the dugout and with no place to hurl it without endangering the other men, Pvt. Ozbourn unhesitatingly grasped it close to his body and fell upon it, sacrificing his own life to absorb the full impact of the explosion, but saving his comrades. His great personal valor and unwavering loyalty reflect the highest credit upon Pvt. Ozbourn and the U.S. Naval Service. He gallantly gave his life for his country.

OFFICIAL COMMUNIQUE:
United States
WASHINGTON July 30, - Pacific Fleet Communique 97:

Tinian Town, on Tinian Island, was captured by United States Marines during the afternoon of July 29 (West Longitude date).

Substantial gains were made along the entire front during the day, and the enemy is now contained in an area of approximately five square miles at the southern tip of the island. enemy resistance increased progressively throughout July 29 as the marines advanced.

Activity on Guam on July 29 (West Longitude date) was limited to clearing local pockets of resistance, and to patrolling. Some of our patrols crossed the island to Ylig and Togcha Bay without meeting resistance.

Our troops to date have counted 4,543 enemy dead and have captured forty-four prisoners of war. At least twenty-eight Japanese tanks have been destroyed. Our own casualties on Guam as of July 29, including both soldiers and marines, totaled 958 killed in action, 4,739 wounded in action, and 290 missing in action.

Our ships now are using Apra Harbor, on the west coast of Guam, site of the former American naval base. Several of our aircraft have landed and taken off from the Orote Peninsula airfield.

Two Liberators of Fleet Air Wing 2 on July 28 strafed Japanese small craft in the Truk Atoll lagoon. Five enemy fighters attempted to intercept our force and two fighters were damaged. The bombers proceeded to Ponape where Japanese gun positions and buildings were bombed. One of our planes was damaged by anti-aircraft fire but both returned to base.

Attacks on remaining Japanese positions in the Marshall Islands were continued on July 28. Fourth Marine Aircraft Wing Corsairs and Dauntless dive bombers and Group 1, Fleet Air Wing 2, Venturas and aircraft gun replacements. A navy Ventura search plane bombed Nauru. Anti-aircraft fire ranged form moderate to meager. Two of our aircraft were damaged but all returned.

RAMAGE, LAWSON PATERSON
Rank and Organization: Commander, U.S. Navy. U.S.S. *Parch.*
Born: January 19, 1920, Monroe Bridge, Massachusetts.
Entered Service At: Vermont.
Place and Date: Pacific, July 31, 1944.
Citation: For conspicuous gallantry and intrepidity at the risk of his life above and beyond the call of duty as commanding officer of the U.S.S. *Parche* in a predawn attack on a Japanese convoy, July 31, 1944. Boldly penetrating the screen of a heavily escorted convoy. Comdr. Ramage launched a perilous surface attack by delivering a crippling stern shot into a freighter and quickly following up with a series of bow and stern torpedoes to sink the leading tanker and damage the second one. Exposed by the light of bursting flares and bravely defiant of terrific shellfire passing close overhead, he struck again, sinking a transport by two forward reloads. In the mounting fury of fire from the damaged and sinking tanker, he calmly ordered his men below, remaining on the bridge to fight it out with an enemy now disorganized and confused. Swift to act as a fast transport closed in to ram, Comdr. Ramage daringly swung the stern of the speeding *Parche* as she crossed the bow of the onrushing ship, clearing by less than 50 feet but placing his submarine in a deadly crossfire from escorts on all sides and with the transport dead ahead. Undaunted, he sent 3 smashing "down the throat" bow shots to stop the target, then scored a killing hit as a climax to 46 minutes of violent action with the *Parche* and her valiant fighting company retiring victorious and unscathed.

OFFICIAL COMMUNIQUE:
United Nations
WASHINGTON July 31 – Pacific Fleet Communique 98:

Marine and Army troops on Guam swept completely across the island during July 30 (West Longitude Date) and established a line form Agana Bay on the west coast to Pago Point on the east coast. Patrols sent out to reconnoiter the southern half of the island have encountered only sporadic resistance.

Through July 30 our troops have counted 6,205 enemy dead and have interned 775 civilians. Close support is being given to advance troops by surface ships, which are now firing from both sides of the island.

Troops of the Second and Fourth Marine Divisions continued their advance on Tinian Island during July 30 and have forced the enemy into a small pocket near Lalo Point at the southern tip of the island. Difficult terrain in this area impeded progress during the day. Our attack on the last enemy defenses began in the early morning and was preceded by more than two hours of bombing and naval gunfire.

On July 29 Liberators of the Seventh AAF dropped nearly seventy-five tons of bombs on Japanese installations and an airfield at Truk. Several enemy fighters attempted to intercept our bombers. One enemy fighter was destroyed, another probably destroyed, and two more damaged. Four of our planes were damaged but all returned.

†WITEK, FRANK PETER

Rank and Organization: Private First Class, U.S. Marine Corps Reserve, 3d Marine Division.
Born: December 1921, Derby, Connecticut.
Entered Service At: Illinois.
Place and Date: Battle of Finegayen, Guam, Marianas Islands, August 3, 1944.
Citation: For conspicuous gallantry and intrepidity at the risk of his life above and beyond the call of duty while serving with the 1st Battalion, 9th Marines, 3d Marine Division, during the battle of Finegayen at Guam, Marianas, on August 3, 1944. When his rifle platoon was halted by heavy surprise fire from well-camouflaged enemy positions, Pfc. Witek daringly remained standing to fire a full magazine from his automatic weapon at point-blank range into a depression housing Japanese Troops, killing 8 of the enemy and enabling the greater part of his platoon to take cover. During his platoon's withdrawal for consolidation of lines, he remained to safeguard a severely wounded comrade, courageously returning the enemy's fire until the arrival of stretcher bearers, and then covering the evacuation by sustained fire as he moved backward toward his own lines. With his platoon again pinned down by a hostile machinegun, Pfc. Witek, on his own initiative, moved forward boldly to the reinforcing tanks and infantry, alternately throwing handgrenades and firing as he advanced to within 5 to 10 yards of the enemy position, and destroying the hostile machinegun emplacement and an additional 8 Japanese before he himself was struck down by an enemy rifleman. His valiant and inspiring action effectively reduced the enemy's firepower, thereby enabling his platoon to attain its objective, and reflects the highest credit upon Pfc. Witek and the U.S. Naval Service. He gallantly gave his life for his country.

†WILSON, ROBERT LEE

Rank and Organization: Private First Class. U.S. Marine Corps, 2d Marine Division.
Born: May 24, 1921, Centralia, Illinois.
Entered Service At: Illinois.

Place and Date: Tinian Island, Marianas Group, August 4, 1944.

Citation: For conspicuous gallantry and intrepidity at the risk of his life above and beyond the call of duty while serving with the 2d Battalion, 6th Marines, 2d Marine Division, during action against enemy Japanese forces at Tinian Island, Marianas Group, on August 4, 1944. As 1 of a group of marines advancing through heavy underbrush to neutralize isolated points of resistance, Pfc. Wilson daringly preceded his companions toward a pile of rocks where Japanese troops were supposed to be hiding. Fully aware of the danger involved, he has moving forward while the remainder of the squad, armed with automatic rifles, closed together in the rear when an enemy grenade landed in the midst of the group. Quick to act, Pfc. Wilson cried a warning to the men and unhesitatingly threw himself on the grenade, heroically sacrificing his own life that the others might live and fulfill their mission. His exceptional valor, his courageous loyalty and unwavering devotion to duty in the face of grave peril reflect the highest credit upon Pfc. Wilson and the U.S. Naval Service. He gallantly gave his life for his country.

Note: The following is a newspaper account of the preceding battle for which both Pfc. Witek and Pfc. Wilson were awarded the Medal of Honor:

AMERICANS THRUST TWO MILES ON GUAM

• • •

Japanese Are Driven Well Into
Third of Island as Carrier
Planes Back Advance

• • •

ENEMY DEAD REACH 7,893

• • •

Stars and Stripes Raised on Tinian
As Marines Mop Up Foe's Remnants

• • •

PEARL HARBOR August 3 – Army and Marine forces on Guam have battered forward for gains averaging two miles against stiffening enemy resistance, Admiral Chester W. Nimitz stated today.

On the west coast of Guam our line advanced farther along the shoreline of Tumon Bay and on the shoreline of Sassayan Point. An important road junction near the town for Finegayan is now under our control.

[The new gains on Guam put the Americans well into the upper third of the island, The Associated Press said.

[The hard-driving Americans were advancing with the continuing support of carrier-based aircraft. Those planes yesterday flew low over enemy fortifications and storage areas in the northern end of Guam to shatter targets with bombs and rocket fire]

Admiral Nimitz said that the enemy dead counted on Guam had mounted to 7,893.

A large number of civilians have sought protection behind American lines, the Admiral said. Guam civilians are considered friendly to us and about 7,000 are now being cared for.

The American flag was raised yesterday on Tinian, adding another thirty-two square miles to American possessions in the western Pacific. Admiral Nimitz said that the flag-raising ceremony eleven days after marines of the Second and Fourth Divisions began the invasion.

He said that scattered remnants of the beaten Japanese garrison were being "dealt with" by the marines, who have thus far killed an estimated 5,000 enemy troops and interned about 4,000 civilians.

Last Stand on Orote

WITH THE MARINES ON OROTE PENINSULA Guam, July 30 (Delayed) – The Japanese defense of the Orote airfield, prize of the peninsula campaign, came to a flaming end yesterday as marine tanks, rifles, machine guns and mortars blasted enemy fortifications and then infantrymen surged along the sides of the field advancing over heaps of blackened, broken corpses, many still burning.

The marines began their advance from the old marine barracks at 8:15 A.M. and by 3 P.M., after seven hours under incessant fire, organized resistance had been completely overcome. At sunset the marines were at the end of the peninsula, about a mile beyond the airfield, this ending the first phase in the recapture of Guam.

During the early afternoon the airfield itself was an island of peace surrounded by the smoke and noise of the battle. Both the marines and the japanese stayed clear of the bare coral strip, which was in some parts mined. Blue smoke of rifle and machine-gun fire and gray dust from shell burst rose over the palms bordering the field as marine riflemen advanced along a line of revetments toward a group of concrete buildings midway along the strip where the Japanese made their last stand.

The doomed Japanese took final refuge in bomb-proof shelters. Grim mud-caked marines under the command of Capt. William Stewart of Binghamton, N. Y., whose company led the advance throughout the peninsula campaign, finally broke the enemy's back by crawling ahead of tanks and tossing grenades into cellars and dugouts, slaughtering Japanese by the score.

Some Japanese, surviving the deadly hall of bursting grenades, ran out among the palms and scurried like moles in a field of knee-high wild poinsettia. Many of these died a sudden, mangling death when a mortar platoon commanded by Lieut. Thomas Daly of Los Angeles opened fire from positions among coconut log and coral revetments screened by coral filled oil drums.

†**LINDSEY, DARRELL R. (Air Mission)**
Rank and Organization: Captain, U.S. Army Air Corps.
Born: Jefferson, Iowa.
Entered Service At: Storm Lake, Iowa.
Place and Date: L'Isle Adam railroad bridge over the Seine in occupied France August 9, 1944.
Citation: On August 9, 1944 Capt. Lindsey led a formation of 30 B-26 medium bombers on a hazardous mission to destroy the strategic enemy-held L'Isle Adam railroad bridge over the Seine in occupied France. With most of the bridges over the Seine destroyed, the heavily fortified L'Isle Adam bridge was of inestimable value to the enemy in moving troops, supplies, and equipment to Paris. Capt. Lindsey was fully aware of the fierce resistance that would be encountered. Shortly after reaching enemy territory the formation was buffeted with heavy and accurate antiaircraft fire. By skillful evasive action, Capt. Lindsey was able to elude much of the enemy flak, but just before entering the bombing run his B-26 was peppered with holes. During the bombing run the enemy fire was even more intense, and Capt. Lindsey's right engine received a direct hit and burst into flames. Despite the fact that his ship was hurled out of formation by the violence of the concussion, Capt. Lindsey brilliantly maneuvered back into the lead position without disrupting the flight. Fully aware that the gasoline tanks might explode at any moment, Capt. Lindsey gallantly elected to continue the perilous bombing run. With fire streaming from his right engine and his right wing half enveloped in flames, he led his formation over the target upon which the bombs were dropped with telling effect. Immediately after the objective was attacked, Capt. Lindsey gave the order for the crew to parachute from the doomed aircraft. With magnificent cool-

ness and superb pilotage, and without regard for his own life, he held the swiftly descending airplane in a steady glide until the members of the crew could jump to safety. With the right wing completely enveloped in flames and an explosion of the gasoline tank imminent, Capt. Lindsey still remained unperturbed. The last man to leave the stricken plane was the bombardier, who offered to lower the wheels so that Capt. Lindsey might escape from the nose. Realizing that this might throw the aircraft into an uncontrollable spin and jeopardize the bombardier's chances of escape, Capt. Lindsey refused the offer. Immediately after the bombardier had bailed out, and before Capt, Lindsey was able to follow, the right gasoline tank exploded. The aircraft sheathed in fire, went into a steep dive and was seen to explode as it crashed. All who are living today from this plane owe their lives to the fact that Capt. Lindsey remained cool and showed supreme courage in this emergency.

OFFICIAL COMMUNIQUE:
UNITED NATIONS
SUPREME HEADQUARTERS Allied Expeditionary Force Communique 123:

Allied forces in Brittany are closing in on the ports of St. Malo, Brest and Lorient. Converging columns have pushed to within five miles of Lorient and other forces have engaged the enemy four miles from Brest. Fighting is now in progress in the outskirts of St. Malo.

Large fires are burning at both St. Malo and Lorient, indicating destruction by the Germans of their supplies in both ports.

Confused fighting is in progress around Mortain on the Normandy front. To the northwest of Mortain a German counter-attack, with tanks and infantry, was broken at Gathemo, which has been freed. The drive penetrated about one mile into our line, but heavy losses were inflicted on the enemy by Allied troops, assisted by planes and artillery.

The front line in this area now extends generally along the road between Gathemo and Vire. In the vicinity of Vire the enemy is offering stubborn resistance south and southwest of the town.

The Allied drive south of Caen progressed some 7,000 yards yesterday. After heavy and accurate preliminary bombing, first objectives were secured by first light and number of pockets of the enemy, which had been by-passed in this first advance, were cleared up during the day.

The advance continued at midday in the face of determined enemy resistance supported by armor. The villages of La Hogue, Hautmesnil, Cintheaux and St. Aignan and the town of Bretteville-sur-Laize are in our hands.

The bridgehead over the River Orne has been extended and local advances were made to improve our positions east of Mount Pincon.

Targets in the immediate support of ground forces southeast of Caen and air-fields at La Perthe, Clastres, Villacoublay and Romilly-sur-Seine were attacked successfully by heavy bombers in a day of great air activity.

By last night and during darkness heavy bombers also attacked fuel dumps in forest at Chantilly, Aire-sur-Lys and Lucheux.

Road and rail bridges were attacked by medium and light bombers, with satis-factory results reported over nine widespread targets, most of them east of the Seine. Rail yards at Igoville, south of Rougen were also attacked.

Long - range and short - range fighters in a considerable numbers swept the area south and east of the battle zone throughout the day, taking heavy toll of enemy transport and attacking gun positions.

Three enemy minesweepers in the Bay of Biscay were attacked by rocket-firing costal aircraft and were left ablaze.

During the night fires were started among oil tanks south of Fontainebleau and a train at Dijon was also set afire by light bombers.

CONNOR, JAMES P.

Rank and Organization: Sergeant, U.S. Army, 7th Infantry, 3d Infantry Division.

Born: Wilmington, Delaware.

Entered Service At: Wilmington, Delaware.

Place and Date: Cape Cavalaire, southern France, August 15, 1944.

Citation: For conspicuous gallantry and intrepidity at the risk of his life above and beyond the call of duty. On August 15, 1944, Sgt. Connor, through sheer grit and determination, led his platoon in clearing an enemy vastly superior in numbers and firepower from strongly entrenched positions on Cape Cavalaire, removing a grave enemy threat to his division during the amphibious landing in southern France, and thereby insured safe and unin-terrupted landings for the huge volume of men and materiel which fol-lowed. His battle patrol landed on "Red Beach" with the mission of de-stroying the strongly fortified enemy positions with utmost speed. From the peninsula the enemy had commanding observation and seriously men-aced the vast landing operations taking place. Though knocked down and seriously wounded in the neck by a hanging mine which killed his platoon lieutenant, Sgt. Connor refused medical aid and with his driving spirit prac-tically carried the platoon across several thousand yards of mine-saturated beach through intense fire from mortars, 20-mm. flak guns, machineguns, and snipers. Enroute to the Cape he personally shot and killed 2 snipers. The platoon sergeant was killed and Sgt. Connor became platoon leader. Receiving a second wound, which lacerated his shoulder and back, he again refused evacuation, expressing determination to carry on until physically unable to continue. He reassured and prodded the hesitating men of his decimated platoon forward through almost impregnable mortar concentrations. Again emphasizing the prevalent urgency of their mission, he impelled his men toward a group of buildings honeycombed with enemy snipers and machineguns. Here he received his third grave wound, this time in the leg, felling him in his tracks. Still resolved to carry on, he relinquished command only after his attempts proved that it was physically impossible to stand. Nevertheless, from his prone position, he gave the orders and directed his men in assaulting the enemy. Infused with Sgt. Connor's dogged determination, the platoon, though reduced to less than one-third of its original 36 men, out-flanked and rushed the enemy with such furiousness that they killed 7, captured 40, and seized 3 machineguns and considerable other materiel, and took all their assigned objectives, successfully completing their mission. By his repeated examples of tenaciousness and indomitable spirit Sgt, Connor transmitted his heroism to his men until they became a fighting team which could not be stopped.

OFFICIAL COMMUNIQUE:
UNITED NATIONS
ROME Aug. 15 – A special communique:

Today American, British and French troops, strongly supported by Allied air forces, are being landed by American, British and French fleets on the southern coast of France.

ROME Aug. 15 – A Headquarters announcement accompanying the special communique:

The assault, which was in strong force, was led by specially trained Allied troops, many of them veterans of previous invasions and campaigns in the Mediterranean theater. Air-borne troops were among those participating. Ground troops went ashore form the invasion fleet at several points along a wide front.

This planning an execution of this operation had the advantage of experience gained in the successful North African, Sicilian, Salerno and Anzio landings.

The invasion troops underwent several weeks of intensive training in amphibious operations in preparation for his latest blow against the enemy, who in less than two years has been driven from North Africa, Sicily, and most of Italy through the combined force of the Allies in the Mediterranean.

A special Navy communique:

Various beaches over which ships of the United states, British and French Navies are landing American and French troops in southern France extended over a considerable part of the coast between Nice and Marsellies. More than 800 ships of all types with many mixed vessels, are taking part in operations, which are wide spread. Warships of the Royal Canadian Navy are participating, and vessels flying the ensigns of the Netherlands, Poland Greece and Belgium also are present.

The assault craft started to move in toward the coast and landed exactly on time this morning in calm clear weather. They were preceded close inshore by minesweepers, and the attack was supported by a heavy covering of gun fire from battleships, cruisers destroyers and other ships and craft of the Allied Navy.

Air craft Royal an United States Navies are cooperating with the Allied Air Forces. Responsibility for landing and establishing the army on shore is naval and the naval commander has ordered the assault pressed home with relentless force. The operations continue.

A later special communique:

By mid-morning all landings were proceeding successfully according to schedule against only light ground opposition and no air opposition. The supporting airborne operation was also successfully executed.

BENDER, STANLEY

Rank and Organization: Staff Sergeant, U.S. Army, Company E, 7th Infantry, 3d Infantry Division.
Born: October 31, 1909, Carlisle, West Verginia.
Entered Service At: Chicago, Illinois.
Place and Date: Near La Lande, France, August 17, 1944.
Citation: For conspicuous gallantry and intrepidity at risk of life above and beyond the call of duty. On August 17 1944, near La Lande, France, S/ Sgt. Bender climbed on top of a knocked-out tank, in the face of withering machinegun fire which had halted the advance of his company, in an effort to locate the source of this fire. Although bullets ricocheted off the turret at his feet, he nevertheless remained upright in full view of the enemy for over 2 minutes. Locating the enemy machineguns on a knoll 200 yards away, he ordered 2 squads to cover him and led his men down an irrigation ditch, running a gauntlet of intense machinegun fire, which completely blanketed 50 yards of his advance and wounded 4 of his men. While the Germans hurled handgrenades at the ditch, he stood his ground until his

squad caught up with him, then advanced alone, in a wide flanking approach, to the rear of the knoll. He walked deliberately a distance of 40 yards, without cover, in full view of the Germans and under a hail of both enemy and friendly fire, to the first machinegun and knocked it out with a single short burst. Then he made his way through the strongpoint, despite bursting handgrenades, toward the second machinegun, 25 yards distant, whose 2-man crew swung the machinegun around and fired two bursts at him, but he walked calmly through the fire and, reaching the edge of the emplacement, dispatched the crew. Signaling his men to rush the rifle pits, he then walked 35 yards further to kill an enemy rifleman and returned to lead his squad in the destruction of the 8 remaining Germans in the strongpoint. His audacity so inspired the remainder of the assault company that the men charged out of their positions, shouting and yelling, to overpower the enemy roadblock and sweep into town, knocking out 2 antitank guns, killing 37 Germans and capturing 26 others. He had sparked and led the assault company in an attack which overwhelmed the enemy, destroying a roadblock, taking a town, seizing intact 3 bridges over the Maravenne River, and capturing commanding terrain which dominated the area.

OFFICIAL COMMUNIQUE:
UNITED NATIONS
SUPREME HEADQUARTERS Allied Expeditionary Force, Aug. 17 –Communique 131:

Allied troops have made further gains in the Normandy pocket. Our forces are clearing the last enemy from the town of Falaise. East of the town heavy fighting continues. Most of the road from Falaise to Conde is in our hands and the town of Conde has been captured.

Forward elements advancing from the west and northwest have reached Flers. To the east enemy opposition was bitter and the Allied advance was made more difficult by the enemy's large-scale use of mines, booby traps and demolition.

Farther west advances have been made east of Tincherbray, which has been freed, and east from Ger. Mopping-up has been completed in the vicinity of Juvigny and in the Forest of Andain, east of Domfront.

North of La Ferte-Macre and northeast of Domfront gains of up to six miles have been made against resistance which varies from light to moderate. North of Ranes, which has been by-passed, our units are encountering heavy opposition. In Argentan the enemy still holds most of the city and fighting is in progress.

In Brittany the port of Dinard has been completely occupied. The German garrison at St. Malo is maintaining stubborn defense in the citadel.

Bad weather limited the Allied air effort over northern France yesterday. Five bridges over the River Risle, which flows parallel to the Seine on the western side, were attacked by our medium bombers and an ammunition dump near Rouen was bombed by light bombers.

Last night crossing points on the Seine and road transport near Dijon were successfully attacked by our light bombers. Night fighters destroyed seven enemy aircraft over the battle area.

HAWK, JOHN D.

Rank and Organization: Sergeant, U.S. Army, Company E, 359th Infantry, 90th Infantry Division.
Born: May 30, 1924, San Francisco, California.
Entered Service At: Bremerton, Washington.
Place and Date: Near Chambois, France, August 20, 1944.
Citation: Sgt. Hawk manned a light machine gun on August 20, 1944, near Chambois, France, a key point in the encirclement which created the Falaise Pocket. During an enemy counterattack, his position was menaced by a strong force of tanks and infantry. His fire forced the infantry to withdraw, but an artillery shell knocked out his gun and wounded him in the right thigh. Securing a bazooka, he and another man stalked the tanks and forced them to retire to a wooded section. In the lull which followed, Sgt. Hawk reorganized 2 machine gun squads and, in the face of intense enemy fire, directed the assembly of one workable weapon from two damaged guns. When another enemy assault developed, he was forced to pull back from the pressure of spearheading armor. Two of our tank destroyers were brought up. Their shots were ineffective because of the terrain until Sgt. Hawk, despite his wound, boldly climbed to an exposed position on a knoll where, unmoved by fusillades from the enemy, he became a human aiming stake for the destroyers. Realizing that his shouted fire directions could not be heard above the noise of battle, he ran back to the destroyers through a concentration of bullets and shrapnel to correct the range. He returned to his exposed position, repeating this performance until 2 of the tanks were knocked out an a third driven off. Still at great risk, he continued to direct the destroyers' fire into the Germans' wooded position until the enemy came out and surrendered. Sgt. Hawk's fearless initiative and heroic conduct, even while suffering from a painful wound, was in large measure responsible for crushing 2 desperate attempts of the enemy to escape from the Falaise Picket and for taking more than 500 prisoners.

OFFICIAL COMMUNIQUE:
UNITED NATIONS
SUPREME HEADQUARTERS Allied Expeditionary Force, Aug 20 –Communique 134:

Allied forces have advanced to the vicinity of the Seine and have closed the enemy corridor south of Falaise. Leading elements moving north and northeast from Dreux have reached a point eighteen miles beyond city to the vicinity of Mantes-Gassicourt.

Allied forces from the north and south have met in Chambois, sealing the exit south of Falaise. The area of the enemy pocket has again been reduced substantially by advances from all directions, particularly southward toward Montbard and north Ecouche, where heavy fighting has taken place.

West of Arfentan, in the are southeast of Putanges, we have completed mopping up of enemy groups behind the southern edge of the pocket.

Farther north, in the area east of St. Pierre-sur-Dives, our troops have continued to thrust eastward and have established three bridges heads over the river Vie and Livarot, Coupesarte and Grandchamp.

No changes are reported in the areas of Chartres and Orleans, or in Brittany Peninsula.

Our Normandy-based planes continued their heavy planes continued their heavy attacks on tanks and motor vehicles of all types retreating eastward and against river barges on the Seine. They also provided close support for our advancing columns.

Roads in the escape corridor in the vicinity of Orbec are strewn with knocked-out vehicle, often making it difficult for our pilots to select active targets. More than 800 motor trucks were destroyed and 600 damaged yesterday from the line Falaise-Argentan northeastward to the Seine in addition to forty tanks destroyed and many others damaged.

ROME, Aug, 20 – Communique:
SOUTHERN FRANCE

Troops of the Seventh Army, in a swift-drive in the northwest sector of the southern France bridgehead, have advanced as much as twenty miles. With American infantry and French armored forces operating together in this area, the towns of St. Maximin Rians and Barpols were liberated.

The total of prisoners taken now numbers more than 12,000. Our casualties continue light.

†CAREY, ALVIN P.

Rank and Organization: Staff Sergeant, U.S. Army, 38th Infantry, 2d Infantry Division.
Born: August 16, 1916, Lycippus, Pennsylvania.
Entered Service At: Laughlinstown, Pennsylvania.
Place and Date: Near Plougastel, Brittany, France, August 23, 1916.
Citation: For conspicuous gallantry and intrepidity at the risk of his life, above and beyond the call of duty, on August 23, 1944. S/Sgt Carey, leader

of a machinegun section, was advancing with his company in the attack on the strongly held enemy Hill 154, near Plougastel, Brittany, France. The advance was held up when the attacking units were pinned down by intense enemy machinegun fire from a pillbox 200 yards up the hill. From his position covering the right flank, S/Sgt. Carey displaced his guns to an advanced position and then, upon his own initiative, armed himself with as many handgrenades as he could carry and without regard for his personal safety started alone up the hill toward the pillbox. Crawling forward under its withering fire, he proceeded 150 yards when he met a German rifleman whom he killed with his carbine. Continuing his steady forward movement until he reached grenade-throwing distance, he hurled his grenades at the pillbox opening in the face of intense enemy fire which wounded him mortally. Undaunted, he gathered his strength and continued his grenade attack until one entered and exploded within the pillbox, killing the occupants and putting their guns out of action. Inspired by S.Sgt. Carey's heroic act, the riflemen quickly occupied the position and overpowered the remaining enemy resistance in the vicinity.

OFFICIAL COMMUNIQUE:
United Nations
SUPREME HEADQUARTERS, Allied Expeditionary Force, Aug. 23 –Communique 137:

Allied forces have liberated Sens on the east bank of the River Yonne. Pithiviers and Etampes are also in our hands.

North of Dreux other units are moving northwestward between the Rivers Seine and Eure. A drive northward between Dreux and Verneuil has liberated Nonancourt, and the advance has carried to a point north of St. Andre-de-l'Eure.

To the west considerable advances have been made along the whole Allied front between Laigle and the Seine. In the center of this wide sweep our forces are fighting in Lisieux.

North of the town our forces have surged forward all along the line and captured Cabourg, Houlgate, Villers-sur-Mer and Deuville along the coast and have reached Trouville, Pont l'Eveque and the line of the River Touques farther south.

South of Lisieux our troops have established a broad bridgehead extending for several miles farther east across the Orbec River. Other troops have advanced across the River Vie through Vimoutiers, crossed the River Touques and have reached the area of the town of Orbec.

Continuing the advance from Gace, our troops have captured Laigle.

The Falaise pocket has been eliminated.

Allied fighter-bombers and fighters continue to pound the enemy at the Seine crossings, destroying more than 200 vehicles, fifteen boats and barges and six tanks. These attacks, made through rain and thick cloud, were often delivered at 200 feet despite heavy anti-aircraft fire and strong air opposition.

More than 150 railway cars were destroyed or damaged by other formations operating to the east and southeast of Paris. Marshaling yards at Dijon and Chagny were attacked with good results.

At least thirty-one enemy aircraft were destroyed in the air and six on the ground. Preliminary reports show two of ours are missing.

During a gun action fought Monday morning south of Cap d'Antifer between light coastal forces of the Royal Navy and an enemy patrol of armed trawlers and R-boats, one trawler was severely damaged and an R-boat destroyed. Two other R-boats received serious damage.

ROME, Aug. 23 – A communique:

FRANCE

American troops of the Seventh Army, in a swift advance northward of some 140 airline miles from their points of landing in southern France, have entered the town of Grenoble. They have had the effective cooperation of French Forces of the Interior in their drive since the early stages of the campaign. Towns taken enroute include Dogne, Sisteron, Aspres, Cap St. Bonnet and L'Argentiere.

French troops have cleared and occupied Hyeres after heavy fighting and have closed in on Toulon from the east. Within Toulon heavy fighting continues. The French have improved their positions and advanced further toward the port area.

The encirclement of Marseille is continuing on a broad front. French forward elements have penetrated to within three miles of the eastern outskirts of the city, while to the northwest, American columns were a similar distance from Etang de Berre.

Further advances have been made in the Durance River valley. More than 17,000 prisoners have been taken.

GARMAN, HAROLD A.
Rank and Organization: Private, U.S. Army, Company B, 5th Medical Battalion, 5th Infantry Division.
Born: February 26, 1918, Fairfield, Illinois.
Entered Service At: Albion, Illinois.
Place and Date: Near Montereau, France, August 25, 1944.
Citation: For conspicuous gallantry and intrepidity at the risk of his life above and beyond the call of duty. On August 25, 1944, in the vicinity of Montereau, France, the enemy was sharply contesting any enlargement of

the bridgehead which our forces had established on the northern bank of the Seine River in this sector. Casualties were being evacuated to the southern shore in assault boats paddled by litter bearers from a medical battalion. Pvt. Garman, also a litter bearer in this battalion, was working on the friendly shore carrying the wounded from the boats to waiting ambulances. As 1 boatload of wounded reached mid-stream, a German machinegun suddenly opened fire upon it from a commanding position on the northern bank 100 yards away. All of the men in the boat immediately took to the water except 1 man who was so badly wounded he could not rise from his litter. Two other patients who were unable to swim because of their wounds clung to the sides of the boat. Seeing the extreme danger of these patients, Pvt. Garman without a moment's hesitation plunged into the Seine. Swimming directly into a hail of machinegun bullets, he rapidly reached the assault boat and then while still under accurately aimed fire towed the boat with great effort to the southern shore. This soldier's moving heroism not only saved the lives of the three patients but so inspired his comrades that additional assault boats were immediately procured and the evacuation of the wounded resumed. Pvt. Garman's great courage and his heroic devotion to the highest tenets of the Medical Corps may be written with great pride in the annals of the corps.

OFFICIAL COMMUNIQUE:
United Nations
SUPREME HEADQUARTERS, Allied Expeditionary Force, Aug. 25 —Communique 139:

After overcoming considerable enemy opposition, elements of the Second French Armored Division under General Leclerc have entered the outskirts of Paris.

South and southeast of the capital Allied troops have crossed the Seine near Melun and in the Fontainebleau area.

Farther up the river we occupied Montereau. East of Montargis, which is now in our hands, our units have made further gains.

Our forces are now closing in toward the Seine estuary and have made further advances. The thrust from the south has brought us to the southern outskirts of Elbeuf and to Gaillon, southeast of Louviers.

The advance from the west gained fresh impetus yesterday after the last enemy resistance at Lisieux and Pont-l'Eveque had been overcome. Allied forces moving northeast from Monnai have reached the area of Broglie.

In a rapid thrust from the Orbec area, our troops have captured Thiberville and advanced several miles to the banks of the river Risle east of Bernay, which is in our hands.

Other troops from Lisieux have reached the Risle near Brionne. Southeast of Pont-l'Eveque our forces, after seizing high ground at Blangy, have advanced to the line of the river Calonne, from the area of Moyaux on the right to Les Authieux on the left.

Farther north we have captured the Foret de St. Gatien and have reached the main road south of Beuzeville. On the coast we have captured Trouville and are approaching Honfleur.

Enemy escape lines in the Seine area were attacked yesterday by fighters and fighter-bombers as weather permitted.

Attacks were continued last night by light bombers, which also struck at motor transport in the Dieppe-Beauvais area and bombed railways in Belgium and northeast France. E-boat and R-boat pens at Ijmuiden, Holland, and shipping at Brest were attacked with good results in daylight yesterday by heavy bombers.

ROME, Aug. 25 – A communique:

FRANCE

American troops of the Seventh Army have occupied Cannes. They also occupied Grasse in an advance on the eastern sector of the southern France bridgehead.

French forces have further tightened their grip on Toulon and occupied the land arsenal inside the Ollioules, to the northwest of Toulon. The enemy is still offering resistance in the port area.

In Marseille, mopping up of enemy resistance near the port is in progress.

To the northwest, American forward armies have advanced to less than ten miles east of Aries, on the Rhone River, and north and south of Salon have also made further progress.

The number of prisoners taken thus far is estimated at 20,000.

GREGG, STEPHEN R.
Rank and Organization: Second Lieutenant, U.S. Army, 143d Infantry, 36th Infantry Division.
Born: New York, New York.
Entered Service At: Bayonne, New Jersey.
Place and Date: Near Montelimar, France, August 27, 1944.
Citation: For conspicuous gallantry and intrepidity at risk of life above and beyond the call of duty on August 27, 1944, in the vicinity of Montelimar, France. As his platoon advanced upon the enemy positions, the leading scout was fired upon and 2d Lt. Gregg (then a Tech. Sgt.) immediately put his machineguns into action to cover the advance of the riflemen. The Germans, who were at close range, threw handgrenades at the

riflemen, killing some and wounding 7. Each time a medical aid man attempted to reach the wounded,the Germans fired a him. Realizing the seriousness of the situation, 2d Lt. Gregg took 1 of the light .30 caliber machineguns, and firing from the hip, started boldly up the hill with the medical aid man following him. Although the enemy was throwing handgrenades at him, 2d Lt. Gregg remained and fired into the enemy positions while the medical aid man removed the 7 wounded men to safety. When 2d Lt. Gregg had expended all his ammunition, he was covered by 4 Germans who ordered him to surrender. Since the attention of most of the Germans had been diverted by watching this action, friendly riflemen were able to maneuver into firing positions. One, seeing 2d Lt. Gregg's situation, opened fire on his captors. The 4 Germans hit the ground and thereupon 2d Lt. Gregg recovered a machine pistol from one of the Germans and managed to escape to his other machinegun positions. He manned a gun, firing at his captors, killed 1 of them and wounded the other. This action so discouraged the Germans that the platoon was able to continue its advance up the hill to achieve its objective. The following morning, just prior to daybreak, the Germans launched a strong attack, supported by tanks, in an attempt to drive Company L from the hill. As these tanks moved along the valley and their foot troops advanced up the hill, 2d Lt. Gregg immediately ordered his mortars into action. During the day, by careful observation, he was able to direct effective fire on the enemy, inflicting heavy casualties, By late afternoon he had directed 600 rounds when his communication to the mortars was knocked out. Without hesitation he started checking his wires, although the area was under heavy enemy small-arms and artillery fire. When he was within 100 yards of his mortar position, 1 of his men informed him that the section had been captured and the Germans were using the mortars to fire on the company. 2d Lt. Gregg with this man and another nearby rifleman started for the gun position where he could see 5 Germans firing his mortars. He ordered the 2 men to cover him, crawled up, threw a handgrenade into the position, and then charged it. The handgrenade killed 1, injured 2; 2d Lt. Gregg took the other 2 prisoners, and put his mortars back into action.

OFFICIAL COMMUNIQUE:
United Nations
SUPREME HEADQUARTERS, Allied Expeditionary Force, Aug. 27 —Communique 141:

Allied troops advancing eastward toward the Upper Seine Valley have reached the river in the northern outskirts of Troyes and at a point twelve miles farther south.

Nearer Paris, armored units have launched an attack between Melun and Corbeil, where a bridgehead had been previously established.

Approximately 10,000 enemy troops, including the German commander and his staff, were taken prisoner in Paris. One enemy strong point has been holding out in Champigny on the southeast edge of the city, and small enemy groups still operate in the northeast and northwest suburbs. Within the city, formal resistance has ceased, but some sniping continues.

In the Seine Valley, armored elements have advanced along the south side of the river in the area between Mantes-Gassicourt and Paris, encountering slight opposition.

Allied forces have closed in toward the south bank of the Seine and have crossed the river at Vernon and Pont-de-l'Arche. Farther west, our troops have captured Bourgtheroulde and are clearing the enemy from the forest of La Londe. In the coastal area, the enemy has driven over the Lower Risle and Pont Audemer is in our hands.

Heavy fighting is in progress in the area north of Brest on the Brittany Peninsula, where the enemy garrison is offering stubborn resistance. Gun positions and fortified targets at Brest again were attacked without loss by escorted heavy bombers.

Attacks on enemy transport in northeast France by our fighter-bombers and fighters are being extended into Belgium and Germany. Locomotives, hundreds of motor vehicles and railway cars, some loaded with ammunition and oil, have been destroyed or damaged during the last twenty-four hours, especially near the Seine at Rouen. Marshaling yards at Gisors and Charleroi also were hit. Rail movements in the Lille-Amiens-Dieppe area have been pounded incessantly.

Concentrations of enemy troops and vehicles seeking passage over the Seine were hit throughout the day by waves of escorted light and medium bombers which dropped fragmentation and high-explosive bombs. Their targets included four fuel dumps in the east and southeast of Rouen.

Enemy air opposition was slight but heavy anti-aircraft fire has been concentrated at many points to the east of the Seine. Six enemy aircraft were shot down and at least twelve others were destroyed on the ground. Seven of our bombers and seventeen fighters are missing.

ROME, Aug. 27 – A communique:

SOUTHERN FRANCE

French forces have completed the occupation of the city of Toulon with the capture of the Six-Fours fortifications and the district of Bregaillon and Marvivo. Enemy resistance continues only on the peninsula south of the city and in the fort south of Six-Fours.

In Marseille, much progress was made in liquidating scattered enemy pockets.

Advances of American troops eastward along the Riviera coast from Antibes continues slowly. The opposition is chiefly artillery fire and dense minefields.

†McVEIGH, JOHN J.

Rank and Organization: Sergeant, U.S. Army, Company H, 23d Infantry, 2d Infantry Division.
Born: Philadelphia, Pennsylvania.
Entered Service At: Philadelphia, Pennsylvania.
Place and Date: Near Brest, France, August 29, 1944.
Citation: For conspicuous gallantry and intrepidity at the risk of his life above and beyond the call of duty near Brest, France, on August 29, 1944. Shortly after dusk an enemy counterattack of platoon strength was launched against 1 platoon of Company G, 23d Infantry. Since the Company G platoon was not dug in and had just begun to assume defensive positions along a hedge, part of the line sagged momentarily under heavy fire from small arms and 2 flak guns, leaving a section of heavy machineguns holding a wide frontage without rifle protection. The enemy drive moved so swiftly that German riflemen were soon almost on top of 1 machinegun position. Sgt. McVeigh, heedless of a tremendous amount of small-arms and flak fire directed toward him, stood up in full view of the enemy and directed the fire of his squad on the attacking Germans until his position was almost overrun. He then drew his trench knife, and singlehanded charged several of the enemy. In a savage hand-to-hand struggle, Sgt. McVeigh killed 1 German with the knife, his only weapon, and was advancing on 3 more of the enemy when he was shot down and killed with small-arms fire at point-blank range. Sgt. McVeigh's heroic act allowed the 2 remaining men in his squad to concentrate their machine-gun fire on the attacking enemy and then turn their weapons on the 3 Germans in the road, killing all 3. Fire from this machinegun and the other gun of the section was almost entirely responsible for stopping this enemy assault, and allowed the rifle platoon to which it was attached time to reorganize, assume positions on and hold the high ground gained during the day.

OFFICIAL COMMUNIQUE:
United Nations
SUPREME HEADQUARTERS, Allied Expeditionary Force, Aug. 30 –Communique 144:

Allied forces, continuing their sweep beyond Paris, have crossed the Aisne and Marne Rivers.

In the upper Marne Valley, mopping up is in progress in Vitry-le-Francois and our troops have reached Marson and Lepine, southeast and east of Chalons-sur-Marne. Other units are less than one mile south of Chalons, on the west side of the river.

Chateau-Thierry, on the Marne, has been occupied and our armored units have moved north to take Soisson and establish a bridgehead across the Aisne at Pont-Arcy, fourteen miles to the east. Our troops are advancing through the area between the Marne and Aisne, north of Meaux and Chateau-Thierry.

In the Paris area advances were made through the northeastern outskirts of the city beyond Le Bourget and Montmorency, and farther west elements cleared the Forest of St. Germain and moved northward to a point less than two miles south of Pontoise.

The bridgehead across the Seine in the vicinity of Mantes-Gassicourt was further enlarged to the north and east beyond Meulan. Contact was made with troops from bridgeheads to the north.

Advancing from the Vernon bridgehead, our troops pushed across the Paris-Rouen road to Etrepagny and from there to Longchamps. The Paris-Rouen road also was cut near the village of Ecouis by troops from the Louviers bridgehead. In the evening, contact was established between these two bridgeheads.

Southeast of Rouen, our forces advanced in the face of persistent opposition and captured the village of Boos, some five miles from the center of Rouen. In the Caudebec area, fighting was heavy, but the Forest of Brotonne was cleared and the whole of this loop of the river is now in our hands.

In Brittany, hard fighting continues at Brest as Allied forces close in slowly on the port.

Air operations yesterday were restricted by the weather.

Fighters and fighter-bombers attacked enemy rail and road movement over a wide area in the Low Countries, western Germany and in France as far south as Lyon. Large numbers of locomotives, railway cars and motor vehicles were attacked successfully and twenty enemy aircraft were destroyed on the ground near Brussels.

Six of our aircraft are missing.

LEE, DANIEL W.

Rank and Organization: First Lieutenant, U.S. Army, Troop A, 117th Cavalry Reconnaissance Squadron.
Born: June 23, 1919, Alma, Georgia.
Entered Service At: Alma, Georgia.
Place and Date: Montreval, France, September 2, 1944.

Citation: 1st Lt. (then 2d Lt.) Daniel W. Lee was leader of Headquarters Platoon, Troop A, 117th Cavalry Reconnaissance Squadron, Mechanized, at Montreval, France, on September 2, 1944, when the Germans mounted a strong counterattack, isolating the town and engaging its outnumbered defenders in a pitched battle. After the fight had raged for hours and our forces had withstood heavy shelling and armor-supported infantry attacks, 2d Lt. Lee organized a patrol to knock out mortars which were inflicting heavy casualties on the beleaguered reconnaissance troops. He led the small group to the edge of the town, sweeping enemy riflemen out of position on a ridge from which he observed 7 Germans manning 2 large mortars near an armored halftrack about 100 yards down the reverse slope. Armed with a rifle and grenades, he left his men on the high ground and crawled to within 30 yards of the mortars, where the enemy discovered him and unleashed machine-pistol fire which shattered his right thigh. Scorning retreat, bleeding and suffering intense pain, he dragged himself relentlessly forward. He killed 5 of the enemy with rifle fire, and the others fled before he reached their position. Fired on by an armored car, he took cover behind the German halftrack and there found a panzerfaust with which to neutralize this threat. Despite his wounds, he inched his way toward the car through withering machinegun fire, maneuvered into range, and blasted the vehicle with a round from the rocket launcher, forcing it to withdraw. Having cleared the slope of hostile troops, he struggled back to his men, where he collapsed from pain and loss of blood. 2d Lt. Lee's outstanding gallantry, willing risk of life, and extreme tenacity of purpose in coming to grips with the enemy, although suffering from grievous wounds, set an example of bravery and devotion to duty in keeping with the highest traditions of the military service.

URBAN, MATT

Rank and Organization: Lieutenant Colonel (then Captain), 2d Battalion, 60th Infantry Regiment, 9th Infantry Division.
Born: August 25, 1919, Buffalo, New York.
Entered Service At: Fort Bragg, North Carolina, July 2, 1941.
Place and Date: Renouf, France, June 14 to September 3, 1944.
Citation: Lieutenant Colonel (then Captain) Matt Urban, United States Army, who distinguished himself by a series of bold, heroic actions, exemplified by singularly outstanding combat leadership, personal bravery, and tenacious devotion to duty, during the period June 14 to September 3, 1944, while assigned to the 2d Battalion, 60th Infantry Regiment, 9th Infantry Division. On June 14, Captain Urban's company, attacking at Renouf, France, encountered heavy enemy small arms and tank fire. The enemy

tanks were unmercifully raking his unit's positions and inflicting heavy casualties. Captain Urban, realizing that his company was in imminent danger of being decimated, armed himself with a bazooka. He worked his way with an ammo carrier thorough hedgerows, under a continuing barrage of fire, to a point near the tanks. He brazenly exposed himself to the enemy fire and, firing the bazooka, destroyed both tanks. Responding to Captain Urban's action, his company moved forward and routed the enemy. Later that same day, still in the attack near Orgalndes, Captain Urban was wounded in the leg by direct fire from a 37mm tank-gun. He refused evacuation and continued to lead his company until they moved into defensive positions for the night. At 0500 hours the next day, still in the attack near Orgalndes, Captain Urban, though badly wounded, directed his company in another attack. One hour later he was again wounded. Suffering from two wounds, one serous, he was evacuated to England. In mid-July, while recovering from his wounds, he learned of his unit's severe losses in the hedgerows of Normandy. Realizing his unit's need for battle-tested leaders, he voluntarily left the hospital and hitchhiked his way back to his unit hear St. Lo, France. Arriving at the 2d Battalion Command Post at 1130 hours, July 25, he found that his unit had jumped-off at 1100 hours in the first attack of "Operation Cobra." Still limping from his leg wound, Captain Urban made his way forward to retake command of his company. He found his company held up by strong enemy opposition. Two supporting tanks had been destroyed and another, intact but with no tank commander or gunner, was not moving. He located a lieutenant in charge of the support tanks and directed a plan of attack to eliminate the enemy strong-point. The lieutenant and a sergeant were immediately killed by the heavy enemy fire when they tried to mount the tank. Captain Urban, though physically hampered by his leg wound and knowing quick action had to be taken, dashed through the scathing fire and mounted the tank. With enemy bullets ricocheting from the tank, Captain Urban ordered the tank forward and, completely exposed to the enemy fire, manned the machine gun and placed devastating fire on the enemy. His action, in the face of enemy fire, galvanized the battalion into action and they attacked and destroyed the enemy position. On August 2, Captain Urban was wounded in the chest by shell fragments and, disregarding the recommendation of the Battalion Surgeon, again refused evacuation. On August 6, Captain Urban became the commander of the 2d Battalion. On August 15, he was again wounded but remained with his unit. On September 3, the 2d Battalion was given the mission of establishing a crossing-point, on the Meuse River near Heer, Belgium. The enemy planned to stop the advance of the Allied Army by concentrating heavy forces at the Meuse. The 2d Battalion, attacking toward the crossing-point, encountered fierce enemy artillery, small arms, and mortar fire which stopped the attack. Captain Urban quickly moved from his command post to the lead position of the battalion. Reorganizing the attacking elements, he personally led a charge toward the enemy's strong-point. As the charge moved across the open terrain, Captain Urban was seriously wounded in the neck. Although unable to talk above a whisper from the paralyzing neck wound, and in danger of losing his life, he refused to be evacuated until the enemy was routed and his battalion had secured the crossing-point on the Meuse River. Captain Urban's personal leadership, limitless bravery and repeated extraordinary exposure to enemy fire served as an inspiration to his entire battalion. His valorous and intrepid actions reflect the utmost credit on him and uphold the noble traditions of the United States Army.

OFFICIAL COMMUNIQUE:
United Nations
SUPREME HEADQUARTERS, Allied Expeditionary Force, Sept. 2 –Communique No. 147:

Dieppe, Arras, and Verdun were liberated yesterday by Allied forces.

On the Channel coast, Allied troops entered Dieppe, where the enemy offered only slight opposition, and pushed northward to Le Treport. Further west, our troops have taken Bolbec, Fauville-en-Caux and have entered Yvetot.

Armored thrusts northward from Amiens passed through Arras soon after midday and by evening were established in strength north of the town. Another thrust captured the town of Doullens and further west our leading elements have reached the Somme southeast of Abbeville.

Light enemy resistance was met by Allied troops advancing northeast of Beauvais, and we have taken Coullemelle and Villers Tournelle, six miles west of Montididier.

Our advance through the Foret de Compiegne and through the southwestern edge of the town of Compiegne met heavy resistance.

North of the Aisne River, armored elements have taken Montcoronet, eighteen miles northeast of Laon. Other units have entered Rethel, twenty miles northeast of Reims, and have made gains to the edge of the Foret de Signy.

Allied troops have occupied Verdun. They have crossed the Meuse River in the town and also between St. Mihiel and Commercy. West of the Meuse, forces which advanced through the Argonne Forest are in areas of Baulny, Varennes and Clermont.

Troops moving through the area north of St. Dizier have reached a point near the Rhine-Marne canal. Southeast of St. Dizier, armored units have advanced through the vicinity of Joinville.

Enemy transport in the Low Countries and northern France was attacked throughout yesterday by fighters and fighter-bombers. Targets included motor and horse drawn vehicles, tanks, locomotives and barges. Fighter-bombers also attacked an ammunition dump near St. Quentin.

Targets for medium bombers were gun positions, strong points, and a motor park in the Brest area, troop concentrations near Abbeville and railway yards at Givet on the France-Belgian border.

Fighter-bombers continued the attack on the island of Cezembre, off St. Malo, which has also been bombarded by H.M.S. Malaya. Air observation was provided.

MERLI, GINO J.

Rank and Organization: Private First Class, U.S. Army, 18th Infantry, 1st Infantry Division.
Born: Scranton, Pennsylvania.
Entered Service At: Peckville, Pennsylvania.
Place and Date: Near Sars la Bruyere, Belguim, September 4-5, 1944.
Citation: Pfc. Merli was serving as a machine gunner in the vicinity of Sars la Bruyere, Belgium, on the night of September 4-5, 1944, when his company was attacked by a superior German force. Its position was overrun and he was surrounded when our troops were driven back by overwhelming numbers and firepower. Disregarding the fury of the enemy fire concentrated on him he maintained his position, covering the withdrawal of our riflemen and breaking the force of the enemy pressure. His assistant machine gunner was killed and the position captured; the other 8 members of the section were forced to surrender. Pfc. Meril slumped down beside the dead assistant gunner and feigned death. No sooner had the enemy group withdrawn then he was up and firing in all directions. Once more his position was taken and the captors found 2 apparently lifeless bodies. Throughout the night Pfc. Merli stayed at his weapon. By daybreak the enemy had suffered heavy losses, and as our troops launched an assault, asked for a truce. Our negotiating party, who accepted the German surrender, found Pfc. Merli still at his gun. On the battlefield lay 52 enemy dead, 19 of whom were directly in front of the gun. Pfc. Meril's gallantry and courage, and the losses and confusion that he caused the enemy, contributed materially to our victory.

OFFICIAL COMMUNIQUE:
United Nations
SUPREME HEADQUARTERS, Allied Expeditionary Force, Sept. 5 –Communique 150:

Antwerp has been liberated. After a two-day drive across Belgium, Allied armor entered the city yesterday and by evening was clearing the dock area.

Early in the day, our troops to the south captured Louvain, Mechlin and Alost. Other forces operating near the Franco-Belgian frontier took Lille.

North of the Somme, steady progress is being made. Our troops reached Hesdin, Montreuil and Etaples.

Allied forces in the Mons area of Belgium have eliminated a large German pocket southwest of the city. An estimated 9,000 prisoners were taken. Forty tanks and 1,500 motor vehicles were captured or destroyed by ground and air forces.

Local enemy pickets were mopped up south of Tournai and in the areas of Marchiennes northwest of Valenciennes, and Villeroe, northwest of Mons. Gains were made south of Charleroi as far as Florennes and Beaumont.

In the Upper Meuse Valley our forces have advanced northeast of St. Mihiel. Farther south there are no changes to report.

Weather restricted air operations yesterday.

MAXWELL, ROBERT D.

Rank and Organization: Technician Fifth Grade, U.S. Army, 7th Infantry, 3d Infantry Division.
Born: Boise, Idaho.
Entered Service At: Larimer County, Colorado.
Place and Date: Near Besancon, France, September 7, 1944.
Citation: For conspicuous gallantry and intrepidity at the risk of his life above and beyond the call of duty on September 7, 1944, near Besancon, France. Technician Fifth Grade Maxwell and 3 other soldiers, armed only with .45 caliber automatic pistols, defended the battalion observation post against an overwhelming onslaught by enemy infantrymen in approximately platoon strength, supported by 20-mm. flak and machinegun fire, who had infiltrated through the battalion's forward companies and were attacking the observation post with machinegun, machine pistol, and grenade fire at ranges as close as 10 yards. Despite a hail of fire from automatic weapons and grenade launchers, Technician Fifth Grade Maxwell aggressively fought off advancing enemy elements and, by his calmness, tenacity, and fortitude, inspired his fellow soldiers to continue the unequal struggle. When an enemy handgrenade was thrown in the midst of his squad, Technician Fifth Grade Maxwell unhesitatingly hurled himself squarely upon it, using his blanket and unprotected body to absorb the full force of the explosion. This act of instantaneous heroism permanently maimed Technician Fifth Grade Maxwell, but saved the lives of his comrades in arms and facilitated maintenance of vital military communications during the temporary withdrawal of the battalion's forward headquarters.

†PRUSSMAN, ERNEST W.

Rank and Organization: Private First Class, U.S. Army, 13th Infantry, 8th Infantry Division.

Born: Baltimore, Maryland.

Entered Service At: Brighton, Massachusetts.

Place and Date: Near Les Coates, Brittany, France, September 8, 1944.

Citation: For conspicuous gallantry and intrepidity at the risk of his life above and beyond the call of duty on September 8, 1944, near Les Coates, Brittany, France. When the advance of the flank companies of 2 battalions was halted by intense enemy mortar, machinegun, and sniper fire from a fortified position on his left, Pfc. Prussman maneuvered his squad to assault the enemy fortifications. Hurdling a hedgerow, he came upon 2 enemy riflemen whom he disarmed. After leading his squad across an open field to the next hedgerow, he advanced to a machinegun position, destroyed the gun, captured its crew and 2 riflemen. Again advancing ahead of his squad in the assault, he was mortally wounded by an enemy rifleman, but as he fell to the ground he threw a handgrenade, killing his opponent. His superb leadership and heroic action at the cost of his life so demoralized the enemy that resistance at this point collapsed, permitting the 2 battalions to continue their advance.

OFFICIAL COMMUNIQUE:

United Nations

SUPREME HEADQUARTERS, Allied Expeditionary Force, Sept. 8 –Communique 153:

Allied forces, pressing northeast from Louvain, crossed the Albert Canal and advanced elements reached the area of Bourg-Leopold yesterday evening.

Ypres has been captured and our forces have advanced to the vicinity of Roulers. Another armored column has reached a point ten miles northwest of the town.

We have continued to close in on Boulogne and Calais. The area of these ports was further sealed off yesterday by an advance of our troops from the area of the Foret de Gravelines.

Troops operating farther south in Belgium have taken Wavre, southeast of Brussels. Other forces moving along the Meuse from Namur have freed Huy and elements are in the area immediately west of Liege.

East of Dinan, gains have been made and troops advancing from the Forest of Ardennes have taken Louette, St. Pierre and Bievre.

Our forces are near the Moselle River a few minutes north of Metz. Farther south, we have crossed the Moselle north of Pont-a-Mousson against stiff enemy resistance.

Adverse weather yesterday restricted air operations.

ROME, Sept. 8 – A communique:

FRANCE

American troops of the Seventh Army have reached Besancon in a rapid advance in eastern France and are meeting stubborn resistance from the enemy, who is trying to protect his line of retreat.

Stiff fighting also is taking place along the Loue River southwest of Besancon.

French troops have made substantial gains and taken Pontarlier near the Swiss border after overcoming enemy opposition. Further progress also was made northeast of Chalon-sur-Saone.

TOMINAC, JOHN J.

Rank and Organization: First Lieutenant, U.S. Army, Company I, 15th Infantry, 3d Infantry Division.
Born: Conemaugh, Pennsylvania.
Entered Service At: Conemaugh, Pennsylvania.
Place and Date: Saulx de Vesoul, France, September 12, 1944.
Citation: For conspicuous gallantry and intrepidity at the risk of his life above and beyond the call of duty on September 12, 1944, in an attack on Saulx de Vesoul, France. 1st Lt. Tominac charged alone over 50 yards of exposed terrain onto an enemy roadblock to dispatch a 3-man crew of German machine-gunners with a single burst from his Thompson submachinegun. After smashing the enemy outpost, he led 1 of his squads in the annihilation of a second hostile group defended by machinegun, mortar, automatic pistol, rifle, and grenade fire, killing about 30 of the enemy. Reaching the suburbs of the town, he advanced 50 yards ahead of his men to reconnoiter a third enemy position which commanded the road with a 77-mm. SP gun supported by infantry elements. The SP gun opened fire on his supporting tank, setting it afire with a direct hit. A fragment from the same shell painfully wounded 1st Lt. Tominac in the shoulder, knocking him to the ground. As the crew abandoned the M-4 tank, which was rolling down hill toward the enemy, 1st Lt. Tominac picked himself up and jumped onto the hull of the burning vehicle. Despite withering enemy machinegun, mortar, pistol, and sniper fire, which was ricocheting off the hull and turret of the M-4, 1st Lt. Tominac climbed to the turret and gripped the 50-caliber antiaircraft machinegun. Plainly silhouetted against the sky, painfully wounded, and the tank burning beneath his feet, he directed bursts of machinegun fire on the roadblock, the SP gun, and the supporting German infantrymen, and forced the enemy to withdraw from his prepared position. Jumping off the tank before it exploded, 1st Lt. Tominac refused evacu-

ation despite his painful wound. Calling upon a sergeant to extract the shell fragments from his shoulder with a pocket knife, he continued to direct the assault, led his squad in a handgrenade attack against a fortified position occupied by 32 of the enemy armed with machineguns, machine pistols, and rifles, and compelled them to surrender. His outstanding heroism and exemplary leadership resulted in the destruction of 4 successive enemy defensive positions, surrender of a vital sector of the city of Saulx de Vesoul, and the death or capture of at least 60 of the enemy.

†ZUSSMAN, RAYMOND

Rank and Organization: Second Lieutenant, U.S. Army, 756th Tank Battalion.
Born: Hamtramck, Michigan.
Entered Service At: Detroit, Michigan.
Place and Date: Noroy le Bourg, France, September 12, 1944.
Citation: On September 12, 1944, 2d Lt. Zussman was in command of 2 tanks operating with an infantry company in the attack on enemy forces occupying the town of Noroy le Bourg, France. At 7 P.M., his command tank bogged down. Throughout the ensuing action, armed only with a carbine, he reconnoitered alone on foot far in advance of his remaining tank and the infantry. Returning only from time to time to designate targets, he directed the action of the tank and turned over to the infantry the numerous German soldiers he had caused to surrender. He located a roadblock and directed his tanks to destroy it. Fully exposed to fire from enemy positions only 50 yards distant, he stood by his tank directing its fire. Three Germans were killed and 8 surrendered. Again he walked before his tank, leading it against an enemy-held group of houses, machinegun and small-arms fire kicking up dust at his feet. The tank fire broke the resistance and 20 enemy surrendered. Going forward again alone he passed an enemy occupied house from which Germans fired at him and threw grenades in his path. After a brief fire fight, he signaled his tank to come up and fire on the house. Eleven German soldiers were killed and 15 surrendered. Going on alone, he disappeared around a street corner. The fire of his carbine could be heard and in a few minutes he reappeared driving 30 prisoners before him. Under 2d Lt. Zussman's heroic and inspiring leadership, 18 enemy soldiers were killed and 92 captured.

FISHER, ALMOND E.
Rank and Organization: Second Lieutenant, U.S. Army, Company E, 157th Infantry, 45th Infantry Division.
Born: Hume, New York.
Entered Service At: Brooklyn, New York.
Place and Date: Near Grammont, France, September 12-13, 1944.
Citation: For conspicuous gallantry and intrepidity at the risk of his life above and beyond the call of duty on the night of September 12-13, 1944, near Grammont, France. In the darkness of early morning, 2nd Lt. Fisher was leading a platoon of Company E, 157th Infantry, in single column to the attack of a strongly defended hill position. At 2:30 A.M., the forward elements were brought under enemy machinegun fire from a distance of not more than 20 yards. Working his way alone to within 20 feet of the gun emplacement, he opened fire with his carbine and killed the entire guncrew. A few minutes after the advance was resumed, heavy machinegun fire was encountered from the left flank. Again crawling forward alone under withering fire, he blasted the gun and crew from their positions with handgrenades. After a halt to replenish ammunition, the advance was again resumed and continued for 1 hour before being stopped by intense machinegun and rifle fire. Through the courageous and skillful leadership of 2d Lt. Fisher, the pocket of determined enemy resistance was rapidly obliterated. Spotting and emplaced machine pistol a short time later, with 1 of his men he moved forward and destroyed the position. As the advance continued the fire fight became more intense. When a bypassed German climbed from his foxhole and attempted to tear an M1 rifle from the hands of 1 of his men, 2d Lt. Fisher whirled and killed the enemy with a burst from his carbine. About 30 minutes later the platoon came under the heavy fire of machineguns from across an open field. 2d Lt. Fisher, disregarding the terrific fire, moved across the field with no cover or concealment to within range, knocked the gun from the position and killed or wounded the crew. Still under heavy fire he returned to his platoon and continued the advance. Once again heavy fire was encountered from a machinegun directly in front. Calling for handgrenades, he found only 2 remaining in the entire platoon. Pulling the pins and carrying a grenade in each hand, he crawled toward the gun emplacement, moving across areas devoid of cover and under intense fire within 15 yards when he threw the grenades, demolished the gun and killed the gun crew. With ammunition low and daybreak near, he ordered his men to dig in and hold the ground already won. Under constant fire from the front and from both flanks, he moved among them directing the preparations for the defense. Shortly after the ammunition supply was replenished, the Germans launched a last determined effort

against the depleted group. Attacked by superior numbers from the front, right, and left flank, and even from the rear, the platoon, in bitter hand-to-hand engagements drove back the enemy at every point. Wounded in both feet by close-range machine pistol fire early in the battle, 2d Lt. Fisher refused medical attention. Unable to walk, he crawled from man to man encouraging them and checking each position. Only after the fighting had subsided did 2d Lt. Fisher crawl 300 yards to the aid station from which he was evacuated. His extraordinary heroism, magnificent valor, and aggressive determination in the face of pointblank enemy fire is an inspiration to his organization and reflects the finest traditions of the U.S. Armed Forces.

†HALLMAN, SHERWOOD H.
Rank and Organization: Staff Sergeant, U.S. Army, 175th Infantry, 29th Infantry Division
Born: Spring City, Pennsylvania.
Entered Service At: Spring City, Pennsylvania.
Place and Date: Brest, Brittany, France, September 13, 1944.
Citation: For conspicuous gallantry and intrepidity at risk of his life above and beyond the call of duty. On September 13, 1944, in Brittany, France, the 2d Battalion in its attack on the fortified city of Brest was held up by a strongly defended enemy position which had prevented its advance despite repeated attacks extending over a 3-day period. Finally, Company F advanced to within several hundred yards of the enemy position but was again halted by intense fire. Realizing that the position must be neutralized without delay, S/Sgt. Hallman ordered his squad to cover his movements with fire while he advanced alone to a point from which he could make the assault. Without hesitating, S/Sgt. Hallman leaped over a hedgerow into a sunken road, the central point of the German defenses which was known to contain an enemy machinegun position and at least 30 enemy riflemen. Firing his carbine and hurling grenades, S/Sgt. Hallman, unassisted, killed or wounded 4 of the enemy, then ordered the remainder to surrender. Immediately 12 of the enemy surrendered and the position was shortly secured by the remainder of his company. Seeing the surrender of this position, about 75 of the enemy in the vicinity surrendered, yielding a defensive organization which the battalion with heavy supporting fires had been unable to take. This single heroic act on the part of S/Sgt. Hallman resulted in the immediate advance of the entire battalion for a distance of 2,000 yards to a position from which Fort Keranroux was captured later the same day. S/Sgt. Hallman's fighting determination and intrepidity in battle exemplify the highest tradition of the U.S. Armed Forces.

OFFICIAL COMMUNIQUE:
United Nations
SUPREME HEADQUARTERS, Allied Expeditionary Forces, Sept. 12 –Communique 157:

Allied troops have crossed the Luxembourg-German frontier and to the south, we have established contacts with our forces advancing from southern France.

In the Moselle Valley, we are continuing to meet stubborn resistance along the river.

Farther north, troops which made a crossing of the German frontier in force are now in the area northwest of Trier. Earlier, forces which liberated the city of Luxembourg had encountered enemy delaying action northeast of Mersch.

In the Ardennes, gains have been made in the vicinity of Bastogne.

Advances south of Liege have taken our troops across the road between Harre and Aywaille. Ten miles east of Liege, we have occupied Herve after encountering scattered enemy resistance. We have also reached Juprelle on the Liege-Tongres road.

The bridgehead over the Albert Canal has been enlarged in spite of stubborn enemy resistance. East of Ghent, we have liberated Lokeren and St. Nicholas.

On the coast, Allied troops have reached Blankenberghe. Between Calais and Cap Gris Nez, we have taken Wissant and Sangatte.

Enemy gun positions and strong points between Metz and Thionville were attacked by strong forces of medium and light bombers yesterday. There was no opposition in the air but heavy flak was encountered. One bomber is missing.

Railway targets from Saarbruecken to Cologne were hit by fighter-bombers which destroyed and damaged many locomotives and railway cars. Other fighter-bombers attacked enemy guns and fortifications in eastern Belgium. The airfield at Leeuwarden and ferry installations at Breskens were targets for medium and light bombers over the Netherlands.

The fortified area of Le Havre was again pounded by heavy bombers, and fighter-bombers continued the attack on Brest.

Coastal aircraft yesterday afternoon attacked four large minesweepers off Christiansand and left them on fire. Late Sunday afternoon a formation of trawler-type auxiliaries was hit with rocket and cannon. One vessel probably was sunk and four others damaged. One coastal aircraft is missing.

During the night, light bombers attacked transportation targets in the Netherlands and Germany.

ROME, Sept. 12 – A communique:

SOUTHERN FRANCE

The Seventh Army has established contact with the Third Army in eastern France, where farther to the north, advances have been made into areas from which the enemy continues trying to withdraw his remaining forces. After occupying the important communications center of Dijon, French troops kept up the momentum of their drive and forward elements reached Is-sur-Tille, fourteen miles beyond. The town of Sombernon in this sector has been occupied with little resistance.

Approximately 3,200 prisoners were taken in a clash with enemy columns in the vicinity of Autun, forty miles southwest of Dijon. American forces reached the outskirts of Vesoul in their northward advance from the Doubs and Ognon Rivers. Substantial progress has been made in this sector against heavy resistance which includes artillery and tanks.

†KEATHLEY, GEORGE D.

Rank and Organization: Staff Sergeant, U.S. Army, 85th Infantry Division.
Born: Olney, Texas.
Entered Service At: Lamesa, Texas.
Place and Date: Mt. Altuzzo, Italy, September 14, 1944.
Citation: For conspicuous gallantry and intrepidity at risk of life above and beyond the call of duty, in action on the western ridge of Mount Altuzzo, Italy. After bitter fighting his company had advanced to within 50 yards of the objective, where it was held up due to intense enemy sniper, automatic, small-arms, and mortar fire. The enemy launched 3 desperate counterattacks in an effort to regain their former positions, but all 3 were repulsed with heavy casualties on both sides. All officers and noncommissioned officers of the 2d and 3d platoons of Company B had become casualties, and S/Sgt. Keathley, guide of the 1st platoon, moved up and assumed command of both the 2d and 3d platoon, reduced to 20 men. The remnants of the 2 platoons were dangerously low on ammunition, so S/Sgt. Keathley, under deadly small-arms and mortar fire, crawled from 1 casualty to another, collecting their ammunition and administering first aid. He then visited each man of his 2 platoons, issuing the precious ammunition he had collected from the dead and wounded, and giving them words of encouragement. The enemy now delivered their fourth counterattack, which was approximately 2 companies in strength. In a furious charge they attacked from the front and both flanks, throwing handgrenades, firing automatic

weapons, and assisted by a terrific mortar barrage. So strong was the enemy counterattack that the company was given up for lost. The remnants of the 2d and 3d platoons of Company B were now looking to S/Sgt. Keathley for leadership. He shouted his orders precisely and with determination and the men responded with all that was in them. Time after time the enemy tried to drive a wedge into S/Sgt. Keathley's position and each time they were driven back, suffering huge casualties. Suddenly an enemy grenade hit and exploded near S/Sgt. Keathley, inflicting a mortal wound in his left side. However, hurling defiance at the enemy, he rose to his feet. Taking his left hand away from his wound and using it to steady his rifle, he fired and killed an attacking enemy soldier, and continued shouting orders to his men. His heroic and intrepid action so inspired his men that they fought with incomparable determination and viciousness. For 15 minutes S/Sgt. Keathley continued leading his men and effectively firing his rifle. He could have sought a sheltered spot and perhaps saved his life, but instead he elected to set an example for his men and make every possible effort to hold his position. Finally, friendly artillery fire helped to force the enemy to withdraw, leaving behind many of their number either dead or seriously wounded. S/Sgt. Keathley died a few moments later. Had it not been for his indomitable courage and incomparable heroism, the remnants of 3 rifle platoons of Company B might well have been annihilated by the overwhelming enemy attacking force. His actions were in keeping with the highest traditions of the military service.

†LLOYD, EDGAR H.

Rank and Organization: First Lieutenant, U.S. Army, Company E, 319th Infantry, 80th Infantry Division.
Born: Blytheville, Arkansas.
Entered service at: Blytheville, Arkansas.
Place and Date: Near Pompey, France, September 14, 1944.
Citation: For conspicuous gallantry and intrepidity at the risk of his life above and beyond the call of duty. On September 14, 1944, Company E, 319th Infantry, with which 1st Lt. Lloyd was serving as a rifle platoon leader, was assigned the mission of expelling an estimated enemy force of 200 men from a heavily fortified position near Pompey, France. As the attack progressed, 1st Lt. Lloyd's platoon advanced to within 50 yards of the enemy position where they were caught in a withering machinegun and rifle crossfire which inflicted heavy casualties and momentarily disorganized the platoon. With complete disregard for his own safety, 1st Lt. Lloyd leaped to his feet and led his men on a run into the raking fire, shouting

encouragement to them. He jumped into the first enemy machine-gun position, knocked out the gunner with his fist, dropped a grenade, and jumped out before it exploded. Still shouting encouragement he went from 1 machinegun nest to another, pinning the enemy down with submachinegun fire until he was within throwing distance, and then destroyed them with handgrenades. He personally destroyed 5 machineguns and many of the enemy, and by his daring leadership and conspicuous bravery inspired his men to overrun the enemy positions and accomplish the objective in the face of seemingly insurmountable odds. His audacious determination and courageous devotion to duty exemplify the highest traditions of the military forces of the United States.

†SADOWSKI, JOSEPH J.

Rank and organization: Sergeant, U.S. Army 37th Tank Battalion, 4th Armored Division.
Born: Perth Amboy, New Jersey.
Entered Service At: Perth Amboy, New Jersey.
Place and Date: Valhey, France, September 14, 1944.
Citation: For conspicuous gallantry and intrepidity at the rise of his life above and beyond the call of duty at Valhey, France. On the afternoon of September 14, 1944, Sgt. Sadowski as a tank commander was advancing with the leading elements of Combat Command A, 4th Armored Division, through an intensely severe barrage of enemy fire from the streets and buildings of the town of Valhey. As Sgt. Sadowski's tank advanced through the hail of fire, it was struck by a shell from a 88-mm. gun fired at a range of 20 yards. The tank was disabled and burst into flames. The suddenness of the enemy attack caused confusion and hesitation among the crews of the remaining tanks of our forces. Sgt. Sadowski immediately ordered his crew to dismount and take cover in the adjoining buildings. After his crew had dismounted, Sgt. Sadowski discovered that 1 member of the crew, the bow gunner, had been unable to leave the tank. Although the tank was being subjected to a withering hail of enemy small-arms, bazooka, grenade, and mortar fire from the streets and from the windows of adjacent buildings, Sgt. Sadowski unhesitatingly returned to his tank and endeavored to pry up the bow gunners hatch. While engaged in this attempt to rescue his comrade from the burning tank, he was cut down by a stream of machinegun fire which resulted in his death. The gallant and noble sacrifice of his life in the aid of his comrade, undertaken in the face of almost certain death, so inspired the remainder of the tank crews that they pressed forward with great ferocity and completely destroyed the enemy forces in his town with-

out further loss to themselves. The heroism and selfless devotion to duty displayed by Sgt. Sadowski, which resulted in his death, inspired the remainder of his force to press forward to victory, and reflected the highest tradition of the armed forces.

†WIGLE, THOMAS W.

Rank and Organization: Second Lieutenant, U.S. Army, Company K. 135th Infantry, 34th Infantry Division.
Born: Indianapolis, Indiana.
Entered Service At: Detroit, Michigan.
Place and Date: Monte Frassino, Italy, September 14, 1944.
Citation: For conspicuous gallantry and intrepidity at the risk of life above and beyond the call of duty in the vicinity of Monte Frassino, Italy. The 3d Platoon, in attempting to seize a strongly fortified hill position protected by 3 parallel high terraced stone walls, was twice thrown back by the withering crossfire. 2d Lt. Wigle, acting company executive, observing that the platoon was without an officer, volunteered to command it on the next attack. Leading his men up the bare, rocky slopes through intense and concentrated fire, he succeeded in reaching the first of the stone walls. Having himself boosted to the top and perching there in full view of the enemy, he drew and returned their fire while his men helped each other up and over. Following the same method, he successfully negotiated the second. Upon reaching the top of the third wall he faced 3 houses which were the key point of the enemy defense. Ordering his men to cover him, he made a dash through a hail of machine-pistol fire to reach the nearest house. Firing his carbine as he entered, he drove the enemy before him out of the back door and into the second house. Following closely on the heels of the foe, he drove them from this house into the third where they took refuge in the cellar. When his men rejoined him, they found him mortally wounded on the cellar stairs which he had started to descend to force the surrender of the enemy. His heroic action resulted in the capture of 36 German soldiers and the seizure of the strongpoint.

OFFICIAL COMMUNIQUE:
United Nations
SUPREME HEADQUARTERS, Allied Expeditionary Force, Sept. 14 –Communique 159:

On the Channel coast mopping up continues. Allied troops have taken a strong point in the vicinity of Nieuport-Bains.

In northeastern Belgium, we enlarged our bridgehead over the Albert Canal at Gheel and to the southeast, more enemy counter-attacks against our bridgehead brought no results. Mopping up in the area of Hechtel was completed and elements reached the Escaut Canal.

Other Allied troops, after crossing the Albert Canal, pushed on to cross the Netherlands frontier. The frontier also was crossed farther south near Maastricht.

In Luxembourg, our forces made gains in the area northeast of the capital.

The bridgehead over the Moselle River continues to be strengthened in the face of heavy enemy resistance, and we now are holding high ground in one area of the east bank.

In Brittany, progress is being made at Brest against stubborn defenses, which include small arms, mortars, machine guns, and some artillery. A fort about two miles east of the town was taken. Fighter-bombers supported yesterday's attack.

Attacks on the Siegfried Line and against strong points near Nancy and Metz were made yesterday by fighter-bombers. Other fighter-bombers hit rail targets in the Nancy area, destroying and damaging a number of locomotives, and railway trucks.

Communications and transportation targets on railways and waterways in the Netherlands were bombed and strafed by medium, light and fighter-bombers. Hits were scored on the causeway between Walcheren and South Beveland. Fortified positions at Boulogne were targets of other medium and light bombers.

Coastal aircraft attacked an enemy convoy anchorage off Den Helder Tuesday night. Five vessels were left afire and a sixth apparently sinking. Shore installations also were hit.

Other formations attacked shipping between the Hook of Holland and Ameland. Two coastal aircraft are missing.

ROME, Sept. 14 – A communique:

ITALY

The advance of British and American troops of the Fifth Army during the past few days has been continued against considerably increased enemy opposition on the forward edge of the Gothic Line north of Florence.

In the Adriatic sector, Eighth Army troops advanced and cleared the enemy from many of his positions on the Coriano-San Savino ridge, where heavy fighting continued.

SOUTHERN FRANCE

American and French troops have advanced several miles farther at a number of points along the front in southern France against varying enemy resistance.

French Army forces occupied Langres and thrust forward elements toward Chaumont in the upper Marne Valley. To the southeast, Gray is clear of the enemy and considerable gains have been made in this sector.

In the advance west of the Belfort Gap, American troops entered Villersexel against considerable opposition. South of Belfort, French troops cleared stiffly defended Pont de Roide, meeting with a strong enemy counter-attack near by.

†BAUSELL, LEWIS KENNETH

Rank and Organization: Corporal, U.S. Marine Corps, 1st Marine Division.
Born: April 17, 1924, Pulaski, Virginia.
Entered Service At: District of Columbia.
Place and Date: Peleliu Island, September 15, 1944.
Citation: For conspicuous gallantry and intrepidity at the risk of his life above and beyond the call of duty while serving with the 1st Battalion, 5th Marines, 1st Marine Division, during action against enemy Japanese forces on Peleliu Island, Palau Group, September 15, 1944. Valiantly placing himself at the head of his squad, Cpl. Bausell led the charge forward against a hostile pillbox which was covering a vital sector of the beach and, as the first to reach the emplacement, immediately started firing his automatic rifle into the aperture while the remainder of his men closed in on the enemy. Swift to act, as a Japanese grenade was hurled into their midst, Cpl. Bausell threw himself on the deadly weapon, taking the full blast of the explosion and sacrificing his own life to save his men. His unwavering loyalty and inspiring courage reflect the highest credit upon Cpl. Bausell and the U.S. Naval Service. He gallantly gave his life for his country.

ROUH, CARLTON ROBERT

Rank and Organization: First Lieutenant, U.S. Marine Corps Reserve, 1st Battalion, 5th Marines, 1st Marine Division.
Born: May 11, 1919, Lindenwold, New Jersey.
Entered Service At: New Jersey.
Place and Date: Peleliu Island, Palau group, September 15, 1944.
Citation: For conspicuous gallantry and intrepidity at the risk of his life above and beyond the call of duty while attached to the 1st Battalion, 5th Marines, 1st Marine Division, during action against enemy Japanese forces on Peleliu Island, Palau group, September 15, 1944. Before permitting his men to use an enemy dugout as a position for an 81mm. mortar observation post, 1st Lt. Rouh made a personal reconnaissance of the pillbox and, upon

entering, was severely wounded by Japanese rifle fire from within. Emerging from the dugout, he was immediately assisted by 2 marines to a less exposed area but, while receiving first aid, was further endangered by an enemy grenade which was thrown into their midst. Quick to act in spite of his weakened condition, he lurched to a crouching position and thrust both men aside, placing his own body between them and the grenade and taking the full blast of the explosion himself. His exceptional spirit of loyalty and self-sacrifice in the face of almost certain death reflects the highest credit upon 1st Lt. Rouh and the U.S. Naval Service.

Note: The following is a newspaper account of the preceding battle for which Cpl. Bausell and Lt. Rouh were awarded the Medal of Honor:

LANDING ON PELELIU

• • •

**Marines Win Beachhead and
Close In on Main Palau Airdrome**

• • •

MOROTAI GOAL TAKEN

• • •

**Airfield in Halmahera Area Swiftly Seized
In Twin Invasion Push**

• • •

PEARL HARBOR, Sept. 15 – United States Marines landed yesterday in the Palau Islands and are closing in on the airport on Peleliu Island after repulsing several Japanese tank attacks. A communique from the headquarters of Admiral Chester W. Nimitz, Commander in Chief of the Pacific Fleet, late today told of the gains. Peleliu, an island about six miles long by two miles wide in the southern part of the Palau group, was the only objective mentioned in the communique. The First Marine Division, which made the first landing on Guadalcanal on Aug. 7, 1942, made the initial assault and established a beachhead about one and a half miles long on the south-western shore facing the airport.

[American troops who landed on Morotai Island, eleven miles north of Halmahera, swiftly captured their first objectives, Dorobu township and Pitu airdrome, against light opposition, and Army engineers were already putting the airfield in shape for our planes.]

Planes Help Marines

The beachhead on Peleliu is now being developed, the communique said. Apparently the strip of sand along the shore had been cleared and the fighting has progressed far enough inland to allow the landing of supplies to support the assault on the airfield.

Despite nine days of bombing and shelling by units of Admiral William F. Halsey's Third Fleet, assisted by heavy bombers from Gen. Douglas MacArthur's area to the southwest, the Japanese were able to make counter-attacks yesterday, apparently after considerable numbers of troops had come ashore. Our ground forces threw back the several counter-thrusts with the assistance of strong air support from carrier planes and by naval gunfire that tore into the enemy positions.

Enemy mortar and artillery fire peppered the landing area sporadically during the day, probably from the wooded hills northwest of the airstrip. Our casualties, however, were light the first day, the communique said.

Japanese installations immediately behind the narrow beaches were severely bombed and strafed by carrier planes during the landing operations, which presumably held back the enemy ground defenders until an effective Marine force was ashore.

Only One Plane Lost

The only American casualties announced in these preparatory activities were one plane and four of the flight personnel. The plane was evidently brought down by anti-aircraft fire, since there has been no Japanese aerial activity over the Palau group since our carrier planes began the assault preparations on Sept. 5.

Support of the landings and the covering operations, including the attacks on the southern and central Philippines during the past week, were carried out by fast carrier task forces commanded by Vice Admiral Marc A. Mitscher, who directed the carriers in the battle of the Philippines Sea. Admiral Halsey as head of the Third Fleet is the over-all commander on the sea under Admiral Nimitz, with Vice Admiral T. S. Wilkinson directing the amphibious phases. Rear Admiral George H. Fort has command of the bombardment units directly supporting the amphibious assaults.

The marines engaged, besides being themselves veterans of South Pacific ground actions dating back to the Guadalcanal campaign, have the experienced leadership of Maj. Gen. William H. Rupertus, the First Division commander. The amphibious assault and all ground action is under Maj. Gen. Roy S. Geiger, commander of the Third Amphibious Corps, who fulfilled the same function in the

Guam battle. Maj. Gen. Julian C. Smith, who led the Second Marine Division at Tarawa, commands the expeditionary force.

Vicious Fighting Expected

Vicious fighting is expected around the airfield, which is the finest in the Palaus and the primary objective on the island. Hills afford the Japanese many positions for mortars and light artillery and these are cut off on the northeast flank by swamps. The landing at Peleliu was simultaneous with the invasion of Morotai Island in the Moluccas by forces of General MacArthur. This timing was the result of conferences among the staffs of General MacArthur and Admiral Nimitz. The two latest amphibious forays into Japan's middle defenses and the air attacks on the Philippines during the past week were really a single operation in which the two widely separated commands were integrated.

For geographical reasons the two invasions will have greater effect in speeding up the Pacific war because they were made simultaneously rather than at different times. American domination of both the Palaus and the Moluccas places our land-based airpower in position to concentrate on the Philippines. Additionally Morotai's Pitu airdrome is less than 600 miles from Balikpapan in Borneo, which with Palembang, Sumatra, supplies the major portion of Japan's aviation gasoline.

4,000 of Foe Believed on Isle

When the airfield to be gained in the Palaus and the Moluccas are developed, which will not take long once the objectives are captured, American airpower will dominate the Macassar Straits and be able to cut one of the Asiatic enemy's most vital sea lanes depriving him of much loot from his stolen empire which he needs to prosecute a war.

While resistance was light at Morotai, where strategic surprise was achieved, the enemy was evidently prepared for landings in the Palau group and therefore is able to give stiff ground opposition.

It has not been announced how many Japanese are fighting the advance on Peleliu but it is estimated that there are 4,000 to 5,000 combat troops and several thousand construction men who are likely to be armed.

The Japanese garrisons in all the Palaus is believed to number 30,000 to 40,000. It is recalled here that the number of prisoners taken on Saipan was only about 2 percent of the number of Japanese killed. The same stubborn character of fighting is expected on Peleliu.

American possession of the Peleliu airfield will come close to sealing the doom of the rest of the group as effective bases. There is another airfield at Angaur and there are seaplane bases at Arakabesan and Koror, the capital.

Another objective at Palau of secondary concern, but of great importance ultimately, is the great Malakal harbor of Peleliu. Possession of Malakal would give the fleet its best basin in the central Pacific forward area within two days leisurely steaming from Davao, the big Japanese base on Mindanao Island in the Philippines.

Meanwhile, the usual daily aerial activity over beleaguered bases continues throughout the central Pacific. Shimushu Island, in the Kuriles, was bombed Tuesday by Navy Ventura search planes. Paramushiru, in the Kuriles, was bombed by Army Liberators the next night.

Iwo in the Volcano Islands was heavily hit Wednesday by Army Liberators from the Marianas.

Pagan and Rota Islands in the Marianas, Mili, Jaluit and Wotje Atolls in the Marshalls and Marcus Island were also bombed with no damage announced to our planes.

PRESTON, ARTHUR MURRAY

Rank and Organization: Lieutenant, U.S. Navy Reserve, Torpedo Boat Squadron 33.
Born: November 1, 1913, Washington, D.C.
Entered Service At: Maryland.
Place and Date: Wasile Bay, Halmahera Island, September 16, 1944.
Citation: For conspicuous gallantry and intrepidity at the risk of his life above and beyond the call of duty as commander, Motor Torpedo Boat Squadron 33, while effecting the rescue of a Navy pilot shot down in Wasile Bay, Halmahera Island, less than 200 yards from a strongly defended Japanese dock and supply area, September 16, 1944. Volunteering for a perilous mission unsuccessfully attempted by the pilot's squadron mates and a PBY plane, Lt. Comdr. (then Lieutenant) Preston led PT-489 and PT-363 through 60 miles of restricted, heavily mined waters. Twice turned back while running the gauntlet of fire from powerful coastal defense guns guarding the 11-mile strait at the entrance to the bay, he was again turned back by furious fire in the immediate area of the downed airman. Aided by an aircraft smokescreen, he finally succeeded in reaching his objective and, under vicious fire delivered at 150-yard range, took the pilot aboard and cleared the area, sinking a small hostile cargo vessel with 40-mm. fire during retirement. Increasingly vulnerable when covering aircraft were forced to leave because of insufficient fuel, Lt. Comdr. Preston raced PT boats 489 and 363 at high speed for 20 minutes through shell-splashed water and across minefields to safety. Under continuous fire for 2 1/2 hours, Lt. Comdr. Preston successfully achieved a mission considered suicidal in its tremen-

dous hazards, and brought his boats through without personnel casualties and with but superficial damage from shrapnel. His exceptional daring and great personal valor enhance the finest tradition of the U.S. Naval Service.

CLARK, FRANCIS J.

Rank and Organization: Technical Sergeant, U.S. Army, Company K, 109th Infantry, 28th Infantry Division.
Born: Whitehall, New York.
Entered Service At: Salem, New York.
Place and Date: Near Kalborn, Luxembourg, September 12, 1944; near Sevenig, Germany, September 17, 1944.
Citation: T/Sgt. Clark fought gallantly in Luxembourg and Germany. On September 12, 1944, Company K began fording the Our River near Kalborn Luxembourg, to take high ground on the opposite bank. Covered by early morning fog, the 3d Platoon, in which T/Sgt. Clark was a squad leader, successfully negotiated the crossing; but when the 2d Platoon reached the shore, withering automatic and small-arms fire ripped into it, eliminating the platoon leader and platoon sergeant and pinning down the troops in the open. From his comparatively safe position, T/Sgt. Clark crawled alone across a field through a hail of bullets to the stricken troops. He led the platoon to safety and then unhesitatingly returned into the fireswept area to rescue a wounded soldier, carrying him to the American line while hostile gunners tried to cut him down. Later, he led his squad and men of the 2d Platoon in dangerous sorties against strong enemy positions to weaken them by lightning-like jabs. He assaulted an enemy machinegun with handgrenades, killing 2 Germans. He roamed the front and flanks, dashing toward hostile weapons, killing and wounding an undetermined number of the enemy, scattering German patrols and, eventually, forcing the withdrawal of a full company of Germans heavily armed with automatic weapons. On September 17, near Sevening, Germany, he advanced alone against an enemy machinegun, killed the gunner and forced the assistant to flee. The Germans counterattacked, and heavy casualties were suffered by Company K. Seeing that 2 platoons lacked leadership, T/Sgt. Clark took over their command and moved among the men to give encouragement. Although wounded on the morning of September 18, he refused to be evacuated and took up a position in a pillbox when night came. Emerging at daybreak, he killed a German soldier setting up a machinegun not more than 5 yards away. When he located another enemy gun, he moved up unobserved and killed 2 Germans with rifle fire. Later that day he voluntarily braved small-arms fire to take food and water to members of an isolated

platoon. T/Sgt. Clark's actions in assuming command when leadership was desperately needed, in aiding his stranded comrades, and in fearlessly facing powerful enemy fire, were strikingly heroic examples and put fighting heart into the hardpressed men of Company K.

†MESSERSCHMIDT, HAROLD O.

Rank and Organization: Sergeant, U.S. Army, Company L, 30th Infantry, 3d Infantry Division.
Born: Grier City, Pennsylvania.
Entered Service At: Chester, Pennsylvania.
Place and Date: Near Radden, France, September 17, 1944.
Citation: Sgt. Messerschmidt displayed conspicuous gallantry and intrepidity above and beyond the call of duty. Braving machinegun, machine pistol, and rifle fire, he moved fearlessly and calmly from man to man along his 40-yard squad front, encouraging each to hold against the overwhelming assault of a fanatical foe surging up the hillside. Knocked to the ground by a burst from an enemy automatic weapon, he immediately jumped to his feet, and ignoring his grave wounds, fired his submachinegun at the enemy that was now upon them, killing 5 and wounding many others before his ammunition was spent. Virtually surrounded by a frenzied foe and all of his squad now casualties, he elected to fight alone, using his empty submachinegun as a bludgeon against his assailants. Spotting 1 of the enemy about to kill a wounded comrade, he felled the German with a blow of his weapon. Seeing friendly reinforcements running up the hill, he continued furiously to wield his empty gun against the foe in a new attack, and it was thus that he made the supreme sacrifice. Sgt. Messerschmidt's sustained heroism in hand-to-hand combat with superior enemy forces was in keeping with the highest tradition of the military service.

OFFICIAL COMMUNIQUE:
United Nations
SUPREME HEADQUARTERS, Allied Expeditionary Force, Sept. 17 –Communique 162:

Advances were made by Allied troops yesterday between Antwerp and the sea. Our bridgehead over the Meuse-Escaut Canal continues to be subjected to enemy counter-attacks, but we are holding firm.

Farther south on the German frontier, our forces are fighting in the southern outskirts of Aachen, and strong elements have broken through the Siegfried defenses east of the city against heavy resistance.

We have also pierced defenses below Rott, southeast of Aachen, and have advanced into the Roetgenwald. Moderate resistance is being met across the frontier east of St. Vith, but our forces farther south near Brandscheid are encountering heavy resistance.

In the Moselle Valley, our forces are now across the river in strength, and elements have advanced a considerable distance east of Nancy.

The advance from southern France is making progress against varying resistance. Elements have pushed without opposition to Chaumont, but advances northeast of Vesoul at the western approach to the Belfort gap were made against defenses which the enemy has been strengthening.

In the Alps, troops have entered Modane at the western entrance of the Modane railway tunnel, linking France and Italy. The enemy is withdrawing in the direction of high Mont Cenis Pass.

The Arnemuiden and Bath dikes linking by road and rail the island of Walcheren to the Netherlands mainland were attacked yesterday by medium and light bombers. Other medium bombers struck at two strong points north of Bonlogne. Fighters and fighter-bombers attacked transportation targets in the Netherlands.

The Monday communique from General Headquarters in the Southwest Pacific as broadcast from Melbourne to North America and recorded by the Federal Communications Commission:

MOLUCCAS

Halmahera: Our ground forces, with negligible opposition, continue their consolidation of Morotai Island positions. Heavy attack and fighter planes neutralized the Halmahera airdromes with over 210 tons of bombs.
Ceram: Our fighters patrolling the coast and nearby islands destroyed or damaged five barges and other small craft. Our air patrols at night dropped a total of fifteen tons upon merchantmen in the Ambon area and destroyed two coastal vessels at Mangole Island in the northwest.

CELEBES

Our air patrols sank a 2,000-ton freighter-transport and bombed Menado, starting fires and explosions.

NETHERLANDS NEW GUINEA

Vogelkop: Fighter-bombers attacked enemy airdromes and further wrecked the defenses at Geelvink Bay and MacCleur Gulf. A large ammunition dump was destroyed at Kokas, with resulting fires visible for fifty miles.

JOHNSON, OSCAR G.

Rank and Organization: Sergeant, U.S. Army, Company B, 363d Infantry, 91st Infantry Division.
Born: Foster City, Michigan.
Entered Service At: Foster City, Michigan.
Place and Date: Near Scarperia, Italy, September 16-18, 1944.
Citation: Sgt. Johnson (then Pfc.) practically singlehanded protected the left flank of his company's position in the offensive to break the German's gothic line. Company B was the extreme left assault unit of the corps. The advance was stopped by heavy fire from Monticelli Ridge, and the company took cover behind an embankment. Sgt. Johnson, a mortar gunner, having expended his ammunition, assumed the duties of a rifleman. As leader of a squad of 7 men he was ordered to establish a combat post 50 yards to the left of the company to cover its exposed flank. Repeated enemy counterattacks, supported by artillery, mortar, and machinegun fire from the high ground to his front, had by the afternoon of September 16, killed or wounded all his men. Collecting weapons and ammunition from his fallen comrades, in the face of hostile fire, he held his exposed position and inflicted heavy casualties upon the enemy, who several times came close enough to throw handgrenades. On the night of September 16-17, the enemy launched his heaviest attack on Company B, putting his greatest pressure against the lone defender of the left flank. In spite of mortar fire which crashed about him and machine-gun bullets which whipped the crest of his shallow trench, Sgt. Johnson stood erect and repulsed the attack with grenades and small-arms fire. He remained awake and on the alert throughout the night, frustrating all attempts at infiltration. On September 17, 25 German soldiers surrendered to him. Two men, sent to reinforce him that afternoon, were caught in a devastating mortar and artillery barrage. With no thought of his own safety, Sgt. Johnson rushed to the shellhole where they lay half buried and seriously wounded, covered their position by fire, and assisted a Medical Corpsman in rendering aid. That night he secured their removal to the rear and remained on watch until his company was relieved. Five companies of a German paratroop regiment had been repeatedly committed to the attack on Company B without success. Twenty dead German were found in front of his position. By his heroic stand and utter disregard for personal safety, Sgt. Johnson was in a large measure responsible for defeating the enemy's attempts to turn the exposed left flank.

†MANN, JOE E.

Rank and Organization: Private First Class, U.S. Army, Company H, 502d Parachute Infantry, 101st Airborne Division.
Born: Rearden, Washington.
Entered Service At; Seattle, Washington.
Place and Date: Best, Holland, September 18, 1944.
Citation: Pfc. Mann distinguished himself by conspicuous gallantry above and beyond the call of duty. On September 18, 1944, in the vicinity of Best, Holland, his platoon, attempting to seize the bridge across the Wilhelmina Canal, was surrounded and isolated by an enemy force greatly superior in personnel and firepower. Acting as lead scout, Pfc. Mann boldly crept to within rocket-launcher range of an enemy artillery position and, in the face of heavy enemy fire, destroyed an 88-mm. gun and an ammunition dump. Completely disregarding the great danger involved, he remained in his exposed position, and, with his M1 rifle, killed the enemy one by one until he was wounded 4 times. Taken to a covered position, he insisted on returning to a forward position to stand guard during the night. On the following morning the enemy launched a concerted attack and advanced to within a few yards of the position, throwing handgrenades as they approached. One of these landed within a few feet of Pfc. Mann. Unable to raise his arms, which were bandaged to his body, he yelled "grenade" and threw his body over the grenade, and as it exploded, died. His outstanding gallantry above and beyond the call of duty and his magnificent conduct were an everlasting inspiration to his comrades for whom he gave his life.

OFFICIAL COMMUNIQUE:
United Nations
SUPREME HEADQUARTERS, Allied Expeditionary Force, Sept. 18 –Communique 163:

Allied airborne troops were landed in the Netherlands yesterday after powerful air operations in which the Allied air forces operated in great strength. First reports show that the operation is going well.

Our ground forces near the Belgium-Netherlands frontier are continuing to make progress.

Farther south we have mopped up pockets of resistance on the outskirts of Aachen. Heavy fighting continues in the city. Elements pushing on east of the town are encountering determined resistance. Advances have also been made across the Luxembourg-German frontier.

In the Moselle Valley, our troops are clearing the area west of the river of isolated enemy groups. North of Nancy, progress has been made and enemy counterattacks near Pont-A-Mousson were repulsed.

The Germans are fighting hard in the Belfort Gap. Our troops have occupied the town of St. Loup-sur-Semouse and cleared Lure of the enemy. North of Lure, the enemy used tanks in resisting the advance. Local engagements took place in the area of Pont de Roide.

In the high Alps, we have driven several miles up the Maurienne Valley after capturing Modane and have reached Lanslebourg after stiff fighting.

Striking in advance of our airborne forces yesterday, heavy, light and fighter-bombers in very great strength attacked anti-aircraft batteries, gun positions, communications, troops and transport throughout a wide area in the Netherlands, while fighters swept a path for the aerial transports and gliders and provided an umbrella of cover for the landings. As the enemy's guns opened fire, our fighters and fighter-bombers dived to silence them in low level strafing and bombing attacks.

Many motor vehicles, locomotives, railway cars and barges were destroyed or damaged and bridges and supply dumps were hit. According to reports so far received, nine enemy aircraft were shot down in combat by our fighters.

Later in the day, gun positions and troops on the Island of Walcheren were attacked by strong forces of heavy bombers. Coastal aircraft struck at shipping off the Frisian Islands.

Fortified positions and garrison troops at Boulogne were bombarded for four hours by other heavy bombers, which dropped more than 3,500 tons of high explosives. Intense anti-aircraft fire was encountered at times, but there was no opposition in the air.

Strong points at Brest were attacked during the day by small forces of fighter-bombers. Other fighter-bombers hit several locomotives and railway cars in western Germany.

ROME, Sept. 15 – A communique:

ARMY

In the Adriatic sector, troops of the Eighth Army made important progress on high ground to the left of the sector and now hold a bridgehead over the River Marano on a frontage of eight miles.

In the Fifth Army sector, American, British, Indian, and Brazilian troops are still engaged in fierce fighting within the enemy's Gothic Line positions.

On the remainder of the front, there is no material change in the situation.

AIR

Medium forces of escorted heavy bombers yesterday attacked rail yards and oil refineries in Budapest.

Tactical aircraft attacked enemy communications, troop concentrations and other military objectives in northern Italy and in the battle areas, as well as Yugoslavia.

Last night our bombers attacked the Brescia rail yards in northern Italy.

In these operations, eleven of our aircraft are missing. The MAAF flew approximately 1,750 sorties.

JACKSON, ARTHUR J.

Rank and Organization: Private First Class, U.S. Marine Corps, 3d Battalion, 7th Marines, 1st Marine Division.
Born: October 18, 1924, Cleveland, Ohio.
Entered Service At: Oregon.
Place and Date: Island of Peleliu in the Palau group, September 18, 1944.
Citation: For conspicuous gallantry and intrepidity at the risk of his life above and beyond the call of duty while serving with the 3d Battalion, 7th Marines, 1st Marine Division, in action against enemy Japanese forces on the Island of Peleliu in the Palau group, September 18, 1944. Boldly taking the initiative when his platoon's left flank advance was held up by the fire of Japanese troops concealed in strongly fortified positions, Pfc. Jackson unhesitatingly proceeded forward of our lines and, courageously defying the heavy barrages, charged a large pillbox housing approximately 35 enemy soldiers. Pouring his automatic fire into the opening of the fixed installation to trap the occupying troops, he hurled white phosphorus grenades and explosive charges brought up by a fellow marine, demolishing the pillbox and killing all of the enemy. Advancing alone under the continuous fire from other hostile emplacements, he employed similar means to smash 2 smaller positions in the immediate vicinity. Determined to crush the entire pocket of resistance although harassed on all sides by the shattering blasts of Japanese weapons and covered only by small rifle parties, he stormed 1 gun position after another, dealing death and destruction to the savagely fighting enemy in his inexorable drive against the remaining defenses, and succeeded in wiping out a total of 12 pillboxes and 50 Japanese soldiers. Stouthearted and indomitable despite the terrific odds, Pfc. Jackson resolutely maintained control of the platoon's left flank movement throughout his valiant 1-man assault and, by his cool decision and relentless fighting spirit during a critical situation, contributed essentially to the complete annihilation of the enemy in the southern sector of the island. His gallant initiative and heroic conducted in the face of extreme peril reflect the highest credit upon Pfc. Jackson and the U.S. Naval Service.

†ROAN, CHARLES HOWARD

Rank and Organization: Private First Class, U.S. Marine Corps Reserve, 1st Marine Division.
Born: August 16, 1923, Claude, Texas.
Entered Service At: Texas.
Place and Date: Peleliu Island, September 18, 1944.
Citation: For conspicuous gallantry and intrepidity at the risk of his life above and beyond the call of duty while serving with the 2d Battalion, 7th Marines, 1st Marine Division, in action against enemy Japanese forces on Peleliu, Palau Islands, September 18, 1944. Shortly after his leader ordered a withdrawal upon discovering that the squad was partly cut off from their company as a result of the rapid advance along an exposed ridge during an aggressive attack on the strongly entrenched enemy, Pfc. Roan and his companions were suddenly engaged in a furious exchange of handgrenades by Japanese forces emplaced in a cave on higher ground and to the rear of the squad. Seeking protection with 4 other marines in a depression in the rocky, broken terrain, Pfc. Roan was wounded by an enemy grenade which fell close to their position and, immediately realizing the eminent peril to his comrades when another grenade landed in the midst of the group, unhesitatingly flung himself upon it, covering it with his body and absorbing the full impact of the explosion. By his prompt action and selfless conduct in the face of almost certain death, he saved the lives of 4 men. His great personal valor reflects the highest credit upon himself and the U.S. Naval Service. He gallantly gave his life for his comrades.

POPE, EVERETT PARKER

Rank and Organization: Captain, U.S. Marine Corps, Company C, 1st Battalion, 1st Marines, 1st Marine Division.
Born: July 16, 1919, Milton, Massachusetts.
Entered Service At: Massachusetts.
Place and Date: Peleliu Island, Palau group, September 19-20, 1944.
Citation: For conspicuous gallantry and intrepidity at the risk of his life above and beyond the call of duty while serving as commanding officer of Company C, 1st Battalion, 1st Marines, 1st Marine Division, against enemy Japanese forces on Peleliu Island, Palau group, on September 19-20, 1944. Subjected to pointblank cannon fire which caused heavy casualties and badly disorganized his company while assaulting a steep coral hill, Capt. Pope rallied his men and gallantly led them to the summit in the face of machinegun, mortar, and sniper fire. Forced by widespread hostile attack to deploy the remnants of his company thinly in order to hold the

ground won, and with his machineguns out of order and insufficient water and ammunition, he remained on the exposed hill with 12 men and 1 wounded officer, determined to hold through the night. Attacked continuously with grenades, machineguns, and rifles from 3 sides, he and his valiant men fiercely beat back or destroyed the enemy, resorting to hand-to-hand combat as the supply of ammunition dwindled, and still maintaining his lines with his 8 remaining riflemen when daylight brought more deadly fire and he was ordered to withdraw. His valiant leadership against devastating odds while protecting the units below from heavy Japanese attack reflects the highest credit upon Capt. Pope and the U.S. Naval Service.

Note: The following is a newspaper account of the preceding battle for which Pfc. Jackson, Pfc. Roan, and Capt. Pope were awarded the Medal of Honor:

CRISIS ON PELELIU BROKEN BY MARINES

• • •

Palau Airfield Threat Erased - Mindanao Bombed - Tokyo Reports Blow at Sumatra

• • •

PEARL HARBOR, Sept. 19 – Advancing slowly against rifle and machine-gun fire from pillboxes and entrenched positions, the First Marine Division has captured a small town on Peleliu Island and made slight gains on the eastern and northeastern fronts while on Angaur, six miles to the south, Army troops have occupied two-thirds of the lightly defended island.

[The marines captured "Bloody Nose Bridge" and seized their primary objectives on Peleliu, passing the crisis of the fighting on the strategic island, a United Press correspondent aboard the expeditionary flagship off the Palaus reported.

[John Cooper, representing the combined American networks, said in a broadcast from Palau received at San Francisco, that the marines on Peleliu had virtually the entire island in their hands, The Associated Press reported. He asserted only the north tip remained to be invested.

[In the Philippines, about 600 miles west of Palau, Far Eastern Air Force bombers started fires on an airdrome and a pier on Mindanao Sunday, General MacArthur's headquarters reported. The Tokyo radio, heard by the Federal Communications Commission, said forty carrier-based bombers struck a Japanese base in northern Sumatra Monday, and fifty planes attacked Davao on Mindanao the same day, when, it reported, Koror, north of Peleliu in the Palaus, was pounded by 100 of our aircraft.}

Admiral Chester W. Nimitz's communique today indicated continued fierce fighting on Peleliu, principal Japanese airbase in the Palau group. The enemy still holds many prepared positions and is using mortars and artillery to support a stubborn defense.

One naval casualty was announced today. This was an infantry landing craft, LCI 459, which had been converted into a gunboat. The small vessel struck a mine while firing rockets in close support of the Marines on Sunday, and sank in twenty minutes. Two of the crew were wounded, the communique said, but all were rescued. An LCI carries four officers and about thirty-six men.

Seabees putting the Peleliu airfield in condition for our fighter planes reported a count of the Japanese aircraft found there, which indicates the air strength based there by the Japanese until the drome was put out of action by carrier planes and Gen. Douglas MacArthur's heavy bombers.

Found on the field badly damaged were seventy-seven single-engine fighters, twenty-eight medium bombers, eight light bombers, and four transport planes.

These 117 planes bring to 820 the total of Japanese aircraft put out of action in the western Pacific since Aug. 30. The count confirms the often remarked inability of the Japanese to get their planes off the ground before an American attack. This is possible due to inferior air warning devices and lack of pilots.

Listing ground gains on Peleliu Monday (United States time), the communique said there had been some advance in the northeastern sector securing Ngardololok town and bringing most of the eastern coastal area under our control. The town, the only settlement of appreciable size on the island, aside from previously captured Asias, is now well inside the marines' perimeter.

East of the airfield, the Marines have crossed one of the largest swamp areas and skirted others.

The regular air strikes in the Kuriles continue unabated. Liberators of the Eleventh Army Air Force, operating from the Aleutians, bombed Shimushu Island the night of Sept. 16. The next day Liberators and Ventura search planes of Fleet Air Wing 4 hit Paramushinu and Shimushu again, setting buildings afire.

A small boat, loaded with enemy personnel, and a warship, presumed to be a destroyer, were strafed off the east coast of Paramushinu. One of several enemy fighter planes that attempted to intercept were shot down. One of our planes was damaged.

Iwo, airbase in the Volcano Islands, was bombed Saturday night by a single plane which met no anti-aircraft fire. Liberators of the Seventh AAF bombed Marcus Island on Sunday. Runways, gun emplacements and bivouac areas on Nauru were bombed by Seventh AAF Mitchells the same day. Wotje and Jaluit, in the Marshalls, were bombed.

†TOWLE, JOHN R.

Rank and Organization: Private, U.S. Army, Company C, 504th Parachute Infantry, 82d Airborne Division.
Born: Cleveland, Ohio.
Entered Service At: Cleveland, Ohio.
Place and Date: Near Oosterhout, Holland, September 21, 1944.
Citation: For conspicuous gallantry and intrepidity at the risk of his life above and beyond the call of duty on September 21, 1944, near Oosterhout, Holland. The rifle company in which Pvt. Towle served as rocket launcher gunner was occupying a defensive position in the west sector of the recently established Nijmegen bridgehead when a strong enemy force of approximately 100 infantry supported by 2 tanks and a half-track formed for a counterattack. With full knowledge of the disastrous consequences resulting not only to his company but to the entire bridgehead by an enemy breakthrough, Pvt. Towle immediately and without orders left his foxhole and moved 200 yards in the face of intense small-arms fire to a position on an exposed dike roadbed. From this precarious position Pvt. Towle fired his rocket launcher at and hit both tanks to his immediate front. Armored skirting on both tanks prevented penetration by the projectiles, but both vehicles withdrew slightly damaged. Still under intense fire and fully exposed to the enemy, Pvt. Towle then engaged a nearby house which 9 Germans had entered and were using as a strongpoint and with 1 round killed all 9. Hurriedly replenishing his supply of ammunition, Pvt. Towle, motivated only by his high conception of duty which called for the destruction of the enemy at any cost, then rushed approximately 125 yards through grazing enemy fire to an exposed position from which he could engage the enemy half-track with his rocket launcher. While in a kneeling position preparatory to firing on the enemy vehicle, Pvt Towle was mortally wounded by a mortar shell. By his heroic tenacity, at the price of his life, Pvt. Towle saved the lives of many of his comrades and was directly instrumental in breaking up the enemy counterattack.

BLOCH, ORVILLE EMIL

Rank and Organization: First Lieutenant, U.S. Army, Company E, 338th Infantry, 85th Infantry Division.
Born: Big Falls, Wisconsin.
Entered Service At: Streeter, North Dakota.
Place and Date: Near Firenzuola, Italy, September 22, 1944.
Citation: For conspicuous gallantry and intrepidity at the risk of life above and beyond the call of duty. 1st Lt. Bloch undertook the task of wiping out

5 enemy machinegun nests that had held up the advance in that particular sector for 1 day. Gathering 3 volunteers from his platoon, the patrol snaked their way to a big rock, behind which a group of 3 buildings and 5 machinegun nests were located. Leaving the 3 men behind the rock, he attacked the first machinegun nest alone charging into furious automatic fire, kicking over the machinegun, and capturing the machinegun crew of 5. Pulling the pin from a grenade, he held it ready in his hand and dashed into the face of withering automatic fire toward this second enemy machinegun nest located at the corner of an adjacent building 15 yards distant. When within 20 feet of the machinegun he hurled the grenade, wounding the machinegunner, the other 2 members of the crew fleeing into a door of the house. Calling one of his volunteer group to accompany him, they advanced to the opposite end of the house, there contacting a machinegun crew of 5 running toward the house. 1st Lt. Bloch and his men opened fire on the enemy crew, forcing them to abandon this machinegun and ammunition and flee into the same house. Without a moment's hesitation, 1st Lt. Bloch, unassisted, rushed through the door into a hail of small-arms fire, firing his carbine from the hip, and captured the 7 occupants, wounding 3 of them. 1st Lt. Bloch with his men then proceeded to a third house where they discovered an abandoned enemy machinegun and detected another enemy machinegun nest at the next corner of the building. The crew of 6 spotted 1st Lt. Bloch the instant he saw them. Without a moment's hesitation he dashed toward them. The enemy fired pistols wildly in his direction and vanished through a door of the house, 1st Lt. Bloch following them through the door, firing his carbine from the hip, wounding 2 of the enemy and capturing 6. Altogether 1st Lt. Bloch had singlehandedly captured 19 prisoners, wounding 6 of them and eliminating a total of 5 enemy machinegun nests. His gallant and heroic actions saved his company many casualties and permitted them to continue the attack with new inspiration and vigor.

OFFICIAL COMMUNIQUE:
UNITED NATIONS
Supreme Headquarters, Allied Expeditionary Force, Sept. 22-Communique 167:

The Allied drive northward through Nijmegen continued yesterday against increasing enemy opposition.

Our armored forces, having captured the bridge at Nijmegen in conjunction with airborne troops, crossed to the north bank of the Waal [Rhine] and pushed on north.

The town of Nijmegen has been cleared of the enemy.

The base of the Allied salient has been widened on both sides of Eindhoven. We have reached Someren on the east and are fighting in the area of Winteire on the west.

Fighters and fighter-bombers supported operations in Holland. Some enemy aircraft were encountered, principally in the areas of Nijmegen and Lochem. Twenty enemy aircraft were shot down for a loss of four of our fighters.

In the Scheide estuary we have captured Ter Neuzen and are steadily mopping up the southern bank east of the Leopold Canal.

In the Boulogne area the enemy has been confined to the high ground south-west of the town. An enemy strongpoint in the Forest of La Creche, on the out-skirts of the town, was attacked by medium and light bombers.

Troops crossing into Germany from southern Holland have advanced to within three miles of Gellenkirchen, in the Stolberg-Busbach area, east of Aachen. Mop-ping up is in progress and we are engaged in house-to-house fighting in Stolberg. East of the town our troops have gained ground.

Farther south Allied troops are clearing the Huertgen Forest against moderate artillery fire and are also mopping up in the area of Lammersdorf.

Numerous counter-attacks have been repulsed near Diekirch and one unit has destroyed twenty-eight enemy tanks.

South of Metz our forces advanced to within six miles of the city.

Along the Meurthe River we have taken the high ground along the west bank, five miles to the southeast.

Other units are in the vicinity of Flin, on the Meurthe River, five miles north-west of Baccarat.

Railway centers at Ehrang, Gerolstein and Pronsfeld, in Germany, were hit yesterday by medium bombers.

ROME, Sept. 22-A communique:

LAND

Allied armies in Italy have still further successes to report. After nearly a month of continuous and bitter fighting, troops of the Eighth Army have driven the enemy from the San Fortunato-Ceriano ridge and have a bridgehead over the River Marecchia.

Rimini has been captured. This is most important, as the town lies at the en-trance to the Po Valley.

The Fifth Army, giving the enemy no respite, has captured the important road center of Firenzuola and dominating hills to the central sector of the Apennines.

SCHAEFER, JOSEPH E.

Rank and Organization: Staff Sergeant, U.S. Army, Company I, 18th Infantry, 1st Infantry Division.
Born: New York, New York.
Entered Service At: Long Island, New York.
Place and Date: Near Stolberg, Germany, September 24, 1944.
Citation: S/Sgt. Schaefer was in charge of a squad of the 2d Platoon in the vicinity of Stolberg, Germany, early in the morning of September 24, 1944, when 2 enemy companies supported by machineguns launched an attack to seize control of an important crossroads which was defended by his platoon. One American squad was forced back, another captured, leaving only S/Sgt. Schaefer's men to defend the position. To shift his squad into a house which would afford better protection, he crawled about under heavy small-arms and machinegun fire, instructed each individual, and moved to the building. A heavy concentration of enemy artillery fire scored hits on his strong point. S/Sgt. Schaefer assigned his men to positions and selected for himself the most dangerous one at the door. With his M1 rifle, he broke the first wave of infantry thrown toward the house. The Germans attacked again with grenades and flame throwers but were thrown back a second time, S/Sgt. Schaefer killing and wounding several. Regrouped for a final assault, the Germans approached from 2 directions. One force drove at the house from the front, while a second group advanced stealthily along a hedgerow. Recognizing the threat, S/Sgt. Scheafer fired rapidly at the enemy before him, killing or wounding all 6; then, with no cover whatever, dashed to the hedgerow and poured deadly accurate shots into the second group, killing 5, wounding 2 others, and forcing the enemy to withdraw. He scoured the area near his battered stronghold and captured 10 prisoners. By this time the rest of his company had begun a counterattack; he moved forward to assist another platoon to regain its position. Remaining in the lead, crawling and running in the face of heavy fire, he overtook the enemy, and liberated the American squad captured earlier in the battle. In all, single-handed and armed only with his rifle, he killed between 15 and 20 Germans, wounded at least as many more, and took 10 prisoners. S/Sgt. Schaefer's indomitable courage and his determination to hold his position at all costs were responsible for stopping an enemy break-through.

†NEW, JOHN DURY

Rank and Organization: Private First Class, U.S Marine Corps, 1st Marine Division.
Born: August 12, 1924, Mobile, Alabama.
Entered Service At: Alabama.

Place and Date: Peleliu Island, September 25, 1944.

Citation: For conspicuous gallantry and intrepidity at the risk of his life above and beyond the call of duty while serving with the 2d Battalion, 7th Marines, 1st Marine Division, in action against enemy Japanese forces on Peleliu Island, Palau Group, September 25, 1944. When a Japanese soldier emerged from a cave in a cliff directly below an observation post and suddenly hurled a grenade into the position from which 2 of our men were directing mortar fire against enemy emplacements, Pfc. New instantly perceived the dire peril to the other marines and, with utter disregard for his own safety, unhesitatingly flung himself upon the grenade and absorbed the full impact of the explosion, thus saving the lives of the 2 observers. Pfc. New's great personal valor and selfless conduct in the face of almost certain death reflect the highest credit upon himself and the U.S. Naval Service. He gallantly gave his life for his country.

OFFICIAL COMMUNIQUE:
UNITED STATES
SUPREME HEADQUARTERS, Allied Expeditionary Force, Sept. 24-Communique 169:

Heavy engagements continued yesterday in the Allied salient in Holland.

Fighting was particularly fierce in the vicinity of Arnhem, where the enemy is exerting very strong pressure. We have increased our hold on the area between the Neder Rijn [Lek] and the Waal [Rhine].

Our position in the Nijmegen area has been improved. We have strengthened a bridgehead over the Bols le Duc Canal near the base of the salient.

Our airborne operations were further reinforced during the day. Ahead of the transport aircraft and gliders, fighters and fighter-bombers in strength dropped fragmentation bombs on numerous gun positions and carried out low-level strafing attacks. Many batteries were silenced. Other fighters provided escort and cover for the airborne operations.

The enemy was active in the air and a number of combats with our fighters resulted. According to reports so far received twenty-seven enemy aircraft were shot down. Fourteen of our fighters are missing.

East of Antwerp our forces advanced after establishing a bridgehead across the Meuse-Escaut Canal. Northwest of the city we have made a slight advance.

The entire front, from the Geilenkirshen area to Meurthe Valley, remains relatively unchanged with stubborn enemy resistance and numerous counter-attacks in all sectors.

In the Aschen are our patrols are meeting fire from the outskirts of the city where the enemy appears to be well entrenched. Stolberg is being cleared of isolated German pockets but southeast of the town our troops are meeting,stubborn resistance in their advance. East of Buesbach a counter-attacking German force was driven off with an estimated loss of 40 percent of its strength.

German pockets are being mopped up in the sector bordering northern Luxembourg and our units along the entire German-Luxembourg frontier are receiving moderate artillery fire from the enemy.

South of Metz stubborn enemy resistance continues and a small counter-attack at Pournoy was broken up by our artillery.

We have made gains nine miles north of Nancy where the town of Morey was freed. Enemy tanks and infantry are offering strong opposition in the area east of Nancy.

Our troops have advanced to the vicinity of Benamenil, ten miles east of Luneville.

Gun emplacements on the Island of Walcheren in the Schelde Estuary were attacked by a small force of heavy bombers.

Strong points at Calais were attacked by medium and light bombers. Fighter bombers hit fortified positions in the Trier area.

A Pacific Fleet announcement:

An attempt by the enemy to reinforce his beleaguered troops in the northern end of Peleliu Island was broken up Sept. 23 (West Longitude date).

A convoy of thirteen barges and one motor sampan carrying men and equipment was sighted northeast of Peleliu. It was immediately brought under fire by United States warships, some of which to close range. A number of the barges were seen to explode. Later, ten wrecked barges were counted on the reefs northeast of Peleliu and the remainder were thought to have sunk. A few of the enemy probably were able to swim ashore without their equipment.

On the same day in Malakai harbor two camouflaged ships previously damaged by a United States cruiser which scored at least one direct hit.

Marine forces on Peleliu made small gains on both the right and left flank during Sept. 23. On Angaur mopping-up operations continue.

FIELDS, JAMES H.

Rank and Organization: First Lieutenant, U.S. Army, 10th Armored Infantry, 4th Armored Division.
Born: Caddo, Texas.
Entered Service At: Houston, Texas.
Place and Date: Rechicourt, France, September 27, 1944.
Citation: For conspicuous gallantry and intrepidity at risk of life above and beyond the call of duty, at Rechicourt, France. On September 27, 1944, during a sharp action with the enemy infantry and tank forces, 1st Lt. Fields

personally led his platoon in a counterattack on the enemy position. Although his platoon had been seriously depleted, the zeal and fervor of his leadership was such as to inspire his small force to accomplish their mission in the face of overwhelming enemy opposition. Seeing that 1 of the men had been wounded, he left his slit trench and with complete disregard for is personal safety attended the wounded man and administered first aid. While returning to his slit trench he was seriously wounded by a shell burst, the fragments of which cut through his face and head, tearing his teeth, gums, and nasal passage. Although rendered speechless by his wounds, 1st Lt. Fields refused to be evacuated and continued to lead his platoon by the use of hand signals. On 1 occasion, when 2 enemy machineguns had a portion of his unit under deadly crossfire, he left his hole, wounded as he was, ran to a light machinegun, whose crew had been knocked out, picked up the gun, and fired it from his hip with such deadly accuracy that both the enemy gun positions were silenced. His action so impressed his men that they found new courage to take up the fire fight, increasing their firepower, and exposing themselves more than ever to harass the enemy with additional bazooka and machinegun fire. Only when his objective had been taken and the enemy scattered did 1st Lt. Fields consent to be evacuated to the battalion command post. At this point he refused to move further back until he had explained to his battalion commander by drawing on paper the position of his men and the disposition of the enemy forces. The dauntless and gallant heroism displayed by 1st Lt. Fields were largely responsible for the repulse of the enemy forces and contributed in a large measure to the successful capture of his battalion objective during this action. His eagerness and determination to close with the enemy and to destroy him was an inspiration to the entire command, and are in the highest traditions of the U.S. Armed Forces.

†ROEDER, ROBERT E.

Rank and Organization: Captain, U.S. Army, Company G, 350th Infantry, 88th Infantry Division.
Born: Summit Station, Pennsylvania.
Entered Service At: Summit Station, Pennsylvania.
Place and Date: Mt. Battaglia, Italy, September 27-28, 1944.
Citation: For conspicuous gallantry and intrepidity at risk of life above and beyond the call of duty. Capt. Roeder commanded his company in defense of the strategic Mount Battaglia. Shortly after the company had occupied the hill, the Germans launched the first of a series of determined counterattacks to regain this dominating height. Completely exposed to

ceaseless enemy artillery and small-arms fire, Capt. Roeder constantly circulated among his men, encouraging them and directing their defense against the persistent enemy. During the sixth counterattack, the enemy, by using flamethrowers and taking advantage of the fog, succeeded in overrunning the position. Capt. Roeder led his men in a fierce battle at close quarters, to repulse the attack with heavy losses to the Germans. The following morning, while the company was engaged in repulsing an enemy counterattack in force, Capt. Roeder was seriously wounded and rendered unconscious by shell fragments. He was carried to the company command post, where he regained consciousness. Refusing medical treatment, he insisted on rejoining his men. Although in a weakened condition, Capt. Roeder dragged himself to the door of the command post and, picking up a rifle, braced himself in a sitting position. He began firing his weapon, shouted words of encouragement, and issued orders to his men. He personally killed 2 Germans before he himself was killed instantly by an exploding shell. Through Capt. Roeder's able and intrepid leadership his men held Mount Battaglia against the aggressive and fanatical enemy attempts to retake this important and strategic height. His valorous performance is exemplary of the fighting spirit of the U.S. Army.

OFFICIAL COMMUNIQUE:
United Nations
SUPREME HEADQUARTERS, Allied Expeditionary Force, Sept. 27-Communique 172:

Allied troops have again repulsed enemy moves threatening our communications along the Eindhoven-Nijmegen road. Our salient has been further secured south of the Meuse by advances to Oss, on the west, and to the area of Boxmeer, on the east. A stretch of some five miles of the Meuse south of Boxmeer is in our hands. Gains have also been made on both sides of the base of the Allied salient. On the west, we have reached the Antwerp-Turnhout Canal along a considerable portion of its length. On the east, around Maeseyck, we control the west bank of the Meuse between Wessem and Dilsen.

To the south, as far as Luneville, active patrolling continues with little change of position. Light to moderate artillery fire was encountered in the Aachen and Stolberg areas, and our units engaged German pillboxes and strong points northeast of Roetgen. In south Luxembourg we occupied Grieveldange.

An enemy counter-attack in the vicinity of Marsal, east of Nancy, was repulsed. Considerable enemy artillery fire has been directed against our troops in the Meurthe Valley. North of Epinal our forces have crossed the Moselle in strength and have occupied Chatelsur-Moselle and a number of towns to the south.

The enemy is fighting stubbornly in the vicinity of Docelles and Tendon to slow our advance east of Epinal. West and northwest of Belfort further progress has been made and several villages have been liberated.

On the Channel coast ground operations against Calais continued successfully. Yesterday, fortified positions in the town and heavy guns and radio installations at Cap Gris Nez were attacked by heavy bombers. Other heavy bombers attacked rail centers at Osnabrueck and Hamm in northwest Germany and industrial targets at Bremen. Twelve bombers are missing.

Fortifications and strong points at Breskens and rail and road targets at Cleve were attacked by medium bombers.

Fighters provided escort for the heavy bombers to Germany and also for supply missions to the Low Countries, while fighters and fighter-bombers gave support to the ground forces and also attacked transportation targets in Holland. Thirty-eight enemy aircraft were destroyed in the air. Seven of our fighters are missing.

Last night light bombers attacked road, rail and river transport in Holland and western Germany.

ROME, Sept. 27-A communique:

LAND

Eighth Army troops have now cleared the last enemy resistance south of the Rubicon, and Dominion troops of the Eighth Army are in the outskirts of Bellaria. On their left British troops in heavy fighting have extended their bridgehead over the Bubicon and are now approaching the town of Savignano.

In the central sector American and British troops of the fifth Army have made slight advances against determined enemy resistance.

CARR, CHRIS (name legally changed from CHRISTOS H. KARABERIS, under which name the medal was awarded)
Rank and Organization: Sergeant, U.S. Army, Company L, 337th Infantry, 85th Infantry Division.
Born: Manchester, New Hampshire.
Entered Service At: Manchester, New Hampshire.
Place and Date: Near Guignola, Italy, October 1-2, 1944.
Citation: Leading a squad of Company L, he gallantly cleared the way for his company's approach along a ridge toward its objective, the Casoni di Remagna. When his platoon was pinned down by heavy fire from enemy mortars, machineguns, machine pistols, and rifles, he climbed in advance of his squad on a maneuver around the left flank to locate an eliminate the enemy gun positions. Undeterred by deadly fire that ricocheted off the bar-

ren rocky hillside, he crept to the rear of the first machinegun and charged, firing his submachinegun. In this surprise attack he captured 8 prisoners and turned them over to his squad before striking out alone for a second machinegun. Discovered in his advance and subjected to direct fire from the hostile weapon, he leaped to his feet and ran forward, weaving and crouching, pouring automatic fire into the emplacement that killed 4 of its defenders and forced the surrender of the lone survivor. He again moved forward through heavy fire to attack a third machinegun. When close to the emplacement, he closed with a nerve-shattering shout and burst of fire. Paralyzed by his whirlwind attack, all 4 gunners immediately surrendered. Once more advancing aggressively in the face of a thoroughly alerted enemy, he approached a point of high ground occupied by 2 machineguns which were firing on his company on the slope below. Charging the first of these weapons, he killed 4 of the crew and captured 3 more. The 6 defenders of the adjacent position, cowed by the savagery of his assault, immediately gave up. By his 1-man attack, heroically and voluntarily undertaken in the face of tremendous risks, Sgt. Karaberis captured 5 enemy machinegun positions, killed 8 Germans, took 22 prisoners, cleared the ridge leading to his company's objective, and drove a deep wedge into the enemy line, making it possible for his battalion to occupy important, commanding ground.

†KINER, HAROLD G.
Rank and Organization: Private, U.S. Army, Company F, 117th Infantry, 30th Infantry Division.
Born: Aline, Oklahoma.
Entered Service At: Enid, Oklahoma.
Place and Date: Near Palenberg, Germany, October 2, 1944.
Citation: With 4 other men, Pvt. Kiner was leading in a frontal assault October 2, 1944, on a Siegfried Line pillbox near Palenberg, Germany. Machinegun fire from the strongly defended enemy position 25 yards away pinned down the attackers. The Germans threw handgrenades, 1 of which dropped between Pvt. Kiner and 2 other men. With no hesitation, Private Kiner hurled himself upon the grenade, smothering the explosion. By his gallant action and voluntary sacrifice of his own life, he saved his 2 comrades from serious injury or death.

OFFICIAL COMMUNIQUE:
UNITED NATIONS
SUPREME HEADQUARTERS, Allied Expeditionary Force, Oct. 2-Communique 177:

Allied troops have strengthened the Dutch salient by an advance north of Oss which cleared the enemy from the banks of the River Maas [Meuse]. Northeast of Mijmegen we have repulsed attacks by enemy infantry and armor. To the southwest, our forces, making further progress west of Turnhout, captured the village of Brecht and are three miles north of Merxplas.

Fighters and fighter-bombers attacked troop concentrations, guns and transportation targets in support of our ground forces in Holland. Other fighters flew offensive patrols.

Active patrolling was maintained along the German border from Aachen to southeastern Luxembourg.

In the area northeast of Nancy our troops advanced into the Forest of Gremecey and occupied the high ground around Fresnes-en-Saunois and Coutures. A strong counter-attack near Jallaucourt was repulsed.

Local gains were made in the Epinal sector against strong resistance. Artillery fire was particularly heavy. The town of St. Jean du Marche is in our hands.

Mopping up at Calais has been completed.

ROME, Oct. 2-A communique:

LAND

In the central sector American and British troops of the Fifth Army met very strong enemy resistance to their drive toward the Po Valley. Some local gains have been made, including the capture of Mount Cappello, an important feature dominating the road to Imola.

In the Adriatic sector there is no appreciable change in our forward positions.

†**PHELPS, WESLEY**
Rank and Organization: Private, U.S. Marine Corps Reserve, 1st Marine Division.
Born: June 12, 1923, Neafus, Kentucky.
Entered Service At: Kentucky.
Place and Date: Peleliu Island, October 4, 1944.
Citation: For conspicuous gallantry and intrepidity at the risk of his life above and beyond the call duty while serving with the 3d Battalion, 7th Marines, 1st Marine Division, in action against enemy Japanese forces on Peleliu Island, Palau Group, during a savage hostile counterattack on the night of October 4, 1944. Stationed with another marine in an advanced position when a Japanese handgrenade landed in his foxhole, Pfc. Phelps instantly shouted a warning to his comrade and rolled over on the deadly bomb, absorbing with his own body the full, shattering impact of the ex-

ploding charge. Courageous and indomitable, Pfc. Phelps fearlessly gave his life that another might be spared serious injury, and his great valor and heroic devotion to duty in the face of certain death reflect the highest credit upon himself and the U.S. Naval Service. He gallantly gave his life for his country.

†DEALEY, SAMUEL DAVID
Rank and Organization: Commander, U.S. Navy.
Born: September 13, 1906, Dallas, Texas.
Entered Service At: Texas.
Other Navy Awards: Navy Cross with 3 Gold Stars, Silver Star Medal.
Place and Date: Near the Philippines, in Japanese-controlled waters, ca. October 1944.
Citation: For conspicuous gallantry and intrepidity at the risk of his life above and beyond the call of duty as Commanding Officer of the *USS Harder* during her 5th War Patrol in Japanese-controlled waters. Flood-lighted by a bright moon and disclosed to an enemy destroyer escort which bore down with the intent to attack, Comdr. Dealey quickly dived to peri-scope depth and waited for the pursuer to close range, then opened fire, sending the target and all aboard down in flames with his third torpedo. Plunging deep to avoid fierce depth charges, he again surfaced and, within 9 minutes after sighting another destroyer, had sent the enemy down tail first with a hit directly amidship. Evading detection, he penetrated the con-fined waters off Tawi Tawi with the Japanese fleet base 6 miles away and scored death blows on 2 patrolling destroyers in quick succession. With his ship heeled over by concussion from the first exploding target and the sec-ond vessel nose-diving in a blinding detonation, he cleared the area at high speed. Sighted by a large hostile fleet force on the following day, he swung his bow toward the lead destroyer for another "down the throat" shot, fired 3 bow tubes and promptly crash-dived to be terrifically rocked seconds later by the exploding ship as the *Harder* passed beneath. This remarkable record of 5 vital Japanese destroyers in 5 short-range torpedo attacks at-tests the valiant spirit of Comdr. Dealey and his indomitable command.

†KRAUS, RICHARD EDWARD
Rank and Organization: Private First Class, U.S. Marine Corps Reserve.
Born: November 24, 1925, Chicago, Illinois.
Entered Service At: Minnesota.
Place and Date: Peleliu Island, October 5, 1944.
Citation: For conspicuous gallantry and intrepidity at the risk of his life

above and beyond the call of duty while serving with the 8th Amphibious Tractor Battalion, Fleet Marine Force, in action against enemy Japanese forces on Peleliu, Palau Islands, on October 5, 1944. Unhesitatingly volunteering for the extremely hazardous mission of evacuating a wounded comrade from the front lines, Pfc. Kraus and 3 companions courageously made their way forward and successfully penetrated the lines for some distance before the enemy opened with an intense, devastating barrage of handgrenades which forced the stretcher party to take cover an subsequently abandon the mission. While returning to the rear, they observed 2 men approaching who appeared to be marines and immediately demanded the password. When, instead of answering, 1 of the 2 Japanese threw a handgrenade into the midst of the group, Pfc. Kraus heroically flung himself upon the grenade and, covering it with his body, absorbed the full impact of the explosion and was instantly killed. By his prompt action and great personal valor in the face of almost certain death, he saved the lives of his 3 companions, and his loyal spirit of self-sacrifice reflects the highest credit upon himself and the U.S Naval Service. He gallantly gave his life for his comrades.

OFFICIAL COMMUNIQUE:
United Nations
WASHINGTON, Oct. 4 – Pacific Fleet communique 140:

Further reducing the remnants of enemy troops still resisting on Peleliu and Angaur Islands. Marine and Army troops destroyed the occupants of a number of enemy held caves on Oct. 3 (West Longitude date). Mopping up operations on Angaur continued. The bodies of more dead Japanese soldiers have been counted, a total of 9,878 on Peleliu and 1,109 on Angaur.

Search Venturas of Fleet Air Wing 4 bombed Parmushiru in the Kuriles on Oct. 2. Meager anti-aircraft fire was encountered. All our planes returned.

Seventh Air Force Liberators on Oct. 1 scored a direct hit on an enemy cargo vessel at Chichi Jima [Island] in the Bonin Islands. Two enemy planes were in the air, but did not attempt interception. Shipping in Chichi Jima harbor was attacked by Seventh Air Force Liberators on Oct. 2. Anti-aircraft fire varied from moderate to meager.

Buildings, gun emplacements and docking facilities at Pagan Island were bombed and rocketed on Oct. 2 by Thunderbolts of the Seventh Air Force. No anti-aircraft fire was encountered.

Seventh Air Force Liberators bombed the runway and installations on Marcus Island on Oct. 2. Anti-aircraft fire was meager.

Corsairs and Venturas of the Fourth Marine Aircraft Wing bombed communications facilities and gun positions at Jaluit Atoll on Oct. 2. Anti-aircraft fire, which was moderate, damaged one Ventura. All our planes returned safely.

Dauntless dive-bombers of the Fourth Marine Aircraft Wing flew through meager anti-aircraft fire to bomb installations at Taroa Island in the Maloelap Atoll.

†HARRIS, JAMES L.

Rank and Organization: Second Lieutenant, U.S. Army, 756th Tank Battalion.

Born: Hillsboro, Texas.

Entered Service At: Hillsboro, Texas.

Place and Date: At Vagney, France, October 7, 1944.

Citation: For conspicuous gallantry and intrepidity at risk of life above and beyond the call of duty on October 7, 1944, in Vagney, France. At 9 p.m. an enemy raiding party, comprising a tank and 2 platoons of infantry, infiltrated through the lines under cover of mist and darkness and attacked an infantry battalion command post with handgrenades, retiring a short distance to an ambush position on hearing the approach of the M4 tank commanded by 2d Lt. Harris. Realizing the need for bold aggressive action, 2d Lt. Harris ordered his tank to halt while he proceeded on foot, fully 10 yards ahead of his 6-man patrol and armed only with a service pistol, to probe the darkness for the enemy. Although struck down and mortally wounded by machinegun bullets which penetrated his solar plexus, he crawled back to his tank, leaving a trail of blood behind him, and, too weak to climb inside it, issued fire orders while lying on the road between the 2 contending armored vehicles. Although the tank which he commanded was destroyed in the course of the fire fight, he stood the enemy off until friendly tanks, preparing to come to his aid, caused the enemy to withdraw and thereby lose an opportunity to kill or capture the entire battalion command personnel. Suffering a second wound, which severed his leg at the hip, in the course of this tank duel, 2d Lt. Harris refused aid until after a wounded member of his crew had been carried to safety. He died before he could be given medical attention.

BROWN, BOBBY E.

Rank and Organization: Captain, U.S. Army, Company C, 18th Infantry, 1st Infantry Division.

Born: September 2, 1903, Dublin, Georgia.

Entered Service At: Atlanta, Georgia.

Place and Date: Crucifix Hill, Aachen, Germany, October 8, 1944.

Citation: Capt. Brown commanded Company C, 18th Infantry Regiment, on October 8, 1944, when it, with the Ranger Platoon of the 1st Battalion, attacked Crucifix Hill, a key point in the enemy's defense of Aachen, Germany. As the leading rifle platoon assaulted the first of many pillboxes studding the rising ground, heavy fire from a flanking emplacement raked it. An intense artillery barrage fell on the American troops which had been pinned down in an exposed position. Seeing that the pillboxes must be neutralized to prevent the slaughter of his men, Capt. Brown obtained a pole charge and started forward alone toward the first pillbox, about 100 yards away. Hugging the ground while enemy bullets whipped around him, he crawled and then ran toward the aperture of the fortification, rammed his explosive inside and jumped back as the pillbox and its occupants were blown up. He rejoined the assault platoon, secured another pole charge, and led the way toward the next pillbox under continuous artillery mortar, automatic, and small-arms fire. He again ran forward and placed his charge in the enemy fortification, knocking it out. He then found that fire from a third pillbox was pinning down his company; so he returned to his men, secured another charge, and began to creep and crawl toward the hostile emplacement. With heroic bravery he disregarded opposing fire and worked ahead in the face of bullets streaming from the pillbox. Finally reaching his objective, he stood up and inserted his explosive, silencing the enemy. He was wounded by a mortar shell but refused medical attention and, despite heavy hostile fire, moved swiftly among his troops exhorting and instructing them in subduing powerful opposition. Later, realizing the need for information of enemy activity beyond the hill, Capt. Brown went out alone to reconnoiter. He observed possible routes of enemy approach and several times deliberately drew enemy fire to locate gun emplacements. Twice more, on this self-imposed mission, he was wounded; but he succeeded in securing information which led to the destruction of several enemy guns and enabled his company to throw back 2 powerful counterattacks with heavy losses. Only when Company C's position was completely secure did he permit treatment of his 3 wounds. By his indomitable courage, fearless leadership, and outstanding skill as a soldier, Capt. Brown contributed in great measure to the taking of Crucifix Hill, a vital link in the American line encircling Aachen.

†KANDLE, VICTOR L.

Rank and Organization: First Lieutenant, U.S. Army, 15th Infantry, 32d Infantry Division.
Born: Roy, Washington.
Entered Service At: Redwood City, California.
Place and Date: Near La Forge, France, October 9, 1944.

Citation: For conspicuous gallantry and intrepidity at risk of his life above and beyond the call of duty. On October 9, 1944, at about noon, near La Forge, France, 1st Lt. Kandle, while leading a reconnaissance patrol into enemy territory, engaged in a duel at pointblank range with a German field officer and killed him. Having already taken 5 enemy prisoners that morning, he led a skeleton platoon of 16 men, reinforced with a light machinegun squad, through fog and over precipitous mountain terrain to fall on the rear of a German quarry stronghold which had checked the advance of an infantry battalion for 2 days. Rushing forward several yards ahead of his assault elements, 1st Lt. Kandle fought his way into the heart of the enemy strongpoint, and, by his boldness and audacity, forced the Germans to surrender. Harassed by machinegun fire from a position which he had bypassed in the dense fog, he moved to within 15 yards of the enemy, killed a German machinegunner with accurate rifle fire and led his men in the destruction of another machinegun crew and its rifle security elements. Finally, he led his small force against a fortified house held by 2 German officers and 30 enlisted men. After establishing a base of fire, he rushed forward alone through an open clearing in full view of the enemy, smashed through a barricaded door, and forced all 32 Germans to surrender. His intrepidity and bold leadership resulted in the capture or killing of 3 enemy officers and 54 enlisted men, the destruction of 3 enemy strongpoints, and the seizure of enemy positions which had halted a battalion attack.

OFFICIAL COMMUNIQUE:
United Nations
SUPREME HEADQUARTERS Allied Expeditionary Force, Oct. 8 –Communique 183:

Allied troops moving toward the southern bank of the Schelde Estuary from our bridgehead over the Leopold Canal are engaged in heavy fighting.

North of Antwerp further progress has been made toward the roads leading to the island of Walcheren, where the sea dikes at Flushing were attacked yesterday without loss of a strong force of escorted heavy bombers.

North of Nijmegen we have freed the village of Halberen. Fighting continues in the area of Opheusden.

Fighters and fighter-bombers closely supported our ground forces in Holland and attacked transportation targets in Holland and western Germany. Rocket-firing fighters sank a medium-sized coastal vessel near the Hook of Holland.

Medium bombers struck at bridges in the Arnhem area and a railway yard at Hengelo. Heavy bombers in very great strength, with escort fighters, struck at enemy supplies and communications at Emmerich and Cleve. Five bombers are missing.

In the Aachen sector, our troops have captured Beggendorf and Baesweiler, east and southeast of Uebach. Forces which advanced to the outskirts of Alsdorf encountered decreasing resistance and lessening artillery fire. On the northern fringe of this advance, we have occupied Waldenrath.

Good progress in the Forest of Huertgen has taken our troops to within less than two miles of the village of Huertgen.

In Luxembourg, we have cleared the enemy from Echternach and Wormeldingen.

North of Metz, our troops have entered Maizieres-les-Metz. Heavy fighting continued in Fort Driant, where we hold the northwest and southwest corners of the fort.

Along the whole front, from Aachen to Nancy, fighter-bombers in strength supported our troops and attacked transportation targets behind the enemy lines. Medium bombers hit railway targets at Euskirchen, Trier, and Dillingen.

In the Vosges foothills, our troops captured two villages, but lost ground to a strong enemy counter-attack northeast of Epinal. Farther south newly won positions in the Le Thillot area were consolidated, and numerous counter-attacks repulsed.

More than 1,400 heavy bombers escorted by 900 fighters hit synthetic oil plants at Politz, Ruhland, Magdeburg, Bohlen, Merseburg, Lutzkendorf; tank plants at Magdeburg and Kassel; aero engine, locomotive and chemical works at Kassel and Clausthal Zellerseldt, an aircraft repair depot and a motor transport plant at Zwickau and an airfield at Norbhausen.

In the course of these operations, thirty-three enemy aircraft were shot down and sixteen destroyed on the ground. Fifty-six bombers and fifteen fighters are missing.

†PENDLETON, JACK J.

Rank and Organization: Staff Sergeant, U. S. Army, Company I, 120th Infantry, 30th Infantry Division.
Born: Sentinel Butte, North Dakota.
Entered Service At: Yakima, Washington.
Place and Date: Bardening, Germany, October 12, 1944.
Citation: For conspicuous gallantry and intrepidity at the risk of his life above and beyond the call of duty on October 12, 1944. When Company I was advancing on the town of Bardening, Germany, they reached a point approximately two-thirds of the distance through the town when they were pinned down by fire from a nest of enemy machineguns. This enemy strongpoint was protected by a lone machinegun strategically placed at an intersection and firing down a street which offered little or no cover or

concealment for the advancing troops. The elimination of this protecting machinegun was imperative in order that the stronger position it protected could be neutralized. After repeated and unsuccessful attempts had been made to knock out this position, S/Sgt. Pendleton volunteered to lead his squad in an attempt to neutralize this strongpoint. S/Sgt. Pendleton started his squad slowly forward, crawling about 10 yards in front of his men in the advance toward the enemy gun. After advancing approximately 130 yards under the withering fire, S/Sgt. Pendleton was seriously wounded in the leg by a burst from the gun he was assaulting. Disregarding his grievous wound, he ordered his men to remain where they were, and with a supply of handgrenades he slowly and painfully worked his way forward alone. With no hope of surviving the veritable hail of machinegun fire which he deliberately drew onto himself, he succeeded in advancing to within 10 yards of the enemy position when he was instantly killed by a burst from the enemy gun. By deliberately diverting the attention of the enemy machinegunners upon himself, a second squad was able to advance, undetected, and with the help of S.Sgt. Pendleton's squad, neutralized the lone machinegun, while another platoon of his company advanced up the intersecting street and knocked out the machinegun nest which the first gun had been covering. S/Sgt. Pendleton's sacrifice enabled the entire company to continue the advance and complete their mission at a critical phase of the action.

BURT, JAMES M.

Rank and Organization: Captain, U.S. Army, Company B, 66th Armored Regiment, 2d Armored Division.
Born: Hinsdale, Massachusetts.
Entered Service At: Lee, Massachusetts.
Place and Date: Near Wurselen, Germany, October 13, 1944.
Citation: Capt. James M. Burt was in command of Company B, 66th Armored Regiment on the western outskirts of Wurselen, Germany, on October 13, 1944, when his organization participated in a coordinated infantry-tank attack destined to isolate the large German garrison which was tenaciously defending the city of Aachen. In the first day's action, when infantrymen ran into murderous small-arms and mortar fire, Capt. Burt dismounted from his tank about 200 yards to the rear and moved forward on foot beyond the infantry positions, where, as the enemy concentrated a tremendous volume of fire upon him, he calmly motioned his tanks into good firing positions. As our attack gained momentum, he climbed aboard his tank and directed the action from the rear deck, exposed to hostile vol-

leys which finally wounded him painfully in the face and neck. He maintained his dangerous post despite pointblank self-propelled gunfire until friendly artillery knocked out these enemy weapons, and then proceeded to the advanced infantry scouts' positions to deploy his tanks for the defense of the gains which had been made. The next day, when the enemy counterattacked, he left cover and went 75 yards through heavy fire to assist the infantry battalion commander who was seriously wounded. For the next 8 days, through rainy, miserable weather and under constant, heavy shelling, Capt. Burt held the combined forces together, dominating and controlling the critical situation through the sheer force of his heroic example. To direct artillery fire, on October 15, he took his tank 300 yards into the enemy lines, where he dismounted and remained for one hour giving accurate data to friendly gunners. Twice more that day he went into enemy territory under deadly fire on reconnaissance. In succeeding days he never faltered in his determination to defeat the strong German forces opposing him. Twice the tank in which he was riding was knocked out by enemy action, and each time he climbed aboard another vehicle and continued the fight. He took great risks to rescue wounded comrades and inflicted prodigious destruction on enemy personnel and material even though suffering from the wounds he received in the battle's opening phase. Capt. Burt's intrepidity and disregard of personal safety were so complete that his own men and the infantry who attached themselves to him were inspired to overcome the wretched and extremely hazardous conditions which accompanied one of the most bitter local actions of the war. The victory achieved closed the Aachen gap.

OFFICIAL COMMUNIQUE:
United Nations
SUPREME HEADQUARTERS, Allied Expeditionary Force, Oct. 13 —Communique 188:

Further reinforcements have been landed on the south shore of the Schelde estuary east of Breskens. In the Leopold Canal bridgehead, the village of Biezen was cleared of the enemy. Heavy fighting continues in both areas. North of Antwerp an enemy counter-attack was repelled.

Fighters and fighter-bombers continued to support our ground forces in the Breskens area. Troops and strongpoints were hit. Fortified positions at Oostburg, Sluis and Schoondijke were again attacked by rocket-firing fighters. Heavy bombers struck at gun emplacements at Fort Frederick-Henrik. Batteries north of Knockeiere were bombed without loss by medium bombers.

Other fighters and fighter-bombers provided support for our troops near Arnhem and Nijmegen and attacked transportation targets in the Amersfoort and Appeldoorn areas and elsewhere in Holland. On the east side of the Dutch salient, Allied troops have retaken Overloon. Medium and light bombers hit road junctions at Venray, south of Overloon.

Aachen was dive-bombed and strafed yesterday by hundreds of fighter-bombers.

Other fighter-bombers attacked tanks east of Aachen. Enemy fighters came up to give battle over the city and twelve were shot down and others were damaged, for the loss of four of our aircraft.

Northeast of Aachen, a heavy enemy counter-attack with infantry and tanks has been launched in the Bardenburg area. Earlier counter-attacks from the east in the vicinity of Verlautenheide and Haaren were repulsed by our artillery. Fighting is still in progress at Haaren and Wuerselen, where an enemy pocket has been cleared up.

Air attacks were made during Wednesday night on our troops in the areas of Schaufenberg and Siersdorf, east of Alsdorf, and increased artillery fire has been encountered in the area southeast of Geilenkirchen.

Four miles east of Stolberg, our forces have advanced slightly against heavy resistance. Farther south in the Huertgen sector, we reached Vossenack, but were pushed back slightly by a counter-attack.

Striking at communications in the Aachen sector, medium and light bombers with fighter escort bombed a railway bridge across the River Erfe at Grevenbroich and the towns of Aldenhoven and Langerwehe. At Ahrweiler, also, a rail bridge was bombed.

South of Monschau, patrol activity continues and our troops are encountering sporadic artillery and mortar fire. Near Nancy, fighter-bombers, in advance of our infantry, dropped fragmentation bombs in wooded country.

East of Luneville, our patrols have advanced to the eastern edge of the Forest of Parroy, and the town of Parroy has been cleared of the enemy. Local counter-attacks have been met near Foincourt. In the Epinal-Belfort sector, our troops have made substantial gains over rugged country in the bend of Moselotte River, north of Le Thillot. Several villages have been taken. Heavy enemy counter-attacks were repulsed in this area as well as in the vicinity of Le Thillot, where our positions were improved.

Elsewhere in the Vosges foothills, activity was limited mostly to artillery exchanges and patrolling.

Strong forces of heavy bombers, with fighter escort, attacked an aircraft component factory at Bremen and other targets in northwest Germany. Other escorted heavy bombers struck at the synthetic oil plant at Wanne-Eickel.

Medium and light bombers attacked targets in Menningen.

THOMPSON, MAX

Rank and Organization: Sergeant, U.S. Army, Company K, 18th Infantry, 1st Infantry Division.
Born: Bethel, North Carolina.
Entered Service At: Prescott, Arizona.
Place and Date: Near Haaren, Germany, October 18, 1944.
Citation: On October 18, 1944, Company K, 18th Infantry, occupying a position on a hill near Haaren, Germany, was attacked by an enemy infantry battalion supported by tanks. The assault was preceded by an artillery concentration, lasting an hour, which inflicted heavy casualties on the company. While engaged in moving wounded men to cover, Sgt. Thompson observed that the enemy had overrun the positions of the 3d Platoon. He immediately attempted to stem the enemy's advance single-handedly. He manned an abandoned machine-gun and fired on the enemy until a direct hit from a hostile tank destroyed the gun. Shaken and dazed, Sgt. Thompson picked up an automatic rifle and although alone against the enemy force which was pouring into the gap in our lines, he fired burst after burst, halting the leading elements of the attack and dispersing those following. Throwing aside his automatic rifle, which had jammed, he took up a rocket gun, fired on a light tank, setting it on fire. By evening the enemy had been driven from the greater part of the captured position but still held 3 pillboxes. Sgt. Thompson's squad was assigned the task of dislodging the enemy from these emplacements. Darkness having fallen and finding that fire of his squad was ineffective from a distance, Sgt. Thompson crawled forward alone to within 20 yards of one of the pillboxes and fired grenades into it. The Germans holding the emplacement concentrated their fire upon him. Though wounded, he forced the enemy to abandon the blockhouse. Sgt. Thompson's courageous leadership inspired his men and materially contributed to the clearing of the enemy from his last remaining hold on this important hill position.

OFFICIAL COMMUNIQUE:
United Nations
SUPREME HEADQUARTERS, Allied Expeditionary Force, Oct. 18 –Communique 193:

In the Schelde pocket, Allied units have reached the area of Ijzendijke. North of the town, we advanced westward about a mile. Good progress also was made farther south. Fighter-bombers gave support to our ground forces, who repulsed counter-attacks against the neck of the Zuid Beveland Peninsula. Escorted heavy bombers, none of which is missing, attacked the sea dike at Westkapelle, on the island of Walcheren. In the Breskens sector, supply dumps, strongpoints, and road transport were hit by fighter-bombers.

Our forces have reached the outskirts of Venray, where heavy fighting continues. In another thrust to the southwest, our units have crossed the Venray-Deurne road.

Rail targets were hit over a wide area in Holland and western Germany by fighter-bombers. Attacks were made in the areas of Venloo and Kempen, east of the Dutch salient; at Neuss, near Duesseldorf; Bad Kreuznach, Bellheim, and Rheinzabern, in the Rhineland, and at Muenster.

Our troops are mopping up northeast of Aachen and are maintaining lines completely encircling the city, where house-to-house fighting continues. Northwest of Aachen, we mopped up segments of the Siegfried Line. Light bombers, without loss, attacked a railway bridge at Euskirchen.

In the Moselle Valley, fighting continues in Maizieres-les-Metz.

Military targets at Cologne were attacked in daylight by more than 1,300 heavy bombers escorted by 800 fighters. Thirteen bombers and three fighters are missing.

In the Vosges foothills, despite stubborn resistance and strong enemy counter-attacks in several areas, our troops made a substantial advance just south of the road junction at Bruyeres and northeast of Le Thillot. Hard fighting continues in both of these areas. The village of Laval, near Bruyeres, was taken. Counter-attacks were repulsed in the Luneville-Epinal sector.

†MOON, HAROLD H., JR.

Rank and Organization: Private, U.S. Army, Company G, 34th Infantry, 24th Infantry Division.
Born: Albuquerque, New Mexico.
Entered Service At: Gardena, California.
Place and Date: Pawig, Leyte, Philippine Islands, October 21, 1944.
Citation: Pvt. Moon fought with conspicuous gallantry and intrepidity when powerful Japanese counter-blows were being struck in a desperate effort to annihilate a newly won beachhead. In a forward position, armed with a submachine-gun, he met the brunt of a strong, well-supported night attack which quickly enveloped his platoon's flanks. Many men in nearby positions were killed or injured, and Pvt. Moon was wounded as his foxhole became the immediate object of a concentration of mortar and machine-gun fire. Nevertheless, he maintained his stand, poured deadly fire into the enemy, daringly exposed himself to hostile fire time after time to exhort and inspire what American troops were left in the immediate area. A Japanese officer, covered by machine-gun fire and hidden by an embankment,

attempted to knock out his position with grenades, but Pvt. Moon, after protracted and skillful maneuvering, killed him. When the enemy advanced a light machine-gun to within 20 yards of the shattered perimeter and fired with telling effects on the remnants of the platoon, he stood up to locate the gun and remained exposed while calling back range corrections to friendly mortars which knocked out the weapon. A little later he killed 2 Japanese as they charged an aid man. By dawn his position, the focal point of the attack for more than 4 hours, was virtually surrounded. In a fanatical effort to reduce it and kill its defender, an entire platoon charged with fixed bayonets. Firing from a sitting position, Pvt. Moon calmly emptied his magazine into the advancing horde, killing 18 and repulsing the attack. In a final display of bravery, he stood up to throw a grenade at a machine-gun which had opened fire on the right flank. He was hit and instantly killed, falling in the position from which he had not been driven by the fiercest enemy action. Nearly 200 dead Japanese were found within 100 yards of his foxhole. The continued tenacity, combat sagacity, and magnificent heroism with which Pvt. Moon fought on against overwhelming odds contributed in a large measure to breaking up a powerful enemy threat and did much to insure our initial successes during a most important operation.

OFFICIAL COMMUNIQUE:
United Nations
GENERAL MacARTHUR'S HEADQUARTERS, the Philippines, Oct. 21 – A communique:

PHILIPPINES

Visayas: Our fighter-bombers, reaching into the central Philippines, attacked or damaged enemy planes caught on the ground. A 1,000-ton freighter and several luggers were set afire. We lost three planes to anti-aircraft defenses. Reconnaissance units destroyed a seaplane to the northeast.
Sulu Islands: Our fighters destroyed or damaged a 6,000-ton freighter transport, three freighters of 1,000 tons, three coastal vessels, and several small craft. Waterfront installations also were attacked and two float planes set afire.

A later communique from General MacArthur's Headquarters, in the Philippines, as recorded by the Columbia Broadcasting System:

LEYTE

Our ground forces have advanced in all sectors an average depth of four miles. Strong enemy defenses carefully prepared with concrete pillboxes and prepared artillery positions were skillfully enveloped by infiltration and the enemy was forced to withdraw. Direct assaults were thereby avoided. Our casualties consequently remained light. The enemy is already showing signs of a lack of maneuverable cohesion in the face of the skillful attacks of our local commanders.

The force to the north has taken Tacloban, the capital of Leyte, and secured Tacloban airfield.

In the southern sector, the Twenty-fourth Corps has seized Dulag and its airdrome and is pushing toward San Pablo in the Leyte valley. Two strong enemy counter-attacks were repulsed. Enemy air activity against our beachhead and shipping was limited to dawn-and-dusk raids by small groups of aircraft. Three enemy bombers were destroyed by ship anti-aircraft fire.

O'KANE, RICHARD HETHERINGTON

Rank and Organization: Commander, U.S. Navy, commanding U.S.S. *Tang*.
Born: February 2, 1911, Dover, New Hampshire.
Entered Service At: New Hampshire.
Place and Date: Vicinity Philippine Islands, October 23 and 24, 1944.
Citation: For conspicuous gallantry and intrepidity at the risk of his life above and beyond the call of duty as commanding officer of the *U.S.S. Tang* operating against 2 enemy Japanese convoys on October 23 and 24, 1944, during her fifth and last war patrol. Boldly maneuvering on the surface into the midst of a heavily escorted convoy, Comdr. O'Kane stood in the fusillade of bullets and shells from all directions to launch smashing hits on 3 tankers, coolly swung his ship to fire at a freighter and, in a split-second decision, shot out of the path of an onrushing transport, missing it by inches. Boxed in by blazing tankers, a freighter, transport, and several destroyers, he blasted 2 of the targets with his remaining torpedoes and, with pyrotechnics bursting on all sides, cleared the area. Twenty-four hours later, he again made contact with a heavily escorted convoy steaming to support the Leyte campaign with reinforcements and supplies and with crated planes piled high on each unit. In defiance of the enemy's relentless fire, he closed the concentration of ships and in quick succession sent 2 torpedoes each into the first and second transports and an adjacent tanker, finding his mark with each torpedo in a series of violent explosions at less than 1,000-yard range. With ships bearing down from all sides, he charged the enemy at high speed, exploding the tanker in a burst of flame, smashing the transport dead in the water, and blasting the destroyer with a mighty roar which rocked the *Tang* from stem to stern. Expending his last 2 torpedoes into the remnants of a once powerful convoy before his own ship when down, Comdr. O'Kane, aided by his gallant command, achieved an

illustrious record of heroism in combat, enhancing the finest traditions of the U.S. Naval Service.

CHOATE, CLYDE L.

Rank and Organization: Staff Sergeant, U.S. Army, Company C, 601st Tank Destroyer Battalion.
Born: June 28, 1920, West Frankfurt, Illinois.
Entered Service At: Anna, Illinois.
Place and Date: Near Bruyeres, France, October 25, 1944.
Citation: S/Sgt. Choate commanded a tank destroyer near Bruyeres, France, on October 25, 1944. Our infantry occupied a position on a wooded hill when, at dusk, an enemy Mark IV tank and a company of infantry attacked, threatening to overrun the American position and capture a command post 400 yards to the rear. S/Sgt. Choate's tank destroyer, the only weapon available to oppose the German armor, was set afire by 2 hits. Ordering his men to abandon the destroyer, S/Sgt. Choate reached comparative safety. He returned to the burning destroyer to search for comrades possibly trapped in the vehicle risking instant death in an explosion which was imminent and braving enemy fire which ripped his jacket and tore the helmet from his head. Completing the search and seeing the tank and its supporting infantry overrunning our infantry in their shallow foxholes, he secured a bazooka and ran after the tank, dodging from tree to tree and passing through the enemy's loose skirmish line. He fired a rocket from a distance of 20 yards, immobilizing the tank but leaving it able to spray the area with cannon and machine-gun fire. Running back to our infantry through vicious fire, he secured another rocket, and, advancing against a hail of machine-gun and small-arms fire reached a position 10 yards from the tank. His second shot shattered the turret. With his pistol he killed 2 of the crew as they emerged from the tank; and then running to the crippled Mark IV while enemy infantry sniped at him, he dropped a grenade inside the tank and completed its destruction. With their armor gone, the enemy infantry became disorganized and was driven back. S/Sgt. Choate's great daring in assaulting an enemy tank single-handed, his determination to follow the vehicle after it had passed his position, and his skill and crushing thoroughness in the attack prevented the enemy from capturing a battalion command post and turned a probable defeat into a tactical success.

†EVANS, ERNEST EDWIN
Rank and Organization: Commander, U.S. Navy.
Born: August 13, 1908, Pawnee, Oklahoma.
Entered Service At: Oklahoma.
Place and Date: Off Samar, October 25, 1944.
Citation: For conspicuous gallantry and intrepidity at the risk of his life above and beyond the call of duty as commanding officer of the *U.S.S. Johnston* in action against major units of the enemy Japanese fleet during the battle off Samar on October 25, 1944. The first to lay a smokescreen and to open fire as an enemy task force, vastly superior in number, firepower and armor, rapidly approached. Comdr. Evans gallantly diverted the powerful blasts of hostile guns from the lightly armed and armored carriers under his protection, launching the first torpedo attack when the *Johnston* came under straddling Japanese shellfire. Undaunted by damage sustained under the terrific volume of fire, he unhesitatingly joined others of his group to provide fire support during subsequent torpedo attacks against the Japanese and, outshooting and outmaneuvering the enemy as he consistently interposed his vessel between the hostile fleet units and our carriers despite the crippling loss of engine power and communications with steering aft, shifted command to the fantail, shouted steering orders through an open hatch to men turning the rudder by hand and battled furiously until the Johnston, burning and shuddering from a mortal blow, lay dead in the water after 3 hours of fierce combat. Seriously wounded early in the engagement, Comdr. Evans, by his indomitable courage and brilliant professional skill, aided materially in turning back the enemy during a critical phase of the action. His valiant fighting spirit throughout this historic battle will venture as an inspiration to all who served with him.

†CARSWELL, HORACE S., JR. (Air Mission)
Rank and Organization: Major, 308th Bombardment Group, U.S. Army Air Corps.
Born: Fort Worth, Texas.
Entered Service At: San Angelo, Texas.
Place and Date: Over South China Sea, October 26, 1944.
Citation: Maj. Carswell piloted a B-24 bomber in a one-plane strike against a Japanese convoy in the South China Sea on the night of October 26, 1944. Taking the enemy force of 12 ships escorted by at least 2 destroyers by surprise, he made one bombing run at 600 feet, scoring a near miss on one warship and escaping without drawing fire. He circled, and fully realizing that the convoy was thoroughly alerted and would meet his next at-

tack with a barrage of anti-aircraft fire, began a second low-level run which culminated in 2 direct hits on a large tanker. A hail of steel from Japanese guns, riddled the bomber, knocking out 2 engines, damaging a third, crippling the hydraulic system, puncturing one gasoline tank, ripping uncounted holes in the aircraft, and wounding the copilot; but by magnificent display of flying skill, Maj. Carswell controlled the plane's plunge toward the sea and carefully forced it into a halting climb in the direction of the China shore. On reaching land, where it would have been possible to abandon the staggering bomber, one of the crew discovered that his parachute had been ripped by flak and rendered useless; the pilot, hoping to cross mountainous terrain and reach a base, continued onward until the third engine failed. He ordered the crew to bail out while he struggled to maintain altitude, and, refusing to save himself, chose to remain with his comrade and attempt a crash landing. He died when the airplane struck a mountainside and burned. With consummate gallantry and intrepidity, Maj. Carswell gave his life in a supreme effort to save all members of his crew. His sacrifice, far beyond that required of him, was in keeping with the traditional bravery of America's war heroes.

OFFICIAL COMMUNIQUE:
United Nations
SUPREME HEADQUARTERS, Allied Expeditionary Force, Oct. 26 –Communique 201:

Allied forces are fighting in 's Hertogenbosch, where they have driven the enemy from the north and east sections of the town. Boxtel has been freed and gains have taken us several miles to the northwest.

On the Oirschot-Tiburg road we have reached the area of Moergestel. There has been general progress northward in the area east of the Antwerp-Breda road.

On the approach to Zuid Beveland we have taken the village of Rilland and have moved forward three miles west along the south side of the isthmus. Further ground has been gained in the area between Pindorp and Woendsdrecht.

In the Schelde pocket, Allied forces have made progress in the direction of Poldertje. Fort Frederik-Hendrik, from which we withdrew after an initial entry four days ago, has been taken. Farther south we have reached the outskirts of Groede. We have also gained some ground west and northwest of Schoondijke.

Northeast of Epinal, our advance was slowed by stiffened resistance. In the Vosges Mountains sector, farther south, counter-attacks were thrown back with severe losses to the enemy.

Fighters and fighter-bombers gave support over the battle zones, and went for road and rail transport in western Germany. In daylight, heavy bombers in very great strength, escorted by fighters, attacked Essen and the synthetic oil plant at Homburg. Four bombers are missing.

More than 1,200 heavy bombers, escorted by some 500 fighters, again in daylight, attacked the railway yards at Hamm, an oil refinery in the Hamburg area and other military targets in northwestern Germany.

ADVANCED HEADQUARTERS, on Leyte, Oct. 26 – A communique:

PHILIPPINES

Mindanao: Heavy and medium units dropped forty tons of bombs on enemy personnel areas at Buayan and communication lines east of Cotabato. Buildings and trucks were destroyed and fires started.

BISMARCK-SOLOMONS

Medium and light bombers started fires in the Kavieng area and bombed enemy concentrations in northern Bougainville. Air and naval patrols harassed shore positions at Gazelle Peninsula, New Ireland, and Choiseul Island.

A later communique:

PHILIPPINES

Leyte: Junction of the Tenth and Twenty-fourth Corps has been established on the coast south of Tanavan. We now control the eastern coastal sector of Leyte from the northern end of San Juanico Strait to Dulag, a distance of forty miles.

Elements of the First Cavalry Division repulsed a small enemy counter-attack at La Paz on Samar Island.

The Twenty-fourth Division is meeting increasing opposition in its advance west of Palo. To the south, in the Twenty-fourth Corps sector, the Ninety-sixth Division captured Tabontabon, three and one-half miles west of Catmon Hill. The Seventh Division, after sharp fighting, captured Buri on the Burauen-Dagami road.

Additional communities freed from the enemy include Anibung, Tigbad, Cannangui, Hindang, Bolongtohan, Kalvasag, Calampanon, Malabka, San Gabriel, Kanmonhag, Telegrafo, San Joaquin, and Diit.

Air activity against shipping in San Pedro Bay and the beachhead areas was again limited to intermittent harassing raids, causing light damage and casualties. Thirty-nine enemy planes were shot down by anti-aircraft fire, fourteen by fighter patrol, and twenty-three by planes from our escort carriers in Leyte Gulf.

Remnants of the enemy's naval forces retreating from Leyte Gulf are being kept under continual attack by our aircraft.

CHUNGKING, China, Oct. 26 – A Fourteenth United States Air Force communique:

SOUTH CHINA AREA

Seventeen missions of P-51's and P-40's of the Fourteenth Air Force continued coordinated air support for Chinese ground forces in the Menghu-Kweiping sector of the West River front on Oct. 25, causing heavy damage and casualties to Japanese forces attempting a breakthrough to the west and north.

Compounds, villages, gun emplacements, and troop positions were bombed and strafed by fighters as directed by ground forces. Wooded areas containing enemy supplies and troop concentrations were repeatedly hit. More than 155 Japanese troops were known to have been killed in the strafing and bombing sorties.

Menghu and Szewang, north of the river, and Kweiping were bombed. Large fires were observed in Kweiping, where all hits were in the target. One extensive Japanese position, four miles northeast of Menghu, was covered by flames when P-40's struck it with incendiaries. West of Tengyun, on the West River, where enemy shipping has declined the past few days, P-40's sank a barge which exploded and then bombed and destroyed enemy material on the river bank.

On Oct. 24, P-51's and P-40's attacked the Amoy area, on the East China coast. They damaged an enemy vessel and strafed barracks areas and warehouses and anti-aircraft positions.

COOLIDGE, CHARLES H.
Rank and Organization: Technical Sergeant, U.S. Army, Company M. 141st Infantry, 36th Infantry Division.
Born: Signal Mountain, Tennessee.
Entered Service At: Signal Mountain, Tennessee.
Place and Date: East of Belmont sur Buttant, France, October 24-27, 1944.
Citation: Leading a section of heavy machine-guns supported by one platoon of Company K, T/Sgt. Coolidge took a position near Hill 623, east of Belmont sur Buttant, France on October 24, 1944, with the mission of covering the right flank of the 3d Battalion and supporting its action. T/Sgt. Coolidge went forward with a sergeant of Company K to reconnoiter positions for coordinating the fires of the light and heavy machine-guns. They ran into an enemy force in the woods estimated to be an infantry company. T/Sgt. Coolidge, attempting to bluff the Germans by a show of assurance and boldness called upon them to surrender, whereupon the enemy opened fire. With is carbine, T/Sgt. Coolidge wounded 2 of them. There being no officer present with the force, T/Sgt. Coolidge at once assumed command.

Many of the men were replacements recently arrived; this was their first experience under fire. T/Sgt. Coolidge, unmindful of the enemy fire delivered at close range, walked along the position, calming and encouraging his men and directing their fire. The attack was thrown back. Through October 25 and 26, the enemy launched repeated attacks against the position of this combat group but each was repulsed due to T/Sgt. Coolidge's able leadership. On October 27, German infantry, supported by 2 tanks, made a determined attack on the position. The area was swept by enemy small-arms, machine-gun, and tank fire. T/Sgt. Coolidge armed himself with a bazooka and advanced to within 25 yards of the tanks. His bazooka failed to function and he threw it aside. Securing all the hand-grenades he could carry, he crawled forward and inflicted heavy casualties on the advancing enemy. Finally it became apparent that the enemy, in greatly superior force, supported by tanks, would overrun the position. T/Sgt. Coolidge, displaying great coolness and courage, directed and conducted an orderly withdrawal, being himself the last to leave the position. As a result of T/Sgt. Coolidge's heroic and superior leadership, the mission of this combat group was accomplished throughout 4 days of continuous fighting against numerically superior enemy troops in rain and cold and amid dense woods.

ADAMS, LUCIAN
Rank and Organization: Staff Sergeant, U.S. Army, 30th Infantry, 3d Infantry Division.
Born: Port Arthur, Texas.
Entered Service At: Port Arthur, Texas.
Place and Date: Near St. Die, France, October 28, 1944.
Citation: For conspicuous gallantry and intrepidity at risk of life above and beyond the call of duty on October 28, 1944, near St. Die, France. When his company was stopped in its effort to drive through the Mortagne Forest to reopen the supply line to the isolated Third Battalion, S/Sgt. Adams braved the concentrated fire of machine-guns in a lone assault on a force of German troops. Although his company had progressed less than 10 yards and had lost 3 killed and 6 wounded, S/Sgt. Adams charged forward dodging from tree to tree firing a borrowed BAR from the hip. Despite intense machine-gun fire which the enemy directed at him and rifle grenades which struck the trees over his head showering him with broken twigs and branches, S/Sgt. Adams made his way to within 10 yards of the closest machine-gun and killed the gunner with a hand-grenade. An enemy soldier threw hand-grenades at him from a position only 10 yards distant; however, S/Sgt. Adams dispatched him with a single burst of BAR fire. Charging into the

vortex of the enemy fire, he killed another machine-gunner at 15 yards range with a hand-grenade and forced the surrender of 2 supporting infantrymen. Although the remainder of the German group concentrated the full force of its automatic weapons fire in a desperate effort to knock him out, he proceeded through the woods to find and exterminate 5 more of the enemy. Finally, when the third German machine-gun opened up on him at a range of 20 yards, S/Sgt. Adams killed the gunner with BAR fire. In the course of the action, he personally killed 9 Germans, eliminated 3 enemy machine-guns, vanquished a specialized force which was armed with automatic weapons and grenade launchers, cleared the woods of hostile elements, and reopened the severed supply lines to the assault companies of his battalion.

OFFICIAL COMMUNIQUE:
United Nations
SUPREME HEADQUARTERS, Allied Expeditionary Force, Oct. 28 –Communique 203:

In South Beveland, Allied forces now hold the south side of the isthmus as far as the canal west of Kruiningen. Our bridgehead on the southern coast of the peninsula has been reinforced and expanded.

Groede in the Schelde pocket is in our hands and we are on the coast to the northwest of the village.

Northeast of the South Beveland Isthmus we have taken Bergen op Zoom.

North of Esschen, our units are within two miles of Roosendaal. On the Antwerp-Breda road, we have progressed to the area of Zundert.

We are in the eastern outskirts of Tilburg, and north of the town, our troops have reached the vicinity of Loon op Zand. To the south, we have made good gains and on the west, forward elements have cut the Tilburg-Breda road.

The enemy has been cleared from 's Hertogenbosch, and we have made some progress farther west.

On the east side of the Dutch salient, we checked a counter-attack in the vicinity of Meijel, where fighting still is in progress.

Light artillery fire was directed against our units in the Aachen area, and along the Belgian-German frontier in the sector east of St. Vith.

Near Rambervillers, we made local gains at several points. The village of Housseras has been taken.

Farther south, limited progress was made between Bruyeres and Le Tholy.

In the Vosges Mountains, attempts to infiltrate our positions were frustrated, and losses were inflicted on the enemy.

Adverse weather restricted air operations yesterday.

ROME, Oct. 28 – A communique:

LAND

The extremely bad weather during the last forty-eight hours brought operations in Italy to a virtual standstill.

†BROSTROM, LEONARD C.

Rank and Organization: Private First Class, U.S. Army, Company F, 17th Infantry, 7th Infantry Division.
Born: Preston, Idaho.
Entered Service At: Preston, Idaho.
Place and Date: Near Dagami, Leyte, Philippine Islands, October 28, 1944.
Citation: Pfc. Brostrom was a rifleman with an assault platoon which ran into powerful resistance near Dagami, Leyte, Philippine Islands, on October 28, 1944. From pillboxes, trenches, and spider holes, so well camouflaged that they could be detected at no more than 20 yards, the enemy poured machine-gun and rifle fire, causing severe casualties in the platoon. Realizing that a key pillbox in the center of the strong point would have to be knocked out if the company were to advance, Pfc. Brostrom, without orders and completely ignoring his own safety, ran forward to attack the pillbox with grenades. He immediately became the prime target for all the riflemen in the area, as he rushed to the rear of the pillbox and tossed grenades through the entrance. Six enemy soldiers left a trench in a bayonet charge against the heroic American, but he killed one and drove the others off with rifle fire. As he threw more grenades from his completely exposed position he was wounded several times in the abdomen and knocked to the ground. Although suffering intense pain and rapidly weakening from loss of blood, he slowly rose to his feet and once more hurled his deadly missiles at the pillbox. As he collapsed, the enemy began fleeing from the fortification and were killed by riflemen of his platoon. Pfc. Brostrom died while being carried from the battlefield, but his intrepidity and unhesitating willingness to sacrifice himself in a one-man attack against overwhelming odds enabled his company to reorganize against attack, and annihilate the entire enemy position.

†THORSON, JOHN F.

Rank and Organization: Private First Class, U.S. Army, Company G, 17th Infantry, 7th Infantry Division.
Born: Armstrong, Iowa.
Entered Service At: Armstrong, Iowa.
Place and Date: Dagami, Leyte, Philippine Islands, October 28, 1944
Citation: Pfc. Thorson was an automatic rifleman on October 28, 1944, in the attack on Dagami, Leyte, Philippine Islands. A heavily fortified enemy position consisting of pillboxes and supporting trenches held up the advance of his company. His platoon was ordered to out-flank and neutralize the strong point. Voluntarily moving well out in front of his group, Pfc. Thorson came upon an enemy fire trench defended by several hostile riflemen and, disregarding the intense fire directed at him, attacked single-handedly. He was seriously wounded and fell about 6 yards from the trench. Just as the remaining 20 members of the platoon reached him, one of the enemy threw a grenade into their midst. Shouting a warning and making a final effort, Pfc. Thorson rolled onto the grenade and smothered the explosion with his body. He was instantly killed, but his magnificent courage and supreme self-sacrifice prevented the injury and possible death of his comrades, and remain with them as a lasting inspiration.

Note: The following is a newspaper account of the preceding battle for which Pfc. Brostrom and Pfc. Thorson were awarded the Medal of Honor:

67-MILE COASTLINE IS SEIZED ON LEYTE

• • •

Americans Drive west and South as Japanese Crumble and Our Samar Drive Gains

• • •

ADVANCED HEADQUARTERS, on Leyte, Sunday, Oct. 29 – American troops driving west and south through rapidly deteriorating Japanese defenses have seized control of a sixty-seven-mile front on Leyte Island, Gen. Douglas MacArthur announced today, as other United States forces on Samar Island to the north reached the last water barrier on the road to Manila, 250 miles away.

Covered by Fifth Air Force fighters and anti-aircraft that shot down twenty-enemy raiders on the American beachhead, dismounted troops of the First Cavalry Division drove into Carigara in a three-mile advance along the bay on the northern sector, while troops of the Twenty-fourth Division picked up four miles in the Leyte Valley, where the enemy now is fighting only a delaying action.

As the Twenty-fourth slashed at Alangalang, ten and a half miles northwest of Palo, and threw back a Jap counter-attack against Santa Fe, six miles southeast of Alangalang, elements of the Seventh Division on the southern sector drove to within a mile of Dagami, key junction of the Burauan-Dagami road, eight miles below Santa Fe, linking the coastal sectors.

On the left flank, patrols broke into the town of Santa Ana, four miles southeast of the key junction of Burauan, and near San Andre and Pangban, south of the Marabang River. Minor contact with the enemy was reported inland from Abuyog, where six coastal guns and forty vehicles gathered in a motor pool were captured, the communique said.

Samar, third largest of the Philippine Islands with an area of 5,124 square miles, was reported in the firm grip of Maj. Gen. Verne D. Mudge's dismounted cavalry.

ROSS, WILBURN K.

Rank and Organization: Private, U.S. Army, Company G, 350th Infantry, 3d Infantry Division.
Born: Strunk, Kentucky.
Entered Service At: Strunk, Kentucky.
Place and Date: Near St. Jacques, France, October 30, 1944.
Citation: For conspicuous gallantry and intrepidity at risk of life above and beyond the call of duty near St. Jacques, France. At 11:30 a.m., on October 30, 1944, after his company had lost 55 out of 88 men in an attack on an entrenched, full-strength German company of elite mountain troops, Pvt. Ross placed his light machine-gun 10 yards in advance of the foremost supporting riflemen in order to absorb the initial impact of an enemy counter-attack. With machine-gun and small-arms fire striking the earth near him, he fired with deadly effect on the assaulting force and repelled it. Despite the hail of automatic fire and the explosion of rifle grenades within a stone's throw of his position, he continued to man his machine-gun alone, holding off 6 more German attacks. When the eighth assault was launched, most of his supporting riflemen were out of ammunition. They took positions in echelon behind Pvt. Ross and crawled up, during the attack, to extract a few rounds of ammunition from his machine-gun ammunition belt. Pvt. Ross fought on virtually without assistance and, despite the fact that enemy grenadiers crawled to within 4 yards of his position in an effort to kill him with hand-grenades, he again directed accurate and deadly fire on the hostile force and hurled it back. After expending his last rounds, Pvt. Ross was advised to withdraw to the company command post, together with 8

surviving riflemen, but, as more ammunition was expected, he declined to do so. The Germans launched their last all-out attack, converging their fire on Pvt. Ross in a desperate attempt to destroy the machine-gun which stood between them and a decisive breakthrough. As his supporting riflemen fixed bayonets for a last-ditch stand, fresh ammunition arrived and was brought to Pvt. Ross just as the advance assault elements were about to swarm over his position. He opened murderous fire on the oncoming enemy; killed 40 and wounded 10 of the attacking force; broke the assault single-handedly, and forced the Germans to withdraw. Having killed or wounded at least 58 Germans in more than 5 hours of continuous combat and saved the remnants of his company from destruction, Pvt. Ross remained at his post that night and the following day for a total of 36 hours. His actions throughout this engagement were an inspiration to his comrades and maintained the high traditions of the military service.

OFFICIAL COMMUNIQUE:
UNITED NATIONS
SUPREME HEADQUARTERS, Allied Expeditionary Force, Oct. 30-Communique 205:

Cadzand and Zuidzane, south of the Schelde, have been taken by Allied troops.

In Zuid Beveland our troops freed Goes and linked up with our seaborne force in the area of Hoedenskerke. The seaborne bridgehead was also enlarged to the westward. Defenses on the island of Walcheren were attacked yesterday by heavy bombers made, one of which is missing, and by fighter-bombers. Fighters which escorted the heavy bombers made low level attack on flak positions.

Allied forces continued their advance along the whole front south of the Maas [Meuse]. Breda was freed by troops advancing from the east. Other forces driving from the south cut the road between Breda and Roosendaal. Fighter-bombers strafed road transport north of these two towns and medium bombers attacked a bridge at Moerdijk.

In the area north of Tilburg our forces are some miles north and west of Loon op Zand. Fighter-bombers cut railway lines between Amersfoort and Zwolle, in the Venlo area, and elsewhere behind the battle areas in Holland.

In southeastern Holland medium bombers also attacked communications at Venlo and a bridge at Roermond. Our ground forces held further enemy attacks in the Meijel area.

Bridges at Konz-Karthaus, Euskirchen, Mayen and Eller were the targets for medium bombers, and fighter-bombers destroyed three bridges and damaged a fourth across the River Ahr, south of Bonn, and sealed two near-by railway tunnels. Fighter-bombers hit highways radiating northward from Dueren, a railway yard at Kerpen, and cut rail lines in many places between Muenster and the Dutch-German frontier, and in the areas of Bonn and Coblenz. They also attacked locomotives, rail cars and barges over a wide area and silenced gun positions.

Our units made slight gains in the Luneville sector. East of Rambervillers we took Fraipertuis and held the village against strong counter-attacks against our positions in the Vosges Mountains were repulsed.

Yesterday morning heavy bombers, one of which is missing, attacked the battleship Tirpitz near Tromsoe.

According to reports so far received, twenty-eight enemy aircraft were shot down during yesterday. One medium bomber and nine fighter-bombers are missing.

BOLTON, CECIL H.
Rank and Organization: First Lieutenant, U.S. Army, Company E, 413th Infantry, 104th Infantry Division.
Born: Crawfordsville, Florida.
Entered Service At: Huntsville, Alabama.
Place and Date: Mark River, Holland, November 2, 1944.
Citation: As leader of the weapons platoon of Company E, 413th Infantry, on the night of November 2, 1944, 1st Lt. Bolton fought gallantly in a pitched battle which followed the crossing of the Mark River in Holland. When 2 machine-guns pinned down his company, he tried to eliminate, with mortar fire, their grazing fire which was inflicting serious casualties and preventing the company's advance from an area rocked by artillery shelling. In the moonlight it was impossible for him to locate accurately the enemy's camouflaged positions, but he continued to direct fire until wounded severely in the legs and rendered unconscious by a German shell. When he recovered consciousness he instructed his unit and then crawled to the forward rifle platoon positions. Taking a two-man bazooka team on his voluntary mission, he advanced chest deep in chilling water along a canal toward one enemy machine-gun. While the bazooka team covered him, he approached alone to within 15 yards of the hostile emplacement in a house. He charged the remaining distance and killed the 2 gunners with hand-grenades. Returning to his men he led them through intense fire over open ground to assault the second German machine-gun. An enemy sniper who tried to block the way was dispatched, and the trio pressed on. When discovered by the machine-gun crew and subjected to direct fire, 1st Lt. Bolton killed one of the 3 gunners with carbine fire, and his 2 comrades shot the others. Continuing to disregard his wounds, he led the bazooka team toward an 88-mm. artillery piece which was having telling effect on

the American ranks, and approached once more through icy canal water until he could dimly make out the gun's silhouette. Under his fire direction, the two soldiers knocked out the enemy weapon with rockets. On the way back to his own lines he was again wounded. To prevent his men being longer subjected to deadly fire, he refused aid and ordered them back to safety, painfully crawling after them until he reached his lines, where he collapsed. 1st Lt. Bolton's heroic assaults in the face of vicious fire, his inspiring leadership, and continued aggressiveness even through suffering from serious wounds, contributed in large measure to overcoming strong enemy resistance and made it possible for his battalion to reach its objective.

†FEMOYER, ROBERT E. (Air Mission)

Rank and Organization: Second Lieutenant, 711th Bombing Squadron, 447th Bomber Group, U.S. Army Air Corps.
Born: October 31, 1921, Huntington, West Virginia.
Entered Service At: Jacksonville, Florida.
Place and Date: Over Merseburg Germany, November 2, 1944.
Citation: For conspicuous gallantry and intrepidity at the risk of his life above and beyond the call of duty near Merseburg, Germany, on November 2, 1944. While on a mission, the bomber, of which 2d Lt. Femoyer was the navigator, was struck by 3 enemy antiaircraft shells. The plane suffered serious damage and 2d Lt. Femoyer was severely wounded in the side and back by shell fragments which penetrated his body. In spite of extreme pain and great loss of blood he refused an offered injection of morphine. He was determined to keep his mental faculties clear in order that he might direct his plane out of danger and so save his comrades. Not being able to rise from the floor, he asked to be propped up in order to enable him to see his charts and instruments. He successfully directed the navigation of his lone bomber for two and one half hours so well it avoided enemy flak and returned to the field without further damage. Only when the plane had arrived in the safe area over the English Channel did he feel that he had accomplished his objective; then, and only then, he permitted an injection of a sedative. He died shortly after being removed from the plane. The heroism and self-sacrifice of 2d Lt. Femoyer are in keeping with the highest traditions of the U.S. Army.

†MOWER, CHARLES E.

Rank and Organization: Sergeant, U.S. Army, Company A, 34th Infantry, 24th Infantry Division.
Born: Chippewa Falls, Wisconsin.
Entered Service At: Chippewa Falls, Wisconsin.
Place and Date: Near Capoocan, Leyte, Philippine Islands, November 3, 1944.
Citation: Sgt. Mower was an assistant squad leader in an attack against strongly defended enemy positions on both sides of a stream running through a wooded gulch. As the squad advanced through concentrated fire, the leader was killed and Sgt. Mower assumed command. In order to bring direct fire upon the enemy, he had started to lead his men across the stream, which by this time was churned by machinegun and rifle fire, but he was severely wounded before reaching the opposite bank. After signaling his unit to halt, he realized his own exposed position was the most advantageous point from which to direct the attack, and stood fast. Half submerged, gravely wounded, but refusing to seek shelter or accept aid of any kind, he continued to shout and signal to his squad as he directed it in the destruction of 2 enemy machineguns and numerous riflemen. Discovering that the intrepid man in the stream was largely responsible for the successful action being taken against them, the remaining Japanese concentrated the full force of their firepower upon him, and he was killed while still urging his men on. Sgt. Mower's gallant initiative and heroic determination aided materially in the successful completion of his squad's mission. His magnificent leadership was an inspiration to those with whom he served.

WAR NEWS SUMMARIZED

• • •

Friday November 3, 1944
Twenty-five hundred war planes battled in the skies over Merseburg, southwest of Berlin, yesterday in one of the greatest air battles ever fought. When it was over the Luftwaffe had lost 208 of its rapidly dwindling air force and the United States Eighth Air Force reported forty-one of 1,100 bombers and twenty-three of 900 fighters missing. Flying Fortresses and Liberators smashed oil and rail targets while flying through solid curtains of flak and still had time to shoot down fifty-three German planes. Our fighters knocked out 130; a new combat record, and destroyed twenty-five more on the ground. A little later the RAF sent more than 1,000 bombers against Duesseldorf.

On the ground the United States First Army went on the move again, smashing through Huertgen Forest, southeast of Aachen, and capturing Vossenack and Germeter. American and British forces joined at Meijel in the eastern Netherlands and pushed the Germans back farther, but two bridgeheads over the Mark River in the west were lost to the enemy. The battles of Walcheren and the Schelde estuary were nearly won. At the southern end of the line the Seventh Army was battering its way into the Vosges passes.

The virtually undamaged port of Antwerp will be used to unload supplies for the march into Germany soon after all enemy gun sites are mopped up.

Eighth Army units consolidated their bridgeheads southwest of Forli and captured half of that Italian city's modern airport.

Russian troops were only twenty-one miles from Budapest, and farther northeast in Hungary they cleared the enemy from the entire left bank of the Tisza river.

Two political developments clouded the European picture. The French Communists broke with the de Gaulle Government over Patriotic Milita, and Lithuanian and Estonian leaders protested against the substitution of what they called Soviet domination for Nazi slavery.

End of the Leyte-Samar campaign in the Philippines was in sight. American troops smashed north to the coast at Carigara and west across the island to Baybay, compressing the Japanese remnants into a narrow pocket near Ormoc. Enemy casualties were estimated at 30,000.

Chinese were battling valiantly to save Kweilin from falling to the Japanese. In Burma the British captured Mawlu, on the railroad to Mandalay.

President Roosevelt, at the personal urging of Generalissimo Chiang Kai-shek, has directed Donald M. Nelson to return to China at the "earliest possible date" to organize a war production board to increase that country's war capacity. Mr. Nelson will be accompanied by technical advisers who will concentrate on explosives and steel production.

Dr. H.L. Hsia, director of the Chinese News Service in this country, said that continued war-time cooperation conditioned upon reforms in the Chinese Government would constitute an indefensible ultimatum.

†LEONARD, TURNEY W.

Rank and Organization: First Lieutenant, U.S. Army, Company C, 893d Tank Destroyer Battalion.
Born: Dallas, Texas.
Entered Service At: Dallas, Texas.
Place and Date: Kommerscheidt, Germany, November 4-6, 1944.
Citation: 1st Lt. Leonard displayed extraordinary heroism while commanding a platoon of mobile weapons at Kommerscheidt, Germany, November 4, 5, and 6, 1944. During the fierce 3-day engagement, he repeatedly braved

overwhelming enemy fire in advance of his platoon to direct the fire of his tank destroyer from exposed, dismounted positions. He went on lone reconnaissance missions to discover what opposition his men faced, and on one occasion, when fired upon by a hostile machine-gun, advanced alone and eliminated the enemy emplacement with a hand-grenade. When a strong German attack threatened to overrun friendly positions, he moved through withering artillery, mortar, and small-arms fire, reorganized confused infantry units whose leaders had become casualties, and exhorted them to hold firm. Although wounded early in battle, he continued to direct fire from his advanced position until he was disabled by a high-explosive shell which shattered his arm, forcing him to withdraw. He was last seen at a medical aid station which was subsequently captured by the enemy. By his superb courage, inspiring leadership, and indomitable fighting spirit, 1st Lt. Leonard enabled our forces to hold off the enemy attack and was personally responsible for the direction of fire which destroyed 6 German tanks.

OFFICIAL COMMUNIQUE:
United Nations
SUPREME HEADQUARTERS, Allied Expeditionary Force, Nov. 6-Communique 212:
Excellent progress has been made in western Holland. Allied forces are approaching the line of the Maas [Meuse] from the Hollandsch Diep. Heusden, Geertruidenberg, Klundert and Dinteloord were cleared of the enemy and we are operating in the island of Tholen and on Filipsland Isthmus.

On Walcheren progress was made northeast of Domburg. Nieuwland yards of Middleburg to the south.

Fighters and fighter-bombers gave support to our forces in this area. Other fighters and fighter-bombers attacked troop concentrations, strongpoints, ammunition dumps and flak positions in the Dunkerque area. Rail lines in northern and eastern Holland were cut.

In southeastern Holland heavy fighting continues in the Meijel area.

In the areas of Aachen, Bonn, Kaiserslautern and Viersen fighter-bombers attacked dumps and military buildings.

Our forces made small gains in the Huertgen forest sector against stubborn resistance. Extensive minefields covered by artillery and small arms fire hindered our progress southwest of the town of Huertgen, and our units near Kommerscheidt, three-quarters of a mile northwest Schmidt, continued to meet strong pressure of tank, infantry and artillery fire. Mopping-up continued in the forest approximately one mile west of Schmidt.

Our fighter-bombers attacked tanks and troops near Schmidt. Other fighter-bombers attacked airfields near Halle, Cralishelm and Sachsenhausen, and a dam near Fritzlar. Rails were cut in several places in the Rhineland. Rail yards near

Duesseldorf were bombed and an ammunition train south of Kassel was blown up.

Medium and light bombers, using pathfinder technique, attacked an ordnance depot at Homburg.

Four enemy aircraft were shot down and thirty-four destroyed on the ground. Seven of our aircraft are missing.

In the Moselle Valley our units freed Berg, on the Moselle River eight miles northeast of Thionville. Farther south our troops maintained their progress in the Baccarat sector and have taken the village of St. Barbe.

†WILSON, ALFRED L.

Rank and Organization: Technician Fifth Grade, U.S. Army, Medical Detachment, 328th Infantry, 26th Infantry Division.
Born: Fairchance, Pennsylvania.
Entered Service At: Fairchance, Pennsylvania.
Place and Date: Near Bezange la Petite, France, November 8, 1944.
Citation: Tech. 5th Grade Wilson volunteered to assist as an aid man to a company other than his own, which was suffering casualties from constant artillery fire. He administered to the wounded and returned to his own company when a shellburst injured a number of its men. While treating his comrades he was seriously wounded, but refused to be evacuated by litter bearers sent to relieve him. In spite of great pain and loss of blood, he continued to administer first aid until he was too weak to stand. Crawling from one patient to another, he continued his work until excessive loss of blood prevented him from moving. He then verbally directed unskilled enlisted men in continuing the first aid for the wounded. Still refusing assistance himself, he remained to instruct others in dressing the wounds of his comrades until he was unable to speak above a whisper and finally lapsed into unconsciousness. The effects of his injury later caused his death. By steadfastly remaining at the scene without regard for his own safety, Cpl. Wilson through distinguished devotion to duty and personal sacrifice helped to save the lives of at least 10 wounded men.

OFFICIAL COMMUNIQUE:
United Nations
SUPREME HEADQUARTERS, Allied Expeditionary Force, Nov. 8-Communique 214:

With the freeing of Willemstad Allied forces now hold the entire south short of the Hollandsch-Diep and the Maas [Meuse} River with the exception of an area south and east of the destroyed Moerdijk bridges, where a small isolated force of the enemy is still holding out.

On Walcheren fighting is continuing northeast of Domburg. Gun positions in this area were hit by rocket-firing fighters. Elsewhere on the island resistance has ceased.

Two military buildings in Dunkerque were destroyed yesterday in attacks by rocket-firing fighters.

Air attacks on enemy communications cut railway lines in the area of Amersfoort, Apeldoorn and Zwolle. The railway bridge at Goch, an oil storage tank and railway buildings at Emmerich were hit by rocket-firing fighters and fighter-bombers. Railway lines were cut in several other places along the Dutch-German frontier.

Action continues in the Huertgen Forest sector with little change in positions. Fighting still is in progress in the village of Vossenack. Farther south we have repulsed two counter-attacks from the vicinity of Schmidt. West of Schmidt our units improved their positions and mopped up pockets of resistance. Enemy defense positions near Schmidt were attacked by fighter-bombers. Other targets were buildings, railways lines and bridges in the Ruhr.

Rain slowed ground operations in the Luneville-Remiremont sector. A strong counter-attack was repulsed west of Gerardmer after stiff fighting.

†GOTT, DONALD J. (Air Mission)

Rank and Organization: First Lieutenant, U.S. Army Air Corps, 729th Bomber Squadron, 452d Bombardment Group.
Born: June 3, 1923, Arnett, Oklahoma.
Entered Service At: Arnett, Oklahoma.
Place and Date: Saarbrucken, Germany, November 9, 1944.
Citation: On a bombing run upon the marshaling yards at Saarbrucken a B-17 aircraft piloted by 1st. Lt. Gott was seriously damaged by anti-aircraft fire. Three of the aircraft's engines were damaged beyond control and on fire; dangerous flames from the No. 4 engine were leaping back as far as the tail assembly. Flares in the cockpit were ignited and a fire raged therein, which was further increased by free-flowing fluid from damaged hydraulic lines. The interphone system was rendered useless. In addition to these serious mechanical difficulties the engineer was wounded in the leg and the radio operator's arm was severed below the elbow. Suffering from intense pain, despite the application of a tourniquet, the radio operator fell unconscious. Faced with the imminent explosion of his aircraft, and death to his entire crew, mere seconds before bombs away on the target, 1st. Lt. Gott and his copilot conferred. Something had to be done immediately to save the life of the wounded radio operator. The lack of a static line and the thought that his unconscious body striking the ground in unknown territory would not bring immediate medical attention forced a quick decision. 1st

Lt. Gott and his copilot decided to fly the flaming aircraft to friendly territory and then attempt to crash land. Bombs were released on the target and the crippled aircraft proceeded alone to Allied-controlled territory. When that had been reached, 1st. Lt. Gott had the copilot personally inform all crewmembers to bail out. The copilot chose to remain with 1st. Lt. Gott in order to assist in landing the bomber. With only one normally functioning engine, and with the danger of explosion much greater, the aircraft banked into an open field, and when it was at an altitude of 100 feet it exploded, crashed, exploded again and then disintegrated. All 3 crewmembers were instantly killed. 1st. Lt. Gott's loyalty to his crew, his determination to accomplish the task set forth to him, and his deed of knowingly performing what may have been his last service to his country was an example of valor at its highest.

†METZGER, WILLIAM E., JR. (Air Mission)
Rank and Organization: Second Lieutenant, U.S. Army Air Corps, 729th Bomber Squadron, 452d Bombardment Group.
Born: February 9, 1922, Lima, Ohio.
Entered Service At: Lima, Ohio.
Place and Date: Saarbrucken, Germany, November 9, 1944.
Citation: On a bombing run upon the marshaling yards at Saarbrucken, Germany, on November 9, 1944, a B-17 aircraft on which 2d Lt. Metzger was serving as copilot was seriously damaged by anti-aircraft fire. Three of the aircraft's engines were damaged beyond control and on fire; dangerous flames from the No. 4 engine were leaping back as far as the tail assembly. Flares in the cockpit were ignited and a fire roared therein which was further increased by free-flowing fluid from damaged hydraulic lines. The interphone system was rendered useless. In addition to these serious mechanical difficulties the engineer was wounded in the leg and the radio operator's arm was severed below the elbow. Suffering from intense pain, despite the application of a tourniquet, the radio operator fell unconscious. Faced with the imminent explosion of his aircraft and death to his entire crew, mere seconds mere seconds before bombs away on the target, 2d Lt. Metzger and his pilot conferred. Something had to be done immediately to save the life of the wounded radio operator. The lack of a static line and the thought that his unconscious body striking the ground in unknown territory would not bring immediate medical attention forced a quick decision. 2d Lt. Metzger and his pilot decided to fly the flaming aircraft to friendly territory and then attempt to crash land. Bombs were released on the target and the crippled aircraft proceeded alone to Allied-controlled territory. When that had been reached, 2d Lt. Metzger personally informed all crewmembers

to bail out upon the suggestion of the pilot. 2d Lt. Metzger chose to remain with the pilot for the crash landing in order to assist him in this emergency. With only one normally functioning engine, and with the danger of explosion much greater, the aircraft banked into an open field, and when it was at an altitude of 100 feet it exploded, crashed, exploded again and then disintegrated. All 3 crewmembers were instantly killed. 2d Lt. Metzger's loyalty to his crew, his determination to accomplish the task set forth to him, and his deed of knowingly performing what may have been his last service to his country was an example of valor at its highest.

OFFICIAL COMMUNIQUE:
United Nations
SUPREME HEADQUARTERS, Allied Expeditionary Force, Nov. 9-Communique 215:

Gun positions at Dunkerque were attacked yesterday by rocket-firing fighters. Fighter-bombers continued the attack on transportation targets in Holland, principally in the Utrecht area. Rail tracks were cut in numerous places, and motor transport destroyed.

The railway station and a factory at Weeze, south of Goch, and strong pints north and south of the Reichswald Forest were attacked by rocket-firing fighters. Fighter-bombers attacked the communications center of Geilenkirchen, where many fires were started; bridges near Duesseldorf and Cologne, and a rail yard near Euskirchen. Locomotives and freight cars in the Rhineland also were attacked. Air fields at Weisbaden and Schsenheim were hit by fighter-bombers.

Between Nancy and Metz nine enemy command posts were bombed and fighter-bombers supporting our ground forces in the area east of Pont-a-Mousson bombed gun positions and troop concentrations.

Eight enemy aircraft were shot down and two destroyed on the ground in tactical air operations yesterday. Seven of our aircraft are missing. Yesterday morning heavy bombers attacked the synthetic oil plant at Homberg in the Ruhr. Fighters escorted the bombers and flew supporting sweeps. From this operation one bomber and one fighter are missing.

EVERHART, FORREST E.
Rank and Organization: Technical Sergeant, U.S. Army, Company H, 359th Infantry, 90th Infantry Division.
Born: Bainbridge, Ohio.
Entered Service At: Texas City, Texas.
Place and Date: Near Kerling, France, November 12, 1944.
Citation: T/Sgt. Everhart commanded a platoon that bore the brunt of a

desperate enemy counter-attack near Kerling, France, before dawn on November 12, 1944. When German tanks and self-propelled guns penetrated his left flank and overwhelming infantry forces threatened to overrun the one remaining machine-gun in that section, he ran 400 yards through woods churned by artillery and mortar concentrations to strengthen the defense. With the one remaining gunner, he directed furious fire into the advancing hordes until they swarmed close to the position. He left the gun, boldly charged the attackers and, after a 15-minute exchange of hand-grenades, forced them to withdraw leaving 30 dead behind. He recrossed the fire-swept terrain to his then threatened right flank, exhorted his men and directed murderous fire from the single machine-gun at that position. There, in the light of bursting mortar shells, he again closed with the enemy in a hand-grenade duel and, after a fierce 30-minute battle, forced the Germans to withdraw leaving another 20 dead. The gallantry and intrepidity of T/Sgt. Everhart in rallying his men and refusing to fall back in the face of terrible odds were highly instrumental in repelling the fanatical enemy counter-attack directed at the American bridgehead across the Moselle River.

†SAYERS, FOSTER J.

Rank and Organization: Private First Class, U.S. Army, Company L, 357th Infantry, 90th Infantry Division.
Born: Marsh Creek, Pennsylvania.
Entered Service At: Howard, Pennsylvania.
Place and Date: Near Thionville, France, November 12, 1944.
Citation: Pfc. Sayers displayed conspicuous gallantry above and beyond the call of duty in combat on November 12, 1944, near Thionville, France. During an attack on strong hostile forces entrenched on a hill he fearlessly ran up the steep approach toward his objective and set up his machine-gun 20 yards from the enemy. Realizing it would be necessary to attract full attention of the dug-in Germans while his company crossed an open area and flanked the enemy, he picked up his gun, charged through withering machine-gun and rifle fire to the very edge of the emplacement, and there killed 12 German soldiers with devastating close-range fire. He took up a position behind a log and engaged the hostile infantry from the flank in an heroic attempt to distract their attention while his comrades attained their objective at the crest of the hill. He was killed by the very heavy concentration of return fire; but his fearless assault enabled his company to sweep the hill with a minimum of casualties, killing or capturing every enemy soldier on it. Pfc. Sayers' indomitable fighting spirit, aggressiveness, and supreme devotion to duty live on as an example of the highest traditions of the military service.

SPURRIER, JUNIOR J.
Rank and Organization: Staff Sergeant, U.S. Army, Company G, 134th Infantry, 35th Infantry Division.
Born: Russell County, Kentucky.
Entered Service At: Riggs, Kentucky.
Place and Date: Achain, France, November 13, 1944.
Citation: For conspicuous gallantry and intrepidity at risk of his life above and beyond the call of duty in action against the enemy at Achain, France, on November 13, 1944. At 2 p.m., Company G attacked the village of Achain from the east. S/Sgt. Spurrier armed with a BAR passed around the village and advanced alone. Attacking from the west, he immediately killed 3 Germans. From this time until dark, S/Sgt. Spurrier, using at different times his BAR and M1 rifle, American and German rocket launchers, a German automatic pistol, and hand-grenades, continued his solitary attack against the enemy regardless of all type of small-arms and automatic-weapons fire. As a result of his heroic actions, he killed an officer and 24 enlisted men and captured 2 officers and 2 enlisted men. His valor has shed fresh honor on the U.S. Armed Forces.

Note: The following is a newspaper account of the preceding battle for which Sgt. Everhart, Pfc. Sayers, and Sgt. Spurrier were awarded the Medal of Honor:

PATTON 5 MILES FROM METZ, CUTS OUTLETS

• • •

6 DIVISIONS PUSH ON

• • •

Main Railway and Roads Into
the Saar Valley Slashed in Advance

• • •

GERMANS FALLING BACK

• • •

Supreme Headquarters, Allied Expeditionary Force, France, November 11 – Six divisions of the American Third Army broke through German rear guards holding the approaches to the Saar Valey and Metz today and cut the main enemy railroad and highway communications with Metz in a day of swift and sure advances.

Attacking on a twenty-mile front Lt.Gen. George S. Patton's tanks and infantry smashed from three to five miles eastward to cut the Metz-Saarebourg railroad, cross the Nied River and, striking up the railroad, from Nancy, move to within four miles of the vital rail junction of Benestroff.

Within 5 Miles of Metz

At the same time infantrymen, pushing north on Metz and its ring of nine forts, advanced within five miles of the city.

The Germans are getting out as fast as they can. Troops of the German 110th and 111th Panzer Grenadier Regiments of the Eleventh Panzer Division are withdrawing from the forest of Chateau Salins under a hail of American shells and bombs, while fifty-one guns have been knocked out or captured in the forest of Gremency.

The main German forces have not yet been encountered, but there is every sign that the covering forces left by Filed Marshal Johannes von Blaskowitz to screen the Maginot Line have been broken and are now withdrawing onto the line itself.

The Third Army had captured 2,440 German prisoners up to midnight last night, a total that points to the small number of German troops left to guard the areas covered by the sustained American advance, extending to fourteen miles in some sectors.

The American Fourth and Sixth Armored Divisions are spearheading the drive east of the Seille River and the Twenty-sixth, Thirty-fifth, Eightieth and Fifth Infantry Divisions are fighting in the same area.

Farther north the Ninetieth and Ninety-fifth Divisions are fighting around Metz and to the north of the fortress.

The Fifth Division fought at Fort Driant in August and September.

Two German divisions thus far identified are among the best enemy units on that sector, the Eleventh Panzer Division, two of whose Panzer Grenadier Regiments have been encountered in the Chateau Salins forest, and the Seventeenth SS Panzer Grenadier Division. Both were in action in Normandy, where the Seventeenth fought at Carentan and the Eleventh between Caen and Caumont.

The Third Army's offensive failed to make headway only in the south today. Troops advancing north of the Rhine-Marne canal were impeded by extensive minefields north of Bezange-la-Petite.

Father north, however, the advance was swift and sure with General Patton using his armor with a master's touch. A column of the Fourth Armored Division, moving along the Nancy-Saarebourg railroad, took the village of Haboudance and smashed on three miles to the area of Conthel, four miles from Benestroff, main junction where the railroad from Nancy joins the main line running from Metz southeast of Saarebourg. Tanks pushed on toward the junction at dark. The cutting of this railroad, main rail line supplying Metz, was a serious blow to the Germans defending Metz.

North of Chateau Salins, the road junction occupied Friday, American tanks were fighting last night around Gerbecoort on the eastern edge of the forest. German Panzer Grenadiers flanked on both sides of the forest are withdrawing, whipped on by artillery shells and fighters who blasted a convoy of fifty-horse drawn guns on a roads in this area today.

The Sixth Armored Division, thrusting northeastward in back of Metz, cut the main railroad and an important highway leading into the fortress from the southeast today. Tanks rumbled through the village of Luppy in the morning, drove the Germans from the village of Aube, and then smashed into the village of Lemund, which is on the railroad and a highway leading from Metz to Saarebourg and Saarbruecken on the banks of the Nied River.

Another armored column pushed on four miles east of Luppy, which is five miles south of Lemund, and reached the area of Han-sur-Nied where the railroad line splits, one branch going southeast to Saarebourg and the other almost due east of Saarbruecken. [Press services said the Americans crossed the Nied River later.]

Lemud, which soldiers find aptly named, marked the deepest penetration of General Patton's drive up to this evening. It is thirteen miles east of the starting line at Chenicourt.

On the left of this armored sweep the Fifth Infantry Division, which was roughly handled by the Germans a month ago and is eager to even the score, tolled up the German flank south of Metz and approached within five miles of the city. One report from the front, which was not confirmed here, said that the doughboys had pushed on another mile and that their guns already were shelling the fortresses that ring the city.

Four Miles From Metz

There was no action today southwest or west of Metz but the Ninety-fifth Infantry Division, fighting north of the city at Maizieres-les-Metz, captured Brieux Chateau, a mile south of it, and advanced within six miles of the city. A front-line report said these troops had pushed through the forest and advancing along the westernmost of two roads running into Metz from the north, had established positions four miles from the city. This report was not confirmed here. Still farther north the Ninetieth Infantry Division, which hammered out the bridgehead over the Moselle at Koenigsmacher, improved its position by wiping out a German salient that an enemy counter-attack had pushed into the center of the bridgehead.

The bloody battle in the Huertgen Forest between troops of the American First Army and its German defenders continued today without mush change. It is obvious, however, that this battle, which seemed a small affair at first, is developing from the German side into a "test case" in which the Wehrmacht's ability to defend the soil of the Fatherland is being held up to the German people as an example of the Nazis' ability to defend the Reich.

Lieut. Gen. Courtney H. Hodges' troops hacked out an advance of 200 yards in the southern part of the forest of Huertgen and also made some progress west of Schmidt in the face of heavy enemy fire. There was no sign of a speedy end to the battle, however, and the enemy continued to fight from prepared positions with skill and bravery.

This is still a tactical battle while the offensive on the Third Army's front, with the approach to Benestroff, which is about seventeen miles from Saarebourg, has become a strategic threat to the entire German position in the west. This advance is still only a threat, however, for until the main enemy positions at Metz and on the Maginot Line have been reached and breached, the principal German barriers to the Fatherland will be intact and Marshal von Blaskowitz's field army will remain unbeaten.

The American Ninth and British Second Tactical Air forces hammered enemy ground forces communications today. The Ninth Air Force carried out 700 individual attacks against the enemy and claimed the destruction of ten German tanks on the Third Army front as well as the destruction of seventy-five trucks, thirty-five horse-drawn guns and eleven enemy gun positions.

Three fighters from one P-47 Thunderbolt squadron engaged twenty-four Focke Wulf 190s over Vigny, southeast of Metz, and destroyed two German planes and damaged three others.

Thunderbolts fell on twenty-five tanks moving west toward the American positions and claimed that ten were knocked out and fifteen damaged. Rocket-firing Thunderbolts hit an underground strong point southeast of Thoinville and bombed Morhange and Uberkinger, northeast of Chateau Salins and the villages of Sorbey, Oron, Fremery and Bous.

On the American First Army front rail facilities around Geilenkirchen, Schleiden, Trier, Euskirchen, Cologne and Grevenbroick were attacked. At Rheydt, eight miles behind the German line, twenty-four newly constructed barracks were destroyed. Roads outside Stockholm, four miles east of Schmidt, were hit and two railroad bridges were destroyed near Sindorf, eight miles west of Cologne.

Fighter bombers of the British Second Tactical Air Force flew more than 800 sorties, concentrating their attacks in the are north and east of the Twenty-first Army Group positions. Typhoons bombed and the train blew up.

BONG, RICHARD I. (Air Mission)
Rank and Organization: Major, U.S. Army Air Corps.
Born: Poplar, Wisconsin.
Entered Service At: Poplar, Wisconsin.
Place and Date: Over Borneo and Leyte, October 10, to November 15, 1944.
Citation: For conspicuous gallantry and intrepidity in action above and beyond the call of duty in the Southwest Pacific area from October 10, to November 15, 1944. Though assigned to duty as gunnery instructor and neither required nor expected to perform combat duty, Maj. Bong voluntarily and at his own urgent request engaged in repeated combat missions, including unusually hazardous sorties over Balikpapan, Borneo, and in the Leyte area of the Philippines. His aggressiveness and daring resulted in his shooting down 8 enemy airplanes during this period.

OFFICIAL COMMUNIQUE:
United Nations
ADVANCED HEADQUARTERS, on Leyte, Thursday, Nov. 16-Communique 953:

PHILIPPINES

Leyte: In the Tenth Corps sector units of the Twenty-fourth Division by a double development have practically severed the Ormoc road in the rear of enemy defense positions at Limon. Elements of the First Cavalry Division, sweeping west and southwest from Jaro, overcame numerous scattered enemy defensive positions to seize Hills 4047 and 4018 and Mount Mamban.

In the Twenty-fourth Corps sector forward elements of the Seventh Division bloodily repulsed an enemy counter-attack at Balogo, ten miles south of Ormoc on the coast road.

Our fighters strafed enemy barges and shore targets near Ormoc. There were several ineffective harassing raids on our ground installations by single enemy planes. Five were shot down.

ADVANCED HEADQUARTERS, on Leyte, Nov. 15-A supplementary communique:

PHILIPPINES

Visayas: Our escorted heavy units struck Alicante airdrome on Negros Island with thirty-six tons of bombs, heavily orating the runaways. Opposition was negligible.

At Cebu our fighters dive-bombed coastal targets, starting large fires and destroying a float plane.

Mindanao: Our escorted medium units bombed Davao airdrome. Air patrols to the northwest left a 4,000-ton freighter in flames from three direct hits.

HORNER, FREEMAN V.

Rank and Organization: Staff Sergeant, U.S. Army, Company K, 119th Infantry, 30th Infantry Division.
Born: Mount Carmel, Pennsylvania.
Entered Service At: Shamokin, Pennsylvania.
Place and Date: Wurselen, Germany, November 16, 1944.
Citation: S/Sgt. Horner and other members of his company were attacking Wurselen, Germany, against stubborn resistance on November 16, 1944, when machine-gun fire from houses on the edge of the town pinned the attackers in flat, open terrain 100 yards from their objective. As they lay in the field, enemy artillery observers directed fire upon them, causing serious casualties. Realizing that the machine-guns must be eliminated in order to permit the company to advance from its precarious positions, S/Sgt. Horner voluntarily stood up with his submachine-gun and rushed into the teeth of concentrated fire, burdened by a heavy load of ammunition and hand-grenades. Just as he reached a position of seeming safety, he was fired on by a machine-gun which had remained silent up until that time. He coolly wheeled in his fully exposed position while bullets barely missed him and killed 2 hostile gunners with a single, devastating burst. He turned to face the fire of the other 2 machine-guns, and dodging fire as he ran, charged the 2 positions 50 yards away. Demoralized by their inability to hit the intrepid infantryman, the enemy abandoned their guns and took cover in the cellar of the house they occupied. S/Sgt. Horner burst into the building, hurled 2 grenades down the cellar stairs, and called for the Germans to surrender. Four men gave up to him. By his extraordinary courage, S/Sgt. Horner destroyed 3 enemy machine-gun positions, killed or captured 7 enemy, and cleared the path for his company's successful assault on Wurselen.

LINDSEY, JAKE W.

Rank and Organization: Technical Sergeant, U.S. Army, 16th Infantry, 1st Infantry Division.
Born: Isney, Alabama.
Entered Service At: Lucedale, Mississippi.
Place and Date: Near Hamich, Germany, November 16, 1944.

Citation: For gallantry and intrepidity in action at the risk of his life above and beyond the call of duty. Technical Sergeant Jake W. Lindsey led a platoon reduced to six of its original strength of forty, in the attack on an enemy position near Hamich, Germany, November 16, 1944. His men had captured their objective and were digging in when counter-attacked by a German infantry company and five tanks. Armed with a rifle and grenades, Sergeant Lindsey took position on the left and in advance of the remnant of his platoon, and though exposed to heavy rifle, machine-gun and tank fire, beat off repeated enemy attacks. Tanks moved to within 50 yards of him but were forced to withdraw because of his accurate rifle grenade fire. After driving off the tanks, he knocked out two machine-guns to his front. Though painfully wounded, Sergeant Lindsey continued firing and throwing grenades until his ammunition was expended. An enemy squad attempted to set up a machine-gun 50 yards from him. Unmindful of his wounds and enemy fire, he rushed these eight German soldiers, single-handedly closed with them, killed three with his bayonet and captured three, the two others escaping. In his fearlessness, inspiring courage and superb leadership, Sergeant Lindsey carried on a brilliant defense of his platoon's hard-won ground, securing the position and inflicting heavy casualties on the numerically superior enemy.

†RAY, BERNARD J.

Rank and Organization: First Lieutenant, U.S. Army, Company F, 8th Infantry, 4th Infantry Division.
Born: Brooklyn, New York.
Entered Service At: Baldwin, New York.
Place and Date: Hurtgen Forest near Schevenhutte, Germany, November 17, 1944.
Citation: 1st Lt. Ray was platoon leader with Company F, 8th Infantry, on November 17, 1944, during the drive through the Hurtgen Forest near Schevenhutte, Germany. The American forces attacked in wet, bitterly cold weather over rough, wooded terrain, meeting brutal resistance from positions spaced throughout the forest behind minefields and wire obstacles. Small arms, machine-gun, mortar, and artillery fire caused heavy casualties in the ranks when Company F was halted by a concertina-type wire barrier. Under heavy fire, 1st. Lt. Ray reorganized his men and prepared to blow a path through the entanglement, a task which appeared impossible of accomplishment and from which others tried to dissuade him. With implacable determination to clear the way, he placed explosive caps in his pockets, obtained several bangalore torpedoes, and then wrapped a length of highly explosive primer cord about his body. He dashed forward under

direct fire, reached the barbed wire and prepared his demolition charge as mortar shells, which were being aimed at him alone, came steadily nearer his completely exposed position. He had placed a torpedo under the wire and was connecting it to a charge he carried when he was severely wounded by a bursting mortar shell. Apparently realizing that he would fail in his self-imposed mission unless he completed it in a few moments, he made a supremely gallant decision. With the primer cord still wound about his body and the explosive caps in his pocket, he completed a hasty wiring system and unhesitatingly thrust down on the handle of the charger, destroying himself with the wire barricade in the resulting blast. By the deliberate sacrifice of his life, 1st Lt. Ray enabled his company to continue its attack, resumption of which was of positive significance in gaining the approaches to the Cologne Plain.

OFFICIAL COMMUNIQUE:
United Nations
SUPREME HEADQUARTERS, Allied Expeditionary Force, Nov. 17 –Communique 223:

The Allied advance toward the Mass [Meuse] in southeastern Holland continued yesterday. Opposition was light and fighter-bombers gave support by attacking enemy positions west of Venlo. We have taken Wessem and are within a mile of Roermond. Three miles farther north Bruggenem has been freed, with other troops reaching the Canal de Derivation in the Borekhide area. Contact was established between forces south of the Noorder Canal and the troops which captured Meijel.

In the Geilenkirchen sector our units launched attacks and made gains of several thousand yards. We are in Loverich and Immendorf. These operations were preceded and supported by air attacks in very great strength by heavy, medium and fighter-bombers. In support of our ground forces in the Geilenkirchen area fighter-bombers attacked at least twelve German towns and bombed and strafed dug-in enemy troops, gun positions and communications.

In the Dueren-Eschweiler area 1,200 heavy bombers, escorted by 480 fighters, attacked enemy strongpoints, field batteries and anti-aircraft guns. Some escorting fighters also strafed enemy transport at Frankfort and in the Giessen region. Bombing generally was in adverse weather, although some crews reported seeing good results through breaks in the clouds.

Medium bombers, none of which are missing, hit gun positions at Eichen and Luchen, east of Eschweiler. Another force of heavy bombers, numbering 1,150, with an escort of 250 fighters, struck the towns of Dueren, Juelich and Heinsberg immediately behind the enemy lines. Bombing was controlled throughout by master bombers, who claim all attacks were highly concentrated.

Striking deeper into Germany, other fighter-bombers attacked railway targets in the vicinity of Cologne. Eight fighters and fighter-bombers are missing from the day's operations. Farther south our forces continue their attack, enlarging the Moselle bridgeheads. We have troops in the vicinity of Monneren, Lacroix and Metzervisse in the Thionville area.

Stuckange is in our hands and our forces are in Augny and Marly, south of Metz. In the Blamont-St. Die area resistance was moderate but progress slow. St. Die and several other villages in the path of our advance were set afire by the enemy and many explosions were heard. In the approaches to Belfort Gap the momentum of our drive was maintained. Several towns have been freed north and south of the Doubs River.

†McGRAW, FRANCIS X.

Rank and Organization: Private First Class, U.S. Army, Company H, 26th Infantry, 1st Infantry Division.
Born: Philadelphia, Pennsylvania.
Entered Service At: Camden, New Jersey.
Place and Date: Near Schevenhutte, Germany, November 19, 1944.
Citation: Pfc. McGraw manned a heavy machine-gun emplaced in a foxhole near Schevenhutte, Germany, on November 19, 1944, when the enemy launched a fierce counter-attack. Braving an intense hour-long preparatory barrage, he maintained his stand and poured deadly accurate fire into the advancing foot troops until they faltered and came to a halt. The hostile forces brought up a machine-gun in an effort to dislodge him but were frustrated when he lifted his gun to an exposed but advantageous position atop a log, courageously stood up in his foxhole and knocked out the enemy weapon. A rocket blasted his gun from position, but he retrieved it and continued firing. He silenced a second machine-gun and then made repeated trips over fireswept terrain to replenish his ammunition supply. Wounded painfully in this dangerous task, he disregarded his injury and hurried back to his post, where his weapon was showered with mud when another rocket barely missed him. In the midst of the battle, with enemy troops taking advantage of his predicament to press forward, he calmly cleaned his gun, put it back into action and drove off the attackers. He continued to fire until his ammunition was expended, when, with a fierce desire to close with the enemy, he picked up a carbine, killed one enemy soldier, wounded another and engaged in a desperate fire-fight with a third until he was mortally wounded by a burst from a machine pistol. The extraordinary heroism and intrepidity displayed by Pfc. McGraw inspired his comrades to great efforts and was a major factor in repulsing the enemy attack.

OFFICIAL COMMUNIQUE:
United Nations
SUPREME HEADQUARTERS, Allied Expeditionary Force, Nov. 19 —Communique 225:

The Allied bridgeheads across the Canal de Derivation have been enlarged. We have cut the Meijel-Panningen road and reached the vicinity of Helden. Opposition was light but many mines were encountered.

Progress north and south of Geilenkirchen has now completed the encirclement of the town, except for a narrow escape corridor northeast along the railway.

Units of the north freed Niederheide and made gains of 1,500 yards farther east. Units of the south launched an attack at first light yesterday, in the face of moderate opposition, and freed Huenshoven and Prummern. We are in the outskirts of Sueggerath.

Farther south we have taken a number of towns, including Puffendorf, and contained two counter-attacks.

Our forces made slight gains against mortar and small-arms fire in the area south of Wuerselen and moderate progress against stubborn resistance in the Stolberg area. Wire obstacles and mine fields delayed our advance.

Farther south Allied forces have entered Germany near the Luxembourg border and are in the town of Bueschdorf. Other elements are at Ritzing and in the Halstroff area. We also have units in Schwerdorf and Heckling.

Our forces are at the north and south edges of Metz.

Gains of up to two miles in the Blamont-St. Die sector have freed twelve towns, including Raon l'Etape, in the Meurthe valley, which was found heavily mined. More villages have been set on fire by the enemy.

Our forces in the Belfort Gap freed many towns and drove to within four miles of Belfort. Along the Swiss border we have advanced nearly twenty miles in three days.

Communications and supply lines behind the enemy lines from Nijmegen to Belfort were attacked by medium and fighter bombers in strength yesterday. Bridges, rail and road focal points and transport vehicles were among the targets.

Muenster, center of rail and water transport, was hit by a strong force of escorted heavy bombers. Close support for our attacking troops was given in all sectors by fighter-bombers.

In the areas of Eschweiler and Dueren, fortified villages, troop concentrations and military barracks were hit by medium and light bombers.

Near the towns of Geilenkirchen, Juelich, Dueren, Stolberg and Grevenbroich, troops, armored units, gun positions and strong points were strafed in low-level attacks by fighter-bombers.

BRILES, HERSCHEL F.
Rank and Organization: Staff Sergeant, U.S. Army, Co. C, 899th Tank Destroyer Battalion.
Born: Colfax, Iowa.
Entered Service At: Fort Des Moines, Iowa.
Place and Date: Near Scherpenseel, Germany, November 20, 1944.
Citation: S/Sgt. Briles was leading a platoon of destroyers across an exposed slope near Scherpenseel, Germany, on November 20, 1944, when they came under heavy enemy artillery fire. A direct hit was scored on one of the vehicles, killing one man, seriously wounding two others, and setting the destroyer afire. With a comrade, S/Sgt. Briles left the cover of his own armor and raced across ground raked by artillery and small-arms fire to the rescue of the men in the shattered destroyer. Without hesitation, he lowered himself into the burning turret, removed the wounded and then extinguished the fire. From a position he assumed the next morning, he observed hostile infantrymen advancing. With his machine-gun, he poured such deadly fire into the enemy ranks that an entire pocket of 55 Germans surrendered, clearing the way for a junction between American units which had been held up for two days. Later that day, when another of his destroyers was hit by a concealed enemy tank, he again left protection to give assistance. With the help of another soldier, he evacuated two wounded under heavy fire and, returning to the burning vehicle, braved death from exploding ammunition to put out the flames. By his heroic initiative and complete disregard for personal safety, S/Sgt. Briles was largely responsible for causing heavy enemy casualties, forcing the surrender of 55 Germans, making possible the salvage of our vehicles, and saving the lives of wounded comrades.

MABRY, GEORGE L., JR.
Rank and Organization: Lieutenant Colonel, U.S. Army, 2d Battalion, 8th Infantry, 4th Infantry Division.
Born: Sumter, South Carolina.
Entered Service At: Sumter, South Carolina.
Place and Date: Hurtgen Forest near Schevenhutte, Germany, November 20, 1944.
Citation: Lt. Col. Mabry was commanding the 2d Battalion, 8th Infantry, in an attack through the Hurtgen Forest near Schevenhutte, Germany, on November 20, 1944. During the early phases of the assault, the leading elements of his battalion were halted by a minefield and immobilized by heavy hostile fire. Advancing alone into the mined area, Col. Mabry estab-

lished a safe route of passage. He then moved ahead of the foremost scouts, personally leading the attack, until confronted by a booby-trapped double concertina obstacle. With the assistance of the scouts, he disconnected the explosives and cut a path through the wire. Upon moving through the opening, he observed 3 enemy in foxholes whom he captured at bayonet point. Driving steadily forward he paced the assault against 3 log bunkers which housed mutually supported automatic weapons. Racing up a slope ahead of his men, he found the initial bunker deserted, then pushed on to the second where he was suddenly confronted by 9 onrushing enemy. Using the butt of his rifle, he felled 1 adversary and bayoneted a second, before his scouts came to his aid and assisted him in overcoming the others in hand-to-hand combat. Accompanied by the riflemen, he charged the third bunker under pointblank small-arms fire and led the way into the fortification from which he prodded 6 enemy at bayonet point. Following the consolidation of this area, he led his battalion across 300 yards of fireswept terrain to seize elevated ground upon which he established a defensive position which menaced the enemy on both flanks, and provided his regiment a firm foothold on the approach to the Cologne Plain. Col. Mabry's superlative courage, daring, and leadership in an operation of major importance exemplify the finest characteristics of the military service.

†MINICK, JOHN W.

Rank and Organization: Staff Sergeant, U.S. Army, Company I, 121st Infantry, 8th Infantry Division.
Born: Wall, Pennsylvania.
Entered Service At: Carlisle, Pennsylvania.
Place and Date: Near Hurtgen, Germany, November 21, 1944.
Citation: S/Sgt. Minick displayed conspicuous gallantry and intrepidity at the risk of his own life, above and beyond the call of duty, in action involving actual conflict with the enemy on November 21, 1944, near Hurtgen, Germany. S/Sgt. Minick's battalion was halted in its advance by extensive minefields, exposing troops to heavy concentrations of enemy artillery and mortar fire. Further delay in the advance would result in numerous casualties and a movement through the minefield was essential. Voluntarily, S/Sgt. Minick led 4 men through hazardous barbed wire and debris, finally making his way through the minefield for a distance of 300 yards. When an enemy machine-gun opened fire, he signaled his men to take covered positions, edged his way alone toward the flank of the weapon and opened fire, killing 2 members of the guncrew and capturing 3 others. Moving forward again, he encountered and engaged single-handedly an entire company kill-

ing 20 Germans and capturing 20, and enabling his platoon to capture the remainder of the hostile group. Again moving ahead and spearheading his battalion's advance, he again encountered machine-gun fire. Crawling forward toward the weapon, he reached a point from which he knocked the weapon out of action. Still another minefield had to be crossed. Undeterred, S/Sgt. Minick advanced forward alone through constant enemy fire and while thus moving, detonated a mine and was instantly killed.

OFFICIAL COMMUNIQUE:
United Nations
SUPREME HEADQUARTERS, Allied Expeditionary Force, Nov. 20 –Communiqué 226:

In the Venlo area of southeastern Holland Allied forces have cleared the wooded area between Helden and Kessel, and reconnaissance elements have reached the Maas [Meuse] at Kessel. North of Meijel crossings were made over the Deurne Canal.

Further progress has been made in our attacks in the Geilenkirchen-Aachen sector. The town of Geilenkirchen was taken yesterday.

Several counter-attacks were contained in the vicinity of Prummern, and we have made gains east of Setterich, which has been cleared of the enemy.

Farther south, Hoengen, Kinzweiler and St. Joeris are in Allied hands. Our patrols advancing through wire entanglements and minefields are in the southern outskirts of Eschweiler and we have reached the town of Roehe. Hamich and Hastenrath, northeast of Stolberg, have been freed and we have made substantial progress in this area.

In close support of our troops in the Geilenkirchen-Aachen sector, fighter bombers dive-bombed and strafed nine towns, including Welz, Gereonsweiler, Aldenhoven, Niedermerz and Guesten. Medium bombers attacked four defended villages near Dueren. Light bombers struck at troop concentrations at Baal.

Northeast of Koenigsmacher our forces have reached Launstroff and advanced across the border at Wellingen.

Medium bombers attacked Merzig, five miles northeast of Launstroff.

Our forces have completed the encirclement of Metz. Troops are on the eastern edge of the city, and units from the north and south have established contact at Vallieres and Vaudreville east of Metz. On the northwestern side of the city our forces are advancing across St. Symphorien Island between the Moselle River and the Laternal Canal, while other units have crossed the Seille River on the northeastern edge of the city.

Farther south we are in the northern outskirts of Dieuze and have reached Gros Tenquin, eleven miles to the north.

Advances of several miles were made against moderate resistance in the offensives north and southeast of Blamont.

Eleven more towns have been freed in the area farther south, including Rechicourt, Harbouey and Badonviller. In the Vosges Mountains Gerardmer has been freed.

Our troops have thrust almost through the Belfort Gap, reaching Seppois, within twenty miles of the Rhine. Other units have driven to within three miles of Belfort.

East of the Belfort Gap medium bombers went for the Rhine bridge at Neurenberg.

A storage depot at Saverne, twenty miles northwest of Strasbourg, an ordnance depot at Pirmasens, and two enemy radio stations were among the day;s targets for other medium, light and fighter bombers and rocket-firing fighters.

From all air operations twenty-nine fighters and three bombers are missing, but four of our fighter pilots are safe.

At least sixteen enemy aircraft were destroyed in the air during the day.

A sharp attack by enemy ground forces on Mardick in the Dunkerque area was firmly repulsed on Saturday morning.

Yesterday strong points and gun positions in the area were attacked by fighter-bombers.

SILK, EDWARD A.

Rank and Organization: First Lieutenant, U.S. Army, Company E, 398th Infantry, 100th Infantry Division.
Born: June 8, 1916, Johnstown, Pennsylvania.
Entered Service At: Johnstown, Pennsylvania.
Place and Date: Near St. Pravel, France, November 23, 1944.
Citation: 1st Lt. Edward A. Silk commanded the weapons platoon of Company E, 398th Infantry, on November 23, 1944, when the end battalion was assigned the mission of seizing high ground overlooking Moyenmoutier, France, prior to an attack on the city itself. His company jumped off in the lead at dawn and by noon had reached the edge of a woods in the vicinity of St. Pravel where scouts saw an enemy sentry standing guard before a farmhouse in a valley below. One squad, engaged in reconnoitering the area, was immediately pinned down by intense machine-gun and automatic-weapons fire from within the house. Skillfully deploying his light machine-gun section, 1st Lt. Silk answered enemy fire, but when 15 minutes had elapsed with no slackening of resistance, he decided to eliminate the strong point by a 1-man attack. Running 100 yards across an open field to the shelter of a low stone wall directly in front of the farmhouse, he fired into the door and windows with his carbine; then, in full view of the enemy, vaulted the

wall and dashed 50 yards through a hail of bullets to the left side of the house, where he hurled a grenade through a window, silencing a machine-gun and killing 2 gunners. In attempting to move to the right side of the house, he drew fire from a second machine-gun emplaced in the woodshed. With magnificent courage he rushed this position in the face of direct fire and succeeded in neutralizing the weapon and killing the 2 gunners by throwing grenades into the structure. His supply of grenades was by now exhausted, but undaunted, he dashed back to the side of the farmhouse and began to throw rocks through a window, demanding the surrender of the remaining enemy. Twelve Germans, overcome by his relentless assault and confused by his unorthodox methods, gave up to the lone American. By his gallant willingness to assume the full burden of the attack and the intrepidity with which he carried out his extremely hazardous mission, 1st Lt. Silk enabled his battalion to continue its advance and seize its objective.

OFFICIAL COMMUNIQUE:
United Nations
SUPREME HEADQUARTERS, Allied Expeditionary Force, Nov. 23-Communique 229:

The Allied advance continued in the Venlo sector. We have captured miles from Venlo. Farther north our forces have taken the village of Amerika, on the Dueren-Venlo railway.

West of Roermond our troops have advanced to the bank of the Meuse River opposite the town and have captured the village of Weerd.

In the Geilenkirchen sector our forces advancing toward the Roer River have taken Hoven and are on the high ground beyond Gereonsweiler. We are approaching Koslar, two miles west of Juelich.

In the area northeast of Eschweiler fighting is in progress in Lohn. Duerwiss and Eschweiler have been cleared of the enemy.

We are making slow gains in the Huertgen Forest against intense small-arms, mortar and artillery fire.

Northeast of Thionville Allied armored elements are advancing northward beyond the German border in the area of Ounsdorf.

Metz has been entirely cleared of the enemy, but several outlying forts continue to resist.

Gains have been made by our forces north of Faulquemont, and east and northeast of Dieuze we have reached Rohrbach, Angviller and Bisping. Forward elements are beyond Cutting and are in the vicinity of Mittersheim.

Our units drove into the lower Alsace plain within twenty miles of Strasbourg and the Rhine. Saverne, eastern gateway of the southern gap, was occupied and our forward elements advanced elsewhere in this area.

St. Die, burned by the enemy, has been entered and extensive gains have made east of the Meurthe River.

In the Belfort Gap a strong enemy counter-attack has been repulsed. Most of Belfort has been cleared. Gains were made in the area of Mulhouse, which has been freed.

Fighter-bombers yesterday attacked road and railway transport in the Colmar and Strasbourg area, but generally had weather throughout the day prevented any other air operations.

†SHERIDAN, CARL V.

Rank and Organization: Private First Class, U.S. Army, Company K, 47th Infantry, 9th Infantry Division.
Born: Baltimore, Maryland.
Entered Service At: Baltimore, Maryland.
Place and Date: Frenzenberg Castle, Weisweiler, Germany, November 26, 1944.
Citation: Attached to the 2d Battalion of the 47th Infantry on November 26, 1944, for the attack on Frenzenberg Castle, in the vicinity of Weisweiler, Germany, Company K, after an advance of 1,000 yards through a shattering barrage of enemy artillery and mortar fire, had captured 2 buildings in the courtyard of the castle but was left with an effective fighting strength of only 35 men. During the advance, Pfc. Sheridan, acting as a bazooka gunner, had braved the enemy fire to stop and procure the additional rockets carried by his ammunition bearer who was wounded. Upon rejoining his company in the captured buildings, he found it in a furious fight with approximately 70 enemy paratroopers occupying the castle gate house. This was a solidly built stone structure surrounded by a deep water-filled moat 20 feet wide. The only approach to the heavily defended position was across the courtyard and over a drawbridge leading to a barricaded oaken door. Pfc. Sheridan, realizing that his bazooka was the only available weapon with sufficient power to penetrate the heavy oak planking, with complete disregard for his own safety left the protection of the buildings and in the face of heavy and intense small-arms and grenade fire, crossed the courtyard to the drawbridge entrance where he could bring direct fire to bear against the door. Although handicapped by the lack of an assistance, and a constant target for the enemy fire that burst around him, he skillfully and effectively handled his awkward weapon to place two well-aimed rockets into the structure. Observing that the door was only weakened, and realizing that a gap must be made for a successful assault, he loaded his last rocket, took careful aim, and blasted a hole through the heavy planks. Turn-

ing to his company he shouted, "Come on, let's get them!" With his .45 pistol blazing, he charged into the gaping entrance and was killed by the withering fire that met him. The final assault on Frenzenberg Castle was made through the gap which Pfc. Sheridan gave his life to create.

GARCIA, MARCARIO

Rank and Organization: Staff Sergeant, U.S. Army, Company B, 22d Infantry, 4th Infantry Division.
Born: January 20, 1920, Villa De Castano, Mexico.
Entered Service At: Sugarland, Texas.
Place and Date: Near Grosshau, Germany, November 27, 1944.
Citation: While an acting squad leader of Company B, 22d Infantry, on November 27, 1944, near Grosshau, Germany, S/Sgt. Garcia single-handedly assaulted 2 enemy machine-gun emplacements. Attacking prepared positions on a wooded hill, which could be approached only through meager cover, his company was pinned down by intense machine-gun fire and subjected to a concentrated artillery and mortar barrage. Although painfully wounded, he refused to be evacuated and on his own initiative crawled forward alone until he reached a position near an enemy emplacement. Hurling grenades, he boldly assaulted the position, destroyed the gun, and with his rifle killed 3 of the enemy who attempted to escape. When he rejoined his company, a second machine-gun opened fire and again the intrepid soldier went forward, utterly disregarding his own safety. He stormed the position and destroyed the gun, killed 3 more Germans, and captured 4 prisoners. He fought on with his unit until the objective was taken and only then did he permit himself to be removed for medical care. S/Sgt. (then private) Garcia's conspicuous heroism, his inspiring, courageous conduct, and his complete disregard for his personal safety wiped out 2 enemy emplacements and enabled his company to advance and secure its objective.

OFFICIAL COMMUNIQUE:

United Nations
SUPREME HEADQUARTERS, Allied Expeditionary Force, Nov. 27 –Communique 233:

Allied forces, continuing to clear the Maas [Meuse] pocket, have reached the river between Blitterswijk and Broekhuizenvorst. North of the Venlo defenses only scattered pockets of enemy remain west of the Maas.

In the area west of Juelich we contained counter-attacks by infantry and tanks. Farther south, Weisweiler has been cleared after stubborn house-to-house fighting and we have advanced to the east. Fighting continues for high ground south of Langerwehe and our forces continued to make slow progress in the forest south of Huertgen.

South of Juelich fighter-bombers broke up a counter-attack by enemy armor. Other fighter-bombers bombed Dueren and Langerwehe and troops and gun positions in the area. Communications and transport behind the enemy line in Germany were attacked by fighter-bombers which hit rolling stock in the Cologne, Coblenz and Giessen areas. Railway yards at Rheydt were the target for escorted medium bombers. Fortified towns along the Saar River were bombed by fighter-bombers.

Southwest of Merzig, in the Saar Valley, our forces have reached Oberesch.

General gains were made in the area east of Metz despite enemy counterattacks. Fort Sommy and Fort. St. Blaize were captured and Fort Marival was abandoned by the enemy. Allied units made gains of one and one-half miles to take Ricrange, seventeen miles northeast of Metz, and other elements are in Zimmingen, northwest of St. Avold. The Gutenbrumner Forest north of Finstingen is being cleared and we have advanced up to three miles to reach Hunkirch. North of Sarrebourg we have repulsed counter-attacks and regained lost ground.

Our forces advancing from the St. Die region have pushed through the Saale Pass in the Vosges Mountains and reached the Alsace Plain west of Strasbourg. Our grip on Strasbourg was tightened with the capture of a dozen forts near the city. Prisoners include two generals.

In the southern Vosges further progress was made toward clearing the enemy from the mountain passes and narrowing the salient in the Belfort Gap.

Ammunition and fuel dumps at Homburg, Giessen and Bergzadern were attacked without loss by medium and light bombers. Escorted heavy bombers without loss attacked objectives in western Germany.

†MILLER, ANDREW

Rank and Organization: Staff Sergeant, U.S. Army, Company G, 377th Infantry, 95th Infantry Division.
Born: Manitowoc, Wisconsin.
Entered Service At: Two Rivers, Wisconsin.
Place and Date: From Woippy, France, through Metz to Kerprich Hemmersdorf, Germany, November 16-29, 1994.
Citation: For performing a series of heroic deeds from November 16-29, 1944, during his company's relentless drive from Woippy, France, through Metz to Kerprich Hemmersdorf, Germany. As he led a rifle squad on November 16, at Woippy, a crossfire from enemy machine-guns pinned down his unit. Ordering his men to remain under cover, he went forward alone,

entered a building housing one of the guns and forced 5 Germans to surrender at bayonet point. He then took the second gun single-handedly by hurling grenades into the enemy position, killing 2, wounding 3 more, and taking 2 additional prisoners. At the outskirts of Metz the next day, when his platoon, confused by heavy explosions and the withdrawal of friendly tanks, retired, he fearlessly remained behind armed with an automatic rifle and exchanged bursts with a German machine-gun until he silenced the enemy weapon. His quick action in covering his comrades gave the platoon time to regroup and carry on the fight. On November 19, S/Sgt. Miller led an attack on large enemy barracks. Covered by his squad, he crawled to a barracks window, climbed in and captured 6 riflemen occupying the room. His men, and then the entire company, followed through the window, scoured the building, and took 75 prisoners. S/Sgt. Miller volunteered, with 3 comrades, to capture Gestapo officers who were preventing the surrender of German troops in another building. He ran a gauntlet of machine-gun fire and was lifted through a window. Inside, he found himself covered by a machine pistol, but he persuaded the 4 Gestapo agents confronting him to surrender. Early the next morning, when strong hostile forces punished his company with heavy fire, S/Sgt. Miller assumed the task of destroying a well-placed machine-gun. He was knocked down by a rifle grenade as he climbed an open stairway in a house, but pressed on with a bazooka to find an advantageous spot from which to launch his rocket. He discovered that he could fire only from the roof, a position where he would draw tremendous enemy fire. Facing the risk, he moved into the open, coolly took aim and scored a direct hit on the hostile emplacement, wreaking such havoc that the enemy troops became completely demoralized and began surrendering by the score. The following day, in Metz, he captured 12 more prisoners and silenced an enemy machine-gun after volunteering for a hazardous mission in advance of his company's position. On November 29, as Company G climbed a hill overlooking Kerprich Hemmersdorf, enemy fire pinned the unit to the ground. S/Sgt. Miller, on his own initiative, pressed ahead with his squad past the company's leading element to meet the surprise resistance. His men stood up and advanced deliberately, firing as they went. Inspired by S/Sgt. Miller's leadership, the platoon followed, and then another platoon arose and grimly closed with the Germans. The enemy action was smothered, but at the cost of S/Sgt. Miller's life. His tenacious devotion to the attack, his gallant choice to expose himself to enemy action rather than endanger his men, his limitless bravery, assured the success of Company G.

OFFICIAL COMMUNIQUE:
United Nations
SUPREME HEADQUARTERS, Allied Expeditionary Force, Nov. 29 –Communique 235:

Allied forces north of Venlo are in contact with the few remaining enemy strong points west of the Maas [Meuse].

Gun positions and defended buildings in Holland were attacked by fighter-bombers yesterday and cover was given to our ground forces. Other fighter-bombers hit railway targets in Holland and over the German frontier to Muenster, and struck at the Ruhr Valley railway system. At Zwolie, the railway yards were bombed and strafed, and near Borken station, buildings were set on fire.

In the Geilenkirchen area, increased mortar fire was encountered by our ground forces. Mortar positions at Birgden were destroyed by rocket-firing fighters.

South of Juelich we have taken high ground and attacked the village of Barmen. Fighting continues in Koslar, and the enemy was cleared from Merzenhausen and Kirchberg. Farther south our units were fighting in five German towns: Inden, Langerwehe, Juengersdorf, Huertgen and Lamersdorf.

In this sector, medium, light, and fighter-bombers destroyed a number of tanks near Barmen and attacked fortified villages including Rurich, Merken, and Birgel. Railway yards at Erkelenz and Elsdorf were among other targets hit.

Our forces have extended their action in the Saar Valley and occupied a number of towns. We have reached Villing and Berus, southwest of Saarlautern.

Gains have been made in the St. Avold area, where we are beyond Hombourg-Haut, and armored elements have reached Vahl-Ebersing and Diffembach. Infantry has advanced to Hinsing, and farther south, armored forces have almost completely cleared Gutenbrunner Forest and cleared Wolfskirchen. Other elements are at Burbach and Berg.

In the northern Alsace Plain, our advances reached to within three miles west of Haguenau. Farther north, the Moder River was crossed, and Ingweiler and the outskirts of Zutzendorf reached. Other elements completed their drive through the Vosges Mountains south of Molsheim.

In the Belfort Gap area, a large enemy salient between Belfort and Mulhouse was cut by forces which joined south of the Dollar River after an eight-mile drive. The main enemy escape routes were severed.

Fighter-bombers attacked strong points and gun positions at Dunkerque. In late evening the industrial town of Nuremberg was bombed by light bombers.

†HENRY, ROBERT T.

Rank and Organization: Private, U.S. Army, 16th Infantry, 1st Infantry Division.
Born: Greenville, Mississippi.
Entered Service At: Greenville, Mississippi.
Place and Date: Luchem, Germany, December 3, 1944.
Citation: Near Luchem, Germany, Pvt. Henry volunteered to attempt the destruction of a nest of 5 enemy machine-guns located in a bunker 150 yards to the flank which had stopped the advance of his platoon. Stripping off his pack, overshoes, helmet, and overcoat, he sprinted alone with his rifle and hand-grenades across the open terrain toward the enemy emplacement. Before he had gone half the distance, he was hit by a burst of machine-gun fire. Dropping his rifle, he continued to stagger forward until he fell mortally wounded only 10 yards from the enemy emplacement. His single-handed attack forced the enemy to leave the machine-guns. During this break in hostile fire, the platoon moved forward and overran the position. Pvt. Henry, by his gallantry and intrepidity and utter disregard for his own life, enabled his company to reach its objective, capturing this key defense and 70 German prisoners.

†WEICHT, ELLIS R.

Rank and Organization: Sergeant, U.S. Army, Company F, 142d Infantry, 36th Infantry Division.
Born: Clearville, Pennsylvania.
Entered Service At: Bedford, Pennsylvania.
Place and Date: St. Hippolyte, France, December 3, 1944.
Citation: For commanding an assault squad in Company F's attack against the strategically important Alsatian town of St. Hippolyte on December 3, 1944. Sgt. Weicht aggressively led his men down a winding street, clearing the houses of opposition as he advanced. Upon rounding a bend, the group was suddenly brought under the fire of 2 machine-guns emplaced in the door and window of a house 100 yards distant. While his squad members took cover, Sgt. Weicht moved rapidly forward to a high rock wall and, fearlessly exposing himself to the enemy action, fired 2 clips of ammunition from his rifle. His fire proving ineffective, he entered a house opposite the enemy gun position, and, firing from a window, killed the 2 hostile gunners. Continuing the attack, the advance was again halted when two 20-mm. guns opened fire on the company. An artillery observer ordered friendly troops to evacuate the area and then directed artillery fire upon the gun positions. Sgt. Weicht remained in the shelled area and continued to

fire on the hostile weapons. When the barrage lifted and the enemy soldiers attempted to remove their gun, he killed 2 crewmembers and forced the others to flee. Sgt. Weicht continued to lead his squad forward until he spotted a road block approximately 125 yards away. Moving to the second floor of a nearby house and firing from a window, he killed 3 and wounded several of the enemy. Instantly becoming a target for heavy and direct fire, he disregarded personal safety to continue his fire, with unusual effectiveness, until he was killed by a direct hit from an anti-tank gun.

OFFICIAL COMMUNIQUE:
United Nations
SUPREME HEADQUARTERS, Allied Expeditionary Force, Dec. 3 –Communique 239:

Allied forces which entered Linnich were mopping up in the town yesterday. To the south, we have cleared Roerdorf and hard fighting continued at Flossdorf and in Inden, where the action was fierce.

Fighter-bombers went for road, river and railway targets over a wide area in the Rhineland. They destroyed or disabled a large quantity of enemy rolling stock and cut railway lines in many places. Fortified towns immediately behind the enemy lines in the Dueren-Linnich areas, and troop concentrations near Dueren, were attacked, and a railway bridge twenty miles east of Euskirchen was destroyed.

Our ground forces enlarged their control of the Saar River bank above and below Merzig and entered the town of Rehlingen. Other forces were in the outskirts of Saarlautern on the west side of the river. Farther south, moderate gains were made and mopping up is in progress in Sarre Union.

Southeast of Sarre Union our forces made gains of approximately two miles and reached the vicinity of Mackwiller. Two enemy counter-attacks were repulsed. The enemy was forced from an area on the west bank of the Rhine near Strasbourg. In his retreat he blew up three bridges across the Rhine.

Fighter-bombers attacked a railway yard at Rastatt and Offenburg.

On the Alsace Plain we have reached Selestat where house-to-house fighting continues.

In the southern High Vosges, our forces pushed into the Upper Ruhr River Valley and occupied several villages. Units which crossed to the north bank of the Dollar River near Mulhouse repulsed a strong counter-attack.

During the day's air operations, which included an attack by rocket-firing fighters on an enemy strong point in the Venlo area of Holland, four enemy aircraft were destroyed in the air and seven on the ground. According to reports so far received, we lost one light bomber and thirteen fighter-bombers.

Yesterday afternoon a force of escorted heavy bombers attacked a plant in the outskirts of Dortmund. Last night heavy bombers were over Germany in strength with Hagen as the main objective.

†McWHORTER, WILLIAM A.
Rank and Organization: Private First Class, U.S. Army, Company M, 126th Infantry, 32d Infantry Division.
Born: Liberty, South Carolina.
Entered Service At: Liberty, South Carolina.
Place and Date: Leyte, Philippine Islands, December 5, 1944.
Citation: Pfc. McWhorter displayed gallantry and intrepidity at the risk of his life above and beyond the call of duty while engaged in operations against the enemy. Pfc. McWhorter, a machine gunner, was emplaced in a defensive position with one assistant when the enemy launched a heavy attack. Manning the gun and opening fire, he killed several members of an advancing demolition squad, when one of the enemy succeeded in throwing a fused demolition charge in the entrenchment. Without hesitation and with complete disregard for his own safety, Pfc. McWhorter picked up the improvised grenade and deliberately held it close to his body bending over and turning away from his companion. The charge exploded, killing him instantly, but leaving his assistant unharmed. Pfc. McWhorter's outstanding heroism and supreme sacrifice in shielding a comrade reflect the highest traditions of the military service.

OFFICIAL COMMUNIQUE:
United Nations
ADVANCED HEADQUARTERS, on Leyte, Wednesday, Dec. 6 – A communique:

PHILIPPINES

Leyte: Rainy weather continues. Local gains were made along the ridges south of Limon. An enemy night tank attack was turned back by our road block south of the Leyte River. Reduction of enemy pockets in the mountains east of the road continues, while our forces on the high ground southwest of Dagami are continuing their step-by-step elimination of enemy positions.

Our fighters continued their attacks on stores and lines of communications in the enemy's rear and sank a small freighter in Ormoc Bay. Naval units bombarded shore targets and intercepted and sank a southbound freighter near Masbate. There were no enemy air attacks.

Luzon: Patrol planes attacking enemy shipping off the southwest coast strafed two coastal vessels and sank a destroyer. Others harassed the Manila airdrome cluster and destroyed barracks at Fort Stotesenburg to the north.

Visayas: Heavy units from Palau dropped twenty-four tons of bombs on Lahug and upon airdromes at Cebu, damaging buildings and supply depots. Fighter-bombers cratered the Masbate airfield and patrol planes sank three small freighters in the Sibuyan Sea, harassed Negros airdromes at night and shot down an enemy float plane.

†FRYAR, ELMER E.

Rank and Organization: Private, U.S. Army, Company E, 511th Parachute Infantry, 11th Airborne Division.
Born: Denver, Colorado.
Entered Service At: Denver, Colorado.
Place and Date: Leyte, Philippine Islands, December 8, 1944.
Citation: For conspicuous gallantry and intrepidity at the risk of his life above and beyond the call of duty. Pvt. Fryar's battalion encountered the enemy strongly entrenched in a position supported by mortars and automatic weapons. The battalion attacked, but in spite of repeated efforts was unable to take the position. Pvt. Fryar's company was ordered to cover the battalion's withdrawal to a more suitable point from which to attack, but the enemy launched a strong counter-attack which threatened to cut off the company. Seeing an enemy platoon moving to outflank his company, he moved to higher ground and opened heavy and accurate fire. He was hit, and wounded, but continuing his attack he drove the enemy back with a loss of 27 killed. While withdrawing to overtake his squad, he found a seriously wounded comrade, helped him to the rear, and soon overtook his platoon leader, who was assisting another wounded. While these 4 were moving to rejoin their platoon, an enemy sniper appeared and aimed his weapon at the platoon leader. Pvt. Fryar instantly sprang forward, received the full burst of automatic fire in his own body and fell mortally wounded. With his remaining strength he threw a hand-grenade and killed the sniper. Pvt. Fryar's indomitable fighting spirit and extraordinary gallantry above and beyond the call of duty contributed outstandingly to the success of the battalion's withdrawal and its subsequent attack and defeat of the enemy. His heroic action in unhesitatingly giving his own life for his comrade in arms exemplifies the highest tradition of the U.S. Armed Forces.

†**KELLEY, OVA A.**
Rank and Organization: Private, U.S. Army, Company A, 382d Infantry, 96th Infantry Division.
Born: Norwood, Missouri.
Entered Service At: Norwood, Missouri.
Place and Date: Leyte, Philippine Islands, December 8, 1944.
Citation: For conspicuous gallantry and intrepidity at the risk of his life above and beyond the call of duty. Before dawn, near the edge of the enemy-held Buri airstrip, the company was immobilized by heavy, accurate rifle and machine-gun fire from hostile troops entrenched in bomb craters and a ditch less than 100 yards distant. The company commander ordered a mortar concentration which destroyed one machine-gun but failed to dislodge the main body of the enemy. At this critical moment Pvt. Kelley, on his own initiative, left his shallow foxhole with an armload of hand-grenades and began a 1-man assault on the foe. Throwing his missiles with great accuracy, he moved forward, killed or wounded 5 men, and forced the remainder to flee in a disorganized route. He picked up a M1 rifle and emptied its clip at the running Japanese, killing 3. Discarding this weapon, he took a carbine and killed 3 more of the enemy. Inspired by his example, his comrades followed him in a charge which destroyed the entire enemy force of 34 enlisted men and 2 officers and captured 2 heavy and 1 light machine-guns. Pvt. Kelley continued to press the attack on to an airstrip, where sniper fire wounded him so grievously that he died 2 days later. His outstanding courage, aggressiveness, and initiative in the face of grave danger was an inspiration to his entire company and led to the success of the attack.

OFFICIAL COMMUNIQUE:
United Nations
ADVANCED HEADQUARTERS, on Leyte, Saturday, Dec. 9 – A communique:

PHILIPPINES

Leyte: The Seventy-seventh Division is now at the outskirts of Ormoc. The Seventh Division, attacking northward from Palanas, has seized Balogo and high ground north of the Tabgas River and is now within five miles of the Seventy-seventh. The substantial enemy forces are caught between these units and face annihilation. Ten miles west of Burauen on the Albuera trail we have captured the mountain pass at Mahomag and are driving westward toward the coast. In X Corps' sector, the Thirty-second Division south of Leyte River, eliminated by-passed enemy pockets and are advancing slowly to the south against stubborn enemy resistance.

Our light naval units operating in the Camotes Sea intercepted and sank six small enemy vessels and left a seventh burning furiously. In the Leyte Gulf area, our fighters and ships' anti-aircraft defenses shot down fourteen enemy planes attacking our shipping. An additional five enemy planes were destroyed by our fighters over western Leyte.

Luzon: Heavy units bombed the Legaspi airdrome without opposition. Night air patrols off Bondoc Peninsula sank a 9,000-ton transport and damaged a small freighter. Others bombed Talisay and harassed the Manila area, destroying an ammunition dump at Clark Field.

NEPPEL, RALPH G.

Rank and Organization: Sergeant, U.S. Army, Company M, 329th Infantry, 83d Infantry Division.
Born: Willey, Iowa.
Entered Service At: Glidden, Iowa.
Place and Date: Birgel, Germany, December 14, 1944.
Citation: Sgt. Neppel was leader of a machine-gun squad defending an approach to the village of Birgel, Germany, on December 14, 1944, when an enemy tank, supported by 20 infantrymen, counter-attacked. He held his fire until the Germans were within 100 yards and then raked the foot soldiers beside the tank, killing several of them. The enemy armor continued to press forward, and, at the pointblank range of 30 yards, fired a high-velocity shell into the American emplacement, wounding the entire squad. Sgt. Neppel, blown 10 yards from his gun, had one leg severed below the knee and suffered other wounds. Despite his injuries and the danger from the onrushing tank and infantry, he dragged himself back to his position on his elbows, remounted his gun and killed the remaining enemy riflemen. Stripped of its infantry protection, the tank was forced to withdraw. By his superb courage and indomitable fighting spirit, Sgt. Neppel inflicted heavy casualties on the enemy and broke a determined counter-attack.

OFFICIAL COMMUNIQUE:
United Nations
SUPREME HEADQUARTERS, Allied Expeditionary Force, Dec. 14 –Communique 250:

In the Juelich-Dueren sector, Allied troops, after overcoming heavy resistance, have cleared Schophoven. The villages of Mariaweiler and Derichsweiler, west of Dueren, and Gey, farther south, are also in our handle.

Gains have been made in the areas north and south of Monschau. East and southeast of Roetgen our troops have taken Rollesbroich and Simmerath. Progress has been made in the forest area about four miles southeast of Monschau.

Supporting our ground forces, medium, light, and fighter-bombers attacked fortified positions at Schoneseiffen, Hellenthal, Blumenthal, Schleiden and Kall. Medium and fighter-bombers struck at targets in the Zuelpich area and a railway yard at Euskirchen.

In the Saar Valley our ground forces in the Dillingen bridgehead and being subjected to considerable enemy artillery fire. We have crossed the Blies River between Habkirchen and Bliesbruck in the area northeast of Sarreguemines. House-to-house fighting continues in Habkirchen.

Fort Jeanne d'Arc, the last of the Metz forts held by the enemy, has been captured.

In northern Alsace, just west of the lower Vosges, gains up to three miles were made. Northwest of Bitche our forces went through the Maginot Line to Kapellenhoff. In Forest, Soultz and several near-by villages were freed and to the east fighting continued at Seltz, near the Rhine.

The attack on the enemy's rail transport and communications in Holland and western Germany was continued yesterday by fighter-bombers.

NETT, ROBERT B.

Rank and Organization: Captain (then Lieutenant), U.S. Army, Company E, 305th Infantry, 77th Infantry Division.
Born: New Haven, Connecticut.
Entered Service At: New Haven, Connecticut.
Place and Date: Near Cognon, Leyte, Philippine Islands, December 14, 1944.
Citation: Lt. Nett commanded Company E in an attack against a reinforced enemy battalion which had held up the American advance for 2 days from its entrenched positions around a 3-story concrete building. With another infantry company and armored vehicles, Company E advanced against heavy machine-gun and other automatic weapons fire with Lt. Nett spearheading the assault against the strongpoint. During the fierce hand-to-hand encounter which ensued, he killed 7 deeply entrenched Japanese with his rifle and bayonet and, although seriously wounded, gallantly continued to lead his men forward, refusing to relinquish his command. Again he was severely wounded, but, still unwilling to retire, pressed ahead with his troops to assure the capture of the objective. Wounded once more in the final assault, he calmly made all arrangements for the resumption of the advance, turned over his command to another officer, and then walked unaided to the rear for medical treatment. By his remarkable courage in con-

tinuing forward through sheer determination despite successive wounds, Lt. Nett provided an inspiring example for his men and was instrumental in the capture of a vital strongpoint.

†JOHNSON, LEROY

Rank and Organization: Sergeant, U.S. Army, Company K, 126th Infantry, 32d Infantry Division.
Born: Caney Creek, Louisiana.
Entered Service At: Oakdale, Louisiana.
Place and Date: Near Limon, Leyte, Philippine Islands, December 15, 1944.
Citation: Sgt. Johnson was squad leader of a 9-man patrol sent to reconnoiter a ridge held by a well-entrenched enemy force. Seeing an enemy machine-gun position, he ordered his men to remain behind while he crawled to within 6 yards of the gun. One of the enemy crew jumped up and prepared to man the weapon. Quickly withdrawing, Sgt. Johnson rejoined his patrol and reported the situation to his commanding officer. Ordered to destroy the gun, which covered the approaches to several other enemy positions, he chose 3 other men, armed them with hand-grenades, and led them to a point near the objective. After taking partial cover behind a log, the men had knocked out the gun and begun an assault when hostile troops on the flank hurled several grenades. As he started for cover, Sgt. Johnson saw 2 unexploded grenades which had fallen near his men. Knowing that his comrades would be wounded or killed by the explosion, he deliberately threw himself on the grenades and received their full charge in his body. Fatally wounded by the blast, he died soon afterward. Through his outstanding gallantry in sacrificing his life for his comrades, Sgt. Johnson provided a shining example of the highest traditions of the U.S. Army.

VLUG, DIRK J.

Rank and Organization: Private First Class, U.S. Army, 126th Infantry, 32d Infantry Division.
Born: Maple Lake, Minnesota.
Entered Service At: Grand Rapids, Michigan.
Place and Date: Near Limon, Leyte, Philippine Islands, December 15, 1944.
Citation: Pfc. Vlug displayed conspicuous gallantry and intrepidity above and beyond the call of duty when an American roadblock on the Ormoc Road was attacked by a group of enemy tanks. He left his covered position,

and with a rocket launcher and 6 rounds of ammunition, advanced alone under intense machine-gun and 37-mm. fire. Loading single-handedly, he destroyed the first tank, killing its occupants with a single round. As the crew of the second tank started to dismount and attack him, he killed one of the foe with his pistol, forcing the survivors to return to their vehicle, which he then destroyed with a second round. Three more hostile tanks moved up the road, so he flanked the first and eliminated it, and then, despite a hail of enemy fire, pressed forward again to destroy another. With his last round of ammunition he struck the remaining vehicle, causing it to crash down a steep embankment. Through his sustained heroism in the face of superior forces, Pfc. Vlug alone destroyed 5 enemy tanks and greatly facilitated successful accomplishment of his battalion's mission.

Note: The following is a newspaper account of the preceding battle for which Capt. Nett, Sgt. Johnson, and Pfc. Vlug were awarded the Medal of Honor:

AMERICANS GAIN ON LEYTE

• • •

ADVANCED HEADQUARTERS on Leyte, Saturday, Dec. 16 – Troops of the United States Seventy-seventh Division, supported by heavy artillery, drove northward from Ormoc today for an inevitable head-on clash with the large body of Japanese caught in the Ormoc corridor of northwestern Leyte Island.

The enemy's main supply depot, a mile north of Ormoc, was in American hands after a bitter struggle.

At the northern end of the corridor, the United States Thirty-second Division tightened its pressure on the hemmed-in enemy force, the only one of any size remaining on Leyte.

McGARITY, VERNON
Rank and Organization: Technical Sergeant, U.S. Army, Company L, 393d Infantry, 99th Infantry Division.
Born: December 1, 1921, Right, Tennessee.
Entered Service At: Model, Tennessee.
Place and Date: Near Krinkelt, Belgium, December 16, 1944.
Citation: T/Sgt. McGarity was painfully wounded in an artillery barrage that preceded the powerful counter-offensive launched by the Germans near Krinkelt, Belgium, on the morning of December 16, 1944. He made his way to an aid station, received treatment, and then refused to be evacuated,

choosing to return to his hard-pressed men instead. The fury of the enemy's great Western Front offensive swirled about the position held by T/Sgt. McGarity's small force, but so tenaciously did these men fight on orders to stand firm at all costs that they could not be dislodged despite murderous enemy fire and the breakdown of their communications. During the day, the heroic squad leader rescued one of his friends who had been wounded in a forward position, and throughout the night he exhorted his comrades to repulse the enemy's attempts at infiltration. When morning came and the Germans attacked with tanks and infantry, he braved heavy fire to run to an advantageous position where he immobilized the enemy's lead tank with a round from a rocket launcher. Fire from his squad drove the attacking infantrymen back, and three supporting tanks withdrew. He rescued, under heavy fire, another wounded American, and then directed devastating fire on a light cannon which had been brought up by the hostile troops to clear resistance from the area. When ammunition began to run low, T/Sgt. McGarity, remembering an old ammunition hole about 100 yards distant in the general direction of the enemy, braved a concentration of hostile fire to replenish his unit's supply. By circuitous route the enemy managed to emplace a machine-gun to the rear and flank of the squad's position, cutting off the only escape route. Unhesitatingly, the gallant soldier took it upon himself to destroy this menace single-handedly. He left cover, and while under steady fire from the enemy, killed or wounded all the hostile gunners with deadly accurate rifle fire and prevented all attempts to re-man the gun. Only when the squad's last round had been fired was the enemy able to advance and capture the intrepid leader and his men. The extraordinary bravery and extreme devotion to duty of T/Sgt. McGarity supported a remarkable delaying action which provided the time necessary for assembling reserves and forming a line against which the German striking power was shattered.

MURRAY, CHARLES P., JR.

Rank and Organization: First Lieutenant, U.S. Army, Company C, 30th Infantry, 3d Infantry Division.
Born: Baltimore, Maryland.
Entered Service At: Wilmington, North Carolina.
Place and Date: Near Kaysersberg, France, December 16, 1944.
Citation: For commanding Company C, 30th Infantry, displaying supreme courage and heroic initiative near Kaysersberg, France, on December 16, 1944, while leading a reinforced platoon into enemy territory. Descending into a valley beneath hilltop positions held by our troops, he observed a

force of 200 Germans pouring deadly mortar, bazooka, machine-gun, and small-arms fire into an American battalion occupying the crest of the ridge. The enemy's position in a sunken road, though hidden from the ridge, was open to a flank attack by 1st Lt. Murray's patrol but he hesitated to commit so small a force to battle with the superior and strongly disposed enemy. Crawling out ahead of his troops to a vantage point, he called by radio for artillery fire. His shells bracketed the German force, but when he was about to correct the range his radio went dead. He returned to his patrol, secured grenades and a rifle to launch them and went back to his self-appointed outpost. His first shots disclosed his position; the enemy directed heavy fire against him as he methodically fired his missiles into the narrow defile. Again he returned to his patrol. With an automatic rifle and ammunition, he once more moved to his exposed position. Burst after burst he fired into the enemy, killing 20, wounding many others. He prevented the removal of three German mortars by knocking out a truck. By that time, a mortar had been brought to his support. 1st Lt. Murray directed fire of this weapon, causing further casualties and confusion in the German ranks. Calling on his patrol to follow, he then moved out toward his original objective, possession of a bridge and construction of a roadblock. He captured 10 Germans in foxholes. An eleventh, while pretending to surrender, threw a grenade which knocked him to the ground, inflicting eight wounds. Though suffering and bleeding profusely, he refused to return to the rear until he had chosen the spot for the block and had seen his men correctly deployed. By his single-handed attack on an overwhelming force and by his intrepid and heroic fighting, 1st Lt. Murray stopped a counter-attack, established an advance position against formidable odds, and provided an inspiring example for the men of his command.

OFFICIAL COMMUNIQUE:
United Nations
SUPREME HEADQUARTERS, Allied Expeditionary Force, Dec. 16 – Communique 252:

Allied progress toward Dueren has given us control of high ground dominating the Roer River on the southwest side of the town. The villages of Guerzenich, Birgel and Kufferath are in our hands and enemy counter-attacks against both Guerzenich and Birgel have been repulsed. Targets in the village of Kreuzau, across the Roer from Kufferath, were hit by fighter-bombers.

Farther north, two remaining pockets of resistance west of the Dueren-Linnich sector of the Roer River have been cleared. Our units mopped up the factor area southeast of Mariaweiler and captured a castle near Schophoven.

Fighter-bombers struck at military objectives in Baal and other villages in the Juelich-Linnich area, Buir, northeast of Dueren, and railway yards at Rheydt, Grevenbroich, Euskirchen and Cologne.

Southeast of Lammersdorf our ground forces are mopping up Kesternich. In this sector we are encountering minefields and wire entanglements.

Medium and light bombers attacked fortifications in five villages in the area east and southeast of Monschau.

In the Saar Valley, the enemy continues to direct heavy artillery fire into our bridgeheads across the river at Dillingen and Saarlautern. A small counter-attack in the Saarlautern area was repulsed by our artillery.

East of Sarreguemines mopping up continues in Habkirchen. We have entered Niedergailbach and Erching.

Fighter-bombers supported our ground forces in the Saar Valley, striking at defended positions and communications behind the enemy line. Farther into Germans ammunition dumps were attacked.

West of the lower Vosges Mountains where the enemy is manning the Maginot fortifications resistance continued to be stubborn.

On the east side of the lower Vosges our units have crossed the Franco-German frontier north of Climbach, which has been freed.

Heavy fire is coming from the Siegfried Line at many points between Wissembourg and the Rhine.

An additional slight advance has been made on the Alsace plain northeast of Selestat.

†COWAN, RICHARD ELLER

Rank and Organization: Private First Class, U.S. Army, Company M, 23d Infantry, 2d Infantry Division.
Born: Lincoln, Nebraska.
Entered Service At: Wichita, Kansas.
Place and Date: Near Krinkelter Wald, Belgium, December 17, 1944.
Citation: Pfc. Cowan was a heavy machine-gunner in a section attached to Company I in the vicinity of Krinkelter Wald, Belgium, December 17, 1944, when that company was attacked by a numerically superior force of German infantry and tanks. The first six waves of hostile infantrymen were repulsed with heavy casualties, but a seventh drive with tanks killed or wounded all but three of his section, leaving Pvt. Cowan to man his gun, supported by only 15 to 20 riflemen of Company I. He maintained his position, holding off the Germans until the rest of the shattered force had set up a new line along a firebreak. Then, unaided, he moved his machine-gun and ammunition to the second position. At the approach of a Royal

Tiger tank, he held his fire until about 80 enemy infantrymen supporting the tank appeared at a distance of about 150 yards. His first burst killed or wounded about half of these infantrymen. His position was rocked by an 88-mm. shell when the tank opened fire, but he continued to man his gun, pouring deadly fire into the Germans when they again advanced. He was barely missed by another shell. Fire from three machine-guns and innumerable small arms struck all about him; an enemy rocket shook him badly, but did not drive him from his gun. Infiltration by the enemy had by this time made the position untenable, and the order was given to withdraw. Pvt. Cowan was the last man to leave, voluntarily covering the withdrawal of his remaining comrades. His heroic actions were entirely responsible for allowing the remaining men to retire successfully from the scene of their last-ditch stand.

LOPEZ, JOSE M.

Rank and Organization: Sergeant, U.S. Army, 23d Infantry, 2d Infantry Division.
Born: Mission, Texas.
Entered Service At: Brownsville, Texas.
Place and Date: Near Krinkelt, Belgium, December 17, 1944.
Citation: On his own initiative, he carried his heavy machine-gun from Company K's right flank to its left, in order to protect that flank which was in danger of being overrun by advancing enemy infantry supported by tanks. Occupying a shallow hole offering no protection above his waist, he cut down a group of 10 Germans. Ignoring enemy fire from an advancing tank, he held his position and cut down 25 more enemy infantry attempting to turn his flank. Glancing to his right, he saw a large number of infantry swarming in from the front. Although dazed and shaken from enemy artillery fire which had crashed into the ground only a few yards away, he realized that his position soon would be outflanked. Again, alone, he carried his machine-gun to a position to the right rear of the sector; enemy tanks and infantry were forcing a withdrawal. Blown over backward by the concussion of enemy fire, he immediately reset his gun and continued his fire. Single-handed he held off the German horde until he was satisfied his company had effected its retirement. Again he loaded his gun on his back and in a hail of small-arms fire he ran to a point where a few of his comrades were attempting to set up another defense against the onrushing enemy. He fired from this position until his ammunition was exhausted. Still carrying his gun, he fell back with his small group to Krinkelt. Sgt. Lopez's gallantry and intrepidity, on seemingly suicidal missions in which he killed

at least 100 of the enemy, were almost solely responsible for allowing Company K to avoid being enveloped, to withdraw successfully and to give other forces coming up in support time to build a line which repelled the enemy drive.

SODERMAN, WILLIAM A.
Rank and Organization: Private First Class, U.S. Army, Company K, 9th Infantry, 2d Infantry Division.
Born: West Haven, Connecticut.
Entered Service At: West Haven, Connecticut.
Place and Date: Near Rocherath, Belgium, December 17, 1944.
Citation: Armed with a bazooka, he defended a key road junction near Rocherath, Belgium, on December 17, 1944, during the German Ardennes counter-offensive. After a heavy artillery barrage had wounded and forced the withdrawal of his assistant, he heard enemy tanks approaching the position where he calmly waited in the gathering darkness of early evening until the five Mark V tanks which made up the hostile force were within pointblank range. He then stood up, completely disregarding the firepower that could be brought to bear upon him, and launched a rocket into the lead tank, setting it afire and forcing its crew to abandon it as the other tanks pressed on before Pfc. Soderman could reload. The daring bazooka-man remained at his post all night under severe artillery, mortar, and machine-gun fire, awaiting the next onslaught, which was made shortly after dawn by five more tanks. Running along a ditch to meet them, he reached an advantageous point and there leaped to the road in full view of the tank gunners, deliberately aimed his weapon and disabled the lead tank. The other vehicles, thwarted by a deep ditch in their attempt to go around the crippled machine, withdrew. While returning to his post Pfc. Soderman, braving heavy fire to attack an enemy infantry platoon from close range, killed at least three Germans and wounded several others with a round from his bazooka. By this time, enemy pressure had made Company K's position untenable. Orders were issued for withdrawal to an assembly area, where Pfc. Soderman was located when he once more heard enemy tanks approaching. Knowing that elements of the company had not completed their disengaging maneuver and were consequently extremely vulnerable to an armored attack, he hurried from his comparatively safe position to meet the tanks. Once more he disabled the lead tank with a single rocket, his last; but before he could reach cover, machine-gun bullets from the tank ripped into his right shoulder. Unarmed and seriously wounded he dragged himself along a ditch to the American lines and was evacuated. Through

his unfaltering courage against overwhelming odds, Pfc. Soderman contributed in great measure to the defense of Rocherath, exhibiting to a superlative degree the intrepidity and heroism with which American soldiers met and smashed the savage power of the last great German offensive.

Note: The following is a newspaper account of the preceding battle (the "Battle of the Bulge") for which Pfc. Cowan, Sgt. Lopez, and Pfc. Soderman were awarded the Medal of Honor:

NAZI OFFENSIVE PIERCES FIRST ARMY LINES; CHUTISTS AND LUFTWAFFE SUPPORT PUSH

• • •

BELGIUM ENTERED

• • •

**Germans Also Push Into Luxembourg
In Attack on 70-Mile Front**

• • •

FOE LOSES 143 WARPLANES

• • •

**Seventh Army Continues Its Advance Into Reich –
Third Breaks Into Siegfried Line**

• • •

SUPREME HEADQUARTERS, Allied Expeditionary Force, Paris, Dec. 17 – A German offensive against the southern flank of the American First Army bit several miles into Belgium today and crashed across the Luxembourg frontier in two areas.

Several German armored infantry divisions are being employed in Field Marshal Karl von Rundstedt's counter-blow, which is described here as a major effort. Parachute troops dropped in small groups behind the First Army front and today the Luftwaffe flew 450 sorties, its largest effort since D-day, in support of the veteran divisions attacking on a seventy-mile front.

The Ninth, Nineteenth and Twenty-ninth Tactical Air Commands of the Ninth Air Force flew 1,120 sorties against the Luftwaffe today, engaging German squadrons in the skies and dive-bombing and strafing enemy troops as they advanced.

Germans Lose 143 Planes

Ninety-seven German planes were destroyed today while eleven more enemy aircraft of about 200 engaged or sighted were destroyed by British fighters of the British Second Tactical Air Force today. All told, the enemy has lost 123 planes in the past twenty-four hours.

[Press services reports late Sunday night raised the German loss to 143 planes, while the American loss was put at thirty-five.]

The size of the air effort and the use of paratroops indicated Marshal von Rundstedt was throwing in every reserve he had into the assault. It is not an offensive that should be underestimated, but as yet there is no cause for alarm, although it should be realized that the German attack has not yet reached its climax.

7th and 3d Armies Gain

The German eruption into Belgium and Luxembourg overshadowed the steady, significant gains made by the American Seventh Army in Wissembourg Gap and on the west bank of the Rhine. Lieut. Gen. Alexander M. Patch's tanks and infantry continued their advance despite the resistance offered by the five German divisions covering the thirty-five-mile front in the south.

At the same time the American Third Army broke into Siegfried Line positions in a 500-yard advance east of Dillingen and pushed on two miles from Gerscheim, northeast of Sarreguemines, capturing Medelsheim, Walsheim and three villages in the area.

The Germans intensified their ground effort all along the First and Ninth Army fronts from Monschau to north of Trier today.

They progressed several miles in the area of Honsfeld and Hepscheid, the former eight miles east of the important road junction of Malmedy in Belgium and seven miles west of the German frontier.

Other thrusts were made into Luxembourg south of Vianden and Echternach. Echternach is eighteen and a half miles northeast of the city of Luxembourg and Vianden is twelve miles northwest of Echternach. The Germans are using armor and infantry on a considerable scale in these attacks.

The intensification of the ground onslaught today was prepared for last night when the Luftwaffe flew an estimated 250 sorties in the First Army sector alone, bombing Kleinhau, Bergstein and Sweifall among other targets.

American Black Widows knocked down five of the night raiders, while First Army anti-aircraft gunners claimed the destruction of twenty-six more.

During these aerial attacks a number of paratroopers dropped behind the American lines in groups of four to eight men. A number of these raiding parties were mopped up today before they could do serious damage to the bridges, roads and other communications behind the First Army's battered front.

Marshal von Rundstedt, always canny, chose to strike at a moment when the American Ninth and First Armies, attacking on the Cologne Plain, had reached the formidable barrier of the Roer River, whose crossing would necessitate a major effort. With Cologne and the Rhine frontier temporarily safe, he chose to strike at a "soft" area, in the hopes of diverting troops from the sector to the north, which presents the greatest threat to the security of western Germany.

In the southern sector of the Allies' front, the Seventh Army has widened its front to eighteen miles, from Berg to a mile east of Bobenthal on he eastern slopes of the Vosges.

The Fourteenth Armored Division smashed north of Wissembourg Gap to enter Schweighofen and Kapsweyer, three and four miles northeast of Wissembourg.

Schweigen and Rechtenbach, two towns north of Wissembourg, also were cleared in the face of fire from small arms and anti-tank guns, while northwest of Wissembourg enemy rearguards were driven from Bobenthal and Nothweiler.

The Seventy-ninth Infantry Division, operating in the area northeast of Lauterbourg, cleared the enemy from Berg on the edge of the Bienwald Forest, eight and one-half miles west of Karlsruhe, despite moderate resistance. [Press services also said the German town of Scheibenhardt was cleared.]

On the left flank of the Seventh Army fighting around Bitche, there was a slight slackening of resistance, although gains were not large, the Germans holding out in four Maginot Line forts south of Bitche. [Press services said General Patch's forces had entered Hottviller, four miles west of Bitche.]

Opposing General Patch's forces here and in the frontier battle are these five German divisions: The Eleventh Panzer, the Twenty-fifth Panzer Grenadier on the left and the 361st Infantry Division around Bitche and the 245th and 256th Infantry Divisions between Wissembourg and Lauterbourg.

The last two named have been fighting a withdrawing action from Haguenau and the 256th has been badly mauled. The same is true of the 361st farther to the west. There are also a number of fortress battalions fighting in this thirty-five-mile-long sector where the Germans have approximately one division to every seven miles of the front, with two divisions in bad shape.

BELL, BERNARD P.

Rank and Organization: Technical Sergeant, U.S. Army, Company I, 142d Infantry, 36th Infantry Division.
Born: Grantsville, West Virginia.
Entered Service At: New York, New York.
Place and Date: Mittelwihr, France, December 18, 1944.
Citation: For fighting gallantly at Mittelwihr, France. On the morning of December 18, 1944, he led a squad against a schoolhouse held by enemy troops. While his men covered him, he dashed toward the building, surprised two guards at the door and took them prisoner without firing a shot. He found that other Germans were in the cellar. These he threatened with hand-grenades, forcing 26 in all to emerge and surrender. His squad then occupied the building and prepared to defend it against powerful enemy action. The next day, the enemy poured artillery and mortar barrages into the position, disrupting communications which T/Sgt. Bell repeatedly repaired under heavy small-arms fire as he crossed dangerous terrain to keep his company commander informed of the squad's situation. During the day, several prisoners were taken and other Germans killed when hostile forces were attracted to the schoolhouse by the sound of captured German weapons fired by the Americans. At dawn the next day the enemy prepared to assault the building. A German tank fired round after round into the structure, partially demolishing the upper stories. Despite this heavy fire, T/Sgt. Bell climbed to the second floor and directed artillery fire which forced the hostile tank to withdraw. He then adjusted mortar fire on large forces of enemy foot soldiers attempting to reach the American position and, when this force broke and attempted to retire, he directed deadly machine-gun and rifle fire into their disorganized ranks. Calling for armored support to blast out the German troops hidden behind a wall, he unhesitatingly exposed himself to heavy small-arms fire to stand beside a friendly tank and tell its occupants where to rip holes in walls protecting approaches to the school building. He then trained machine-guns on the gaps and mowed down all hostile troops attempting to cross the openings to get closer to the school building. By his intrepidity and bold, aggressive leadership, T/Sgt. Bell enabled his 8-man squad to drive back approximately 150 of the enemy, killing at least 87 and capturing 42. Personally, he killed more than 20 and captured 33 prisoners.

OFFICIAL COMMUNIQUE:

United Nations
SUPREME HEADQUARTERS, Allied Expeditionary Force, Dec. 18 –Communique 254:

Fighting has increased in intensity from the Monschau area southward to the southern end of the Luxembourg-German border, with the enemy continuing his attacks. Both infantry and armor now are in action and in some sectors the enemy has made use of small groups of parachutists. Gains were made by the Germans near Honsfeld, southwest of Vianden and south of Echternach.

During the enemy's efforts to give air support to his attacking ground forces we destroyed 108 of his aircraft for a loss of thirty-three of our fighters. Most of the action took place over the Monschau Forest and adjoining areas, though combats also developed farther north in the Rheine, Muenster and Bocholt regions. This resulted in aerial battles in the course of which fighter-bombers, operating mainly against road traffic in the Monschau Forest area, and rail traffic radiating from Cologne, destroyed or damaged large numbers of locomotives, railcars, armored fighting vehicles and motor and horse-drawn vehicles. Much of the road traffic was moving eastward on a road running along the Roer River to the east of Monschau. Other operations against road traffic were carried out between Monschau and Pruem.

In the Saar Valley Allied forces are making steady progress in the Dillingen and Saarlautern areas. Northeast of Sarreguemines we have made gains north of Walsheim. Fighter-bombers attacked fortified towns in the Saar region and bombed an ammunition dump east of Coblenz.

In the Bitche area heavy fighting continues around the Maginot forts. Enemy resistance slackened slightly but remains stubborn. Northeast of Wissembourg our units have captured half a dozen villages inside Germany including Schweighofen and Kapsweyer. Our forces now are facing the Siegfried Line at many points.

Medium bombers, two of which are missing, attacked Siegfried Line defenses between Ober-Otterbach and Steinfeld, including fortification pillboxes, tank traps and wire entanglements. Fighter-bombers operating in the Kaiserslautern, Speyer and Pforzheim areas shot down four enemy aircraft and attacked rail lines, locomotives, railyards and cars and motor transport.

In the high Vosges Mountains our ground forces freed Kaysersberg. On the Alsace Plain some ground was lost to strong enemy counter-attacks.

GERSTUNG, ROBERT E.

Rank and Organization: Technical Sergeant, U.S. Army, Company H, 313th Infantry, 79th Infantry Division.
Born: August 6, 1915, Chicago, Illinois.
Entered Service At: Chicago, Illinois.
Place and Date: Siegfried Line near Berg, Germany, December 19, 1944.
Citation: On December 19, 1944, he was ordered with his heavy machine-gun squad to the support of an infantry company attacking the outer de-

fense of the Siegfried Line near Berg, Germany. For eight hours he maintained a position made almost untenable by the density of artillery and mortar fire concentrated upon it and the proximity of enemy troops who threw hand-grenades into the emplacement. While all other members of his squad became casualties, he remained at his gun. When he ran out of ammunition, he fearlessly dashed across bullet-swept, open terrain to secure a new supply from a disabled friendly tank. A fierce barrage pierced the water jacket of his gun, but he continued to fire until the weapon overheated and jammed. Instead of withdrawing, he crawled 50 yards across coverless ground to another of his company's machine-guns which had been silenced when its entire crew was killed. He continued to man this gun, giving support vitally needed by the infantry. At one time he came under direct fire from a hostile tank, which shot the glove from his hand with an armor-piercing shell but could not drive him from his position or stop his shooting. When the American forces were ordered to retire to their original positions, he remained at his gun, giving the only covering fire. Finally withdrawing, he cradled the heavy weapon in his left arm, slung a belt of ammunition over his shoulder, and walked to the rear, loosing small bursts at the enemy as he went. One hundred yards from safety, he was struck in the leg by a mortar shell; but, with a supreme effort, he crawled the remaining distance, dragging along the gun which had served him and his comrades so well. By his remarkable perseverance, indomitable courage, and heroic devotion to his task in the face of devastating fire, T/Sgt. Gerstung gave his fellow soldiers powerful support in their encounter with formidable enemy forces.

†KIMBRO, TRUMAN

Rank and Organization: Technician Fourth Grade, U.S. Army, Company C, 2d Engineer Combat Battalion, 2d Infantry Division.
Born: Madisonville, Texas.
Entered Service At: Houston, Texas.
Place and Date: Near Rocherath, Belgium, December 19, 1944.
Citation: On December 19, 1944, as scout, he led a squad assigned to the mission of mining a vital crossroads near Rocherath, Belgium. At the first attempt to reach the objective, he discovered it was occupied by an enemy tank and at least 20 infantrymen. Driven back by withering fire, Technician 4th Grade Kimbro made two more attempts to lead his squad to the crossroads but all approaches were covered by intense enemy fire. Although warned by our own infantrymen of the great danger involved, he left his squad in a protected place and, laden with mines, crawled alone toward the crossroads. When nearing his objective he was severely wounded, but he

continued to drag himself forward and laid his mines across the road. As he tried to crawl from the objective his body was riddled with rifle and machine-gun fire. The mines laid by his act of indomitable courage delayed the advance of enemy armor and prevented the rear of our withdrawing columns from being attacked by the enemy.

OFFICIAL COMMUNIQUE:
United Nations
SUPREME HEADQUARTERS, Allied Expeditionary Force, Dec. 19 –Communique 255:

Heavy fighting continues in the sectors where the enemy launched his attack between the Monschau area and the southern part of the German-Luxembourg border. Supporting Allied ground forces, fighter-bombers knocked out ninety-five enemy armored vehicles and struck at road and rail transport.

Medium and light bombers attacked targets at Herhahn, Olff, Harperscheid, Blumenthal and Hellenthal, east of Monschau. Forty-six enemy aircraft were shot down in the air. From these operations eleven fighters are missing. All the bombers returned.

Our forces in the Linnich area are mopping up in Wuerm and Mullendorf.

In the Dillengen and Saarlautern bridgeheads our troops continued to make slow progress in wiping out enemy strongpoints. In the area northeast of Sarreguemines we have reached a wooded area one mile north of Habkirchen and gains were made in the vicinity of Walsheim and Medelsheim.

Fighter-bombers destroyed or damaged many fortified buildings and attacked road and rail transport in the area of Landau.

In the vicinity of Bitche our units have taken a large portion of two stubbornly defended Maginot fortifications.

Northwest of Wissembourg we advanced two miles and entered the German villages of Bundenthal and Nieder-Schlettenbach. Farther east heavy fire was received from the Siegfried Line.

Stiff fighting continues northwest of Colmar. Further limited advances have been made in the high Vosges Mountains.

Last night a strong force of heavy bombers attacked enemy ships in the Baltic port of Gydnia.

†**WARNER, HENRY F.**
Rank and Organization: Corporal, U.S. Army, Antitank Company, 2d Battalion, 26th Infantry, 1st Infantry Division.
Born: August 23, 1923, Troy, North Carolina.
Entered Service At: Troy, North Carolina.

Place and Date: Near Dom Butgenbach, Belgium, December 20-21, 1944.
Citation: Serving as 57-mm. antitank gunner with the 2d Battalion, he was a major factor in stopping enemy tanks during heavy attacks against the battalion position near Dom Butgenbach, Belgium, on December 20-21, 1944. In the first attack, launched in the early morning of the 20th, enemy tanks succeeded in penetrating parts of the line. Cpl. Warner, disregarding the concentrated cannon and machine-gun fire from two tanks bearing down on him, and ignoring the imminent danger of being overrun by the infantry moving under tank cover, destroyed the first tank and scored a direct and deadly hit upon the second. A third tank approached to within five yards of his position while he was attempting to clear a jammed breach lock. Jumping from his gun pit, he engaged in a pistol duel with the tank commander standing in the turret, killing him and forcing the tank to withdraw. Following a day and night during which our forces were subjected to constant shelling, mortar barrages, and numerous unsuccessful infantry attacks, the enemy struck in great force on the early morning of the 21st. Seeing a Mark IV tank looming out of the mist and heading toward his position. Cpl. Warner scored a direct hit. Disregarding his injuries, he endeavored to finish the loading and again fire at the tank, whose motor was now aflame, when a second machine-gun burst killed him. Cpl. Warner's gallantry and intrepidity at the risk of life above and beyond the call of duty contributed materially to the successful defense against the enemy attacks.

CURREY, FRANCIS S.
Rank and Organization: Sergeant, U.S. Army, Company K, 120th Infantry, 30th Infantry Division.
Born: Loch Sheldrake, New York.
Entered Service At: Hurleyville, New York.
Place and Date: Malmedy, Belgium, December 21, 1944.
Citation: Sgt. Currey was an automatic rifleman with the 3d Platoon defending a strong point near Malmedy, Belgium, on December 21, 1944, when the enemy launched a powerful attack. Overrunning tank destroyers and antitank guns located near the strong point, German tanks advanced to the 3d Platoon's position, and, after prolonged fighting, forced the withdrawal of this group to a nearby factory. Sgt. Currey found a bazooka in the building and crossed the street to secure rockets meanwhile enduring intense fire from enemy tanks and hostile infantrymen who had taken up a position at a house a short distance away. In the face of small-arms, machine-gun, and artillery fire, he, with a companion, knocked out a tank with one shot. Moving to another position, he observed three Germans in

the doorway of an enemy-held house. He killed or wounded all three with his automatic rifle. He emerged from cover and advanced alone to within 50 yards of the house, intent on wrecking it with rockets. Covered by friendly fire, he stood erect, and fired a shot which knocked down half of one wall. While in this forward position, he observed five Americans who had been pinned down for hours by fire from the house and three tanks. Realizing that they could not escape until the enemy tank and infantry guns had been silenced, Sgt. Currey crossed the street to a vehicle, where he procured an armful of antitank grenades. These he launched while under heavy enemy fire, driving the tankmen from the vehicles into the house. He then climbed onto a half-track in full view of the Germans and fired a machine-gun at the house. Once again changing his position, he manned another machine-gun whose crew had been killed; under his covering fire, the five soldiers were able to retire to safety. Deprived of tanks and with heavy infantry casualties, the enemy was forced to withdraw. Through his extensive knowledge of weapons and by his heroic and repeated braving of murderous enemy fire, Sgt. Currey was greatly responsible for inflicting heavy losses in men and material on the enemy, for rescuing five comrades, two of whom were wounded, and for stemming an attack which threatened to flank his battalion's position.

†THORNE, HORACE M.

Rank and Organization: Corporal, U.S. Army, Troop D, 89th Cavalry Reconnaissance Squadron, 9th Armored Division.
Born: Keansburg, New Jersey.
Entered Service At: Keyport, New Jersey.
Place and Date: Near Grufflingen, Belgium, December 21, 1944.
Citation: Cpl. Thorne was the leader of a combat patrol on December 21, 1944, near Grufflingen, Belgium, with the mission of driving German forces from dug-in positions in a heavily wooded area. As he advanced his light machine-gun, a German Mark III tank emerged from the enemy position and was quickly immobilized by fire from American light tanks supporting the patrol. Two of the enemy tankmen attempted to abandon their vehicle but were killed by Cpl. Thorne's shots before they could jump to the ground. To complete the destruction of the tank and its crew, Cpl. Thorne left his covered position and crept forward alone through intense machine-gun fire until close enough to toss two grenades into the tank's open turret, killing two more Germans. He returned across the same fire-beaten zone as heavy mortar fire began falling in the area, seized his machine-gun and, without help, dragged it to the knocked-out tank and set it up on the vehicle's rear

deck. he fired short rapid bursts into the enemy positions from his advantageous but exposed location, killing or wounding eight. Two enemy machine-gun crews abandoned their positions and retreated in confusion. His gun jammed; but rather than leave his self-chosen post, he attempted to clear the stoppage; enemy small-arms fire, concentrated on the tank, killed him instantly. Cpl. Thorne, displaying heroic initiative and intrepid fighting qualities, inflicted costly casualties on the enemy and insured the success of his patrol's mission by the sacrifice of his life.

Note: The following is a newspaper account of the preceding battle (the "Battle of the Bulge") for which Cpl. Warner, Sgt. Currey, and Cpl. Thorne were awarded the Medal of Honor:

AMERICANS TAKING, GIVING RECORD LOSS

• • •

Belgium Battle Dwarfs All Their Experiences in This War – Foe Uses Every Ruse

• • •

IN THE STAVELOT SECTOR, Belgium, Dec. 20 – American troops bearing the brunt of an attack by at least thirteen German divisions are suffering and inflicting their greatest single-battle losses of the war on the Western Front.

This northern flank held firm today as a new series of German tank and infantry attacks shattered in bloody waves, vainly trying to breach the positions held by the American veterans. To the south, however, elements of five German armored divisions and eight infantry divisions surged forward in new advances and the end was not in sight.

More American troops are involved in this struggle than in any single battle of the war. They are opposed by the most powerful punching force that they have yet encountered. The price on both sides is heavy. The struggle thus far dwarfs the two other main American setbacks, at Kasserine Pass in North Africa and at the Rapido River in Italy.

Along this sector the German advance has been stemmed and broken. It was hurled back this morning when the Germans launched a series of violent attacks at points on a twenty-mile front. These blows failed in piles of broken bodies and twisted metal.

One veteran American unit knocked out eight Mark V and Mark VI tanks in two hours this morning. Farther south, however, the German advance was showing the professional punch that the enemy exhibited in 1940.

As various units fought their way back to this sector through the German lines, it was becoming possible to piece together a picture of the early fighting. One infantry unit returned to the American lines in bits and pieces, but its losses were amazingly small in view of the fact the group claimed to have killed 1,200 Germans. The unit had lost much of its equipment, except for rifles and bazookas.

Another badly mauled American formation, which bore the full fury of the German assault, claimed to have stopped sixty German tanks in three days. But it, too, had lost a great deal of its artillery and motorized equipment.

The German troops are using every trick ever tried during this war. There have been several authenticated cases in the last forty-eight hours in which the Germans used the old trick of waving a white flag as if they were going to surrender and then advancing near the American lines to a favorable position, dropping down and opening fire. Several miles to the south the Germans operated four American Sherman tanks, calling American troops to come up close for support and then opening fire on them with machine guns.

[Near one Belgian city, American flame-thrower crews battling German tanks found at least ten dead Germans dressed in civilian clothes, The United Press reported. The Germans sent captured jeeps into the American lines, manned by men in American uniforms and carrying captured American credential, a Columbia Broadcasting System correspondent said.].

The weather has been almost as much an enemy to the Allies as the Germans. It is apparent that Field Marshal Gen. Karl von Rundstedt picked the time for his attack to coincide with a run of bad weather. Today the weather along the entire front is appalling. A pea-soup fog, which was almost turned to sleet by low temperatures, clung close to the ground. Automobiles had to be driven with their headlights on at noon and the roads were slippery from the fog and slimy mud.

It is impossible for the Allies' air arm to operate, but two clear days might change the complexion of the battle.

In this weird hell of fog and mud and mountains, one of the oddest battles is being fought several miles behind the lines by an infantry force led by Lieut. Col. Elisha Peckham of Narragansett, R.I. "This is a regular Indian war," he said. "My men have a look behind every tree and creep through the woods like Indians to hunt out German paratroopers."

Colonel Peckham's forces surrounded 200 last night and attacked this morning, but in the fog the paratroopers escaped despite considerable losses. "They were getting hungry and running out of ammunition," Colonel Peckham said. "We will get them all. We just have to keep chasing them. We rescued twenty-three of our GI's from a laundry the paratroopers had captured."

Colonel Peckham's executive officer, Major Samuel Carter of North Attleboro, Mass., said that a good number of the German paratroopers had overshot their landings and been found hanging in trees, some with their legs broken. Colonel Peckham said that this particular group of paratroopers was from a "new crop."

"They all are around 21, in good health and full of fight," he said.

A typical experience of some of the units overrun by the Germans was that of an anti-aircraft outfit that landed in France on D-day and has been fighting ever since. After having been overrun and forced to flee in trucks without their equipment, the crews organized salvage parties and crept back under machine-gun and artillery fire to salvage some of their guns.

"We got out several half-tracks, but the machine-gun fire drove us away. We were operating ahead of what is now the front line," Lieut. John Conroy of 2290 University Avenue, New York, said.

"Anyway, before we were knocked out we got twenty-three Jerry planes and would have gotten more," Capt. Spencer Calderwood of Logan, Utah, added.

The unit's chaplain, Lieut. Fred Steen, standing in ankle-deep mud with troops crowded all around him, told how the outfit had originally been overrun:

"The first we knew we heard shooting and saw German tanks coming down the main street of the town where we were quartered. The colonel crowded us into trucks and we took off. Some of the trucks went up one street while tanks came down another.

"I had a lot of Christmas packages from my congregation and I didn't open them and now the Germans have them. The next time I get a package it's going to be opened on the spot."

Corp, Warren Holden of Florence, Ore., was saved because a lieutenant insisted that he save the lieutenant's bedding roll.

"I was just putting on my shoes when I heard a burp gun and I finished dressing in a hurry," he said. "I was stopped by the lieutenant, who insisted I go back and get his bedroll, so I turned around and hurried to his house. I was lucky I did because later I found out that Tiger tanks were coming down the street I was going to take."

Corp. Holden had barely got in the house and started hunting for the bedroll when another tank came down the street and the rest of the American jumped out of the truck and dived into the cellar of the house. While Corp. Holden and the others watched, the tanks rumbled by. One blasted the truck and knocked the top off the house, but the cellar was safe. For the rest of the day, the Americans peered out the cellar window while tanks and German half-tracks rolled by. That night they made a run for it and reached the American lines.

†BENJAMIN, GEORGE, JR.

Rank and Organization: Private First Class, U.S. Army, Company A, 306th Infantry, 77th Infantry Division.
Born: Philadelphia, Pennsylvania.
Entered Service At: Carney's Point, New Jersey.
Place and Date: Leyte, Philippine Islands, December 21, 1944.

Citation: Pfc. Benjamin was a radio operator, advancing in the rear of his company as it engaged a well-defended Japanese strongpoint holding up the progress of the entire battalion. When a rifle platoon supporting a light tank hesitated in its advance, he voluntarily and with utter disregard for personal safety left his comparatively secure position and ran across bullet-whipped terrain to the tank, waving and shouting to the men of the platoon to follow. Carrying his bulky radio and armed only with a pistol, he fearlessly penetrated intense machine-gun and rifle fire to the enemy position, where he killed one of the enemy in a foxhole and moved on to annihilate the crew of a light machine-gun. Heedless of the terrific fire now concentrated on him, he continued to spearhead the assault, killing two more of the enemy and exhorting the other men to advance, until he fell mortally wounded. After being evacuated to an aid station, his first thought was still of the American advance. Overcoming great pain he called for the battalion operations officer to report the location of enemy weapons and valuable tactical information he had secured in his heroic charge. The unwavering courage, the unswerving devotion to the task at hand, the aggressive leadership of Pfc. Benjamin were a source of great and lasting inspiration to his comrades and were to a great extent responsible for the success of the battalion's mission.

OFFICIAL COMMUNIQUE:
United Nations
ADVANCED HEADQUARTERS on Leyte, Friday, Dec. 22 – A communique:

PHILIPPINES

Mindoro: There was no ground activity, but air activity increased sharply. Twenty-nine enemy planes attempting an attack on ground installations were intercepted by our fighters. Eleven raiders were definitely destroyed and three others probably. We lost one fighter.

Planes of the Far East Air Forces are already operating from local bases. One of our heavy reconnaissance units damaged a 6,000-ton freighter-transport off the northwest coast, leaving the vessel in flames.

Leyte: The pincers along the Ormoc corridor from the north and south have now closed, the Tenth and Twenty-fourth Corps being in contact. Destruction of enemy pockets continues. Enemy remnants are desperately but futilely trying to cut their way out to the west. An additional 2,032 abandoned enemy dead were counted during the day. Our fighters effectively supported ground operations.

Luzon: Our fighters attacked Batangas, damaging three parked planes on the airdrome and barges in the Batangas River.

Visayas: Following night harassing attacks, our fighters swept over Negros airdromes, destroying three enemy planes and damaging others. We lost one plane. Mindanao: Medium bombers and patrol planes attacked enemy shipping at Davao and off the north coast. Four coastal vessels and five barges were destroyed and a 1,000-ton freighter and other small craft damaged. Two enemy planes on Cagayan airdrome were destroyed by strafing and a building was set afire at Tawi Tawi.

DALESSONDRO, PETER J.

Rank and Organization: Technical Sergeant, U.S. Army, Company E, 39th Infantry, 9th Infantry Division.
Born: May 19, 1918, Watervliet, New York.
Entered Service At: Watervliet, New York.
Place and Date: Near Kalterherberg, Germany, December 22, 1944.
Citation: T/Sgt. Dalessondro was with the 1st Platoon holding an important road junction on high ground near Kalterherberg, Germany, on December 22, 1944. In the early morning hours, the enemy, after laying down an intense artillery and mortar barrage, followed through with an all-out attack that threatened to overwhelm the position. T/Sgt. Dalessondro, seeing that his men were becoming disorganized, braved the intense fire to move among them with words of encouragement. Advancing to a fully exposed observation post, he adjusted mortar fire upon the attackers, meanwhile firing upon them with his rifle and encouraging his men in halting and repulsing the attack. Later in the day the enemy launched a second determined attack. Once again, T/Sgt. Dalessondro, in the face of imminent death, rushed to his forward position and immediately called for mortar fire. After exhausting his rifle ammunition, he crawled 30 yards over exposed ground to secure a light machine-gun, returned to his position, and fired upon the enemy at almost pointblank range until the gun jammed. He managed to get the gun to fire one more burst, which used up his last round, but with these bullets he killed four German soldiers who were on the verge of murdering an aid man and two wounded soldiers in a nearby foxhole. When the enemy had almost surrounded him, he remained alone, steadfastly facing almost certain death or capture, hurling grenades and calling for mortar fire closer and closer to his outpost as he covered the withdrawal of his platoon to a second line of defense. As the German hordes swarmed about him, he was last heard calling for a barrage, saying, "OK, mortars, let me have it – right in this position!" The gallantry and intrepidity shown by T/Sgt. Dalessondro against an overwhelming enemy attack saved his company from complete rout.

OFFICIAL COMMUNIQUE:
United Nations
SUPREME HEADQUARTERS, Allied Expeditionary Force, Dec. 22 –Communique 258:

Several small enemy attacks have been repulsed by Allied forces in the vicinity of Monschau, and we have regained a few small towns in that area.

On the north flank of the German thrust we have stemmed the enemy advance and have retaken Stavelot, southwest of Malmedy.

Fighting is in progress for Malmedy itself.

Enemy armored elements have reached Habiemont, eight miles west of Stavelot, and enemy parachutists were dropped a few miles to the southwest of Habiemont.

Our forces have slowed down the enemy pincer movement directed at St. Vith, which is still in our hands.

The enemy drive west from Vianden has penetrated to a point just east of Wiltz and a force operating about six miles farther north reached the vicinity of Clervaux.

Fighting continues in the Echternach area, where our troops have denied the enemy control of Echternach and other towns in the immediate vicinity. An enemy thrust to Consdorf, southwest of Echternach, made further progress to the west.

In the Saar Valley our forces have cleared Dillingen. North and northwest of Wissembourg town counter-attacks, one supported by tanks, were beaten off. Repeated patrol clashes took place farther east nearer the Rhine.

Further slight gains were made in the high Vosges. We are now two miles north of Lake Noir, near Muenster.

Weather restricted air operations yesterday. Targets in Trier were attacked by heavy bombers. Fighter-bombers, which provided escort, also truck at objectives in the city and at Speicher, a main road junction twelve miles north.

Anti-aircraft positions east of Lebach were targets for other fighter-bombers. From these operations one fighter-bomber is missing.

Last evening heavy bombers attacked marshaling yards at Cologne and Bonn.

BOLDEN, PAUL L.
Rank and Organization: Staff Sergeant, U.S. Army, Company I, 120th Infantry, 30th Infantry Division.
Born: Hobbes Island, Iowa.
Entered Service At: Madison, Alabama.
Place and Date: Petit-Coo, Belgium, December 23, 1944.
Citation: S/Sgt. Bolden voluntarily attacked a formidable enemy strongpoint in Petit-Coo, Belgium, on December 23, 1944, when his com-

pany was pinned down by extremely heavy automatic and small-arms fire coming from a house 200 yards to the front. Mortar and tank artillery shells pounded the unit, when S/Sgt. Bolden and a comrade, on their own initiative, moved forward into a hail of bullets to eliminate the ever-increasing fire from the German position. Crawling ahead to close with what they knew was a powerfully armed, vastly superior force, the pair reached the house and took up assault positions, S/Sgt. Bolden under a window, his comrade across the street where he could deliver covering fire. In rapid succession, S/Sgt. Bolden hurled a fragmentation grenade and a white phosphorous grenade into the building; and then, fully realizing that he faced tremendous odds, rushed to the door, threw it open and fired into 35 SS troopers who were trying to reorganize themselves after the havoc wrought by the grenades. Twenty Germans died under fire of his submachine-gun before he was struck in the shoulder, chest, and stomach by part of a burst which killed his comrade across the street. He withdrew from the house, waiting for the surviving Germans to come out and surrender. When none appeared in the doorway, he summoned his ebbing strength, overcame the extreme pain he suffered and boldly walked back into the house, firing as he went. He had killed the remaining 15 soldiers when his ammunition ran out. S/Sgt. Bolden's heroic advance against great odds, his fearless assault, and his magnificent display of courage in re-entering the building where he had been severely wounded cleared the path for his company and insured the success of its mission.

BIDDLE, MELVIN E.

Rank and Organization: Private First Class, U.S. Army, Company B, 517th Parachute Infantry Regiment.
Born: Daleville, Indiana.
Entered Service At: Anderson, Indiana.
Place and Date: Near Soy, Belgium, December 23-24, 1944.
Citation: Pfc. Biddle displayed conspicuous gallantry and intrepidity in action against the enemy near Soy, Belgium, on December 23 and 24, 1944. Serving as lead scout during an attack to relieve the enemy-encircled town of Hotton, he aggressively penetrated a densely wooded area, advanced 400 yards until he came within range of intense enemy rifle fire, and within 20 yards of enemy positions killed three snipers with unerring marksmanship. Courageously continuing his advance an additional 200 yards, he discovered a hostile machine-gun position and dispatched its 2 occupants. He then located the approximate position of a well-concealed enemy machine-gun nest, and crawling forward, threw hand-grenades which killed two

Germans and fatally wounded a third. After signaling his company to advance, he entered a determined line of enemy defense, coolly and deliberately shifted his position, and shot three more enemy soldiers. Undaunted by enemy fire, he crawled within 20 yards of a machine-gun nest, tossed his last hand-grenade into the position, and after the explosion charged the emplacement firing his rifle. When night fell, he scouted enemy positions alone for several hours and returned with valuable information which enabled our attacking infantry and armor to knock out two enemy tanks. At daybreak he again led the advance and, when flanking elements were pinned down by enemy fire, without hesitation made his way toward a hostile machine-gun position and from a distance of 50 yards killed the crew and two supporting riflemen. The remainder of the enemy, finding themselves without automatic weapon support, fled panic stricken. Pfc. Biddle's intrepid courage and superb daring during his 20-hour action enabled his battalion to break the enemy grasp on Hotton with a minimum of casualties.

†KEFURT, GUS
Rank and Organization: Staff Sergeant, U.S. Army, Company K, 15th Infantry, 3d Infantry Division.
Born: Greenville, Pennsylvania.
Entered Service At: Youngstown, Ohio.
Place and Date: Near Bennwihr, France, December 23-24, 1944.
Citation: S/Sgt. Kefurt distinguished himself by conspicuous gallantry and intrepidity above and beyond the call of duty on December 23 and 24, 1944, near Bennwihr, France. Early in the attack S/Sgt. Kefurt jumped through an opening in a wall to be confronted by about 15 Germans. Although outnumbered he opened fire, killing 10 and capturing the others. During a seesaw battle which developed he effectively adjusted artillery fire on an enemy tank close to his position although exposed to small-arms fire. When night fell he maintained a 3-man outpost in the center of the town in the middle of the German positions and successfully fought off several hostile patrols attempting to penetrate our lines. Assuming command of his platoon the following morning he led it in hand-to-hand fighting through the town until blocked by a tank. Using rifle grenades he forced surrender of its crew and some supporting infantry. He then continued his attack from house to house against heavy machine-gun and rifle fire. Advancing against a strongpoint that was holding up the company, his platoon was subjected to a strong counter-attack and infiltration to its rear. Suffering heavy casualties in their exposed position, the men remained there due

to S/Sgt. Kefurt's personal example of bravery, determination and leadership. He constantly exposed himself to fire by going from man to man to direct fire. During this time he killed approximately 15 of the enemy at close range. Although severely wounded in the leg, he refused first aid and immediately resumed fighting. When the forces to his rear were pushed back three hours later, he refused to be evacuated, but, during several more counter-attacks, moved painfully about under intense small-arms and mortar fire, stiffening the resistance of his platoon by encouraging individual men and by his own fire until he was killed. As a result of S/Sgt. Kefurt's gallantry, the position was maintained.

†CASTLE, FREDERICK W. (Air Mission)

Rank and Organization: Brigadier General, Assistant Commander, 4th Bomber Wing, U.S. Army Air Corps.
Born: October 14, 1908, Manila, Philppine Islands.
Entered Service At: Mountain Lake, New Jersey.
Place and Date: Germany, December 24, 1944.
Citation: Brig. Gen. Castle was air commander and leader of more than 2,000 heavy bombers in a strike against German airfields on December 24, 1944. En route to the target, the failure of one engine forced him to relinquish his place at the head of the formation. In order not to endanger friendly troops on the ground below, he refused to jettison his bombs to gain speed maneuverability. His lagging, unescorted aircraft became the target of numerous enemy fighters which ripped the left wing with cannon shells, set the oxygen system afire, and wounded two members of the crew. Repeated attacks started fires in two engines, leaving the Flying Fortress in imminent danger of exploding. Realizing the hopelessness of the situation, the bail-out order was given. Without regard for his personal safety he gallantly remained alone at the controls to afford all other crewmembers an opportunity to escape. Still another attack exploded gasoline tanks in the right wing, and the bomber plunged earthward, carrying Gen. Castle to his death. His intrepidity and willing sacrifice of his life to save members of the crew were in keeping with the highest traditions of the military service.

OFFICIAL COMMUNIQUE:

United Nations
SUPREME HEADQUARTERS, Allied Expeditionary Force, Dec. 24 –Communique 260:

There have been no substantial changes in the Allied positions in the Monschau sector.

In the area northeast of Marche, enemy forces have cut the road northeast of Hotton. The town of Hotton remains in our hands but there is considerable resistance south of the road between Hotton and Soy, three miles to the northeast. Farther south enemy forces have reached Morhet, six miles southwest of Bastogne.

In the area north of Mersch, our troops have made gains on the southern flank of the enemy penetrations.

Allied forces in the Saar Valley repulsed a counter-attack by enemy infantry who crossed the Saar River south of Saarlautern. East of Wissembourg enemy artillery and mortars were active. More than 1,000 rounds fell on Berg within a few hours. Slight further progress was made in the Vosges west of Colmar.

Improved weather yesterday permitted the resumption of air operations on a large scale. Fighter-bombers in great strength struck at motor transport, tanks, rolling stock, troop concentrations, gun positions and other targets in and behind the area of the enemy counter-offensive, while fighters flew offensive sweeps. Medium and light bombers in force attacked bridges, railheads and communications centers behind this area. Great numbers of aerial combats ensued in the course of these operations.

The targets for the medium and light bombers were rail bridges at Euskirchen, Ahrweiler, Mayer and Eller, railheads at Zuelpich, Pruem, and Tilburg, and communications centers in the neighborhood of St. Vith and at Hergarten, Luenebach, Waxweiler and Neuerburg. Farther to the south medium bombers attacked bridges at Neckargemuend and Breisach, also dropping anti-personnel bombs on enemy troops in the latter area.

Fighter-bombers went for rail yards, rolling stock and rail lines in the area of Landau, Ringsheim and Colmar, destroying locomotives and rolling stock.

Escorted heavy bombers attacked objectives in the railway and garrison town of Trier and seven other air and road communication centers in western Germany, including railway yards at Ehrang, Kaiserslautern, Homberg, and rail and road junctions in an area between Coblenz and the Belgian border.

Last night light bombers attacked rail targets near Bonn and Coblenz.

In the course of all these operations 178 enemy aircraft were shot down and nine destroyed on the ground. Eight of our heavy bombers, twenty-six fighters and fighter-bombers, and thirty-nine medium and light bombers are not yet reported, though some of the medium bombers may have landed away from base.

During the night, our night fighters shot down nine enemy aircraft.

WIEDORFER, PAUL J.

Rank and Organization: Staff Sergeant (then Private), U.S. Army, Company G, 318th Infantry, 80th Infantry Division.
Born: Baltimore, Maryland.
Entered Service At: Baltimore, Maryland.
Place and Date: Near Chaumont, Belgium, December 25, 1944.
Citation: Pvt. Wiedorfer alone made it possible for his company to advance until its objective was seized. Company G had cleared a wooded area of snipers, and one platoon was advancing across an open clearing toward another woods when it was met by heavy machine-gun fire from two German positions dug in at the edge of the second woods. These positions were flanked by enemy riflemen. The platoon took cover behind a small ridge approximately 40 yards from the enemy position. There was no other available protection and the entire platoon was pinned down by the German fire. It was about noon and the day was clear, but the terrain extremely difficult due to a 3-inch snowfall the night before over ice-covered ground. Pvt. Wiedorfer, realizing that the platoon advance could not continued until the two enemy machine-gun nests were destroyed, voluntarily charged alone across the slippery open ground with no protecting cover of any kind. Running in a crouched position, under a hail of enemy fire, he slipped and fell in the snow, but quickly rose and continued forward with the enemy concentrating automatic and small-arms fire on him as he advanced. Miraculously escaping injury, Pvt. Wiedorfer reached a point some 10 yards from the first machine-gun emplacement and hurled a hand-grenade into it. With his rifle he killed the remaining Germans, and, without hesitation, wheeled to the right and attacked the second emplacement. One of the enemy was wounded by his fire and the other six immediately surrendered. This heroic action by one man enabled the platoon to advance from behind its protecting ridge and continue successfully to reach its objective. A few minutes later, when both the platoon leader and the platoon sergeant were wounded, Pvt. Wiedorfer assumed command of the platoon, leading it forward with inspired energy until the mission was accomplished.

OFFICIAL COMMUNIQUE:
United Nations
SUPREME HEADQUARTERS, Allied Expeditionary Force, Dec. 25 —Communique 261:

The Monschau and Stavelot sectors have been relatively quiet, although both Allied and enemy artillery fire has been heavy. No further progress has been made by the enemy in these sectors. The Germans dropped parachutists in small groups in several places in the area north and northwest of Stavelot. These are being dealt with.

Very heavy enemy attacks directed to the northwest in the areas of Hotton and Marche have been successfully held. Enemy forward elements have moved westward, and tanks and troop carrying vehicles have been reported between Marche and Rochefort.

There has been only local ground activity in the area of Bastogne, but enemy pressure continues to be strong just southwest of the town. German tanks are in the vicinity of Rosieres, seven miles southwest of Bastogne. Chaumond, about six miles south of Bastogne, has been cleared, and fighting continues near the town following an enemy counter-attack.

Farther to the south, Martelange, on the Bastogne-Arlon road, is half cleared of the enemy, and we have made gains to the vicinity of Bigonville, three miles northeast.

In the area west and northwest of Diekirch, our troops have cleared the enemy from Heiderscheid. A German counter-attack launched with tanks and infantry near Tadler resulted in heavy fighting. Further progress has been made by our forces a few miles west of Diekirch.

There have been no substantial changes in the area south and southwest of Echternach, where fighting is under way in the vicinity of Consdorf.

More than 2,000 heavy bombers, escorted by over 900 fighters, attacked eleven airfields in the Frankfort-on-the-Main area and road and rail junctions, bridges and supply centers from Euskirchen south to Trier. Seventy enemy aircraft were shot down by the escorting fighters and eighteen by the bombers. From incomplete reports, thirty-nine bombers and six fighters are missing, but some of them are believed to have landed away from their bases.

Enemy patrols which crossed the Rhine northeast of Strasbourg were repulsed. North of Colmar a counter-attack forced a slight withdrawal of our forward elements at Sigolsheim.

Medium bombers, striking deep into Germany, attacked a bridge at Langenargen, on the north shore of Lake Constance, and hit railway yards at Emmendingen, north of Freiburg.

Night fighters shot down six enemy aircraft last night.

†McGUIRE, THOMAS B., JR. (Air Mission)
Rank and Organization: Major, U.S. Army Air Corps, 13th Air Force.
Born: Ridgewood, New Jersey.
Entered Service At: Sebring, Florida.
Place and Date: Over Luzon, Philippine Islands, December 25-26, 1944.
Citation: Maj. McGuire fought with conspicuous gallantry and intrepidity

over Luzon, Philippine Islands. Voluntarily, he led a squadron of 15 P-38's as top cover for heavy bombers striking Mabalacat Airdrome, where his formation was attacked by 20 aggressive Japanese fighters. In the ensuing action he repeatedly flew to the aid of embattled comrades, driving off enemy assaults while himself under attack and at times outnumbered three to one, and even after his guns jammed, continuing the fight by forcing a hostile plane into his wingman's line of fire. Before he started back to his base, he had shot down three Zeros. The next day, he again volunteered to lead escort fighters on a mission to strongly defended Clark Field. During the resultant engagement he again exposed himself to attacks so that he might rescue a crippled bomber. In rapid succession, he shot down one aircraft, parried the attack of four enemy fighters, one of which he shot down, single-handedly engaged three more Japanese, destroying one, and then shot down still another, his 38th victory in aerial combat. On January 7, 1945, while leading a voluntary fighter sweep over Los Negros Island, he risked an extremely hazardous maneuver at low altitude in an attempt to save a fellow flyer from attack, crashed, and was reported missing in action. With gallant initiative, deep and unselfish concern for the safety of others, and heroic determination to destroy the enemy at all costs. Maj. McGuire set an inspiring example in keeping with the highest traditions of the military service.

HENDRIX, JAMES R.

Rank and Organization: Private, U.S. Army, Company C, 53d Armored Infantry Battalion, 4th Armored Division.
Born: Lepanto, Arkansas.
Entered Service At: Lepanto, Arkansas.
Place and Date: Near Assenois, Belgium, December 26, 1944.
Citation: On the night of December 26, 1944, near Assenois, Belgium, he was with the leading element engaged in the final thrust to break through to the besieged garrison at Bastogne when halted by a fierce combination of artillery and small-arms fire. He dismounted from his half-track and advanced against two 88-mm. guns, and, by the ferocity of his rifle fire, compelled the guncrews to take cover and then to surrender. Later in the attack, he again left his vehicle, voluntarily, to aid two wounded soldiers, helpless and exposed to intense machine-gun fire. Effectively silencing two hostile machine-guns, he held off the enemy by his own fire until the wounded men were evacuated. Pvt. Hendrix again distinguished himself when he hastened to the aid of still another soldier who was trapped in a burning half-track. Braving enemy sniper fire and exploding mines and ammuni-

tion in the vehicle, he extricated the wounded man and extinguished his flaming clothing, thereby saving the life of his fellow soldier. Pvt. Hendrix, by his superb courage and heroism, exemplified the highest traditions of the military service.

WARE, KEITH L.

Rank and Organization: Lieutenant Colonel, U.S. Army, 1st Battalion, 15th Infantry, 3d Infantry Division.
Born: November 23, 1915, Denver, Colorado.
Entered Service At: Glendale, California.
Place and Date: Near Sigolsheim, France, December 26, 1944.
Citation: Commanding the 1st Battalion attacking a strongly held enemy position on a hill near Sigolsheim, France, on December 26, 1944, found that one of his assault companies had been stopped and forced to dig in by a concentration of enemy artillery, mortar, and machine-gun fire. The company had suffered casualties in attempting to take the hill. Realizing that his men must be inspired to new courage, Lt. Col. Ware went forward 150 yards beyond the most forward elements of his command, and for two hours reconnoitered the enemy positions, deliberately drawing fire upon himself which caused the enemy to disclose his dispositions. Returning to his company, he armed himself with an automatic rifle and boldly advanced upon the enemy, followed by two officers, nine enlisted men, and a tank. Approaching an enemy machine-gun, Lt. Col. Ware shot two German riflemen and fired tracers into the emplacement, indicating its position to his tank, which promptly knocked the gun out of action. Lt. Col. Ware turned his attention to a second machine-gun, killing two of its supporting riflemen and forcing the others to surrender. The tank destroyed the gun. Having expended the ammunition for the automatic rifle, Lt. Col. Ware took up an M1 rifle, killed a German rifleman, and fired upon a third machine-gun 50 yards away. His tank silenced the gun. Upon his approach to a fourth machine-gun, its supporting riflemen surrendered and his tank disposed of the gun. During this action, Lt. Col. Ware's small assault group was fully engaged in attacking enemy positions that were not receiving his direct and personal attention. Five of his party of 11 were casualties and Lt. Col. Ware was wounded, but refused medical attention until this important hill position was cleared of the enemy and securely occupied by his command.

WHITELEY, ELI

Rank and Organization: First Lieutenant, U.S. Army, Company L, 15th Infantry, 3d Infantry Division.

Born: Florence, Texas.

Entered Service At: Georgetown, Texas.

Place and Date: Sigolsheim, France, December 27, 1944.

Citation: While leading his platoon on December 27, 1944, in savage house-to-house fighting through the fortress town of Sigolsheim, France, he attacked a building through a street swept by withering mortar and automatic weapons fire. He was hit and severely wounded in the arm and shoulder; but he charged into the house alone and killed its two defenders. Hurling smoke and fragmentation grenades before him, he reached the next house and stormed inside, killing two and capturing 11 of the enemy. He continued leading his platoon in the extremely dangerous task of clearing hostile troops from strong points along the street until he reached a building held by fanatical Nazi troops. Although suffering from wounds which had rendered his left arm useless, he advanced on this strongly defended house, and after blasting out a wall with bazooka fire, charged through a hail of bullets. Wedging his submachine-gun under his uninjured arm, he rushed into the house through the hole torn by his rockets, killed five of the enemy and forced the remaining 12 to surrender. As he emerged to continue his fearless attack, he was again hit and critically wounded. In agony and with one eye pierced by a shell fragment, he shouted for his men to follow him to the next house. He was determined to stay in the fighting, and remained at the head of his platoon until forcibly evacuated. By his disregard for personal safety, his aggressiveness while suffering from severe wounds, his determined leadership and superb courage, 1st Lt. Whiteley killed nine Germans, captured 23 more and spearheaded an attack which cracked the core of enemy resistance in a vital area.

WAR NEWS SUMMARIZED

• • •

WEDNESDAY, DECEMBER 26, 1944

Germany's offensive in Belgium was under way again and, despite increasing Allied resistance, had reached Celles, four miles southeast of Dinant on the Meuse, and Ciney, eight miles northeast of the city. This situation, as of Christmas morning, recorded a new gain of more than ten miles for a total advance from the Reich frontier of fifty-one miles. The two salients west of St. Vith had been joined.

Two, and maybe three, armies have been thrown into the drive by Field Marshal von Rundstedt and they were expected to make more progress before being stopped. American gains, particularly along the southern flank east of the Arlon-Bastogne road, were not deemed sufficient to halt the enemy. One of the relief columns hacking its way to the encircled Americans at Bastogne was last reported six miles away.

Once again Allied fliers spilled death and destruction upon the Germans, who continued to advance nevertheless. Some 4,000 tactical sorties were flown yesterday, with the RAF sending its heavy bombers to the St. Vith area. Eighth Air Force Flying Fortresses and Liberators attacked rail yards and bridges in the Coblenz region. During the day sixty-nine German planes were shot down.

Paris was bombed with little damage and few casualties in a minor German raid.

Russian troops completed the encirclement of Budapest and carried the fighting into the Hungarian capital. Beyond Sahy, they expanded the front along the Hron River in Czechoslovakia pointing toward Vienna, and farther north they were clearing the Germans from the last bit of Hungary east of the Danube.

Canadians in Italy captured a rail junction ten miles northwest of Ravenna. The Eighth Army also advanced in the Senio River area.

Greek leaders of all factions met Prime Minister Churchill and conferred in an attempt to "put an end to the fratricidal strife." Nearly a ton of explosives was found in sewers near the British-Green headquarters in Athens.

American bombers and fighters cutting down Japanese air strength in the Philippines again attacked Clark Field near Manila, shooting down thirty-nine of fifty enemy planes; four more were probably destroyed. We lost four fighters.

B-29's bombed Tokyo again today. Two dozen Japanese planes attacked the Superfortress base of Saipan Christmas Eve; four were shot down. One of our planes was destroyed on the ground and several were damaged.

In the continuing battle of the Philippines, some American surface craft have been lost, Navy Secretary Forrestal said, but details were being withheld to keep information from the Japanese. The United States Navy now controls the waters around the Philippines, he added.

Fourteenth Air Force Mustangs, making the first American flights from bases in North China, hit the Tsinan airfield in Shantung Province, destroying thirty-eight planes.

CHAPTER 5

1945

MacGILLIVARY, CHARLES A.
Rank and Organization: Sergeant, U.S. Army, Company I, 71st Infantry, 44th Infantry Division.
Born: Charlottetown, Prince Edward Island, Canada.
Entered Service At: Boston, Massachusetts.
Place and Date: Near Woelfling, France, January 1, 1945.
Citation: Sgt. MacGillivary led a squad when his unit moved forward in the darkness to meet the threat of a breakthrough by elements of the 17th German Panzer Grenadier Division. Assigned to protect the left flank, he discovered hostile troops digging in. As he reported this information several German machineguns opened fire, stopping the American advance. Knowing the position of the enemy, Sgt. MacGillivary volunteered to knock out 1 of the guns while another company closed in from the right to assault the remaining strong points. He circled from the left through woods and snow, carefully worked his way to the emplacement and shot the 2 camouflaged gunners at a range of 3 feet as other enemy forces withdrew. Early in the afternoon of the same day, Sgt. MacGillivary was dispatched on reconnaissance and found that Company I was being opposed by about 6 machineguns reinforcing a company of fanatically fighting Germans. His unit began an attack but was pinned down by furious automatic and small-arms fire. With a clear idea of where the enemy guns were placed, he voluntarily embarked on a lone combat patrol. Skillfully taking advantage of all available cover, he stalked the enemy, reached a hostile machinegun and blasted its crew with a grenade. He picked up a submachinegun from the battlefield and pressed on to within 10 yards of another machinegun, where the enemy crew discovered him and feverishly tried to swing their weapon into line to cut him down. He charged ahead, jumped into the midst of the Germans and killed them with several bursts. Without hesitation, he moved on to still another machinegun, creeping, crawling, and rushing from tree to tree, until close enough to toss a grenade into the emplacement and

close with its defenders. He dispatched this crew also, but was himself seriously wounded. Through his indomitable fighting spirit, great initiative, and utter disregard for personal safety in the face of powerful enemy resistance, Sgt. MacGillivary destroyed four hostile machine guns and immeasurably helped his company to continue on it mission with minimum casualties.

OFFICIAL COMMUNIQUE:
United Nations
SUPREME HEADQUARTERS, Allied Expeditionary Force, Dec. 31 –Communique 267:

The enemy has continued sending patrols across the River Maas [Meuse] north of Tilburg. These withdrew when fired upon by Allied forces.

The northern flank of the Ardennes salient has been quiet. A small enemy pocket west of Grandmenil is surrounded and is being mopped up. At Rochefort our troops still are meeting strong opposition and enemy artillery and mortar fire is heavy.

On the southern flank of the Salient, we have reached the vicinity of Lavaselle and Chenogne and we are near Senonchamps, two and a half miles west of Bastogne. The enemy is strongly dug in along the line St. Hubert-Moircy-Remagne-Lavaselle, where he is supported by tanks and self-propelled guns.

Continued strong enemy resistance is being met by our forces widening the corridor into Bastogne. The Arlon-Bastogne road was cleared and we have taken Remofosse, Marvie and Lutrebois. Our units have reached the south-eastern edge of Harlange. The enemy in this area is taking advantage of high ground to fight a delaying action.

We have made gains in the vicinity of Berle, southwest of Wiltz, and have cleared Nothum.

In the Diekirch area we have cleared the enemy from highground just north of Ettelbruck. Most of the right bank of the Sauer River between Diekirch and Echternach now is in our hands with the exception of a short stretch northwest of Bigelbach.

There has been only patrol activity and sporadic enemy artillery fire in the Saar Valley.

Yesterday heavy bombers in very great strength with a strong escort of fighters attacked a number of bridges and marshaling yards in western Germany, including those at Kaiserslautern, Mannheim and Kassel.

Weather prevented the full employment of our medium and fighter bombers.

Thirty-two tanks were knocked out and others were damaged, mostly in the Bastogne area. Enemy road transport also was hit. Fighter-bombers struck at railway stock and communications between Bonn and Kaiserslautern and farther south in the areas of Homburg, Landau, Karlsruhe and Colmar.

Active patrolling and artillery exchanges continue in the Wissembourg sector. Several towns in the Alsace plain were shelled by the enemy.

TURNER, GEORGE B.

Rank and Organization: Private First Class, U.S. Army, Battery C, 499th Armored Field Artillery Battalion, 14th Armored Division.
Born: June 27, 1899, Longview, Texas.
Entered Service At: Los Angeles, California.
Place and Date: Philippsbourg, France, January 3, 1945.
Citation: At Philippsbourg, France, Pfc. Turner was cut off from his artillery unit by an enemy armored infantry attack. Coming upon a friendly infantry company withdrawing under the vicious onslaught, he noticed 2 German tanks and approximately 75 supporting foot soldiers advancing down the main street of the village. Seizing a rocket launcher, he advanced under intense small-arms and cannon fire to meet the tanks and, standing in the middle of the road, fired at them, destroying 1 and disabling the second. From a nearby half-track he then dismounted a machinegun, placed it in the open street and fired into the enemy infantrymen, killing or wounding a great number and breaking up the attack. In the American counterattack which followed, 2 supporting tanks were disabled by an enemy antitank gun. Firing a light machinegun from the hip, Pfc. Turner held off the enemy so that the crews of the disabled vehicles could extricate themselves. He ran through a hail of fire to one of the tanks which had burst into flames and attempted to rescue a man who had been unable to escape; but an explosion of the tanks ammunition frustrated his effort and wounded him painfully. Refusing to be evacuated, he remained with the infantry until the following day, driving off an enemy patrol with serious casualties, assisting in capturing a hostile strong point, and voluntarily and fearlessly driving a truck through heavy enemy fire to deliver wounded men to the rear aid station. The great courage displayed by Pfc. Turner and his magnificently heroic initiative contributed materially to the defense of the French town and inspired the troops about him.

†JACHMAN, ISADORE S.

Rank and Organization: Staff Sergeant, U.S. Army, Company B, 513th Parachute Infantry Regiment.
Born: Berlin, Germany.
Entered Service At: Baltimore, Maryland.
Place and Date: Flamierge, Belgium, January 4, 1945.
Citation: For conspicuous gallantry and intrepidity above and beyond the call of duty at Flamierge, Belgium, on January 4, 1945, when his company was pinned down by enemy artillery, mortar, and small-arms fire, 2 hostile tanks attacked the unit, inflicting heavy casualties. S/Sgt. Jachman, seeing the desperate plight of his comrades, left his place of cover and with total disregard for his own safety dashed across open ground through a hail of fire and seizing a bazooka from a fallen comrade advanced on the tanks, which concentrated their fire on him. Firing the weapon alone, he damaged one and forced both to retire. S/Sgt. Jachman's heroic action, in which he suffered fatal wounds, disrupted the entire enemy attack, reflecting the highest credit upon himself and the parachute infantry.

OFFICIAL COMMUNIQUE:
United Nations
SUPREME HEADQUARTERS, Allied Expeditionary Force, Jan. 3 –Communique 270:

Allied forces in the Ardennes salient have made some gains and repulsed a number of enemy counter-attacks.

In the St. Hubert-Bastogne sector on the southern flank we have made progress in the areas of Bonnerue and Hubermont against resistance varying from moderate to heavy. We have taken Gerimont and Mande. Fighting is in progress in Senonchamps.

Northeast of Bastogne, we have reached a point on the railway three miles beyond the town. Mageret is in our hands and we are in the immediate vicinity of Michamps. Heavy fighting is going on in he areas of Neffe and Wardin. We have made some gains east and south of Lutrebois and are encountering heavy shelling in Honville.

In the Saar Valley enemy activity has increased. Southeast of Saarlautern a small-scale infantry attack in the area of Geislautern was repulsed and our units cleared the area northeast of Sarreguemines. Near Neunkirchen an infantry attack supported by one tank was contained.

Between Habkirchen and Bliesbruecken enemy attempts to cross the Blies River were repulsed. German units are across the Blies River. Farther east five companies of German infantry gained about one kilometer from the area south of Obergailbach to a point just west of Rimlingen.

Enemy attacks supported by tanks southeast of Bitche forced our units to give some ground initially, but all thrusts either were slowed down or halted.

Strong enemy pressure continued in the lower Vosges Mountains, where hostile attacks were launched and attempts to infiltrate were made at several points in the area about five miles north of Reipertsweiler. Farther east patrolling was active and particularly aggressive in the vicinity of Berg, near the Rhine. The enemy pocket west of the Rhine farther south was generally quiet. Our troops captured a strong point north of Kembs and held it against a counter-attack.

Inn the Ardennes salient fighter-bombers attacked enemy armor in the Bastogne and St. Vith areas. Medium and fighter-bombers struck at communications and transport in the salient, including a rail junction at Couvy. Other medium bombers bombed railway bridges at Eimmern and Bad-Muenster.

Fighters and fighter-bombers attacked troop concentrations and defense positions in the Neunkirchen and Kaiserslautern areas, destroyed several tanks near Pirmasens and struck at rail and road transport and communications in the Homburg and Kaiserslautern area. Medium bombers attacked supply dumps and troop barracks at Nunschweiler, Thaleischweiler and Oos.

In the course of these operations, thirteen enemy aircraft were shot down. Eleven of our fighters and ten bombers are missing, according to reports so far received.

†DAVIS, GEORGE FLEMING

Rank and Organization: Commander, U.S. Navy.
Born: March 23, 1911, Manila, Philippine Islands.
Entered Service At: Philippine Islands.
Other Navy Awards: Silver Star Medal, Legion of Merit.
Place and Date: Lingayen Gulf, Luzon, Philippine Islands, January 6, 1945.
Citation: For conspicuous gallantry and intrepidity at the risk of his life above and beyond the call of duty as Commanding Officer of the U.S.S. *Walke* engaged in a detached mission in support of minesweeping operations to clear the waters for entry of our heavy surface and amphibious forces preparatory to the invasion of Lingayen Gulf, Luzon, Philippine Islands, January 6, 1945. Operating without gun support of other surface ships when 4 Japanese suicide planes were detected flying low overland to attack simultaneously, Comdr. Davis boldly took his position in the exposed wings of the bridge and directed control to pick up the leading plane and open fire. Alert and fearless as the *Walke's* deadly fire sent the first target crashing into the water and caught the second as it passed over the bridge to plunge into the sea on portside, he remained steadfast in the path of the third plane plunging swiftly to crash into the after end of the bridge

structure. Seriously wounded when the craft struck, drenched with gasoline and immediately enveloped in flames, he conned the *Walke* in the midst of the wreckage; he rallied his command to heroic efforts; he exhorted his officers and men to save the ship and, still on his feet, saw the barrage from his guns destroy the fourth suicide bomber. With the fires under control and the safety of the ship assured, he consented to be carried below. Succumbing several hours later, Comdr. Davis by his example of valor and his unhesitating self-sacrifice, steeled the fighting spirit of his command into unyielding purpose in completing a vital mission. He gallantly gave his life in the service of his country.

OFFICIAL COMMUNIQUE:
United States
PEARL HARBOR, Jan. 6 – A Pacific Fleet communique:

1. Carrier-based aircraft of the United States Pacific Fleet destroyed 111 enemy aircraft and damaged 220 more in attacks on Formosa and Okinawa in the Ryukyus Jan. 2 and 3 (West Longitude date). Twenty-seven ships were sunk and an additional sixty-eight damaged. The enemy offered ineffective air opposition to our aircraft.
2. Surface units of the United States Pacific Fleet bombarded enemy installations at Chichi Jima [Island] and Haha Jima, in the Bonin Islands, Jan. 5.
3. The shelling was concentrated on facilities around the harbor of Futami Ko on Chichi Jima and on other targets in Okimura town and Higashi harbor on Haha Jima. Fires were started in Okimura town and an enemy cargo ship was sunk west of Haha Jima. Answering the attack with meager gunfire, defending shore batteries inflicted minor damage to units of our forces. A single enemy fighter was observed airborne.

A later Pacific Fleet communique:

1. On Jan. 3 and 4 [United States time] Army Liberators of the Strategic Air Force, Pacific Ocean Areas, bombed the airstrips and installations on Iwo Jima [Island] in the Volcano Islands.
2. Surface units of the United States Pacific Fleet bombarded coast defenses and airstrip installations at Iwo Jima in the Volcanos Jan. 1. Numerous fires were observed on the island. Fire from enemy shore batteries was meager.

†SHOUP, CURTIS F.

Rank and Organization: Staff Sergeant, U.S. Army, Company I, 346th Infantry, 87th Infantry Division.
Born: Napenoch, New York.
Entered Service At: Buffalo, New York.
Place and Date: Near Tillet, Belgium, January 7, 1945.
Citation: On January 7, 1945, near Tillet, Belgium, his company attacked German troops on rising ground. Intense hostile machinegun fire pinned down and threatened to annihilate the American unit in an exposed position where frozen ground made it impossible to dig in for protection. Heavy mortar and artillery fire from enemy batteries was added to the storm of destruction falling on the Americans. Realizing that the machinegun must be silenced at all cost, S/Sgt. Shoup, armed with an automatic rifle, crawled to within 75 yards of the enemy emplacement. He found that his fire was ineffective from this position, and completely disregarding his own safety, stood up and grimly strode ahead into the murderous stream of bullets, firing his low-held weapon as he went. He was hit several times and finally was knocked to the ground. But he struggled to his feet and staggered forward until close enough to hurl a grenade, wiping out the enemy machinegun nest with his dying action. By his heroism, fearless determination, and supreme sacrifice, S/Sgt. Shoup eliminated a hostile weapon which threatened to destroy his company and turned a desperate situation into victory.

OFFICIAL COMMUNIQUE:
United Nations
SUPREME HEADQUARTERS, Allied Expeditionary Force, Jan. 7 –Communique 274:

Allied forces continued to maintain pressure on the northern flank of the Ardennes salient southwest of Stavelot. An attack across the River Ambleve by our units achieved an initial gain of 3,000 yards. Farther west, the villages of Odeigne and Lierneux have been taken.

We have made small gains north of the St. Hubert-Bastogne road, two miles east of St. Hubert, and have reached Tillet. Two miles southeast of Tillet, our artillery broke up a counter-attack by enemy infantry.

Northeast of Bastogne, an enemy counter-attack with eight tanks and an estimated battalion of infantry was broken up by fire from our tanks and artillery just north of Mageret.

Probing activity by enemy tanks and infantry continues along the east side of the Bastogne bulge, particularly in the Mageret area.

South of Wiltz, our troops have crossed the Sauer River one and one half miles northeast of Eschdorf, and have cleared Goesdorf and Dahl.

Our units made progress toward reducing the enemy salient southeast of Bitche against strong resistance. We made gains of more than 1,000 yards in an attack north of Reipertswiller near the southernmost point to the salient. Remaining elements of the enemy force which infiltrated Wingen were surrounded.

On the west bank of the Rhine, enemy units which crossed the river on Thursday were mopped up at all points of penetration except at Gambsheim, where stubborn opposition is being met.

Early last night, heavy bombers, again in great strength, were over Germany, with the important railway and industrial center of Hanau as their main objective.

DUNHAM, RUSSEL E.
Rank and Organization: Technical Sergeant, U.S. Army, Company I, 30th Infantry, 3d Infantry Division.
Born: February 23, 1920, East Carondelet, Illinois.
Entered Service At: Brighton Illinois.
Place and Date: Near Kayserberg, France, January 8, 1945.
Citation: For conspicuous gallantry and intrepidity at risk of life above and beyond the call of duty. At about 1430 hours on January 8, 1945, during an attack on Hill 616, near Kayserberg, France, T/Sgt. Dunham singlehandedly assaulted 3 enemy machineguns. Wearing a white robe made of a mattress cover, carrying 12 carbine magazines and with a dozen handgrenades snagged in his belt, suspenders, and buttonholes, T/Sgt Dunham advanced in the attack up a snow-covered hill under fire from 2 machineguns supporting riflemen. His platoon 35 yards behind him, T/Sgt. Dunham crawled 75 yards under heavy direct fire toward the timbered emplacement shielding the left machinegun. As he jumped to his feet 10 yards from the gun and charged forward machinegun fire tore through his camouflage robe and a rifle bullet seared a 10-inch gash across his back sending him spinning 15 yards down hill into the snow. When the indomitable sergeant sprang to his feet to renew his 1-man assault, a German egg grenade landed beside him. He kicked it aside, and as it exploded 5 yards away, shot and killed the German machinegunner and assistant gunner. His carbine empty, he jumped into the emplacement and hauled out the third member of the gun crew by the collar. Although his back wound was causing him excruciating pain and blood was seeping through his white coat, T/Sgt. Dunham proceeded 50 yards through a storm of automatic and rifle fire to attack the second machinegun. Twenty-five yards from the emplacement he hurled 2 grenades, destroying the gun and its crew; then fired down into the supporting foxholes with his carbine, dispatching and dispersing the enemy riflemen. Although his coat was so thoroughly

bloodsoaked that he was a conspicuous target against the white landscape, T/Sgt. Dunham again advanced ahead of his platoon in an assault on enemy positions farther up the hill. Coming under machinegun fire from 65 yards to his front, while rifle grenades exploded 10 yards from his positions, he hit the ground and crawled forward. At 15 yards range, he jumped to his feet, staggered a few paces toward the timbered machinegun emplacement and killed the crew with handgrenades. An enemy rifleman fired at point blank range but missed him. After killing the rifleman, T/Sgt. Dunham drove others from their foxholes with grenades and carbine fire. Killing 9 Germans – wounding 7 and capturing 2 – firing about 175 rounds of carbine ammunition, and expending 11 grenades, T/Sgt. Dunham, despite a painful wound, spearheaded a spectacular and successful diversionary attack.

†TURNER, DAY G.
Rank and Organization: Sergeant, U.S. Army, Company B, 319th Infantry, 80th Infantry Division.
Born: Berwick, Pennsylvania.
Entered Service At: Nescopek, Pennsylvania.
Place and Date: At Dahl, Luxembourg, January 8, 1945.
Citation: Sgt. Turner commanded a 9-man squad with the mission of holding a critical flank position. When overwhelming numbers of the enemy attacked under cover of withering artillery, mortar, and rocket fire, he withdrew his squad into a nearby house, determined to defend it to the last man. The enemy attacked again and again and were repulsed with heavy losses. Supported by direct tank fire, they finally gained entrance, but the intrepid sergeant refused to surrender although 5 of his men were wounded and 1 was killed. He boldly flung a can of flaming oil at the first wave of attackers, dispersing them, and fought doggedly from room to room closing with the enemy in fierce hand-to-hand encounters. He hurled handgrenade for handgrenade, bayoneted 2 fanatical Germans who rushed a doorway he was defending and fought on with the enemy's weapon when his own ammunition was expended. The savage fight raged for 4 hours, and finally, when only 3 men of the defending squad were left unwounded, the enemy surrendered. Twenty-five prisoners were taken, 11 enemy dead and a great number of wounded were counted. Sgt. Turner's valiant stand will live on as a constant inspiration to his comrades. His heroic, inspiring leadership, his determination and courageous devotion to duty exemplify the highest tradition of the military service.

†CAREY, CHARLES F., JR.

Rank and Organization: Technical Sergeant, U.S. Army, 379th Infantry, 100th Infantry Division.
Born: Canadian, Oklahoma.
Entered Service At: Cheyenne, Wyoming.
Place and Date: Rimling, France, January 8-9, 1945.
Citation: T/Sgt. Carey was in command of an antitank platoon when about 200 enemy infantrymen and 12 tanks attacked his battalion, overrunning parts of its position. After losing his guns, T/Sgt. Carey, acting entirely on his own initiative, organized a patrol and rescued 2 of his squads from the threatened sector, evacuating those who had been wounded. He organized a second patrol and advanced against an enemy-held house from which vicious fire issued, preventing the free movement of our troops. Covered by fire from his patrol, he approached the house, killed 2 snipers with his rifle, and threw a grenade in the door. He entered alone and a few minutes later emerged with 16 prisoners. Acting on information he furnished, the American forces were able to capture an additional 41 Germans in adjacent houses. He assembled another patrol, and, under covering fire, moved to within a few yards of an enemy tank and damaged it with a rocket. As the crew attempted to leave their burning vehicle, he calmly shot them with his rifle, killing 3 and wounding a fourth. Early in the morning of January 9, German infantry moved into the western part of town and encircled a house in which T/Sgt. Carey had previously posted a squad. Four of the group escaped to the attic. By maneuvering an old staircase against the building, T/Sgt. Carey was able to rescue these men. Later that day, when attempting to reach an outpost, he was struck down by sniper fire. The fearless and aggressive leadership of T/Sgt. Carey, his courage in the face of heavy fire from superior enemy forces, provided an inspiring example for his comrades and materially helped his battalion to withstand the German onslaught.

OFFICIAL COMMUNIQUE:
United Nations
SUPREME HEADQUARTERS, Allied Expeditionary Force, Jan. 8 –Communique 275:

Along the Maas [Meuse] River there have been some short patrol clashes. East of Geertruidenberg, an enemy outpost on the south bank of the river was attacked by Allied forces and after spirited fighting; mopping up is in progress.

On the northern flank of the Ardennes salient, our attack has been continued with advances in both sectors against stubborn enemy resistance. South of Lierneux, we have gained two miles. Farther west, we have captured La Falaise and Fraiture, and cut the St. Vith-La Roche highway in three places. Southeast of Marche, our units gained 2,000 yards. Under heavy enemy pressure, the village of Bure was evacuated.

Northwest of Bastogne, our forces have cleared the enemy from Flamierge, one and one-half miles northwest of Mande. Southeast of Bastogne, we have made limited gains in the area one to two miles east of Harlange. In the Wiltz area, a small counter-attack moving from the vicinity of Nocher toward Dahl was repulsed by our artillery.

In the salient south of Bitche, we continued mopping up enemy groups and made small local gains. German troops surrounded in Wingen attempted to escape. Many were captured.

South of Wissembourg, enemy infantry supported by tanks made four attacks, in which some ground was lost by our forward elements. In one attack, three of nine tanks were knocked out. On the west bank of the Rhine, an attack against Rohrwiller by enemy units that had crossed the river was repulsed. Other hostile elements entered Drusenheim near by after we had inflicted losses and destroyed three of five enemy tanks. Fighting continues at Gambsheim. Enemy transport near Gambsheim was attacked by a small number of bombers.

In the Alsace Plain, twenty miles south of Strasbourg, an enemy force supported by tanks, which drove northward along the Rhine-Rhone Canal, forced our troops from Witternheim and Friesenheim. Fighting continued north of these towns.

Weather again restricted air operations over the battle zone yesterday.

More than 1,000 heavy bombers, escorted by 650 fighters, attacked railway yards, bridges, and communications in western Germany from Hamm in the north to Rastatt in the south. Among targets attacked were railway yards at Hamm, Bielefeld, Paderborn, Cologne, and Rastatt, and road and rail junctions east of the Ardennes salient.

Heavy bombers in great strength attacked the industrial and railway center of Munich last night.

BERTOLDO, VITO R.

Rank and Organization: Master Sergeant. U.S. Army, Company A, 242d Infantry, 42d Infantry Division.
Born: December 1, 1916, Decatur, Illinois.
Entered Service At: Decatur, Illinois.
Place and Date: Hatten, France, January 9-10, 1945.
Citation: M/Sgt. Bertoldo fought with extreme gallantry while guarding 2 command posts against the assault of powerful infantry and armored forces which had overrun the battalion's main line of resistance. On the close approach of enemy soldiers, he left the protection of the building he de-

fended and set up his gun in the street, there to remain for almost 12 hours driving back attacks while in full view of his adversaries and completely exposed to 88-mm., machinegun and small-arms fire. He moved back inside the command post, strapped his machinegun to a table and covered the main approach to the building by firing through a window, remaining steadfast even in the face of 88-mm. fire from tanks only 75 yards away. One shell blasted him across the room, but he returned to his weapon. When 2 enemy personnel carries led by a tank moved toward his position, he calmly waited for troops to dismount and then, with the tank firing directly at him, leaned out of the window and mowed down the entire group of more than 20 Germans. Some time later, removal of the command post to another building was ordered. M/Sgt. Bertoldo voluntarily remained behind, covering the withdrawal of his comrades and maintaining his stand all night. In the morning he carried his machinegun to an adjacent building used as the command post of another battalion and began a day-long defense of that position. He broke up a heavy attack, launched by self-propelled 88-mm. gun covered by a tank and about 15 infantrymen. Soon afterward another 88-mm. weapon moved up to within a few feet of his position, and, placing the muzzle of its gun almost inside the building, fired into the room, knocking him down and seriously wounding others. An American bazooka team set the German weapon afire, and M/Sgt. Bertoldo went back to his machinegun dazed as he was and killed several of the hostile troops as they attempted to withdraw. It was decided to evacuate the command post under the cover of darkness, but before the plan could be put into operation the enemy began an intensive assault supported by fire from their tanks and heavy guns. Disregarding the devastating barrage, he remained at his post and hurled white phosphorous grenades into the advancing enemy troops until they broke and retreated. A tank less than 50 yards away fired at his stronghold, destroyed the machinegun and blew him across the room again but he once more returned to the bitter fight and, with a rifle, singlehandedly covered the withdrawal of his fellow soldiers when the post was finally abandoned. With inspiring bravery and intrepidity M/Sgt. Bertoldo withstood the attack of vastly superior forces for more than 48 hours without rest or relief, time after time escaping death only by the slightest margin while killing at least 40 hostile solders and wounding many more during his grim battle against the enemy hordes.

OFFICIAL COMMUNIQUE:
United Nations
SUPREME HEADQUARTERS, Allied Expeditionary Force, Jan. 10 –Communique 277:

Allied forces in the Ardennes salient continued to make progress. In some sectors of the northern flank, notably south of Dochamps, where enemy armor has been engaged by our artillery, operations have been hampered by deep snow.

Around Marcourt, mopping up has continued, while the village of Cielle, to the south, has been taken and Allied units now are thrusting in the direction of La Roche. Southeast of Marche, we have cleared the Nolaumont Forest and have occupied the village of Forrieres, southeast of Rochefort.

West of Bastogne, bitter fighting continues in the area of Bonnerue and Tillet. About two miles west of Mande, an enemy counter-attack was repulsed with destruction of nine of eighteen enemy tanks engaged. Southeast of Bastogne, our troops have made gains against strongly defended enemy positions.

Enemy attacks were broken up in the Rimling area and near Reyersweiler and Lemberg in the enemy's lower Vosges salient. In the Rhine Valley, north of Haguenau Forest, a strong enemy attack supported by tanks was repulsed. Heavy losses were inflicted on the enemy and he withdrew northward. We made some progress on the Rhine River bank and re-entered Gambsheim.

Weather severely restricted air operations yesterday, but a small force of medium bombers attacked the railway embankment and bridge at Rimmthal, west of Landau, and fighter-bombers attacked rail yards at Neustadt and Rastatt.

South of Strasbourg the enemy continued aggressive attempts to exploit the gains he made on Sunday. We have withdrawn from Boofzheim. In the Vosges west of Colmar our troops occupied high ground near Turckheim.

An enemy ground force attack on the outskirts of Mulhouse was beaten off.

In all air operations five enemy aircraft were shot down and one of our fighters is missing.

†GAMMON, ARCHER T.

Rank and Organization: Staff Sergeant, U.S. Army, Company A, 9th Armored Infantry Battalion, 6th Armored Division.
Born: September 11, 1918, Chatham, Virginia.
Entered Service At: Roanoke, Virginia.
Place and Date: Near Bastogne, Belgium, January 11, 1945.
Citation: S/Sgt. Gammon charged 30 yards through hip-deep snow to knock out a machinegun and its 3-man crew with grenades, saving his platoon from being decimated and allowing it to continue its advance from an open field into some nearby woods. The platoon's advance through the woods had only begun when a machinegun supported by riflemen opened fire and a Tiger Royal tank sent 88-mm. shells screaming at the unit from the left flank. S/Sgt. Gammon, disregarding all thoughts of personal safety, rushed forward, then cut to the left, crossing the width of the platoon's skirmish

line in an attempt to get within grenade range of the tank and its protecting foot troops. Intense fire was concentrated on him by riflemen and the machinegun emplaced near the tank. He charged the automatic weapon, wiped out its crew of 4 with grenades, and, with supreme daring, advanced to within 25 yards of the armored vehicle, killing 2 hostile infantrymen with rifle fire as he moved forward. The tank had started to withdraw, backing a short distance, then firing, backing some more, and then stopping to blast out another round, when the man whose singlehanded relentless attack had put the ponderous machine on the defensive was struck and instantly killed by a direct hit from the Tiger Royal's heavy gun. By his intrepidity and extreme devotion to the task of driving the enemy back no matter what the odds, S/Sgt. Gammon cleared the woods of German forces, for the tank continued to withdraw, leaving open the path for the gallant squad leader's platoon.

SHOMO, WILLIAM A.

Rank and Organization: Major, U.S. Army Air Corps, 82d Tactical Reconnaissance Squadron.
Born: Jeannette, Pennsylvania.
Entered Service At: Westmoreland County, Pennsylvania.
Place and Date: Over Luzon, Philippine Islands, January 11, 1945.
Citation: For conspicuous gallantry and intrepidity at the risk of his life above and beyond the call of duty. Maj. Shomo was lead pilot of a flight of 2 fighter planes charged with an armed photographic and strafing mission against the Aparri and Laoag airdromes. While en route to the objective, he observed an enemy twin engine bomber, protected by 12 fighters, flying about 2,500 feet above him and in the opposite direction. Although the odds were 13 to 2, Maj. Shomo immediately ordered an attack. Accompanied by his wingman he closed on the enemy formation in a climbing turn and scored hits on the leading plane of the third element, which exploded in midair. Maj. Shomo then attacked the second element from the left side of the formation and shot another fighter down in flames. When the enemy formed for a counterattack, Maj. Shomo moved to the other side of the formation and hit a third fighter which exploded and fell. Diving below the bomber, he put a burst into its underside and it crashed and burned. Pulling up from this pass he encountered a fifth plane firing head on and destroyed it. He next dived upon the first element and shot down the lead plane; then diving to 300 feet in pursuit of another fighter he caught it with his initial burst and it crashed in flames. During this action his wingman had shot down 3 planes, while the 3 remaining enemy fighters had fled into a

cloudbank and escaped. Maj. Shomo's extraordinary gallantry and intrepidity in attacking such a far superior force and destroying 7 enemy aircraft in one action is unparalleled in the southwest Pacific area.

LAWS, ROBERT E.

Rank and Organization: Staff Sergeant, U.S. Army, Company G, 169th Infantry, 43d Infantry Division.
Born: Altoona, Pennsylvania.
Entered Service At: Altoona, Pennsylvania.
Place and Date: Pangasinan Province, Luzon, Philippine Islands, January 12, 1945.
Citation: S/Sgt. Laws led the assault squad when Company G attacked enemy hill positions. The enemy force, estimated to be a reinforced infantry company, was well supplied with machineguns, ammunition, grenades, and blocks of TNT and could be attacked only across a narrow ridge 70 yards long. At the end of this ridge an enemy pillbox and rifle positions were set in rising ground. Covered by his squad, S/Sgt. Laws traversed the hogback through vicious enemy fire until close to the pillbox, where he hurled grenades at the fortification. Enemy grenades wounded him, but he persisted in his assault until 1 of his missiles found its mark and knocked out the pillbox. With more grenades, passed him by members of his squad who had joined him, he led the attack on the entrenched riflemen. In the advance up the hill, he suffered additional wounds in both arms and legs, about the body and in the head, as grenades and TNT charges exploded near him. Three Japs rushed him with fixed bayonets, and he emptied the magazine of his machine pistol at them, killing 2. He closed in hand-to-hand combat with the third, seizing the Jap's rifle as he met the onslaught. The 2 fell to the ground and rolled some 50 or 60 feet down a bank. When the dust cleared the Jap lay dead and the valiant American was climbing up the hill with a large gash across the head. He was given first aid and evacuated from the area while his squad completed the destruction of the enemy position. S/Sgt. Laws' heroic actions provided great inspiration to his comrades, and his courageous determination, in the face of formidable odds and while suffering from multiple wounds, enabled them to secure an important objective with minimum casualties.

OFFICIAL COMMUNIQUE:
United Nations
SUPREME HEADQUARTERS, Allied Expeditionary Force, Jan. 11 –Communique 278:

On the northern flank of the Ardennes salient, Allied forces have cleared the west bank of the Salm River as far south as Salm Chateau. The village of Samree has been taken after heavy fighting.

Farther west our units continued to follow up the withdrawing enemy. Hodister has been captured and we are patrolling forward to the La Roche-Marche road. South of Marche we have crossed the River Homme and occupied Ambly. Opposition has been slight, but mines are plentiful.

On the southern flank of the salient, Tillet is in our hands after hard fighting. In the wooded area just west of the town, our troops have made gains of about a quarter of a mile. We have been forced back from Flamierge.

Our units have reached points four and one-half miles directly north of Bastogne and have taken Recogne.

In the sector south and east of Bastogne, our forces have cleared the enemy from Villers-la-Bonne Eau and Harlange. Farther east we have taken Berle and our units are one-half miles north of the town.

We hold high ground one and one-half miles southwest of Wiltz. Fighter-bombers operating in this sector attacked enemy transport and troop barracks.

Southwest of Saarbruecken we gained more than 200 yards against moderate resistance and entered Oeting. Progress also was made on the east side of the enemy wedge in the lower Vosges Mountains, where Obermuhlithal was occupied by our forces.

In the Rhine Valley north of Haguenau Forest fighting continues at Hatten, where a strong enemy thrust was turned back Tuesday. Along the Rhine near by there was fighting at several points in the enemy bridgehead north of Strasbourg. Enemy attacks were repulsed in the Alsace Plain between Strasbourg and Colmar.

ADVANCED HEADQUARTERS, on Luzon, Friday, Jan. 12 – A communique:

PHILIPPINES

Luzon: Our ground forces are advancing rapidly in all sectors. On our right, our troops are beyond Umanday, seven miles inland. A parallel column to the east has passed through Calasiao and Bulog, five miles inland from Dagupan.

On the extreme west flank, we occupied Labrador and secured the mouth of the Agno River.

In our left sector, our forward elements have seized Manaoag and are in combat contact along the Pozorrubio road nine miles from the coast.

The enemy still is suffering from the effects of surprise caused by our landing in this sector in his rear, and has as yet been unable to displace the mass of his forces forward from the south in sufficient strength to offer serious resistance.

Our air forces continue to sweep the air. Our heavy bombers struck Clark, Nielson, and Nichols Fields with ninety tons of bombs, starting many large fires.

Intense anti-aircraft fire was encountered, but no interception. Our medium, attack and fighter planes swept enemy airdromes and lines of communications from Bicol Peninsula, in southern Luzon, to the Lingayen Plains area. Many enemy planes caught on the ground were destroyed.

Northbound artillery and supply columns on the main highway were strafed and dispersed. Railroad installations and bridges were wrecked. Many locomotives and 100 freight cars were destroyed or damaged.

At night, our patrol planes continued their harassment.

Enemy air activity was negligible. Enemy light naval craft raided our anchorage under cover of darkness, causing damage to our shipping.

BEYER, ARTHUR O.

Rank and Organization: Corporal, U.S. Army, Company C, 603d Tank Destroyer Battalion.
Born: May 20, 1909, Rock Township, Mitchell County, Iowa.
Entered Service At: St. Ansgar, Iowa.
Place and Date: Near Arloncourt, Belgium, January 15, 1945.
Citation: Cpl. Beyer displayed conspicuous gallantry in action. His platoon, in which he was a tank-destroyer gunner, was held up by antitank, machine gun, and rifle fire from enemy troops dug in along a ridge about 200 yards to the front. Noting a machinegun position in this defense line, he fired upon it with his 76-mm. gun killing 1 man and silencing the weapon. He dismounted from his vehicle and, under direct enemy observation, crossed open ground to capture the 2 remaining members of the crew. Another machinegun, about 250 yards to the left, continued to fire on him. Through withering fire, he advanced on the position. Throwing a grenade into the emplacement, he killed 1 crewmember and again captured the 2 survivors. He was subjected to concentrated small-arms fire but, with great bravery, he worked his way a quarter mile along the ridge, attacking hostile soldiers in their foxholes with his carbine and grenades. When he had completed his self-imposed mission against powerful German forces, he had destroyed 2 machinegun positions, killed 8 of the enemy and captured 18 prisoners, including 2 bazooka teams. Cpl. Beyer's intrepid action and unflinching determination to close with and destroy the enemy eliminated the German defense line and enabled his task force to gain its objective.

OFFICIAL COMMUNIQUE:
United Nations
SUPREME HEADQUARTERS, Allied Expeditionary Force, Jan. 15 –Communique 282:

On the northern flank of the Ardennes salient, south of Stavelot and Malmedy, opposition has stiffened. Allied forces have taken the villages of Henumont, Hedomont, and Thirimont. To the southwest, we have cleared Mont-le-Ban and cut the main Houffalize-Cherain road south of Cherain. In the area west of the La Roche-Bertogne road, mopping up operations continued and reconnaissance elements have reached the River Orthe and contacted Allied patrols from the southern flank of the salient.

Northwest of Bastogne, Allied units advancing against moderate resistance captured Givroulle and Bertogne and pushed two miles beyond both towns to a point on the Orthe River. Earlier, an enemy counter-attack made by a force of infantry and twenty-five tanks was repulsed east of Bertogne. Farther east, we advanced to the edge of Compogne and have entered the town of Noville, four and one-half miles northeast of Bastogne.

East of Bastogne, our forces pushed one mile past Mageret. We have made additional gains on high ground just southwest of Wiltz.

Southeast of Remich, near the Luxembourg-German border, we have cleared the enemy from Tettingen.

Against stubborn resistance in rugged terrain, we made gains up to 1,000 yards at the southern edge of the Lower Vosges salient. Fighting continues in the Maginot Line in Upper Alsace, and we made headway despite intermittent enemy attacks. Part of Hatten has been cleared, and in Rittershofen, the enemy still holds one strong point. In Saturday's fighting in this area, seventeen tanks and six other armored vehicles were knocked out.

In the day's air operations, 235 enemy aircraft were shot down and eight others destroyed on the ground. Nineteen of our heavy bombers, one medium bomber, and thirty-three of our fighters are missing.

ORESKO, NICHOLAS
Rank and Organization: Master Sergeant, U.S. Army, Company C, 302d Infantry, 94th Infantry Division.
Born: Bayonne, New Jersey.
Entered Service At: Bayonne, New Jersey.
Place and Date: Near Tettington, Germany, January 23, 1945.
Citation: M/Sgt. Oresko was a platoon leader with Company C, in an attack against strong enemy positions. Deadly automatic fire from the flanks pinned down his unit. Realizing that a machinegun in a nearby bunker must be eliminated, he swiftly worked ahead alone, braving bullets which struck about him, until close enough to throw a grenade into the German position. He rushed the bunker and, with pointblank rifle fire, killed all the hostile occupants who survived the grenade blast. Another machinegun opened up

on him, knocking him down and seriously wounding him in the hip. Refusing to withdraw from the battle, he placed himself at the head of his platoon to continue the assault. As withering machinegun and rifle fire swept the area, he struck out alone in advance of his men to a second bunker. With a grenade, he crippled the dug-in machinegun defending this position and then wiped out the troops manning it with his rifle, completing his second self-imposed, 1 man attack. Although weak from loss of blood, he refused to be evacuated until assured the mission was successfully accomplished. Through quick thinking, indomitable courage, and unswerving devotion to the attack in the face of bitter resistance and while wounded, M/Sgt. Oresko killed 12 Germans, prevented a delay in the assault, and made it possible for Company C to obtain its objective with minimum casualties.

OFFICIAL COMMUNIQUE:
United Nations
SUPREME HEADQUARTERS, Allied Expeditionary Force, Jan. 23 –Communique 290:

North of Zetten, Allied forces have driven the enemy across the De Linge Canal. Northeast of Echt, heavy fighting continues in the area of St. Joost, where the enemy has reinforced his units with local reserves. We have repulsed counterattacks against Waldfeucht, and farther to the southeast, our units have occupied the villages of Hontem and Selsten.

Our forces have cleared Born and against light resistance, have pushed to a point two miles north of St. Vith. We have entered Hinderhausen, three and a half miles west of St. Vith, and our troops, meeting slightly stiffening opposition, have taken the high ground southwest of Hinderhausen. We have gained up to 1,500 yards east of a line Hinderhausen-Rogery, and our elements east and southeast of Bovigny have driven 3,000 yards eastward, meeting little resistance.

Along the Houffalize-St. Vith road, our units have cleared Gouvy, three miles east of Cherain. Other elements, moving northeast from the Bastogne area, took Hachiville and advanced one-half mile to the northeast. Our units on the Bastogne-St. Vith road are less than a mile southwest of Trois Vierges. Boevange, three miles west of Clervaux, has been taken.

Wiltz has been cleared of the enemy and our troops have taken Noertrange, two miles to the northwest. Northeast of Bourscheid, our forces east of the Sure [Sauer] River have taken Lipperscheid and have gained more than a mile farther north.

The rail yards at Neuss, on the route from the Ruhr to Dueren, where there was a heavy concentration of rail cars, were attacked by fighter-bombers. In the course of this and other attacks, more than 650 rail cars were destroyed and many others damaged.

In the area southeast of Remich, more enemy counter-attacks have been repulsed in the vicinity of Tettingen.

In the Bitche salient, the enemy made aggressive attempts to infiltrate. Our forces mopped up hostile elements which had penetrated our forward positions.

Patrols were active on the Rhine west bank north of Strasbourg but no major fighting developed. Late reports disclosed that twelve, rather than four, tanks were knocked out in Sunday's actions.

On the south side of the Colmar sector, the principal suburbs of Mulhouse have been cleared in our attacks of the last three days and gains have been made in the vicinity of Cernay. This progress was made against stiff enemy resistance, through snow storms and over icy roads.

The forest of Nonnenbruch, south of Cernay, has been cleared. More than 1,000 prisoners have been counted.

Medium and light bombers attacked the rail head of Blankenheim, rail bridges at Sinzig, Slimmer and Bullay, and rail yards and a supply depot at Gerolstein. Farther south, fighter-bombers struck at rail yards at Homburg, Elmstein, Bergzabern, and Neustadt, and fuel dumps near Kaiserslautern and Bergzabern.

Escorted heavy bombers attacked the synthetic oil plant at Sterkrade, in the Ruhr. Some of the escorting fighters also strafed an airfield and rail targets in he Hanover area.

During the day, seven enemy aircraft were shot down and eight destroyed on the ground. From the day's operations, nine heavy bombers, two medium bombers and twenty-one fighters are missing.

†PARRISH, LAVERNE

Rank and Organization: Technician 4th Grade, U.S. Army, Medical Detachment, 161st Infantry, 25th Infantry Division.
Born: Knox City, Missouri.
Entered Service At: Ronan, Montana.
Place and Date: Binalonan, Luzon, Philippine Islands, January 18-24, 1945.
Citation: Tech 4th Grade Parrish was medical aid man with Company C during the fighting in Binalonan, Luzon, Philippine Islands. On the 18th, he observed 2 wounded men under enemy fire and immediately went to their rescue. After moving 1 to cover, he crossed 25 yards of open ground to administer aid to the second. In the early hours of the 24th, his company, crossing an open field near San Manuel, encountered intense enemy fire and was ordered to withdraw to the cover of a ditch. While treating the casualties, Technician Parrish observed 2 wounded still in the field. With-

out hesitation he left the ditch, crawled forward under enemy fire, and in 2 successive trips he brought both men to safety. He next administered aid to 12 casualties in the same field, crossing and recrossing the open area raked by hostile fire. Making successive trips, he then brought 3 wounded in to cover. After treating nearly all of the 37 casualties suffered by his company, he was mortally wounded by mortar fire, and shortly after was killed. The indomitable spirit, intrepidity, and gallantry of Technician Parrish saved many lives at the cost of his own.

OFFICIAL COMMUNIQUE:
United Nations
ADVANCED HEADQUARTERS on Luzon, Thursday, Jan. 25 – A communique:

PHILIPPINES

Luzon: Leading elements of the Fourteenth Corps, driving swiftly southward into the central plain in Pampanga, captured the town of Bamban and its near-by airfield, one of the major satellite airdromes of the Clark air center. Strong motorized patrols pressed on south of Mabalacat and are now operating near Clark Field, itself, and Fort Stotsenburg. Small enemy motorized patrols and harassing snipers were dispersed.

Troops of the First Corps seized Mount Balungao and pushed patrols eastward. On the left flank, our forces, supported by heavy naval bombardment, continued the reduction of the enemy's fixed defenses around Rosario.

Our heavy units dropped forty-five tons of bombs on enemy installations at Corregidor, causing large explosions and fires. Our fighters and bombers hit enemy-occupied Baguio, destroying many enemy installations. Other planes struck enemy coastal defenses in Subic Bay, damaged barges in Dasol Bay, and executed close-support attack for our ground forces.

Enemy casualties for the two weeks since the landing are estimated at approximately 14,000. Of these, 6,449 are counted killed, 423 prisoners, and an estimated 7,200 wounded. Our casualties are 657 killed, 187 missing, and 2,301 wounded, a total of 3,145. Every possible strategical and tactical ingenuity is being successfully employed to hold our losses in men to an absolute minimum.

†VALDEZ, JOSE F.
Rank and Organization: Private First Class, U.S. Army, Company B, 7th Infantry, 3d Infantry Division.
Born: Governador, New Mexico.
Entered Service At: Pleasant Grove, Utah.
Place and Date: Near Rosenkrantz, France, January 25, 1945.
Citation: Pfc. Valdez was on outpost duty with 5 others when the enemy counterattacked with overwhelming strength. From his position near some woods 500 yards beyond the American lines he observed a hostile tank about 75 yards away, and raked it with automatic rifle fire until it withdrew. Soon afterward he saw 3 Germans stealthily approaching through the woods. Scorning cover as the enemy soldiers opened up with heavy automatic weapons fire from a range of 30 yards, he engaged in a fire fight with the attackers until he had killed all 3. The enemy quickly launched an attack with 2 full companies of infantrymen, blasting the patrol with murderous concentrations of automatic and rifle fire and beginning an encircling movement which forced the patrol leader to order a withdrawal. Despite the terrible odds, Pfc. Valdez immediately volunteered to cover the maneuver, and as the patrol 1 by 1 plunged through a hail of bullets toward the American lines, he fired burst after burst into the swarming enemy. Three of his companions were wounded in their dash for safety and he was struck by a bullet that entered his stomach and, passing through his body, emerged from his back. Overcoming agonizing pain, he regained control of himself and resumed his firing position, delivering a protective screen of bullets until all others of the patrol were safe. By field telephone he called for artillery and mortar fire on the Germans and corrected the range until he had shells falling within 50 yards of his position. For 15 minutes he refused to be dislodged by more than 200 of the enemy; then, seeing that the barrage had broken the counter attack, he dragged himself back to his own lines. He died later as a result of his wounds. Through his valiant, intrepid stand and at the cost of his own life, Pfc. Valdez made it possible for his comrades to escape, and was directly responsible for repulsing an attack by vastly superior enemy forces.

MURPHY, AUDIE L.
Rank and Organization: Second Lieutenant, U.S. Army, Company B, 15th Infantry, 3d Infantry Division.
Born: Hunt County, near Kingston, Texas.
Entered Service At: Dallas, Texas.
Place and Date: Near Holtzwihr, France, January 26, 1945.
Citation: 2d Lt. Murphy commanded Company B, which was attacked by

6 tanks and waves of infantry. 2d Lt. Murphy ordered his men to withdraw to prepared positions in a woods, while he remained forward at his command post and continued to give fire directions to the artillery by telephone. Behind him, to his right, 1 of our tank destroyers received a direct hit and began to burn. Its crew withdrew to the woods. 2d Lt. Murphy continued to direct artillery fire which killed large numbers of the advancing enemy infantry. With the enemy tanks abreast of his position, 2d Lt. Murphy climbed on the burning tank destroyer, which was in danger of blowing up at any moment, and employed its .50 caliber machinegun against the enemy. He was alone and exposed to German fire from 3 sides, but his deadly fire killed dozens of Germans and caused their infantry attack to waver. The enemy tanks, losing infantry support, began to fall back. For an hour the Germans tried every available weapon to eliminate 2d Lt. Murphy, but he continued to hold his position and wiped out a squad which was trying to creep up unnoticed on his right flank. Germans reached as close as 10 yards, only to be mowed down by his fire. He received a leg wound, but ignored it and continued the singlehanded fight until his ammunition was exhausted. He then made his way to his company, refused medical attention, and organized the company in a counterattack which forced the Germans to withdraw. His directing of artillery fire wiped out many of the enemy; he killed or wounded about 50. 2d Lt. Murphy's indomitable courage and his refusal to give an inch of ground saved his company from possible encirclement and destruction, and enabled it to hold the woods which had been the enemy's objective.

OFFICIAL COMMUNIQUE:
United Nations
SUPREME HEADQUARTERS, Allied Expeditionary Force, Jan. 26 –Communique 293:

Allied forces wiped out an enemy party which crossed the Maas [Meuse] River near Boxmeer, south of Nijmegen.

Farther south our forces occupied the line north of Montfort. The wooded area south of Montfort was cleared of the enemy. Across the German border, mopping up operations in Heinsberg were completed and the town is in our hands. A crossroads at the German town of Birgelen, southeast of Roermond, was attacked by rocket-firing fighters.

Our forces between Bullange and St. Vith gained half a mile southeast of Moderscheid and have taken high ground approximately two miles east of Born. Deep snow continued to hamper our operations in this area. We made small gains just southeast of St. Vith. Southwest of St. Vith, we cleared Audrange and Wattermal.

To the southeast, Wilwerdange was taken despite strong resistance from the enemy, and we occupied Breidfeld, one mile east of Binfield. We crossed the Clerve River north and south of Clervaux. North of the town, our troops have taken Hupperdange and are in the vicinity of Urspelt. One and a half miles south of Clervaux, our units gained high ground across the river. Farther south, we cleared the enemy from Alscheid, three miles east of Wiltz. We captured Hoscheidt, four miles west of Vianden, after a battle in which three enemy tanks were knocked out. Four other enemy tanks were destroyed when we repulsed a counter-attack at Putscheid, two miles northwest of Vianden. House-to-house fighting is in progress in Wasserbillig, at the junction of the Sauer and Moselle Rivers.

East of Saareguemines, our ground patrols destroyed five enemy-held bunkers, and inflicted personnel losses. In the northern Alsace Plain, a reinforced enemy launched a series of attacks against our new positions and scored initial gains, but by the end of the day, these were largely offset by our counter-attacks. Hostile forces penetrated more than a mile to Schillersdorf, and occupied near-by Muhlhausen. They were halted in hard fighting, which continued in Schillersdorf.

West of Haguenau, our counter-attacks resulted in retaking sections of the wooded area which the enemy entered after crossing the Moder River. East of Haguenau, eighty of an enemy company which crossed the river were captured, and the rest forced back. Stiff fighting continued north of Colmar, and along the southern edge of the Colmar sector with little change in the situation.

FUNK, LEONARD A., JR.
Rank and Organization: First Sergeant, U.S. Army, Company C, 508th Parachute Infantry, 82nd Airborne Division.
Born: Braddock Township, Pennsylvania.
Entered Service At: Wilkinsburg, Pennsylvania.
Place and Date: Holzheim, Belgium, January 29, 1945.
Citation: First Sergeant Funk distinguished himself by gallant, intrepid actions against the enemy. After advancing 15 miles in a driving snowstorm, the American force prepared to attack through waist deep drifts. The company executive officer became a casualty, and 1st Sgt. Funk immediately assumed his duties, forming headquarters soldiers into a combat unit for an assault in the face of direct artillery shelling and harassing fire from the right flank. Under his skillful and courageous leadership, this miscellaneous group and the 3rd Platoon attacked 15 houses, cleared them, and took 30 prisoners without suffering a casualty. The fierce drive of Company C quickly overran Holzheim, netting some 80 prisoners, who were placed under a 4-man guard, all that could be spared, while the rest of the understrength unit went about mopping up isolated points of resistance. An

enemy patrol, by means of a ruse, succeeded in capturing the guards and freeing the prisoners, and had begun preparations to attack Company C from the rear when 1st Sgt. Funk walked around the building and into their midst. He was ordered to surrender by a German officer who pushed a machine pistol into his stomach. Although overwhelmingly outnumbered and facing almost certain death, 1st Sgt. Funk, pretending to comply with the order, began slowly to unsling his submachinegun from his shoulder and then, with lightning motion, brought the muzzle into line and riddled the German officer. He turned upon the other Germans, firing and shouting to the other Americans to seize the enemy's weapons. In the ensuing fight 21 Germans were killed, many wounded, and the remainder captured. 1st Sgt. Funk's bold action and heroic disregard for his own safety were directly responsible for the recapture of a vastly superior enemy force, which, if allowed to remain free, could have taken the widespread units of Company C by surprise and endangered the entire attack plan.

OFFICIAL COMMUNIQUE:
United Nations
SUPREME HEADQUARTERS, Allied Expeditionary Force, Jan. 29 –Communique 296:

Allied forces launched an attack in the area northeast of St. Vith against light to moderate resistance. We have captured Hepscheid and Heppenbach. Gains also were made east of Ambleve and to high ground two miles southeast of St. Vith. Southwest of St. Vith, we have cleared the enemy from Gruflange. Farther southeast, our units have advanced to the vicinity of Bracht after encountering enemy mines and road blocks west of the town.

Northeast of Weiswampach, we have made gains to within one mile of the Our River, and our patrols have reached Kalborn, five miles northeast of Clervaux. Munshausen, southeast of Clervaux, is in our hands.

In the area four miles northwest of Vianden, our units have occupied Wahlhausen and Weiler and have reached high ground northeast of Weiler. In the area southeast of Remich, we repulsed a small enemy counter-attack in the vicinity of Sinz.

From the Saarbruecken area, across the Lower Vosges and northern Alsace, a lull in activity continued. Heavy snowfalls hampered operations. Northeast of Colmar, our forces have reached the east-west Colmar Canal. On the southern edge of the Colmar sector, we have made further limited gains.

Mortar positions southwest of Meeuwen, and a strong point south of Nijmegen were attacked by fighter-bombers yesterday. Communications in Holland and northwest Germany also were targets for fighter-bombers. Rail lines were cut in the

Utrecht-Deventer area, and, also to the northwest of Rheine, while locomotives and rolling stock in the north and northeast of the Ruhr were attacked.

Last night heavy bombers were over Germany in great strength with railway communications near Stuttgart as the main objective. Berlin also was bombed.

†KELLEY, JONAH E.

Rank and Organization: Staff Sergeant, U.S. Army, 311th Infantry, 78th Infantry Division.
Born: Roda, West Virginia.
Entered Service At: Keyser, West Virginia.
Place and Date: Kesternich, Germany, January 30-31, 1945.
Citation: In charge of the leading squad of Company E, S/Sgt. Kelley heroically spearheaded the attack in furious house-to-house fighting. Early on January 30, he led his men through intense mortar, and small arms fire in repeated assaults on barricaded houses. Although twice wounded, once when struck in the back, the second time when a mortar shell fragment passed through his left hand and rendered it practically useless, he refused to withdraw and continued to lead his squad after hasty dressings had been applied. His serious wounds forced him to fire his rifle with 1 hand, resting it on rubble or over his left forearm. To blast his way forward with handgrenades, he set aside his rifle to pull the pins with his teeth while grasping the missiles with his good hand. Despite these handicaps, he created tremendous havoc in the enemy ranks. He rushed 1 house, killing 3 of the enemy and clearing the way for his squad to advance. On approaching the next house, he was fired upon from an upstairs window. He killed the sniper with a single shot and similarly accounted for another enemy soldier who ran from the cellar of the house. As darkness came, he assigned his men to defensive positions, never leaving them to seek medical attention. At dawn the next day, the squad resumed the attack, advancing to a point where heavy automatic and small-arms fire stalled them. Despite his wounds, S/Sgt. Kelley moved out alone, located an enemy gunner dug in under a haystack and killed him with rifle fire. He returned to his men and found that a German machine-gun, from a well-protected position in a neighboring house, still held up the advance. Ordering the squad to remain in comparatively safe positions, he valiantly dashed into the open and attacked the position singlehandedly through a hail of bullets. He was hit several times and fell to his knees when within 25 yards of his objective; but he summoned his waning strength and emptied his rifle into the machinegun nest, silencing the weapon before he died. The superb courage, aggressiveness, and utter disregard for his own safety displayed by S/Sgt. Kelley

inspired the men he led and enabled them to penetrate the last line of defense held by the enemy in the village of Kesternich.

OFFICIAL COMMUNIQUE:
United Nations
SUPREME HEADQUARTERS, Allied Expeditionary Force, Jan. 30 –Communique 297:

Allied forces continuing their eastward drive have taken Bullange. In the area northeast of St. Vith, we have made gains of nearly two miles against scattered resistance to take Herresbach and have reached the vicinity of Holzheim, three miles northeast of Herresbach.

Our units have made gains in the vicinity of Maspelt, four miles south of St. Vith. Farther south, we have taken Oberhausen, on the Our River, and some of our elements have crossed the river in the Oberhausen area against very strong resistance. Kalborn has been cleared of the enemy and we have taken Roder, Putscheid, three miles northwest of Vianden, is in our hands.

West of the Lower Vosges Mountains, and in northern Alsace, a lull continued for the third day with heavy snow hampering all movement. Long-range enemy artillery fire fell in the vicinity of Saverne.

Northeast of Colmar, we made local gains. Our forces drew close to Cernay from the west and east of the town.

Rail transportation targets over a wide area in western Germany were under air attack yesterday. Fighter-bombers struck at rail traffic in the region of Rheine, Osnabrueck, and Herford in northwest Germany, railway yards in the areas of Duesseldorf, Dueren, Cologne and Pruem, and farther south in the areas of Trier, Frankford-on-the-Main, Kaiserslautern, Pirmasens, Mannheim and Stuttgart.

During the day, seven enemy aircraft were destroyed on the ground. According to reports so far received, five of our heavy bombers and ten fighters are missing.

Last night objectives in Berlin were bombed.

BENNETT, EDWARD A.
Rank and Organization: Corporal, U.S. Army, Company B, 358th Infantry, 90th Infantry Division.
Born: Middleport, Ohio.
Entered Service At: Middleport, Ohio.
Place and Date: Heckhuscheid, Germany, February 1, 1945.
Citation: Cpl. Bennett was advancing with Company B across open ground to assault Heckhuscheid, Germany, just after dark when vicious enemy

machinegun fire from a house on the outskirts of the town pinned down the group and caused several casualties. He began crawling to the edge of the field in an effort to flank the house, persisting in this maneuver even when the hostile machinegunners located him by the light of burning buildings and attempted to cut him down as he made for the protection of some trees. Reaching safety, he stealthily made his way by a circuitous route to the rear of the building occupied by the German gunners. With his trench knife he killed a sentry on guard there and then charged into the darkened house. In a furious hand-to-hand struggle he stormed about a single room which harbored 7 Germans. Three he killed with rifle fire, another he clubbed to death with the butt of his gun, and the 3 others he dispatched with his.45 caliber pistol. The fearless initiative, stalwart combat ability, and outstanding gallantry of Cpl. Bennett eliminated the enemy fire which was decimating his company's ranks and made it possible for the Americans to sweep all resistance from the town.

†DELEAU, EMILE, JR.

Rank and Organization: Sergeant, U.S. Army, Company A, 142d Infantry, 36th Infantry Division.
Born: Lansing, Ohio.
Entered Service At: Blaine, Ohio.
Place and Date: Oberhoffen, France, February 1-2, 1945.
Citation: Sgt. Deleau led a squad in the night attack on Oberhoffen, France, where fierce house-to-house fighting took place. After clearing 1 building of opposition, he moved his men toward a second house from which heavy machine-gun fire came. He courageously exposed himself to hostile bullets and, firing his submachinegun as he went, advanced steadily toward the enemy position until close enough to hurl grenades through a window, killing 3 Germans and wrecking their gun. His progress was stopped by heavy rifle and machinegun fire from another house. Sgt. Deleau dashed through the door with his gun blazing. Within, he captured 10 Germans. The squad then took up a position for the night and awaited daylight to resume the attack. At dawn of February 2, Sgt. Deleau pressed forward with his unit, killing 2 snipers as he advanced to a point where machinegun fire from a house barred the way. Despite vicious small-arms fire, Sgt. Deleau ran across an open area to reach the rear of the building, where he destroyed 1 machinegun and killed its 2 operators with a grenade. He worked to the front of the structure and located a second machinegun. Finding it impossible to toss a grenade into the house from his protected position, he fearlessly moved away from the building and was about to hurl his explo-

sive when he was instantly killed by a burst from the gun he sought to knock out. With magnificent courage and daring aggressiveness, Sgt. Deleau cleared 4 well-defended houses of Germans, inflicted severe losses on the enemy and at the sacrifice of his own life aided his battalion to reach its objective with a minimum of casualties.

OFFICIAL COMMUNIQUE:
United Nations
SUPREME HEADQUARTERS, Allied Expeditionary Force, Feb. 1 –Communique 299:

Allied forces have completely cleared the enemy from the island of Kapelsheveer in the River Maas [Meuse], east of Geertruidenberg, after heavy and prolonged fighting.

Farther south our units continued their attack northeast of Monschau and have captured Eichersheid and Imgenbroich. Between Monschau and the area northeast of Clervaux, we have made general gains, advancing 5,000 yards in some places. In the forest southeast of Hofen, our forces gained up to 4,000 yards and pushed 1,000 yards east of Rocherath through deep snow and occasional minefields.

Our infantry elements have crossed the Belgian-German border on a 5,000-yard advance to within a mile west of Udenbreith. Another crossing of the border was made five miles southeast of Bullange.

East and southeast of St. Vith, our units have taken Setz, Schlierbach and Lommersweiler, and have cleared the enemy from Steffeshausen, three miles farther south.

In the bridgeheads across the Our River, east of Weiswampach, our artillery repulsed an infantry counter-attack, and we have advanced to a point one and a half miles northeast of Welchenhausen, on the east bank of the river.

West of the lower Vosges Mountains, and in northern Alsace, activity was confined to patrolling and exchanges of small-arms fire.

Northeast of Strasbourg, we have occupied Gambsheim and Bettenhoffen against light resistance. South of Strasbourg, our forces progressed about four miles to the Rhine-Rhone Canal in the area east of Benfeld.

Our bridgehead south of the Colmar Canal was enlarged with the aid of armor to a depth of approximately three miles. Resistance was spotty. On the southern edge of the Colmar sector, the enemy continued to defend Cernay and Wittlesheim stubbornly. Violent street fighting has been in progress in both towns.

Weather drastically restricted air operations yesterday.

†KNIGHT, JACK L.

Rank and Organization: First Lieutenant, U.S. Army, 124th Cavalry Regiment, Mars Task Force.
Born: Garner, Texas.
Entered Service At: Weatherford, Texas.
Place and Date: Near Loi-Kang, Burma, February 2, 1945.
Citation: 1st Lt. Knight led his cavalry troop against heavy concentrations of enemy mortar, artillery, and small-arms fire. After taking the troop's objective and while making preparations for a defense, he discovered a nest of Japanese pillboxes and foxholes to the right front. Preceding his men by at least 10 feet, he immediately led an attack. Singlehandedly he knocked out 2 enemy pillboxes and killed the occupants of several foxholes. While attempting to knock out a third pillbox, he was struck and blinded by an enemy grenade. Although unable to see, he rallied his platoon and continued forward in the assault on the remaining pillboxes. Before the task was completed he fell mortally wounded. 1st Lt. Knight's gallantry and intrepidity were responsible for the successful elimination of most of the Jap positions and served as an inspiration to officers and men of his troops.

OFFICIAL COMMUNIQUE:
United Nations
KANDY, Ceylon, Feb. 1 – A communique:

LAND

Fifteenth Indian Corps: Our troops took Kangaw on Jan. 30 after heavy fighting. The enemy has a strong artillery concentration in this sector and s counter-attacking fiercely despite his severe losses. Farther north, West African troops continue to drive the enemy southward. They are approaching Minbya and have reached Hpontha, east of the Yamaung River, east of Minbya.

Fourteenth Army: Mopping up of the enemy remaining around the village of Kyaukse, southwest of Ondaw, is proceeding. West of the Irrawaddy, enemy resistance near Kabwet has ceased.

Northern Combat Area Command: In patrol clashes near the Burma Road, troops of the Mars Task Force yesterday inflicted numerous casualties on the enemy.

AIR

Heavy bombers of the Eastern Air Command attacked the Japanese headquarters area near Mandalay in strength yesterday, starting many fires. Other aircraft hit a railway bridge south of the city and bombed targets to the west.

All buildings in a depot in the Northern Combat Area were destroyed. Stores areas were hit, and in cooperation with the Thirty-sixth British Division, enemy positions were attacked.

In Arakan, fighter-bombers hit gun positions, strong points, and trenches. Rivercraft on the Irrawaddy were damaged and aircraft pens on an enemy airfield strafed.

†PEDEN, FORREST E.

Rank and Organization: Technician 5th Grade, U.S. Army, Battery C, 10th Field Artillery Battalion, 3d Infantry Division.
Born: St. Joseph, Missouri.
Entered Service At: Wathena, Kansas.
Place and Date: Near Biesheim, France, February 3, 1945.
Citation: Technician 5th Grade Peden was a forward artillery observer when the group of about 45 infantrymen with whom he was advancing was ambushed in the uncertain light of a waning moon. Enemy forces outnumbering the Americans by 4 to 1 poured withering artillery, mortar, machinegun and small-arms fire into the stricken unit from the flanks, forcing our men to seek the cover of a ditch which they found already occupied by enemy foot troops. As the opposing infantrymen struggled in hand-to-hand combat, Tech. Peden courageously went to the assistance of 2 wounded soldiers and rendered first-aid under heavy fire. With radio communications inoperative, he realized that the unit would be wiped out unless help could be secured from the rear. On his own initiative, he ran 800 yards to the battalion command post through a hail of bullets which pierced his jacket and there secured 2 light tanks to go to the relief of his hard-pressed comrades. Knowing the terrible risk involved, he climbed upon the hull of the lead tank and guided it into battle. Through a murderous concentration of fire the tank lumbered onward, bullets and shell fragments ricocheting from its steel armor within inches of the completely exposed rider, until it reached the ditch. As it was about to go into action it was turned into a flaming pyre by a direct hit which killed Tech. Peden. However, his intrepidity and gallant sacrifice was not in vane. Attracted by the light from the burning tank, reinforcements found the beleaguered Americans and drove off the enemy.

OFFICIAL COMMUNIQUE:
United Nations

SUPREME HEADQUARTERS, Allied Expeditionary Force, Feb. 3 —Communique 301:

Allied infantry gained from 1,500 to 2,000 yards in the Monschau forest against light to moderate resistance to points three and a half miles east of Hofen.

Other infantry elements reached the eastern edge of the forest along the main road running southeast from Monschau.

Farther to the south, we pushed eastward through the dragon's teeth obstacles of the Siegfried Line, against increasing resistance from small-arms and machine-gun fire, and reached the high ground west of Ramscheid.

Five and a half miles east of Bullange, the German town of Neuhof has been taken and heavy fighting is in progress in Udenbreth to the north.

Across the German boarder, east and southeast of St. Vith, we have captured Auw, Mutzenich, and have reached the vicinity of Bleialf after taking Gross-Langenfeld.

Heckhusscheid, three miles southwest of Gross-Langenfeld, also is in our hands.

At Oberoffen, southeast of Haguenau, we made slow progress in fighting, which continued to be heavy for the second day.

Our infantry and tanks drove to the center of Colmar, and we also made gains on the eastern and western sides of the city.

To the east, near Huenheim, our units reached the Rhine. We now hold the west bank of the Rhine for about thirty-five miles south of Strasbourg. Progress was made in the Colmar forest, while heavy fighting took place at near-by Appenwihr and Biesheim.

Local gains were made on the southern side of the Colmar sector against strong resistance.

Continuing the offensive against the enemy's communications and transport, medium and fighter-bombers in strength struck at targets from Groningen, in the north of Holland, to Neuf-Brisach, southeast of Colmar.

They operated in the battle areas and eastward into Germany. Railway yards and bridges were bombed, rail lines were cut at many places and large numbers of locomotives and railway cars were destroyed or damaged. A considerable number of motor and armored vehicles also were hit.

In the Colmar area, fighter-bombers bombed and strafed the enemy from dawn to dusk and inflicted heavy losses on his transport. An oil refinery and fuel dump near Emmerich and targets at Euskirchen, Gemuend, Stadtkyll and Hillesheim were attacked by other medium bombers.

Last night heavy bombers in very great strength attacked Wiesbaden, Karlsruhe, and the synthetic oil plant at Wanne-Eickel. Light bombers struck at rail transport over wide areas in Germany.

RUDOLPH, DONALD E.

Rank and Organization: Second Lieutenant, U.S. Army, Company E, 20th Infantry, 6th Infantry Division.
Born: South Haven, Minnesota.
Entered Service At: Minneapolis, Minnesota.
Place and Date: Munoz, Luzon, Philippine Islands, February 5, 1945.
Citation: 2d Lt. Rudolph (then T/Sgt.) was acting as platoon leader at Munoz, Luzon, Philippine Islands. While administering first-aid on the battlefield, he observed enemy fire issuing from a nearby culvert. Crawling to the culvert with rifle and grenades, he killed 3 of the enemy concealed there. He then worked his way across open terrain toward a line of enemy pillboxes which had immobilized his company. Nearing the first pillbox, he hurled a grenade through its embrasure and charged the position. With his bare hands he tore away the wood and tin covering, then dropped a grenade through the opening, killing the enemy gunners and destroying their machinegun. Ordering several riflemen to cover his further advance, 2d Lt. Rudolph seized a pick mattock and made his way to the second pillbox. Piercing its top with the mattock, he dropped a grenade through the hole, fired several rounds from his rifle into it and smothered any surviving enemy by sealing the hole and the embrasure with earth. In quick succession he attacked and neutralized 6 more pillboxes. Later, when his platoon was attacked by an enemy tank, he advanced under covering fire, climbed to the top of the tank and dropped a white phosphorus grenade through the turret, destroying the crew. Through his outstanding heroism, superb courage, and leadership, and complete disregard for his own safety, 2d Lt. Rudolph cleared a path for an advance which culminated in one of the most decisive victories of the Philippine campaign.

†VIALE, ROBERT M.

Rank and Organization: Second Lieutenant, U.S. Army, Company K, 148th Infantry, 37th Infantry Division.
Born: Bayside, California.
Entered Service At: Ukiah, California.
Place and Date: Manila, Luzon, Philippine Islands, February 5, 1945.
Citation: 2d Lt. Viale displayed conspicuous gallantry and intrepidity above and beyond the call of duty. Forced by the enemy's detonation of prepared demolitions to shift the course of his advance through the city, he led the 1st platoon toward a small bridge, where heavy fire from 3 enemy pillboxes halted the unit. With 2 men he crossed the bridge behind screening grenade smoke to attack the pillboxes. The first he knocked out himself

while covered by his men's protecting fire; the other 2 were silenced by 1 of his companions and a bazooka team which he had called up. He suffered a painful wound in the right arm during the action. After his entire platoon had joined him, he pushed ahead through mortar fire and encircling flames. Blocked from the only escape route by an enemy machinegun placed at a street corner, he entered a nearby building with his men to explore possible means of reducing the emplacement. In one room he found civilians huddled together, in another, a small window placed high in the wall and reached by a ladder. Because of the relative positions of the window, ladder, and enemy emplacement, he decided that he, being left-handed, could better hurl a grenade than one of his men who had made an unsuccessful attempt. Grasping an armed grenade, he started up the ladder. His wounded right arm weakened, and, as he tried to steady himself, the grenade fell to the floor. In the 5 seconds before the grenade would explode, he dropped down, recovered the grenade and looked for a place to dispose of it safely. Finding no way to get rid of the grenade without exposing his own men or the civilians to injury of death, he turned to the wall, held it close to his body and bent over it as it exploded. 2d Lt. Viale died in a few minutes, but his heroic act saved the lives of others.

OFFICIAL COMMUNIQUE:
United Nations
ADVANCED HEADQUARTERS on Luzon, Tuesday, Feb. 6 – A communique:

PHILIPPINES

Luzon: Our forces are rapidly clearing the enemy from Manila. Our converging columns of the First Cavalry Division from the east, the Thirty-seventh Infantry Division from the north, and the Eleventh Airborne Division from the south, after an overnight thirty-five-mile advance from Tagaytay, simultaneously entered the city and surrounded the Japanese defenders. Their complete destruction is imminent.

Two of the four bridges over the Pasig River, the Quezon and the Ayala, were blown up by the enemy in a futile effort to block our advance.

The Thirty-seventh Infantry Division, in capturing Bilibid Prison, released more than 800 prisoners of war and about 550 civilian internees, including women and children. With the 3,700 internees from Santo Tomas released by the First Cavalry Division, this brings the total rescued to approximately 5,000. About 4,000 were Americans and the rest British, Australian, and other Allied nationalities. Every facility of the armed forces is being devoted to the care and attention of those who have been rescued. All names will be made public as quickly as they are tabulated.

In the First Corps sector, our troops occupied most of San Jose and cut the main road leading into Balete Pass and the Cagayan Valley. At Munoz, we are reducing an isolated enemy strong point. Twenty-five tanks, many trucks, pillboxes, and artillery pieces were destroyed in these sectors. We have secured he San Jose-Lupao road, we are engaging he enemy in Lupao, and have advanced five miles along the Villa Verde trail into the Caraballo Mountains.

In the Eleventh Corps sector, our troops have affected a junction with the Fourteenth Corps at Dinalupihan. We control all roads loading into Bataan.

Our heavy bombers struck the naval base at Cavite and defense positions on Corregidor, while attack bombers swept Lipa and Calingatan airdromes in Batangas. Other planes hi enemy installations in Ipo and San Jose del Norte, northeast of Manila. Fighters supported ground operations in all sectors.

Leyte: An additional 733 enemy have been killed or found dead or captured in the Ormoc Barrio and northwest coastal hills.

McGAHA, CHARLES L.

Rank and Organization: Master Sergeant, U.S. Army, Company G, 35th Infantry, 25th Infantry Division.
Born: Crosby, Tennessee.
Entered Service At: Crosby, Tennessee.
Place and Date: Near Lupao, Luzon, Philippine Islands, February 7, 1945.
Citation: M/Sgt. McGaha displayed conspicuous gallantry and intrepidity. His platoon and one other from Company G were pinned down in a roadside ditch by heavy fire from 5 Japanese tanks supported by 10 machineguns and a platoon of riflemen. When one of his men fell wounded 40 yards away, he unhesitatingly crossed the road under a hail of bullets and moved the man 75 yards to safety. Although he had suffered a deep arm wound, he returned to his post. Finding the platoon leader seriously wounded, he assumed command and rallied his men. Once more he braved the enemy fire to go to the aid of a litter party moving another wounded soldier. A shell exploded in their midst, wounding him in the shoulder and killing 2 of the party. He picked up the remaining man, carried him to cover, and then moved out in front deliberately to draw the enemy fire while the American forces, thus protected, withdrew to safety. When the last man had gained the new position, he rejoined his command and there collapsed from loss of blood and exhaustion. M/Sgt. McGaha set an example of courage and leadership in keeping with the highest traditions of the service.

OFFICIAL COMMUNIQUE:
United Nations
ADVANCED HEADQUARTERS on Luzon, Thursday, Feb. 8 – A communique:

PHILIPPINES

Luzon: The thirty-seventh Infantry Division and the First Cavalry Division have cleared north Manila and Quezon City. In south Manila, the Eleventh Airborne Division continued mopping up in the vicinity of Nichols Field. All bridges on the Pasig River have been blown up by the enemy.

In the First Corps sector, elements of the Thirty-second Division cut the Balete Pass road leading to the Cagayan Valley, twenty-four miles north of San Jose. The Sixth and Twenty-fifth Divisions made steady progress in attacks on Lupao, Munoz and along the San Jose road. Forward elements are operating in the vicinity of Rizal, nine miles southeast of San Jose. The enemy tanks and many heavily defended pillboxes were destroyed or captured in this area.

In the air, our heavy units dropped 204 tons of bombs on Corregidor while our attack-bombers hit Caballa Island, destroying a coast defense battery. medium units and fighters bombed and strafed enemy installations at Echague in the Cagayan Valley. Patrol planes on low-level sweeps over the east coast sank twenty-eight enemy barges and several speedboats. Fighters, light bombers, and attack-planes supported ground operations in all sectors.

Enemy casualties for the four weeks of the campaign are approximately 48,000. Our own casualties are 1,609 killed, 191 missing, and 5,276 wounded, a total of 7,076.

†CICCHETTI, JOSEPH J.

Rank and Organization: Private First Class, U.S. Army, Company A, 148th Infantry, 37th Infantry Division.
Born: Waynesburg, Ohio.
Entered Service At: Waynesburg, Ohio.
Place and Date: South Manila, Luzon, Philippine Islands, February 9, 1945.
Citation: Pfc. Cicchetti was with troops assaulting the first important line of enemy defenses. The Japanese had converted the partially destroyed Manila Gas Works and adjacent buildings into a formidable system of mutually supporting strongpoints from which they were concentrating machinegun, mortar, and heavy artillery fire on the American forces. Casualties rapidly mounted, and the medical aid men, finding it increasingly difficult to evacuate the wounded, called for volunteer litter bearers. Pfc.

Cicchetti immediately responded, organized a litter team and skillfully led it for more than 4 hours in rescuing 14 wounded men, constantly passing back and forth over a 400-yard route which was the impact area for a tremendous volume of the most intense enemy fire. On one return trip the path was blocked by machinegun fire, but Pfc. Cicchetti deliberately exposed himself to draw the automatic fire which he neutralized with his own rifle while ordering the rest of the team to rush past to safety with the wounded. While gallantly continuing his work, he noticed a group of wounded and helpless soldiers some distance away and ran to their rescue although the enemy fire had increased to new fury. As he approached the casualties, he was struck in the head by a shell fragment, but with complete disregard for his gaping wound he continued to his comrades, lifted 1 and carried him on his shoulders 50 yards to safety. He then collapsed and died. By his skilled leadership, indomitable will, and dauntless courage, Pfc. Cicchetti saved the lives of many of his fellow soldiers at the cost of his own.

†REESE, JOHN N. JR.

Rank and Organization: Private First Class, U.S. Army, Company B, 148th Infantry, 37th Infantry Division.
Born: Muskogee, Oklahoma.
Entered Service At: Pryor, Oklahoma.
Place and Date: Paco Railroad Station, Manila, Philippine Islands, February 9, 1945.
Citation: Pfc. Reese was engaged in the attack on the Paco Railroad Station, which was strongly defended by 300 determined enemy soldiers with machine-guns and rifles, supported by several pillboxes, three 20-mm. guns, one 37-mm. gun and heavy mortars. While making a frontal assault across an open field, his platoon was halted 100 yards from the station by intense enemy fire. On his own initiative, he left the platoon, accompanied by a comrade, and continued forward to a house 60 yards from the objective. Although under constant enemy observation, the two men remained in this position for an hour, firing at targets of opportunity, killing more than 35 Japanese and wounding many more. Moving closer to the station and discovering a group of Japanese replacements attempting to reach pillboxes, they opened heavy fire, killed more than 40 and stopped all subsequent attempts to man the emplacements. Enemy fire became more intense as they advanced to within 20 yards of the station. From that point, Pfc. Reese provided effective covering fire and courageously drew enemy fire to himself while his companion killed seven Japanese and destroyed a 20-mm.

gun and heavy machine-gun with hand-grenades. With their ammunition running low, the two men started to return to the American lines, alternately providing covering fire for each other as they withdrew. During this movement, Pfc. Reese was killed by enemy fire as he reloaded his rifle. The intrepid team in 2-1/2 hours of fierce fighting, killed more than 82 Japanese, completely disorganized their defense and paved the way for subsequent complete defeat of the enemy at this strong point. By his gallant determination in the face of tremendous odds, aggressive fighting spirit, and extreme heroism at the cost of his life, Pfc. Reese materially aided the advance of our troops in Manila and provided a lasting inspiration to all those with whom he served.

RODRIGUEZ, CLETO

Rank and Organization: Technical Sergeant (then Private), U.S. Army, Company B, 148th Infantry, 37th Infantry Division.
Born: San Marcos, Texas.
Entered Service At: San Antonio, Texas.
Place and Date: Paco Railroad Station, Manila, Philippine Islands, February 8, 1945.
Citation: Pvt. Rodriguez was an automatic rifleman when his unit attacked the strongly defended Paco Railroad Station during the battle for Manila, Philippine Islands. While making a frontal assault across an open field, his platoon was halted 100 yards from the station by intense enemy fire. On his own initiative, he left the platoon, accompanied by a comrade, and continued forward to a house 60 yards from the objective. Although under constant enemy observation, the two men remained in this position for an hour, firing at targets of opportunity, killing more than 35 hostile soldiers and wounding many more. Moving closer to the station and discovering a group of Japanese replacements attempting to reach pillboxes, they opened heavy fire, killed more than 40 and stopped all subsequent attempts to man the emplacements. Enemy fire became more intense as they advanced to within 20 yards of the station. Then, covered by his companion, Pvt. Rodriguez boldly moved up to the building and threw five grenades through a doorway killing seven Japanese, destroying a 20-mm. gun and wrecking a heavy machine-gun. With their ammunition running low, the two men started to return to the American lines, alternately providing covering fire for each other's withdrawal. During this movement, Pvt. Rodriguez' companion was killed. In 2-1/2 hours of fierce fighting the intrepid team killed more than 82 Japanese, completely disorganized their defense, and paved the way for the subsequent overwhelming defeat of the enemy at this strong

point. Two days later, Pvt. Rodriguez again enabled his comrades to advance when he single-handedly killed six Japanese and destroyed a well-placed 20-mm. gun. By his outstanding skill with his weapons, gallant determination to destroy the enemy, and heroic courage in the face of tremendous odds, Pvt. Rodriguez, on two occasions, materially aided the advance of our troops in Manila.

Note: the following is a newspaper account of the preceding battle for which Pfc. Cicchetti, Pfc. Reese, and Sgt. Rodriguez were awarded the Medal of Honor:

MANILA ENEMY LINE BREACHED BY 37TH

• • •

Division Crosses Pasig River to Join
11th Airborne in Clearing City of Japanese

• • •

ADVANCED HEADQUARTERS, on Luzon, Friday, Feb. 9 – American troops in a fleet of amphitracks crossed the Pasig River into southern Manila and moved southward to assist the Eleventh Airborne Division, which is clearing an area north of Nichols Field.

The crossing was made by advance elements of the Thirty-seventh Division against light resistance, the enemy using mortars, machine guns and light mobile guns to supplement the rifle fire of his snipers.

The Pasig was crossed in the vicinity of Malacanan Palace despite the enemy destruction of the bridges across the river, which is deep enough to be navigable by ocean-going steamers some distance up from its mouth.

According to reports from the front, the enemy has done little damage to the city in he region where the crossing was made, the most extensive demolitions and fires being along the waterfront north of the Pasig, in the Escolta business district and in the Intramuros, the old walled city.

Meanwhile, the population of Manila has been assured of at least partial functioning of the precious water supply. When the First Cavalry crossed the Novaliches watershed, the site of the reservoir that supplies the city, in its dash to the Santo Tomas internment camp, the Americans found the dam mined for demolition but the speed of the advance apparently drove off the Japanese before they had time to explode their mines. The pumping station was somewhat damaged, according to reports, but a large part of the usual water supply probably remains available.

In the First Corps section on the northeastern flank of our deep Luzon wedge, the Sixth and Twenty-fifth Divisions last night and this morning effected the capture of three bastions where the enemy has been offering perhaps his stubbornness resistance in this campaign – the villages of Munoz, Rizal, and Lupzo.

Munoz and Rizal were entered about midnight and Lupzo this morning at 11:30 against stiff resistance. Forty-two enemy tanks were destroyed in this sector, bringing to eighty-six the total reported since Feb. 4 in Gen. Douglas MacArthur's communiques. It was along the northeastern flank that the enemy had concentrated the bulk of his armor – the Second Armored Division. These medium tanks, armed with 37-mm. guns, and in many instances, the Japanese had buried them to the turrets, carefully camouflaged them, and used them as pillboxes, which opened up on the Americans at close range. These were blasted by incendiary bombs dropped by planes in close support of the ground troops, the heat and resulting fires driving the enemy from the steel shells of the tanks. Then the area was shelled by artillery to catch the defenders who had been driven out, and the final attack was delivered by charging infantrymen.

The communique reported enemy losses in the northeastern areas to be "very heavy in personnel, guns and armor." At Munoz, the Sixth Division counted 1,242 enemy dead and sixty-two armored cars and twenty-two guns were found wrecked as we occupied he village.

In the whole campaign, it was announced, more than 200 tanks of the Second Armored Division had been destroyed, representing more than two-thirds its striking power and the balance "now is so scattered that this division is no longer an effective fighting unit." The capture of three villages represented a considerable strategic blow to the Japanese since it further strengthens the American grip on the last remaining road over which parties of Japanese could move from the south to join with their forces concentrated around Baguio and in the Cagayan Valley. According to reports from the scene, no large bodies of the enemy have been able to use the road for the past several days, and small bodies of stragglers are now making their way northward along trails through foothills of the Caraballo Mountains, which do not accommodate heavy vehicles.

The heavy attack from the air on the fortress of Corregidor continued. Bombers struck coastal defenses and gun positions and started large fires north and south of our ground positions, while patrol planes attacked buildings and supply dumps on Divilacan Bay on the northeast coast and at Hondagua on the Bicol Peninsula.

A strong flight of attack planes bombed and strafed the Fabrica airdrome on Negros Island from low levels, causing wide destruction and fires, some of which were seen still burning seven hours later.

Japanese Are Trapped

MANILA, Friday, Feb. 9 – Remaining Japanese units in southern Manila are trapped between the thirty-seventh Division forces which crossed the river, and Maj. Gen. Joseph M. Swing's Eleventh airborne coming up from the south. American artillery firing from northern Manila paved the way for the Pasig River crossing, blasting Japanese batteries that have been setting fires in northern Manila.

DAHLGREN, EDWARD C.
Rank and Organization: Second Lieutenant (then Sergeant), U.S. Army, Company E, 142d Infantry, 36th Infantry Division.
Born: Perham, Maine.
Entered Service At: Portland, Maine.
Place and Date: Oberhoffen, France, February 11, 1945.
Citation: Sgt. Dahlgren led the 3d Platoon to the rescue of a similar unit which had been surrounded in an enemy counter-attack at Oberhoffen, France. As he advanced along a street, he observed several Germans crossing a field about 100 yards away. Running into a barn, he took up a position in a window and swept the hostile troops with submachine-gun fire, killing six, wounding others, and completely disorganizing the group. His platoon then moved forward through intermittent sniper fire and made contact with the besieged Americans. When the two platoons had been reorganized, Sgt. Dahlgren continued to advance along the street until he drew fire from an enemy-held house. In the face of machine-pistol and rifle fire, he ran toward the building, hurled a grenade through the door, and blasted his way inside with his gun. This aggressive attack so rattled the Germans that all eight men who held the strong point immediately surrendered. As Sgt. Dahlgren started toward the next house, hostile machine-gun fire drove him to cover. He secured rifle grenades, stepped to an exposed position, and calmly launched his missiles from a difficult angle until he had destroyed the machine-gun and killed its two operators. He moved to the rear of the house and suddenly came under the fire of a machine-gun emplaced in a barn. Throwing a grenade into the structure, he rushed the position, firing his weapon as he ran; within, he overwhelmed five Germans. After reorganizing his unit he advanced to clear hostile riflemen from the building where he had destroyed the machine-gun. He entered the house by a window and trapped the Germans in the cellar, where he tossed grenades into their midst, wounding several and forcing ten more to surrender. While reconnoitering another street with a comrade, he heard German voices in a house. An attack with rifle grenades drove the hostile troops to the cellar.

Sgt. Dahlgren entered the building, kicked open the cellar door, and, firing several bursts down the stairway, called for the trapped enemy to surrender. Sixteen soldiers filed out with their hands in the air. The bold leadership and magnificent courage displayed by Sgt. Dahlgren in his heroic attacks were in a large measure responsible for repulsing an enemy counterattack and saving an American platoon from great danger.

OFFICIAL COMMUNIQUE:
United Nations
SUPREME HEADQUARTERS, Allied Expeditionary Force, Feb. 11 –Communique 309:

The Allied offensive southeast of Nijmegen continues over very difficult terrain. South of Wyler, the town of Heikant has been captured and our units have penetrated the Reichswald [Forest] and captured Schottheide. More than 3,000 prisoners have been captured.

In the Nijmegen sector, supply dumps, gun positions, and enemy troops and transport south and southeast of the Reichswald and between Goch and Geldern were attacked by fighter-bombers. Farther to the rear of the enemy lines, factory buildings near Wesel and Bocholt were hit by rocket-firing fighters, while medium and fighter-bombers struck at communications at Xanten and Borken and attacked rail and road transport in the Gutersloh and Bielefeld areas.

Allied forces have reached the northern end of the Schwammenauel Dam despite heavy artillery and mortar fire. All flood gates have been blown by the enemy, but the dam itself remains intact. Conduits leading from the back-up waters of the Urftalsperre Dam to a point downstream from the Schwammenauel Dam have been blown open, causing a rise of three feet in the Roer River. The town of Hasenfeld, 1,200 yards east of Schwammenauel Dam, has been captured and patrols have pushed to the Roer River east and northeast of the town.

In the area north of Pruem, we have captured Neuendorf and have reached Willwerath. Other units made gains up to three quarters of a mile and are little more than a half mile northwest of Pruem, and have also reached the high ground two and a half miles northeast of the town.

In the Nieder Mehlen area, two enemy counter-attacks, each made by two to three infantry companies and led by five tanks, were repulsed. Four of the ten tanks were knocked out. allied elements, across the Sure [Sauer] River in the area two and a half miles northwest of Bollendorf have gained three quarters of a mile to the northeast.

Southeast of Haguenau near the Rhine, our forces crossed the Moder River and captured the railway station northwest of Oberhoffen. Further progress was made toward clearing Oberhoffen. Our attack on nearby Drushenheim was met by determined resistance and a strong tank-supporting counter-attack which forced us to withdraw.

Several groups of prisoners were taken in mopping up operations in the Colmar area.

†PEREZ, MANUEL, JR.

Rank and Organization: Private First Class, U.S. Army, Company A, 511th Parachute Infantry, 11th Airborne Division.
Born: March 3, 1923, Oklahoma City, Oklahoma.
Entered Service At: Chicago, Illinois.
Place and Date: Fort William McKinley, Luzon, Philippine Islands, February 13, 1945.
Citation: Pfc. Perez was lead scout for Company A, which had destroyed 11 of 12 pillboxes in a strongly fortified sector defending the approach to enemy-held Fort William McKinley on Luzon, Philippine Islands. In the reduction of these pillboxes, he killed five Japanese in the open and blasted others in pillboxes with grenades. Realizing the urgent need for taking the last emplacement, which contained two twin-mount .50-caliber dual-purpose machine-guns, he took a circuitous route to within 20 yards of the position, killing four of the enemy in his advance. He threw a grenade into the pillbox, and, as the crew started withdrawing through a tunnel just to the rear of the emplacement, shot and killed four before exhausting his clip. He had reloaded and killed four more when an escaping Japanese threw his rifle with fixed bayonet at him. In warding off this thrust, his own rifle was knocked to the ground. Seizing the Jap rifle, he continued firing, killing two more of the enemy. He rushed the remaining Japanese, killed three of them with the butt of the rifle and entered the pillbox, where he bayoneted the one surviving hostile soldier. Single-handedly, he killed 18 of the enemy in neutralizing the position that had held up the advance of his entire company. Through his courageous determination and heroic disregard of grave danger, Pfc. Perez made possible the successful advance of his unit toward a valuable objective and provided a lasting inspiration for his comrades.

OFFICIAL COMMUNIQUE:
United Nations
ADVANCED HEADQUARTERS, on Luzon, Wednesday, Feb. 14 – A communique:

PHILIPPINES

Luzon: In Manila the end of the enemy's trapped garrison is in sight.

The Eleventh Airborne Division cleared Nichols airdrome and occupied the naval base at Cavite. Ten enemy seaplanes and a battery of 3-inch guns were captured intact. First Cavalry Division units, sweeping through the Pasay district, penetrated to Manila Bay, while troops on the left cleared Nielson airfield. the Thirty-seventh Division is closing on Intramuros and the dock area where the enemy makes his final stand.

In the First Corps sector, troops of the Sixth Division reached Baler, on Luzon's east coast, securing the abandoned airfield. Extensive patrolling continues in the Carballo Mountains. Enemy troops, attempting to raid Rosario at night, were quickly dispersed. The Fortieth Division continued systematic mopping up operations in the Zambales range foothills.

Our heavy units dropped over 150 tons of bombs on Corregidor coastal defenses, scoring hits on four heavy gun batteries. Attack-bombers again hit enemy installations near Mariveles, while fighter and low-level sweeps strafed enemy concentrations in central Bataan and sank six enemy fuel and ammunition barges. Patrol planes wrecked enemy communication installations and motor vehicles in Balete Pass. Fighters and light bombers supported all ground operations.

For the five weeks of the Luzon campaign, enemy casualties exceed 68,000. Our own casualties are 2,102 killed, 192 missing, and 7,389 wounded – a total of 9,683.

Mindanao: Medium bombers swept the waterfront at Zamboanga from minimum altitude. Four small vessels were destroyed or damaged and a fuel tank exploded. Near Davao, fighter-bombers attacked Padao airdrome, scoring hits on the runway.

†BIGELOW, ELMER CHARLES
Rank and Organization: Watertender First Class, U.S. Naval Reserve.
Born: July 12, 1920, Hebron, Illinois.
Entered Service At: Illinois.
Place and Date: Corregidor Island, Philippines, February 14, 1945.
Citation: For conspicuous gallantry and intrepidity at the risk of his life above and beyond the call of duty while serving on board the *U.S.S. Fletcher* during action against enemy Japanese forces off Corregidor Island in the Philippines, February 14, 1945. Standing topside when an enemy shell struck the *Fletcher*, Bigelow, acting instantly as the deadly projectile exploded into fragments which penetrated the No. 1 gun magazine and set fire to several powder cases, picked up a pair of fire extinguishers and rushed

below in a resolute attempt to quell the raging flames. Refusing to waste the precious time required to don rescue-breathing apparatus, he plunged through the blinding smoke billowing out of the magazine hatch and dropped into the blazing compartment. Despite the acrid, burning powder smoke which seared his lungs with every agonizing breath, he worked rapidly and with instinctive sureness and succeeded in quickly extinguishing the fires and in cooling the cases and bulkheads, thereby preventing further damage to the stricken ship. Although he succumbed to his injuries on the following day, Bigelow, by his dauntless valor, unfaltering skill and prompt action in the critical emergency, had averted a magazine explosion which undoubtedly would have left his ship wallowing at the mercy of the furiously pounding Japanese guns on Corregidor, and his heroic spirit of self-sacrifice in the face of almost certain death enhanced and sustained the highest traditions of the U.S. Naval Service. He gallantly gave his life in the service of his country.

FLUCKEY, EUGENE BENNET

Rank and Organization: Commander, U.S. Navy, Commanding U.S.S. *Barb.*
Born: October 5, 1913, Washington, D.C.
Entered Service At: Illinois.
Other Navy Awards: Navy Cross with 3 Gold Stars.
Place and Date: Along coast of China, December 19, 1944 to February 15, 1945.
Citation: For conspicuous gallantry and intrepidity at the risk of his life above and beyond the call of duty as commanding officer of the *U.S.S. Barb* during her 11th war patrol along the east coast of China from December 19, 1944, to February 15, 1945. After sinking a large enemy ammunition ship and damaging additional tonnage during a running two hour night battle on January 8, Comdr. Fluckey, in an exceptional feat of brilliant deduction and bold tracking on January 25, located a concentration of more than 30 enemy ships in the lower reaches of Nankuan Chiang (Mamkwan Harbor). Fully aware that a safe retirement would necessitate an hour's run at full speed through the uncharted, mined, and rock-obstructed waters, he bravely ordered, "Battle station – torpedoes!" In a daring penetration of the heavy enemy screen, and riding in five fathoms of water, he launched the *Barb's* last forward torpedoes at 3,000-yard range. Quickly bringing the ship's stern tubes to bear, he turned loose four more torpedoes into the enemy, obtaining eight direct hits on six of the main targets to explode a large ammunition ship and cause inestimable damage by the resultant fly-

ing shells and other pyrotechnics. Clearing the treacherous area at high speed, he brought the *Barb* through to safety and four days later sank a large Japanese freighter to complete a record of heroic combat achievement, reflecting the highest credit upon Comdr. Fluckey, his gallant officers and men, and the U.S. Naval Service.

OFFICIAL COMMUNIQUE:
United Nations
ADVANCED HEADQUARTERS, on Luzon, Thursday, Feb. 15 – A communique:

PHILIPPINES

Luzon: In Manila we are gradually compressing the circle on the trapped enemy garrison.

In the Zambales foothills the Fortieth Division captured a great quantity of supplies after inflicting heavy casualties.

Patrols from the Sixth, Twenty-fifth and Thirty-second Divisions are probing deep into the southern Caraballo Mountains, where additional large stores of enemy equipment, including four tanks, were found abandoned.

The Eleventh Corps has cleaned the entire length of the Olongapo-Dinalupihan road across Bataan Peninsula and has advanced eleven miles south to seize Abucay, the eastern anchor of our first defense line in the 1942 campaign.

In the air our heavy units dropped 107 tons of bombs on Corregidor's coastal batteries. Fighters at minimum altitude swept the east coast of Bataan, destroying an additional twenty-four enemy positions in the Zambales foothills and artillery positions in Fort McKinley.

Visayas: Naval patrol craft operating at night off the Cebu coast destroyed a small freighter, sank two supply-laden barges and engaged enemy concentrations on shore. Air patrols bombed Sogod, on the northeast coast.

†HAMMERBERG, OWEN FRANCIS PATRICK
Rank and Organization: Boatswain's Mate Second Class, U.S. Navy.
Born: May 31, 1920, Daggett, Michigan.
Entered Service At: Michigan.
Place and Date: West Loch, Pearl Harbor, February 17, 1945.
Citation: For conspicuous gallantry and intrepidity at the risk of his life above and beyond the call of duty as a diver engaged in rescue operations at West Loch, Pearl Harbor, February 17, 1945. Aware of the danger when two fellow divers were hopelessly trapped in a cave-in of steel wreckage

while tunneling with jet nozzles under an LST sunk in 40 feet of water and 20 feet of mud. Hammerberg unhesitatingly went overboard in a valiant attempt to effect their rescue despite the certain hazard of additional cave-ins and the risk of fouling his lifeline on jagged pieces of steel imbedded in the shifting mud. Washing a passage through the original excavation, he reached the first of the trapped men, freed him from the wreckage and, working desperately in pitch-black darkness, finally effected his release from fouled lines, thereby enabling him to reach the surface. Wearied but undaunted after several hours of arduous labor, Hammerberg resolved to continue his struggle to wash through the oozing submarine, subterranean mud in a determined effort to save the second diver. Venturing still farther under the buried hulk, he held tenaciously to his purpose, reaching a place immediately above the other man just as another cave-in occurred and a heavy piece of steel pinned him crosswise over his shipmate in a position which protected the man beneath from further injury while placing the full brunt of terrific pressure on himself. Although he succumbed in agony 18 hours after he had gone to the aid of his fellow divers, Hammerberg, by his cool judgment, unfaltering professional skill and consistent disregard of all personal danger in the face of tremendous odds, had contributed effectively to the saving of his two comrades. His heroic spirit of self-sacrifice throughout enhanced and sustained the highest traditions of the U.S. Naval Service. He gallantly gave his life in the service of his country.

HERRING, RUFUS G.
Rank and Organization: Lieutenant, U.S. Naval Reserve, LCI (G) 449.
Born: June 11, 1921, Roseboro, North Carolina.
Entered Service At: North Carolina.
Place and Date: Iwo Jima, February 17, 1945.
Citation: For conspicuous gallantry and intrepidity at the risk of his life above and beyond the call of duty as commanding officer of LCI (G) *449* operating as a unit of LCI (G) Group 8, during the pre-invasion attack on Iwo Jima on February 17, 1945. Boldly closing the strongly fortified shores under the devastating fire of Japanese coastal defense guns. Lt. (then Lt. [jg.]) Herring directed shattering barrages of 40-mm. and 20-mm. gunfire against hostile beaches until struck down by the enemy's savage counter-fire which blasted the *449's* heavy guns and whipped her decks into sheets of flame. Regaining consciousness despite profuse bleeding he was again critically wounded when a Japanese mortar crashed the conning station, instantly killing or fatally wounding most of the officers and leaving the ship wallowing without navigational control. Upon recovering the second

time, Lt. Herring resolutely climbed down to the pilothouse and, fighting against his rapidly waning strength, took over the helm, established communication with the engine room, and carried on valiantly until relief could be obtained. When no longer able to stand, he propped himself against empty shell cases and rallied his men to the aid of the wounded; he maintained position in the firing line with his 20-mm. guns in action in the face of sustained enemy fire, and conned his crippled ship to safety. His unwavering fortitude, aggressive perseverance, and indomitable spirit against terrific odds reflect the highest credit upon Lt. Herring and uphold the highest traditions of the U.S. Naval Service.

OFFICIAL COMMUNIQUE:
United States
ADVANCED HEADQUARTERS, Guam, Sunday, Feb. 18 – Pacific Fleet Communique 261:

(1) Further reports on the attacks on Tokyo by aircraft of the Fifth Fleet under Admiral R. A. Spruance on Feb. 16 and 17 [East Longitude time] are unavailable.
(2) Bombardment of Iwo Jima [Island] in the Volcano Islands by battleships and cruisers of the Pacific Fleet is continuing. On Feb. 17 carrier aircraft and Army Liberators of the Strategic Air Force, Pacific Ocean Areas, bombed targets on the island through intense anti-aircraft fire. One of our ships was damaged during the attack by shore-based gunfire, which was intense.
(3) Five aircraft were strafed on the ground at Chichi Jima in the Bonin Islands and eighteen small craft were strafed and an ammunition barge exploded at Haha Jima in the same group on Feb. 17. Enemy anti-aircraft fire was intense over both targets. Ships' anti-aircraft batteries shot down two enemy planes.
(4) Army Liberators of the Strategic Air Force bombed Marcus Island on Feb. 16.
(5) Fighters of the Fourth Marine Aircraft Wing attacked targets on Babelthuap in the Palaus and Yap in the western Carolines on the same date.

McCARTER, LLOYD G.

Rank and Organization: Private, U.S. Army, 503d Parachute Infantry Regiment.
Born: May 11, 1917, St. Maries, Idaho.
Entered Service At: Tacoma, Washington.
Place and Date: Corregidor, Philippine Islands, February 16-19, 1945.
Citation: Pvt. McCarter was a scout with the regiment which seized the fortress of Corregidor, Philippine Islands. Shortly after the initial parachute assault on February 16, 1945, he crossed 30 yards of open ground under

intense enemy fire, and at point-blank range silenced a machine-gun with hand-grenades. On the afternoon of February 18, he killed six snipers. That evening, when a large force attempted to bypass his company, he voluntarily moved to an exposed area and opened fire. The enemy attacked his position repeatedly throughout the night and was each time repulsed. By 2 o'clock in the morning, all the men about him had been wounded; but shouting encouragement to his comrades and defiance at the enemy, he continued to bear the brunt of the attack, fearlessly exposing himself to locate enemy soldiers and then pouring heavy fire on them. He repeatedly crawled back to the American line to secure more ammunition. When his submachine-gun would no loner operate, he seized an automatic rifle and continued to inflict heavy casualties. This weapon, in turn, became too hot to use and, discarding it, he continued with an M1 rifle. At dawn the enemy attacked with renewed intensity. Completely exposing himself to hostile fire, he stood erect to locate the most dangerous enemy positions. He was seriously wounded; but, though he had already killed more than 30 of the enemy, he refused to evacuate until he had pointed out immediate objectives for attack. Through his sustained and outstanding heroism in the face of grave and obvious danger, Pvt. McCarter made outstanding contributions to the success of his company and to the recapture of Corregidor.

OFFICIAL COMMUNIQUE:
United Nations
ADVANCED HEADQUARTERS on Luzon, Tuesday, Feb. 20 – A Communique

PHILIPPINES

Luzon: On Corregidor our troops continue the reduction of enemy strong points and mopping-up in the rear of the batteries. On Bataan we are combing the peninsula for enemy remnants. In south Manila the steady reduction of the final enemy positions continue. We have captured Fort McKinley. The town of Hagonoy and Tagig, on the northwest shore of Laguna de Bay has been taken.

To the north, near Novaliches and Norzagaray, frequent patrol clashes continued.

Elements of the Fortieth Division continued mopping-up of enemy remnants in the Zambales Mountains. In the First Corps sector activity was limited to patrolling.

Our Air Forces supported all ground activity. Our light naval units, operating in Manila Bay, sank four enemy barges.

Visayas: Motor-torpedo boats at night destroyed a small cruiser off Cebu; while patrolling fighters sank two barges, burned a fuel-laden vessel and strafed short defenses.

Leyte: An additional 616 enemy have been killed during the past weeks by our troops methodically sweeping the hills along the northwest coast.

Mindanao: Heavy bombers covered bivouac areas near Davao with thirty-five tons of bombs, while fighter-bombers hit Sasa airdrome. Enemy supplies concentrated at Butuan on north coast were effectively attacked by fighter-bombers with forty-five tons of bombs.

†COLE, DARRELL SAMUEL

Rank and Organization: Sergeant, U.S. Marine Corps Reserve.
Born: July 20, 1920, Flat River, Missouri.
Entered Service At: Esther, Missouri.
Other Navy Award: Bronze Star Medal.
Place and Date: Iwo Jima, Volcano Islands, February 19, 1945.
Citation: For conspicuous gallantry and intrepidity at the risk of his life above and beyond the call of duty while serving as leader of a Machinegun Section of Company B, 1st Battalion, 23d Marines, 4th Marine Division, in action against enemy Japanese forces during the assault on Iwo Jima in the Volcano Islands, February 19, 1945. Assailed by a tremendous volume of small-arms, mortar and artillery fire as he advanced with 1 squad of his section in the initial assault wave, Sgt. Cole boldly led his men up the sloping beach toward Airfield No. 1 despite the blanketing curtain of flying shrapnel and, personally destroying with handgrenades 2 hostile emplacements which menaced the progress of his unit, continued to move forward until a merciless barrage of fire emanating from 3 Japanese pillboxes halted the advance. Instantly placing his 1 remaining machinegun in action, he delivered a shattering fusillade and succeeded in silencing the nearest and most threatening emplacement before his weapon jammed and the enemy, reopening fire with knee mortars and grenades, pinned down his unit for the second time. Shrewdly gaging the tactical situation and evolving a daring plan of counterattack, Sgt. Cole, armed solely with a pistol and 1 grenade, coolly advanced alone to the hostile pillboxes. Hurling his 1 grenade at the enemy in sudden, swift attack, he quickly withdrew, returned to his own lines for additional grenades and again advanced, attacked, and withdrew. With enemy guns still active, he ran the gauntlet of slashing fire a third time to complete the total destruction of the Japanese strong point and the annihilation of the defending garrison in this final assault. Although instantly killed by an enemy grenade as he returned to his squad, Sgt. Cole had eliminated a formidable Japanese position, thereby enabling his company to storm the remaining fortifications, continue the advance, and seize the objective. By his dauntless initiative, unfaltering

courage, and indomitable determination during a critical period of action, Sgt. Cole served as an inspiration to his comrades, and his stouthearted leadership in the face of almost certain death sustained and enhanced the highest tradition of the U.S. Naval Service. He gallantly gave his life for his country.

†STEIN, TONY

Rank and Organization: Corporal, U.S. Marine Corps Reserve.
Born: September 30, 1921, Dayton, Ohio.
Entered Service At: Ohio.
Place and Date: Iwo Jima, Volcano Islands, February 19, 1945.
Citation: For conspicuous gallantry and intrepidity at the risk of his life above and beyond the call of duty while serving with Company A, 1st Battalion, 28th Marines, 5th Marine Division, in action against enemy Japanese forces on Iwo Jima, in the Volcano Islands, February 19, 1945. The first man of his unit to be on station after hitting the beach in the initial assault, Cpl. Stein, armed with a personally improvised aircraft-type weapon, provided rapid covering fire as the remainder of his platoon attempted to move into position. When his comrades were stalled by a concentrated machinegun and mortar barrage, he gallantly stood upright and exposed himself to the enemy's view, thereby drawing the hostile fire to his own person and enabling him to observe the location of the furiously blazing hostile guns. Determined to neutralize the strategically placed weapons, he boldly charged the enemy pillboxes 1 by 1 and succeeded in killing 20 of the enemy during the furious singlehanded assault. Cool and courageous under the merciless hail of exploding shells and bullets which fell on all sides, he continued to deliver the fire of his skillfully improvised weapon at a tremendous rate of speed which rapidly exhausted his ammunition. Undaunted, he removed his helmet and shoes to expedite his movements and ran back to the beach for additional ammunition, making a total of 8 trips under intense fire and carrying or assisting a wounded man back each time. Despite the unrelenting savagery and confusion of battle, he rendered prompt assistance to his platoon whenever the unit was in position, directing the fire of a half-track against a stubborn pillbox until he had effected the ultimate destruction of the Japanese fortification. Later in the day, although his weapon was twice shot from his hands, he personally covered the withdrawal of his platoon to the company position. Stouthearted and indomitable, Cpl. Stein, by his aggressive initiative, sound judgement, and unwavering devotion to duty in the face of terrific odds, contributed materially to the fulfillment of his mission, and his outstanding valor through-

out the bitter hours of conflict sustains and enhances the highest traditions of the U.S. Naval Service.

†RUHL, DONALD JACK

Rank and Organization: Private First Class, U.S. Marine Corps Reserve.
Born: July 2, 1923, Columbus, Montana.
Entered Service At: Montana.
Place and Date: Iwo Jima, Volcano Islands, February 19 to 21, 1945.
Citation: For conspicuous gallantry and intrepidity at the risk of his life above and beyond the call of duty while serving as a rifleman in an assault platoon of Company E, 28th Marines, 5th Marine Division, in action against enemy Japanese forces on Iwo Jima, Volcano Islands, from February 19 to 21, 1945. Quick to press the advantage after 8 Japanese had been driven from a blockhouse on D-day, Pfc. Ruhl singlehandedly attacked the group, killing 1 of the enemy with his bayonet and another by rifle fire in his determined attempt to annihilate the escaping troops. Cool and undaunted as the fury of hostile resistance steadily increased throughout the night, he voluntarily left the shelter of his tank trap early in the morning of D-day plus 1 and moved out under a tremendous volume of mortar and machinegun fire to rescue a wounded marine lying in an exposed position approximately 40 yards forward of the line. Half pulling and half carrying the wounded man, he removed him to a safe position, called for an assistant and a stretcher and, again running the gauntlet of hostile fire, carried the casualty to an aid station some 300 yards distant on the beach. Returning to his platoon, he continued his valiant efforts, volunteering to investigate an apparently abandoned Japanese gun emplacement 75 yards forward of the right flank during consolidation of the front lines, and subsequently occupying the position through the night to prevent the enemy from repossessing the valuable weapon. Pushing forward in the assault against the vast network of fortifications surrounding Mt. Suribachi the following morning, he crawled with his platoon guide to the top of a Japanese bunker to bring fire to bear on enemy troops located on the far side of the bunker. Suddenly a hostile grenade landed between the 2 marines. Instantly Pfc. Ruhl called a warning to his fellow marine and dived on the deadly missile, absorbing the full impact of the shattering explosion in his own body and protecting all within range from the danger of flying fragments although he might easily have dropped from his position on the edge of the bunker to the ground below. An indomitable fighter, Pfc. Ruhl rendered heroic service toward the defeat of a ruthless enemy, and his valor, initiative and unfaltering spirit of self-sacrifice in the face of almost certain death sustain and enhance the

highest traditions of the U.S. Naval Service. He gallantly gave his life for his country.

LUCAS, JACKLYN HAROLD

Rank and Organization: Private First Class, U.S. Marine Corps Reserve, 1st Battalion, 26th Marines, 5th Marine Division.
Born: February 14, 1928, Plymouth, North Carolina.
Entered Service At: Norfolk, Virginia.
Place and Date: Iwo Jima, Volcano Islands, February 20, 1945.
Citation: For conspicuous gallantry and intrepidity at the risk of his life above and beyond the call of duty while serving with the 1st Battalion, 26th Marines, 5th Marine Division, during action against enemy Japanese forces on Iwo Jima, Volcano Islands, February 20, 1945. While creeping through a treacherous, twisting ravine which ran in close proximity to a fluid and uncertain frontline on D-plus-1 day, Pfc. Lucas and 3 other men were suddenly ambushed by a hostile patrol which savagely attacked with rifle fire and grenades. Quick to act when the lives of the small group were endangered by 2 grenades which landed directly in front of them, Pfc. Lucas unhesitantly hurled himself over his comrades upon 1 grenade and pulled the other under him, absorbing the whole blasting forces of the explosions in his own body in order to shield his companions from the concussion and murderous flying fragments. By his inspiring action and valiant spirit of self-sacrifice, he not only protected his comrades from certain injury or possible death but also enabled them to rout the Japanese patrol and continue the advance. His exceptionally courageous initiative and loyalty reflect the highest credit upon Pfc. Lucas and the U.S. Naval Service.

DUNLAP, ROBERT HUGO

Rank and Organization: Captain, U.S. Marine Corps Reserve, Company C, 1st Battalion, 26th Marines, 5th Marine Division.
Born: October 19, 1920, Abingdon, Illinois.
Entered Service At: Illinois.
Place and Date: On Iwo Jima, Volcano Islands, February 20-21, 1945.
Citation: For conspicuous gallantry and intrepidity at the risk of his life above and beyond the call of duty as commanding officer of Company C, 1st Battalion, 26th Marines, 5th Marine Division, in action against enemy Japanese forces during the seizure of Iwo Jima in the Volcano Islands, on February 20-21, 1945. Defying uninterrupted blasts of Japanese artillery, mortar, rifle and machinegun fire, Capt. Dunlap led his troops in a deter-

mined advance from low ground uphill toward the steep cliffs from which the enemy poured a devastating rain of shrapnel and bullets, steadily inching forward until the tremendous volume of enemy fire from the caves located high to his front temporarily halted his progress. Determined not to yield, he crawled alone approximately 200 yards forward of his front lines, took observation at the base of the cliff 50 yards from Japanese lines, located the enemy gun positions and returned to his own lines where he relayed the vital information to supporting artillery and naval gunfire units. Persistently disregarding his own personal safety, he then placed himself in an exposed vantage point to direct more accurately the supporting fire and, working without respite for 2 days and 2 nights under constant enemy fire, skillfully directed a smashing bombardment against the almost impregnable Japanese positions despite numerous obstacles and heavy marine casualties. A brilliant leader, Capt. Dunlap inspired his men to heroic efforts during this critical phase of the battle and by his cool decision, indomitable fighting spirit, and daring tactics in the face of fanatic opposition greatly accelerated the final decisive defeat of Japanese countermeasures in his sector and materially furthered the continued advance of his company. His great personal valor and gallant spirit of self-sacrifice throughout the bitter hostilities reflect the highest credit upon Capt. Dunlap and the U.S. Naval Service.

†GRAY, ROSS FRANKLIN
Rank and Organization: Sergeant, U.S. Marine Corps Reserve.
Born: August 1, 1920, Marvel Valley, Alabama.
Entered Service At: Alabama.
Place and Date: Iwo Jima, Volcano Islands, February 21, 1945.
Citation: For conspicuous gallantry and intrepidity at the risk of his life above and beyond the call of duty as a Platoon Sergeant attached to Company A, 1st Battalion, 25th Marines, 4th Marine Division, in action against enemy Japanese forces on Iwo Jima, Volcano Islands, February 21, 1945. Shrewdly gaging the tactical situation when his platoon was held up by a sudden barrage of hostile grenades while advancing toward the high ground northeast of Airfield No. 1, Sgt. Gray promptly organized the withdrawal of his men from enemy grenade range, quickly moved forward alone to reconnoiter and discovered a heavily mined area extending along the front of a strong network of emplacements joined by covered trenches. Although assailed by furious gunfire, he cleared a path leading through the minefield to one of the fortifications, then returned to the platoon position and, informing his leader of the serious situation, volunteered to initiate an attack

under cover of 3 fellow marines. Alone and unarmed but carrying a huge satchel charge, he crept up on the Japanese emplacement, boldly hurled the short-fused explosive and sealed the entrance. Instantly taken under machinegun fire from a second entrance to the same position, he unhesitatingly braved the increasingly vicious fusillades to crawl back for another charge, returned to his objective and blasted the second opening, thereby demolishing the position. Repeatedly covering the ground between the savagely defended enemy fortifications and his platoon area, he systematically approached, attacked, and withdrew under blanketing fire to destroy a total of 6 Japanese positions, more than 25 troops and a quantity of vital ordnance gear and ammunition. Stouthearted and indomitable, Sgt. Gray had singlehandedly overcome a strong enemy garrison and had completely disarmed a large minefield before finally rejoining his unit. By his great personal valor, daring tactics and tenacious perseverance in the face of extreme peril, he had contributed materially to the fulfillment of his company mission. His gallant conduct throughout enhanced and sustained the highest traditions of the U.S. Naval Service.

McCARTHY, JOSEPH JEREMIAH

Rank and Organization: Captain, U.S. Marine Corps Reserve, 2d Battalion, 24th Marines, 4th Marine Division.
Born: August 10, 1911, Chicago, Illinois.
Entered Service At: Illinois.
Place and Date: Iwo Jima, Volcano Islands, February 21, 1945.
Citation: For conspicuous gallantry and intrepidity at the risk of his life above and beyond the call of duty as commanding officer of a rifle company attached to the 2d Battalion, 24th Marines, 4th Marine Division, in action against enemy Japanese forces during the seizure of Iwo Jima, Volcano Islands, February 21, 1945. Determined to break through the enemy's cross-island defenses, Capt. McCarthy acted on his own initiative when his company's advance was held up by uninterrupted Japanese rifle, machinegun, and high-velocity 47-mm. fire during the approach to Motoyama Airfield No.2. Quickly organizing a demolitions and flamethrower team to accompany his picked rifle squad, he fearlessly led the way across 75 yards of fire-swept ground, charged a heavily fortified pillbox on the ridge of the front and, personally hurling handgrenades into the emplacement as he directed the combined operations of his small assault group, completely destroyed the hostile installation. Spotting 2 Japanese soldiers attempting an escape from the shattered pillbox, he boldly stood upright in full view of the enemy and dispatched both troops before

advancing to a second emplacement under greatly intensified fire and then blasted the strong fortifications with a well-planned demolitions attack. Subsequently entering the ruins, he found a Japanese taking aim at one of our men and, with alert presence of mind, jumped the enemy, disarmed and shot him with his own weapon. Then, intent on smashing through the narrow breach, he rallied the remainder of his company and pressed a full attack with furious aggressiveness until he had neutralized all resistance and captured the ridge. An inspiring leader and indomitable fighter, Capt. McCarthy consistently disregarded all personal danger during the fierce conflict and, by his brilliant professional skill, daring tactics, and tenacious perseverance in the face of overwhelming odds, contributed materially to the success of his division's operations against this savagely defended outpost of the Japanese Empire. His cool decision and outstanding valor reflect the highest credit upon Capt. McCarthy and enhance the finest traditions of the U.S. Naval Service.

CHAMBERS, JUSTICE M.

Rank and Organization: Colonel, U.S. Marine Corps Reserve, 3rd Assault Battalion Landing Team, 25th Marines, 4th Marine Division.
Born: February 2, 1908, Huntington, West Virginia.
Entered Service At: Washington, D.C.
Place and Date: On Iwo Jima, Volcano Islands, February 19-22, 1945.
Citation: For conspicuous gallantry and intrepidity at the risk of his life above and beyond the call of duty as commanding officer of the 3d Assault Battalion Landing Team, 25th Marines, 4th Maine Division, in action against enemy Japanese forces on Iwo Jima, Volcano Islands, from February 19 to 22, 1945. Under a furious barrage of enemy machinegun and small-arms fire from the commanding cliffs on the right, Col. Chambers (then Lt. Col.) landed immediately after the initial assault waves of his battalion on D-day to find the momentum of the assault threatened by heavy casualties from withering Japanese artillery, mortar rocket, machinegun, and rifle fire. Exposed to relentless hostile fire, he coolly reorganized his battle-weary men, inspiring them to heroic efforts by his own valor and leading them in an attack on the critical, impregnable high ground from which the enemy was pouring an increasing volume of fire directly onto troops ashore as well as amphibious craft in succeeding waves. Constantly in the frontlines encouraging his men to push forward against the enemy's savage resistance, Col. Chambers led the 8-hour battle to carry the flanking ridge top and reduce the enemy's fields of aimed fire, thus protecting the vital foothold gained. In constant defiance of hostile fire while reconnoitering the entire regi-

mental combat team zone of action, he maintained contact with adjacent units and forwarded vital information to the regimental commander. His zealous fighting spirit undiminished despite terrific casualties and the loss of most of his key officers, he again reorganized his troops for renewed attack against the enemy's main line of resistance and was directing the fire of the rocket platoon when he fell, critically wounded. Evacuated under heavy Japanese fire, Col. Chambers, by forceful leadership, courage, and fortitude in the face of staggering odds, was directly instrumental in insuring the success of subsequent operations of the 5th Amphibious Corps on Iwo Jima, thereby sustaining and enhancing the finest traditions of the U.S. Naval Service.

Note: The following is a newspaper account of the preceding battle for which Sgt. Cole, Cpl. Stein, Pfc. Ruhl, Pfc. Lucas, Capt. Dunlap, Sgt. Gray, Capt. McCarthy, and Col. Chambers were awarded the Medal of Honor:

AMERICANS STRIKE FROM IWO FOXHOLES

• • •

Marines Edge Ahead on Wings, Then Beat Off Japanese Night Counter-Attack.

• • •

IWO JIMA, Volcano Islands, Feb. 20 (11 A.M.) – The battle that may shorten the Iwo campaign began today when the Fourth and Fifth Marine Divisions came out of their foxholes, dug laboriously in the brittle volcanic ash, and attacked on both flanks in the face of heavy artillery and mortar fire.

The marines, who were in the narrow neck of Iwo yesterday, pushed south to envelop Mount Suribachi, grim, 511-foot volcanic cone whence enemy emplacements in caves and brown rock continue to pepper our beachhead despite fierce bombing and strafing. The Leathernecks now hold the southern airfield and are attempting to move northward into the boulder strewn badlands and Airfield No. 2.

The Japanese suffered minimum losses yesterday in the most overwhelming initial assault of the Pacific war. Only fifty enemy dead were counted, though there must be many more.

The American losses are severe in some sectors, but not so heavy as expected. Our progress yesterday, while satisfactory, was not what we had hoped.

The enemy counter-attacked conservatively at 2:30 A.M. today, sending about 500 men against our perimeter on the airfield. They hit what they might have considered a soft spot, but their attack was repulsed in a sharp battle fought under the cold light of starshells lofted over the island by our ships to expose enemy movements. [The blow was smashed by the Twenty-seventh Regiment.]

Throughout the night our ships poured harassing fire into enemy positions, hoping to keep the Japanese off balance and disorganized. The enemy answered occasionally. We could see their white tracers arching high toward the ships, but they landed harmlessly in the water.

The Japanese attempted a barge landing at 5 A.M. today. Twenty-five men got ten yards in and but then were wiped out.

Bloody Battle for Field

Two days of torturous fighting has given the United States Marines a strong toehold on Iwo from which to push the conquest of this strategic island to its final, expectedly bloody finish in the rocky northern terrain.

The southernmost of three shellpocked airfields fell to the leathernecks yesterday in a drive that at times caused heavy American casualties. Every yard of the way from the beachheads they met enemy fire.

The going was described as extremely tough on the right flank of the American line running from the northern slope of Suribachi to the curving east-west line, which traverses the northern end of the airfield runways and then dips down to the northern limit of the beachhead.

The Navy unleashed the power of its stand-by fleet, bombarding the island for the sixth straight day while the marines' own artillery began to function in strength. An entire battery under command of Captain James B. McDermott of Topeka, Kan., registered hits on caves on the steep sides of Suribachi.

Challenged in their strongest fortress this side of Honshu Island, and with the empire-guarding defense system threatened, thousands of Japanese are fighting back with everything at their command – with rockets, mortars, artillery, machine guns and the ever present sniper fire.

Early, on the third day of the invasion not a single enemy plane had penetrated the combat air patrol maintained around the island and the hundreds of ships that carried men and supplies to Iwo. Several Japanese aircraft attempted to attack the previous night, but were turned back by carrier-based fighters.

Mist and light rain fell yesterday and mixed with clouds and smoke. The weather still favored the Americans however.

Col. Harry B. Liversedge of Pine Grove, Calif., reported that there were pillboxes every ten feet in the sector around Suribachi.

But the marines are cracking Iwo; there's no mistaking that.

No Room for Both Sides

The Fifth Marine Division, with which I went ashore on Iwo on D-day, is little more than a year old and is fighting its first battle. But many of its men and officers are veterans of Pacific campaigns with other outfits. They behaved like veterans in this operation, the toughest of the war.

Coming in fast behind the terrific bombardment by Navy surface and aircraft on the south beaches under the shadow of the volcano of Mount Suribachi, they stalked swiftly up the ridges, their carbines and machine guns pitted against Japanese small arm and mortar fire that increased as the battle wore on.

While the Japanese, with mortars and artillery on the high ground to the south and north of the Fifth Division, plastered their supplies and reinforcements along the shore, our forward battalions attacked the vital airstrip, which will soon speed the work of the B-29's in their lathering of the Japanese homeland.

Iwo is part of the Japanese homeland. We are as close to Tokyo as to the nearest American naval base in the Pacific.

The first day and a half of fighting indicates that the Japanese garrison is one as strong as an island five miles by two will accommodate. Since two divisions of Marines as well are on it, someone has to give ground. Until now the enemy has done so, but grudgingly.

If the Japanese cannot hold this important base, which Vice Admiral Richmond Kelly Turner considers one of the strongest small defense points in the world, and are unwilling to send what is left of the Imperial Fleet to help, then the war in the Pacific has entered a new and epochal phase in which the sad conditions of Singapore and Java three years ago this month are directly reversed.

†**GRABIARZ, WILLIAM J.**
Rank and Organization: Private First Class, U.S. Army, Troop E, 5th Calvary, 1st Calvary Division.
Born: Buffalo, New York.
Entered Service At: Buffalo, New York.
Place and Date: Manila, Luzon, Philippine Islands, February 23, 1945.
Citation: Pfc. Grabiarz was a scout when the unit advanced with tanks along a street in Manila, Luzon, Philippine Islands. Without warning, enemy machinegun and rifle fire from concealed positions in the Customs building swept the street, striking down the troop commander and driving his men to cover. As the officer lay in the open road, unable to move and completely exposed to the point-blank enemy fire, Pfc. Grabiarz voluntarily ran from behind a tank to carry him to safety, but was himself wounded in the shoulder. Ignoring both the pain in his injured useless arm and his

comrades' shouts to seek the cover which was only a few yards distant, the valiant rescuer continued his efforts to drag his commander out of range. Finding this impossible, he rejected the opportunity to save himself and deliberately covered the officer with his own body to form a human shield, calling as he did so for a tank to maneuver into position between him and the hostile emplacement. The enemy riddled him with concentrated fire before the tank could interpose itself. Our troops found that he had been successful in preventing bullets from striking his leader, who survived. Through his magnificent sacrifice in gallantly giving his life to save that of his commander, Pfc. Grabiarz provided an outstanding and lasting inspiration to his fellow soldiers.

OFFICIAL COMMUNIQUE:
United Nations
ADVANCED HEADQUARTERS, on Luzon, Saturday, Feb. 24 – A communique:

PHILIPPINES

Our troops have seized Biri Island, at the eastern entrance of San Bernardino Strait. Luzon: In the Fourteenth Corps sector the destruction of the final remnants of the enemy's trapped garrison in South Manila is in its final phases. Troops of the Thirty seventh Division breached the walled city and in fierce hand-to-hand fighting are successfully seizing all remaining points of resistance. Among the brutalities practiced by the enemy during the clearing of Manila was the shelling of the internees at Santo Tomas several days after its recapture by the First Calvary Division. Casualties fortunately were very light and families have now all been informed. First Cavalry and Sixth Division units, pushing toward the Marikina watershed reservation, captured San Mateo and Taytay. Our air force was active throughout all sectors.
Visayas: Fighter-bombers attacked enemy concentrations on Cebu and Negros.
Mindanao: Heavy units and fighter-bombers struck Sasa and Licanan airdromes at Davao, dropping sixty-two tons of explosives followed by low-level strafing. Many fires and explosions were observed. At Surigao and Lumbia airfields to the north patrolling fighters exploded a fuel and ammunition dump, destroyed a parked plane and started fires.

WILLIAMS, HERSHEL WOODROW

Rank and Organization: Corporal, U.S. Marine Corps Reserve, 21st Marines, 3d Marine Division.
Born: October 2, 1923, Quiet Dell, West Virginia.
Entered Service At: West Virginia.
Place and Date: Iwo Jima, Volcano Islands, February 23, 1945.
Citation: For conspicuous gallantry and intrepidity at the risk of his life above and beyond the call of duty as demolition sergeant serving with the 21st Marines, 3d Marine Division, in action against enemy Japanese forces on Iwo Jima, Volcano Islands, February 23, 1945. Quick to volunteer his services when our tanks were maneuvering vainly to open a lane for the infantry through the network of reinforced concrete pillboxes, buried mines, and black volcanic sands, Cpl. Williams daringly went forward alone to attempt the reduction of devastating machinegun fire from the yielding positions. Covered only by 4 riflemen, he fought desperately for 4 hours under terrific enemy small-arms fire and repeatedly returned to his own lines to prepare demolition charges and obtain serviced flamethrowers, struggling back, frequently to the rear of hostile emplacements, to wipe out 1 position after another. On 1 occasion, he daringly mounted a pillbox to insert the nozzle of his flamethrower through the air vent, killing the occupants and silencing the gun; on another he grimly charged enemy riflemen who attempted to stop him with bayonets and destroyed them with a burst of flame from his weapon. His unyielding determination and extraordinary heroism in the face of ruthless enemy resistance were directly instrumental in neutralizing one of the most fanatically defended Japanese strong points encountered by his regiment and aided vitally in enabling his company to reach its objective. Cpl. Williams' aggressive fighting spirit and valiant devotion to duty throughout this fiercely contested action sustain and enhance the highest traditions of the U.S. Naval Service.

OFFICIAL COMMUNIQUE:
United States
ADVANCED HEADQUARTERS, Guam, Saturday, Feb. 24-Pacific Fleet communique 275:

(1) The Fifth Amphibious Corps attacking northward on Iwo Island made limited gains against elaborate enemy defenses by 1800 [6 P.M.] on Feb. 23 (East Longitude date). On the right flank the Fourth Marine Division advanced a maximum of 300 yards. In the center elements of the Third Marine Division occupied the southern tip of the central Iwo airfield. There was no appreciable change in the positions of the Fifth Marine Division on the left flank. In all sectors the enemy is resisting our advance from concrete pillboxes, entrenchments and caves.

(2) In the area of Mount Suribachi mopping-up operations are being carried out against block-houses and pillboxes on the slopes of the volcano. Similar defenses have been reported inside the crater. A total of 717 enemy dead have been counted in the Suribachi sector.

COOLEY, RAYMOND H.

Rank and Organization: Staff Sergeant, U.S. Army, Company B, 27th Infantry, 25th Infantry Division.
Born: May 7, 1914, Dunlap, Tennessee.
Entered Service At: Richard City, Tennessee.
Place and Date: Near Lumboy, Luzon, Philippine Islands, February 24, 1945.
Citation: S/Sgt. Cooley was a platoon guide in an assault on a camouflaged entrenchment defended by machineguns, rifles, and mortars. When his men were pinned down by 2 enemy machineguns, he voluntarily advanced under heavy fire to within 20 yards of 1 of the guns and attacked it with a handgrenade. The enemy, however, threw the grenade back at him before it could explode. Arming a second grenade, he held it for several seconds of the safe period and then hurled it into the enemy position, where it exploded instantaneously, destroying the gun and crew. He then moved toward the remaining gun, throwing grenades into enemy foxholes as he advanced. Inspired by his actions, 1 squad of his platoon joined him. After he had armed another grenade and was preparing to throw it into the second machinegun position, 6 enemy soldiers rushed at him. Knowing he could not dispose of the armed grenade without injuring his comrades, because of the intermingling in close combat of the men of his platoon and the enemy in the melee which ensued, he deliberately covered the grenade with his body and was severely wounded as it exploded. By his heroic actions, S/Sgt. Cooley not only silenced a machinegun and so inspired his fellow soldiers that they pressed the attack and destroyed the remaining enemy emplacements, but also, in complete disregard of his own safety, accepted certain injury and possible loss of life to avoid wounding his comrades.

OFFICIAL COMMUNIQUE:
United Nations
ADVANCED HEADQUARTERS, on Luzon, Sunday, Feb. 25 – A communique:

PHILIPPINES

Luzon: Troops of the Thirty-seventh Infantry and First Cavalry Divisions of the Fourteenth Corps overwhelmed the enemy's final positions in South Manila and completed the destruction of the trapped garrison.

More than 12,000 enemy bodies have already been counted in Manila, with many more to come. It was here the enemy apparently expected to turn the tide of battle in a supreme effort.

Three thousand civilians caught in the walled city and held there by this incorrigible enemy were successfully released by our troops in the final onslaught. They comprised many nationalities, the bulk being Filipinos. A number of Catholic priests and nuns were included. All had suffered unbelievable indignities and dangers.

This operation and the tremendous and disproportionate losses in men and material sustained during the progress of our advance through Luzon following the catastrophic defeat in Leyte dooms General Yamashita's Philippine campaign and presages the early clearance of the entire archipelago.

Elements of the First Cavalry and Sixth Divisions, driving into the Marikina watershed area, penetrated to within two miles of Montalban and reached Angono on the north shore of Laguna de Bay.

On Corregidor known enemy dead now total 2,309, while other enemy troops, estimated to be several thousand, have been destroyed underground by the blasting and closing of 132 tunnels. Nineteen serviceable motor torpedo boats of Q class have been captured around Corregidor.

In the First Corp sector units of the Twenty-fifth Division captured Pantanbangan in the Caraballo Mountains, ten miles north of Rizal. The Thirty-second and Thirty-third Divisions are probing northward.

Our attack bombers and fighters struck enemy concentrations south of Bagulo and in Baleta Pass. Others supported ground operations of the Eleventh and Fourteenth Corps.

JACOBSON, DOUGLAS THOMAS

Rank and Organization: Private First Class, U.S. Marine Corps Reserve, 3d Battalion, 23d Marines, 4th Marine Division.
Born: November 25, 1925, Rochester, New York.
Entered Service At: New York.
Place and Date: Iwo Jima, Volcano Islands, February 26, 1945.
Citation: For conspicuous gallantry and intrepidity at the risk of his life above and beyond the call of duty while serving with the 3d Battalion, 23d Marines, 4th Marine Division, in combat against enemy Japanese forces during the seizure of Iwo Jima in the Volcano Island, February 26, 1945.

Promptly destroying a stubborn 20-mm. antiaircraft gun and its crew after assuming the duties of a bazooka man who had been killed, Pfc. Jacobson waged a relentless battle as his unit fought desperately toward the summit of Hill 382 in an effort to penetrate the heart of Japanese cross-island defense. Employing his weapon with ready accuracy when his platoon was halted by overwhelming enemy fire on February 26, he first destroyed 2 hostile machinegun positions, then attacked a large blockhouse, completely neutralizing the fortification before dispatching the 5-man crew of a second pillbox and exploding the installation with a terrific demolitions blast. Moving steadily forward, he wiped out an earth-covered rifle emplacement and, confronted by a cluster of similar emplacements which constituted the perimeter of enemy defenses in his assigned sector, fearlessly advanced, quickly reduced all 6 positions to a shambles, killed 10 of the enemy, and enabled our forces to occupy the strong point. Determined to widen the breach thus forced, he volunteered his services to an adjacent assault company, neutralized a pillbox holding up its advance, opened fire on a Japanese tank pouring a steady stream of bullets on 1 of our supporting tanks, and smashed the enemy tank's gun turret in a brief but furious action culminating in a singlehanded assault against still another blockhouse and the subsequent neutralization of its firepower. By his dauntless skill and valor, Pfc. Jacobson destroyed a total of 16 enemy positions and annihilated approximately 75 Japanese, thereby contributing essentially to the success of his division's operations against this fanatically defended outpost of the Japanese Empire. His gallant conduct in the face of tremendous odds enhanced and sustained the highest traditions of the U.S. Naval Service.

WATSON, WILSON DOUGLAS
Rank and Organization: Private, U.S. Marine Corps Reserve, 2d Battalion, 9th Marines, 3d Marine Division.
Born: February 18, 1921, Tuscumbia, Alabama.
Entered Service At: Arkansas.
Place and Date: Iwo Jima, Volcano Islands, February 26-27, 1945.
Citation: For conspicuous gallantry and intrepidity at the risk of his life above and beyond the call of duty as automatic rifleman serving with the 2d Battalion, 9th Marines, 3d Marine Division, during action against enemy Japanese forces on Iwo Jima, Volcano Islands, February 26-27, 1945. With his squad abruptly halted by intense fire from the enemy fortifications in the high rocky ridges and crags commanding the line of advance, Pvt. Watson boldly rushed 1 pillbox and fired into the embrasure with his

weapon, keeping the enemy pinned down singlehandedly until he was in a position to hurl in a grenade, and then running to the rear of the emplacement to destroy the retreating Japanese and enable his platoon to take its objective. Again pinned down at the foot of a small hill, he dauntlessly scaled the jagged incline under fierce mortar and machinegun barrages and, with his assistant BAR man, charged the crest of the hill, firing from his hip. Fighting furiously against Japanese troops attacking with grenades and knee mortars from the reverse slope, he stood fearlessly erect in his exposed position to cover the hostile entrenchments and held the hill under savage fire for 15 minutes, killing 60 Japanese before his ammunition was exhausted and his platoon was able to join him. His courageous initiative and valiant fighting spirit against devastating odds were directly responsible for the continued advance of his platoon, and his inspiring leadership throughout this bitterly fought action reflects the highest credit upon Pvt. Watson and the U.S. Naval Service.

OFFICIAL COMMUNIQUE:
United States
GUAM, Tuesday, Feb. 27-Pacific Fleet Communique 280:

(1) Elements of the Third Marine Division, constituting the center of our lines on Iwo Island, advanced about 400 yards through extremely heavy enemy defenses on Feb. 26 (East Longitude date), seized the high ground of the central plateau and by nightfall brought most of the island's second airfield into our possession.
Fighting along the entire line was very heavy, with enemy resistance mounting before our attack throughout the day. Our troops were subjected to artillery and rocket fire and a very heavy volume of small-arms fire during the advance.
The Fourth Marine Division on the east and the Fifth Marine Division on the west advanced during the day, the Fourth Division capturing a commanding hill near the east coast. The attack by our forces was supported by marine artillery, naval gunfire and carrier aircraft.
(2) Mopping-up operations continued in the south around Mount Suribachi. Little enemy fire fell on the interior of our beachhead during the day.
(3) By 1200 [noon] of Feb. 26 our forces counted 3,568 enemy dead and nine enemy prisoners in eight days of fighting on Iwo Island.
(4) Marine observation planes, the first United States aircraft to land, began operating on the southern Iwo airstrip during the morning while restoration of the runways to operational conditions continued.
(5) Supplies and equipment were landed in increasing quantities as road and beach conditions continued to improve.
(6) Carrier aircraft strafed targets in and around Chichi Jima [Island] in the Bonins,

burning one plane on the ground, sinking a small merchant vessel and burning two medium merchant ships. Oil storage facilities were destroyed.

†WALLACE, HERMAN C.
Rank and Organization: Private First Class, U.S. Army, Company B, 301st Engineer Combat Battalion, 76th Infantry Division.
Born: Marlow, Oklahoma.
Entered Service At: Lubbock, Texas.
Place and Date: Near Prumzurley, Germany, February 27, 1945.
Citation: Pfc. Wallace displayed conspicuous gallantry and intrepidity above and beyond the call of duty. While helping clear enemy mines from a road, he stepped on a well-concealed S-type antipersonnel mine. Hearing the characteristic noise indicating that the mine had been activated and, if he stepped aside, would be thrown upward to explode above ground and spray the area with fragments, surely killing 2 comrades directly behind him and endangering other members of his squad, he deliberately placed his other foot on the mine even though his best chance for survival was to fall prone. Pvt. Wallace was killed when the charge detonated, but his supreme heroism at the cost of his life confined the blast to the ground and his own body and saved his fellow soldiers from death or injury.

OFFICIAL COMMUNIQUE:
United Nations
PARIS, Feb. 27-Communique 325 of Supreme Headquarters, Allied Expeditionary Force:

Allied infantry supported by tanks advanced against strong opposition to Keppeln, southwest of Calcar, where heavy fighting continues.

Enemy gun positions west of Xanten were attacked by medium bombers. East of the Roer our troops have made further good progress. In the area north of Linnich we have captured Golkrath, Granterath and Kuckhoven. Northeast of Juelich we have occupied Ameln and Oberembt and to the east most of the Hambach Forest is in our hands.

In the Juelich-Dueren area we have reached the outskirts of Elsdorf and have entered Blatzheim, Eschweiler and Frauwuellesheim. A number of towns were captured, including Buir, Golzheim, Rommersheim, Drove and Boich. Dueren has been completely cleared of the enemy. Resistance in the area was centered mainly in the towns.

Armored elements have crossed the Nims River in the vicinity of Bitburg. In this area we have captured Liessem, Oberweis, Bettingen and Messerich and have entered Wolfeld. A strong enemy counter-attack was repulsed six miles southwest of Bitburg.

Northeast of Saarburg our armored units have cleared Schoden and we have reached a point five and a half miles east of Saarburg. We repulsed a strong tank-supported counter-attack five miles east of Saarburg.

North of Forbach our forces repulsed two attacks near Stiring-Wendel. Enemy patrols were turned back in the northern Alsace plain and farther south along the west bank of the Rhine.

Allied forces in the west captured 3,500 prisoners on Feb. 24.

†WALSH, WILLIAM GARY

Rank and Organization: Gunnery Sergeant, U.S. Marine Corps Reserve.
Born: April 7, 1922, Roxbury, Massachusetts.
Entered Service At: Massachusetts.
Place and Date: Iwo Jima, Volcano Islands, February 27, 1945.
Citation: For extraordinary gallantry and intrepidity at the risk of his life above and beyond the call of duty as leader of an assault platoon, attached to Company G, 3d Battalion, 27th Marines, 5th Marine Division, in action against enemy Japanese forces at Iwo Jima, Volcano Islands, on February 27, 1945. With the advance of his company toward Hill 362 disrupted by vicious machinegun fire from a forward position which guarded the approaches to this key enemy stronghold, G/Sgt. Walsh fearlessly charged at the head of his platoon against the Japanese entrenched on the ridge above him, utterly oblivious to the unrelenting fury of hostile automatic weapons fire and handgrenades employed with fanatic desperation to smash his daring assault. Thrown back by the enemy's savage resistance, he once again led his men in a seemingly impossible attack up the steep, rocky slope, boldly defiant of the annihilating streams of bullets which saturated the area. Despite his own casualty losses and the overwhelming advantage held by the Japanese in superior numbers and dominant position, he gained the ridge's top only to be subjected to an intense barrage of handgrenades thrown by the remaining Japanese staging a suicidal last stand on the reverse slope. When 1 of the grenades fell in the midst of his surviving men, huddled together in a small trench, G/Sgt. Walsh, in a final valiant act of complete self-sacrifice, instantly threw himself upon the deadly bomb, absorbing with his own body the full and terrific force of the explosion. Through his extraordinary initiative and inspiring valor in the face of almost certain death, he saved his comrades from injury and possible loss of life and enabled his company to seize and hold this vital enemy position. He gallantly have his life for his country.

†WILLIS, JOHN HARLAN

Rank and Organization: Pharmacist's Mate First Class, U.S. Navy.
Born: June 10, 1921, Columbia, Tennessee.
Entered Service At: Tennessee.
Place and Date: Iwo Jima, Volcano Islands, February 28, 1945.
Citation: For conspicuous gallantry and intrepidity at the risk of his life above and beyond the call of duty as Platoon Corpsman serving with the 3d Battalion, 27th Marines, 5th Marine Division, during operations against enemy Japanese forces on Iwo Jima, Volcano Islands, February 28, 1945. Constantly imperiled by artillery and mortar fire from strong and mutually supporting pillboxes and caves studding Hill 362 in the enemy's cross-island defenses, Willis resolutely administered first aid to the many marines wounded during the furious close-in fighting until he himself was struck by shrapnel and was ordered back to the battle-aid station. Without waiting for official medical release, he quickly returned to his company and, during a savage hand-to-hand enemy counterattack, daringly advanced to the extreme frontlines under mortar and sniper fire to aid a marine lying wounded in a shellhole. Completely unmindful of his own danger as the Japanese intensified their attack, Willis calmly continued to administer blood plasma to his patient, promptly returning the first hostile grenade which landed in the shell-hole while he was working and hurling back 7 more in quick succession before the ninth 1 exploded in his hand and instantly killed him. By his great personal valor in saving others at the sacrifice of his life, he inspired his companions, although terrifically outnumbered, to launch a fiercely determined attack and repulse the enemy force. His exceptional fortitude and courage in the performance of duty reflect the highest credit upon Willis and the U.S. Naval Service. He gallantly gave his life for his country.

Note: The following is a newspaper account of the preceding battle for which Sgt. Walsh and Pharmacist's Mate First Class Willis were awarded the Medal of Honor:

3-PLY MARINE PUSH
WINS MORE OF IWO

• • •

Ground Gained in Center and East –
Navy Backs Attack – Enemy on Airstrip Tip

• • •

GUAM, Wednesday, Feb. 28 – Two of the three marine divisions battling side by side toward the high north part of Iwo gnawed out small gains yesterday through thickly studded Japanese defenses, but enemy resistance remains high and still includes tanks after nine days of ceaseless hammering.

The Japanese grimly clung to one tip of the central airfield after a week of flaming action concentrated on and around that two-runway fighter base.

Admiral Chester W. Nimitz announced in a communique today that the marines resumed a power-packed push from the south half of Iwo yesterday morning after artillery had broken up a tank-led counter-attack on Monday night. Enemy infiltration attempts were repulsed.

The gains were registered in the center by Maj. Gen. Graves B. Erskine's Third Division, which holds virtually all of the central airfield, and on the east shore by Maj. Gen. Clifton B. Cates' Fourth Division.

No mention was made of any gain on the west by Maj. Gen. Keller E. Rockey's Fifth Division.

Warships Aid Strike

The fiercely resisted advance was supported by marine artillery, carrier-based planes and warships of the Fifth Fleet.

Mortar units blew up two Japanese ammunition dumps to further lessen the fighting power of a garrison that is receiving no reinforcements, no naval support and little support from the air.

The Third Division has counted 800 enemy pillboxes in its zone of action, indicating the tough type of battle that must be waged.

Land-based Army Liberators, flying from the Marianas, joined with carrier planes in bombing Japanese Iwo positions on Tuesday.

Other Seventh Force Liberators attacked the Bonin Islands north of Iwo.

General Erskine's Third Division straightened its line north and west of the central airfield. The enemy fingertip grasp is on the northeast corner.

Just east of those Japanese, the Fourth Division pushed bulges into enemy lines right and left of seized Hill No. 382.

The Japanese are running short of water and probably of food and ammunition. In contrast, American supply forces are landing ammunition, water and food.

The enemy still has considerable artillery and mortar in action. Their fire was heavy throughout yesterday, some of it directed at rear areas and the unloading beaches.

Admiral Nimitz' communique bristled with terms that left no doubt about the viciousness of the fight that has raged for more than a week on this volcanic island at the southern threshold of Japan.

The Pacific areas commander, who believes in powerhouse tactics, gave an idea of what the devildogs are up against by such descriptive terms as "extremely heavy enemy defenses," "very heavy" fighting, "enemy resistance mounting" and "a very heavy volume of small arms fire."

One Airstrip Already in Use

Iwo's most important airdrome, the bomber field near the southern end of the island, already was being used by Marine observation planes. Later, this field will mount medium, heavy and superfort forays against Tokyo.

Mopping up continued along fortress - Mount Suribachi, now firmly in American hands. Tokyo, which only Monday claimed the peak had been recaptured, yesterday conceded loss of the whole southern area. The enemy radio, however, broadcast that its southern force had broken through the Yank lines to rejoin Japanese locked in a death struggle in the northern sector.

Enemy dead totaling 3,568 had been counted up to noon Monday, Admiral Nimitz reported. Nine Japanese had been taken prisoner –the first report in eight days of fighting that any of them had surrendered.

†BERRY, CHARLES JOSEPH
Rank and Organization: Corporal, U.S. Marine Corps.
Born: July 10, 1923, Lorain, Ohio.
Entered Service At: Ohio.
Place and Date: Iwo Jima, Volcano Islands, March 3, 1945.
Citation: For conspicuous gallantry and intrepidity at the risk of his life above and beyond the call of duty as a member of a machinegun crew, serving with the 1st Battalion, 26th Marines, 5th Marine Division, in action against enemy Japanese forces during the seizure of Iwo Jima in the Volcano Islands, on March 3, 1945. Stationed in the front lines, Cpl. Berry manned his weapon with alert readiness as he maintained a constant vigil with other members of his guncrew during the hazardous night hours. When infiltrating Japanese soldiers launched a surprise attack shortly after midnight in an attempt to overrun his position, he engaged in a pitched handgrenade duel, returning the dangerous weapons with prompt and deadly accuracy until an enemy grenade landed in the foxhole. Determined to save his comrades, he unhesitatingly chose to sacrifice himself and immediately dived on the deadly missile, absorbing the shattering violence of the exploding charge in his own body and protecting the others from serious injury. Stouthearted and indomitable, Cpl. Berry fearlessly yielded his own life that his fellow marines might carry on the relentless battle against a

ruthless enemy and his superb valor and unfaltering devotion to duty in the face of certain death reflect the highest credit upon the U.S. Naval Service. He gallantly gave his life for his country.

†CADDY, WILLIAM ROBERT

Rank and Organization: Private First Class, U.S. Marine Corps Reserve.
Born: August 8, 1925, Quincy, Massachusetts.
Entered Service At: Massachusetts.
Place and Date: Iwo Jima, Volcano Islands, March 3, 1945.
Citation: For conspicuous gallantry and intrepidity at the risk of his life above and beyond the call of duty while serving as a rifleman with Company I, 3d Battalion, 26th Marines, 5th Marine Division, in action against enemy Japanese forces during the seizure of Iwo Jima in the Volcano Islands, March 3, 1945. Consistently aggressive, Pfc. Caddy boldly defied shattering Japanese machinegun and small-arms fire to move forward with his platoon leader and another marine during the determined advance of his company through an isolated sector and, gaining the comparative safety of a shell hole, took temporary cover with his comrades. Immediately pinned down by deadly sniper fire from a well-concealed position, he made several unsuccessful attempts to again move forward and then, joined by his platoon leader, engaged the enemy in a fierce exchange of handgrenades until a Japanese grenade fell beyond reach in the shell hole. Fearlessly disregarding all personal danger, Pfc. Caddy instantly dived on the deadly missile, absorbing the exploding charge in his own body and protecting the others from serious injury. Stouthearted and indomitable, he unhesitatingly yielded his own life that his fellow marines might carry on the relentless battle against a fanatic enemy. His dauntless courage and valiant spirit of self-sacrifice in the face of certain death reflect the highest credit upon Pfc. Caddy and upon the U.S. Naval Service. He gallantly gave his life for his comrades.

HARRELL, WILLIAM GEORGE

Rank and Organization: Sergeant, U.S. Marine Corps, 1st Battalion, 28th Marines, 5th Marine Division.
Born: June 26, 1922, Rio Grande City, Texas.
Entered Service At: Mercedes, Texas.
Place and Date: Iwo Jima, Volcano Islands, March 3, 1945.
Citation: For conspicuous gallantry and intrepidity at the risk of his life above and beyond the call of duty as leader of an assault group attached to

the 1st Battalion, 28th Marines, 5th Marine Division during hand-to-hand combat with enemy Japanese at Iwo Jima, Volcano Islands, on March 3, 1945. Standing watch alternately with another marine in a terrain studded with caves and ravines, Sgt. Harrell was holding a position in a perimeter defense around the company command post when Japanese troops infiltrated our lines in the early hours of dawn. Awakened by a sudden attack, he quickly opened fire with his carbine and killed 2 of the enemy as they emerged from a ravine in the light of a shellburst. Unmindful of his danger as hostile grenades fell closer, he waged a fierce lone battle until an exploding missile tore off his left hand and fractured his thigh. He was vainly attempting to reload the carbine when his companion returned from the command post with another weapon. Wounded again by a Japanese who rushed the foxhole wielding a saber in the darkness, Sgt. Harrell succeeded in drawing his pistol and killing his opponent and then ordered his wounded companion to a place of safety. Exhausted by profuse bleeding but still unbeaten, he fearlessly met the challenge of 2 more enemy troops who charged his position and placed a grenade near his head. Killing 1 man with his pistol, he grasped the sputtering grenade with his good right hand, and, pushing it painfully toward the crouching soldier, saw his remaining assailant destroyed but his own hand severed in the explosion. At dawn Sgt. Harrell was evacuated from a position hedged by the bodies of 12 dead Japanese, at least 5 of whom he had personally destroyed in his self-sacrificing defense of the command post. His grim fortitude, exceptional valor, and indomitable fighting spirit against almost insurmountable odds reflect the highest credit upon himself and enhance the finest traditions of the U.S. Naval Service.

WAHLEN, GEORGE EDWARD

Rank and Organization: Pharmacist's Mate Second Class, U.S. Navy, serving with 2d Battalion, 26th Marines, 5th Marine Division.
Born: August 8, 1924, Ogden, Utah.
Entered Service At: Utah.
Place and Date: Iwo Jima, Volcano Islands, March 3, 1945.
Citation: For conspicuous gallantry and intrepidity at the risk of his life above and beyond the call of duty while serving with the 2d Battalion, 26th Marines, 5th Marine Division, during action against enemy Japanese forces on Iwo Jima, in the Volcano group on March 3, 1945. Painfully wounded in the bitter action on February 26, Wahlen remained on the battlefield, advancing well forward of the front lines to aid a wounded marine and carrying him back to safety despite a terrific concentration of fire. Tireless in his

ministrations, he consistently disregarded all danger to attend his fighting comrades as they fell under the devastating rain of shrapnel and bullets, and rendered prompt assistance to various elements of his combat group as required. When an adjacent platoon suffered heavy casualties, he defied the continuous pounding of heavy mortars and deadly fire of enemy rifles to care for the wounded, working rapidly in an area swept by constant fire and treating 14 casualties before returning to his own platoon. Wounded again on March 2, he gallantly refused evacuation, moving out with his company the following day in a furious assault across 600 yards of open terrain and repeatedly rendering medical aid while exposed to the blasting fury of powerful Japanese guns. Stouthearted and indomitable, he persevered in his determined efforts as his unit waged fierce battle and, unable to walk after sustaining a third agonizing wound, resolutely crawled 50 yards to administer first aid to still another fallen fighter. By his doubtless fortitude and valor, Wahlen served as a constant inspiration and contributed vitally to the high morale of his company during critical phases of this strategically important engagement. His heroic spirit of self-sacrifice in the face of overwhelming enemy fire upheld the highest traditions of the U.S. Naval Service.

†WILLIAMS, JACK

Rank and Organization: Pharmacist's Mate Third Class, U.S. Naval Reserve.
Born: October 18, 1924, Harrison, Arkansas.
Entered Service At: Arkansas.
Place and Date: Iwo Jima, Volcano Islands, March 3, 1945.
Citation: For conspicuous gallantry and intrepidity at the risk of his life above and beyond the call of duty while serving with the 3d Battalion, 28th Marines, 5th Marine Division, during the occupation of Iwo Jima, Volcano Islands, March 3, 1945. Gallantly going forward on the frontlines under intense enemy small-arms fire to assist a marine wounded in a fierce grenade battle, Williams dragged the man to a shallow depression and was kneeling, using his own body as a screen from the sustained fire as he administered first aid, when struck in the abdomen and groin 3 times by hostile rifle fire. Momentarily stunned, he quickly recovered and completed his ministration before applying battle dressing to his own multiple wounds. Unmindful of his own urgent need for medical attention, he remained in the perilous fire-swept area to care for another marine casualty. Heroically completing his task despite pain and profuse bleeding, he then endeavored to make his way to the rear in search of adequate aid for himself when

struck down by a Japanese sniper bullet which caused his collapse. Succumbing later as a result of his self-sacrificing service to others, Williams, by his courageous determination, unwavering fortitude and valiant performance of duty, served as an inspiring example of heroism, in keeping with highest traditions of the U.S. Naval Service. He gallantly gave his life for his country.

Note: The following is a newspaper account of the preceding battle for which Cpl. Berry, Pfc. Caddy, Sgt. Harrell, Pharmacist's Mate Wahlen, and Pharmacist's Mate Williams were awarded the Medal of Honor:

MARINES ADVANCE
400 YARDS ON IWO

• • •

Deepen Salient Threatening to Cut Enemy in Two Despite Heavy Fire – Flank Lags

• • •

GUAM, Sunday, March 4 – Struggling forward under intense enemy fire that shows little decrease as yet, the Marines made further gains on Iwo, Admiral Chester W. Nimitz announced in his communique today covering operations to 6 P.M. yesterday.

While mortars and rifles poured in a furious blast from the Japanese lines, the Fifth Marine Division on the left flank and the Third Marines in the center pushed for ward 200 to 400 yards in desperate fighting up, into and around stout pillboxes and other defenses.

[The Third Marine Division drove to within 300 yards of the edge of cliffs sloping down to the sea on the northeastern coast of Iwo in a move to cut the Japanese garrison in two, The Associated Press said.

[The Japanese are compressed into a gourd-shaped area around Iwo's northeastern and northern rim. The area is 1,500 yards wide at the widest point on the east and 1,400 yards at the widest point on the north.]

Fourth's Task Is Toughest

Our men were helped to some extent by artillery dropping shells closely ahead of our lines and airplanes plummeting down release bombs on Japanese nests, but these aids have not diminished the deadly flow of bullets from the enemy.

The hardest of all the positions remaining to be taken by the marines is the northeast sector allotted to the Fourth division. Ahead of the Fourth's lines are terraces covered with low, sparse, vividly green vegetation, just enough to color the ground, but not enough to cover the men. Ahead, dimly observable, lies Higashi, thatched-roof village of a few houses. Throughout the vegetation, pillboxes and other strongpoints, jammed with Japanese, await inevitable capture. An exceptionally strong pocket of Japanese in the Fourth's sector, near Minami, is proving tough. There, although the marines have attacked again and again, the enemy has not budged.

Wounded Evacuated by Air

As proof, however, that we are on "the last mile," came a reassuring report on beach supplies. Up to now this has been a bitter matter. Today's communique disclosed that we are handling food, munitions and guns on both the west and east beaches of the island. And the boys are moving supplies straight to the line where they are needed.

Another encouraging item was the fact that Seabees and marines have patched the southern Iwo airfield to the point where it is nearing full use. For example bit transport planes are now landing to evacuate wounded who are flown back to other points where greater hospitalization is obtainable.

While the Iwo operations have driven forward, carrier airplanes swung off our ships and hit the town of Omura on Chichi Island and harbor installations at Haha, both in the Bonins. At Haha our bombs hit a small ship lying offshore and when the planes turned to administer a second dose the ship was going down nicely.

On Friday Omura and its airfield were heavily bombed by Seventh Army Air Force Liberators. Two bridges were destroyed and fires were started.

Thunderbolts hit the airfield on Pagan in the Marianas on Saturday, while twenty-four hours earlier Navy search Venturas of Fleet Air Wing 2 pock-marked the airstrip on Wake Island, while marine fliers were on neutralizing missions over enemy bases in the Marshalls.

'Phantoms' Around Caves

The Japanese on Iwo are by no means "through." They have the capacity still to inflict many casualties – which they are doing as the marines fight their way deeper into the enemy's last ditch defenses.

Late yesterday afternoon about 150 Japanese rushed our left flank held on the western side of the island. The attack was repulsed and most of the Japanese were killed. As evening approached at an hour when both sides usually solidify positions for the night another counter-attack hit the marines in the center. It, too, was thrown back.

There was some infiltration Thursday night in the front lines and down near Mount Suribachi far behind the front, where some Japanese hurled a few grenades. Any outfit here can tell a story of sudden attack by the Japanese appearing like phantoms among caves that the marines believed they had cleared some time before. This is a long-familiar experience with veteran marine divisions.

A curious point of interest on Motoyama Airfield No. 1 is a captured wooden sign transplanted from Airfield No. 2. In black lettering over white paint it warns in both Japanese and English that there must be no trespassing, photographing and so forth on the airfield premises without official permission – by order of the Ministry of the Navy in October, 1937.

American planes dropped propaganda leaflets yesterday behind the enemy lines. However, there is apparently no civilian problem here, as on Saipan. In fact, Iwo is an older and closer part of the empire than the Marianas were. No civilians have been seen to date. They probably were evacuated.

LEIMS, JOHN HAROLD

Rank and Organization: Second Lieutenant, U.S. Marine Corps Reserve, Company B, 1st Battalion, 9th Marines, 3d Marine Division.
Born: June 8, 1921, Chicago, Illinois.
Entered Service At: Chicago, Illinois.
Place and Date: Iwo Jima, Volcano Islands, March 7, 1945.
Citation: For conspicuous gallantry and intrepidity at the risk of his life above and beyond the call of duty as commanding officer of Company B, 1st Battalion, 9th Marines, 3d Marine Division, in action against enemy Japanese forces on Iwo Jima in the Volcano Islands, March 7, 1945. Launching a surprise attack against the rock-imbedded fortifications of a dominating Japanese hill position, 2d Lt. Leims spurred his company forward with indomitable determination and, skillfully directing his assault platoons against the cave-emplaced enemy troops and heavily fortified pillboxes, succeeded in capturing the objective in the late afternoon. When it became apparent that his assault platoons were cut off in this newly won position, approximately 400 yards forward of adjacent units and lacked all communication with the command post, he personally advanced and laid telephone lines across the isolated expanse of open, fire-swept terrain. Ordered to withdraw his command after he had joined his forward platoons he immediately complied, arriving at the rear, he was informed that several casualties had been left at the abandoned ridge position beyond the frontlines. Although suffering acutely from the strain and exhaustion of battle, he instantly went forward despite darkness and the slashing fury of hostile machinegun fire, located and carried to safety 1 seriously wounded marine

and then, running the gauntlet of enemy fire for the third time that night, again made his tortuous way into the bullet-riddled deathtrap and rescued another of his wounded men. A dauntless leader, concerned at all times for the welfare of his men, 2d Lt. Leims soundly maintained the coordinated strength of his battle-wearied company under extremely difficult conditions and, by his bold tactics, sustained aggressiveness, and heroic disregard of all personal danger, contributed essentially to the success of his division's operations against this vital Japanese base. His valiant conduct in the face of fanatic opposition sustains and enhances the highest traditions of the U.S. Naval Service.

†LaBELLE, JAMES DENNIS

Rank and Organization: Private First Class, U.S. Marine Corps Reserve.
Born: November 22, 1925, Columbia Heights, Minnesota.
Entered Service At: Minnesota.
Place and Date: Iwo Jima, Volcano Islands, March 8, 1945.
Citation: For conspicuous gallantry and intrepidity at the risk of his life above and beyond the call of duty while attached to the 27th Marines, 5th Marine Division, in action against enemy Japanese forces during the seizure of Iwo Jima in the Volcano Islands, March 8, 1945. Filling a gap in the front lines during a critical phase of the battle, Pfc. LaBelle had dug into a foxhole with 2 other marines and, grimly aware of the enemy's persistent attempts to blast a way through our lines with handgrenades, applied himself with steady concentration to maintaining a sharply vigilant watch during the hazardous night hours. Suddenly a hostile grenade landed beyond reach in his foxhole. Quickly estimating the situation, he determined to save the others if possible, shouted a warning, and instantly dived on the deadly missile, absorbing the exploding charge in his own body and thereby protecting his comrades from serious injury. Stouthearted and indomitable, he had unhesitatingly relinquished his own chance of survival that his fellow marines might carry on the relentless fight against a fanatic enemy. His dauntless courage, cool decision and valiant spirit of self-sacrifice in the face of certain death reflect the highest credit upon Pfc. LaBelle and upon the U.S. Naval Service. He gallantly gave his life in the service of his country.

†LUMMUS, JACK

Rank and Organization: First Lieutenant, U.S. Marine Corps Reserve.
Born: October 22, 1915, Ennie, Texas.
Entered Service At: Texas.
Place and Date: Iwo Jima, Volcano Islands, March 8, 1945.
Citation: For conspicuous gallantry and intrepidity at the risk of his life above and beyond the call of duty as leader of a Rifle Platoon attached to the 2d Battalion, 27th Marines, 5th Marine Division, in action against enemy Japanese forces on Iwo Jima in the Volcano Islands, March 8, 1945. Resuming his assault tactics with bold decision after fighting without respite for 2 days and nights, 1st Lt. Lummus slowly advanced his platoon against an enemy deeply entrenched in a network of mutually supporting positions. Suddenly halted by a terrific concentration of hostile fire, he unhesitatingly moved forward of his front lines in an effort to neutralize the Japanese position. Although knocked to the ground when an enemy grenade exploded close by, he immediately recovered himself and, again moving forward despite the intensified barrage, quickly located, attacked, and destroyed the occupied emplacement. Instantly taken under fire by the garrison of a supporting pillbox and further assailed by the slashing fury of hostile rifle fire, he fell under the impact of a second enemy grenade but, courageously disregarding painful shoulder wounds, staunchly continued his heroic 1-man assault and charged the second pillbox, annihilating all the occupants. Subsequently returning to his platoon position, he fearlessly traversed his lines under fire, encouraging his men to advance and directing the fire of supporting tanks against other stubbornly holding Japanese emplacements. Held up again by a devastating barrage, he again moved into the open, rushed a third heavily fortified installation and killed the defending troops. Determined to crush all resistance, he led his men indomitably, personally attacking foxholes and spider traps with his carbine and systematically reducing the fanatic opposition, until, stepping on a land mine, he sustained fatal wounds. By his outstanding valor, skilled tactics, and tenacious perseverance in the face of overwhelming odds, 1st Lt. Lummus had inspired his stouthearted marines to continue the relentless drive northward, thereby contributing materially to the success of his regimental mission. His dauntless leadership and unwavering devotion to duty throughout sustain and enhance the highest traditions of the U.S. Naval Service. He gallantly gave his life in the service of his country.

†JULIAN, JOSEPH RODOLPH

Rank and Organization: Platoon Sergeant, U.S. Marine Corps Reserve.
Born: April 3, 1918, Sturbridge, Massachusetts.
Entered Service At: Massachusetts.
Place and Date: Iwo Jima, Volcano Islands, March 9, 1945.
Citation: For conspicuous gallantry and intrepidity at the risk of his life above and beyond the call of duty as a P/Sgt. serving with the 1st Battalion, 27th Marines, 5th Marine Division, in action against enemy Japanese forces during the seizure of Iwo Jima in the Volcano Islands, March 9, 1945. Determined to force a breakthrough when Japanese troops occupying trenches and fortified positions on the left front laid down a terrific machinegun and mortar barrage in a desperate effort to halt his company's advance, P/Sgt. Julian quickly established his platoon's guns in strategic supporting positions, and then, acting on his own initiative, fearlessly moved forward to execute a 1-man assault on the nearest pillbox. Advancing alone, he hurled deadly demolitions and white phosphorus grenades into the emplacement, killing 2 of the enemy and driving the remaining 5 out into the adjoining trench system. Seizing a discarded rifle, he jumped into the trench and dispatched the 5 before they could make an escape. Intent on wiping out all resistance, he obtained more explosives and, accompanied by another marine, again charged the hostile fortifications and knocked out 2 more cave positions. Immediately thereafter, he launched a bazooka attack unassisted, firing 4 rounds into the 1 remaining pillbox and completely destroying it before he fell, mortally wounded by a vicious burst of enemy fire. Stouthearted and indomitable, P/Sgt. Julian consistently disregarded all personal danger and, by his bold decision, daring tactics, and relentless fighting spirit during a critical phase of the battle, contributed materially to the continued advance of his company and to the success of his division's operations in the sustained drive toward the conquest of this fiercely defended outpost of the Japanese Empire. His outstanding valor and unfaltering spirit of self-sacrifice throughout the bitter conflict sustained and enhanced the highest traditions of the U.S. Naval Service. He gallantly gave his life for his country.

Note: The following is a newspaper account of the preceding battle for which 2d Lt. Leims, Pfc. LaBelle, Lt. Lummus, and Sgt. Julian were awarded the Medal of Honor:

MARINES HEW OUT 500-YARD GAINS
IN HAND-TO-HAND FIGHTING ON IWO

• • •

GUAM, Thursday, March 8 – The fighting on Iwo Island has reached the hand-to-hand stage as the tired marines battle desperately to bring the prolonged encounter to an end.

The Japanese, fighting equally furiously, continue to hang on to each acre of land, but are slowly being pushed back. Today's communique from Admiral Chester W. Nimitz showed the largest forward push by the marines in three days, but there was no claim that Japanese defenses had finally cracked.

On the northwest shoulder of the island the Fifth Marine Division fought its way down ridges sloping to the sea, gaining as much as 500 yards at one point on the extreme left of the American line, with smaller gains registered in the center and right.

The Third Marine Division, which entered the battle as reserves on D-day plus two, and has borne the brunt of the offensive since then, hacked out an equal 500-yard gain on its front between the Fifth and Fourth Marines in the center of the island.

Veterans of the Bougainville and Guam campaigns knocked out Japanese pillboxes with grenades, wrestled and bayoneted the enemy as he was driven from caves.

The Fourth Division, holding the line to the east, made advances of 400 to 200 yards in local areas, but in other places gained not all in the face of intense enemy small-arms and machine-gun fire that the Japanese are now using in place of mortar fire in the earlier stages of the campaign.

The possibility now is that the Japanese are running out of mortars either as a result of their being knocked out by our bombardment or because they are short of mortar ammunition as a result of the stores in caves we have overrun or captured.

There is no danger of the Americans on the island running short. Weather conditions have continued to improve and the landing of supplies is now almost routine.

While the fighting is going on, transport planes continue to evacuate the wounded at an increasing pace from the southernmost airfield. This field is also being used by Army fighter planes.

Carrier planes of the fleet, still supporting the Iwo operation, continue using rockets as well as bombs.

Enemy cargo ships supplying the Bonins came in for their share of attention. A Liberator search plane, looking for just such a target, found it after hours of roaming the lonesome seas, once full of Japanese shipping. It found three enemy vessels and bombed one and strafed two north of the Bonins on March 6. The damage was not specified.

Miles to south, Fourth Marine aircraft Wing Corsair, Hellcat and Avenger torpedo planes destroyed a bridge and set buildings afire in bomb and rocket attacks on the Palaus on March 6.

Other marine planes hit installations on Yap, in the western Carolines, the same day, as well as Ponape, in the eastern Carolines. Moderate ack-ack greeted the planes over Ponape.

Schmidt Calls It 'Tough'

Maj. Gen. Harry Schmidt, Fifth Marine Amphibious Corps commander, said today that the battle for Iwo has been tougher than the American command figured, and it was expected to be tough from the start.

"Victory here will be obtained by slow, pulverizing pressure on the Japanese defenses," he said.

"This is no smack-bang campaign. It is a matter of slowly crowding them out of their holes one by one and killing them one by one. The Japanese have made a skillful defense. It ought to be skillful. They have owned it ever since it was an island."

ATKINS, THOMAS E.

Rank and Organization: Private First Class, U.S. Army, Company A, 127th Infantry, 32d Infantry Division.
Born: Campobello, South Carolina.
Entered Service At: Campobello, South Carolina.
Place and Date: Villa Verde Trail, Luzon, Philippine Islands, March 10, 1945.
Citation: Pfc. Atkins fought gallantly on the Villa Verde Trail, Luzon, Philippine Islands. With 2 companions he occupied a position on a ridge outside the perimeter defense established by the 1st Platoon on a high hill. At about 3 a.m., 2 companies of Japanese attacked with rifle and machinegun fire, grenades, TNT charges, and land mines, severely wounding Pfc. Atkins and killing his 2 companions. Despite the intense hostile fire and pain from his deep wound, he held his ground and returned heavy fire. After the attack was repulsed, he remained in his precarious position to repel any subsequent assaults instead of returning to the American lines for medical treatment. An enemy machinegun, set up within 20 yards of his foxhole, vainly attempted to drive him off or silence his gun. The Japanese repeatedly made fierce attacks, but for 4 hours Pfc. Atkins determinedly, remained in his foxhole, bearing the brunt of each assault and maintaining steady and accurate fire until each charge was repulsed. At 7 a.m., 13 enemy dead lay in front of his position; he had fired 400 rounds, all he and his 2 dead companions possessed, and had used 3 rifles until each had jammed too badly for

further operation. He withdrew during a lull to secure a rifle and more ammunition, and was persuaded to remain for medical treatment. While waiting, he saw a Japanese within the perimeter and, seizing a nearby rifle, killed him. A few minutes later, while lying on a litter, he discovered an enemy group moving up behind the platoon's lines. Despite his severe wound, he sat up, delivered heavy rifle fire against the group and forced them to withdraw. Pfc. Atkins' superb bravery and his fearless determination to hold his post against the main force of repeated enemy attacks, even though painfully wounded, were major factors in enabling his comrades to maintain their lines against a numerically superior enemy force.

OFFICIAL COMMUNIQUE:
United Nations
ADVANCED HEADQUARTERS, on Luzon, Sunday, March 11 – A communique:

PHILIPPINES

Luzon: In the Fourteenth Corps sector, forward elements of the First Cavalry Division have driven into Antipolo while the Sixth Division advanced southwest of Montalban. In Batangas, the 158th Regimental Combat Team advanced nine miles to secure the road net between Lake Taal and Batangas Bay.

In the First Corps sector, the Forty-third and Thirty-eighth Divisions continued their two-pronged drive through rugged mountain terrain toward Balete Pass.

In the same corps sector, the Forty-third and Thirty-eighth Divisions carried on the destruction of the enemy remnants. Indicative of the deadly effectiveness of our concentrated bombing and artillery fire was the discovery of over 900 enemy bodies in one locality in the Zambales foothills.

Our heavy units with 247 tons of bombs destroyed enemy installations in Balete Pass. Medium and attack bombers destroyed enemy installations in the Cagayan Valley and swept over Aparri airfield. Light bombers and fighters attacked targets of opportunity in central Luzon and supported ground operations.

Visayas: Fighters bombed enemy concentrations near Cebu City and north of Iloilo on Panay. Light naval units on night patrol sank a barge.

†CRAIN, MORRIS E.
Rank and Organization: Technical Sergeant, U.S. Army, Company E, 141st Infantry, 36th Infantry Division.
Born: Bandana, Kentucky.
Entered Service At: Paducah, Kentucky.
Place and Date: Haguenau, France, March 13, 1945.

Citation: T/Sgt. Crain led his platoon against powerful German forces during the struggle to enlarge the bridgehead across the Moder River. With great daring and aggressiveness he spearheaded the platoon in killing 10 enemy soldiers, capturing 12 more and securing its objective near an important road junction. Although heavy concentrations of artillery, mortar, and self-propelled gunfire raked the area, he moved about among his men during the day, exhorting them to great efforts and encouraging them to stand firm. He carried ammunition and maintained contact with the company command post, exposing himself to deadly enemy fire. At nightfall the enemy barrage became more intense and tanks entered the fray to cover foot troops while they bombarded our positions with grenades and rockets. As buildings were blasted by the Germans, the Americans fell back from house to house. T/Sgt. Crain deployed another platoon which had been sent to his support and then rushed through murderous tank and small-arms fire to the foremost house, which was being defended by 5 of his men. With the enemy attacking from an adjoining room and a tank firing pointblank at the house, he ordered the men to withdraw while he remained in the face of almost certain death to hold the position. Although shells were crashing through the walls and bullets were hitting all around him, he held his ground and with accurate fire from his submachinegun killed 3 Germans. He was killed when the building was destroyed by the enemy. T/Sgt. Crain's outstanding valor and intrepid leadership enabled his platoon to organize a new defense, repel the attack and preserve the hard-won bridgehead.

†MICHAEL, HARRY J.

Rank and Organizations: Second Lieutenant, U.S. Army, Company L, 318th Infantry, 80th Infantry Division.
Born: Milford, Indiana.
Entered Service At: Milford, Indiana.
Place and Date: Near Neiderzerf, Germany, March 14, 1945.
Citation: 2d Lt. Michael was serving as a rifle platoon leader when his company began an assault on a wooded ridge northeast of the village of Neiderzerf, Germany, early on March 13, 1945. A short distance up the side of the hill, 2d Lt. Michael, at the head of his platoon, heard the click of an enemy machinegun bolt. Quietly halting the company, he silently moved off into the woods and discovered 2 enemy machineguns and crews. Executing a sudden charge, he completely surprised the enemy and captured the guns and crews. At daybreak, enemy voices were heard in the thick woods ahead. Leading his platoon in a flanking movement, they charged the enemy with handgrenades and, after a bitter fight, captured 25 mem-

bers of an SS mountain division, 3 artillery pieces, and 20 horses. While his company was establishing its position, 2d Lt. Michael made 2 personal reconnaissance missions of the wood on his left flank. On his first mission he killed 2, wounded 4, and captured 6 enemy soldiers singlehandedly. On the second mission he captured 7 prisoners. During the afternoon he led his platoon on a frontal assault of a line of enemy pillboxes, successfully capturing the objective, killing 10 and capturing 30 prisoners. The following morning the company was subjected to sniper fire and 2d Lt. Michael, in an attempt to find the hidden sniper, was shot and killed. The inspiring leadership and heroic aggressiveness displayed by 2d Lt. Michael upheld the highest traditions of the military service.

OFFICIAL COMMUNIQUE:
United Nations
PARIS, March 13 – Communique 339 of Supreme Headquarters, Allied Expeditionary Force:

The Allied bridgehead across the Rhine has been extended against increasing enemy resistance to a depth of four miles and a length of ten miles.

In the northern part of the bridgehead fighting continues in Honnef. Our units cleared the towns of Hargarten and Ginsterhahn, northeast of Linz, and fighting is in progress in Hoenningen, in the southern portion of the bridgehead.

Enemy artillery directed at the bridgehead decreased after we captured several hills which were being used for observation. Fighter aircraft continued to provide umbrella cover for the bridgehead.

On the west bank of the Rhine, our units continued to reduce the enemy pocket in the Laacher See [Lake] area, southwest of Andernach, clearing the towns of Eich, Nickenich and Kretz.

We now control all the north bank of the Moselle River between Trier and Coblenz; with the exception of a ten-mile stretch between Cochem and Reil. West of Cochem we captured Driesch and Lutzerath and our armor reached the vicinity of Reil to the south.

Southeast of Wittlich we captured Urzig and cleared Maring.

Northeast of Trier our forces south of the Moselle captured Riol in a one-mile gain. An enemy counter-attack with armor and infantry succeeded in recapturing some high ground in the area of Walbach, five miles east of Trier.

In the Saarbruecken area and the Hardt Mountain sector farther east, our troops repulsed several small enemy attacks and attempts at infiltration. Harassing enemy artillery fire fell along the Rhine.

Allied forces in the West captured 4,980 prisoners on March 11.

The enemy's communications in and around the Ruhr were subjected to heavy air attacks yesterday.

The communications center of Dortmund was attacked by escorted heavy bombers in very great strength. Four thousand nine hundred tons of bombs were dropped in a concentrated attack which lasted less than half an hour. Other escorted heavy bombers in great strength struck at rail yards at Betzdorf, Siegen, Dillenburg, Wetzlar, Marburg and Friedberg.

†PHILLIPS, GEORGE

Rank and Organizations: Private, U.S. Marine Corps Reserve.
Born: July 14, 1926, Rich Hill, Missouri.
Entered Service At: Labadie, Missouri.
Place and Date: Iwo Jima, Volcano Islands, March 14, 1945.
Citation: For conspicuous gallantry and intrepidity at the risk of his life above and beyond the call of duty while serving with the 2d Battalion, 28th Marines, 5th Marine Division, in action against enemy Japanese forces during the seizure of Iwo Jima in the Volcano Islands, on March 14 1945. Standing the foxhole watch while other members of his squad rested after a night of bitter handgrenade fighting against infiltrating Japanese troops, Pvt. Phillips was the only member of his unit alerted when an enemy handgrenade was tossed into their midst. Instantly shouting a warning, he unhesitatingly threw himself on the deadly missile, absorbing the shattering violence of the exploding charge in his own body and protecting his comrades from serious injury. Stouthearted and indomitable, Pvt. Phillips willingly yielded his own life that his fellow marines might carry on the relentless battle against a fanatic enemy. His superb valor and unfaltering spirit of self-sacrifice in the face of certain death reflect the highest credit upon himself and upon the U.S. Naval Service. He gallantly gave his life for his country.

SIGLER, FRANKLIN EARL

Rank and Organization: Private, U.S. Marine Corps Reserve, 2d Battalion, 26th Marines, 5th Marine Division.
Born: November 6, 1924, Glen Ridge, New Jersey.
Entered Service At: New Jersey.
Place and Date: Iwo Jima, Volcano Islands, March 14, 1945.
Citation: For conspicuous gallantry and intrepidity at the risk of his life above and beyond the call of duty while serving with the 2d Battalion, 26th Marines, 5th Marine Division, in action against enemy Japanese forces during the seizure of Iwo Jima in the Volcano Islands on March 14, 1945. Voluntarily taking command of his rifle squad when the leader became a

casualty, Pvt. Sigler fearlessly led a bold charge against an enemy gun installation which had held up the advance of his company for several days and, reaching the position in advance of the others, assailed the emplacement with handgrenades and personally annihilated the entire crew. As additional Japanese troops opened fire from concealed tunnels and caves above, he quickly scaled the rocks leading to the attacking guns, surprised the enemy with a furious 1-man assault and, although severely wounded in the encounter, deliberately crawled back to his squad position where he steadfastly refused evacuation, persistently directing heavy machinegun and rocket barrages on the Japanese cave entrances. Undaunted by the merciless rain of hostile fire during the intensified action, he gallantly disregarded his own painful wounds to aid casualties, carrying 3 wounded squad members to safety behind the lines and returning to continue the battle with renewed determination until ordered to retire for medical treatment. Stouthearted and indomitable in the face of extreme peril, Pvt. Sigler, by his alert initiative, unfaltering leadership, and daring tactics in a critical situation, effected the release of his besieged company from enemy fire and contributed essentially to its further advance against a savagely fighting enemy. His superb valor, resolute fortitude, and heroic spirit of self-sacrifice throughout reflect the highest credit upon Pvt. Sigler and the U.S. Naval Service.

Note: The following is a newspaper account of the preceding battle for which Pvt. Phillips and Pvt. Sigler were awarded the Medal of Honor:

VICTORY FLAG RAISED ON IWO;
AIRFIELD IS USED BY BOMBERS

GUAM, Thursday, March 15 – The United States flag was formally raised over Iwo at 9:30 A.M. yesterday, although fighting continued unabated in the northern sector and in a small pocket inn the northeastern part of the island, Pacific Fleet headquarters announced today. The communique gave 20,000 as a "very close approximation" of the Japanese dead in the twenty-three days of the Iwo battle through yesterday. Marine casualties were not mentioned.

Army, Navy and Marine planes are now operating from Iwo, using No. 1 airfield, which is far behind the lines. The second airfield is being worked into condition meanwhile. This strip has a hump in the middle and from there runs uphill. Seabees and engineers are leveling that. No. 1 strip is already a very busy airport, taking all sizes of planes.

Army fighters based on Iwo bombed and strafed airfield installations on Chichi Island in the Bonin group yesterday. On the previous day Army Liberators of the Strategic Air Force of the Pacific Ocean areas bombed the Chichi airstrip.

Ceremony Held During Battle

Rifle fire in the embattled area to the north was faintly audible as Col. D.A. Stafford of Spokane, Wash., Fiftieth Amphibious Corps personnel officer, read Admiral Chester W. Minitz's proclamation suspending Japanese rule in the Volcano Islands –an integral part of the Japanese Empire. Near-by Marine artillery pieces roared as Colonel Stafford read, drowning his voice.

The flag was raised on a Japanese anti-aircraft gun emplacement at the foot of Mount Suribachi and simultaneously the flag raised by the Marines during the fifth day of the battle on top of Suribachi's 551-foot active cone was lowered. marine Pfc. John Glynn, 21, of New Orleans sounded "Colors" as the Stars and Stripes were pulled to the top of the flagstaff by Pfcs. Thomas J. Casale, 20, of Herkimer, N.Y., and Albert B. Bush, 24, of Cleveland. Sgt. Anthony Yusi, 25, of Port Chester, N.Y., was in charge of the color detail. They were chosen from the corps military police company for "general efficiency and military bearing."

High ranking officers of the Army, Navy, and Marine Corps were present at the ceremony.

Booby-traps have been found attached to the bodies of marine dead, the bulletin revealed. On Iwo, marines for the first time encountered systematic booby-trapping and placement of mines.

The battle situation on Iwo has been little changed for several days. The Fifth Marine Division, attacking the last prepared enemy defenses at the northern tip of the island, gained 200 to 400 yards yesterday. "At nightfall," the communique said, "the battle was continuing in this sector and in small pockets on the Fourth Marine Division zone of action."

Lieut. Gen. Tadamichi Kurisayashi, the Japanese commander on Iwo, according to the Tokyo radio, is apparently making his last stand just where he had thought he would have to make it, and that accounts for the difficulty the Fifth Division is encountering in its attempt to reach the remaining two miles of coastline still held by the foe. This part of the island is unbelievably rugged country of high-peaked rocks ridden with hundreds of fortified caves and pillboxes.

Some delay occurs when the infantry must wait while armored bulldozers clear the roads for tanks to move in and blast the Japanese positions with cannon. another factor is the short distance of the Marine front line from the sea, which inhibits the use of supporting artillery. The Japanese are using mortars on nearly flat trajectory, firing point blank into the advancing Marines.

The pocket holding out in the Fourth Division sector is a high butte with almost vertical sides. The marines have it surrounded, but they can't overrun it.

Air activities in other corners of the vast Central Pacific theatre went as usual. Eleventh Army Air Force Liberators from Aleutians bases bombed airfield facilities at Kurabu Point on the southern part of Paramushiru Island in the Kuriles on

Tuesday. There was meager anti-aircraft fire. Marine Corsairs and Hellcats destroyed a bridge, damaged two piers and fired fuel dumps and motor facilities in the Palaus yesterday.

Garrison forces are still killing and capturing Japanese in the Marianas and the Palaus. During the week of March 4, through March 10, forty-eight Japanese were killed on Saipan, Tinian, and Guam, and thirteen were captured on Saipan, Guam, and Peleliu.

HERRERA, SILVESTRE S.
Rank and Organization: Private First Class, U.S. Army, Company E, 142d Infantry, 36th Infantry Division.
Born: El Paso, Texas.
Entered Service At: Phoenix, Arizona.
Place and Date: Near Mertzwiller, France, March 15, 1945.
Citation: Pfc. Herrera advanced with a platoon along a wooded road until stopped by heavy enemy machinegun fire. As the rest of the unit took cover, he made a 1-man frontal assault on a strongpoint and captured 8 enemy soldiers. When the platoon resumed its advance and was subjected to fire from a second emplacement beyond an extensive minefield, Pvt. Herrera again moved forward, disregarding the danger of exploding mines, to attack the position. He stepped on a mine and had both feet severed; but, despite intense pain and unchecked loss of blood, he pinned down the enemy gun by skirting the minefield and rushing in from the flank. The magnificent courage, extraordinary heroism, and willing self-sacrifice displayed by Pvt. Herrera resulted in the capture of 2 enemy strongpoints and the taking of 8 prisoners.

OFFICIAL COMMUNIQUE:
United Nations
PARIS, March 15 – Communique 341 of Supreme Headquarters, Allied Expeditionary Force:

Allied forces have increased the depth of the bridgehead over the Rhine at Remagen to more than five miles. In the northern portion of the bridgehead, our infantry advanced 1,500 yards northward to reach a point one and a half miles northeast of Honnef. Other elements drove to a point one and a fourth miles from the Autobahn [superhighway] in the area three miles east of Honnef.

Northeast of Linz, our units are in the outskirts of Kalenborn and Notscheid. Our infantry pushed into the wooded area three and a half miles due east of Linz against stiff resistance.

Mopping up operations continue along the north side of the Moselle River. South of Cochem we have captured Eller, Bremm and Aldegund. Three more bends in the river northeast of Trier have been cleared with the taking of Cues, Minheim, and Trittenheim.

Southeast of Trier, our infantry made gains of one and one-half miles eastward, capturing Morscheid, Holzerath, Hentern, and Frommersbach. Enemy Nebelwerfer and artillery fire against our forces increased in the area southeast of Trier.

West of Saarbruecken our forces advanced up to three miles on a five-mile front. The Franco-German border was crossed and the Saar River reached at several points. Towns occupied include Schaffhausen, Wehrden, Geislautern, Fuerstenhausen, Clarenthal, and Schoenecken. Farther east, at Haguenau, an armor-supported enemy attack failed to dislodge our units from newly won positions on the north side of the Moder River.

Allied forces in the West captured 2,413 prisoners on March 13.

PIERCE, FRANCIS JUNIOR

Rank and Organization: Pharmacist's Mate First Class, U.S. Navy, serving with 2d Battalion, 24th Marines, 4th Marine Division.
Born: December 7, 1924, Earlville, Iowa.
Entered Service At: Iowa.
Place and Date: Iwo Jima, March 15-16, 1945.
Citation: For conspicuous gallantry and intrepidity at the risk of his life above and beyond the call of duty while attached to the 2d Battalion, 24th Marines, 4th Marine Division, during the Iwo Jima campaign, March 15 and 16, 1945. Almost continuously under fire while carrying out the most dangerous volunteer assignments, Pierce gained valuable knowledge of the terrain and disposition of troops. Caught in heavy enemy rifle and machinegun fire which wounded a corpsman and 2 of the 8 stretcher bearers who were carrying 2 wounded marines to a forward aid station on March 15, Pierce quickly took charge of the party, carried the newly wounded men to a sheltered position, and rendered first aid. After directing the evacuation of 3 of the casualties, he stood in the open to draw the enemy's fire and, with his weapon blasting, enabled the litter bearers to reach cover. Turning his attention to the other 2 casualties, he was attempting to stop the profuse bleeding of 1 man when a Japanese fired from a cave less than 20 yards away and wounded his patient again. Risking his own life to save his patient, Pierce deliberately exposed himself to draw the attacker from the cave and destroyed him with the last of his ammunition. Then lifting the wounded man to his back, he advanced unarmed through deadly rifle fire

across 200 feet of open terrain. Despite exhaustion and in the face of warnings against such a suicidal mission, he again traversed the same fire-swept path to rescue the remaining marine. On the following morning, he led a combat patrol to the sniper nest and, while aiding a stricken marine, was seriously wounded. Refusing aid for himself, he directed treatment for the casualty, at the same time maintaining protective fire for his comrades. Completely fearless, completely devoted to the care of his patients, Pierce inspired the entire battalion. His valor in the face of extreme peril sustains and enhances the finest traditions of the U.S. Naval Service.

OFFICIAL COMMUNIQUE:
United States
GUAM, Friday, March 16 – Pacific Fleet communique 299:

(1) The Fifth Marine Division on March 15, continued to reduce further the area held by the enemy at the northern tip of Iwo Island. Our forces encountered intense small-arms and mortar fire throughout the day. Mopping up operations were continued in the Third and Fourth Marine Division zones of action.
(2) Planes of the Seventh Army Fighter Command bombed airfields and installations on Chichi Jima [Island] in the Bonins on the same day.
(3) On March 14, Liberators of the Seventh Army Air Force, operating under the Strategic Air Force, Pacific ocean Areas, bombed Chichi Jima airfield.
(4) Navy search Privateers of Fleet Air Wing 2 bombed Wake Island through meager anti-aircraft fire on March 14.
(5) On the same date, Corsair fighters of the Fourth Marine Aircraft Wing continued neutralizing attacks on enemy held bases in the Marshals.

†McGEE, WILLIAM D.
Rank and Organization: Private, U.S. Army, Medical Detachment, 304th Infantry, 76th Infantry Division.
Born: Indianapolis, Indiana.
Entered Service At: Indianapolis, Indiana.
Place and Date: Near Mulheim, Germany, March 18, 1945.
Citation: A medical aid man, Pvt. McGee made a night crossing of the Moselle River with troops endeavoring to capture the town of Mulheim. The enemy had retreated in the sector where the assault boats landed, but had left the shore heavily strewn with antipersonnel mines. Two men of the first wave attempting to work their way forward detonated mines which wounded them seriously, leaving them bleeding and in great pain beyond the reach of their comrades. Entirely on his own initiative, Pvt. McGee

entered the minefield, brought out 1 of the injured to comparative safety, and had returned to rescue the second victim when he stepped on a mine and was severely wounded in the resulting explosion. Although suffering intensely and bleeding profusely, he shouted orders that none of his comrades was to risk his life by entering the death-sown field to render first aid that might have saved his life. In making the supreme sacrifice, Pvt. McGee demonstrated a concern for the well-being of his fellow soldiers that transcended all considerations for his own safety and a gallantry in keeping with the highest traditions of the military service.

†MURPHY, FREDERICK C.
Rank and Organization: Private First Class, U.S. Army, Medical Detachment, 259th Infantry, 65th Infantry Division.
Born: Boston, Massachusetts.
Entered Service At: Weymouth, Massachusetts.
Place and Date: Siegfried Line at Saarlautern, Germany, March 18, 1945.
Citation: An aid man, Pfc. Murphy was wounded in the right shoulder soon after his comrades had jumped off in a dawn attack March 18, 1945, against the Siegfried Line at Saarlautern, Germany. He refused to withdraw for treatment and continued forward, administering first aid under heavy machinegun, mortar, and artillery fire. When the company ran into a thickly sown antipersonnel minefield and began to suffer more and more casualties, he continued to disregard his own wound and unhesitatingly braved the danger of exploding mines, moving about through heavy fire and helping the injured until he stepped on a mine which severed one of his feet. In spite of his grievous wounds, he struggled on with his work, refusing to be evacuated and crawling from man to man administering to them while in great pain and bleeding profusely. He was killed by the blast of another mine which he had dragged himself across in an effort reach still another casualty. With indomitable courage, and unquenchable spirit of self-sacrifice and supreme devotion to duty which made it possible for him to continue performing his tasks while barely able to move, Pfc. Murphy saved many of his fellow soldiers at the cost of his own life.

TREADWELL, JACK L.
Rank and Organization: Captain, U.S. Army, Company F, 180th Infantry, 45th Infantry Division.
Born: Ashland, Alabama.
Entered Service At: Snyder, Oklahoma.
Place and Date: Near Nieder-Wurzbach, Germany, March 18, 1945.

Citation: Capt. Treadwell (then 1st Lt.), commanding officer of Company F, near Nieder-Wurzbach, Germany, in the Siegfried line, singlehandedly captured 6 pillboxes and 18 prisoners. Murderous enemy automatic and rifle fire with intermittent artillery bombardments had pinned down his company for hours at the base of a hill defended by concrete fortifications and interlocking trenches. Eight men sent to attack a single point had all become casualties on the bare slope when Capt. Treadwell, armed with a submachinegun and handgrenades, went forward alone to clear the way for his stalled company. Over the terrain devoid of cover and swept by bullets, he fearlessly advanced, firing at the aperture of the nearest pillbox and, when within range, hurling grenades at it. He reached the pillbox, thrust the muzzle of his gun through the port, and drove 4 Germans out with their hands in the air. A fifth was found dead inside. Waving these prisoners back to the American line, he continued under terrible, concentrated fire to the next pillbox and took it in the same manner. In this fort he captured the commander of the hill defenses, whom he sent to the rear with the other prisoners. Never slackening his attack, he then ran across the crest of the hill to a third pillbox, traversing this distance in full view of hostile machinegunners and snipers. He was again successful in taking the enemy position. The Germans quickly fell prey to his further rushes on 3 more pillboxes in the confusion and havoc caused by his whirlwind assaults and capture of their commander. Inspired by the electrifying performance of their leader, the men of Company F stormed after him and overwhelmed resistance on the entire hill, driving a wedge into the Siegfried line and making it possible for their battalion to take its objective. By his courageous willingness to face nearly impossible odds and by his overwhelming one-man offensive, Capt. Treadwell reduced a heavily fortified, seemingly impregnable enemy sector.

† **WILKIN, EDWARD G.**
Rank and Organization: Corporal U.S. Army, Company C, 157th Infantry, 45th Infantry Division.
Born: Burlington, Vermont.
Entered Service At: Longmeadow, Massachusetts.
Place and Date: Siegfried Line in Germany, March 18, 1945.
Citation: Cpl. Wilkin spearheaded his unit's assault of the Siegfried Line in Germany. Heavy fire from enemy riflemen and camouflaged pillboxes had pinned down his comrades when he moved forward on his own initiative to reconnoiter a route of advance. He cleared the way into an area studded with pillboxes, where he repeatedly stood up and walked into vicious enemy fire, storming 1 fortification after another with automatic rifle

fire and grenades, killing enemy troops, taking prisoners as the enemy defense became confused, and encouraging his comrades by his heroic example. When halted by heavy barbed wire entanglements, he secured bangalore torpedoes and blasted a path toward still more pillboxes, all the time braving bursting grenades and mortar shells and direct rifle and automatic-weapons fire. He engaged in fierce fire fights, standing in the open while his adversaries fought from the protection of concrete emplacements, and on one occasion pursued enemy soldiers across an open field and through interlocking trenches, disregarding the crossfire from 2 pillboxes until he had penetrated the formidable line 200 yards in advance of any American element. That night, although terribly fatigued, he refused to rest and insisted on distributing rations and supplies to his comrades. Hearing that a nearby company was suffering heavy casualties, he secured permission to guide litter bearers and assist them in evacuating the wounded. All that night he remained in the battle area on his mercy missions, and for the following 2 days he continued to remove casualties, venturing into enemy-held territory, scorning cover and braving devastating mortar and artillery bombardments. In 3 days he neutralized and captured 6 pillboxes singlehandedly, killed at least 9 Germans, wounded 13, took 13 prisoners, aided in the capture of 14 others, and saved many Americans lives by his fearless performance as a litter bearer. Through his superb fighting skill, dauntless courage, and gallant, inspiring actions, Cpl. Wilkin contributed in large measure to his company's success in cracking the Siegfried Line. One month later he was killed in action while fighting deep in Germany.

BURR, HERBERT H.
Rank and Organization: Staff Sergeant, U.S. Army, Company C, 41st Tank Battalion, 11th Armored Division.
Born: St. Joseph, Missouri.
Entered Service At: Kansas City, Missouri.
Place and Date: Near Dorrmoschel, Germany, March 19, 1945.
Citation: S/Sgt. Burr displayed conspicuous gallantry during action when the tank in which he was bow gunner was hit by an enemy rocket, which severely wounded the platoon sergeant and forced the remainder of the crew to abandon the vehicle. Deafened, but otherwise unhurt, S/Sgt. Burr immediately climbed into the driver's seat and continued on the mission of entering the town to reconnoiter road conditions. As he rounded a turn he encountered an 88-mm. antitank gun at pointblank range. Realizing that he had no crew, no one to man the tank's guns, he heroically chose to disregard his personal safety in a direct charge on the German weapon. At con-

siderable speed he headed straight for the loaded gun, which was fully manned by enemy troops who had only to pull the lanyard to send a shell into his vehicle. So unexpected and daring was his assault that he was able to drive his tank completely over the gun, demolishing it and causing its crew to flee in confusion. He then skillfully sideswiped a large, truck overturned it, and wheeling his lumbering vehicle, returned to his company. When medical personnel who had been summoned to treat the wounded sergeant could not locate him, the valiant soldier ran through a hail of sniper fire to direct them to his stricken comrade. The bold, fearless determination of S/Sgt. Burr, his skill and courageous devotion to duty, resulted in the completion of his mission in the face of seemingly impossible odds.

Note: The following is a newspaper account of the preceding battle for which Pvt. McGee, Pfc. Murphy, Capt. Tredwell, Cpl. Wilkin, and Sgt. Burr were awarded the Medal of Honor:

3D AND 7TH ARMIES CUT DEEP INTO SAAR POCKET, REMAGEN BRIDGE FALLS, BUT REPAIR IS SPEEDED

• • •

46 TOWNS OVERRUN

• • •

New Armored Division Joins Drive to Trap 80,000 Germans

• • •

SIEGFRIED KEY FALLS

• • •

1st Army Captures One German Airfield East of the Rhine

• • •

PARIS, March 18 – Lieut. Gen. George S. Patton Jr. hurled four armored divisions and ten tank battalions into battle today in a bold effort to cut off and destroy

80,000 soldiers of the German First Army struggling against the United States Third and Seventh Armies in the Saar-Moselle-Rhine triangle.

Third and Seventh Army units have entered, captured or cleared no fewer than forty-six German towns and villages in the past twenty-four hours. The most notable of these was storied Bingen on the Rhine, entered by doughboys of the Ninetieth Infantry Division on the northern flank of the two salients that General Patton is driving southeastward and eastward across the triangle.

The United States First Army's attacks from the bridgehead at Remagen diminished somewhat today. A stroke of bad luck hampered the efforts there slightly yesterday when the central span of the Ludendorff Bridge collapsed. Sizable forces, however, are across the Rhine and reinforcements can use the pontoon bridges that have been set up there.

Near Plain East of Bonn

The Seventh-eighth Infantry Division on the north of the bridgehead, advanced five-eighths of a mile today to enter Niederdollendorf and Oberdollendorf opposition Bad Godesberg, across the Rhine. In the north, the doughboys are almost on the plain east of Bonn.

Other infantrymen in this sector occupied high ground a mile north of Brungsberg.

The Ninth Infantry Division, fighting in the center, crossed the Wied River in the vicinity of Niederhoppen and overran an airstrip east of the Autobahn near Windhagen. The First Army now controls six miles of the Autobahn. [Press services said Hill 329, east of Hoenningen, was captured.]

In their dash toward the Rhine, two of the Third Army armored divisions, the Fourth and the Eleventh, are striking southeast toward the Rhine while two others, the Tenth and another division whose identity has not yet been disclosed, are smashing eastward in the rear of the Siegfried Line.

Infantry Captures Merzig

Meanwhile, infantry of the third Army has captured Merzig, a bulwark of the Siegfried Line where forward line switchback positions that defend the Saar Basin join to the west of it, and doughboys of the Seventh Army are slugging their way forward afoot through the forward positions of the line from Saarbruecken to the Hardt Mountains.

The Germans fighting between the Hardt Mountains and the Rhine on the northern extremity of the Alsace Plain evidently have given up plans for fighting in the open and have withdrawn into the Siegfried Line positions defending the Wissembourg Gap. If the enemy is to salvage anything out of the tactical defeat he has already suffered, these positions must be held to the last to prevent Lieut. Gen. Alexander M. Patch's Seventh Army troops from driving northward along the west bank of the Rhine toward a possible junction with Third Army forces.

From all accounts of airmen, the westernmost section of the triangle is in a state of confusion. German troops and civilian refugees crowd the roads and, although the weather again limited aerial activity, fighter-bombers took a heavy toll of German vehicles moving eastward toward the Rhine again today.

The Fourth Armored Division crossed the Nahe River and seized most of Bad Kreuznach. This important communications center is now being mopped up. The Germans counter-attacked once this morning, but after an hour and forty-five minutes of hard fighting, the enemy thrust was broken up and no damage was done.

[Simultaneously other units of the Fourth crossed the Nahe and entered Bad Muenster-am-Stein, an Associated Press dispatch from the front said.]

Ninth Captures Bingen

The Fifth Infantry Division cleared seven towns within a seven-mile radius of Simmern after advances of from two to four miles while the Ninetieth Infantry Division on the eastern side of the salient advanced six miles into Bingen, on the Rhine west of Mainz. [The Fifth Division took Fronhofen, press services said.]

The Eleventh Armored Division advanced in two columns, one of which reached a point five miles northwest of Kirn, a road junction on the Nahe River, eighteen miles southwest of Bad Kreuznach, after an eight-mile drive. The other column drove on seven miles southeast to reach Kellenbach, due north of Kirn.

The Eleventh Armored Division also sent out a column that cleared the important road center of Kirchberg.

Behind this advance, the Eighty-seventh Infantry Division, one unit of which was mopping up the last few blocks in Coblenz, extended its front down the west bank of the Rhine until it controlled a seventeen-mile stretch from Boppard to a point six miles northwest of Bingen. Another element, operating between Boppard and Coblenz, also reached the Rhine and Brey and Rhens, the former five miles south of Coblenz, were cleared of the enemy. Boppard was captured yesterday.

The capture of Merzig by the Twenty-sixth Infantry Division on the right flank of the salient moving eastward along the Siegfried Line was the most notable victory in this sector today. Following up their victory, the doughboys of this division gained three miles on a two-mile front in an area twelve miles east of Merzig, capturing Aussen and Huettersdorf and entering Greasaubach in an advance that flanked Saarbruecken. This advance is part of a converging movement, for the Sixty-fifth Infantry Division crossed the Saar River a mile north of Dillingen this morning, and then swung south to enter and clear half of that town, which is two miles north of Saarlautern.

To the north, the Tenth Armored Division gained eight miles in the latest spurt to reach a point twenty-seven miles southeast of Saarburg, while other elements advanced into Lochweiler. [Press services said other Tenth Division units were near Walhausen and Kastel.]

These advances place General Patton's tanks inn an area twenty to twenty-five miles north of Saarbruecken, central citadel of the Siegfried Line inn that area. The other armored division in this sector is fighting in the vicinity of Nohen, three miles east of Birkenfeld, which was reached by the Tenth Armored Division yesterday.

The Ninety-fourth Infantry Division, wheelhorse of this salient, is pressing on to the north. One column advanced five miles northeast of St. Wendel, yet another important railroad center, and took 700 prisoners. Another column progressed two and a half miles to the northeast to capture Soetern.

Eisenhower Visits Patton

The Third Army sector was visited yesterday by Gen. Dwight D. Eisenhower, who conferred with General Patton on the progress of his offensive.

Progress on the Seventh Army front was greatest east of Saarbruecken. Doughboys of the Sixty-third Infantry Division repulsed a counter-attack y 200 German infantrymen north of Ensheim, eight miles southeast of Saarbruecken, and then pushed on to the east of this sector to occupy Mimbach. [Press services said Heckendalheim and Niederwuerzbach were reached.]

The Third Infantry Division advanced within three miles of the industrial city of Zweibruecken, one of the centers of Saar industry. Third Division veterans took Alten Hornbach and reached Mittelbach in this advance, which carried them well through one sector of the Siegfried Line.

The 100th Infantry Division crossed the border into the Reich, captured Walschbronn and Liederschiedt, and reached Schweix. Walschbronn is only eight miles from Pirmasens, chief communications center of the eastern Saar basin.

Dambach and Neunhoffen in the Hardt Mountains fell to the Forty-second Infantry Division, which then pushed on to Steinbach on the frontier. [Press services said other elements of this division cleared Phillipsbourg.]

GARY, DONALD ARTHUR

Rank and Organization: Lieutenant, Junior Grade, U.S. Navy, U.S.S. *Franklin*.

Born: July 23, 1903, Findlay, Ohio.

Entered Service At: Ohio.

Place and Date: Japanese Home Islands near Kobe, Japan, March 19, 1945.

Citation: For conspicuous gallantry and intrepidity at the risk of his life

above and beyond the call of duty as an engineering officer attached to the U.S.S. *Franklin* when that vessel was fiercely attacked by enemy aircraft during the operations against the Japanese Home Islands near Kobe, Japan, March 19, 1945. Stationed on the third deck when the ship was rocked by a series of violent explosions set off in her own ready bombs, rockets, and ammunition by the hostile attack, Lt. (jg.) Gary unhesitatingly risked his life to assist several hundred men trapped in a messing compartment filled with smoke, and with no apparent egress. As the imperiled men below decks became increasingly panic stricken under the raging fury of incessant explosions, he confidently assured them he would find a means of effecting their release and, groping through the dark, debris-filled corridors, ultimately discovered an escapeway. Staunchly determined, he struggled back to the messing compartment 3 times despite menacing flames, flooding water, and the ominous threat of sudden additional explosions, on each occasion calmly leading his men through the blanketing pall of smoke until the last one had been saved. Selfless in his concern for his ship and his fellows, he constantly rallied others about him, repeatedly organized and led fire fighting parties into the blazing inferno on the flight deck and, when firerooms 1 and 2 were found to be inoperable, entered the No. 3 fireroom and directed the raising of steam in 1 boiler in the face of extreme difficulty and hazard. An inspiring and courageous leader, Lt. (jg.) Gary rendered self-sacrificing service under the most perilous conditions and, by his heroic initiative, fortitude, and valor, was responsible for the saving of several hundred lives. His conduct throughout reflects the highest credit upon himself and upon the U.S. Naval Service.

O'CALLAHAN, JOSEPH TIMOTHY
Rank and Organization: Commander (Chaplain Corps), U.S. Naval Reserve, U.S.S. *Franklin.*
Born: May 14, 1904, Boston, Massachusetts.
Entered Service At: Massachusetts.
Place and Date: Near Kobe, Japan, March 19, 1945.
Citation: For conspicuous gallantry and intrepidity at the risk of his life above and beyond the call of duty while serving as chaplain on board the U.S.S. *Franklin* when that vessel was fiercely attacked by enemy Japanese aircraft during offensive operations near Kobe, Japan, on March 19, 1945. A valiant and forceful leader, calmly braving the perilous barriers of flame and twisted metal to aid his men and his ship, Lt. Comdr. O'Callahan groped his way through smoke-filled corridors to the open flight deck and into the midst of violently exploding bombs, shells, rockets, and other armament. With the ship rocked by incessant explosions, with debris and fragments

raining down and fires raging in ever-increasing fury, he ministered to the wounded and dying, comforting and encouraging men of all faiths; he organized and led firefighting crews into the blazing inferno on the flight deck; he directed the jettisoning of live ammunition and the flooding of the magazine; he manned a hose to cool hot, armed bombs rolling dangerously on the listing deck, continuing his efforts, despite searing, suffocating smoke which forced men to fall back gasping and imperiled others who replaced them. Serving with courage, fortitude, and deep spiritual strength, Lt. Comdr. O'Callahan inspired the gallant officers and men of the *Franklin* to fight heroically and with profound faith in the face of almost certain death and to return their stricken ship to port.

OFFICIAL COMMUNIQUE:
United States
WASHINGTON, March 19 – Twentieth Air Force communique 73:
For the second time in eight days, Superfortresses of the Twenty-first Bomber Command on Sunday bombed urban industrial targets in Nagoya, Japan's principal aircraft production center, in an incendiary attack. The strike was made by B-29's under Maj. Gen. Curtis E. LeMay in very great strength early on March 19 (Japanese time).
Returning air crewmen reported huge fires in the industrial heart of the city, with dense smoke rising to 6,000 feet. Results generally were described as ranging from good to excellent.
Fighter opposition was meager and ineffective, but anti-aircraft fire was more intense tan on the last attack on Nagoya just a week earlier. There were no losses due to enemy action.

Navy communique 585:

PACIFIC AREA

(1) United States submarines operating in Far Eastern waters have sunk fifteen enemy vessels, including two escort vessels and three destroyers. The vessels sunk were: Three destroyers, two escort vessels, one large tanker, one large cargo transport, six medium cargo vessels, one medium transport, one small cargo vessel.
(2) These actions have not been announced in any previous Navy Department communique.

GUAM, Tuesday, March 20 – Pacific Feet communique 304:

(1) Carrier aircraft of the Pacific Fleet continued their attacks on Japan on March

19 (East Longitude date). They attacked Kobe, Kure, and other objectives in and around the Inland Sea.

(2) The Marines on Iwo Island continued to search out snipers and isolated remnants of the enemy garrison on March 19,

(3) On the same date, Army fighters from Iwo bombed and strafed the airfield and radio station on Chichi Jima [Island] in the Bonins.

(4) Army Liberators of the Strategic Air Force bombed targets on Chichi Jima and Haha Jima on March 18. One enemy fighter was observed in the air at Chichi.

(5) A single Navy search Ventura of Fleet Air Wing 4 made rocket attacks on small craft and buildings in the Torishima group, southeast of Paramushiru, on March 18. On the same date, Liberators of the Eleventh Army Air Force bombed Matsuwa in the Kuriles without opposition.

(6) A navy search Privateer of Fleet Air Wing 1 sank a lugger and four small craft in the anchorage at Truk in the Carolines on March 19,

†VILLEGAS, YSMAEL R.

Rank and Organization: Staff Sergeant, U.S. Army, Company F, 127th Infantry, 32d Infantry Division.
Born: Casa Blanca, California.
Entered Service At: Casa Blanca, California.
Place and Date: Villa Verde Trail, Luzon, Philippine Islands, March 20, 1945.
Citation: S/Sgt. Villegas was a squad leader when his unit, in a forward position, clashed with an enemy strongly entrenched in connected caves and foxholes on commanding ground. He moved boldly from man to man, in the face of bursting grenades and demolition charges, through heavy machinegun and rifle fire, to bolster the spirit of his comrades. Inspired by his gallantry, his men pressed forward to the crest of the hill. Numerous enemy riflemen, refusing to flee, continued firing from their foxholes. S/Sgt. Villegas, with complete disregard for his own safety and the bullets which kicked up the dirt at his feet, charged an enemy position, and, firing at point-blank range killed the Japanese in a foxhole. He rushed a second foxhole while bullets missed him by inches, and killed 1 more of the enemy. In rapid succession he charged a third, a fourth, a fifth foxhole, each time destroying the enemy within. The fire against him increased in intensity, but he pressed onward to attack a sixth position. As he neared his goal, he was hit and killed by enemy fire. Through his heroism and indomitable fighting spirit, S.Sgt. Villegas, at the cost of his life, inspired his men to a determined attack in which they swept the enemy from the field.

OFFICIAL COMMUNIQUE:
United Nations
MANILA, Tuesday, March 20 – A communique:

PHILIPPINES

Panay: We have landed in Panay. With naval and air support, the Fortieth Division of the Eighth Army seized a beachhead at Tigbauan on the south coast fourteen miles west of the capital city of Iloilo. Complete tactical as well as strategic surprise was accomplished and our troops went ashore with practically no loss. They immediately drove inland four miles to Cordova and eastward along the coast seven miles to Oton, midway between the beachhead and Iloilo. They are rapidly closing in on the city.

Luzon: In the Eleventh Corps sector, forward elements of the Forty-third Division entered Tanay, four miles southeast of Maybancal. Pushing up the Morong River Valley against scattered resistance, they are now within a mile of Pantay, four miles northeast of Teresa. The Sixth Division on the north flank sharply repulsed an enemy counter-attack southwest of Mount Baytangan. In recent mopping up in the Zambales range, the Thirty-eighth Division killed an additional 2,654 of the enemy.

In the First Corps sector, the Twenty-fifth and thirty-second Divisions continued their converging drives on Balete Pass against increasing opposition.

Our medium and attack bombers struck Baguio City and troop concentrations to the north. Fighters sweeping the Cagayan Valley wrecked bridges and gun positions at Bagabag. Air units supporting ground operations sank several enemy barges and small craft on Laguna de Bay.

†PETERS, GEORGE J.

Rank and Organization: Private, U.S. Army, Company G, 507th Parachute Infantry, 17th Airborne Division.
Born: Cranston, Rhode Island.
Entered Service At: Cranston, Rhode Island.
Place and Date: Near Fluren, Germany, March 24, 1945.
Citation: Pvt. Peters, a platoon radio operator with Company G, made a descent into Germany near Fluren, east of the Rhine. With 10 others, he landed in field about 75 yards from a German machinegun supported by riflemen, and was immediately pinned down by heavy, direct fire. The position of the small unit seemed hopeless with men struggling to free themselves of their parachutes in a hail of bullets that cut them off from their nearby equipment bundles, when Pvt. Peters stood up without orders and

began a 1-man charge against the hostile emplacement armed only with rifle and grenades. His singlehanded assault immediately drew the enemy fire away from his comrades. He had run halfway to his objective, pitting rifle fire against that of the machinegun, when he was struck and knocked to the ground by a burst. Heroically, he regained his feet and struggled onward. Once more he was torn by bullets, and this time he was unable to rise. With gallant devotion to his self-imposed mission, he crawled directly into the fire that had mortally wounded him until close enough to hurl grenades which knocked out the machinegun, killed 2 of its operators, and drove protecting riflemen from their positions into the safety of a woods. By his intrepidity and supreme sacrifice, Pvt. Peters saved the lives of many of his fellow soldiers and made it possible for them to reach their equipment, organize, and seize their first objective.

†STRYKER, STUART S.

Rank and Organization: Private First Class, U.S. Army, Company E, 513th Parachute Infantry, 17th Airborne Division.
Born: Portland, Oregon.
Entered Service At: Portland, Oregon.
Place and Date: Near Wesel, Germany, March 24, 1945.
Citation: Pfc. Stryker was a platoon runner, when the unit assembled near Wesel, Germany, after a descent east of the Rhine. Attacking along a railroad, Company E reached a point about 250 yards from a large building used as an enemy headquarters and manned by a powerful force of Germans with rifles, machineguns, and 4 field pieces. One platoon made a frontal assault but was pinned down by intense fire from the house after advancing only 50 yards. So badly stricken that it could not return the raking fire, the platoon was at the mercy of German machine gunners when Pfc. Stryker voluntarily left a place of comparative safety, and, armed with a carbine, ran to the head of the unit. In full view of the enemy and under constant fire, he exhorted the men to get to their feet and follow him. Inspired by his fearlessness, they rushed after him in a desperate charge through an increased hail of bullets. Twenty-five yards from the objective the heroic soldier was killed by the enemy fusillades. His gallant and wholly voluntary action in the face of overwhelming firepower, however, so encouraged his comrades and diverted the enemy's attention that other elements of the company were able to surround the house, capturing more than 200 hostile soldiers and much equipment, besides freeing 3 members of an American bomber crew held prisoner there. The intrepidity and unhesitating self-sacrifice of Pfc. Strkyer were in keeping with the highest traditions of the military service.

OFFICIAL COMMUNIQUE:
United Nations
PARIS, March 24 – A special communique from Supreme Headquarters, Allied Expeditionary Force:

The Allied force today are crossing the Rhine River on a wide front north of the Ruhr.

Elements of the First Allied Airborne Army have also been landed east of the Rhine.

The operations are being assisted by the Allied navies and air forces following an intensive aerial preparation.

Communique 350 of Supreme Headquarters, Allied Expeditionary Force:

Allied forces have established another bridgehead across the Rhine in an area south of the Remagen bridgehead. The crossing was made at 2500 hours [10 P.M.] Thursday without air or artillery preparation and our forces have since been engaged in enlarging the bridgehead.

Meanwhile, other forces are in the process of mopping up the remaining German pocket in the Saar. The last such pocket between Coblenz and Ludwigshafen is being reduced at a point eight miles north of Worms. Fighting continues in Ludwigshafen, and Rhein-Gonheim, on the southern edge of the city, has been cleared.

Speyer and Landau have been captured and our units are mopping up in Edenkoben, north of Landau, and in Stirkelbach, to the east.

Our forces have broken through another section of the remaining Siegfried defenses and are rapidly reducing the last enemy elements along the Alsace border near the Rhine.

Klingenmuenster, Bergzabern, and Oberhausen have been captured and our units have reached Windem. Enemy elements remaining in this area have been squeezed into a strip ten miles deep along the Rhine east and southeast of Landau. Resistance is stubborn and we repulsed a counter-attack near Steinfeld, five miles west of Wissembourg.

Honnnef, in he northern part of our Remagen bridgehead, has been captured. In the central sector we reached the Autobahn east of Rahms, extending the Bridgehead to a depth of ten miles at that point. Farther south our units are across the Wied River on a fourteen-mile front north of Neuwied. Breitscheid, Waldbreitbach, Niederbreitbach, Niederbieber, and Segendorf have been captured, and Neuwied has been cleared. enemy artillery fire was heavy in the vicinity of Breitscheid.

Enemy armor and road transport northeast of the bridgehead were bombed by fighter-bombers.

Allied forces in the West captured 14,056 prisoners on March 22.

†MARTIN, HARRY LINN

Rank and Organization: First Lieutenant, U.S. Marine Corps Reserve.
Born: January 4, 1911, Bucyrus, Ohio.
Entered Service At: Ohio.
Place and Date: Iwo Jima, Volcano Islands, March 26, 1945.
Citation: For conspicuous gallantry and intrepidity at the risk of his life above and beyond the call of duty as platoon leader attached to Company C, 5th Pioneer Battalion, 5th Marine Division, in action against enemy Japanese forces on Iwo Jima, Volcano Islands, March 26, 1945. With his sector of the 5th Pioneer Battalion bivouac area penetrated by a concentrated enemy attack launched a few minutes before dawn, 1st Lt. Martin instantly organized a firing line with the marines nearest his foxhole and succeeded in checking momentarily the headlong rush of the Japanese. Determined to rescue several of his men trapped in positions overrun by the enemy, he defied intense hostile fire to work his way through the Japanese to the surrounded marines. Although sustaining 2 severe wounds, he blasted the Japanese who attempted to intercept him, located his beleaguered men and directed them to their own lines. When 4 of the infiltrating enemy took possession of an abandoned machinegun pit and subjected his sector to a barrage of handgrenades, 1st Lt. Martin, alone and armed only with a pistol, boldly charged the hostile position and killed all of its occupants. Realizing that his few remaining comrades could not repulse another organized attack, he called to his men to follow and then charged into the midst of the strong enemy force, firing his weapon and scattering them until he fell, mortally wounded by a grenade. By his outstanding valor, indomitable fighting spirit and tenacious determination in the face of overwhelming odds, 1st Lt. Martin permanently disrupted a coordinated Japanese attack and prevented a greater loss of life in his own and adjacent platoons. His inspiring leadership and unswerving devotion to duty reflect the highest credit upon himself and the U.S. Naval Service. He gallantly gave his life in the service of his country.

OFFICIAL COMMUNIQUE:
United States
GUAM, Monday, March 26 – Pacific Fleet communique 309:

(1) Avenger torpedo planes and Helldiver bombers of the Fifth Fleet, covered by Corsair and Hellcat fighters, destroyed a convoy of three large cargo ships, two destroyers and three other escort vessels west of the Amami Gunto [group] in the Ryukyus on March 24 (East Longitude date).

(2) On the same date, Navy search Liberators of Fleet Air Wing 1 attacked a medium-sized cargo ship in the northern Ryukyus. Navy search Venturas strafed two

small cargo ships north of the Bonins on March 25, leaving one ship dead in the water and the other damaged.

(3) Liberators of the Seventh Army Air Force bombed the airfield on Chichi Jima [Island] in the Bonins on March 23. Naval installations and air facilities were bombed and strafed by Army Mustang fighters on March 23 and 24.

(4) Storage areas on Marcus Island were bombed by Seventh Army Air Force Liberators on March 24.

(5) Attacking through intense anti-aircraft fire, planes of the Fourth Marine Aircraft Wing destroyed a bridge and a large building and started fires on Babelthuap in the Palaus on March 25.

(6) On the same date, installations on Yap, in the western Carolines, were bombed by Marine Corsair fighters.

†HEDRICK, CLINTON M.

Rank and Organization: Technical Sergeant, U.S. Army, Company I, 194th Glider Infantry, 17th Airborne Division.
Born: Cherrygrove, West Virginia.
Entered Service At: Riverton, West Virginia.
Place and Date: Near Lembeck, Germany, March 27-28, 1945.
Citation: T/Sgt. Hedrick displayed extraordinary heroism and gallantry in action on March 27-28, 1945, in Germany. Following an airborne landing near Wesel, his unit was assigned as the assault platoon for the assault on Lembeck. Three times the landing elements were pinned down by intense automatic weapons fire from strongly defended positions. Each time, T/Sgt. Hedrick fearlessly charged through heavy fire, shooting his automatic rifle from his hip. His courageous action so inspired his men that they reduced the enemy positions in rapid succession. When 6 of the enemy attempted a surprise, flanking movement, he quickly turned and killed the entire party with a burst of fire. Later, the enemy withdrew across a moat into Lembeck Castle. T/Sgt. Hedrick, with utter disregard for his own safety, plunged across the drawbridge alone in pursuit. When a German soldier, with hands upraised, declared the garrison wished to surrender, he entered the castle yard with 4 of his men to accept the capitulation. The group moved through a sally port, and was met by fire from a German self-propelled gun. Although mortally wounded, T/Sgt. Hedrick fired at the enemy gun and covered the withdrawal of his comrades. He died while being evacuated after the castle was taken. His great personal courage and heroic leadership contributed in large measure to the speedy capture of Lembeck and provided an inspiring example to his comrades.

OFFICIAL COMMUNIQUE:
United Nations
PARIS, March 27 – Communique 353 of Supreme Headquarters, Allied Expeditionary Force:

Allied forces continued to strengthen their bridgehead over the Rhine north of the Ruhr. Rees has been completely cleared and to the north, Bienen has been captured. North of Wesel, we occupied Hamminkelnn and advanced beyond it. Good progress has been made between the Lippe Canal and Dinslaken, and Bruckhausen and Hiesfeld have been captured.

In the Wesel area, enemy armor, gun positions, and troops were attacked by medium, light, and fighter-bombers operating in strength immediately ahead f our ground forces. Single enemy tanks being used as forward gun positions were hit by rocket-firing fighters. Other fighter-bombers took a heavy toll of motor transport in and behind the battle area and attacked airfields at Dorsten and Dortmund.

Our forces have broken out of the Remagen bridgehead. In the north, we gained 4,000 yards to reach the outskirts of Fitorf, on the Sieg River, and to the southeast other elements advanced up to seven miles to reach a point one miles southeast of Altenkirchen. Tanks and armored vehicles north of Altenkirchen were attacked by fighter-bombers.

In the central sector of the bridgehead, we pushed eight miles eastward and reached Maxsain, while to the south, our units gained fifteen miles to reach Staudt, two miles north of Montabaur. Our forces, in a twenty-two miles advance, drove east of Hohr-Grenzhausen and then southeastward along the Cologne-Frankfort Autobahn to Limburg.

East of the Rhine, between Coblenz and Boppard, we cleared Filsen and advanced southeast against varying resistance to take Lykershausen.

Our units, pushing out seven miles to the northeast from the bridgehead in the Mainz-Worms area, have entered the outskirts of Frankfort. We now control the south bank of the Main River for a stretch of seven miles upstream from its junction with the Rhine.

East of Frankfort, our units reached the Main River opposite Hanau. Two enemy counter-attacks, one to the south of Hanau, and the other at Aschaffenburg, were repulsed. Targets at Aschaffenburg were bombed by aircraft cooperating closely with our ground forces.

In the area between Frankfort and Darmstadt, we have entered Langen and have cleared Wixhausen. Farther south our units made another Rhine crossing without air or artillery preparation.

Allied forces in the west captured 15,132 prisoners on March 25.

†**DIETZ, ROBERT H.**
Rank and Organization: Staff Sergeant, U.S. Army, Company A, 38th Armored Infantry Battalion, 7th Armored Division.
Born: Kingston, New York.
Entered Service At: Kingston, New York.
Place and Date: Kirchain, Germany, March 29, 1945.
Citation: S/Sgt. Dietz was a squad leader when the task force to which his unit was attached encountered resistance in its advance on Kirchain, Germany. Between the town's outlying buildings 300 yards distant, and the stalled armored column were a minefield and 2 bridges defended by German rocket-launching teams and riflemen. From the town itself came heavy small-arms fire. Moving forward with his men to protect engineers while they removed the minefield and the demolition charges attached to the bridges, S/Sgt. Dietz came under intense fire. On his own initiative he advanced alone, scorning the bullets which struck all around him, until he was able to kill the bazooka team defending the first bridge. He continued ahead and had killed another bazooka team, bayoneted an enemy soldier armed with a panzerfaust and shot 2 Germans when he was knocked to the ground by another blast of another panzerfaust. He quickly recovered, killed the man who had fired at him and then jumped into waist-deep water under the second bridge to disconnect the demolition charges. His work was completed; but as he stood up to signal that the route was clear he was killed by another enemy volley from the left flank. S/Sgt. Dietz by his intrepidity and valiant effort on his self-imposed mission, singlehandedly opened the road for the capture of Kirchain and left with his comrades an inspiring example of gallantry in the face of formidable odds.

OFFICIAL COMMUNIQUE:
United Nations
PARIS, March 29-Communique 355 of Supreme Headquarters, Allied Expeditionary Force:

Allied forces breaking out of their bridgehead across the Rhine north of the Ruhr have made good progress in all sectors.

North of Rees our units reached the outskirts of Emmerich and captured Isselburg. Farther east we advanced rapidly to Borken, Erie and the part of Dorsten that is north of the Lippe Canal. South of the canal we occupied Besten and Kirchhellen and cleared Hamborn.

In the northern sector of our lower Rhine bridgehead fighter-bombers attacked enemy transport, troops, tanks and guns. At Ahaus a petrol-laden convoy was destroyed. Other fighter-bombers bombed an artillery observation post east of Isselburg.

Farther south our armored units, driving eastward, have entered Giessen, sixty-five miles east of the Rhine River, and Bellnhausen, eight miles north of Giessen. One unit reached the vicinity of Lich, six miles southeast of Giessen, after an advance of twenty-seven miles. Weilburg, southwest of Giessen, has been captured and our armor crossed the Lahn River there and at Amenau, six miles farther south. Infantry units mopping up behind the armor west of the Giessen-Weilburg area reduced enemy strongpoints and units by-passed by the armor.

Our forces across the Rhine east of Boppard reached the vicinity of Hennethal, ten miles northwest of Wiesbaden. Farther south our units, after making another crossing of the Rhine, have cleared Kastel, Kocheim and Biebrich and have entered Wiesbaden.

Our infantry and armor have half of Frankfort cleared against stiff opposition. Hanau and Aschaffenburg, farther to the east, have been cleared. North of Hanau our armor reached the vicinity of Nieder-Florstadt six miles southeast of Bad-Nauheim.

Road and rail transport and communications south and east of the Ruhr in the areas of Hagen, Wipperfurth, Berg, Neustadt and Warburg and south and east of Giessen were struck at by fighter-bombers. Rail yards at Engelskirchen and Olpe, targets at Attendorf, a road junction at Kitzingen and oil-storage depots at Neuenheerse and Ebrach were bombed by medium and light bombing.

We continued to expand our bridgehead in the Darmstadt-Mannheim area. The bridgehead area is now more than 200 square miles. Several bridges are in operation across the Rhine. Units pushing out of the bridgehead reached Niedernberg, on the Main River south of Aschaffenburg, after occupying Gross-Urmstadt.

Progress was slower in the Odenwald area, but more than a score of towns were taken. The northern half of Mannheim has been cleared. Fourteen hundred additional prisoners have been taken in this area east of the Rhine. On the west bank of the Rhine some 700 more enemy stragglers have been picked up.

Allied forces in the West captured 17,039 prisoners on March 27.

†**PETERSON, GEORGE**
Rank and Organization: Staff Sergeant, U.S. Army, Company D, 18th Infantry, 1st Infantry Division.
Born: Brooklyn, New York.
Entered Service At: Brooklyn, New York.
Place and Date: Near Eisern, Germany, March 30, 1945.
Citation: S/Sgt. Peterson was an acting platoon sergeant with Company K, near Eisern, Germany. When his company encountered an enemy battalion and came under heavy small-arms, machinegun, and mortar fire, the 2d Platoon was given the mission of flanking the enemy positions while

the remaining units attacked frontally. S/Sgt. Peterson crept and crawled to a position in the lead and motioned for the 2d Platoon to follow. A mortar shell fell close by and severely wounded him in the legs, but, although bleeding and suffering intense pain, he refused to withdraw and continued forward. Two hostile machineguns went into action at close range. Braving this grazing fire, he crawled steadily toward the guns and worked his way alone to a shallow draw, where, despite the hail of bullets, he raised himself to his knees and threw a grenade into the nearest machinegun nest, silencing the weapon and killing or wounding all its crew. The second gun was immediately turned on him, but he calmly and deliberately threw a second grenade which rocked the position and killed all 4 Germans who occupied it. As he continued forward he was spotted by an enemy rifleman, who shot him in the arm. Undeterred, he crawled some 20 yards until a third machinegun opened fire on him. By almost superhuman effort, weak from loss of blood and suffering great pain, he again raised himself to his knees and fired a grenade from his rifle, killing 3 of the enemy guncrew and causing the remaining one to flee. With the first objective seized, he was being treated by the company aid man when he observed 1 of his outpost men seriously wounded by a mortar burst. He wrenched himself from the hands of the aid man and began to crawl forward to assist his comrade, whom he had almost reached when he was struck and fatally wounded by an enemy bullet. S/Sgt. Peterson, by his gallant, intrepid actions, unrelenting fighting spirit, and outstanding initiative, silenced 3 enemy machineguns against great odds and while suffering from severe wounds, enabling his company to advance with minimum casualties.

†WILL, WALTER J.

Rank and Organization: First Lieutenant, U.S. Army, Company K, 18th Infantry, 1st Infantry Division.
Born: Pittsburgh, Pennsylvania.
Entered Service At: West Winfield, New York.
Place and Date: Near Eisern, Germany, March 30, 1945.
Citation: 1st Lt. Will displayed conspicuous gallantry during an attack on powerful enemy positions. He courageously exposed himself to withering hostile fire to rescue 2 wounded men and then, although painfully wounded himself, made a third trip to carry another soldier to safety from an open area. Ignoring the profuse bleeding of his wound, he gallantly led men of his platoon forward until they were pinned down by murderous flanking fire from 2 enemy machineguns. He fearlessly crawled alone to within 30 feet of the first enemy position, killed the crew of 4 and silenced the gun with accurate grenade fire. He continued to crawl through intense enemy

fire to within 20 feet of the second position where he leaped to his feet, made a lone, ferocious charge and captured the gun and its 9-man crew. Observing another platoon pinned down by 2 more German machineguns, he led a squad on a flanking approach and, rising to his knees in the face of direct fire, coolly and deliberately lobbed 3 grenades at the Germans, silencing 1 gun and killing its crew. With tenacious aggressiveness, he ran toward the other gun and knocked it out with grenade fire. He then returned to his platoon and led it in a fierce, inspired charge, forcing the enemy to fall back in confusion. 1st Lt. Will was mortally wounded in this last action, but his heroic leadership, indomitable courage, and unflinching devotion to duty live on as a perpetual inspiration to all those who witnessed his deeds.

OFFICIAL COMMUNIQUE:
United Nations
PARIS, March 30-Communique 356 of Supreme Headquarters, Allied Expeditionary Force:

North of Ruhr, Allied forces continued to make good progress in the break-out from their Rhine bridgehead. Several armored thrusts have achieved gains of more than ten miles. In the area of Emmerich heavy fighting continues.

Gun positions north of Emmerich were attacked by medium and light bombers.

Our armored units, thrusting deeper into Germany over a wide area east and southeast of the Ruhr, have reached numerous points on a line extending roughly from Paderborn to the north to Aschaffenburg to the south. One unit driving north advanced fifty-five miles to reach a point ten miles south of Paderborn. To the south other units have reached Lelbach, Titmaringhausen, Langewiese and Hallenberg.

Walbach, south of Siegen and northwest of Giessen, has been cleared by our infantry. Northeast of Giessen our armor has captured Marburg and reached Amoeneburg, eighty-five miles east of the Rhine.

East of Giessen we have entered Ulrichstein and Lauterbach. Small arms and sniper fire, scattered mines and road blocks were encountered in this advance.

To the south, between Giessen and Frankfort [on the Main], our units have entered Lang-Goens and Bad Nauheim and cleared up a number of towns, including Rendel and Massenheim. The city of Frankfort has been cleared.

In the areas between the Rhine and the Giessen-Frankfort road units moving from the north and from the south linked up along the Cologne-Frankfort Autobahn at Kamberg, Idstein and Niederhausen.

The city of Wiesbaden has been cleared.

East of Darmstadt our units reached the Main River on a twelve-mile front and hold the east bank for a distance of eight miles south of Aschaffenburg. Resistance stiffened in this area, with the enemy fighting from prepared positions.

Farther south armored elements advanced beyond Michelstadt. Other units are northeast of Beerfelden. Mannheim, on the Rhine, has been captured. The Neckar River has been crossed at several points in this area. Ladenburg, to the east, has been cleared and our units are within three miles of Heidelberg.

Allied forces in the west captured 18,819 prisoners March 29.

†SHOCKLEY, WILLIAM R.

Rank and Organization: Private First Class, U.S. Army, Company L, 128th Infantry, 32d Infantry Division.
Born: Bokoshe, Oklahoma.
Entered Service At: Selma, California.
Place and Date: Villa Verde Trail, Luzon, Philippine Islands, March 31, 1945.
Citation: Pfc. Shockley was in position with his unit on a hill when the enemy, after a concentration of artillery fire, launched a counterattack. He maintained his position under intense enemy fire and urged his comrades to withdraw, saying that he would "remain to the end" to provide cover. Although he had to clear two stoppages which impeded the reloading of his weapon, he halted one enemy charge. Hostile troops then began moving in on his left flank, and he quickly shifted his gun to fire on them. Knowing that the only route of escape was being cut off by the enemy, he ordered the remainder of his squad to withdraw to safety and deliberately remained at his post. He continued to fire until he was killed during the ensuing enemy charge. Later, 4 Japanese were found dead in front of his position. Pfc. Shockley, facing certain death, sacrificed himself to save his fellow soldiers, but the heroism and gallantry displayed by him enabled his squad to reorganize and continue its attack.

OFFICIAL COMMUNIQUE:
United Nations
MANILA, Saturday, March 31-A communique:

PHILIPPINES

Visayas: We have landed on the west coast of Negros near Bago. The Fortieth Division of the Eighth Army, with air and naval support, crossed Guimaras Strait and seized Pulupandan and the Bago River bridge. Quickly brushing aside enemy opposition, one of the columns drove fourteen miles to the northeast, capturing the Bacolod airstrip and reaching the outskirts of the capital at Bacolod.

A second column, sweeping south eleven miles, captured Ponte Verdra and, pushing inland along the Bago River, secured Santa Aniceta and made contact with the guerrilla forces under Colonel Abcede.

On Cebu the Americal Division, with air support, advancing to the northeast, is clearing up enemy resistance north of Guadalupe. Along the coast Mandaue and Manda have been taken. Our forces have made junction with the guerrillas under Colonel Cushing and are rapidly securing all areas to the south.

Throughout the entire Visayan area, comprising the central portion of the Phillippines, the enemy seems bewildered and his defense is rapidly collapsing. Preoccupied to the north in Luzon and fearful of his position to the south in Mindanao, he has neglected his center and left it exposed to a series of divergent thrusts, which are proving vital.

Mindanao: Fighter-bombers, with sixty-six tons, struck the Sulu Archipelago. Air and naval patrols harassed coastal sectors.

Luzon: In the south, with Lipa as a base, the Fourteenth Corps continues its advance to the east. In the center the Eleventh Corps continues mopping up in the mountains of the Sierra Madre and Zambales Ranges. Elements of the Thirty-eighth Division landed and secured Caballo Island, south of Corregidor. In the north the First Corps continued pressure on Balete Pass.

Our air force bombed enemy installations in the north and supported all ground operations.

†WETZEL, WALTER C.

Rank and Organization: Private First Class, U.S. Army, 13th Infantry, 8th Infantry Division.
Born: Huntington, West Virginia.
Entered Service At: Roseville, Michigan.
Place and Date: Birken, Germany, April 3, 1945.
Citation: Pfc. Wetzel, an acting squad leader with the Antitank Company of the 13th Infantry, was guarding his platoon's command post in a house at Birken, Germany, during the early morning hours of April 3, 1945, when he detected strong enemy forces moving in to attack. He ran into the house, alerted the occupants and immediately began defending the post against heavy automatic weapons fire coming from the hostile troops. Under cover of darkness the Germans forced their way close to the building where they hurled grenades, 2 of which landed in the room where Pfc. Wetzel and the others had taken up firing positions. Shouting a warning to his fellow soldiers, Pfc. Wetzel threw himself on the grenades and, as they exploded,

absorbed their entire blast, suffering wounds from which he died. The supreme gallantry of Pfc. Wetzel saved his comrades from death or serious injury and made it possible for them to continue the defense of the command post and break the power of a dangerous local counterthrust by the enemy. His unhesitating sacrifice of his life was in keeping with the U.S. Army's highest traditions of bravery and heroism.

OFFICIAL COMMUNIQUE:
United Nations
PARIS, April 3-Communique 360 of Supreme Headquarters, Allied Expeditionary Force:

Allied forces north and west of Emmerich continue to make good progress and in some areas have reached points fifteen miles north of the Dutch-German border. Farther north the line of the Twente Canal has been reached. To the east we captured Enschede and reached the outskirts of Rheine.

East of the Dortmund-Ems Canal our troops are fighting in the Ibbenbuergen and Lengerich areas. North of the Lippe River our armor reached Lippstadt and made substantial gains to the north and east.

Our forces are consolidating rear positions and closing in on the sides of the Ruhr pocket. Our armor cleared Paderborn, and infantry units advancing to the west reached Altenruethen, southwest of Paderborn.

Farther south our units are clearing the enemy from the vicinity of Winterberg and Langewiese and from the woods four miles southwest of Berleburg. We are fighting in Siegen and repulsed a counter-attack at Netphen, northeast of Siegen.

East of the Ruhr pocket our units repulsed a tank-supported counter-attack north of Warburg and reached Peckelsheim and Borgentreich.

We are fighting in the outskirts of Kassel and our units have reached the vicinity of Melsungen, twelve miles to the south. Resistance southeast of Kassel along the east bank of the Fulda River continues to be strong.

Our armor crossed the Fulda River and reached the Werra River at a point seventeen miles northwest of Eisenach. Other armored elements reached a point three miles northwest of Eisenach. Our infantry entered Fulda and very severe street fighting is in progress. Armored units which by-passed Fulda on the south advanced twenty-five miles eastward to the area of Mittlesdorf and Kaltennordenheim. Farther east our armor reached the Werra River at a point two miles north of Meiningen.

Our units continue to mop up in the area north and northeast of Frankfort. Groups of the enemy are ambushing supply lines along the Autobahn.

Northeast of Aschaffenburg we drove twelve miles to Bad Orb, where some 6,500 Allied personnel prisoner of war camp. Hard fighting continued in Aschaffenburg, which is almost completely destroyed.

Substantial advances were made northwest of Wuerzburg. To the southeast we are along the Main River almost to Marktbreit. The Giebelstadt airfield south of Wuerzburg was captured. In the drive up the Neckar River our armor and infantry reached the vicinity of Wimpfen, eight miles north of Heilbronn.

South of Heidelberg approximately 100 anti-tank and other artillery pieces were knocked out in heavy fighting. Our advance in this area has reached Unterowisheim, and we are near Bruchsal.

Allied forces in the west captured 12,446 prisoners on April 1.

KELLY, THOMAS J.
Rank and Organization: Corporal, U.S. Army, Medical Detachment, 48th Armored Infantry Battalion, 7th Armored Division.
Born: Brooklyn, New York.
Entered Service At: Brooklyn, New York.
Place and Date: Alemert, Germany, April 5, 1945.
Citation: Cpl. Kelly was an aid man with the 1st Platoon of Company C during an attack on the town of Alemert, Germany. The platoon, committed in a flanking maneuver, had advanced down a small, open valley overlooked by wooded slopes hiding enemy machineguns and tanks, when the attack was stopped by murderous fire that inflicted heavy casualties in the American ranks. Ordered to withdraw, Cpl. Kelly reached safety with uninjured remnants of the unit, but, on realizing the extent of casualties suffered by the platoon, voluntarily retraced his steps and began evacuating his comrades under direct machinegun fire. He was forced to crawl, dragging the injured behind him for most of the 300 yards separating the exposed area from a place of comparative safety. Two other volunteers who attempted to negotiate the hazardous route with him were mortally wounded, but he kept on with his herculean task after dressing their wounds and carrying them to friendly hands. In all, he made 10 separate trips through the brutal fire, each time bringing out a man from the death trap. Seven more casualties who were able to crawl by themselves he guided and encouraged in escaping from the hail of fire. After he had completed his heroic, self-imposed task and was near collapse from fatigue, he refused to leave his platoon until the attack had been resumed and the objective taken. Cpl. Kelly's gallantry and intrepidity in the face of seemingly certain death saved the lives of many of his fellow soldiers and was an example of bravery under fire.

†MUNEMORI, SADAO S.

Rank and Organization: Private First Class, U.S. Army, Company A, 100th Infantry Battalion, 442d Combat Team.
Born: Los Angeles, California.
Entered Service At: Los Angeles, California.
Place and Date: Near Seravezza, Italy, April 5, 1945.
Citation: Pfc. Munemori fought with great gallantry and intrepidity near Seravezza, Italy. When his unit was pinned down by grazing fire from the enemy's strong mountain defense and command of the squad devolved on him with the wounding of its regular leader, he made frontal, 1-man attacks through direct fire and knocked out 2 machineguns with grenades. Withdrawing under murderous fire and showers of grenades from other enemy emplacements, he had nearly reached a shell crater occupied by 2 of his men when an unexploded grenade bounced on his helmet and rolled toward his helpless comrades. He arose into the withering fire, dived for the missile and smothered its blast with his body. By his swift, supremely heroic action Pfc. Munemori saved 2 of his men at the cost of his own life and did much to clear the path for his company's victorious advance.

OFFICIAL COMMUNIQUE:
United Nations
PARIS, April 5-Communique 362 of Supreme Headquarters, Allied Expeditionary Force:

Allied forces north of Nijmegen reached the line of the Neder Rijn [Lek] on a broad front. In the Zevenaar area, north of Emmerich, we made further progress to the northwest. North of the Twente Canal we cleared Hengelo and made gains to the north and west. Farther north armored units advancing northeast from Nordhorn reached the line of the Ems River at several points.

Southeast of Rheine our troops crossed the Dortmund-Ems Canal. Northeast of Osnabrueck we crossed the Ems-Weser Canal and advanced beyond it. Osnabrueck has been entered, but is not yet clear. Other units by-passed the town to the south and reached a point seven miles east of it.

Muenster has been cleared, with the exception of snipers. Over 1,700 prisoners were taken in the city.

Our armor reached the Weser River in the vicinity of Bad Oeynhausen and other elements reached a point five miles northeast of Salzuflen. Other armored units reached the Bega River on the outskirts of Lemgo, capturing more than 4,000 prisoners.

Our infantry is mopping up a by-passed hill in the Teutoberg Forest. In the Detmold area we are meeting resistance from the remnants of an S.S. tank battalion.

Enemy strongpoints near Guetersloh were attacked by fighter-bombers.

Kassel has been cleared after heavy house-to-house fighting.

Our armor reached the vicinity of Oberdoria, four miles south of Mulhausen. Other armored elements are in the vicinity of Heldra, northwest of Creuzburg. Infantry advancing beyond the armor crossed the Fula River and reached a point fourteen miles northwest of Eisenach. Eisenach, by-passed by our spearhead, is an enemy strongpoint defended by tanks and infantry.

Armored spearheads cleared Gotha and entered Ohrdruf, seven miles to the south. Farther south of Gotha our armored units reached the vicinity of Oberhof and cleared Suhl.

German troop concentrations at Nordhausen were attacked by escorted heavy bombers. Fighter-bombers hit enemy airfields at Schweinfurt and Jena.

On the northern side of the Ruhr pocket our infantry crossed the Dortmund-Ems Canal, captured Ickern and Waltrop and advanced to a point one and a half miles west of Luenem after repulsing several small counter-attacks. Resistance continues in Hamm, with considerable artillery fire coming from the city.

†BEAUDOIN, RAYMOND O.

Rank and Organization: First Lieutenant, U.S. Army, Company F, 119th Infantry, 30th Infantry Division.
Born: Holyoke, Massachusetts.
Entered Service At: Holyoke, Massachusetts.
Place and Date: Hamelin, Germany, April 6, 1945.
Citation: 1st Lt. Beaudoin was leading the 2d Platoon of Company F over flat, open terrain to Hamelin, Germany, when the enemy went into action with machineguns and automatic weapons, laying down a devastating curtain of fire which pinned his unit to the ground. By rotating men in firing positions he made it possible for his entire platoon to dig in, defying all the while the murderous enemy fire to encourage his men and to distribute ammunition. He then dug in himself at the most advanced position, where he kept up a steady fire, killing 6 hostile soldiers, and directing his men in inflicting heavy casualties on the numerically superior opposing force. Despite these defensive measures, however, the position of the platoon became more precarious, for the enemy had brought up strong reinforcements and was preparing a counterattack. Three men, sent back at intervals to obtain ammunition and reinforcements, were killed by sniper fire. To relieve his command from the desperate situation, 1st Lt. Beaudoin decided to make a 1-man attack on the most damaging enemy sniper nest 90 yards to the right flank, and thereby divert attention from the runner who would attempt to pierce the enemy's barrier of bullets and secure help. Crawling over completely exposed ground, he relentlessly advanced, un-

deterred by 8 rounds of bazooka fire which threw mud and stones over him or by rifle fire which ripped his uniform. Ten yards from the enemy position he stood up and charged. At point-blank range he shot and killed 2 occupants of the nest; a third, who tried to bayonet him, he overpowered and killed with the butt of his carbine; and the fourth adversary was cut down by the platoon's rifle fire as he attempted to flee. He continued his attack by running toward a dugout, but there he was struck and killed by a burst from a machinegun. By his intrepidity, great fighting skill, and supreme devotion to his responsibility for the well-being of his platoon, 1st Lt. Beaudoin singlehandedly accomplished a mission that enabled a messenger to secure help which saved the stricken unit and made possible the decisive defeat of the German forces.

†ROBINSON, JAMES E., JR.

Rank and Organization: First Lieutenant, U.S. Army, Battery A, 861st Field Artillery Battalion, 63d Infantry Division.
Born: Toledo, Ohio.
Entered Service At: Waco, Texas.
Place and Date: Near Untergriesheim, Germany, April 6, 1945.
Citation: 1st Lt. Robinson was a field artillery forward observer attached to Company A, 253d Infantry, near Untergriesheim, Germany, on April 6, 1945. Eight hours of desperate fighting over open terrain swept by German machinegun, mortar, and small-arms fire had decimated Company A, robbing it of its commanding officer and most of its key enlisted personnel when 1st Lt. Robinson rallied the 23 remaining uninjured riflemen and a few walking wounded, and, while carrying his heavy radio for communication with American batteries, led them through intense fire in a charge against the objective. Ten German infantrymen in foxholes threatened to stop the assault, but the gallant leader killed them all at point-blank range with rifle and pistol fire and then pressed on with his men to sweep the area of all resistance. Soon afterward he was ordered to seize the defended town of Kressbach. He went to each of the 19 exhausted survivors with cheering words, instilling in them courage and fortitude, before leading the little band forward once more. In the advance he was seriously wounded in the throat by a shell fragment, but, despite great pain and loss of blood, he refused medical attention and continued the attack, directing supporting artillery fire even though he was mortally wounded. Only after the town had been taken and he could no longer speak did he leave the command he had inspired in victory and walk nearly 2 miles to an aid station where he died from his wound. By his intrepid leadership 1st Lt. Robinson was di-

rectly responsible for Company A's accomplishing its mission against tremendous odds.

COLALILLO, MIKE
Rank and Organization: Private First Class, U.S. Army, Company C, 398th Infantry, 100th Infantry Division.
Born: Hibbing, Minnesota.
Entered Service At: Duluth, Minnesota.
Place and Date: Near Untergriesheim, Germany, April 7, 1945.
Citation: Pfc. Colalillo was pinned down with other members of his company during an attack against strong enemy positions in the vicinity of Untergriesheim, Germany. Heavy artillery, mortar, and machinegun fire made any move hazardous when he stood up, shouted to the company to follow, and ran forward in the wake of a supporting tank, firing his machine pistol. Inspired by his example, his comrades advanced in the face of savage enemy fire. When his weapon was struck by shrapnel and rendered useless, he climbed to the deck of a friendly tank, manned an exposed machinegun on the turret of the vehicle, and, while bullets rattled about him, fired at an enemy emplacement with such devastating accuracy that he killed or wounded at least 10 hostile soldiers and destroyed their machinegun. Maintaining his extremely dangerous post as the tank forged ahead, he blasted 3 more positions, destroyed another machinegun emplacement and silenced all resistance in his area, killing at least 3 and wounding an undetermined number of riflemen as they fled. His machinegun eventually jammed; so he secured a submachinegun from the tank crew to continue his attack on foot. When our armored forces exhausted their ammunition and the order to withdraw was given, he remained behind to help a seriously wounded comrade over several hundred yards of open terrain rocked by an intense enemy artillery and mortar barrage. By his intrepidity and inspiring courage Pfc. Colallilo gave tremendous impetus to his company's attack, killed or wounded 25 of the enemy in bitter fighting, and assisted a wounded soldier in reaching the American lines at great risk of his own life.

CREWS, JOHN R.
Rank and Organization: Staff Sergeant, U.S. Army, Company F, 253d Infantry, 63d Infantry Division.
Born: Golden, Oklahoma.
Entered Service At: Bowlegs, Oklahoma.
Place and Date: Near Lobenbacherhof, Germany, April 8, 1945.

Citation: S/Sgt. Crews displayed conspicuous gallantry and intrepidity at the risk of his life above and beyond the call of duty on April 8, 1945, near Lobenbacherhof, Germany. As his company was advancing toward the village under heavy fire, an enemy machinegun and automatic rifle with rifle support opened up on it from a hill on the right flank. Seeing that his platoon leader had been wounded by their fire, S/Sgt. Crews, acting on his own initiative, rushed the strongpoint with 2 men of his platoon. Despite the fact that 1 of these men was killed and the other was badly wounded, he continued his advance up the hill in the face of terrific enemy fire. Storming the well-dug-in position singlehandedly, he killed 2 of the crew of the machinegun at pointblank range with his M1 rifle and wrested the gun from the hands of the German whom he had already wounded. He then with his rifle charged the strongly emplaced automatic rifle. Although badly wounded in the thigh by crossfire from the remaining enemy, he kept on and silenced the entire position with his accurate and deadly rifle fire. His actions so unnerved the remaining enemy soldiers that 7 of them surrendered and the others fled. His heroism caused the enemy to concentrate on him and permitted the company to move forward into the village.

OFFICIAL COMMUNIQUE:
United Nations
PARIS, April 7-Communique 364 of Supreme Headquarters, Allied Expeditionary Force:

Allied forces have broken out of their bridgehead across the Twente Canal and are astride the Zutphen-Deventer highway, within two miles of Deventer.

To the northeast our forward elements captured Meppen following a fifteen-mile advance. Lingen has been cleared and we have gained a bridgehead across the Ems River in the Lingen area.

We captured Ibbenbueren, east of Rheine, and reached Deipholz, northeast of Osnabruick.

Our forces are at a point five miles south of Bueckeberg. We are fighting in Hamein, and to the south we have crossed the Weser River near Tundern and continued eastward.

In the area northeast of Warburg our unites reached the vicinity of Bruechhausen and we are at Tietelsen and Borgentreich.

We captured Hofgeismar, ten miles east of Warburg, and to the southeast we reached Hann Mueden after repulsing a counter-attack.

Our forces advanced twelve miles on a five-mile front east and southeast of Kassel. We repulsed a counter-attack in the vicinity of Ungsterode, thirteen miles southwest of Kassel.

Our infantry entered Langensalza and other elements are in the area four to seven miles north of Gotha.

We cleared Eisenach and Meiningen and our armored elements have reached the vicinity of Stuetzerbach.

We made gains into the Ruhr pocket from the north and east. Hamm has been cleared and to the east we captured Nordinker and Sudinker. Our armor took Bettinghausen and Schmerlecke, northeast of Soest.

We reached Olsberg and captured Siedlinghausen, north of Winterburg, and our armor is beyond Winkhausen, west of the city. Considerable opposition is being met in the Siegin area.

We advanced to the outskirts of Fulda and cleared a substantial area to the south. Wuerzburg has been cleared and gains were made north and south of the city. Farther south our units gained more than six miles south of Bad Mergentheim. We cleared one-third of Heilbronn. East and southeast of Karlsruhe we captured Bretten and reached Stein.

Allied forces in the west captured 40,107 prisoners on April 5.

†MOSKALA, EDWARD J.

Rank and Organization: Private First Class, U.S. Army, Company C, 383d Infantry, 96th Infantry Division.
Born: November 6, 1921, Chicago, Illinois.
Entered Service At: Chicago, Illinois.
Place and Date: Kakazu Ridge, Okinawa, Ryukyu Islands, April 9, 1945.
Citation: Pfc. Moskala was the leading element when grenade explosions and concentrated machinegun and mortar fire halted the unit's attach on Kakazu Ridge, Okinawa, Ryukyu Islands. With utter disregard for his personal safety, he charged 40 yards through withering, grazing fire and wiped out 2 machinegun nests with well-aimed grenades and deadly accurate fire from his automatic rifle. When strong counterattacks and fierce enemy resistance from other positions forced his company to withdraw, he voluntarily remained behind with 8 others to cover the maneuver. Fighting from a critically dangerous position for 3 hours, he killed more than 25 Japanese before following his surviving companions through screening smoke down the face of the ridge to a gorge where it was discovered that one of the group had been left behind, wounded. Unhesitatingly, Pvt. Moskala climbed the bullet-swept slope to assist in the rescue, and, returning to lower ground, volunteered to protect other wounded while the bulk of the troops quickly took up more favorable positions. He had saved another casualty and killed 4 enemy infiltrators when he was struck and mortally wounded himself while aiding still another disabled soldier. With gallant initiative, unfaltering

courage, and heroic determination to destroy the enemy, Pvt. Moskala gave his life in his complete devotion to his company's mission and his comrades' well-being. His intrepid conduct provided a lasting inspiration for those with whom he served.

Note: The following is a newspaper account of the preceding battle for which Pfc. Moskala was awarded the Medal of Honor:

JAPANESE RETAKE HEIGHT ON OKINAWA

• • •

Americans Forced to Give Up Captured Hill in the South by Fierce Artillery Fire

• • •

OKINAWA, April 9 – In the now bitter fighting under way in southern Okinawa doughboys of the Twenty-fourth Army Corps slowly punching the Japanese backwards are being halted time and time again by the heaviest concentrations of Japanese artillery fire encountered so far in the Pacific.

In the drive down the western coast this morning a no man's land was created as we drove the enemy off a ridge that is part of his main defense line only to find it too hot to hold in the face of the Japanese artillery fire. For a long time we centered on the Japanese guns while they centered on our positions but now a straight artillery duel is in progress.

Our casualties are believed to have risen sharply as we pushed into Japanese positions prepared long in advance, which may make the Okinawa campaign as long as we originally feared before our easy time in the center and northern part of the island made us wonder whether the enemy intended to fight for it at all.

In addition to the determined artillery fire the enemy is using heavy mortar projectiles weighing possibly 1,000 pounds. But we have the biggest guns and the greatest number and more and more are being placed into position for the drive southward.

All day long as the infantry gained only a bit here and a bit there on either side of the island, trucks bringing up supplies and reinforcements churned up the dusty island roads.

Three Counter-Attacks Smashed

Three counter-attacks were made on our right flank in the late afternoon, all of which were beaten off, and the Japanese tried numerous infiltrations along the eastern shore. Three Japanese, one nude and two other covered only by camouflage cloth, were discovered among reeds and shot down.

Rising hill masses face our forces on both sides of the island with the Japanese positions protected in both cases by Japanese guns, operated, probably on tracks, from caves.

Rising hill masses face our forces on both sided of the island with the Japanese positions protected in both cases by Japanese guns, operated, probably on tracks, from caves.

Two main ridges held by the Japanese dominate all the area crossing the island. In the front of these ridges are lower ones. Every morning our patrols start forward accompanied usually by tanks. They hit strong points consisting of anti-tank ditches, in some cases 2,000 yards long, and barbed wire and pillboxes. Supporting these positions the Japanese artillery works from its caves, the enemy artillerymen moving the guns out, firing, then drawing them back into the caves.

In some cases our Piper Cub planes hovering overhead spot the Japanese guns. Our heavy artillery led by Long Toms, the big 155 mm. guns, blast away again and again till the Japanese position is either no more or so weakened the infantry patrols can rush the pillboxes and caves. In this artillery duel so far our firepower and fire direction are clearly superior to those of the enemy.

Japanese Defense Line

Most of this is going on along the west coast of the island, were the Japanese first main line of defense was reached several days ago. On the east coast, where the Seventh Division was held up by more difficult terrain, the main line has just about been reached by now. It is a straight line on the ridge crossing the island starting just north of Machinato on the west coast to a point 3,000 yards north of the Yonabaru airstrip on the east coast.

We have taken the lower ridges of this line in the west and our patrols have pushed down toward the north end of the Yonabaru air strip in the east, but the enemy line cannot yet be called broken.

South of this is the apparent second line of Japanese defense running east from the northern edge of Naha, the island's capital and largest city, through Shuri to the village of Yonabaru in the east. Shuri is believed to be the key to this line, with Japanese artillery heavily concentrated there. Once Shuri is in our hands we would have an observation point over-looking the entire southern end of the island and Japanese positions probably would crumble rapidly.

All evidence indicates that the Japanese expected landings by us from the south rather than through the difficult reef barrier on the western shore. therefore their defense positions pointed that way and also toward domination of the eastern beaches that guard Nakagusuku Bay, Okinawa's great anchorage.

Engineers Handle a Situation

The Japanese cannot always be counted out of a position even after it has been taken. We took a village on the eastern coast in the central part of the island the third day of the invasion. The village was deserted then, but valuable to us because of sand pits. Last night small Japanese forces, presumably coming out of caves, made an attack on our engineers, attempting to destroy heavy equipment we had there. The Japanese were wiped out by the engineers.

How many Japanese troops are in the southernmost ten miles of the island is undetermined, but estimates continue to go downward rather than upward.

ERWIN, HENRY E. (Air Mission)
Rank and Organization: Staff Sergeant, U.S. Army Air Corps, 52d Bombardment Squadron, 29th Bombardment Group, 20th Air Force.
Born: May 8, 1921, Adamsville, Alabama.
Entered Service At: Bessemer, Alabama.
Place and Date: Koriyama, Japan, April 12, 1945.
Citation: S/Sgt. Erwin was the radio operator of a B-29 airplane leading a group formation to attack Koriyama, Japan. He was charged with the additional duty of dropping phosphorous smoke bombs to aid in assembling the group when the launching point was reached. Upon entering the assembly area, anti-aircraft fire and enemy fighter opposition was encountered. Among the phosphorous bombs launched by S/Sgt. Erwin, 1 proved faulty, exploding in the launching chute, and shot back into the interior of the aircraft, striking him in the face. The burning phosphorous obliterated his nose and completely blinded him. Smoke filled the plane, obscuring the vision of the pilot. S/Sgt. Erwin realized that the aircraft and crew would be lost if the burning bomb remained in the plane. Without regard for his own safety, he picked it up and feeling his way, instinctively, crawled around the gun turret and headed for the copilot's window. He found the navigator's table obstructing his passage. Grasping the burning bomb between his forearm and body, he unleashed the spring lock and raised the table. Struggling through the narrow passage he stumbled forward into the smoke-filled pilot's compartment. Groping with his burning hands, he located the window and threw the bomb out. Completely aflame, he fell back upon the floor. The smoke cleared, the pilot, at 300 feet, pulled the plane out of its dive. S/Sgt. Erwin's gallantry and heroism above and beyond the call of duty saved the lives of his comrades.

OFFICIAL COMMUNIQUE:
United States
Washington April 12, Twentieth Air Force communique 84:

In the longest mission yet flown by the Twenty-first Bomber Command from its bases in the Marianas a very large task force of B-29's under Maj: Gen. Curtis E. LeMay, delivered a three-way attack upon industrial targets on the Japanese island of Honshu Wednesday (April 12, Japanese time).

The Superfortresses, escorted by fighter planes of the Seventh Air Force, attacked the Hodagaya chemical industry at Koriyama, the Koriyama chemical industries and the Nakajima aircraft engine plant at Tokyo.

Bombing was carried out by visual means in clear weather, and crew members reported results ranged from good to excellent. Enemy fighter opposition was slight and anti-aircraft fire was moderate. Bombers crews reported destroying ten enemy planes and probably destroying four others.

None of our planes was lost to enemy action.

†**HASTINGS, JOE R.**
Rank and Organization: Private First Class, U.S. Army, Company C, 386th Infantry, 97th Infantry Division.
Born: Malvern, Ohio.
Entered Service At: Magnolia, Ohio.
Place and Date: Drabenderhohe, Germany, April 12, 1945.
Citation: Pfc. Hastings fought gallantly during an attack against strong enemy forces defending Drabenderhohe, Germany, from the dug-in positions on commanding ground. As squad leader of a light machinegun section supporting the advance of the 1st and 3d Platoons, he braved direct rifle, machinegun, 20-mm, and mortar fire, some of which repeatedly missed him only by inches, and rushed forward over 350 yards of open, rolling fields to reach a position from which he could fire on the enemy troops. From this vantage point he killed the crews of a 20-mm. gun and a machinegun, drove several enemy riflemen from their positions, and so successfully shielded the 1st Platoon, that it had time to reorganize and remove its wounded to safety. Observing that the 3d Platoon to his right was being met by very heavy 40-mm. and machinegun fire, he ran 150 yards with his gun to the leading elements of that unit, where he killed the crew of the 40-mm.gun. As spearhead of the 3d Platoon's attack, he advanced, firing his gun held at hip height, disregarding the bullets that whipped past him, until the assault had carried 175 yards to the objective. In this charge he and the riflemen he led killed or wounded many of the

fanatical enemy and put 2 machineguns out of action. Pfc. Hastings, by his intrepidity, outstanding leadership, and unrelenting determination to wipe out the formidable German opposition, cleared the path for his company's advance into Drabenderhohe. He was killed 4 days later while again supporting the 3d Platoon.

OFFICIAL COMMUNIQUE:
United Nations
PARIS, April 12 - Communique 369 of Supreme Headquarters, allied Expeditionary Force:

Allied forces have launched an attack westward across the Ijasel River. We pushed beyond Furstenau, crossed the Hass Canal and captured Badbergen, Ankum and Bersenbrusche and Vorden.

Southeast of Bremen our forces are in Wildeshausen and Harpstedt, but farther east we are meeting strong enemy opposition.

Our armored elements, advancing more than fifty miles eastward, reached the Elbe River at Magdeburg after enveloping Wolfenbuettel, just south of Brunswick, and passing through Eilenstadt and Wulferstedt, southwest of Oscheraleben. Other armored units have reached Meine, north of Brunswick, while infantry is heavily engaged in and around the city against stubborn enemy delaying action. Our infantry made rapid progress to the vicinity of Halberstadt.

Armored and infantry units reached Herzberg and Osterhagen, northwest of Duderstadt. Armored elements cleared Nordhausen, and Bilsingsleben, eight miles northeast of Clingen, and are one mile from Koelleda to the southwest after a twenty-two-mile advances.

Southwest of Coburg we made limited advances against scattered resistance.

Schweinfurt was entered after it was practically surrounded and heavy house-to-house fighting is in progress. Armored units pushed along the Main River to the east and also made gains to the south. To the southeast we advanced four miles along the highway between Ochenfurt and Ansbach, occupied Uffenheim and Rudolzhofen.

Our armor withdrew from a part of the Crailsheim wedge after more than 1,500 prisoners and important enemy material were taken. Our bridgehead over the Kocher in the vicinity of Neiderhall was extended to a depth of three miles. Progress was made in Heimbronn, and north of the city two bridgeheads over the Neckar River have been joined.

We made advances up to three miles southeast of Karlsruhe and have reached the Black Forest. Our bridgehead across the Enz River east of Pforzheim has been extended.

Allied forces in the west captured 25,846 prisoners on April 10.

In the Ruhr pocket our infantry cleared Essen, captured Gelsenkirchen and entered Bochum. We took Frondenberg, south of Unna. West of Meschede we captured Freienohl. Our infantry advancing in the area north of Siegen took Attendorf, while armored elements made limited gains north of Siegburg. Enemy armor and artillery around Dortmund and in the triangle formed by Remsheid, Gummersbach and Meschede were attacked by fighter-bombers.

ANDERSON, BEAUFORT T.

Rank and Organization: Technical Sergeant, U.S. Army, 381st Infantry, 96th Infantry Division.
Born: Eagle, Wisconsin.
Entered Service At: Soldiers Grove, Wisconsin.
Place and Date: Okinawa, April 13, 1945.
Citation: T/Sgt. Anderson displayed conspicuous gallantry and intrepidity above and beyond the call of duty. When a powerfully conducted predawn Japanese counterattack struck his unit's flank, he ordered his men to take cover in an old tomb, and then, armed only with a carbine, faced the on-slaught alone. After emptying 1 magazine at pointblank range into the screaming attackers, he seized an enemy mortar dud and threw it back among the charging Japs, killing several as it burst. Securing a box of mortar shells, he extracted the safety pins, banged the bases upon a rock to arm them and proceeded alternately to hurl shells and fire his piece among the fanatical foe, finally forcing them to withdraw. Despite the protests of his comrades, and bleeding profusely from a severe shrapnel wound, he made his way to his company commander to report the action. T/Sgt. Anderson's intrepid conduct in the face of overwhelming odds accounted for 25 enemy killed and several machineguns and knee mortars destroyed, thus singlehandedly removing a serious threat to the company's flank.

OFFICIAL COMMUNIQUE:
UNITED STATES
GUAM, Friday, April 13-Pacific Fleet communique 330:

(1) The Sixth Marine Division on Okinawa moved forward against sporadic resistance by the enemy on Motobu Peninsula on April 12 (East Longitude date). On Ishikawa Isthmus our troops continued to press northward over rugged terrain and extremely poor roads. The First Marine Division continued mopping up in its zone of action.
(2) There was virtually no change in the lines in the southern sector of Okinawa, where the Twenty-four Army Corps, including elements of the Twenty-seventh

and Ninety-sixth Divisions, continued to meet strong enemy resistance on April 12.

(3) On April 12 large numbers of enemy aircraft made desperate suicidal attacks on our forces in the Okinawa area. Early in the morning seven enemy aircraft were shot down in the vicinity of the Hagushi beaches. During the afternoon ships' guns, carrier aircraft and shore-based anti-aircraft shot down 111 of the attackers. One of our destroyers was sunk during these attacks and several other surface units were damaged but remained in operation.

KERSTETTER, DEXTER J.

Rank and Organization: Private First Class, U.S. Army, Company C, 130th Infantry, 33d Infantry Division.
Born: Centralia, Washington.
Entered Service At: Centralia, Washington.
Place and Date: Near Galiano, Luzon, Philippine Islands, April 13, 1945.
Citation: Pfc. Kerstetter was with his unit in a dawn attack against hill positions approachable only along a narrow ridge paralleled on each side by steep cliffs which were heavily defended by enemy mortars, machineguns, and rifles in well-camouflaged spider holes and tunnels leading to caves. When the leading element was halted by intense fire that inflicted 5 casualties, Pfc. Kerstetter passed through the American line with his squad. Placing himself well in advance of his men, he grimly worked his way up the narrow steep hogback, meeting the brunt of enemy action. With well-aimed shots and rifle-grenade fire, he forced the Japs to take cover. He left the trail and moving down a cliff that offered only precarious footholds, dropped among 4 Japs at the entrance to a cave, fired his rifle from his hip and killed them all. Climbing back to the trail, he advanced against heavy enemy machinegun, rifle, and mortar fire to silence a heavy machinegun by killing its crew of 4 with rifle fire and grenades. He expended his remaining ammunition and grenades on a group of approximately 20 Japs, scattering them, and returned to his squad for more ammunition and first aid for his left hand, which had been blistered by the heat from his rifle. Resupplied, he guided a fresh platoon into a position from which a concerted attack could be launched, killing 3 hostile soldiers on the way. In all, he dispatched 16 Japs that day. The hill was taken and held against the enemy's counterattacks, which continued for 3 days. Pfc. Kerstetter's dauntless and gallant heroism was largely responsible for the capture of this key enemy position, and his fearless attack in the face of great odds was an inspiration to his comrades in their dangerous task.

OFFICIAL COMMUNIQUE:
UNITED NATIONS
MANILA, Friday, April 13-A communique:

PHILIPPINES

Visayas: In another thrust in the swift campaign to clear the bewildered enemy from the Visayas, we have landed on Bohol, last of the Visayan Islands not yet liberated. Elements of the American Division of the Eighth Army went ashore near Tagbilaran under cover of naval and air support and rapidly drove inland in an endeavor to secure control of the entire island before the surprised enemy could rally his strength. Local guerrilla forces are acting in coordination.

On Cebu our troops, clearing the hills to the northeast, made substantial gains against moderate resistance.

Luzon: In south Luzon the Fourteenth Corps swept forward thirty miles form Atimonan to Calauag, on the east coast of the Bicol opposite the Bondoc Peninsula, closing the trap on enemy left in the peninsula. At Legaspi the other prong of the pincer advanced five miles to Camalig.

In the center the Eleventh Corps steadily continued the reduction of fixed enemy positions in the upper Marikina River area, sealing many caves, and advanced in the Angat weathershed toward Ipo. Investigation of one cave recently sealed in the Bosoboso River sector practically without loss on our part revealed 257 enemy dead inside.

In the north troops of the First Corps continued the pressure on enemy cave defenses in the Balete Pass-Villa Verde Trail areas. Several enemy counter-attacks in the vicinity of Highway 5 were repulsed.

In the air attack bombers and fighters closely supported ground operations in all sectors.
Mindanao: Dive and medium bombers and fighters attacked enemy defense positions and supply areas near Davao and in the interior, causing much damage.

†MAGRATH, JOHN D.

Rank and Organization: Private First Class, U.S. Army, Company G, 85th Infantry, 10th Mountain Division.
Born: East Norwalk, Connecticut.
Entered Service At: East Norwalk, Connecticut.
Place and Date: Near Castel d'Aiano, Italy, April 14, 1945.
Citation: Pfc. Magrath displayed conspicuous gallantry and intrepidity above and beyond the call of duty when his company was pinned down by heavy artillery, mortar, and small-arms fire, near Castel d'Aiano, Italy.

Volunteering to act as a scout, armed with only a rifle, he charged headlong into withering fire, killing 2 Germans and wounding 3 in order to capture a machinegun. Carrying this enemy weapon across an open field through heavy fire, he neutralized 2 more machinegun nests; he then circled behind 4 other Germans, killing them with a burst as they were firing on his company. Spotting another dangerous enemy position to this right, he knelt with the machinegun in his arms and exchanged fire with the Germans until he had killed 2 and wounded 3. The enemy now poured increased mortar and artillery fire on the company's newly won position. Pfc. Magrath fearlessly volunteered again to brave the shelling in order to collect a report of casualties. Heroically carrying out this task, he made the supreme sacrifice - a climax to the valor and courage that are in keeping with highest traditions of the military service.

STREET, GEORGE LEVICK, III

Rank and Organization: Commander, U.S. Navy, U.S.S. *Tirante*.
Born: July 27, 1913, Richmond, Virginia.
Entered Service At: Virginia.
Place and Date: Harbor of Quelpart Island, off the coast of Korea, April 14, 1945.
Citation: For conspicuous gallantry and intrepidity at the risk of his life above and beyond the call of duty as commanding officer of the U.S.S. *Tirante* during the first war patrol of that vessel against enemy Japanese surface forces in the harbor of Quelpart Island, off the coast of Korea, on April 14, 1945. With the crew at surface battle stations, Comdr. (then Lt. Comdr.) Street approached the hostile anchorage from the south within 1,200 yards of the coast to complete a reconnoitering circuit of the island. Leaving the 10-fathom curve far behind, he penetrated the mined and shoal-obstructed waters of the restricted harbor despite numerous patrolling vessels and in defiance of 5 shorebased radar stations and menacing aircraft. Prepared to fight it out on the surface if attacked, Comdr. Street went into action, sending 2 torpedoes with deadly accuracy into a large Japanese ammunition ship and exploding the target in mountainous and blinding glare of white flames. With the *Tirante* instantly spotted by the enemy as she stood out plainly in the flare of light, he ordered the torpedo data computer set up while retiring and fired his last 2 torpedoes to disintegrate in quick succession the leading frigate and a similar flanking vessel. Clearing the gutted harbor at emergency full speed ahead, he slipped undetected along the shoreline, diving deep as a pursuing patrol dropped a pattern of depth charges at the point of submergence. His illustrious record of combat

achievement during the first war patrol of the *Tirante* characterizes Comdr. Street as a daring and skilled leader and reflects the highest credit upon himself, his valiant command, and the U.S. Naval Service.

OFFICIAL COMMUNIQUE:
UNITED NATIONS
ROME, April 14-An Allied Mediterranean communique:

LAND

In spite of increasing enemy resistance, the Eighth Army has made further gains along its entire front.

Our troops are in the outskirts of Imol and are within two miles of Bastia.

On the west coast American troops of the Fifth Army have continued their advance.

A supplementary communique of the Allied Mediterranean Command, as recorded by the Federal Communications Commission:

West of Massa Lombarda troops of the Eighth Army have reached the River Siliaro and at some points have forced crossings against strong resistance. On the remainder of the Eighth Army front progress continues to be made.

Fifth Army patrols have been active.

MANILA, Sunday, April 15-A communique:

PHILIPPINES

Luzon: In southern Luzon our troops landed on Rapu Rapu and Batan Islands, in Albay Gulf, quickly eliminating the enemy garrison.

In the First Corps sector our troops are closing in on Bagulo. In the air numerous bomber and fighter missions were flown in local support of ground troops and in attacks on rear installations. Five hundred and forty tons of bombs were dropped, followed by low-level strafing.

Visayas: On Cebu the enemy's hill positions are rapidly being outflanked and enveloped, while constant air strikes by our bombers and fighters are sapping his meager reserves of men and material.

Mindanao: Heavy bombers struck enemy installations at Davao, starting large fires.

FORMOSA

Patrol planes bombed and strafed the west coast.

CHINA COAST

Our air blockade wrecked six small freighters and swept rail facilities in Indo-China.

†**GONSALVES, HAROLD**
Rank and Organization: Private First Class, U.S. Marine Corps Reserve.
Born: January 28, 1926, Alameda, California.
Entered Service At: California.
Place and Date: Okinawa, April 15, 1945.
Citation: For conspicuous gallantry and intrepidity at the risk of his life above and beyond the call of duty while serving as Acting Scout Sergeant with the 4th Battalion, 15th Marines, 6th Marine Division, during action against enemy Japanese forces on Okinawa Shima in the Ryukyu Chain, April 15, 1945. Undaunted by the powerfully organized opposition encountered on Motobu Peninsula during the fierce assault waged by his battalion against the Japanese stronghold at Mount Yaetake, Pfc. Gonsalves repeatedly braved the terrific enemy bombardment to aid his forward observation team in directing well-placed artillery fire. When his commanding officer determined to move into the front lines in order to register a more effective bombardment in the enemy's defensive position, he unhesitatingly advanced uphill with the officer and another Marine despite a slashing barrage of enemy mortar and rifle fire. As they reached the front and a Japanese grenade fell close within the group, instantly Pfc. Gonsalves dived on the deadly missile, absorbing the exploding charge in his own body and thereby protecting the others from serious and perhaps fatal wounds. Stouthearted and indomitable, Pfc. Gonsalves readily yielded his own chances of survival that his fellow marines might carry on the relentless battle against a fanatic enemy and his cool decision, prompt action and valiant spirit of self-sacrifice in the face of certain death reflect the highest credit upon himself and upon the U.S. Naval Service.

BUSH, RICHARD EARL

Rank and Organization: Corporal, U.S. Marine Corps Reserve, 1st Battalion, 4th Marines, 6th Marine Division.
Born: December 23, 1923, Glasgow, Kentucky.
Entered Service At: Kentucky.
Place and Date: Mount Yaetake on Okinawa, Ryukyu Islands, April 16, 1945.
Citation: For conspicuous gallantry and intrepidity at the risk of his life above and beyond the call of duty as a squad leader serving with the 1st Battalion, 4th Marines, 6th Marine Division, in action against enemy Japanese forces, during the final assault against Mount Yaetake on Okinawa, Ryukyu Islands, April 16, 1945. Rallying his men forward with indomitable determination, Cpl. Bush boldly defied the slashing fury of concentrated Japanese artillery fire pouring down from the gun-stunned mountain fortress to lead his squad up the face of the rocky precipice, sweep over the ridge, and drive the defending troops from their deeply entrenched position. With his unit, the first to break through to the inner defense of Mount Yaetake, he fought relentlessly in the forefront of the action until seriously wounded and evacuated with others under protecting rocks. Although prostrate under medical treatment when a Japanese handgrenade landed in the midst of the group, Cpl. Bush, alert and courageous in extremity as in battle, unhesitantly pulled the deadly missile to himself and absorbed the shattering violence of the exploding charge in his body, thereby saving his fellow marines from severe injury or death despite the certain peril to his own life. By his valiant leadership and aggressive tactics in the face of savage opposition, Cpl. Bush contributed materially to the success of the sustained drive toward the conquest of this fiercely defended outpost of the Japanese Empire. His constant concern for the welfare of his men, his resolute spirit of self-sacrifice, and his unwavering devotion to duty throughout the bitter conflict enhance and sustain the highest traditions of the U.S. Naval Service.

Note: The following is a newspaper account of the preceding battle for which Pvt. Gonsalves and Cpl. Bush were awarded the Medal of Honor:

MARINES OVERRUN BIG OKINAWA AREA

• • •

**Go within 12 Miles of North Tip of Island,
Win Most of Motobu Peninsula**

• • •

GUAM, Sunday, April 15 – While American Army troops beat off a small counter-attack in the southern part of Okinawa, marines of the Third Amphibious Corps continued their northward advance to a point about twelve miles from the northern tip of the island, Fleet Admiral Chester W. Nimitz announced today. Meantime American and British carrier units continued their attacks on near-by islands with new aerial blows against the Sakishima Islands and Formosa.

Marine forward patrol reached the towns of Momobaru on the west coast and Arakawa on the east coast against "negligible resistance." In this area the terrain is rough and largely undeveloped. The advance northward has so far been virtually unopposed, with marine units feeling their way through the rough terrain and at-tempting to cover as much area as possible.

A similar situation prevails on Motobu Peninsula, which juts out from the northwestern coast of Okinawa. Here, according to the communique, the Marines "are attacking small concentrations of enemy troops which continue to resist." The marines now have virtually completed occupation of the peninsula.

While these advances have been made against little opposition and in an area not susceptible to a long-range military development, they will serve the highly useful purpose of securing the northern half of the island and preventing infiltra-tion from the north into the more important areas of Okinawa farther south.

BURKE, FRANK (also known as FRANCIS X. BURKE)
Rank and Organization: First Lieutenant, U.S. Army, 15th Infantry, 3d Infantry Division.
Born: September 29, 1918, New York, New York.
Entered Service At: Jersey City, New Jersey.
Place and Date: Nuremberg, Germany, April 17, 1945.
Citation: 1st Lt. Burke fought with extreme gallantry in the streets of war torn Nuremberg, Germany, where the 1st Battalion, 15th Infantry, was en-gaged in rooting out fanatical defenders of the citadel of Nazism. As battal-ion transportation officer he had gone forward to select a motor-pool site, when, in a desire to perform more than his assigned duties and participate in the fight, he advanced beyond the lines of the forward riflemen. Detect-ing a group of about 10 Germans making preparations for a local counter-attack, he rushed back to a nearby American company, secured a light machinegun with ammunition, and daringly opened fire on this superior force, which deployed and returned his fire with machine pistols, rifles, and rocket launchers. From another angle a German machinegun tried to blast him from his emplacement, but 1st Lt. Burke killed this guncrew and

drove off the survivors of the unit he had originally attacked. Giving his next attention to enemy infantrymen in ruined buildings, he picked up a rifle dashed more than 100 yards through intense fire and engaged the Germans from behind an abandoned tank. A sniper nearly hit him from a cellar only 20 yards away, but he dispatched this adversary by running directly to the basement window, firing a full clip into it and then plunging through the darkened aperture to complete the job. He withdrew from the fight only long enough to replace his jammed rifle and secure grenades, then reengaged the Germans. Finding his shots ineffective, he pulled the pins from 2 grenades, and holding 1 in each hand, rushed the enemy-held building, hurling his missiles just as the enemy threw a potato masher grenade at him. In the triple explosion the Germans were wiped out and 1st Lt Burke was dazed; but he emerged from the shower of debris that engulfed him, recovered his rifle, and went on to kill 3 more Germans and meet the charge of a machine pistolman, who he cut down with 3 calmly delivered shots. He then retired toward the American lines and there assisted a platoon in a raging, 30-minute fight against formidable armed hostile forces. This enemy forum was repulsed, and the intrepid fighter moved to another friendly group which broke the power of a German unit armed with a 20-mm. gun in a fierce fire fight. In 4 hours of heroic action, 1st Lt. Burke singlehandedly killed 11 and wounded 3 enemy soldiers and took a leading role in engagements in which an additional 29 enemy were killed or wounded. His extraordinary bravery and superb fighting skill were an inspiration to his comrades, and his entirely voluntary mission into extremely dangerous territory hastened the fall of Nuremberg, in his battalion's sector.

DALY, MICHAEL J.

Rank and Organization: Captain (then Lieutenant), U.S. Army, Company A, 15th Infantry, 3d Infantry Division.
Born: September 15, 1924, New York, New York.
Entered Service At: Southport, Connecticut.
Place and date: Nuremberg, Germany, April 18, 1945.
Citation: Early in the morning of April 18, 1945, Lt. Daly led his company through the shell-battered, sniper-infested wreckage of Nuremberg, Germany. When blistering machinegun fire caught his unit in an exposed position, he ordered his men to take cover, dashed forward alone, and, as bullets whined about him, shot the 3-man guncrew with his carbine. Continuing the advance at the head of his company, he located an enemy patrol armed with rocket launchers which threatened friendly armor. He again went forward alone, secured a vantage point and opened fire on the Ger-

mans. Immediately he became the target for concentrated machine-pistol and rocket-fire, which blasted the rubble about him. Calmly, he continued to shoot at the patrol until he had killed all 6 enemy infantrymen. Continuing boldly far in front of his company, he entered a park, where as his men advanced, a German machinegun opened up on them without warning. With his carbine, he killed the gunner; and then, from a completely exposed position, he directed machinegun fire on the remainder of the crew until they were all dead. In a final duel, he wiped out a third machinegun emplacement with rifle fire at a range of 10 yards. By fearlessly engaging in 4 singlehanded fire fights with a desperate, powerfully armed enemy, Lt. Daly, voluntarily taking all major risk himself and protecting his men at every opportunity, killed 15 Germans, silenced 3 enemy machineguns and wiped out an entire enemy patrol. His heroism during the lone bitter struggle with fanatical enemy forces was an inspiration to the valiant Americans who took Nuremberg.

†MERRELL, JOSEPH F.

Rank and Organization: Private, U.S. Army, Company I, 15th Infantry, 3d Infantry Division.
Born: Staten Island, New York.
Entered Service At: Staten Island, New York.
Place and date: Near Lohe, Germany, April 18, 1945.
Citation: Pvt. Merrell made a gallant, 1-man attack against vastly superior enemy forces near Lohe, Germany. His unit, attempting a quick conquest of hostile-hill positions that would open the route to Nuremberg before the enemy could organize his defense of that city, was pinned down by brutal fire from rifles, machine pistols, and 2 heavy machineguns. Entirely on his own initiative, Pvt. Merrell began a singlehanded assault. He ran 100 yards through concentrated fire, barely escaping death at each stride, and at point-blank range engaged 4 German machine pistolmen with his rifle, killing all of them while their bullets ripped his uniform. As he started forward again, his rifle was smashed by a snipers bullet, leaving him armed only with 3 grenades. But he did not hesitate. He zigzagged 200 yards through a hail of bullets to within 10 yards of the first machinegun, where he hurled 2 grenades and then rushed the position ready to fight with his bare hands if necessary. In the emplacement he seized a Luger pistol and killed what Germans had survived the grenade blast. Rearmed, he crawled toward the second machinegun located 30 yards away, killing 4 Germans in camouflaged foxholes on the way, but himself receiving a critical wound in the abdomen. And yet he went on, staggering, bleeding, disregarding bullets which tore through the folds of his clothing and glanced off his helmet. He

threw his last grenade into the machinegun nest and stumbled on to wipe out the crew. He had completed this self-appointed task when a machine pistol burst killed him instantly. In his spectacular 1-man attack Pvt. Merrell killed 6 Germans in the first machinegun emplacement, 7 in the next, and an additional 10 infantrymen who were astride his path to the weapons which would have decimated his unit had he not assumed the burden of the assault and stormed the enemy positions with utter fearlessness, intrepidity of the highest order, and a willingness to sacrifice his own life so that his comrades could go on to victory.

OFFICIAL COMMUNIQUE:
United Nations
PARIS, April 18 - Communique 375 Supreme Headquarters, Allied Expeditionary force:

Allied forces south of the Ijsselmeer, in Holland, captured Barneveld and Voorthuizen and occupied Apeldoorn. In North Holland we captured Harlingen and cleared the last of the enemy from Groningen.

North of Friesoythe, in Germany, we established a bridgehead over the Kuesten canal against which the enemy launched two unsuccessful counter-attacks, South of hamburg our armor advanced across the Luneburg Moor and captured Schnevedingen and Ebstorf. Fighting continues in Uelze, but we have advanced beyond the town to the northeast.

Our infantry and armor launched an attack on Magdeburg following a heavy bombardment by artillery and medium, light and fighter-bombers. In the bridgehead area south of Magdeburg our forces east of the Elbe repulsed a heavy counterattack and destroyed fifteen to twenty of the estimated thirty enemy tanks participating. There were no changes in the Dessau area, where we are meeting resistance from German civilians as well as troops. Farther south our forces advanced to Bitterfeld, where we have been held up by enemy tanks and artillery fire. Halle is half cleared.

The enemy commander at Chemnitz refused a surrender demand by our forces, which are two miles west of the city. To the southwest we have taken Werdau and cleared Greiz after heavy street fighting. Our units are enveloping Leizig from the west, south and east.

In the Harz pocket our forces on the north side captured Wernigerode and are meeting stiff resistance as they push southward from the town. Other elements advancing from the southern edge entered Braulage and pushed four miles northeast form Guentersberge.

Our armor reached Hopfenche, fifteen miles southeast of Bayreuth, in an advance of some ten miles. Nuremberg was almost encircled, while stubborn resistance continued in the outskirts. To the north Eriangen was captured. Rothenburg was taken after negotiations for surrender failed. Farther west made against varying resistance.

Strong points near Rothenburg and in the Heilbronn and Halle area, and a troop concentration northwest of Cralisheim, were hit by fighter-bombers.

Southwest of Stuttgart, Nagold was reached after an advance of some twelve miles. In the Black Forest and the Rhine plain upriver from Strasbourg further gains were scored.

In the Maritime Alps several peaks have been taken and Briel, near the Italian border, was entered.

Allied forces in the west captured 112,033 prisoners on April 16.

In the Ruhr the enemy has been confined to a single pocket of about 125 square miles in the Duesseldorf area. We are fighting in the eastern section of Duesseldorf. To the northeast our armor advanced to a point just south of Kettwig and met our units moving from the north.

On the French Atlantic coast the enemy pockets at Pointe de Grave and Points de la Coubre were subjected to heavy artillery concentrations and were bombed by medium bombers. Our ground forces made a deep penetration into the La Coubre Forest, where enemy resistance was broken and mopping-up is proceeding rapidly. The German admiral commanding enemy forces in the Royan pocket and his entire staff were captured.

†MAY, MARTIN O.

Rank and Organization: Private First Class, U.S. Army, 307th Infantry, 77th Infantry Division.
Born: Phillipsburg, New Jersey.
Entered Service At: Phillipsburg, New Jersey.
Place and Date: Iegusuku-Yama, Ie Shima, Ryuku Islands, April 19-21, 1945.
Citation: Pfc. May gallantry maintained a 3-day stand in the face of terrible odds when American troops fought for possession of the rugged slopes of Iegusuku-Yama on Ie Shima, Ryukyu Island. After placing his heavy machinegun in an advantageous yet vulnerable position on a ridge to support riflemen, he became the target of fierce mortar and small arms fire from counterattacking Japanese. He repulsed this assault by sweeping the enemy with accurate bursts while explosions and ricocheting bullets threw blinding dust and dirt about him. He broke up a second counterattack by hurling grenades into the midst of the enemy forces, and then refused to withdraw, volunteering to maintain his post and cover the movement of American riflemen as they reorganized to meet any further hostile action. The major effort of the enemy did not develop until the morning of April 21. It found Pfc. May still supporting the rifle company in the face of dev-

astating rifle, machinegun, and mortar fire. While many of the friendly troops about him became casualties, he continued to fire his machinegun until he was severely wounded and his gun rendered useless by the burst of a mortar shell. Refusing to withdraw from the violent action, he blasted fanatical Japanese troops with handgrenades until wounded again, this time mortally. By his intrepidity and the extreme tenacity with which he held firm until death against overwhelming forces, Pfc. May killed at least 16 Japanese, was largely responsible for maintaining the American lines, and inspired his comrades to efforts which later resulted in complete victory and seizure of the mountain stronghold.

OFFICIAL COMMUNIQUE:
United States
GUAM, Saturday, April 21 – Pacific Fleet communique 388:

(1) After a day of heavy attacks on the enemy's fortified positions in the southern Okinawa sector, the Twenty-fourth Army Corps had advanced about 1,000 yards generally by the morning of April 20 [East Longitude date]. The Seventh Infantry Division penetrated enemy defenses up to 1,400 yards in its zone of action near the east coast. Heavy naval guns continued to bombard enemy strongpoints, and marine and Army artillery supported the advancing infantry, with carrier aircraft delivering close support. Most of Yonabaru town was destroyed. The enemy resisted our attacks bitterly in all sectors of the fighting in the south.
(2) On Ie Shima [Island] Tenth Army troops continued to drive eastward against strong resistance from isolated enemy positions on April 20. Simultaneously operations were begun to destroy enemy forces holding Iegrusugu Peak. At the end of April 17, 736 of the enemy had been killed on the island.
(3) Patrols of the Marine Third Amphibious Corps continued to cover the rugged country in northern Okinawa on April 20, which operations against small groups of the enemy on Motobu Peninsula were continued.
(4) In the early morning hours of April 20, several small groups of enemy aircraft approached our forces in the Okinawa area and retired without causing damage.

†**THOMAS, WILLIAM H.**
Rank and Organization: Private First Class, U.S. Army, 149th Infantry, 38th Infantry Division.
Born: Wynne, Arkansas.
Entered Service At: Ypsilanti, Michigan.
Place and Date: Zambales Mountains, Luzon, Philippine Islands, April 22, 1945.
Citation: Pfc. Thomas was a member of the leading squad of Company B,

which was attacking along a narrow, wooded ridge. The enemy strongly entrenched in camouflaged emplacements on the hill beyond directed heavy fire and hurled explosive charges on the attacking riflemen. Pfc. Thomas, an automatic rifleman, was struck by 1 of these charges, which blew off both his legs below the knees. He refused medical aid and evacuation, and continued to fire at the enemy until his weapon was put out of action by an enemy bullet. Still refusing aid, he threw his last 2 grenades. He destroyed 3 of the enemy after suffering the wounds from which he died later that day. The effective fire of Pfc. Thomas prevented the repulse of his platoon and assured the capture of the hostile position. His magnificent courage and heroic devotion to duty provided a lasting inspiration for his comrades.

OFFICIAL COMMUNIQUE:
UNITED NATIONS
MANILA, Sunday, April 22-A communique:

PHILIPPINES

Mindanao: In a swift amphibious advance up the Mindanao River our southern column has secured the Paidu Pulanga road terminus, thirty-two miles inland. An enemy force southeast of Lomopog was being driven back into the surrounding marshes. Our center column continued to press eastward. In the north our patrols are fanning out throughout the province of Lanao. Heavy and medium units, dive-bombers and fighters, carrying 150 tons, continued disruption of the enemy's lines of communication, attacked troop centers at Davao, Kabacan and Cagayan and closely supported ground forces.
Luzon: In a bitterly contested advance through mountainous terrain the Twenty-fifth Division has secured Kapintal and the adjacent high ground commanding the Cagayan Valley road two miles south of the crest of Balete Pass. Other forces, closing from the west along the Villa Verde trail, report a definite weakening in the enemy's defense. Our medium, attack and fighter-bombers dropped 500 tons in support missions, destroying enemy fortifications and ammunition dumps and heavily strafing troop concentrations.

†KNIGHT, RAYMOND L. (Air Mission)
Rank and Organization: First Lieutenant, U.S. Army Air Corps.
Born: Texas.
Entered Service At: Houston, Texas.
Place and Date: In Northern Po Valley, Italy, April 24-25, 1945.
Citation: 1st Lt. Knight piloted a fighter-bomber aircraft in a series of low-level strafing missions, destroying 14 grounded enemy aircraft and

leading attacks which wrecked 10 others during a critical period of the Allied drive in northern Italy. On the morning of April 23, he volunteered to lead 2 other aircraft against the strongly defended enemy airdrome at Ghedi. Ordering his fellow-pilots to remain aloft, he skimmed the ground through a deadly curtain of antiaircraft fire to reconnoiter the field, locating 8 German aircraft hidden beneath heavy camouflage. He rejoined his flight, briefed them by radio, and then led them with consummate skill through the hail of enemy fire in a low-level attack, destroying 5 aircraft, while his flight accounted for 2 others. Returning to his base, he volunteered to lead 3 other aircraft in reconnaissance of Bergamo airfield, an enemy base near Ghedi and one known to be equally well defended. Again ordering his flight to remain out of range of antiaircraft fire, 1st Lt. Knight flew through an exceptionally intense barrage, which heavily damaged his Thunderbolt, to observe the field at minimum altitude. He discovered a squadron of enemy aircraft under heavy camouflage and led his flight to the assault. Returning alone after this strafing, he made 10 deliberate passes against the field despite being hit by antiaircraft fire twice more, destroying 6 fully loaded enemy twin-engine aircraft and 2 fighters. His skillfully led attack enabled his flight to destroy 4 other twin-engine aircraft and a fighter plane. He then returned to his base in his seriously damaged plane. Early the next morning, when he again attacked Bergamo, he sighted an enemy plane on the runway. Again he led 3 other American pilots in a blistering low-level sweep through vicious antiaircraft fire that damaged his plane so severely that it was virtually non-flyable. Three of the few remaining enemy twin-engine aircraft at that base were destroyed. Realizing the critical need for aircraft in his unit, he declined to parachute to safety over friendly territory and unhesitatingly attempted to return his shattered plane to his home field. With great skill and strength, he flew homeward until caught by treacherous air conditions in the Apennines Mountains, where he crashed and was killed. The gallant action of 1st Lt. Knight eliminated the German aircraft which were poised to wreak havoc on Allied forces pressing to establish the first firm bridgehead across the Po River; his fearless daring and voluntary self-sacrifice averted possible heavy casualties among ground forces and the resultant slowing on the German drive culminated in the collapse of enemy resistance in Italy.

OFFICIAL COMMUNIQUE:
UNITED NATIONS
ROME, April 24-An Allied Mediterranean communique:

ARMY

The Fifth and Eighth Armies are now generally along the Po River on a wide front. Eighth Army troops are still engaged in heavy fighting in the Ferrara area.

On the Ligurian coast Fifth Army troops are closing in on the naval base of La Spezia.

AIR

Road bridges on the Adige River and at Padua were the main targets yesterday for strong forces of escorted Fifteenth United States Army Air Force heavy bombers. Fighters bombed and strafed communications targets, including bridges, in the eastern Italian battle area.

Last night heavy bombers of the RAF bombed the Verona-Perona rail bridge.

Medium bombers of the Mediterranean Allied Tactical Air Force bombed rail bridges and rail fills on the Brenner route, and a road bridge north of Padua, and made many attacks on the Pro Valley, hitting airdromes, dumps, river crossings and rail lines.

Fighter-bombers and fighters, coordinating with the ground forces, concentrated their entire force on battle area attacks, harassing communications and retreating enemy columns, and doing great damage to road and rail transport.

Coastal Air Force mediums attacked small shipping in the Gulf of Genoa, while fighters struck at guns, enemy positions and communications in northwest Italy. Rocket-firing Beaufighters of the Balkan Air Force hit enemy positions and occupied buildings in northern Yugoslavia, and fighters and fighter-bombers bombed and strafed rail lines and rolling stock in the same area.

The Mediterranean Allied Air Force flew more than 3,400 sorties. From all these operations twenty-three of our aircraft, including one heavy bomber, are missing.

†GONZALES, DAVID M.

Rank and Organization: Private First Class, U.S. Army, Company A, 127th Infantry, 32d Infantry Division.
Born: Pacoima, California.
Entered Service At: Pacoima, California.
Place and Date: Villa Verde Trail, Luzon, Philippine Islands, April 25, 1945.
Citation: Pfc. Gonzales was pinned down with his company. As enemy fire swept the area, making any movement extremely hazardous, a 500-pound bomb smashed into the company's perimeter, burying 5 men with

its explosion. Pfc. Gonzales, without hesitation, seized an entrenching tool and under a hail of fire crawled 15 yards to his entombed comrades, where his commanding officer, who had also rushed forward, was beginning to dig the men out. Nearing his goal, he saw the officer struck and instantly killed by machinegun fire. Undismayed, he set to work swiftly and surely with his hands and the entrenching tool while enemy sniper and machinegun bullets struck all about him. He succeeded in digging one of the men out of the pile of rock and sand. To dig faster he stood up regardless of the greater danger from so exposing himself. He extricated a second man, and then another. As he completed the liberation of the third, he was hit and mortally wounded, but the comrades for whom he so gallantly gave his life were safely evacuated. Pfc. Gonzales' valiant and intrepid conduct exemplifies the highest tradition of the military service.

OFFICIAL COMMUNIQUE:
UNITED NATIONS
MANILA, Thursday, April 26-A communique:

PHILIPPINES

Mindanao: The Twenty-fourth Division with air support swept forward sixteen miles on Highway 1 against scattered enemy resistance. We have now reached the hill country.
Luzon: Our guerrilla forces with air support have captured Vigan, its adjacent airfield and Bantay, along the northwest coast. Except for scattered enemy remnants now being mopped up, the entire province of Ilocos Sur is cleared. Attack bombers and fighters carrying over 140 tons bombed and strafed in other sectors.

RUIZ, ALEJANDRO R. RENTERIA
Rank and Organization: Private First Class, U.S. Army, 165th Infantry, 27th Infantry Division.
Born: Loving, New Mexico.
Entered Service At: Carlsbad, New Mexico.
Place and Date: Okinawa, Ryukyu Islands, April 28, 1945.
Citation: When his unit was stopped by a skillfully camouflaged enemy pillbox, Pfc Ruiz displayed conspicuous gallantry and intrepidity above and beyond the call of duty. His squad, suddenly brought under a hail of machinegun fire and a vicious grenade attack, was pinned down. Jumping to his feet, Pfc. Ruiz seized an automatic rifle and lunged through the flying grenades and rifle and automatic fire for the top of the emplacement.

When an enemy soldier charged him, his rifle jammed. Undaunted, Pfc. Ruiz whirled on his assailant and clubbed him down. Then he ran back through bullets and grenades, seized more ammunition and another automatic rifle, and again made for the pillbox. Enemy fire was concentrated on him, but he charged on, miraculously reaching the position, and in plain view he climbed to the top. Leaping from 1 opening to another, he sent burst after burst into the pillbox, killing 12 of the enemy and completely destroying the position. Pfc. Ruiz's heroic conduct, in the face of overwhelming odds, saved the lives of many comrades and eliminated an obstacle that long would have checked his unit's advance.

OFFICIAL COMMUNIQUE:
UNITED STATES
GUAM, Sunday, April 29-Pacific Fleet communique 346:
(1) Troops of the Twenty-fourth Army Corps moved slowly forward in the southern sector of Okinawa on April 27, destroying pillboxes, caves and strong points. Heavy artillery was employed to break up troop concentrations in the enemy's rear areas and planes of the Second Marine Aircraft Wing joined with carrier aircraft of the Pacific Fleet to give close support to the troops. Naval gunfire continued to be effective in destroying enemy fortified positions.
(2) During the night of April 27-28, two groups of enemy aircraft attacked United States shipping off Okinawa beaches, causing some damage and sinking one auxiliary surface unit. Twenty-five, enemy aircraft were shot down and two were probably destroyed. Enemy small craft activity increased during the night and a number of small boats were destroyed by our forces.

BUSH, ROBERT EUGENE
Rank and Organization: Hospital Apprentice First Class, U.S. Naval Reserve, serving as Medical Corpsman with a rifle company, 2d Battalion, 5th Marines, 1st Marine Division.
Born: October 4, 1926, Tacoma, Washington.
Entered Service At: Washington.
Place and Date: Okinawa Jima, Ryukyu Islands, May 2, 1945.
Citation: For conspicuous gallantry and intrepidity at the risk of his life above and beyond the call of duty while serving as Medical Corpsman with a rifle company, in action against enemy Japanese forces on Okinawa Jima, Ryukyu Islands, May 2, 1945. Fearlessly braving the fury of artillery, mortar, and machinegun fire from strongly entrenched hostile positions, Bush constantly and unhesitatingly moved from 1 casualty to another to attend the wounded falling under the enemy's murderous barrages. As the

attack passed over a ridge top, Bush was advancing to administer blood plasma to a marine officer lying wounded on the skyline when the Japanese launched a savage counterattack. In this perilously exposed position, he resolutely maintained the flow of lifegiving plasma. With the bottle held high in 1 hand, Bush drew his pistol with the other and fired into the enemy's ranks until his ammunition was expended. Quickly seizing a discarded carbine, he trained his fire on the Japanese charging pointblank over the hill, accounting for 6 of the enemy despite his own serious wounds and the loss of 1 eye suffered during his desperate battle in defense of the helpless man. With the hostile force finally routed, he calmly disregarded his own critical condition to complete his mission, valiantly refusing medical treatment for himself until his officer patient had been evacuated, and collapsing only after attempting to walk to the battle aid station. His daring initiative, great personal valor, and heroic spirit of self-sacrifice in service of others reflect great credit upon Bush and enhance the finest traditions of the U.S. Naval Service.

†FOSTER, WILLIAM ADELBERT

Rank and Organization: Private First Class, U.S. Marine Corps Reserve.
Born: February 17, 1915, Cleveland, Ohio.
Entered Service At: Ohio.
Place and Date: Okinawa, Ryukyu Islands, May 2, 1945.
Citation: For conspicuous gallantry and intrepidity at the risk of his life above and beyond the call of duty while serving as a rifleman with the 3d Battalion, 1st Marines, 1st Marine Division, in action against enemy Japanese forces on Okinawa Shima in the Ryukyu Chain, May 2, 1945. Dug in with another marine on the point of the perimeter defense after waging a furious assault against a strongly fortified Japanese position, Pfc. Foster and his comrade engaged in a fierce handgrenade duel with infiltrating enemy soldiers. Suddenly an enemy grenade landed beyond reach in the foxhole. Instantly diving on the deadly missile, Pfc. Foster absorbed the exploding charge in his own body, thereby protecting the other marine from serious injury. Although mortally wounded as a result of his heroic action, he quickly rallied, handed his own remaining 2 grenades to his comrade and said, "Make them count." Stouthearted and indomitable, he had unhesitatingly relinquished his own chance of survival that his fellow marine might carry on relentless fight against a fanatic enemy, and his dauntless determination, cool decision and valiant spirit of self-sacrifice in the face of certain death reflect the highest credit upon Pfc. Foster and upon the U.S. Naval Service. He gallantly gave his life in the service of his country.

OFFICIAL COMMUNIQUE:
UNITED STATES
GUAM, Thursday, May 3-Pacific Fleet communique 350:

(1) The Seventh Infantry Division which captured Kuhazu village during the late afternoon of April 30 continued to advance southward on Okinawa on May 1 (East Longitude date). No substantial change was made in other sectors of the lines where our troops were under enemy artillery, mortar and small arms fire. On May 2 ships' guns destroyed a number of enemy emplacements, strong points and boat pens, and carrier and land-based aircraft bombed enemy defenses.

The infantry resumed the attack during the hours of darkness on the morning of May 2 and elements of the Seventh Division moved 1,400 yards forward to the vicinity of Gaja Hill, approximately one mile north of the town of Yonabaru. Tanks and flame-throwers were being employed to develop this salient. The Seventy-seventh Infantry Division and the First Marine Division launched an attack in the center and on the right flank and were moving forward during the morning of May 2.

(2) Targets on Kume Island, west of Okinawa, and in the Sakishima group in the Ryukyus were attacked by aircraft of the United States Pacific Fleet on May 2.

(3) Search aircraft of Fleet Air Wing 1 sank a medium transport south of Korea on May 1. On the following day planes of this wing sank two small cargo ships off the coast of central Honshu and one off the coast of Kyushu. Two small cargo ships were damaged near Honshu and a number of fishing and small craft were struck off Kyushu on the same date.

†KINSER, ELBERT LUTHER

Rank and Organization: Sergeant, U.S. Marine Corps Reserve.
Born: October 21, 1922, Greenville, Tennessee.
Entered Service At: Tennessee.
Place and Date: Okinawa Shima in the Ryukyu Chain, May 4, 1945.
Citation: For conspicuous gallantry and intrepidity at the risk of his life above and beyond the call of duty while acting as leader of a Rifle Platoon, serving with Company I, 3d Battalion, 1st Marines, 1st Marine Division, in action against Japanese forces on Okinawa Shima in the Ryukyu Chain, May 4, 1945. Taken under sudden, close attack by hostile troops entrenched on the reverse slope while moving up a strategic ridge along which his platoon was holding newly won positions, Sgt. Kinser engaged the enemy in a fierce handgrenade battle. Quick to act when a Japanese grenade landed in the immediate vicinity, Sgt. Kinser unhesitatingly threw himself on the deadly missile, absorbing the full charge of the shattering explosion in his

own body and thereby protecting his men from serious injury and possible death. Stouthearted and indomitable, he had yielded his own chance of survival that his comrades might live to carry on the relentless battle against a fanatic enemy. His courage, cool decision and valiant spirit of self-sacrifice in the face of certain death sustained and enhanced the highest traditions of the U.S. Naval Service. He gallantly gave his life for his country.

OFFICIAL COMMUNIQUE:
UNITED STATES
GUAM, Friday, May 4-Pacific Fleet communique 351:

(1) The Tenth Army resumed the attack in southern Okinawa on May 3, (East Longitude date), meeting artillery, mortar and small-arms fire from the enemy's fortified line. The First Marine Division made a limited advance in its zone of action, while other sectors remained stable. The attack was supported by ships, guns and aircraft.

(2) In the early evening hours of May 3 four small groups of enemy aircraft attacked our shipping off the coast of Okinawa, inflicting some damage on our forces and sinking two light units. Seventeen enemy aircraft were destroyed.

(3) Planes from escort carriers of the United States Pacific Fleet continue neutralizing attacks on airfields and air installations in the Sakishima group on May 2.

(4) As of May 2, according to the most recent reports available, 1,131 officers and men of the United States pacific Fleet had been killed in action in the Okinawa operation and associated operations against japan. A total of 2,816 were wounded and 1,604 were missing. All figures are preliminary and incomplete.

†**FARDY, JOHN PETER**
Rank and Organization: Corporal, U.S. Marine Corps.
Born: August 8, 1922, Chicago, Illinois.
Entered Service At: Illinois.
Place and Date: Okinawa Shima, in the Ryukyu Islands, May 7, 1945.
Citation: For conspicuous gallantry and intrepidity at the risk of his life above and beyond the call of duty as a squad leader, serving with Company C, 1st Battalion, 1st Marines, 1st Marine Division, in action against enemy Japanese forces on Okinawa Shima in the Ryukyu Islands, May 7, 1945. When his squad was suddenly assailed by extremely heavy small-arms fire from the front during a determined advance against strongly fortified, fiercely defended Japanese positions, Cpl. Fardy temporarily deployed his men along a nearby drainage ditch. Shortly thereafter, an enemy grenade fell among the marines in the ditch. Instantly throwing himself upon the

deadly missile, Cpl. Fardy absorbed the exploding blast in his own body, thereby protecting his comrades from certain and perhaps fatal injuries. Concerned solely for the welfare of his men, he willingly relinquished his own hope of survival that his fellow marines might live to carry on the fight against a fanatic enemy. A stouthearted leader and indomitable fighter, Cpl. Fardy, by his prompt decision and resolute spirit of self-sacrifice in the face of certain death, had rendered valiant service, and his conduct throughout reflects the highest credit upon himself and the U.S. Naval Service. He gallantly gave his life for his country.

†HANSEN, DALE MERLIN

Rank and Organization: Private, U.S. Marine Corps.
Born: December 13, 1922, Wisner, Nebraska.
Entered Service At: Nebraska.
Place and Date: Okinawa Shima, in the Ryukyu Chain, May 7, 1945.
Citation: For conspicuous gallantry and intrepidity at the risk of his life above and beyond the call of duty while serving with Company E, 2d Battalion, 1st Marines, 1st Marine Division, in action against enemy Japanese forces on Okinawa Shima in the Ryukyu Chain, May 7, 1945. Cool and courageous in combat, Pvt. Hansen unhesitatingly took the initiative during a critical stage of action and, armed with a rocket launcher, crawled to an exposed position where he attacked and destroyed a strategically located hostile pillbox. With his weapon subsequently destroyed by enemy fire, he seized a rifle and continued his 1-man assault. Reaching the crest of a ridge, he leaped across, opened fire on 6 Japanese and killed 4 before his rifle jammed. Attacked by the remaining 2 Japanese, he beat them off with the butt of his rifle and them climbed back to cover. Promptly returning with another weapon and supply of grenades, he fearlessly advanced, destroyed a strong mortar position and annihilated 8 more of the enemy. In the forefront of battle throughout this bitterly waged engagement, Pvt. Hansen, by his indomitable determination, bold tactics and complete disregard of all personal danger, contributed essentially to the success of his company's mission and to the ultimate capture of this fiercely defended outpost of the Japanese Empire. His great personal valor in the face of extreme peril reflects the highest credit upon himself and the U.S. Naval Service.

†SCHWAB, ALBERT EARNEST

Rank and Organization: Private First Class, U.S. Marine Corps Reserve.
Born: July 17, 1920, Washington, D.C.
Entered Service At: Tulsa, Oklahoma.
Place and Date: Okinawa Shima, in the Rykuyu Islands, May 7, 1945.
Citation: For conspicuous gallantry and intrepidity at the risk of his life above and beyond the call of duty as a flamethrower operator in action against enemy Japanese forces on Okinawa Shima in the Rykuyu Islands, May 7, 1945. Quick to take action when his company was pinned down in a valley and suffered resultant heavy casualties under blanketing machinegun fire emanating from a high ridge to the front, Pfc. Schwab, unable to flank the enemy emplacement because of steep cliffs on either side, advanced up the face of the ridge in bold defiance of the intense barrage and, skillfully directing the fire of his flamethrower, quickly demolished the hostile gun position, thereby enabling his company to occupy the ridge. Suddenly a second enemy machinegun opened fire, killing and wounding several marines with its initial bursts. Estimating with split-second decision the tactical difficulties confronting his comrades, Pfc. Schwab elected to continue his 1-man assault despite a diminished supply of fuel for his flamethrower. Cool and indomitable, he moved forward in the face of a direct concentration of hostile fire, relentlessly closed the enemy position and attacked. Although severely wounded by a final vicious blast from the enemy weapon, Pfc. Schwab had succeeded in destroying 2 highly strategic Japanese gun positions during a critical stage of the operation and, by his dauntless, singlehanded efforts, had materially furthered the advance of his company. His aggressive initiative, outstanding valor and professional skill throughout the bitter conflict sustain and enhance the highest traditions of the U.S. Naval Service.

Note: The following is a newspaper account of the preceding battle for which Cpl. Fardy, Pvt. Hansen, and Pfc. Schwab were awarded the Medal of Honor:

NEW OKINAWA ATTACK

• • •

TWENTY-FOURTH CORPS HEADQUARTERS, Okinawa, May 7 (Delayed-In football parlance the Japanese sent a power drive at the left guard and left tackle of our line early today and managed to break through. Some of the interference was 1,500 yards deep before it was knocked down by machine-gun and rifle fire.

It was the second big Japanese counter-attack within twenty-four hours, but by mid-afternoon we had cleaned it up fairly well, and the Army commanders, who are interested primarily in reducing the number of resisting Japanese on this island, were able to count it a success although it disrupted our attack plans on all except the First Marine Division front. With 3,134 counted dead recorded yesterday, we killed several hundred more today.

An enemy force estimated at between 800 and 1,200 launched its attack at the Seventh and Seventy-seventh Divisions at 2 A. M. It slowed down after some slight gains had been made, but was resumed in full fury at dawn, with the Seventy-seventh bearing the brunt of the drive.

Communications between forward observation posts and division headquarters were cut and it was impossible to rush up reserves before the Japanese had managed to break through. Some got as far as 1,500 yards behind the front, and one group of ninety Japanese was mowed down in the immediate vicinity of a regimental command post, which was undoubtedly the Japanese objective. The Japanese were supported by a number of tanks in the smash against our lines.

It is evident that the Japanese have planned carefully this series of counterattacks, to which they were giving heavy artillery support from new positions that our counter-batteries are having difficulty in locating.

The only appreciable United States gains recorded today were on the First Marine Division front. On the far western side of the island, our front line was brought to the Asa River area, gain of about 500 to 600 yards. On the marines' left flank where they have joined with the Seventy-seventh Division in the assault on Hill 187, our troops made considerable progress on the west side of that bastion.

†KROTIAK, ANTHONY L.

Rank and Organization: Private First Class, U.S. Army, Company I, 148th Infantry, 37th Infantry Division.
Born: August 15, 1915, Chicago, Illinois.
Entered Service At: Chicago, Illinois.
Place and Date: Balete Pass, Luzon, Philippine Islands, May 8, 1945.
Citation: Pfc. Krotiak was an acting squad leader, directing his men in consolidating a newly won position on Hill B when the enemy concentrated small-arms fire and grenades upon him and 4 others, driving them to cover in an abandoned Japanese trench. A grenade thrown from above landed in the center of the group. Instantly pushing his comrades aside and jamming the grenade into the earth with his rifle butt, he threw himself over it, making a shield of his body to protect the other men. The grenade exploded under him, and he died a few minutes later. By his extraordinary heroism in deliberately giving his life to save those of his comrades, Pfc. Krotiak set an inspiring example of utter devotion and self-sacrifice which reflects the highest traditions of the military service.

OFFICIAL COMMUNIQUE:
UNITED NATIONS
MANILA, Tuesday, May 8-A communique:

PHILIPPINES

Minanao: In the Davao area we have carried the assault against enemy positions in the hills to the west, while in the central sector our forces advanced another eight miles to the Maramag airfield. Dive-bombers gave support to both armies.
Luzon: Reduction continues of isolated enemy pockets in the northern hills where patrols have reached the edge of the highway leading over Balete Pass. Attack-planes and fighter-bombers with 285 tons of bombs hit enemy concentrations and lines of communication in the Cagayan Valley.

Note: The following newspaper article appeared on the front page of The New York Times May 8, 1945:

THE WAR IN EUROPE IS ENDED!
SURRENDER IS UNCONDITIONAL;
V-E WILL BE PROCLAIMED TODAY.

• • •

GERMANS CAPITULATE ON ALL FRONTS

• • •

American, Russian and French Generals Accept Surrender
in Eisenhower Headquarters, a Reims School

• • •

REICH CHIEF OF STAFF ASKS FOR MERCY

• • •

Doenitz Orders All Military Forces of Germany To Drop Arms –Troops in
Norway Give Up – Churchill and Truman on Radio Today

• • •

REIMS, France, May 7 – Germany surrendered unconditionally to the Western Allies and the Soviet Union at 2:41 A.M. French time today. [This was at 8:41 P.M., Eastern Wartime Sunday.]

The surrender took place at a little red schoolhouse that is the headquarters of Gen. Dwight D. Eisenhower.

The surrender, which brought the war in Europe to a formal end after five years, eight months and six days of bloodshed and destruction, was signed for Germany by Col. Gen. Gustav Jodl. General Jodl is the new Chief of Staff of the German Army.

The surrender was signed for the Supreme Allied Command by Lieut. Gen. Walter Bedell Smith, Chief of Staff for General Eisenhower.

It was also signed by Gen. Ivan Susloparoff for the Soviet Union and by Gen. Francois Sevez for France.

[The official Allied announcement will be made at 9 o'clock Tuesday morning when President Truman will broadcast a statement and Prime Minister Churchill will issue a V-E Day proclamation. Gen. Charles de Gaulle also will address the French at the same time.]

General Eisenhower was not present at the signing, but immediately afterward General Jodl and his fellow delegate, Gen. Admiral Hans Georg Friedeburg, were received by the Supreme Commander.

Germans Say They Understand Terms

They were asked sternly if they understood the surrender terms imposed upon Germany and if they would be carried out by Germany.

They answered Yes.

Germany, which began the war with a ruthless attack upon Poland, followed by successive aggressions and brutality in internment camps, surrendered with an appeal to the victors for mercy toward the German people and armed forces.

After having signed the full surrender, General Jodl said he wanted to speak and received leave to do so.

"With this signature," he said in soft-spoken German, "the German people and armed forces are for better or worse delivered into the victors' hands.

"In this war, which has lasted more than five years, both have achieved and suffered more than perhaps any other people in the world."

LONDON, May 7 – Complete victory in Europe was won by the Allies today with the unconditional surrender of Germany.

[The first announcement that Germany had capitulated came at 8:09 A.M., Eastern Wartime, when German Foreign Minister Count Lutz Schwerin von Krosigk stated in a broadcast over the Flensburg radio that Grand Admiral Karl Doenitz, new Chancellor of Germany, had ordered the unconditional surrender of all German armed forces.

[In his broadcast announcing the German surrender, Count Schwerin von Krosigk called upon the Germans "to stand loyally by the obligations we have undertaken."

["Then we may hope that the atmosphere of hatred which today surrounds Germany all over the world will give place to a spirit of reconciliation among the nations, without which the world cannot recover," he added. "Then we may hope that our freedom will be restored to us, without which no nation can lead a bearable and dignified existence."]

Germany's formal capitulation marked the official end of war in Europe, but it did not silence all the guns, for battles went on in Czechoslovakia.

Boehme Says Troops Were Unbeaten

In Norway, however, Gen. Franz Boehme, German Commander in Chief, broadcast an order of the Day over the Oslo radio tonight commanding his troops to lay down their arms in obedience to Count Schwerin von Krosigk's "announcement of unconditional surrender of all German fighting troops."

The Norwegian garrison surrendered at the order of Boehme, who said that the capitulation "hits us very hard because we are unbeaten and in full possession of our strength in Norway and no enemy has dared to attack us."

"In spite of all that," he added, "in the interests of all that is German we also shall have to obey the dictate of our enemies. We hope that in the future we shall have to deal with men on the other side who respect a soldier's honor, clench your teeth and keep discipline and order. Obey your superiors. Remain what you have been up to now – decent German soldiers who love their people and homeland more than anything in the world."

He said he also "expected" that the Norwegian population "will keep the discipline with respect to the Germans that the German soldiers in Norway always kept toward the Norwegians."

Under the terms of the capitulation, the Germans will march across the border into internment in Sweden.

The Swedish Telegraph Agency in a broadcast said an Allied naval force of forty-eight ships had been sighted at the entrance of Oslo Fjord and a landing was expected "at any moment."

†HALYBURTON, WILLIAM DAVID, JR.
Rank and Organization: Pharmacist's Mate Second Class, U.S. Naval Reserve.
Born: August 2, 1924, Canton, North Carolina.
Entered Service At: North Carolina.
Place and Date: Okinawa, Ryukyu Islands, May 10, 1945.

Citation: For conspicuous gallantry and intrepidity at the risk of his life above and beyond the call of duty while serving with a Marine Rifle Company in the 2d Battalion, 5th Marines, 1st Marine Division, during action against enemy Japanese forces on Okinawa Shima in the Ryukyu Chain, May 10, 1945. Undaunted by the deadly accuracy of Japanese counterfire as his unit pushed the attack through a strategically important draw, Halyburton unhesitatingly dashed across the draw and up the hill into an open fireswept field where the company advance squad was suddenly pinned down under a terrific concentration of mortar, machinegun and sniper fire with resultant severe casualties. Moving steadily forward despite the enemy's merciless barrage, he reached the wounded marine who lay farthest away and was rendering first aid when his patient was struck for the second time by a Japanese bullet. Instantly placing himself in the direct line of fire, he shielded the fallen fighter with his own body and staunchly continued his ministrations although constantly menaced by the slashing fury of shrapnel and bullets falling on all sides. Alert, determined and completely unselfish in his concern for the helpless marine, he persevered in his efforts until he himself sustained mortal wounds and collapsed, heroically sacrificing himself that his comrade might live. By his outstanding valor and unwavering devotion to duty in the face of tremendous odds, Halyburton sustained and enhanced the highest traditions of the U.S. Naval Service. He gallantly gave his life in the service of his country.

OFFICIAL COMMUNIQUE:
GUAM, Thursday, May 10-Pacific Fleet communique 357:

(1) Carrier-based aircraft, marine aircraft based ashore and ships' guns continued to support the troops of the Tenth Army with heavy bombing and gunfire on enemy positions in southern Okinawa on May 8 [East Longitude date]. Adverse weather continued in the Okinawa area through may 8 and no enemy aircraft were active over the Ryukus on that date. The troops continued to move southward on May 9.

(2) At noon on May 9 every gun ashore and every gun afloat which bore on the enemy on Okinawa fired one round simultaneously in recognition of the victory of the United Nations in Europe.

(3) From the beginning of operations against Okinawa through May 7, the Tenth Army lost 2,107 soldiers and 577 marines killed in action. A total of 10,402 soldiers and 2,800 marines were wounded and 501 soldiers and thirty-eight marines were missing.

(4) Aircraft from carriers of the British Pacific Fleet bombed the airfields and defenses on Miyako and Ishigaki in the Sakishima group on May 9, destroying

two planes on the ground and shooting one out of the air. Two units of the force suffered minor damage during an air raid but remained operational.

McKINNEY, JOHN R.
Rank and Organization: Sergeant (then Private), U.S. Army, Company A, 123d Infantry, 33d Infantry Division.
Born: Woodcliff, Georgia.
Entered Service At: Woodcliff, Georgia.
Place and Date: Tayabas Province, Luzon, Philippine Islands, May 11, 1945.
Citation: Pvt. McKinney fought with extreme gallantry to defend the outpost which had been established near Dingalan Bay. Just before daybreak approximately 100 Japanese stealthily attacked the perimeter defense, concentrating on a light machinegun position manned by 3 Americans. Having completed a long tour of duty at this gun, Pvt. McKinney was resting a few paces away when an enemy soldier dealt him a glancing blow on the head with a saber. Although dazed by the stroke, he seized his rifle, bludgeoned his attacker, and then shot another assailant who was charging him. Meanwhile, 1 of his comrades at the machinegun had been wounded and his other companion withdrew carrying the injured man to safety. Alone, Pvt. McKinney was confronted by 10 infantrymen who had captured the machinegun with the evident intent of reversing it to fire into the perimeter. Leaping into the emplacement, he shot 7 of them at pointblank range and killed 3 more with his rifle butt. In the melee the machinegun was rendered inoperative, leaving him only his rifle with which to meet the advancing Japanese, who hurled grenades and directed knee mortar shells into the perimeter. He warily changed position, secured more ammunition, and reloading repeatedly, cut down waves of the fanatical enemy with devastating fire or clubbed them to death in hand-to-hand combat. When assistance arrived, he had thwarted the assault and was in complete control of the area. Thirty-eight dead Japanese around the machinegun and 2 more at the side of a mortar 45 yards distant was the amazing toll he had exacted singlehandedly. By his indomitable spirit, extraordinary fighting ability, and unwavering courage in the face of tremendous odds, Pvt. McKinney saved his company from possible annihilation and set an example of unsurpassed intrepidity.

†TERRY, SEYMOUR W.

Rank and Organization: Captain, U.S. Army, Company B, 382d Infantry, 96th Infantry Division.
Born: Little Rock, Arkansas.
Entered Service At: Little Rock, Arkansas.
Place and Date: Zebra Hill, Okinawa, Ryukyu Islands, May 11, 1945.
Citation: 1st Lt. Terry was leading an attack against heavily defended Zebra Hill when devastating fire from 5 pillboxes halted the advance. He braved the hail of bullets to secure satchel charges and white phosphorus grenades, and then ran 30 yards directly at the enemy with an ignited charge to the first stronghold, demolished it, and moved on to the other pillboxes, bombarding them with his grenades and calmly cutting down their defenders with rifle fire as they attempted to escape. When he had finished this job by sealing the 4 pillboxes with explosives, he had killed 20 Japanese and destroyed 3 machineguns. The advance was again held up by an intense grenade barrage which inflicted several casualties. Locating the source of enemy fire in trenches on the reverse slope of the hill, 1st Lt. Terry, burdened by 6 satchel charges, launched a 1-man assault. He wrecked the enemy's defenses by throwing explosives into their positions and himself accounted for 10 of the 20 hostile troops killed when his men overran the area. Pressing forward again toward a nearby ridge, his 2 assault platoons were stopped by slashing machinegun and mortar fire. He fearlessly ran across 100 yards of fire-swept terrain to join the support platoon and urge it on in a flanking maneuver. This thrust, too, was halted by stubborn resistance. 1st Lt. Terry began another 1-man drive, hurling grenades upon the strongly entrenched defenders until they fled in confusion, leaving 5 dead behind them. Inspired by this bold action, the support platoon charged the retreating enemy and annihilated them. Soon afterward, while organizing his company to repulse a possible counterattack, the gallant company commander was mortally wounded by the burst of an enemy mortar shell. By his indomitable fighting spirit, brilliant leadership, and unwavering courage in the face of tremendous odds, 1st Lt. Terry made possible the accomplishment of his unit's mission and set an example of heroism in keeping with the highest traditions of the military service.

OFFICIAL COMMUNIQUE:
UNITED NATIONS
MANILA, Friday, May 11-A communique:

SOUTH SEAS AIR BLOCKADE

For the four months of January, February, March and April our Allied air forces of this area in blockade of all southern sea lanes have sunk or severely damaged 1,892,082 tons of enemy shipping. Enemy-organized commerce in these lanes only sporadic traffic is now attempted.

PHILIPPINES

Mindanao: The Twenty-fourth Division is systematically reducing enemy strong points and penetrating his positions in the Talomo River area, making steady gains against stubborn resistance. In the interior the Thirty-first Division is rapidly consolidating its advances. Heavy units and dive-bombers continued their effective support in all sectors, dropping 125 tons.
Luzon: In the Angat watershed the Forty-third Division is rapidly closing on Ipo from the north and south following a siege by land and air which is costing us remarkably few casualties, but has seriously depleted the enemy's irreplaceable stocks of ammunition, food and medical supplies and cost him heavy losses in personnel. Our heavy, medium, attack and fighter-bombers, carrying 300 tons, bombed and strafed in close support and hit targets in rear areas, destroying a number of grounded planes in the Cagayan Valley.

GUAM, Friday, May 11-Pacific Fleet communique 358:

(1) Enemy installations in southern Okinawa were bombarded by ships of the United States Pacific Fleet and carrier and marine aircraft on May 9 (East Longitude date). Ships' gunfire broke up a number of troop concentrations in the enemy's rear areas and destroyed pillboxes, emplacements and motor transport.

During the evening of May 9 several groups of enemy aircraft attacked our shipping off the Okinawa coast, damaging two auxiliaries and bombing Yontan airfield without success. Early the following morning another attack was made on our ships and ground installations but we suffered no damage. Six enemy aircraft were shot down during these actions. A Second Marine Aircraft Wing fighter, with guns inoperative, destroyed a Japanese bomber by cutting off its tail assemble with his propeller in these attacks.
(2) Elements of the Sixth Marine Division bridged and crossed the estuary of the Asa River in southern Okinawa on May 10. construction of the bridge was delayed temporarily by the enemy's use of two human bombs, which caused some damage during the early morning hours. Limited gains were made on the remainder of the southern front, where hand-to-hand fighting was in progress in some sectors. The enemy on Okinawa lost 38,857 killed through May 9.

(3) The area of Okinawa from the central sector of the island near the Hagushi beaches northward to the extremity of the island was passed to the control of the island commander, Maj. Gen. F. G. Wallace, United States Army, on May 4. About 135,000 civilians were under the jurisdiction of the United States Military Government on May 8.

†DIAMOND, JAMES H.

Rank and Organization: Private First Class, U.S. Army, Company D, 21st Infantry, 24th Infantry Division.
Born: New Orleans, Louisiana.
Entered Service At: Gulfport, Mississippi.
Place and Date: Mintal, Mindanao, Philippine Islands, May 8-14, 1945.
Citation: As a member of the machinegun section, Pfc. Diamond displayed extreme gallantry and intrepidity above and beyond the call of duty. When a Japanese sniper rose from his foxhole to throw a grenade into their midst, this valiant soldier charged and killed the enemy with a burst from his submachine-gun; then by delivering sustained fire from his personal arm and simultaneously directing the fire of 105-mm. and .50 caliber weapons upon the enemy pillboxes immobilizing this and another machinegun section, he enabled them to put their guns into action. When 2 infantry companies established a bridgehead, he voluntarily assisted in evacuating the wounded under heavy fire; and then, securing an abandoned vehicle, transported casualties to the rear through mortar and artillery fire so intense as to render the vehicle inoperative and despite the fact he was suffering from a painful wound. The following day he again volunteered, this time for the hazardous job of repairing a bridge under heavy enemy fire. On May 14, 1945, when leading a patrol to evacuate casualties from his battalion, which was cut off, he ran through a virtual hail of Japanese fire to secure an abandoned machine gun. Though mortally wounded as he reached the gun, he succeeded in drawing sufficient fire upon himself so that the remaining members of the patrol could reach safety. Pfc. Diamond's indomitable spirit, constant disregard of danger, and eagerness to assist his comrades, will ever remain a symbol of selflessness and heroic sacrifice to those for whom he gave his life.

OFFICIAL COMMUNIQUE:
United Nations
MANILA, Monday, May 14 – A Communique:

PHILIPPINES

Mindanao: Driving southward along the central highway our northern column has captured the Del Monte airdrome and advanced two miles beyond. An enemy force east of the drome was defeated and dispersed. Moving up from the south the Thirty-first division is making steady gains against moderate resistance. In the Davao area the Twenty-fourth Division scattered an enemy group in the Mount Apo region northwest of Digos and scored advances in the Talomo River sector.

Luzon: Sixth Army forces continue constant pressure on enemy position in the Balete Pass sector and in the vicinity of Ipo. Attack planes and fighters with 150 tons provided close support for troops and caused widespread damage in enemy rear areas.

†HAUGE, LOUIS JAMES, Jr.

Rank and Organization: Corporal, U.S. Marine Corps Reserve.
Born: December 12, 1924, Ada, Minnesota.
Entered Service At: Minnesota.
Place and Date: Okinawa Shima, in the Ryukyu Chain, May 14, 1945.
Citation: For conspicuous gallantry and intrepidity at the risk of his life above and beyond the call of duty as leader of a machinegun squad serving with Company C, 1st Battalion, 1st Marines, 1st Marine Division, in action against enemy Japanese forces on Okinawa Shima in the Ryukyu Chain on May 14, 1945. Alert and aggressive during a determined assault against a strongly fortified Japanese hill position, Cpl. Hauge boldly took the initiative when his company's left flank was pinned down under a heavy machinegun and mortar barrage with resultant severe casualties and, quickly locating the 2 machineguns which were delivering the uninterrupted stream of enfilade fire, ordered his squad to maintain a covering barrage as he rushed across an exposed area toward the furiously blazing enemy weapons. Although painfully wounded as he charged the first machinegun, he launched a vigorous singlehanded grenade attack, destroyed the entire hostile gun position and moved relentlessly forward toward the other emplacement despite his wounds and the increasingly heavy Japanese fire. Undaunted by the savage opposition, he again hurled his deadly grenades with unerring aim and succeeded in demolishing the second enemy gun before he fell under the slashing fury of Japanese sniper fire. By his ready grasp of the critical situation and his heroic 1-man assault tactics, Cpl. Hauge had eliminated 2 strategically placed enemy weapons, thereby releasing the besieged troops from an overwhelming volume of hostile fire and enabling his company to advance. His indomitable fighting spirit and decisive valor

in the face of almost certain death reflect the highest credit upon Cpl. Hauge and the U.S. Naval Service. He gallantly gave his life in the service of his country.

†COURTNEY, HENRY ALEXIUS, Jr.
Rank and Organization: Major, U.S. Marine Corps Reserve.
Born: January 6, 1916, Duluth, Minnesota.
Entered Service At: Minnesota.
Place and Date: Okinawa Shima, Ryukyu Islands, May 14-15, 1945.
Citation: For conspicuous gallantry and intrepidity at the risk of his life above and beyond the call of duty as Executive Officer of the 2d Battalion, 22d Marines, 6th Marine Division, in action against enemy Japanese forces on Okinawa Shima in the Ryukyu Islands, May 14-15, 1945. Ordered to hold for the night in static defense behind Sugar Loaf Hill after leading the forward elements of his command in a prolonged fire fight, Maj. Courtney weighed the effect of a hostile night counterattack against the tactical value of an immediate marine assault, resolved to initiate the assault, and promptly obtained permission to advance and seize the forward slope up the hill. Quickly explaining the situation to his small remaining force, he declared his personal intention of moving forward and then proceeded on his way, boldly blasting nearby cave positions and neutralizing enemy guns as he went. Inspired by his courage, every man followed without hesitation, and together the intrepid marines braved a terrific concentration of Japanese gunfire to skirt the hill on the right and reach the reverse slope. Temporarily halting, Maj. Courtney sent guides to the rear for more ammunition and possible replacements. Subsequently reinforced by 26 men and an LVT load of grenades, he determined to storm the crest of the hill and crush any planned counterattack before it could gain sufficient momentum to effect a breakthrough. Leading his men by example rather than by command, he pushed ahead with unrelenting aggressiveness, hurling grenades into cave openings on the slope with devastating effect. Upon reaching the crest and observing large numbers of Japanese forming for action less than 100 yards away, he instantly attacked, waged a furious battle and succeeded in killing many of the enemy and in forcing the remainder to take cover in the caves. Determined to hold, he ordered his men to dig in and, coolly disregarding the continuous hail of flying enemy shrapnel to rally his weary troops, tirelessly aided casualties and assigned his men to more advantageous positions. Although instantly killed by a hostile mortar burst while moving among his men, Maj. Courtney, by his astute military acumen, indomitable leadership and decisive action in the face of overwhelming odds, had con-

tributed essentially to the success of the Okinawa campaign. His great personal valor throughout sustained and enhanced the highest traditions of the U.S. Naval Service. He gallantly gave his life for his country.

†MULLER, JOSEPH E.

Rank and Organization: Sergeant, U.S. Army, Company B, 305th Infantry, 77th Infantry Division.
Born: Holyoke, Massachusetts.
Entered Service At: New York, New York.
Place and Date: Near Ishimmi, Okinawa, Ryukyu Islands, May 15-16, 1945.
Citation: Sgt. Muller displayed conspicuous gallantry and intrepidity above and beyond the call of duty. When his platoon was stopped by deadly fire from a strongly defended ridge, he directed men to points where they could cover his attack. Then through the vicious machinegun and automatic fire, crawling forward alone, he suddenly jumped up, hurled his grenades, charged the enemy, and drove them into the open where his squad shot them down. Seeing enemy survivors about to man a machinegun, he fired his rifle at point-blank range, hurled himself upon them, and killed the remaining 4. Before dawn the next day, the enemy counterattacked fiercely to retake the position. Sgt. Muller crawled forward through the flying bullets and explosives, then leaping to his feet, hurling grenades and firing his rifle, he charged the Japs and routed them. As he moved into his foxhole shared with 2 other men, a lone enemy, who had been feigning death, threw a grenade. Quickly seeing the danger to his companions, Sgt. Muller threw himself over it and smothered the blast with his body. Heroically sacrificing his life to save his comrades, he upheld the highest traditions of the military service.

OFFICIAL COMMUNIQUE:
Unites States
GUAM, Tuesday, May 15 – Pacific Fleet communique 362:

(1) About thirty-five enemy aircraft in three groups attacked our ships off the coast of Okinawa on the evening of May 13, East Longitude date, causing some damage to two light units. Twenty-five of the planes were shot down, one of our destroyers accounting for eight aircraft. Early in the morning of May 14 a few planes dropped bombs ashore on Okinawa, but failed to damage any installations.
(2) On the afternoon of May 13 two rifle companies of the Ninety-sixth Division reached the summit of Conical Hill, 2,500 yards east of Shuri, holding the position

despite Japanese counter-attacks. The 383d Infantry Regiment of the Ninety-sixth Division completed capture of the hill on May 14. dominations of this high ground Permitted our left flank to advance 2,400 yards southward along the east coast, bringing Yonabaru airfield into our possession.

In other sectors of the line advances were limited generally to 100 to 200 yards as troops of the Tenth Army met stiff opposition. The ground forces were supported by heavy gunfire from ships of the Pacific Fleet and by bombing and strafing attacks on enemy positions by carrier aircraft and planes of the Second Marine Aircraft Wing.

(3) Since April 1 our forces on Okinawa have captured or destroyed 386 enemy guns of 70 mm caliber or larger.

(4) Several groups of enemy aircraft made a series of attacks on the fast carrier task forces of the United States Pacific Fleet during the morning of May 14, causing some damage to one major unit. Preliminary reports show that twenty-one enemy planes were shot down by combat air patrols and ships' gunfire.

DOSS, DESMOND T.

Rank and Organization: Private First Class, U.S.Army, Medical Detachment, 307th Infantry, 77th Infantry Division.

Born: Lynchburg, Virginia.

Entered Service At: Lynchburg, Virginia.

Place and Date: Near Urasoe-Mura, Okinawa, Ryukyu Islands, April 29-May 21, 1945.

Citation: Pfc. Doss was a company aid man when the 1st Battalion assaulted a jagged escarpment 400 feet high. As our troops gained the summit, a heavy concentration of artillery, mortar and machinegun fire crashed into them, inflicting approximately 75 casualties and driving the others back. Pfc. Doss refused to seek cover and remained in the fire-swept area with the many stricken, carrying them 1 by 1 to the edge of the escarpment and there lowering them on a rope-supported litter down the face of a cliff to friendly hands. On May 2, he exposed himself to heavy rifle and mortar fire in rescuing a wounded man 200 yards forward of the lines on the same escarpment; and 2 days later he treated 4 men who had been cut down while assaulting a strongly defended cave, advancing through a shower of grenades to within 8 yards of enemy forces in a cave's mouth, where he dressed his comrades' wounds before making 4 separate trips under fire to evacuate them to safety. On May 5, he unhesitatingly braved enemy shelling and small-arms fire to assist an artillery officer. He applied bandages, moved his patient to a spot that offered protection from small-arms fire and, while artillery and mortar shells fell close by, painstakingly administered plasma. Later that day, when an American was severely wounded by fire from a cave, Pfc. Doss crawled to him where he had fallen 25 feet from the enemy position, rendered aid, and carried him 100 yards to safety while continually exposed to enemy fire. On May 21, in a night attack on high ground near Shuri, he remained in exposed territory while the rest of his company took cover, fearlessly risking the chance that he would be mistaken for an infiltrating Japanese and giving aid to the injured until he was himself seriously wounded in the legs by the explosion of a grenade. Rather than call another aid man from cover, he cared for his own injuries and waited 5 hours before litter bearers reached him and started carrying him to cover. The trio was caught in an enemy tank attack and Pfc. Doss, seeing a more critically wounded man nearby, crawled off the litter and directed the bearers to give their first attention to the other man. Awaiting the litter bearers' return, he was again struck, this time suffering a compound fracture of 1 arm. With magnificent fortitude he bound a rifle stock to his shattered arm as a splint and then crawled 300 yards over rough terrain to the aid station. Through his outstanding bravery and unflinching determination in the face of desperately dangerous conditions Pfc. Doss saved the lives of many soldiers. His name became a symbol throughout the 77th Infantry Division for outstanding gallantry far above and beyond the call of duty.

OFFICIAL COMMUNIQUE:
United States
GUAM, Monday, May 21 – Pacific Fleet communique 368:

(1) The Tenth Army in southern Okinawa gained ground slowly against the heaviest kind of resistance in the central and western sectors as it enveloped the enemy citadel of Shuri on May 20 [East Longitude date]. The First Marine Division established its first forward elements at a point about 800 yards south of Dakeshi town and the Seventy-seventh Infantry Division, after repulsing three enemy counter-attacks, captured a strongpoint 900 yards northeast of Shuri.

In the Sixth Marine Division's zone of the west coast, local progress was made east of Takamotoji. Moving against intense fire, the Ninety-sixth Infantry Division reached an elevation about 1,600 yards east of Ishimmi town.

Throughout the day, our troops in all sectors met strong resistance from caves, pillboxes and intense small-arms fire. Fleet aircraft and naval gunfire continued to support the troops.

SJOGREN, JOHN C.

Rank and Organization: Staff Sergeant, U.S. Army, Company I, 160th Infantry, 40th Infantry Division.
Born: Rockford, Michigan.
Entered Service At: Rockford, Michigan.
Place and Date: Near San Jose Hacienda, Negros, Philippine Islands, May 23, 1945.
Citation: S/Sgt. Sjogren led an attack against a high precipitous ridge defended by a company of enemy riflemen, who were entrenched in spider holes and supported by well-sealed pillboxes housing automatic weapons with interlocking bands of fire. The terrain was such that only 1 squad could advance at one time; and from a knoll atop a ridge a pillbox covered the only approach with automatic fire. Against this enemy stronghold, S/Sgt. Sjogren led the first squad to open the assault. Deploying his men, he moved forward and was hurling grenades when he saw that his next in command, at the opposite flank, was gravely wounded. Without hesitation he crossed 20 yards of exposed terrain in the face of enemy fire and exploding dynamite charges, moved the man to cover and administered first aid. He then worked his way forward and, advancing directly into the enemy fire, killed 8 Japanese in spider holes guarding the approach to the pillbox. Crawling to within a few feet of the pillbox while his men concentrated their bullets on the fire port, he began dropping grenades through the narrow firing slit. The enemy immediately threw 2 or 3 of these unexploded grenades out, and fragments from one wounded him in the hand and back. However, by hurling grenades back through the embrasure faster then the enemy could return them, he succeeded in destroying the occupants. Despite his wounds, he directed his squad to follow him in a systematic attack on the remaining positions, which he eliminated in like manner, taking tremendous risks, overcoming bitter resistance, and never hesitating in relentless advance. To silence one of the pillboxes, he wrenched a light machinegun out through the embrasure as it was firing before blowing up the occupants with hand grenades. During this action. S/Sgt. Sjogren, by his heroic bravery, aggressiveness, and skill as a soldier, singlehandedly killed 43 enemy soldiers and destroyed 9 pillboxes, thereby paving the way for his company's successful advance.

OFFICIAL COMMUNIQUE:
United Nations
MANILA, Wednesday, May 23 – A communique:

PHILIPPINES

Mindanao: The Thirty-first Division has liberated Malaybalay, provincial capital of Bukidnon, and secured the near-by airfield against scattered enemy resistance. North of Davao, the Twenty-fourth Division advanced four miles against moderate opposition to the northern outskirts of Bunawan and is less than two miles from Licanan airdrome, only remaining Davao air installation in enemy hands. Our heavy units, dive-bombers, and fighters hit enemy defenses in support.

Luzon: The Sixth Army continues steady pressure on enemy defenses in the rugged Sierra Madre Mountains in eastern Luzon and at the southern entrance to the Cagayan Valley. Our medium, attack and fighter-bombers dropped 325 tons in support of ground troops and on enemy rear installations. Our light naval units bombarded shore positions along the eastern coast.

CRAFT, CLARENCE B.

Rank and Organization: Private First Class, U.S. Army, Company G. 382d Infantry, 96th Infantry Division.
Born: San Bernardino, California.
Entered Service At: Santa Ana, California.
Place and Date: Hen Hill, Okinawa, May 31, 1945.
Citation: Pfc. Craft was a rifleman when his platoon spearheaded an attack on Hen Hill, the tactical position on which the entire Naha-Shuri-Yonabure line of Japanese defense on Okinawa, Ryukyu Islands, was hinged. For 12 days our forces had been stalled, and repeated, heavy assaults by 1 battalion and then another had been thrown back by the enemy with serious casualties. With 5 comrades, Pfc. Craft was dispatched in advance of Company G to feel out the enemy resistance. The group had proceeded only a short distance up the slope when rifle and machinegun fire, coupled with a terrific barrage of grenades, wounded 3 and pinned down the others. Against odds that appeared suicidal, Pfc. Craft launched a remarkable 1-man attack. He stood up in full view of the enemy and began shooting with deadly marksmanship whenever he saw a hostile movement. He steadily advanced up the hill, killing Japanese soldiers with rapid fire, driving others to cover in their strongly disposed trenches, unhesitatingly facing alone the strength that had previously beaten back attacks in battalion strength. He reached the crest of the hill, where he stood silhouetted against the sky while quickly throwing grenades at extremely short range into the enemy positions. His extraordinary assault lifted the pressure from his company for the moment, allowing members of his platoon to comply with his motions to advance and pass him more grenades. With a chain of his comrades

supplying him while he stood atop the hill, he furiously hurled a total of 2 cases of grenades into a main trench and other positions on the reverse slope of Hen Hill, meanwhile directing the aim of his fellow soldiers who threw grenades from the slope below him. He left his position, where grenades from both sides were passing over his head and bursting on either slope, to attack the main enemy trench as confusion and panic seized the defenders. Straddling the excavation, he pumped rifle fire into the Japanese at pointblank range, killing many and causing the others to flee down the trench. Pursuing them, he came upon a heavy machinegun which was still creating havoc in the American ranks. With rifle fire and a grenade he wiped out this position. By this time the Japanese were in complete rout and American forces were swarming over the hill. Pfc. Craft continued down the central trench to the mouth of a cave where many of the enemy had taken cover. A satchel charge was brought to him, and he tossed it into the cave. It failed to explode. With great daring the intrepid fighter retrieved the charge from the cave, relighted the fuse and threw it back, sealing up the Japs in a tomb. In the local action, against tremendously superior forces heavily armed with rifles, machineguns, mortars, and grenades, Pfc. Craft killed at least 25 of the enemy; but his contribution to the campaign on Okinawa was of much more far reaching consequence for Hen Hill was the key to the entire defense line, which rapidly crumbled after his utterly fearless and heroic attack.

OFFICIAL COMMUNIQUE:
United States
GUAM, Thursday, May 31 – Communique 378:

(1) Adverse weather conditions prevailing over the area of Okinawa reduced enemy aircraft activity on May 29. Several isolated raids were made on ships of the fleet, resulting in damage to two light units. Eight enemy planes were shot down during the day.

(2) Escort carrier aircraft attacked targets in the Sakishima group and aircraft from the fast carrier task forces were over the Amamas group on May 29.

(3) Tenth Army troops continued the attack to encircle and reduce the enemy stronghold of Shuri in southern Okinawa on May 30. Despite adverse weather and ground conditions, Sixth marine Division infantrymen advanced southward toward the Kokuba River.

Strong patrols of the First Marine Division moved into Shuri from the west. On the northeast of the enemy fortress, the Seventh Infantry Division was meeting stiff resistance in its zone of action. The Seventh Infantry Division on our left flank advanced westward to capture high ground in the vicinity of Yonawa.

†HARR, HARRY R.

Rank and Organization: Corporal, U.S. Army, Company D, 124th Infantry, 31st Infantry Division.
Born: Pine Croft, Pennsylvania.
Entered Service At: East Freedom, Pennsylvania.
Place and Date: Near Maglamin, Mindanao, Philippine Islands, June 5, 1945.
Citation: Cpl. Harr displayed conspicuous gallantry and intrepidity. In a fierce counterattack, the Japanese closed in on his machinegun emplacement, hurling handgrenades, 1 of which exploded under the gun, putting it out of action and wounding 2 of the crew. While remaining gunners were desperately attempting to repair their weapon another grenade landed squarely in the emplacement. Quickly realizing he could not safely throw the unexploded missile from the crowded position, Cpl. Harr unhesitatingly covered it with his body to smother the blast. His supremely courageous act, which cost him his life, saved 4 of his comrades and enabled them to continue their mission.

†WOODFORD, HOWARD E.

Rank and Organization: Staff Sergeant, U.S. Army, Company I, 30th Infantry, 33d Infantry Division.
Born: Barberton, Ohio.
Entered Service At: Barberton, Ohio.
Place and Date: Near Tabio, Luzon, Philippine Islands, June 6, 1945.
Citation: S/Sgt. Woodford volunteered to investigate the delay in a scheduled attack by an attached guerrilla battalion. Reaching the line of departure, he found the lead company, in combat for the first time, was immobilized by intense enemy mortar, machinegun, and rifle fire which had caused casualties to key personnel. Knowing that further failure to advance would endanger the flanks of adjacent units, as well as delay capture of the objective, he immediately took command of the company, evacuated the wounded, reorganized the unit under fire, and prepared to attack. He repeatedly exposed himself to draw revealing fire from the Japanese strong-points, and then moved forward with a 5-man covering force to determine exact enemy positions. Although intense enemy machine fire killed 2 and wounded his other 3 men. S/Sgt. Woodford resolutely continued his patrol before returning to the company. Then, against bitter resistance, he guided the guerrillas up a barren hill and captured the objective, personally accounting for 2 hostile machinegunners and courageously reconnoitering strong defensive positions before directing neutralizing fire. After organizing a

perimeter defense for the night, he was given permission by radio to return to his battalion, but, feeling that he was needed to maintain proper control, he chose to remain with the guerrillas. Before dawn the next morning the enemy launched a fierce suicide attack with mortars, grenades, and small-arms fire, and infiltrated through the perimeter. Though wounded by a grenade, S/Sgt. Woodford remained at his post calling for mortar support until bullets knocked out his radio. Then, seizing a rifle he began working his way around the perimeter, encouraging the men until he reached a weak spot where 2 guerrillas had been killed. Filling this gap himself, he fought off the enemy. At daybreak he was found dead in his foxhole, but 37 enemy dead were lying in and around his position. By his daring, skillful, and inspiring leadership, as well as by his gallant determination to search out and kill the enemy, S/Sgt. Woodford led an inexperienced unit in capturing and securing a vital objective, and was responsible for the successful continuance of a vitally important general advance.

OFFICIAL COMMUNIQUE:
United Nations
MANILA, Wednesday, June 6 – A communique:

PHILIPPINES
Luzon: The Thirty-seventh Division continued its drive down the upper portion of the Cagayan Valley, advanced elements reaching Aritao, ten miles north of Santa Fe. North of Baguio, progress was made in the direction of Tabio. Medium bombers, attack planes, and fighters with 250 tons of bombs destroyed further enemy supply dumps and bivouacs in the Cagayan Valley and supported ground forces in the central sector. Light naval units on night patrol attacked enemy shore positions on the north coast.
Mindanao: In the Davao area, we extended our gains five miles northwest of Mintal. Dive-bombers supported our ground forces in both central and eastern sectors.

†McTUREOUS, ROBERT MILLER, Jr.
Rank and Organization: Private, U.S. Marine Corps.
Born: March 26, 1924, Altoona, Florida.
Entered Service At: Florida.
Place and Date: Okinawa, June 7, 1945.
Citation: For conspicuous gallantry and intrepidity at the risk of his life above and beyond the call of duty, while serving with the 3d Battalion, 29th Marines, 6th Marine Division, during action against enemy Japanese forces on Okinawa in the Ryukyu Chain, June 7, 1945. Alert and ready for

any hostile counteraction following his companies seizure of an important hill objective, Pvt McTureous was quick to observe the plight of company stretcher bearers who were suddenly assailed by slashing machine-gun fire as they attempted to evacuate wounded at the rear of the newly won position. Determined to prevent further casualties, he quickly filled his jacket with handgrenades and charged the enemy occupied caves from which the concentrated barrage was emanating. Coolly disregarding all personal danger as he waged his furious 1-man assault, he smashed grenades into the cave entrances, thereby diverting the heaviest fire from the stretcher bearers to his own person and, resolutely returning to his own lines under a blanketing hail of rifle and machinegun fire to replenish his supply of grenades, dauntlessly continued his systematic reduction of Japanese strength until he himself sustained serious wounds after silencing a large number of the hostile guns. Aware of his own critical condition and unwilling to further endanger the lives of his comrades, he stoically crawled a distance of 200 yards to a sheltered position within friendly lines before calling for aid. By his fearless initiative and bold tactic, Pvt. McTureous had succeeded in neutralizing the enemy fire, killing 6 Japanese troops and effectively disorganizing the remainder of the savagely defending garrison. His outstanding valor and heroic spirit of self-sacrifice during a critical stage of operations reflect the highest credit upon himself and the U.S. Naval Service.

†LESTER, FRED FAULKNER

Rank and Organization: Hospital Apprentice First Class, U.S. Navy.
Born: April 29, 1926, Downers Grove, Illinois.
Entered Service At: Illinois.
Place and Date: Okinawa, June 8, 1945.
Citation: For conspicuous gallantry and intrepidity at the risk of his life above and beyond the call of duty while serving as a Medical Corpsman with an Assault Rifle Platoon, attached to the 1st Battalion, 22d Marines, 6th Marine Division, during action against enemy Japanese forces on Okinawa Shima in the Ryukyu Chain, June 8, 1945. Quick to spot a wounded marine lying in an open field beyond the front lines following the relentless assault against a strategic Japanese hill position, Lester unhesitatingly crawled toward the casualty under a concentrated barrage from the hostile machineguns, rifles, and grenades. Torn by enemy rifle bullets as he inched forward he stoically disregarded the mounting fury of Japanese fire and his own pain to pull the wounded man toward a covered position. Struck by enemy fire a second time before he reached cover, he exerted tremendous

effort and succeeded in pulling his comrade to safety where, too seriously wounded himself to administer aid, he instructed 2 of his squad in proper medical treatment of the rescued marine. Realizing that his own wounds were fatal, he staunchly refused medical attention for himself and gathering his fast-waning strength with calm determination, coolly and expertly directed his men in the treatment of 2 other wounded marines, succumbing shortly thereafter. Completely selfless in his concern for the welfare of his fighting comrades, Lester, by his indomitable spirit, outstanding valor, and competent direction of others, had saved the life of 1 who otherwise might have perished and had contributed to the safety of countless others. Lester's fortitude in the face of certain death sustains and enhances the highest traditions of the U.S. Naval Service. He gallantly gave his life for his country.

OFFICIAL COMMUNIQUE:
United States
GUAM, Thursday, June 7 – Pacific Fleet communique 385:

(1) Despite weather which imposed severe difficulties on ground troops, soldiers and marines of the Tenth Army continued to advance in all sectors on Okinawa on June 5 and 6 (East Longitude date).

The Sixth Marine Division captured Naha airfield and was driving southeastward on June 6, toward a junction with the First Marine Division in the center of the island.

After sweeping over all the Chinen Peninsula the Twenty-fourth Army Corps turned its main weight southwestward toward the area of the Yaeju-dake escarpment and was driving in that direction on the evening of June 6.

(2) After reducing resistance from numerous strong points and fortified caves on Naha airfield on June 5, the Sixth Marine Division captured the field the following day and expanded its area of control on Oroku Peninsula. Moving directly south, the First Marine Division encountered considerable resistance from enemy strong points during June 5 and 6. By-passing Tomui town, which was in the process of being reduced, the left flank of the division reached Shindawaku on June 6.

(3) Elements of the Ninety-sixth Division captured hill positions south of Iwa on June 5, and on the following day, the division's left flank advanced to the outskirts of Yunagusuku town and the northwest edge of Tomura town on the approaches to the Yaeju-dake escarpments.

In the area of Gushichan town, the Seventh Infantry Division was meeting stiffening resistance on June 6, after capturing Aragusuku the previous day. Enemy defenses in this area appeared to be strong. The capture of Chinen Peninsula was completed by the Seventh Division on June 5.

McCOOL, RICHARD MILES, Jr.

Rank and Organization: Lieutenant, U.S. Navy, U.S.S. *LSC(L)(3) 122*.
Born: January 4, 1922, Tishomingo, Oklahoma.
Entered Service At: Oklahoma.
Place and Date: Off Okinawa, June 10th and 11th, 1945.
Citation: For conspicuous gallantry and intrepidity at the risk of his life above and beyond the call of duty as commanding office of the U.S.S. *LSC(L)(3) 122* during operations against enemy Japanese forces in the Ryukyu chain, June 10 and 11, 1945. Sharply vigilant during hostile air raids against Allied ships on radar picket duty off Okinawa on June 10, Lt. McCool aided materially in evacuating all survivors from a sinking destroyer which had sustained mortal damage under the devastating attacks. When his own craft was attacked simultaneously by 2 of the enemy's suicide squadron early in the evening of June 11, he instantly hurled the full power of his gun batteries against the plunging aircraft, shooting down the first and damaging the second before it crashed his station in the conning tower and engulfed the immediate area in a mass of flames. Although suffering from shrapnel wounds and painful burns, he rallied his concussion-shocked crew and initiated vigorous firefighting measures and then proceeded to the rescue of several trapped in a blazing compartment, subsequently carrying 1 man to safety despite the excruciating pain of additional severe burns. Unmindful of all personal danger, he continued his efforts without respite until aid arrived from other ships and he was evacuated. By his staunch leadership, capable direction, and indomitable determination throughout the crisis, Lt. McCool saved the lives of many who otherwise might have perished and contributed materially to the saving of his ship for further combat service. His valiant spirit of self-sacrifice in the face of extreme peril sustains and enhances the highest traditions of the U.S. Naval Service.

OFFICIAL COMMUNIQUE:
United States
GUAM, Monday, June 11 - Pacific Fleet communique 389:

(1) A few enemy planes were over our forces in the Okinawa area on June 9, east longitude date. Our aircraft and anti-aircraft guns shot down six of them. Planes from escort carriers damaged three enemy aircraft on the ground in the Sakishima on the same date.
(2) One light unit of the fleet was sunk by enemy action off Okinawa on June 30.
(3) On the morning of June 10 Thunderbolts of the 318th Army fighter Group shot down seventeen enemy planes over Kyushu.

(4) The Tenth Army launched a heavy attack against the enemy escarpment positions in southern Okinawa on June 10 and continued its efforts to eliminate the enemy on Oroku Peninsula, southeast of the Naha airfield.

(5) Meeting heavy resistance , the Ninety-sixth Infantry Division made gains of 800 to 1,000 yards in the Twenty-fourth Corps zone of action and was moving up the slopes of the escarpment at the end of the day. The Seventh Infantry Division repulsed two strong counter-attacks on its right and made limited advances on the left in its effort to capture Hill 95.

(6) The First Marine Division, abreast of the Ninety-sixth, moved its right elements through Itoman town and attacked the approaches to Kunishi ridge, east of the town, making gains of 200 to 500 yards on its left. Substantial progress was made by the Sixth Marine Division in further compressing the remainder of the enemy troops on Oroku Peninsula. Gains up to 1,000 yards were made in this area.

(7) The attacks of the Tenth Army ground troops were supported by tanks, artillery, aircraft and heavy gun fire from the fleet.

(8) Search Mariners of Fleet Air Wing 1 sank a small cargo ship on June 10 in the waters around Korea. On the same date Privateers of the same wing damaged three small cargo ships in the Tsushima Strait.

(9) Planes of the Fourth Marine Aircraft Wing bombed targets in the Palaus on June 10.

MEAGHER, JOHN

Rank and Organization: Technical Sergeant, U.S. Army, Company E, 305th Infantry, 77th Infantry Division.
Born: Jersey City, New Jersey.
Entered Service At: Jersey City, New Jersey.
Place and Date: Near Ozanto, Okinawa, June 19, 1945.
Citation: T/Sgt. Meagher displayed conspicuous gallantry and intrepidity above and beyond the call of duty. In the heat of the fight, he mounted an assault tank, and, with bullets splattering about him, designated targets to the gunner. Seeing an enemy solider carrying an explosive charge dash for the tank treads, he shouted fire orders to the gunner, leaped from the tank, and bayonetted the charging solider. Knocked unconscious and his rifle destroyed, he regained consciousness, secured a machinegun from the tank, and began a furious 1-man assault on the enemy. Firing from his hip, moving through vicious crossfire that ripped through his clothing, he charged the nearest pillbox, killing 6. Going on amid the hail of bullets and grenades, he dashed for a second enemy gun, running out of ammunition just as he reached the position. He grasped his empty gun by the barrel and in a violent onslaught killed the crew. By his fearless assaults T/Sgt. Meagher

singlehandedly broke the enemy resistance, enabling his platoon to take its objective and continue the advance.

OFFICIAL COMMUNIQUE:
United States
GUAM, Tuesday, June 19 - Pacific Fleet communique 397:

(1) Lieut. Gen. Simon Bolivar Buckner Jr., United States Army, commander General Tenth Army and the Ryukyus Forces, was killed in action at 1:15 P.M., local time on June 18 (East Longitude date), while observing the attack of the Marine Eighth Regimental Combat Team on Okinawa. His death was instantaneous and resulted from the burst of an enemy shell. Maj. Gen. Roy S. Geiger, United States Marine Corps, has assumed command of the Ryukys Forces.
General Buckner's death occurred as enemy resistance on Okinawa was breaking and Japanese troops were fleeing in the open toward the cliffs at the southern end of the island.
(2) The troops of the Tenth Army broke through Japanese defense lines in all sectors of the front during the day against resistance which was crumbling and diminishing at nightfall.
(3) In the Marine Third Amphibious corps zone of action the Eighth Marine Regiment, reinforced, of the Second Marine Division, moved into the lines to attack before dawn. At nightfall this regiment, commanded by Brig. Gen. L.P. Hunt, USMC, with elements of the Twenty-second Marine Division regiment, was in the area of the Nagausuku-Makable highway. On the corps' left flank the First Marine Division seized ground southeast of Mezado.

MAYFIELD, MELVIN
Rank and Organization: Corporal, U.S. Army, Company D, 20th Infantry, 6th Infantry Division.
Born: Salem, West Virginia.
Entered Service At: Nashport, Ohio.
Place and Date: Cordillera Mountains, Luzon, Philippine Islands, July 29, 1945.
Citation: Cpl. Mayfield displayed conspicuous gallantry and intrepidity above and beyond the call of duty while fighting in the Cordillera Mountains of Luzon, Philippine Islands. When 2 Filipino companies were pinned down under a torrent of enemy fire that converged on them from a circular ridge commanding their position, Cpl. Mayfield, in a gallant single-handed effort to aid them, rushed from shellhole to shellhole until he reached 4 enemy caves atop the barren fire swept hill. With grenades and his carbine,

he assaulted each of the caves while enemy fire pounded about him. However, before he annihilated the last hostile redoubt, a machinegun bullet destroyed his weapon and slashed his left hand. Disregarding his wound, he secured more grenades and dauntlessly charged again into the face of pointblank fire to help destroy a hostile observation post. By his gallant determination and heroic leadership, Cpl. Mayfield inspired the men to eliminate all remaining pockets of resistance in the area and to press the advance against the enemy.

OFFICIAL COMMUNIQUE:
United Nations
MANILA, Monday, July 30 - A communique:

In northern Luzon elements from the Thirty-second, Thirty-seventh and thirty-eighth divisions and units of the Philippine Army and guerrilla forces under our Fourteenth Corps continue the reduction of enemy stragglers. The bulk of the remaining Japanese is surrounded and compressed within the Kiangan-Daklian-Loo sector of the southern Cordillera Mountain ranges and in the foothills of the Sierra Nadres.

In Mindanao the Twenty-fourth and Thirty-first Divisions with supporting Philippine units under our Tenth corps reported sporadic patrol clashes in widely scattered sectors, mainly the upper reaches of the Agusan River Valley and along the Kibawe-Tolomo trail.

During the past week our ground forces killed an additional 4,477 and captured 587 in mopping-up operations. Our own casualties were thirty-four killed and seventy-three wounded.

Note: The following article appeared on the front page of The New York Times on September 2, 1945:

JAPAN SURRENDERS TO ALLIES,
SIGNS RIGID TERMS ON WARSHIP;
TRUMAN SETS TODAY AS V-J DAY

• • •

WAR COMES TO END

• • •

Articles of Capitulation Endorsed by
Countries in Pacific Conflict

• • •

MACARTHUR SEES PEACE

• • •

Emperor Orders Subjects to Obey
All Commands Issued by General

• • •

ABOARD THE U.S.S. MISSOURI in Tokyo Bay, Sunday, Sept. 2 - Japan surrendered formally and unconditionally to the Allies today in a twenty-minute ceremony which ended just as the sun burst through low-hanging clouds as a shining symbol to a ravaged world now done with war.

[A United Press dispatch said the leading Japanese delegate signed the articles at 9:03 a.m. Sunday, Tokyo time, and that General MacArthur signed them at 9:07 a.m.]

Twelve signatures, requiring only a few minutes to inscribe on the articles of surrender, end the bloody Pacific conflict.

On behalf of Emperor Hirohito, Foreign Minister Mamoru Shigemitsu signed for the government and Gen. Yoshijiro Umezu for the Imperial General Staff.

MacArthur Voices Peace Hope

Gen. Douglas MacArthur then accepted in behalf of the United Nations, declaring: "It is my earnest hope and indeed the hope of all mankind that from this solemn occasion a better world shall emerge out of the blood and carnage of the past."

One by one the Allied representatives stepped forward and signed the document that blighted japan's dream of empire built on bloodshed and tyranny.

First was Admiral Chester W. Nimitz for the Unite States, then the representatives of China, the United Kingdom the Soviet, Australia, Canada, and New Zealand.

The flags of the United States, Britain, the Soviet and China fluttered from the veranda deck of the famed superdreadnought, polished and scrubbed as never before. More than 100 high-ranking military and naval officers watched.

Pledges Justice and Tolerance

"As Supreme Commander for the Allied powers," General MacArthur told the Japanese, "I announce it my firm purpose, in the tradition of the countries I represent, to proceed in the discharge of my responsibilities with justice and tolerance, while taking all necessary dispositions to insure that the terms of surrender are fully, promptly and faithfully complied with."

All through this dramatic half hour, only those aboard the battleship knew of what was taking place, because the Missouri has no broadcasting facilities.

But recordings were rushed to the near-by communications ship Ancon, and the solemn words of General MacArthur beginning the ceremony-"We are gathered here, representatives of the major warring powers"-were flashed around the world.

The Japanese representatives were present at the command of Emperor Hirohito contained in a proclamation issued by order of the Supreme Allied Commander.

The Emperor further commanded his officials "to issue general orders to the military and naval forces in accordance with the direction of the Supreme Commander of the Allied Powers." The imperial General Headquarters issued the order later.

Thus Emperor Hirohito formally acknowledged that General MacArthur's word in Japan would come foremost of all Japanese officialdom during the Allies' occupation of the country, which never before had been occupied by an alien force.

"I command all my people forth-with cease hostilities," the Emperor said, "to lay down their arms and faithfully to carry out all the provisions of the instrument of surrender and the general orders issued by the Imperial General Headquarters hereunder."

All issues have been "determined on the battlefields of the world and hence are not for our discussion or debate," General MacArthur said before he invited all representatives to sign the surrender instrument.

"Nor is it for us here to meet, representing as we do the majority of the peoples of the earth, in a spirit of distrust, malice or hatred," he added. "But rather it is for us, both visitors and vanquished, to rise to that higher dignity which alone benefits the sacred purposes we are about to serve."

General MacArthur and Admiral Nimitz paid deep tribute to Allied dead and to the people of all Allied nations whose blood, work and sacrifices helped bring victory.

Admiral Nimitz said he took "great pride in the American forces which have helped to win this victory," and declared that "America can be proud of them."

"The officers and men of the United States Army, Navy, Marine Corps, Coast Guard and Merchant Marine who fought in the Pacific have written heroic new chapters in this Nation's military history," Admiral Nimitz said. "I have infinite respect for their courage, resourcefulness and devotion to duty. We also acknowledge the great contribution to this victory made by our valiant allies. United we fought and united we prevail."

Admiral Nimitz observed that "the long and bitter struggle, which Japan started so treacherously on the seventh of December, 1941, was at an end.

Recalls Our Dark Days

General MacArthur touched obliquely on the bitter days of the early Philippine fighting when he said:

"As I look back on the long, tortuous trail from those grim days of Bataan and Corregidor, when an entire world lived in fear, when democracy was on the defensive everywhere, when modern civilization trembled in the balance. I thank a merciful God that He has given us the faith, the courage and the power from which to mould victory." General MacArthur told of the Allies' plans to help Japan take her place among peaceful nations.

Summary

Medals of Honor By Service

Army 256
Navy 57
Marines 81
Air Force 38
Coast Guard 1

244 Medals of Honor were awarded posthumously

Maj.Gen. G.B. Erskin U.S.M.C. summed it up best after the battle of Iwo Jima, and I think it holds true for every service and every battle in World War II, when he said, "only the accumulated praise of time will pay proper tribute to our valiant dead. Long after those who lament their immediate loss are themselves dead, these men will be mourned by the nation. They are the nation's loss! There is talk of great history, of unheard-of sacrifice, and unheard-of courage. These phrases are correct. Victory was never in doubt. Its cost was."

Index

Adams, Lucian, 363
Agerholm, Harold Christ, 259
Anderson, Beaufort T., 563
Anderson, Richard Beatty, 173
Antolak, Sylvester, 209
Antrim, Richard Nott, 35
Atkins, Thomas E., 518

Bailey, Kenneth D., 49
Baker, Addison E., 108
Baker, Thomas A., 260
Barfoot, Van T., 202
Barrett, Carlton W., 226
Basilone, John, 54
Bauer, Harold William, 64
Bausell, Lewis Kenneth, 319
Beaudoin, Raymond O., 553
Bell, Bernard P., 416
Bender, Stanley, 291
Benjamin, George, Jr., 424
Bennett, Edward A., 464
Bennion, Mervyn Sharp, 16
Berry, Charles Joseph, 507
Bertoldo, Vito R., 448
Beyer, Arthur O., 454
Bianchi, Willibald C., 29
Biddle, Melvin E., 428
Bigelow, Elmer Charles, 481
Bjorklund, Arnold L., 123
Bloch, Orville Emil, 334
Bolden, Paul L., 427
Bolton, Cecil H., 369
Bong, Richard I., 383

Bonnyman, Alexander, Jr., 152
Booker, Robert D., 84
Bordelon, William James, 151
Boyce, George W. D., Jr., 274
Boyington, Gregory, 158
Briles, Herschel F., 389
Britt, Maurice L., 144
Brostrom, Leonard C., 365
Brown, Bobby E., 347
Bulkeley, John Duncan, 35
Burke, Frank, 570
Burr, Elmer J., 67
Burr, Herbert H., 530
Burt, James M., 351
Bush, Richard Earl, 569
Bush, Robert Eugene, 580
Butts, John E., 251

Caddy, William Robert, 508
Callaghan, Daniel Judson, 62
Calugas, Jose, 28
Cannon, George Ham, 16
Carey, Alvin P., 294
Carey, Charles F., Jr., 447
Carr, Chris, (legally changed from
    Christos H. Karaberis), 342
Carswell, Horace S., Jr., 359
Casamento, Anthony, 57
Castle, Frederick W., 430
Chambers, Justice M., 493
Cheli, Ralph, 117
Childers, Ernest, 130
Choate, Clyde L., 358

Christensen, Dale Eldon, 268
Christian, Herbert F., 218
Cicchetti, Joseph J., 473
Clark, Francis J., 324
Colalillo, Mike, 555
Cole, Darrell Samuel, 487
Cole, Roberᴛ G., 242
Connor, James P., 289
Cooley, Raymond H., 499
Coolidge, Charles H., 362
Courtney, Henry Alexius, Jr., 596
Cowan, Richard Eller, 410
Craft, Clarence B., 601
Craig, Robert, 96
Crain, Morris E., 519
Craw, Demas T., 60
Crawford, William J., 124
Crews, John R., 555
Cromwell, John Philip, 149
Currey, Francis S., 420

Dahlgren, Edward C., 478
Dalessondro, Peter J., 426
Daly, Michael J., 571
Damato, Anthony Peter, 185
David, Albert LeRoy, 223
Davis, Charles W., 74
Davis, George Fleming, 442
Dealey, Samuel David, 345
DeBlanc, Jefferson Joseph, 77
DeFranzo, Arthur F., 239
DeGlopper, Charles N., 236
Deleau, Emile, Jr., 465
Dervishian, Ernest H., 203
Diamond, James H., 594
Dietz, Robert H., 544
Doolittle, James H., 37
Doss, Desmond T., 598
Drowley, Jesse R., 169
Dunham, Russell E., 445
Dunlap, Robert Hugo, 490
Dutko, John W., 204
Dyess, Aquilla James, 175

Edson, Merritt Austin, 50
Ehlers, Walter D., 239
Elrod, Henry Talmage, 24
Endl, Gerald L., 265
Epperson, Harold Glenn, 254
Erwin, Henry E., 560
Eubanks, Ray E., 275
Evans, Ernest Edwin, 359
Everhart, Forrest E., 377

Fardy, John Peter, 583
Femoyer, Robert E., 370
Fields, James H., 339
Finn, John William, 17
Fisher, Almond E., 311
Flaherty, Francis C., 17
Fleming, Richard E., 44
Fluckey, Eugene Bennett, 482
Foss, Joseph Jacob, 75
Foster, William Adelbert, 581
Fournier, William G., 73
Fowler, Thomas W., 205
Fryar, Elmer E., 402
Funk, Leonard A., Jr., 461
Fuqua, Samuel Glenn, 17

Galer, Robert Edward, 50
Galt, William Wylie, 215
Gammon, Archer T., 450
Garcia, Marcario, 395
Garman, Harold A., 296
Gary, Donald Arthur, 534
Gerstung, Robert E., 417
Gibson, Eric G., 167
Gilmore, Howard Walter, 79
Gonsalves, Harold, 568
Gonzales, David M., 578
Gordon, Nathan Green, 183
Gott, Donald J., 375
Grabiarz, William J., 496
Gray, Ross Franklin, 491
Gregg, Stephen R., 298
Gruennert, Kenneth E., 68
Gurke, Henry, 142

Hall, George J., 206
Hall, Lewis, 73
Hall, William E., 41
Hallman, Sherwood H., 312
Halyburton, William David, Jr., 589
Hamilton, Pierpont M., 61
Hammerberg, Owen Francis Patrick, 483
Hansen, Dale Merlin, 584
Hanson, Robert Murray, 165
Harmon, Roy W., 267
Harr, Harry R., 603
Harrell, William George, 508
Harris, James L., 347
Hastings, Joe R., 561
Hauge, Louis James, Jr., 595
Hawk, John D., 293
Hawkins, William Dean, 152
Hawks, Lloyd C., 168
Hedrick, Clinton M., 542
Hendrix, James R., 434
Henry, Robert T., 399
Herrera, Silvestre S., 525
Herring, Rufus G., 484
Hill, Edwin Joseph, 18
Horner, Freeman V., 384
Howard, James H., 161
Huff, Paul B., 180
Hughes, Lloyd H., 109
Hutchins, Johnnie David, 120

Jachman, Isadore S., 441
Jackson, Arthur J., 330
Jacobson, Douglas Thomas, 500
Jerstad, John L., 110
Johnson, Elden H., 219
Johnson, Leon W., 110
Johnson, Leroy, 406
Johnson, Oscar G., 327
Johnston, William J., 184
Jones, Herbert Charpoit, 19
Julian, Joseph Rodolph, 516

Kandle, Victor L., 348
Kane, John R., 111
Kearby, Neel E., 132

Keathley, George D., 314
Kefurt, Gus, 429
Kelley, Jonah E., 463
Kelley, Ova A., 403
Kelly, Charles E., 124
Kelly, John D., 255
Kelly, Thomas J., 551
Keppler, Reinhardt John, 63
Kerstetter, Dexter J., 564
Kessler, Patrick L., 207
Kidd, Isaac Campbell, 19
Kimbro, Truman, 418
Kiner, Harold G., 343
Kingsley, David R., 253
Kinser, Elbert Luther, 582
Kisters, Gerry H., 106
Knappenberger, Alton W., 172
Knight, Jack L., 467
Knight, Raymond L., 576
Kraus, Richard Edward, 345
Krotiak, Anthony L., 586

LaBelle, James Dennis, 514
Lawley, William R., 187
Laws, Robert E., 452
Lee, Daniel W., 302
Leims, John Harold, 513
Leonard, Turney W., 372
Lester, Fred Faulkner, 605
Lindsey, Darrell R., 287
Lindsey, Jake W., 384
Lindstrom, Floyd K., 144
Lloyd, Edgar H., 315
Lobaugh, Donald R., 274
Logan, James M., 121
Lopez, Jose M., 411
Lucas, Jacklyn Harold, 490
Lummus, Jack, 515

Mabry, George L., Jr., 389
MacArthur, Douglas, 26
MacGillivary, Charles A., 438
Magrath, John D., 565
Mann, Joe E., 328
Martin, Harry Linn, 541

Martinez, Joe P., 90
Mason, Leonard Foster, 270
Mathies, Archibald, 187
Mathis, Jack W., 81
Maxwell, Robert D., 307
May, Martin O., 574
Mayfield, Melvin, 609
McCall, Thomas E., 163
McCampbell, David, 249
McCandless, Bruce, 63
McCard, Robert Howard, 246
McCarter, Lloyd G., 485
McCarthy, Joseph Jeremiah, 492
McCool, Richard Miles, Jr., 607
McGaha, Charles L., 472
McGarity, Vernon, 407
McGee, William D., 527
McGill, Troy A., 193
McGraw, Francis X., 387
McGuire, Thomas B., Jr., 433
McKinney, John R., 591
McTureous, Robert Miller, Jr., 604
McVeigh, John J., 301
McWhorter, William A., 401
Meagher, John, 608
Merli, Gino J., 306
Merrell, Joseph F., 572
Messerschmidt, Harold O., 325
Metzger, William E., Jr., 376
Michael, Edward S., 194
Michael, Harry J., 520
Miller, Andrew, 396
Mills, James H., 209
Minick, John W., 390
Minue, Nicholas, 87
Monteith, Jimmie W., Jr., 226
Montgomery, Jack C., 192
Moon, Harold H., Jr., 355
Morgan, John C., 102
Moskala, Edward J., 557
Mower, Charles E., 371
Muller, Joseph E., 597
Munemori, Sadao S., 552
Munro, Douglas Albert, 53
Murphy, Audie L., 459

Murphy, Frederick C., 528
Murray, Charles P., Jr., 408

Nelson, William L., 86
Neppel, Ralph G., 404
Nett, Robert B., 405
New, John Dury, 337
Newman, Beryl R., 213
Nininger, Alexander R., Jr., 26

O'Brien, William J., 261
O'Callahan, Joseph Timothy, 535
Ogden, Carlos C., 256
O'Hare, Edward Henry, 30
O'Kane, Richard Hetherington, 357
Olson, Arlo L., 133
Olson, Truman O., 170
Oresko, Nicholas, 455
Owens, Robert Allen, 136
Ozbourn, Joseph William, 281

Paige, Mitchell, 55
Parle, John Joseph, 95
Parrish, Laverne, 457
Pease, Harl, Jr., 46
Peden, Forrest E., 468
Pendleton, Jack J., 350
Peregory, Frank D., 235
Perez, Manuel, Jr., 480
Peters, George J., 538
Peterson, George, 545
Peterson, Oscar Verner, 40
Petrarca, Frank J., 102
Pharris, Jackson Charles, 19
Phelps, Wesley, 344
Phillips, George, 522
Pierce, Francis Junior, 526
Pinder, John J., Jr., 227
Pope, Everett Parker, 331
Power, John Vincent, 174
Powers, John James, 41
Powers, Leo J., 178
Preston, Arthur Murray, 323
Prussman, Ernest W., 308
Pucket, Donald D., 264

Ramage, Lawson Paterson, 283
Ray, Bernard J., 385
Reese, James W., 114
Reese, John N., Jr., 474
Reeves, Thomas James, 20
Ricketts, Milton Ernest, 42
Riordan, Paul F., 179
Roan, Charles Howard, 331
Robinson, James E., Jr., 554
Rodriguez, Cleto, 475
Roeder, Robert E., 340
Rooks, Albert Harold, 32
Roosevelt, Theodore, Jr., 228
Ross, Donald Kirby, 20
Ross, Wilburn K., 367
Rouh, Carlton Robert, 319
Rudolph, Donald E., 470
Ruhl, Donald Jack, 489
Ruiz, Alejandro R. Renteria, 579

Sadowski, Joseph J., 316
Saronski, Joseph R., 91
Sayers, Foster J., 378
Schaefer, Joseph E., 337
Schauer, Henry, 208
Schonland, Herbert Emery, 147
Schwab, Albert Earnest, 585
Scott, Norman, 64
Scott, Robert R., 21
Scott, Robert S., 103
Shea, Charles W., 199
Sheridan, Carl V., 394
Shockley, William R., 548
Shomo, William A., 451
Shoup, Curtis F., 444
Shoup, David Monroe, 153
Sigler, Franklin Earl, 522
Silk, Edward A., 392
Sjogren, John C., 600
Skaggs, Luther, Jr., 270
Slaton, James D., 130
Smith, Furman L., 217
Smith, John Lucian, 51
Smith, Maynard H., 88
Soderman, William A., 412

Sorenson, Richard Keith, 174
Specker, Joe C., 160
Spurrier, Junior J., 379
Squires, John C., 198
Stein, Tony, 488
Street, George Levick, III, 566
Stryker, Stuart S., 539
Swett, James Elms, 82

Terry, Seymour W., 592
Thomas, Herbert Joseph, 140
Thomas, William H., 575
Thomason, Clyde, 47
Thompson, Max, 354
Thorne, Horace M., 421
Thorson, John F., 366
Timmerman, Grant Frederick, 262
Tomich, Peter, 21
Tominac, John J., 309
Towle, John R., 334
Treadwell, Jack L., 528
Truemper, Walter E., 188
Turner, Day G. , 446
Turner, George B., 440

Urban, Matt, 303

Valdez, Jose F., 459
Vance, Leon R., Jr., 224
Vandegrift, Alexander Archer, 66
Van Noy, Junior, 135
Van Valkenburgh, Franklin, 22
Van Voorhis, Bruce Avery, 93
Viale, Robert M., 470
Villegas, Ysmael R., 537
Vlug, Dirk J., 406
Vosler, Forrest T., 156

Wahlen, George Edward, 509
Wainwright, Jonathan M., 40
Walker, Kenneth N., 72
Wallace, Herman C., 503
Walsh, Kenneth Ambrose, 118
Walsh, William Gary, 504
Ward, James Richard, 22

Ware, Keith L., 435
Warner, Henry F., 419
Watson, Wilson Douglas, 501
Waugh, Robert T., 201
Waybur, David C., 101
Weicht, Ellis R., 399
Wetzel, Walter C., 549
Whiteley, Eli, 436
Whittington, Hulon B., 280
Wiedorfer, Paul J., 432
Wigle, Thomas W., 317
Wilbur, William H., 60
Wilkin, Edward G., 529
Wilkins, Raymond H., 137
Will, Walter J., 546

Williams, Hershel Woodrow, 498
Williams, Jack, 510
Willis, John Harlan, 505
Wilson, Alfred L., 374
Wilson, Louis Hugh, Jr., 277
Wilson, Robert Lee, 284
Wise, Homer L., 244
Witek, Frank Peter, 284
Woodford, Howard E., 603

Young, Cassin, 22
Young, Rodger W., 106

Zeamer, Jay, Jr., 91
Zussman, Raymond, 310

Also from the publisher

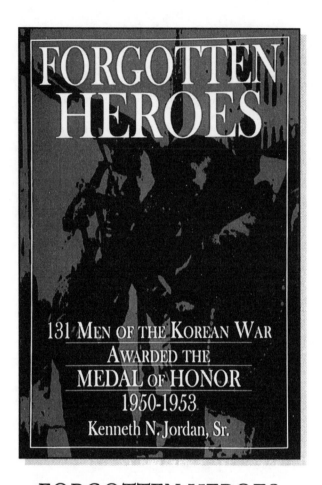

FORGOTTEN HEROES
131 MEN OF THE KOREAN WAR
AWARDED THE MEDAL OF HONOR 1950-1953

KENNETH N. JORDAN, SR.

Forgotten Heroes contains all 131 Medal of Honor citations, along with official communiqués for that day and newspaper accounts of various battles.

Size: 6" x 9" b/w photographs
352 pages, hard cover
ISBN: 0-88740-807-9 $24.95

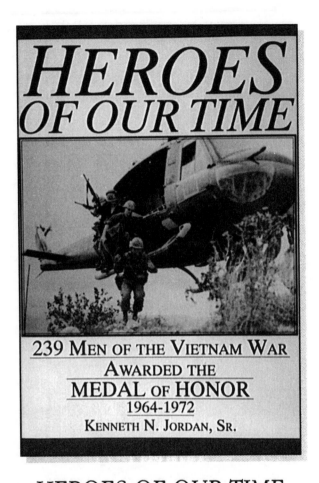

HEROES OF OUR TIME
239 MEN OF THE VIETNAM WAR
AWARDED THE MEDAL OF HONOR 1964-1972

KENNETH N. JORDAN SR.

Heroes of Our Time contains all 239 Medal of Honor citations, along with newspaper accounts of various battles.

Size: 6" x 9"   16 pages of photographs
368 pages, hard cover
ISBN: 0-88740-741-2 $24.95

CHENNAULT'S FORGOTTEN WARRIORS
THE SAGA OF THE 308TH BOMB GROUP IN CHINA
Carroll V. Glines

Chennault's Forgotten Warriors combine political intrigue, military valor and personal hardships to a degree not found elsewhere. The 308th's wide-ranging activities through nearly three years of bitter air warfare are described here by reknowned author C.V. Glines.
Size: 6" x 9"   over 130 b/w photographs
416 pages, hard cover
ISBN: 0-88740-809-5 $29.95